BETWEEN SCHOLARSHIP AND CHURCH POLITICS

The scholar in his study. A portrait of John Prideaux, painted for his family, probably in the late 1620s, and now hanging in Exeter College hall. Artist unknown. See page 193.

BETWEEN SCHOLARSHIP AND CHURCH POLITICS

THE LIVES OF JOHN PRIDEAUX, 1578–1650

JOHN MADDICOTT

OXFORD
UNIVERSITY PRESS

OXFORD
UNIVERSITY PRESS

Great Clarendon Street, Oxford, OX2 6DP,
United Kingdom

Oxford University Press is a department of the University of Oxford.
It furthers the University's objective of excellence in research, scholarship,
and education by publishing worldwide. Oxford is a registered trade mark of
Oxford University Press in the UK and in certain other countries

First Edition published in 2022

Impression: 1

Published in the United States of America by Oxford University Press
198 Madison Avenue, New York, NY 10016, United States of America

British Library Cataloguing in Publication Data
Data available

Library of Congress Control Number: 2021940781

ISBN 978–0–19–289610–0

DOI: 10.1093/oso/9780192896100.001.0001

Printed and bound by
CPI Group (UK) Ltd, Croydon, CR0 4YY

IN MEMORY OF JAMES CAMPBELL
AND HARRY PITT
the best of tutors

Preface and Acknowledgements

John Prideaux is an undeservedly neglected figure. Growing up in Elizabeth's reign, the son of a Devonshire yeoman farmer living on the edge of Dartmoor, he rose under the early Stuart kings to become one of the main actors in both the church politics and the academic world of his day. As the head of his Oxford college for thirty years, he held office at a particularly significant time, when an expanding university stood higher in prosperity and public esteem than at any point before the mid-nineteenth century. As regius professor of divinity, he was Oxford's leading theologian and so inevitably drawn into the widening religious divisions within the nation which would contribute eventually to the coming of civil war. During the war he served as bishop of Worcester, losing his title when the episcopate was abolished in 1646 and dying in relative poverty a few years later. Born in one country parish in 1578, he died in another, at Bredon in Worcestershire in 1650.

Prideaux's public life was informed by two particular loyalties: to the Calvinistic doctrines which inspired his theology and religious teaching, and to Exeter College, his Oxford home. His attachments to creed and college ran in parallel throughout his career. But while the unfettered expression of his religious opinions came to be thwarted by politics and circumstance, within his College, on the other hand, he moved more freely and ruled with striking success, increasing its numbers, endowing it with grand new buildings, and raising its reputation to new heights. Beyond these public roles lay more private affections, especially for his family—his natal family in Devon and, in Oxford, his two wives, and his nine children, only two of whom survived him. Caught up in the conflicts of the time, two of his sons were casualties of the Civil War. He was hardly less firmly attached to his native county, from one of whose gentry families came his second wife. An 'Anglo-Devonian', as he once styled himself, in his allegiance he exemplified those strong bonds of locality which were so marked a feature of early seventeenth-century society. He did not always cut a sympathetic figure.

Both as a theologian and as a powerful man within the university, five times vice-chancellor, he could be irascible, domineering, and a bully to his juniors. Yet if some of his traits were unattractive, he was also, and contrastingly, a man of real humanity whose biography is almost as much a study in character as an essay in religious and political history.

Given the interest of Prideaux's life and career, it remains surprising that a biography has not previously been attempted, either in Prideaux's own day or more recently. The two best lives, no more than brief ones, are by men of the next generation: Anthony Wood, the great memorialist of seventeenth-century Oxford, and John Prince, a Devonshire clergyman with a personal interest in his subject. Wood's account is particularly valuable for what he has to say about Prideaux's college activities: his skill in governing, his care in selecting tutors, his nurturing of foreign scholars at Exeter, and his general enhancement of his College's place in the university. In more modern times Prideaux has, of course, entered into general accounts of the period, though not perhaps to the extent that might have been expected. Anthony Milton's book *Catholic and Reformed* is the exception in the attention which it gives to Prideaux's theological attitudes and ideas. But the lack of a general biography has remained.

This is the gap which the present book attempts to fill. It does so in the first place by providing a narrative account of Prideaux's life, with a special concentration on one of its main themes: Prideaux's relations with allies and opponents within the Church of England, and especially with the supposedly Romanizing Arminians and their leader, Archbishop Laud. Between traditionalists and Arminians there was a real ideological conflict, to whose explication Prideaux's biography can contribute. It also attempts to expound and explain Prideaux's complex theology, though this is a subject on which more remains to be said. Finally, and following the lead set by Wood, it explores in some detail Prideaux's management of his College, his relations with fellows and undergraduates, and the qualities which made him a successful head. Here, for the first time, the college archives have been drawn on to supplement other more familiar sources. The archival documents compiled by Prideaux himself and in his own hand, notably his memorandum book, his survey of the college buildings and their contents, and his correspondence with potential benefactors, supply a particularly sharp insight into some of his leading qualities and concerns. For all Prideaux's primary concern with Calvinistic theology and its implications, until his promotion to a bishopric in 1641 the College was the stabilizing background to all that he did, and its management a central and time-consuming task which helped to make his reputation. No biography should allow the regius professor of divinity to edge out the rector of Exeter.

In writing this book I have been fortunate enough to have been able to draw on advice, information, and general help from many friends and colleagues: from Simon Bailey, Penny Baker, Joanna Bowring, Mary Clapinson, Robin Darwall-Smith, Kenneth Fincham, Stephen Hampton, Andrew Hegarty, Anne Hudson, Anthony Milton, David Morrison, David Pearson, Chris Penny, William Poole, Michael Reeve, Paul Slack, and Robert Witts. Two scholars deserve a special mention and special thanks. John Blair prepared the beautiful plan of Exeter College which appears on page 124; while Moti Feingold, the general editor of the series in which this book appears, read the whole text, commented on it, and offered words of encouragement and sometimes, most helpfully, of correction. He also suggested the book's title. To all of these I owe a large debt of gratitude. Any mistakes are, of course, my own responsibility.

To Hilary, as always, I owe more than I can say.

For kind permission to publish photographs and other material I am greatly indebted to the following:

To the Rector and Scholars of Exeter College, Oxford, for the reproductions of the portraits of John Prideaux and George Hakewill and of Joseph Nash's painting of the old college chapel. Copyright remains with the College.

To Martin Stuchfield of the Monumental Brass Society for the reproduction of the Prideaux brass in Harford church, reproduced from *The Monumental Brasses of Devonshire*, by William Lack, H. Martin Stuchfield, and Philip Whittemore. Copyright remains with the Society.

To the Trustees of the British Museum for the reproduction of Claude Warin's medal depicting Prideaux. Copyright remains with the Trustees.

A final word of thanks should go to those at OUP who have seen this book through the press; in particular, to Cathryn Steele, commissioning editor, and Vaishnavi Subramanyam, production editor. Their efficiency, helpfulness, and willingness to accommodate an author unversed and unskilled in the latest techniques of modern book production has greatly eased an otherwise arduous process. I owe them much.

John Maddicott

Contents

III. EVENTS, 1624–50

List of Illustrations

Abbreviations

BL	British Library
BLR	*Bodleian Library Record*
Boase, *Commoners*	C. W. Boase, *Registrum Collegii Exonienis*. Pars II: *An Alphabetical Register of the Commoners of Exeter College, Oxford* (Oxford, 1894)
Boase, *Register*	C. W. Boase, *Registrum Collegii Exonienis: Register of the Rector, Fellows and other Members on the Foundation of Exeter College, Oxford*, new edn (OHS, 27, 1894)
Bodl.	Bodleian Library
Butcher, 'Dr John Prideaux'	A. V. Butcher, 'Dr John Prideaux (1578–1650)'
CCEd	Clergy of the Church of England Database
CJ	House of Commons Journals
Clark, *Register*	A. Clark (ed.), *Register of the University of Oxford.* Vol. II: *1571–1622*, 4 parts (OHS, 10–14, 1887–9)
CS	*Certaine Sermons Preached by John Prideaux* (Oxford, 1637)
CSPD	*Calendar of State Papers, Domestic*
DHC	Devon Heritage Centre, Exeter
ECA	Exeter College Archives
ECL	Exeter College Library
EHR	*English Historical Review*
ESC	K. Fincham (ed.), *The Early Stuart Church, 1603–1642* (Basingstoke, 1893)
Gadd (ed.), *OUP*	I. Gadd (ed.), *The History of Oxford University Press.* Vol. I: *Beginnings to 1780* (Oxford, 2013)
Gardiner, *History*	S. R. Gardiner, *History of England from the Accession of James I to the Outbreak of the Civil War, 1603–1642*, 10 vols. (London, 1883–4)
Hegarty, 'Prideaux'	A. J. Hegarty, ' Prideaux, John (1578–1650), bishop of Worcester', *Oxford Dictionary of National Biography*

Heylin, *Cyprianus Anglicus*	P. Heylin, *Cyprianus Anglicus, or, The History of the Life and Death of the Most Reverend and Renowned Prelate William, by Divine Providence Lord Archbishop of Canterbury* (London, 1668)
Hist. Parl., 1558–1603	P. W. Hasler, *The History of Parliament: The House of Commons, 1558–1603*, 3 vols. (London, 1981)
Hist. Parl., 1604–1629	A. Thrush and J. P. Ferris (eds.), *The History of Parliament: The House of Commons, 1604–1629*, 6 vols. (Cambridge, 2010)
HMC	Historical Manuscripts Commission
HUO, iii	*The History of the University of Oxford*. Vol. III: *The Collegiate University*, ed. J. McConica (Oxford, 1986)
HUO, iv	*The History of the University of Oxford*. Vol. IV: *Seventeenth-Century Oxford*, ed. N. Tyacke (Oxford, 1997)
LJ	*House of Lords Journals*
Madan	F. Madan, *Oxford Books: A Bibliography of Printed Works Relating to the University and City of Oxford or Printed and Published There*, 3 vols. (Oxford, 1895–1931)
Maddicott, *Founders*	J. Maddicott, *Founders and Fellowship: The Early History of Exeter College, Oxford* (Oxford, 2014)
NUL	Nottingham University Library
ODCC	*The Oxford Dictionary of the Christian Church*, ed. F. L. Cross and E. A. Livingstone, 3rd edn, revised (Oxford, 2005)
ODNB	*Oxford Dictionary of National Biography*
OHA	*The Oxford History of Anglicanism*. Vol. I: *Reformation and Identity, c. 1520–1662*, ed. A. Milton (Oxford, 2017)
OHS	Oxford Historical Society
OUA	Oxford University Archives
Statutes	*The Statutes of Exeter College, Oxford* (London, 1854)
SUL	Sheffield University Library
TNA	The National Archives
Ussher, *Correspondence*	*The Correspondence of James Ussher, 1600–1656*, ed. E. Boran, 3 vols. (Dublin, 2015)

VDL	J. Prideaux, *Viginti-duae Lectiones de totidem religionis capitibus praecipue hoc tempore controversis* (Oxford, 1648)
WCL	Worcester Cathedral Library
WHS	Worcestershire Historical Society
Wood, *Athenae*	A. Wood, *Athenae Oxonienses*, 3rd edn, ed. P. Bliss, 4 vols. (London, 1813–20)
Wood, *Colleges*	A. Wood, *The History and Antiquities of the Colleges and Halls in the University of Oxford*, ed. J. Gutch, 2 vols. (Oxford, 1786–90)
Wood, *Fasti*	*The Fasti*, in Wood, *Athenae*, Vols. 2 and 4.
Wood, *History*	A. Wood, *The History and Antiquities of the University of Oxford now first published in English by John Gutch*, 3 vols. (Oxford, 1792–6).
Wood, *Life and Times*	A. Clark, *The Life and Times of Anthony Wood, Antiquary, of Oxford, 1632–1695, described by himself*, 5 vols. (OHS, 19, 21, 26, 30, 40, 1891–1900)
Works of Laud	*The Works of the Most Reverend Father in God William Laud, sometime Lord Archbishop of Canterbury*, ed. W. Scott and J. Bliss, 7 vols. (Oxford, 1847–60)

Notes

In quotations from contemporary sources, manuscript and printed, the original spelling has been retained, but capitalization and punctuation have been modernized.

All books are published in London unless otherwise stated.

PART I

Events, 1578–1624

I

Climbing the Ladder, 1578–1612

1. Home, 1578–96

The precise birthdates of ordinary men and women are rarely recorded in the sixteenth century, but here, as in many other ways, John Prideaux was unusual. We know that he was born on 17 September 1578 at Stowford, a township in the parish of Harford in South Devon: facts set down on the Latin inscription which Prideaux himself drafted for the brass lying above his grave in the parish church of Bredon in Worcestershire, where he was buried in 1650.[1] The Bredon memorial was a tribute to his later fame. Some of the reasons for that fame he provided almost incidentally in another memorial which he erected in the church at Harford in 1639 to honour his deceased parents. There he described himself as 'Doctor of Divinity and the King's Majesties Professor thereof in the University of Oxford, Rector of Exeter College Oxford, and Chaplaine to Prince Henry, King James the First and King Charles the First'.[2] A few years later, from 1641, he would have been able to add 'Bishop of Worcester' to this tally of achievements.

Both these memorials tell us a little more about Prideaux's family background. Noting his birth, Prideaux on his Bredon memorial describes Stowford as 'an obscure village (*pagus obscurus*)', and his parents as '*ingenui*', meaning something like 'freeborn', 'honest' and 'upright', and implying that although they had no pretensions to gentility, they were by no means among the unregarded rural poor. On the Harford memorial, he names

---

1. J. Prince, *Danmonii Orientales Illustres, or The Worthies of Devon*, new edn (1810), 661; Wood, *Athenae*, iii. 265, 269; below, 375–6.
2. The brass is reproduced in W. Lack, H. M. Stuchfield, and P. Whitemore, *The Monumental Brasses of Devonshire* (London, 2000), 156, and shown below, Figure 4, 165.

Between Scholarship and Church Politics: The Lives of John Prideaux, 1578–1650. John Maddicott, Oxford University Press. © John Maddicott 2022. DOI: 10.1093/oso/9780192896100.003.0001

them as John and Agnes, parents of seven sons and three daughters, among whom our John Prideaux was the fourth son. John Prideaux senior would probably have described himself as a yeoman, one of the many moderately prosperous farmers below the level of the gentry who populated the countryside of Elizabethan England. He had a small farm of some 60 acres, mainly meadow and pasture, and worth about £30 a year by the end of the seventeenth century. Harford lay on the southern edge of Dartmoor, and Stowford in the south of the parish, towards the county's coastal fringe; and it is likely that John Prideaux's livelihood was bolstered by the grazing rights on Dartmoor which the farmers of such moorside parishes customarily enjoyed. He held his lands on lease from the major landholders in Stowford, Thomas Williams and his sons. Williams, who died in 1566, was a person of consequence, several times MP for West Country towns, and speaker for the Commons in the parliament of 1563.[3] Indications of their tenant's relative prosperity come from the subsidy assessment of 1581, which places John Prideaux third equal among the eight parishioners assessed on their goods, and from the will of John Prideaux's widow Agnes, drafted in 1620, which mentions monetary bequests amounting to £7 10s., two silver cups, two great brass pans, a great brass crock, and a chestful of linen.[4] All the evidence goes to suggest that the Prideaux family enjoyed a respectable living.

About the young Prideaux's early years, before he reached Oxford, we know a surprising amount, and more than is known about the upbringing of most future heads of Oxford colleges. It derives almost entirely from a single source: John Prince's great biographical work, *The Worthies of Devon*, first published in 1701. Prince (1643–1723), an Oxford graduate and a Devonshire parish priest, had a particular interest in Prideaux and gave him one of the longest entries among his 'worthies'. That interest, and Prince's close knowledge of Prideaux, probably stemmed from his family connections with those in his subject's circle. Prince married Gertrude Salter, niece of another Devonian, Baldwin Acland, who had been a fellow of Exeter from 1626 to 1652, an exceptionally long period and most of it falling within Prideaux's rectorship. Acland was another of Prince's 'worthies'; and since Prince came to know him well during Acland's later years, he quite possibly

3. R. M. Prideaux, *Prideaux: A Westcountry Clan* (Chichester, 1989), 62–3, 116–17; L. Ryan, *An Obscure Place: A History of Stowford in the Parish of Harford, Devon* (privately printed, Stowford Court, 1973), 23–6, 28–9, 35–7; Prince, *Worthies*, 654.
4. *Devon Taxes, 1581–1660*, ed. T. L. Stoate (Almondsbury, 1988), 57; Prideaux, *Prideaux*, 116.

drew on Prideaux's table talk, transmitted via Acland, for his knowledge of Prideaux's early life. A second link was provided by Gertrude Salter's father, Anthony Salter, born in Exeter city and an Exeter College student from 1617 to 1624, again under Prideaux. These possible informants may have stimulated Prince's curiosity about Prideaux. At any rate he was sufficiently interested in Prideaux's background to pay a visit to Stowford, where he found the family house 'a decent dwelling, healthfully situated': a further pointer to Prideaux's sturdy yeoman origins.[5]

Brief but circumstantial, Prince's account of Prideaux's boyhood has some important bearings on his later career. His parents, says Prince, saw that he was taught to read and write. While he was growing up, and presumably in his teens, the parish clerkship in the neighbouring parish of Ugborough became vacant. Young John had a good voice and came forward for the post, but he had a rival, and in a psalm-singing contest with his competitor Prideaux lost, 'to his very great grief and trouble'. Later in life, in high office, 'he would frequently make this reflection, saying "If I could have been clerk of Ugborow, I had never been bishop of Worcester."' But after this setback he was rescued by 'a good gentlewoman of the parish', identified by Prince as the mother of Sir Edmund Fowell, who took pity on him and, 'seeing him to be a bookish youth', kept him at school until he had learnt Latin and so provided him with the education which he needed if he was to go forward to Oxford.[6]

This rings true. The Ugborough story may well have come to Prince from Acland. But more securely rooted are the identity and family of Prideaux's benefactor, the 'good gentlewoman' who was Sir Edmund Fowell's mother and whose opportune intervention gave him his start in life. The Fowells of Fowlescombe were the leading gentry family in Ugborough. Sir Edmund Fowell, born in 1593, would later become MP for Ashburton in the Long Parliament, and it was very probably at Ashburton grammar school, well regarded in the county and only about ten miles from Ugborough, that Prideaux was a pupil. Edmund Fowell's mother, Mary, who was responsible for his schooling and to whom he owed so much, was the daughter of Richard Reynell of East Ogwell, member of another leading county family, and had been married since 1574 to Arthur Fowell,

5. Prince, *Worthies*, 7–8, 654; Boase, *Register*, 100–1; Boase, *Commoners*, 284; I. Maxted, ' Prince, John (1643–1723), Church of England clergyman and author', *ODNB*.
6. Prince, *Worthies*, 654.

Edmund's father, while Mary's niece, another Mary, daughter of her brother Sir Thomas Reynell, was to become Prideaux's second wife in 1628.[7] Almost from the start Prideaux was adventitiously entangled with a family, the Reynells, which, as we shall see, was to play a large part in the web of Devonshire connections he cultivated throughout his life.

Mary Fowell's generosity had a sequel. In 1606, after Arthur Fowell's death, his widow went on to marry Edmund Prideaux of Netherton, another leading Devonshire landowner, and it was to these two that Prideaux dedicated his first substantial publication, his *Eight Sermons* of 1621. Alluding to 'the many kindnesses I have heretofore received from you both', the dedication names Edmund as 'my very worthy kinsman' (though the family connection is impossible to substantiate) and Mary as 'his vertuous and religious wife'.[8] The dedication was some small recognition of a large debt. But equally large, though of a different kind, was the debt which he owed to his parents. Besides what Prince has to say, the only other insight into Prideaux's upbringing comes from his *Euchologia*, a devotional treatise which he wrote for his two surviving daughters at the very end of his life in the late 1640s. He concludes his book with a moral and a reminiscence of a kind rare at any point in his writings. Citing in full the Collect for the fourth Sunday after Epiphany, 'which especially sorts with the times wherein we live' (the disastrous years after the Civil War), he told his daughters that 'the collect was commended unto me by your grandfather John Prideaux, my dear father, when I was a boy, in the time of a plague'. Evidently, and as we might assume, Prideaux came from a soundly Protestant family and one intimately familiar with the Book of Common Prayer. His early education in his country's religion must have been one reason for his devotion and gratitude to his parents, visible in their Harford memorial and shown too in Prince's account of the regular and sometimes unannounced visits which he paid them from Oxford.[9] With his humble origins he never lost touch.

---

7. J. L. Vivian, *The Visitations of the County of Devon* (Exeter, 1895), 370, 643; W. G. Hoskins, *Devon* (1954), 508–9; W. S. Graf, *Ashburton Grammar School, 1314–1938* (Ashburton [1939]), 4–7; N. Orme, *Education in the West of England, 1066–1548* (Exeter, 1976), 111–12; Hegarty, 'Prideaux'. For Prideaux and the Reynells, see below, 161–4.

8. Vivian, *Visitations*, 370, 621; Prideaux, *Prideaux*, 110; J. Prideaux, *Eight Sermon, preached by John Prideaux, Doctor of Divinity, Regius Professor, Vice-Chancellor of the University of Oxford and Rector of Exeter Colledge* (1621), sig. A2. Note the flourish of titles. Was this intended to show Mary Prideaux how far, with her initial help, he had gone?

9. J. Prideaux, *Euchologia: or, The Doctrine of Practical Praying* (1655), 303–5; below, 368–9.

Prideaux left home for Oxford in 1596, walking all the way. His destination was Exeter College. When he was bishop of Worcester, by now an elderly man, he still kept in his wardrobe, alongside his bishop's vestments, the leather breeches which he had worn on the journey, sometimes showing them to undergraduates 'for their encouragement in studying'. The story was a famous one, used by at least one author to demonstrate Prideaux's humility.[10] But it also testified to the reverse: a justifiable pride in his ascent from the Devonshire yeomanry to a place in the highest ranks of the church.

2. Rector Holland's Exeter

In the twenty years prior to Prideaux's arrival in 1596 his new College had been transformed. Formerly a Catholic redoubt, relatively impoverished, and governed by archaic statutes unchanged since the College's foundation in the early fourteenth century, Exeter had become a Protestant stronghold, its fellowship enlarged, its endowment strengthened, and its constitution rewritten. The agent of change here, in part an unwitting one, was Sir William Petre, lawyer, diplomat, counsellor to four Tudor monarchs, and covert Catholic. Between 1566 and 1568 he established eight new fellowships, provided the means to support them, and drafted a new set of statutes, virtually refounding the College. His intention was seemingly to strengthen Exeter's position as a Catholic base and a future training ground for the Roman priesthood. But in fact his actions had the opposite effect. Within a few years of his death in 1572 they had provoked the intervention of Queen Elizabeth's government, fearful, here as elsewhere, of a resurgent Catholicism which seemed to threaten both the throne and the Protestant Reformation. The result was the appointment, effectively by the Crown, of two new College heads, both soundly Protestant—Thomas Glasier, rector from 1578 to 1592, and Thomas Holland, 1592–1612. Under their leadership Exeter became as strongly committed to the Church of England as, twenty years earlier, it had been committedly Catholic.[11]

10. D. Lloyd, *Memoires of the Lives, Actions, Sufferings and Deaths of those Noble, Reverend and Excellent Personages that suffered by Death, Sequestration, Decimation or otherwise for the Protestant Religion* (1668), 536; W. Turner, *A Compleat History of the most Remarkable Providences both of Judgement and Mercy which have hapned in this Present Age*, 2 vols. (1697), i. 138; Prince, *Worthies*, 658.
11. Maddicott, *Founders*, 255–322.

In this process Rector Holland was much the more significant of the two. Holland was a theologian of the first rank, at a time when post-Reformation disputes, factional divisions within the English church, the continuing challenge posed by Catholicism, and religious wars on the Continent all gave theological learning a polemical and practical value in the affairs of church and state. He was rated highly enough to be named in 1624 by Joseph Hall, the future bishop of Exeter, as one of the twenty 'great lights' of the church, along with such other Anglican luminaries as Jewel and Hooker.[12] Appointed regius professor of divinity in 1589, over the head of the still more learned John Rainolds, fellow of Corpus Christi College, who had been the university's choice (but not the queen's), Holland effectively became the university's senior theologian, holding the post until his death in 1612.[13] Unlike Prideaux, himself regius professor from 1615, Holland wrote and published little, and his reputation was founded mainly on his scriptural learning and on his complementary skills as a linguist. These two qualities account for his membership of the team set up in 1604 to prepare what became the Authorized Version of the Bible. His co-translator and neighbour, Richard Kilbye, rector of Lincoln College, spoke of him in his funeral sermon as 'an Apollos, mighty in the Scriptures . . . familiarly conversant with the fathers', and the reincarnation of Jerome and Augustine. More than any other single figure, he established his College's reputation not only as a bastion of the Protestant establishment but as a centre of learning.[14]

Holland's Protestantism stood four-square with the accepted doctrines of the contemporary Church of England. This was especially true of his, and its, adherence to the seemingly harsh tenets of Calvinism. Under Queen Elizabeth and to a large extent under her successor, James I, the Church of England was predominantly a Calvinist body, its senior members, and many of their subordinates too, holding beliefs which derived from Calvin and other sixteenth-century Protestant reformers and ultimately from Augustine.[15] They were beliefs to which Prideaux may have been introduced in his

12. P. Collinson, *The Religion of Protestants* (Oxford, 1982), 92 n. 1.
13. M. Feingold, 'Rainolds [Reynolds], John (1549–1607), theologian and college head', *ODNB*.
14. J. A. Löwe, 'Holland, Thomas (d.1612), theologian', *ODNB*; V. Westbrook, 'Authorized Version of the Bible, translators of (*act.*1604–1611)', *ODNB*; R. Kilbye, *A Sermon Preached in Saint Maries Church in Oxford March 26. 1612 at the Funerall of Thomas Holland* (Oxford, 1613), 15–16.
15. For this paragraph, see esp. N. Tyacke, *Anti-Calvinists: The Rise of English Arminianism, c.1590–1640*, new paperback edn (Oxford, 1990), 1–4; Collinson, *Religion of Protestants*, 81–2; K. Fincham, 'Introduction', in *ESC*, 4–6.

home parish at Harford, but which he would more certainly have absorbed in his undergraduate years at Exeter from 1596 onwards; and they were grounded on the doctrine of predestination. As a result of the Fall all men were sinners; but it was God's merciful will that some, the elect, should be saved and that others, the reprobate, should be eternally damned. The elect would know and declare themselves by their virtuous lives and Christian conduct: these were the marks of their salvation. Yet even if they fell away into sin and unrighteousness, they remained predestined to salvation, the continuing beneficiaries of God's grace. This doctrine of perseverance, as it was called, was 'the coping stone of Calvinist predestinarian teaching'.[16] Grace was thus bestowed selectively and reserved for the elect, for whom alone Christ had died, though an alternative and slightly more liberal doctrine, that of 'hypothetical universalism', held that in theory Christ had died for all. It was only through the bestowal of grace that free will became possible. As for the reprobate, nothing that they were able to do could alter their fate. Salvation was not to be won by good works, without the assistance of grace—the heresy of Pelagius. Rather, it was wholly dependent on God's will.

These uncompromising beliefs were held by almost all members of the church's governing hierarchy, Calvinists almost to a man.[17] The episcopate from George Abbot, archbishop of Canterbury (1611–33) downwards was very largely Calvinist; so were Prideaux's three predecessors in the regius chair, Robert Abbot, the archbishop's brother, Thomas Holland, and Laurence Humfrey, holder of the chair from 1560 to 1589; and so too were the heads of most Oxford and Cambridge colleges. Under Humfrey, Calvinism had come to dominate Oxford teaching,[18] and this it continued to do. Through the education of a graduate clergy in the university, now more numerous than at any previous time, the means existed to spread these

16. N. Tyacke, 'Archbishop Laud', in his *Aspects of English Protestantism, c.1580–1700* (Manchester, 2001), 213. Cf. P. G. Lake, 'Calvinism and the English Church, 1570–1635', *Past and Present*, 114 (1987), 40–1.

17. R. Muller, *Post-Reformation Reformed Dogmatics*, 2nd edn, 4 vols. (Grand Rapids, MI, 2003), i. 30–1, followed by S. Hampton, *Anti-Arminians: The Anglican Reformed Tradition from Charles II to George I* (Oxford, 2008), 6–8, argues for substituting the term 'Reformed' for 'Calvinist', largely on the grounds that 'Calvinists' by no means derived all their views from Calvin. While we may admit this, 'Calvinist' has the weight of historiographical tradition and convention behind it and will be used throughout what follows. Muller had been partly anticipated by A. Milton, *Catholic and Reformed* (Cambridge, 1997), 407–9.

18. *HUO*, iv. 7.

doctrines into cathedral chapters and parishes.[19] The pulpit was the means to their propagation, and the Calvinist hierarchy, evangelical in outlook, placed a particular emphasis on sermons as a means of spreading the faith. Preaching was particularly directed against *papismus*, popery. That the pope was the Antichrist of the Apocalypse was a commonplace of Anglican-Calvinist discourse, and one complemented by the denunciation of Catholic paraphernalia and superstitions: images, relics, the cult of the Virgin, and the invocation of saints. But Rome was seen as more than a doctrinal rival and a source of false religion. After the Armada of 1588 and, to look ahead, the Gunpowder Plot of 1605, the assassination of Henri IV of France in 1610, the outbreak of religious wars on the Continent in 1618, and the papacy's continuing claim to superiority over secular rulers, it was also regarded as a dangerous national enemy.

With another largely Anglican grouping, the puritans, Calvinists shared much common ground, notably a fierce anti-Catholicism and a belief in predestination and in the gift of God's grace to the elect alone. But they were not 'terms convertible' (to quote Peter Heylyn, Laud's biographer), for while all puritans were Calvinist, not all Calvinists were puritans.[20] What separated the godly, as the puritans called themselves, from middle-of-the-road Calvinist Anglicans was largely a matter of degree. Puritans urged the need for further reform of the church; they were opposed to ceremonies and to what they viewed as the popish elements in conventional Anglican practice, such as the wearing of the surplice; they were strict sabbatarians, wanting to reserve Sundays exclusively for religion rather than recreation; and they encouraged a personal piety which placed an exceptional emphasis on the spiritual benefits to be derived from preaching and sermons. To their opponents many of these traits smacked of killjoy hypocrisy. A small minority, the radical puritans, diverged more sharply from Anglican orthodoxy by challenging the notion of hierarchy within church government, discounting the need for bishops, and substituting instead the Presbyterian ideal of government by local ministers and congregations. It was this aspect of puritanism which was seen as the greatest threat to the established order

---

19. Collinson, *Religion of Protestants*, 94–5; below, 45–6, 207–8.
20. Heylyn, *Cyprianus Anglicus*,124. Cf. H. Trevor-Roper, 'Laudianism and Political Power', in his *Catholics, Anglicans and Puritans: Seventeenth Century Essays* (1987), 44; Tyacke, 'Archbishop Laud', 67; Milton, *Catholic and Reformed*, 26. For what follows, see P. Collinson, *The Elizabethan Puritan Movement* (Oxford, 1990), 103–6, 448–67; Fincham, 'Introduction', in *ESC*, 7–8; and Milton, *Catholic and Reformed*, 12–13, 22–3, 36, 45–7, 78.

and in particular to the Crown: 'No bishop, no king', as James I had famously said at the Hampton Court conference of 1604. But most puritans tolerated the existence of bishops, even though their presence was what most clearly separated the Church of England from the reformed churches of the Continent. In general they remained within the Anglican fold, held together with the orthodox by the Calvinism which was 'the theological cement of the Jacobean Church'.[21]

Potentially more subversive of Calvinist orthodoxy was another set of theological ideas and their corresponding religious practices. This came to be known as Arminianism, so called from the teaching and writings of the Dutch theologian Jacob Arminius (1560–1609). Although English scholars and divines were unfamiliar with Arminius's view before about 1610,[22] much of what was later recognized as Arminian had been anticipated from the 1590s onwards, mainly in the writings and sermons of Richard Hooker and Lancelot Andrewes. Their *avant la lettre* Arminianism broke with the dominant mode of Calvinist churchmanship on some crucial points.[23] Andrewes in particular, dean of Westminster from 1601, then successively bishop of Ely, Chichester, and Winchester before his death in 1626, has a strong claim to be regarded as the morning star of Arminianism. He saw both the sacraments and prayer as providing a more assured entry than preaching into the Christian life; he emphasized the value of Holy Communion as a means of access to God's grace, which was freely available to all and not merely to the elect; he questioned the Calvinist doctrines of predestination and perseverance as things unknowable; he attached a high value to reverence and ceremonial observances in matters of worship; and he detested puritanism, which he saw as a threat to order and a potentially subversive force in church and state. In most of these ways he anticipated the views of William Laud and the direction in which Laud attempted to lead the church in the 1630s. But it has to be stressed that Andrewes's beliefs and values remained those of a very small minority in the English church. Before the mid-1620s they barely encroached on the sovereignty of Calvinism.

21. Collinson, *Religion of Protestants*, 82.
22. Tyacke, *Anti-Calvinists*, 38, 65–6; *HUO*, iv. 578.
23. For what follows, see especially P. Lake, 'Lancelot Andrewes, John Buckeridge, and Avant-Garde Conformity at the Court of James I', in L. Levy Peck (ed.), *The Mental World of the Jacobean Court* (Cambridge, 1991), 113–33; and P. McCullough, '"Avant-Garde Conformity" in the 1590s', in *OHA*, 380–93.

At Oxford Arminianism had its proto-adherents, but they were few.[24] One such was John Howson, canon of Christ Church and vice-chancellor in 1602–3, whose heterodox preaching, defence of ceremony, and relaxed attitude to popery got him into trouble with the university authorities on several occasions. Another was John Buckeridge, Laud's tutor at St John's College in the 1590s, his predecessor as the college's president from 1606 to 1610, a man with 'an exalted view of the sacraments', and the theological ally of Lancelot Andrewes. Laud himself was marked out as a possible papist sympathizer from 1606, if not earlier, though at this stage he still adhered to the Calvinist doctrines of predestination and perseverance.[25] These three did not form a coherent group, nor at this stage did they do much to dent the university's four-square Calvinism. But their opinions and the opprobrium which those opinions attracted showed that other standpoints were becoming possible.

Holland would have had no sympathy with the incipient Arminianism which was beginning to appear in Oxford by the time of his death. As chaplain to the fiercely Protestant, even puritanical Robert Dudley, earl of Leicester, from 1585 to 1589, Holland had been at the heart of the Calvinist establishment, and his Calvinist convictions were unwavering. In his one published sermon he laid stress on the value of preaching, especially when fortified by theological scholarship, and justified the observance of the Sabbath, while he also recognized that the validity of the overseas Protestant churches was not impugned by their lacking bishops (a point which on one occasion put him at odds with the young William Laud).[26] To that extent he was an internationalist, judging all the reformed churches by the common ground on which they stood: a line that Prideaux was also to follow.[27] But most characteristic of Holland's churchmanship was the fierce anti-Catholicism found throughout the Anglican establishment. His customary farewell to the fellows of Exeter when embarking on a journey was to say 'I

---

24. *HUO*, iv. 576–8.
25. N. W. S. Cranfield, 'Howson, John (1556/7–1632), bishop of Durham', *ODNB*; 'John Howson's Answers to Archbishop Abbot's Accusations at his "Trial" before James I at Greenwich, 10 June 1615', ed. N. Cranfield and K. Fincham, in *Camden Miscellany*, 29 (Camden 4th ser., 34, 1987), 320–41; P. E. McCullough, 'Buckeridge, John (d.1631), bishop of Ely', *ODNB*; A. Milton, 'Laud, William (1573–1645), archbishop of Canterbury', *ODNB*.
26. C. M. Dent, *Protestant Reformers in Elizabethan Oxford* (Oxford, 1983), 207–8. The clash with Laud came during Laud's defence of his BD theses in 1604: see Heylin, *Cyprianus Anglicus*, 54.
27. Below, 276–7.

commend you to the love of God and to the hatred of all popery and superstition.'[28]

Prideaux's religious convictions may have been born in Devon, but they were given substance by his early years at Exeter, first as an undergraduate and then as a young fellow and tutor. The religious milieu of Holland's Exeter was vital to his intellectual and moral development. As an undergraduate, he would have been regularly exposed to the doctrines put across in the various Latin and Greek catechisms which since 1579 had been a compulsory feature of the religious instruction given in colleges and halls and in the wider university: part of the government's attempts to ensure Protestant conformity in the face of the Catholic threat. Exeter, like other colleges, had a catechist, elected annually from among the fellows, and the catechisms compiled by Alexander Nowell and by Calvin himself, with their emphasis on scripture, election, and predestination, together with the more popular Heidelberg Catechism, may have helped to mould the pattern of Prideaux's mature theology. He would have been familiar too with the catechism attached to the Genevan Bible, which embodied the core of predestinarian beliefs.[29] But his own future brand of evangelical Calvinism, combined with denunciation of Catholicism and the papacy, owed as much to Holland as to any catechism. He was by no means the only man of subsequent eminence to have been heavily influenced by this seminal College figure. Kilbye spoke of Holland as 'a father of many sons, by scholastical creation of them in the highest degrees of learning', including 'a great part of the reverend bishops of the land'.[30] It is no surprise that the two whom he names, George Abbot, archbishop of Canterbury, 1611–33, and John King, bishop of London, 1611–21, were both evangelical Calvinists and stridently anti-Catholic.

The embryonic distinction of the Exeter fellowship under Holland points in the same direction. One crude measure of that distinction is the appearance in the *Oxford Dictionary of National Biography* of eight men elected to fellowships during Holland's rectorship. Most of the eight gained their reputations as high-ranking churchmen, scholars, and preachers. They

---

28. Kilbie, *A Sermon*, 18.
29. Clark, *Register*, i. 155–6; Dent, *Protestant Reformers*, 87–92, 185–8; A. Milton, 'The Church of England and the Palatinate, 1566–1642', in P. Ha and P. Collinson (eds.), *The Reception of Continental Reformation in Britain* (Oxford, 2010), 139–42; Boase, *Register*, xciii n. 1; Tyacke, *Anti-Calvinists*, 2–3
30. Kilbie, *A Sermon*, 16.

included Thomas Winniffe (fellow, 1595–1609), later dean of Gloucester, John Donne's successor as dean of St Paul's, and bishop of Lincoln;[31] George Hakewill (1596–1611), one of the cleverest, most learned, and most influential intellectuals and writers of early seventeenth-century Oxford, and Prideaux's successor as rector in 1642;[32] and Anthony Lapthorne (1593–1600) and Richard Carpenter (1596–1606), both of them to become famous for their godly preaching.[33] Some made their names in different ways. Degory Wheare (1602–8) was William Camden's choice as his first professor of history in 1622 and was later nominated as principal of Gloucester Hall,[34] while Simon Baskerville (1595–1609) and Robert Vilvaine (1599–1611) became eminent medical men.[35] Other fellows, not public figures but central to the College's work, left a less durable mark. One leading figure here was William Helme, fellow for twenty-eight years from 1587 to 1615, dean of the College from 1595 to 1598 and again in 1600–1, and sub-rector—under the Petrean statutes the rector's second in command— from 1601 to 1611.[36] As dean at the time of Prideaux's arrival, he was in effect the general director of studies. But he was also Prideaux's own tutor and one on whom his pupil looked back with gratitude and affection: 'my faithfull and deserving tutor, ever with thankfulnesse of me to be remembered'. Like many other tutors since, Helme wrote nothing and was unknown outside his College, but, again like other tutors, he was a pillar of his small society and an enduring influence on those who knew him.[37]

Like the fellowship, the undergraduate body under Holland contained men who would later make their mark on English society, and particularly on the church.[38] Edward Chetwynd (matriculated, 1592; DD, 1616) later became dean of Bristol and 'a pillar of the evangelical revival in the West country'.[39] Daniel Price (BA, 1601; DD, 1613), another evangelical

---

31. A. F. Pollard, rev. P. E. McCullough, 'Winniffe, Thomas (bap.1576, d. 1654), bishop of Lincoln', *ODNB*.
32. P. E. McCullough, 'Hakewill, George (bap.1578, d.1649), Church of England clergyman and author', *ODNB*; below, 167–9.
33. K. Fincham, 'Lapthorne, Anthony (1572–1658/9), Church of England clergyman', *ODNB*; J. Benedict, 'Carpenter, Richard' (1575–1627), Church of England clergyman', *ODNB*.
34. J. H. M. Salmon, 'Wheare, Diagory [Degory] (1573–1627), historian', *ODNB*.
35. T. Cooper, rev. B. Nance, 'Baskerville, Sir Simon (bap. 1574, d. 1641), physician', *ODNB*. For Vilvaine, see Boase, *Register*, 88.
36. ECA, A.I.5 (College Register, 1539–1619), 177–239.
37. Boase, *Register*, 83; J. Prideaux, 'Epistle Dedicatory', in his *A Sermon Preached on the fifth of October 1624: at the Consecration of St James Chappel in Exeter Colledge* (Oxford, 1625).
38. Cf. Dent, *Protestant Reformers*, 178.
39. J. M. Rigg, rev. V. Larminie, 'Chetwynd, Edward (1576/7–1639), dean of Bristol', *ODNB*.

Calvinist, became dean of Hereford, while his brother Sampson Price (matric. 1602; DD, 1617) became chaplain to James I and a fierce opponent of both papists and puritans.[40] Nicholas Byfield (matric.1597) was another Calvinist preacher, with many publications, mainly biblical commentaries, to his name.[41] William Smyth (matric. 1599) became the third warden of Wadham College, succeeding another Exonian, John Fleming, fellow of Exeter from 1595 to 1613.[42] Of the undergraduates who embarked on secular careers, the two most conspicuous in later public life were William Noye (matric. 1593), Charles I's Attorney General, 1631–4, and, on the opposite political side, William Hakewill, George Hakewill's brother, who never matriculated but was at Exeter from c.1601 to 1603, and who went on to become one of the most prominent parliamentary and constitutional lawyers of the age.[43]

The rise of the College under Holland, as a cradle for the church and a training ground for preachers, scholars, and talents of all kinds, was recognized by Prideaux himself in a striking passage from the dedicatory letter to George Hakewill which prefaced his consecration sermon for the new chapel in 1624:[44]

> It was the honor of my eminent predecessour Dr Holland, His Majestie's Professor in Divinity, and father of so many bishops and doctors [and here he echoed Kilbye's funeral sermon], to be Rector here at that time when Dr Chetwind and Dr Dan. Price, now both deans, the one of Bristol, the other of Hereford, Dr Carpenter, Dr Fleming, Dr Winnyf, Dr Whetcomb,[45] Dr Standard,[46] Dr Sampson Price, besides Dr Baskerville and Dr Vilvayn, known to be worthy physicians, laid those grounds which, improved since, have attained that height the world now takes notice of.

40. P. E. McCullough, 'Price, Daniel (1581–1631), dean of Hereford', *ODNB*; N. W. S. Cranfield, 'Price, Sampson (1585/6–1630), Church of England clergyman and religious writer', *ODNB*.
41. B. W. Ball, 'Byfield, Nicholas (1578/9–1622), Church of England clergyman and religious writer', *ODNB*.
42. A. J. Hegarty, 'Smyth, William (1582–1658), college head', *ODNB*; Boase, *Register*, 86.
43. J. S. Hart Jr, 'Noy [Noye], William (1577–1634), lawyer and politician', *ODNB*; S. Doyle, 'Hakewill, William (bap.1574, d.1655), lawyer and politician', *ODNB*.
44. Prideaux, *A Sermon Preached*, sig. ¶4r.
45. John Whetcombe, fellow, 1602–10; DD, 1612; married Ann, Holland's daughter; holder of various livings in Dorset (Boase, *Register*, 90). Prideaux seems to have singled out for mention not only those who went on to high office in the church but also those awarded the doctorate in divinity.
46. John Standard, fellow, 1600–14; DD, 1617; JP; rector of Tackley, Oxon., and lord of a manor in Tackley (Boase, *Register*, 89).

Prideaux himself, a missing name but a member of the same generation, was to become the most eminent of the entire company. It was one united, not only by collegiate circumstance but by a vehement brand of evangelical and Protestant churchmanship which owed much to Holland's own beliefs and leadership and which Prideaux would continue to promote. By his own not entirely modest estimation his predecessor had provided the foundation for a college which had risen to even greater fame under his own leadership.

These were the College figures among whom Prideaux found himself in his early years at Exeter.

3. Undergraduate, graduate, fellow, 1596–1610

Prideaux arrived in Oxford in the summer of 1596, a popular time of the year for undergraduates to come into residence. He was one of twenty-five young men matriculating at Exeter in that year, sixteen of them from Devon, and fourteen from landed families. Noted in the university records as one of six 'sons of plebeians', Prideaux was among a small minority of the socially undistinguished when he matriculated on 14 October 1596.[47] Although the choice of Exeter as his College would have been an obvious one for any Devonian, it may also have owed something to the advice of his patron, Mary Fowell, two of whose nephews, Richard and Thomas Reynell, came up to Exeter in 1602.[48] Like all undergraduates, he embarked on the BA course, but, unlike many, he completed the degree, graduating in January 1600.[49] He then started on the MA course, which entailed a further three years of study. The BA demanded the mastering of Aristotelian logic and philosophy, together with grammar and rhetoric, and a supplementary humanistic study of some classical authors. In addition, by the early seventeenth century more informal instruction was offered in a range of subjects outside the statutory syllabus, including history, ancient and modern, and geography. The pupil's general progress was supervised by his tutor, in Prideaux's case William Helme, and proceeded partly by disputations, formal debates on set topics, and partly by attendance at lectures, both in

---

47. Clark, *Register*, ii. 212, 214–18.
48. Wood, *Athenae*, ii. 266; Boase, *Commoners*, 270; below, 162
49. Clark, *Register*, ii. 216, iii. 219; *HUO*, iv, 90.

College and from the university's professors and lecturers.[50] Students made notes (and many student notebooks survive) and occasionally submitted written work.[51]

Prideaux was poor. Rather than his plebeian status, a better indication of his poverty was his humble role as a poor scholar or servitor: technical terms defining an indigent undergraduate who largely paid his way through College by service, often service to a particular fellow or a wealthy undergraduate. In Prideaux's case we know that from the time of his arrival he acted as 'sub-promus', or under-butler, fetching and carrying food and drink in hall. It was not uncommon for those working for degrees, or even those already possessing them, to hold service posts of this sort: James Prideaux, a distant relative, was both an MA and also College butler when he made his will in 1626.[52] But it was not a comfortable way to finance one's studies. In his satirical 'Black Booke', the dramatist Thomas Middleton, as a young man a contemporary of Prideaux's at Queen's College, gives us a glimpse of the humiliations and deprivations which service might involve:

> Lastly, not least, I give and bequeath to thee, Pierce Penniless, exceeding poor scholar, that hath made clean shoes in both universities, and . . . full often heard with this lamentable cry at the butt'ry hatch: "Ho, Lancelot! A cue of bread and a cue of beer", never passing beyond the confines of a farthing nor once munching commons, but only upon gaudy days.[53]

Exposed though he may have been to lamentable cries at the buttery hatch, the impoverished Prideaux was also ambitious. Almost from the start of his College career he showed confidence in his abilities and a determination to do well. Within a few years of his arrival he had set his sights on the acquisition of a College fellowship which would give him security, a respectable income, and the opportunity to make his mark as a scholar. His aspirations in this direction were first made clear in a remarkable Latin letter which he wrote on 6 May 1600, within a few months of taking his BA, to Kenelm Carter, a former fellow of the College.[54] Presented to his fellowship by Sir William Petre, Carter was a devout Catholic, whose

---

50. *HUO*, iv. 211–448.

51. R. O'Day, *Education and Society, 1500–1800* (Harlow, 1982), 118.

52. Boase, *Register*, 89; ECA, L.III.10 (College History box).

53. Middleton, 'The Black Booke', in *Thomas Middleton: The Collected Works*, ed. G. Taylor and J. Lavagnino (Oxford, 2007), 218. A 'cue' is half a farthing.

54. This letter was originally published in the *Gentleman's Magazine*, 1836, part 1, 482, from an original then in the possession of George Oliver and now no longer extant. It was reprinted,

religious convictions had caused him to resign his College place in 1583, during the rectorship of the protestantizing Thomas Glasier, and to take up a post in the household of a more prominent Catholic, Sir John Petre, Sir William's son. There he acted as tutor to John Petre's son. Prideaux's purpose in approaching Carter, whom he seems to have known beforehand, was to ask him to use his influence with Sir John in order to help Prideaux to a fellowship. In deferential and almost abject terms, he wrote to tell Carter that a fellowship at the College was about to become vacant (and since fellowship numbers were strictly limited, a new fellow could be elected only when another had died or departed). Mr Anthony Lapthorne had married and secured a parish, and his place would shortly be filled. Since the College Register tells us that Lapthorne's marriage had taken place on 25 April[55] and Prideaux's letter followed only eleven days later, he had not wasted much time; but since elections to fellowships took place at the mid-year College meeting on 30 June, there was not much time to waste. Certain men, wrote Prideaux, were striving to secure the fellowship through favour, cunning, and solicitation. He judged this to be his opportunity. He had sounded out the fellows and had found them very partial and friendly. A word from Sir John would be greatly to his advantage. He had neither friends nor wealth to carry him forward. His mother, seven years a widow and with ten children, could do little or nothing to sustain him. He yearned to become learned (*'cupio me fieri doctum'*) and, after four years burdened with hard work and turmoil in the College and the buttery (and here we might think again of Middleton's Pierce Penniless), to sail into a tranquil port and to redeem lost time. He was precisely fitted for this place, his last hope. If Sir John could not help him, whose ancestors had lived on the Petre estates at South Brent in Devon, he would have to leave the university, an infant torn from his mother's breast, and his ardour for learning would be extinguished.

The complex, neo-Ciceronian (and sometimes barely intelligible) Latin of this letter was designed to impress and to serve as an advertisement for Prideaux's learning. It was to that extent a self-testimonial. But its heavy

---

with many errors, in *Devon and Cornwall Notes and Gleanings*, 5 (1892), 134–5. The addressee's name is given as 'Reanelm' or 'Reaullme' Carter, clearly a mistake for 'Kenelm' and the result probably of a misreading of Prideaux's intractable hand. For Kenelm Carter, see Boase, *Register*, 75; Maddicott, *Founders*, 219, 298, 300, 302–3, 305, 322; and N. Briggs, 'William, 2nd Lord Petre (1575–1637)', *Essex Recusant*, 10/2 (1968), 52. I am very grateful to Robin Darwall-Smith for his help in translating this difficult letter.

55. ECA, A.I.5, 195.

elements of rhetoric and hyperbole hardly limit its value as a guide to
Prideaux's hopes and fears at a crucial moment in his early Oxford years.
He had set his heart on a university career devoted to learning and there are
no signs that he had any aspirations towards a scholar's alternative pathway in
the wider church.[56] But competition for fellowships was fierce and unscrupulous, and although Prideaux had confidence in his own abilities and in
the support for him within the College, circumstances were against him.
His emphasis on the degree to which he was held back by his College
labours as a poor scholar was almost certainly justified—poor scholars serving
breakfast, for example, often had to miss the university lectures scheduled
for 8 a.m.[57]—and he was justified too in stressing the financial difficulties in
the way of his staying on at College long enough to gain a footing on the
academic ladder. His appeal to Carter, and thence to Petre, was one measure
of his desperation, for their resolute Catholicism must have jarred with the
strongly Protestant tone of Holland's Exeter and what we can assume to
have been Prideaux's own religious convictions. There must always have
been a certain awkwardness in the relations between a Protestant college and
its Catholic patron. But Prideaux had to take his patrons where he could find
them, even perhaps at the cost of his principles. The vacant fellowship,
however, was not in Petre's gift, for Lapthorne was one of the College's
eight Devon fellows, whose place would indeed be reserved for another
Devonian but one elected by the College and not nominated by Petre. All
that Prideaux could expect from Petre (and even this was optimistic) was the
exercise of influence.

Whether this letter elicited any response is not known, but in the event
none was needed. Lapthorne's formal letter of resignation was not submitted
until 3 July 1600, too late to trigger any election at the mid-year meeting,
now past. It was not until next year, on 30 June, that John Trelawny,
another Devonian and some three years senior to Prideaux, was elected in
Lapthorne's place. Prideaux, however, was elected at the same meeting, to a
fellowship vacated by Thomas Dennys, who had recently been presented to
the College living at Menheniot in Cornwall. A year later, on 2 July 1602,
after having served his year of probation, Prideaux was admitted as a

56. Note Prideaux's mildly scathing remark about the recently married Lapthorn's now giving
    himself not so much to books as to children: 'non tantum liberis [sic] sed liberis operam dari'
    (*Gentleman's Magazine*, 482). This play on the double meaning of 'liberis' was an early example
    of the puns for which Prideaux became well known.
57. Clark, *Register*, i. 12.

perpetual fellow.[58] The great ambition which he had set out in his letter to Carter he had now achieved.

After his election Prideaux's formal progress through the university can be charted in its records. He incepted as MA in 1603, the year in which, supposedly, he also took orders,[59] and he then started on the baccalaureate in divinity (BD). This normally took seven years and entailed attendance at the theology lectures given by the two professors, the Lady Margaret professor and the regius professor, participation in theological disputations, and the delivery of a Latin sermon within a year of admission to the degree. Prideaux was admitted in 1611.[60] At a time when theology was the pre-eminent discipline in the two universities, he had now acquired the essential grounding in theological scholarship which was necessary for any College fellow who wished to continue in academic life. Never more numerous than between 1610 and 1639, the holders of the BD represented 'the elite of their profession'.[61]

Prideaux's activities within the College provide a better guide to his ambitions and qualities than the dry record of courses pursued and degrees taken. From the time of his election in 1601, and probably before, if his letter to Carter can be relied on, it was clear that he was an able man and that his abilities lay in some particular directions. But he made his first mark within a university rather than a college context. In 1603 the university offered its congratulations to Elizabeth's successor, James I, in one of the occasional volumes of verses by its members which were commonly published to commemorate important royal events—accessions, births, marriages, and deaths. Among the contributors of the mainly Latin verses which appeared in this one, the *Academiae Oxoniensis Pietas*, were Thomas Holland, rector of Exeter, eight Exeter fellows, including Prideaux and Helme, and eleven other Exonians, mainly well-born undergraduates. Prideaux's offering comprised a conventional enough set of Latin hexameters deploring Elizabeth's death and joining other local poets, the 'Heliconis alumni', in welcoming the new king, the harbinger of a golden age. It was, however, remarkable for

58. ECA, A.I.5, 195, 196, 206.
59. Thus, Wood, *Athenae*, iii. 265. But if so, he can only have been ordained deacon, since we know that he was ordained priest in 1609 (below, 26)—and a six-year gap between minor orders and the priesthood seems unlikely.
60. Boase, *Register*, 89; Clark, *Register*, i. 132–8
61. L. Stone, 'The Size and Composition of the Oxford Student Body, 1580–1910', in L. Stone (ed.), *The University in Society*, Vol. I: *Oxford and Cambridge from the 14th to the Early 19th Century* (1975), 21–2; HUO, iv. 16–17.

its length. At 147 lines Prideaux's was the third longest of all the nearly five hundred contributions, and considerably longer than any other from Exeter, including Holland's, which ran to only twelve lines.[62] It is difficult not to see Prideaux's magniloquent first appearance in print, at the age of 25, as part of a self-conscious advertisement intended to draw attention to an emerging talent. In that respect it resembled the elaborate Latin of his letter to Kenelm Carter.

But it was on College teaching that Prideaux made his firmest impression in these early years. He held his fair share of the main teaching offices which were filled annually by election at each mid-year College meeting. He was chosen as moderator in philosophy for 1603-4, as Greek lecturer (*praelector*) in 1605–6, 1606–7, and 1608–9, and as dean in 1611–12, shortly before his election as rector.[63] If the first of these posts gave him experience in adjudicating undergraduate disputations, his triple appointment as Greek lecturer points to a more particular area of expertise. Later, as dean, a post created under the Petrean statutes, he was effectively the supervisor of the arts course, as his own tutor (and now his colleague), William Helme, had been. The whole *cursus honorum* was an incidental testimony to the degree to which formal teaching, via disputations and lectures, as well as the informal teaching provided by tutors and tutorials, was now in the hands of the colleges.

Additional pointers to Prideaux's growing reputation as a teacher come from two sources. The first is a notebook, now in the Exeter College archives, covering the period from 1606 to 1630 and providing termly lists of tutors and the named pupils for whom they took responsibility.[64] In revealing the number of pupils assigned to each tutor, it allows us to identify the most popular tutors and those most trusted and favoured by the rector, since it was he who normally allocated pupils to tutors. Prideaux is the star of the notebook's early entries. In almost every term from 1606 until his election as rector in 1612, he has more pupils than any other tutor, usually by a large margin. In the first recorded term, Lent 1606, he had some seventeen pupils. Of the fifteen other fellows then acting as tutors, none had more than thirteen (Thomas Winniffe), and most had between three

62. *Academiae Oxoniensis Pietas erga Serenissimum et Potentissimum Jacobum* (Oxford, 1603), 184–7; Madan, i. 56.
63. ECA, A.I.5, 208, 221, 223, 227, 239.
64. ECA, H.II.11 (Tutor-Pupil Lists), unfoliated. For tutors' financial responsibility for their pupils, see below, 106, 115.

and five. Only in the autumn term of 1606, when Prideaux had thirteen pupils to Winniffe's fourteen, did another tutor have more. Towards the end of this short period the numbers assigned to Prideaux rose sharply: in autumn term 1609 he had twenty-six; in Lent term 1610, thirty; in Lent term 1611, thirty-four; in summer term 1611, thirty-five; and in Lent term 1612, his last term as a fellow-tutor before his election as rector, thirty-four. No other tutor approached these numbers. In that particular term his nearest rivals were John Vivian (always a sought-after tutor), with fourteen, and William Battishill, with thirteen. These figures suggest not only the high regard in which Prideaux was held as a teacher—a central feature of his whole career—but also the considerable income which teaching must have brought him. Since fees paid by pupils for teaching went directly to the tutor and were often in the range of £2 to £4 a year, depending on the undergraduate's status, thirty pupils may have brought in as much as an annual £80 or £90.[65] By the time of his election as rector, and long before the accumulation of benefices which marked his mature years, Prideaux may well have been on the way to becoming a rich man, the poverty of his pre-fellowship years put behind him.

Prideaux's first book provides the second source which points to his interest in teaching. This was a short introduction to the essentials of Greek grammar, the *Tabulæ ad Grammatica Graeca Introductoriæ*, published at Oxford in 1607.[66] Some undergraduates arrived at Oxford proficient in Greek, but many did not (Prideaux himself had probably been among them), and it was for their instruction, 'for the private guidance of beginners *(ad tyrunculos privatim manuducendos)*', and partly, it seems, at their request, that Prideaux wrote. No doubt his current experiences as the College's Greek lecturer had shown him where the need lay. In a revealing dedicatory letter addressed to his 'venerable patron' Thomas Holland, he wrote that the task had been assigned to him by Holland (another mark of Holland's faith in him) and that he had completed it during the Whitsun holidays of the previous year. Prideaux credited Holland with being its part author, but by this he probably meant 'initiator' rather than 'writer'. The work was divided into six sections, each of them intended to be mastered in a day; and in two lines of

---

65. For tuition fees, see *HUO*, iv. 85. Teaching and its rewards are considered in more detail below, 108–9.
66. Madan, i. 68. The work was reprinted, with supplements, in 1629 and 1639: below, 213. For undergraduates' knowledge of Greek, see *HUO*, iv. 256–8.

Latin verse written as an envoi to his former pupil's little book, William Helme expressed amazement that 'others with difficulty give up a year to what must be learnt, to which by your book (O Prideaux) you give six days'.

Prideaux's introduction to Greek grammar was his first essay in a genre which he was to make very much his own and which he continued to produce even during his years of eminence as rector and then bishop: an explanatory work written in simple terms for beginners. In the same year as its publication another book appeared, without his name on the title-page but which would also typify some of his later publications. Robert Stafforde, the author of *A Geographicall and Anthologicall Description of all the Empires and Kingdomes both of Continent [sic] and Ilands in this Terrestriall Globe* (1607), was an Exeter undergraduate, listed as a pupil of Prideaux's for five terms in 1606–7. His work was a fairly jejune assemblage of elementary geographical information covering such topics as the countries of the world, their natural features, their products, and so on. Since the author had matriculated in March 1605, aged 16,[67] and so cannot have been more than 18 when he published, little can have been expected of him, and in a jaunty address 'to the reader', Stafforde disarmingly admits that the work was not of much value and had been put together from others' books. More relevant is Prideaux's role. Anthony Wood wrote that Prideaux 'was supposed to have had a chief hand in compiling the said book, as the tradition goes in Exeter Coll', and Stafforde himself says as much, acknowledging that he had borrowed from his tutor and that the whole work was in part 'but the gleanings of his plentifull harvest'.[68] Prideaux was also one of three authors to supply commendatory verses. In allowing an undergraduate pupil to pass off his work as theirs, he showed a generosity of spirit which was sometimes less evident in his later dealings with his fellow theologians.

It was while Prideaux was building a reputation as a fellow, tutor, and occasional author that an extraordinary episode disrupted the routines and rhythms of College life, plunging some of the fellows, including Prideaux, into the middle of what became a notorious case supposedly concerning witchcraft. The College's involvement sprang from the rector's marriage. In 1593 Thomas Holland, then aged about 40, had married Susan Gunter, the 19-year-old daughter of Brian Gunter, a litigious, ill-natured, and sometimes violent member of the Berkshire gentry, and the wealthiest resident in the

67. Boase, *Commoners*, 305; ECA, H.II.11.
68. Wood, *Athenae*, ii. 291.

village of North Moreton, some twelve miles from Oxford.[69] In the course of a brawl at a football match in 1598 Brian Gunter had struck John and Richard Gregory, sons of a less wealthy yeoman family, causing their deaths and initiating a long feud between Gunter and the Gregorys.[70] In 1604, during its course, a scarcely credible plot was hatched by Gunter. Anne, his youngest child, then aged about 19, was both persuaded and bullied by her father, largely against her will, to feign the dramatic symptoms of a woman bewitched.[71] These included convulsions, the vomiting of pins, and the mysterious shedding of Anne's clothes without manual intervention—all attested by many witnesses. Gunter's intention was to claim that Anne had been bewitched and to lay the blame on three village women, Elizabeth Gregory, sister-in-law of the dead Gregory boys and a person with a local reputation as a bad-tempered scold, Agnes Pepwell, already suspected to be a witch, and Mary, her illegitimate daughter.[72] But in his attempts to secure their conviction, he failed. In 1605 Elizabeth Gregory and Mary Pepwell were put on trial and acquitted. Agnes Pepwell had fled.[73] Rashly going on to bring his case before the king during James I's visit to Oxford in 1605, Gunter was confounded by his daughter's confessing in the king's presence that her antics were mere simulation.[74] In 1606 Gunter's actions rebounded on him when he and Anne were brought before Star Chamber and charged with making false accusations against the three women. Most of our evidence comes from witness statements made during the hearing, but there is no record of its conclusion.[75]

Part of Gunter's plan seems to have been to attract the support of the Oxford scholars gathered around his father-in-law, Thomas Holland, in order to add weight and respectability to the case for Anne's bewitchment. Here he was successful. His supporters included not only his daughter Susan but also five fellows of the College: Prideaux himself; William Helme, Prideaux's former tutor; Thomas Winniffe, the future bishop of Lincoln; Robert Vilvaine, later the famous physician; and John Whetcombe, who went on to marry Holland's daughter, Ann. Also involved was William

69. J. Sharpe, *The Bewitching of Anne Gunter* (1999), 33–9, 91–4, 186. I have followed Professor Sharpe's account throughout.
70. Ibid., 17–19.
71. Ibid., 5–7.
72. Ibid., xi–xii, 8–9.
73. Ibid., 127–38.
74. Ibid., 178–82.
75. Ibid., xii, 190–4.

Harvey, an Oxford graduate then reading for his MA.[76] All these men gave
evidence in Gunter's favour, vouching for the authenticity of Anne's dis-
tressing experiences, which they had witnessed either at her family home at
North Moreton or at her brother's house at Stanton St John, a few miles
from Oxford, or in the rector's lodgings in the College. In his own deposition in Star Chamber Prideaux gave an especially detailed account of what
he had seen and heard during Anne's 'fits and passions'. He had seen her
vomiting pins and had witnessed the withdrawal of a pin from her breast
without producing blood. He had tried to move her head during one of her
fits, but found it so heavy that he could not lift it. He had heard her
declaiming against the three women and uttering the names of their famil-
iars. He had noticed 'a strange kind of swelling in her body . . . as great
almost as a man's head'. During an unusually violent fit, when Prideaux
thought that her bones would become disjointed, she had wept so bitterly at
her torments that Prideaux and the other witnesses had wept with her.
Supposedly second-sighted, she had reported on a private conversation
between Prideaux and another man, although she had no informant.[77]
Anne was evidently something of a conjuror and a gymnast, adept at sleight
of hand and perhaps capable of imposing a form of hypnosis on her
credulous audience.

The Gunter affair gives us a rare glimpse of the familial dynamics which
might operate within a college community. Although Holland himself
seems to have stood aside throughout the proceedings, the five fellows
rallied round their head's wife and her sister, as no doubt Brian Gunter
intended them to do. It is worth noting that, leaving Prideaux himself aside,
the remaining four were mentioned by Prideaux in his chapel consecration
sermon of 1625 as being among the College's most distinguished fellows.[78]
Most of them seem to have first come into contact with Gunter when, as
they said in their depositions, he lay 'dangerously sick' at Oxford around
midsummer 1604.[79] It is most likely that his illness laid him up in his
daughter's home in the lodgings at Exeter, that the fellows met him there,
and it was there that he conceived his plan to bind them to his daughter's
supposed bewitchment. Anne's first fits followed soon afterwards in the

76. Ibid., 101–4, 111–12; Boase *Commoners*, 145
77. Sharpe, *Bewitching*, 103–4, 106. Prideaux's original deposition is TNA, STAC 8/4/10, fos.
    143–7.
78. Above, 15–16.
79. Sharpe, *Bewitching*, 91.

same year. They proved as gullible as he could have hoped, Prideaux perhaps more than most. The leading sceptic among the witnesses was no Oxford don, but a well-connected Wiltshire gentleman, Thomas Hinton,[80] and the wider scepticism which was a feature of the judicial proceedings, both against the accused 'witches' and in Star Chamber, was not shared by the fellows of Exeter. That Prideaux, already a respected teacher and a rising scholar, should have had no doubts about the reality of witchcraft throws an interesting light on his mentality and thought-world. For all his growing academic prowess, he shared in some of the norms of popular culture and belief.

In the years which followed, two other episodes marked Prideaux's advancement. In 1609 or 1610 the College paid him £2 for his expenses 'in prosecuting a law suit over our rectory of Merton', one of the Oxfordshire properties given to the College by Sir William Petre.[81] In addition to his other qualities, Prideaux was clearly regarded as a man of business, an asset which must have counted in his favour a few years later when he came to be elected rector. More significant in the long term was his ordination as priest at Silverton in East Devon in September 1609 by William Cotton, bishop of Exeter. As a graduate, Prideaux was not subject to the usual rule that men must be ordained in the diocese where they had been born or long resident,[82] and his ordination in his native diocese, rather than in Oxford, is likely to have been a deliberate choice for this staunch Devonian, especially since he might have been expected to be ordained by John Bridges, the current bishop of Oxford and a loyal Calvinist,[83] whom Prideaux cannot have disfavoured.

He now possessed the final qualification needed for his progress in the church.

4. The road to the rectorship, 1610–12

The Gunter episode may have revealed something of Prideaux's assumptions and beliefs, but it was of no long-term importance for his career. A later

---

80. Ibid., 107–14.
81. ECA, A.II.9 (Rector's Accounts, 1564–1639), fo. 207r.
82. CCEd, Person ID 14698; Record ID 89557; R. O'Day, *The English Clergy, 1558–1642* (Leicester, 1979), 50; Dent, *Protestant Reformers*, 165. For Prideaux's Devonshire affiliations, see below, 89–90.
83. N. Tyacke, 'Religious Controversy during the Seventeenth Century', in his *Aspects*, 273.

staging post in his life was much more portentous. In 1610 his name appears on a list of the twenty-four chaplains attending 'two by two each month' on Prince Henry, James I's elder son, and heir to the throne.[84] It provides us with our first evidence that Prideaux had spread his wings beyond the confines of the College, a move which would lead directly to his election as rector two years later. Although it is just possible that he had become the prince's chaplain prior to 1610, by which time Henry certainly had his own clerical entourage, it was only in that year, when Henry was made prince of Wales, that his household was established on a new footing and in all probability a place found for Prideaux. He can in any case hardly have been a chaplain before his ordination to the priesthood in September 1609.

His entry into the prince's household, based usually at St James's Palace, represented a new opening for his ambition. The formal duties of the prince's chaplains were straightforward. During each chaplain's month of service he was expected to administer Holy Communion once, to preach two sermons, to say divine service daily, and to spend time in reading and study. But from the chaplain's point of view, more materially attractive than the honour these duties conveyed were the opportunities offered by attendance on the prince to secure the attention and favour of both Henry and his father the king, who almost certainly oversaw the appointment of chaplains. Such an appointment might set the beneficiary on the road to high office in the church, and often to a bishopric. Five of the twenty-four chaplains of 1610 eventually became bishops, while James I's chaplains were still more clearly in line for promotion: nineteen of the forty-eight chaplains serving James I in 1621 went on to bishoprics.[85] For part of each year, Prideaux's new post now took him to London, away from the routines of College life, and placed him on this larger and more promising stage.

Prideaux was proud of his new position. That he had been 'chaplain to Prince Henry, King James I, and King Charles I' was an achievement which

---

84. T. Birch, *The Life of Henry Prince of Wales* (1760), 443, 454; T. V. Wilks, 'The Court Culture of Prince Henry and his Circle, 1603–1613' (DPhil thesis, Oxford University, 1987), 277; N. W. S. Cranfield, 'Chaplains in Ordinary at the Early Stuart Court: The Purple Road', in C. Cross (ed.), *Patronage and Recruitment in the Tudor and Early Stuart Church* (York, 1996), 142; P. E. McCullough, *Sermons at Court: Politics and Religion in Elizabethan and Jacobean Preaching* (Cambridge, 1998), 183, 187 and n. 66, 188, 197.

85. N. W. S. Cranfield, 'Early Seventeenth-Century Developments and Change in the Doctrine of [Episcopacy] and Understanding of the Office of Bishop in the Church of England, 1603–1645' (DPhil thesis, Oxford University, 1988), 199, 200, 202, 215, 221; McCullough, *Sermons at Court*, 187–8.

he recorded on the memorial to his parents in their parish church at Harford, along with his doctorate in divinity, his regius chair, and his rectorship of Exeter. Although no source directly reveals the reasons for his appointment, these are not hard to detect. One important general factor was the identity of religious affiliation and outlook between the prince, his household, and Prideaux's College. Henry's court 'offered an unambiguous agenda of anti-Catholic militant Protestantism' and the prince himself was seen as the potential leader of European Protestantism, a Calvinist messiah.[86] This was very much the milieu of Exeter College under Rector Holland (as it would be under his successor), and the common ground shared by court and College largely explains the remarkable degree to which Henry drew upon the College for his chaplains.[87] Prideaux was only one of several Exonians in his household. Among the other chaplains on the 1610 list was Lewis Bayly, later bishop of Bangor, who took his BD from Exeter in 1611 and whose son John was elected to a fellowship in the following year.[88] Henry's other chaplains included the brothers Daniel and Sampson Price, the former also taking his BD from Exeter in 1611, the latter his MA from Exeter in 1608 and his BD in 1615. Daniel Price was already among the prince's chaplains by 1608, when he preached a sermon before the king. Subsequently published, it had a dedication dated from Exeter College.[89] Thomas Winniffe, unlike the others (but like Prideaux) a fellow of the College, may also have served as chaplain.[90] No other Oxford college had the same multiple links with the prince's household.

The choice of Prideaux as chaplain was a testimony not only to the strength of this connection but also to Prideaux's personal qualities. By the time of his appointment, he was probably beginning to establish a reputation both as a preacher and also, and more particularly, as a scholar. Like his father, Prince Henry placed a high value on preaching and on attendance at sermons. He had 'an especiall regard of honest sermons', Daniel Price wrote in 1613, and had requested a copy of one of Price's own sermons.[91] In 1610

86. McCullough, *Sermons at Court*, 187, 192.
87. Ibid., 197, 200.
88. Ibid., 187–8; Wood, *Athenae*, ii. 525; Boase, *Commoners*, 19; Boase, *Register*, 95–6.
89. Boase, *Commoners*, 260–1; McCullough, *Sermons at Court*, 166, 189–91; Daniel Price, *Praelium & Praemium* (Oxford, 1608), dedication to the archbishop of Canterbury dated from Exeter College, 19 June 1608.
90. Wood, *Athenae*, iv. 813; Boase, *Register*, 86.
91. D. Price, *Prince Henry his First Anniversary* (Oxford, 1613), 7–8; McCullough, *Sermons at Court*, 183, 190.

Prideaux had been given a formal preaching role in his College when he was elected for a year to the office of 'concionator' or 'preacher', with the obligation to preach four sermons a year in each of the College's five Oxfordshire parishes.[92] For a major part of the chaplain's role the College would seem to have thought him well qualified.

In the eyes of the king, if perhaps less emphatically than in those of the prince, Prideaux's growing reputation for learning would have been an equally important qualification for his new post. By 1610 he had published nothing besides his verses for James I's accession and his elementary Greek textbook. This mattered little, however, at a time when scholarly reputations were established not only by publications but also by reportage, word of mouth, correspondence, and the multifarious personal contacts between the scholars who constituted the European republic of letters. That Prideaux was coming to be known in this wider world, both as a learned man and as a distinguished teacher, was shown by the foreign students whom he was beginning to attract to the College. This was a much more conspicuous feature of his early years as rector, discussed in more detail later. But it was already in evidence during his last years as a fellow between 1610 and 1612— proof enough of his growing fame beyond his own university. From this period three particular scholars whom he attracted were singled out by Anthony Wood: John Combachius, from the university of Marburg, who came to Exeter in 1610 and was listed as one of Prideaux's pupils in Lent term of that year; Philip Cluvier, born in Danzig but a student at Leiden and already on the way to becoming an expert geographer, who occurs as a pupil from 1610 to 1612; and Louis Cappell, a Frenchman from Sedan, who came to Exeter in 1610 and later returned to France to become professor of Hebrew at the Protestant academy of Saumur. Combachius was said by Wood to have been 'a great admirer of Holland and Prideaux, especially the last', and the other two to have come to Exeter 'for the sake of Holland and Prideaux'.[93] But by 1609 Holland had held the regius chair of divinity for twenty years, without, so far as we can see, attracting any overseas students, and it is likely to have been Prideaux's rising eminence that primarily brought these foreigners to Exeter. His ability to draw in such men,

92. ECA, A.I.5, 234, 247.
93. Wood, *Athenae*, ii. 329–30, 335–7, iii. 463; ECA, H.II.11; M. Feingold, *The Mathematicians' Apprenticeship* (Cambridge, 1984), 58 (for '1619' read '1609'); *HUO*, iv. 457–8; P. R. Sellin, *Daniel Heinsius and Stuart England* (Leiden, 1968), 86.

demonstrating his qualities as it did, helps to explain why he himself was drawn into the larger community of the prince's household.

The household has been aptly termed a 'collegiate society', its clerical members bound together not only by a common churchmanship but also by ties of friendship and mutual respect, even admiration.[94] His chaplaincy thus brought Prideaux for the first time into the company of like-minded churchmen beyond the Exeter circle: men such as Joseph Hall, chaplain since 1607 and a future bishop of Exeter (and thereby Visitor of the College), and Andrew Willet, author of the vast and fiercely anti-papal *Synopsis Papismi*.[95] Among these men, Prideaux was a relatively junior figure. Most of the twenty-four identifiable chaplains of 1610—they are listed only by their surnames—were older than he was and already possessed the doctorate in divinity, while at this stage Prideaux had yet to acquire even the inferior BD.[96] His presence among other Calvinist clerics who were largely his elders, senior theologians, and some of them established authors is likely to have reinforced the religious views which had emerged from his fourteen years as a student and fellow of Exeter.

There is just enough evidence to go further and to suggest that Prideaux was particularly closely engaged with the prince and his court, perhaps more so than his fellow chaplains. It may be significant that on 2 May 1612 he was excused some of the obligatory exercises needed for the completion of his BD because he had been 'unexpectedly impeded by necessary business in the household of the illustrious prince': a reason which seems to point to some unusual activity beyond that arising from his one month's annual attendance.[97] One special link came through Sir Thomas Chaloner, initially the prince's governor, his chamberlain from 1610, and effectively the head of his household. Chaloner sent his third son, another Thomas, to Exeter in 1611, where for four terms in 1611–12 he was under Prideaux's tutelage.[98] This was an expression of confidence in Prideaux by a leading figure who was as

94. McCullough, *Sermons at Court*, 183, 190–2.
95. Ibid., 187–8; A. Milton, 'Willet, Andrew (1561/2–1621), church of England clergyman and religious controversialist', *ODNB*.
96. A conclusion based on biographical material in *ODNB*, CCEd, and McCullough, *Sermons at Court*. Prideaux was awarded the BD on 6 May 1611: Wood, *Fasti*, i. 343.
97. Clark, *Register*, i. 138.
98. McCullough, *Sermons at Court*, 187; C. Macleod (ed.), *The Lost Prince: The Life and Death of Henry Stuart* (2012), 11, 14, 24–5; Boase, *Commoners*, 55; ECA, H.II.11. Prideaux would not have been happy to see his former pupil Chaloner's name among the signatories to Charles I's death warrant in 1648.

close as anyone to the prince. But more interesting still are the few traces we have of Prideaux's links with the prince himself. On 24 August 1612, a few months after Prideaux's election to the rectorship, Henry wrote to the city of Coventry to say that he had asked Dr Prideaux, 'one of our chaplaines and Rector of Excester Colledge in Oxford', to admit to the College a certain unnamed 'poor blinde scholler' on the city's nomination. This favour to the city was apparently given as a thanks offering for the prince's 'worthy intertaynement' during a visit to Coventry. Shortly afterwards, on 5 September, Prideaux himself wrote to the mayor of Coventry, saying that he had spoken about the case with the prince during Henry's recent stay at Woodstock and that he was 'ever readye to performe whatsoever it pleaseth my royall master to command, as havinge the place I inioye by his late procurement'. The 'poor blind scholar', later named as James Illedge, was subsequently admitted to the College, took his BA in 1616, and went on to hold various clerical posts in the Coventry area.[99]

Prideaux here acknowledged a debt that would be otherwise unknown: his owing to the prince's intervention 'the place I enjoy', which can only mean the rectorship of the College. Although there is nothing in the College Register, where the election is recorded, to support or deny this, Henry's patronage was frequently exercised in this way. In 1612, for example, he had secured the chair in divinity at Gresham's College for another chaplain, Samuel Brooke, and given all that we know about Prideaux's general standing and his place among Henry's chaplains, it seems entirely plausible that he had done the same for Prideaux.[100] The case is strengthened by the allusive remark made by Prideaux in the brief Latin verse which he contributed to the university's commemorative volume, published late in 1612, for the prince's recent and grievously lamented death. 'I above the rest have cause to mourn,' wrote Prideaux.[101] And if the prince had gained him the rectorship, so he did.

99. Coventry History Centre, BA/H/17/A79/36, 106, 108 (photocopies in ECA, H.III.11, Correspondence); Boase, *Commoners*, 170. I am grateful to Robert Witts, of the Coventry History Centre, for providing information about Illedge's later career. For his financial difficulties as an undergraduate, see below, 115–16.

100. ECA, A.I.5, 242; C. S. Knighton, 'Brooke, Samuel (c.1575–1631), college head', *ODNB*. Cf. Hegarty, 'Prideaux'.

101. 'Est mihi prae reliquis lugendi causa': *Iusta Oxoniensium* (1612), sig. B2v.

A combination of good fortune and natural talent underlay Prideaux's rise from his boyhood as a farmer's son in rural Devonshire to his election as the head of his Oxford College. He was fortunate in having found two patrons who had recognized his qualities: Mary Fowell, who had given him the preliminary education needed for study at Oxford, and Prince Henry, whose religious sympathies Prideaux wholeheartedly endorsed, so helping to secure his election as Exeter's rector. Between Lady Fowell's intervention and Prince Henry's came his sixteen years under Thomas Holland, first as an undergraduate and then a fellow of Holland's College. It was another piece of good fortune that he had entered Exeter rather than any other house, for Holland's pre-eminence as a theologian, the galaxy of gifted men who gathered around him, and his College's resolutely Calvinist and anti-Catholic milieu, all gave Exeter a leading place in the university and made it a congenial home for a serious student. Although ideologically militant, Holland himself appears in other ways to have been an eirenic paterfamilias. He stood aside when the Gunter case lined up a substantial part of the fellowship behind his litigious brother-in-law; and no appeals to the Visitor, often a sign of factious disputes from within or unwanted interference from without, disturbed the peace of the College in his time, as they frequently did under Rector Kilbye at neighbouring Lincoln.[102] William Helme's role as a friendly father figure, first Prideaux's tutor and then his colleague, was additionally conducive to a stable social and working environment.

Besides good fortune, Prideaux's own qualities provided the driving force behind his ascent. Apart from his innate intelligence, spotted early on by his first patron, those qualities comprised ambition, determination, and a relentless capacity for work. It is not too far-fetched to see all these qualities represented on a small scale by his inaugural walk in his leather breeches from South Devon to Oxford. His subsequent ability to combine the drudgery of his labours as under-butler with his progress towards the BA, which he completed within the statutory four years, was a mark both of his stamina and of his will to succeed. Although nothing seems to have come of the elaborate letter which he wrote to Kenelm Carter, in an attempt to secure the fellowship on which he had set his heart, it illustrated another side of his intellectual development: his forensic power, the ability to present a case, honed no doubt throughout his undergraduate years by his role in the oral disputations which were an essential part of the arts course. Then, once

---

102. V. H. H. Green, *The Commonwealth of Lincoln College, 1427–1977* (Oxford, 1979), 169–70.

established as a fellow, his further gifts as a teacher were given the space to emerge. He must also have had a certain attractiveness of personality, charm even, now irrecoverable but seen perhaps in the favour shown to him by Prince Henry, in his appeal to foreign scholars, and in his willingness to put himself out for his undergraduate pupils. The 'winning and pleasing' ways which Anthony Wood saw in his later government of his College may already have been in evidence.[103]

It remains to be seen how these qualities were reflected in his public career as theologian, academic leader, and College head, which in 1612 was about to begin.

103. Wood, *Athenae*, iii. 266.

2

Halcyon Years, 1612–24

1. Defender of the Faith

Prideaux's election as rector inaugurated twelve years of achievement and, probably, personal happiness. The election itself seems to have provoked no discussion or lengthy debate. Holland died on 17 March 1612, and Prideaux was elected just eighteen days later on 4 April.[1] At the time he had no clear precedence among the fellows. Five men had been elected to their fellow-ships before him, William Orford as long ago as 1580, and Prideaux's own tutor, William Helme, in 1587. Nor was he particularly advanced in years. His two predecessors, Glasier and Holland, had been aged about 38 and 45 respectively when they became rectors, while Prideaux was only 33. Yet compliance with Prince Henry's wishes cannot have been the sole reason for the election of this relatively young and junior figure. Prideaux's established reputation both as a tutor and as a scholar, and one already known on the Continent, gave him independent qualifications, and these can only have been augmented by connections at court which might bring benefits to his College. Unlike the elections of his two predecessors, who had been nominated to fellowships by Sir John Petre with the sole aim of making them eligible for the rectorship, to which they were elected within weeks of receiving their fellowships,[2] Prideaux's election was that of a long-standing fellow, well known to his colleagues. His success here was capped on 30 June, when he was awarded his doctorate in divinity, having taken his BD only in the previous year: a breach of the university's statutes justified as being 'for the dignity of the College over which he presides and for the

---

1. ECA, A.I.5, 241, 242.
2. Maddicott, *Founders*, 305–7.

Between Scholarship and Church Politics: The Lives of John Prideaux, 1578–1650. John Maddicott, Oxford University Press. © John Maddicott 2022. DOI: 10.1093/oso/9780192896100.003.0002

honour of this university'.[3] Without this accolade and professional qualification no head of house could be expected to take office.

The first major task which came Prideaux's way after his election was unrelated to his rectorship. Bringing him into contact with Isaac Casaubon, the greatest scholar of the age after the death of Scaliger in 1609, it showed something more of the high regard in which he was already held by those outside the College. Philologist, editor and emender of classical texts, a pioneer in his exploration of the sources for early church history, and a sharply intelligent critic and religious controversialist, Casaubon had come to England in 1610 as a Huguenot refugee after the murder of Henri IV by a Catholic assassin.[4] Once in England, he was taken up by James I, provided with an income, and expected to partner James in the theological discussions which James loved but which Casaubon found a tiresome distraction from his scholarly work.[5] From his close relationship with the king, and through the medium of a pamphlet war characteristic of the period, came his further relationship with Prideaux. In 1611 Casaubon had published his *Epistola ad Frontonem Ducaeum*: in effect, a defence of James's ecclesiastical policy, shaped as it was by Catholic plots, of the king's demand for an oath of allegiance in 1606 (an oath enforced on new categories of takers after the French king's assassination in 1610), and of the execution of Henry Garnett, the leading Jesuit in England, who had learnt in advance of the Gunpowder Plot in the secrecy of the confessional but who had failed to reveal this to the authorities.[6] Casaubon's work was in turn attacked by another Jesuit, Andreas Eudaemon-Joannes, in his *Responsio ad Epistolam Isaaci Casauboni*. This combined a defence of Garnett's refusal to break the seal of the confessional with slanders on Casaubon's father, including the false statement that he had been hanged, and a scurrilous attack on Casaubon himself,

---

3. Clark, *Register*, i. 139.
4. For an excellent summary of Casaubon's achievements, see A. Grafton and J. Weinberg, '*I have always loved the Holy Tongue': Isaac Casaubon, the Jews and a Forgotten Chapter in Renaissance Scholarship* (Cambridge, MA, 2011), 4–8, 11–12, 177–9. For his flight from Paris, see M. Pattison, *Isaac Casaubon, 1559–1614*, 2nd edn (Oxford, 1892), 267–75.
5. Pattison, *Casaubon*, 284–7.
6. *The Correspondence of Isaac Casaubon in England*, ed. P. Botley and M. Vince, 4 vols. (Geneva, 2018), i. 18–24; Pattison, *Casaubon*, 311–13, 389; Madan, i. 98; M. C. Questier, 'Loyalty, Religion and State Power in Early Modern England: English Romanism and the Jacobean Oath of Allegiance', *The Historical Journal*, 40 (1997), 323; T. M. McCoog, 'Garnett, Henry (1555–1606), Jesuit', *ODNB*; J. Considine, 'Casaubon, Isaac (1559–1614), classical scholar and ecclesiastical historian', *ODNB*.

which accused him of siding with James for money and, still more outra-geously, disparaged his claims to learning.[7]

James did not wish Casaubon to waste time in answering this farrago, and by March 1613 it had been decided by the king and Archbishop Abbot that Prideaux should respond on Casaubon's behalf.[8] What resulted was a lengthy tract of some 242 pages, completed by Prideaux at the end of the year and published early in 1614.[9] It provided a refutation of the Jesuit's charges, a defence of Casaubon's integrity, an attack on papal claims to temporal sovereignty over princes (in which he spoke of the Pope as Antichrist[10]), and a chapter-long discussion of Garnett's case. Particularly hard-hitting was Prideaux's assault on the Jesuits and especially on their defence of equivocation, the use of ambiguous statements in order to mislead—and therefore close to lying. Garnett had been closely associated with the defence of this practice. Both these themes continued to weigh heavily with Prideaux, and in returning to them in his Act lecture of 1625 'On Jesuitical Equivocation', he made a number of further hostile references to Eudaemon-Joannes.[11] Almost as notable as the subject matter of the *Castigatio* was the range of learning which Prideaux drew on to support his case. He cited not only the obvious classical authors (Aristotle, Cicero, etc.), but also many of the Fathers from Augustine onwards, the medieval canon-ists and canon law collections (Gratian, Hostiensis, the *Extravagantes*), some medieval historians (Marianus Scotus, Sigebert of Gembloux), and other more modern philosophers and historians, including Zabarella and Hol-inshed. The most recent work to be cited was the Spanish Dominican Juan de la Puente's *Tomo primero de la conveniencia de las dos monarquias catolicas, la de la Iglesia romana y la del imperio español*, published at Madrid only in the previous year, 1612. For this sort of enterprise the resources of Bodley's new library proved their value.[12]

---

7. A. Eudaemon-Joannes, *Responsio ad Epistolam Isaaci Casauboni* (Cologne, 1613); Pattison, *Casaubon*, 390–3; Considine, 'Casaubon'.

8. Casaubon, *Correspondence*, iii. 414–18, 577; Pattison, *Casaubon*, 365, 393.

9. J. Prideaux, *Castigatio Cuiusdam Circulatoris qui R. P. Andream Eudaemon-Johannem Cydonum e Societate Jesu seipsum Nuncupat* (Oxford, 1614); Madan, i. 98. The best analysis is M. Vince, 'Isaac Casaubon, Andreas Eudaemon-Joannes, John Prideaux, and Tarnished Reputations: A (not Entirely) Scholarly Controversy', *Erudition and the Republic of Letters*, 4 (2019), 376–80, 390–3. Prideaux's dedication to Archbishop Abbot is dated from Exeter College on 24 December 1613. He gave a copy to the College library, now ECL, 9M 20344.

10. Prideaux, *Castigatio*, 31.

11. Ibid., 13–18; *VDL*, 155, 156, 158; Vince, 'Isaac Casaubon', 356, 390–1.

12. *Castigatio*, 38. De la Puente's book is listed in the 1620 Bodleian catalogue.

Prideaux's work for Casaubon forged a close bond between the two men. Before the king and the archbishop made Prideaux's services available to Casaubon, the older scholar had apparently known nothing of the younger.[13] But between March 1613 and March 1614 they became regular correspondents and friends. Fifteen letters survive from Casaubon to Prideaux, and three from Prideaux to Casaubon, though there were certainly others which have been lost.[14] Most of Casaubon's side of the correspondence is taken up with denunciations of 'the Cretan' or 'the Greek', as he usually termed Eudaemon-Joannes, and with the supply of factual ammunition, often of an interesting autobiographical sort, for Prideaux's tract; and most of Prideaux's with accounts of his proposed methods and his progress. The two men met for the first time in May 1613, when Casaubon visited Oxford for a few weeks. He was full of admiration for all that he saw. 'The heads of the colleges live splendidly, like noblemen,' he wrote in a paean of praise to Oxford generally; but it was not this that attracted him to the head of Exeter. Casaubon was clearly impressed by Prideaux, referring to him in a letter of 26 June as 'a most learned man (*vir eruditissimus*)'.[15] It was Prideaux, sharp of eye, who pointed out to Casaubon the slanders again his father in Eudaemon-Joannes's book, which Casaubon, remarkably, had overlooked. And it was in Prideaux's lodgings at Exeter that he first met Jacob Barnet, a Jew who almost certainly fostered Casaubon's (and Prideaux's) studies in Hebrew and Talmudic learning and who accompanied him on his return to London.[16] Along with Richard Kilbye, another former chaplain of Prince Henry and now rector of Lincoln and professor of Hebrew, and Robert Abbot, regius professor of divinity, Prideaux was one of only three 'men of learning' whom Casaubon professed to be able to find in Oxford.[17] Their correspondence continued after Casaubon's return to London, characterized by a tone of friendly respect on both sides. Written a few months before his death in June 1614, Casaubon's last letter accompanied a copy of his latest work, the *Exercitationes*, a fierce attack on the *Annals* of the Catholic historian Baronius. That it was sent 'as a token of my deep-seated love'

13. Casaubon, *Correspondence*, iii. 414–16.
14. Casaubon to Prideaux, in Casaubon, *Correspondence*, iii. 414, 420, 449, 472, 486, 548; iv. 1, 16, 36, 125, 133, 151, 180, 188, 329; Prideaux to Casaubon, ibid., iii. 419; iv. 176, 203.
15. Ibid., iii. 576–7.
16. Ibid., iii. 539, iv. 1, Vince, 'Isaac Casaubon', 374. For Barnet, see Grafton and Weinberg, '*I have always loved the Holy Tongue*', 253–67, and *HUO*, iv. 459–60.
17. Thus Pattison, *Casaubon*, 364–5. But I have been unable to find the original source for this statement.

and came with a request for Prideaux's corrections was a mark of Casaubon's regard for his friendship, learning, and critical acumen.[18]

The Casaubon episode confirmed more generally the reputation which Prideaux now enjoyed as a scholar, a leading anti-Catholic polemicist, a favoured figure at court, and, reciprocally, a strong supporter of the king. His attacks on the Jesuits and on their backing for papal claims to be able to depose kings must have appealed greatly to James, and may indeed have been played up by Prideaux partly with the king's favour in mind; for James loathed the Jesuits, whose papalist views he saw, after the Gunpowder Plot, as one of the greatest threats to his throne.[19] It was significant that he, rather than any other of the well-qualified Oxford theologians, should have been chosen by king and archbishop to provide the counterblast to Eudaemon-Joannes's polemic, and Prideaux handsomely repaid the trust placed in him. Taken together with his friendly relations with Casaubon, his authorship of the *Castigatio* marked a further step towards Prideaux's establishment both in the republic of letters and as a dependable royalist.

It is easy to see why, when Robert Abbot, the archbishop's brother and regius professor of divinity, was elected as bishop of Salisbury in October 1615, Prideaux should have been chosen as his successor in the regius chair. His links with the king and the court stretched back to his appointment as Prince Henry's chaplain in 1610, a role perpetuated by his subsequent appointment as James I's chaplain.[20] Besides his success in carrying through their commission regarding Casaubon, the favour of both king and archbishop which he enjoyed must have largely rested on his commitment to the Calvinist cause which was also their cause. His theological opinions had been publicly revealed for the first time—beyond what might be assumed from his membership of Holland's Exeter—by the theses which he had defended for his DD in 1612. That grace sufficient for salvation was not conceded to all (but only by implication to the elect); that the regenerate (i.e. the elect) could not wholly fall from grace (the doctrine of perseverance); and that the conferring of grace through the sacraments did not rest on works performed (so denying justification by works): all this represented the pure milk of the Calvinist word.[21] Although it may have had a stronger appeal to Archbishop

---

18. Casaubon, *Correspondence*, iv. 329–30.
19. P. Croft, *King James* (Basingstoke, 2003), 161; Questier, 'Loyalty, Religion and State Power', 314–16.
20. McCullough, *Sermons at Court*, 196–7; Cranfield, 'Chaplains in Ordinary', 142.
21. Clark, *Register*, i. 209; Tyacke, *Anti-Calvinists*, 72; Hegarty, 'Prideaux'.

Abbot, a dyed-in-the-wool Calvinist, than to James, whose Calvinism was more moderate than his archbishop's,[22] on one other occasion Prideaux's views were more completely aligned with those of James. In his sermon 'Ephesus Backsliding', preached in the university church in July 1614 and the first of his sermons to be published, he spoke out against the leading Dutch Arminians, Arminius himself, Petrus Bertius, and Conrad Vorstius, the first of these stigmatized by James as 'an enemy of God'; attacked the extreme puritans and sectaries, 'fanatical spirits' who 'retire themselves into conventicles', and a group whom James both detested and feared for the subversive implications of their beliefs; called for conformity in religion, one of the main planks of James's religious programme; and praised the king for his resolute stand against popery.[23] Had James read the sermon he would have been reassured to find that Prideaux's public pronouncements mirrored his own beliefs and policies.

Prideaux was appointed as regius professor in December 1615. In the same month his first child, William, was baptized, which suggests that his marriage to Anne Goodwin, daughter of the dean of Christ Church, had taken place early in that year or in the last months of 1614.[24] The birth of a son must have provided the couple with a double cause for rejoicing. Prideaux was to hold the regius chair for nearly twenty-seven years. Since he and his College were then embroiled in a bitter and expensive struggle with Lord Petre, grandson of the refounder, over Petre's claim to nominate to fellowships (as we shall see), it was not the most timely of promotions.[25] But while concurrently managing the dispute with Petre, he was now able to put his learning and forensic skills to good use in defending Anglican orthodoxy and in attacking the forces which he saw as its enemies: Catholicism, Arminianism, and, to a lesser extent, puritanism. His opportunities came mainly through his new duties as lecturer and moderator, carefully prescribed by statute. The regius professor was expected to lecture on the Scriptures for four days a week at 9 a.m., later reduced to twice a week by the Laudian statutes of 1636. Any member of the university might attend, though the

22. K. Fincham and P. Lake, 'The Ecclesiastical Policy of King James I', *Journal of British Studies*, 24 (1985), 189–91.
23. J. Prideaux, *Ephesus Backsliding Considered and Applyed to these Times, in a sermon preached at Oxford, in St Maries, the Tenth of July, being the Act Sunday, 1614* (Oxford, 1614), 10, 12–14, 16, 36; Madan, i. 98–9; Tyacke, *Anti-Calvinists*, 88; Fincham and Lake, 'Ecclesiastical Policy', 172, 176–7.
24. Below, 158.
25. For the dispute with Petre, see below, 63–74.

majority of the audience would have comprised those working for the MA or for the two higher degrees in theology, the BD and the DD. For the BD students, attendance was compulsory. The professor also acted as moderator, presiding and summing up in the theology disputations which were an essential part in the student's progress towards those degrees. In addition, he gave special addresses at the high points of the university's year, notably at the Act celebrations in July which marked the year's end; and he was also expected to preach, sometimes in English, at other points in the year.[26]

These formal duties provided the regius professor with the means to shape and dominate theological discussion within the university; and at a time when Oxford had something of the character of a clerical seminary, a training school for the clergy, this gave him a vicarious influence in the parishes of England. No other senior member of the university enjoyed quite the same opportunity to mould opinion. That the views of the second theology professor, Sebastian Benefield, Lady Margaret professor of divinity, were almost identical to those of Prideaux reinforced the Calvinist position within the university.[27] More circumscribed but equally important was Prideaux's similar role as moderator in disputations. These again were public occasions, where the presiding professor was able to bring forward his own conclusions and to take apart those of the disputants, sometimes mercilessly, before an audience. Prideaux's later use of his office and authority to lay down the law at disputations was to make him notorious.[28]

Prideaux's elevation allowed him to become the leader of the university's anti-Arminians. His first opportunity to demonstrate the strength of his convictions came in 1617, and in reaction, perhaps surprisingly, to the injunctions of a king whose religious opinions he generally revered and endorsed. Essentially a Calvinist for much of his life, James consistently saw his position under threat both from potentially disloyal papists and from puritans, from the papists' acknowledgement of the temporal sovereignty of the Pope and from the desire of the more extreme puritans for a less hierarchical form of church government, more presbyterian than episcopal. Each was an implicit challenge to the authority of the Crown. Moderate

---

26. Clark, *Register*, i. 132–3; *HUO*, iii. 307–8; *Statutes of the University of Oxford codified in the year 1636 under the Authority of Archb. Laud*, ed. J. Griffiths (Oxford, 1888), 40, 70, 156, 158.
27. Wood, *Athenae*, ii. 487–9; Tyacke, *Anti-Calvinists*, 61–2, 72; J. S. Macauley, 'Benefield [Benfield], Sebastian (1568/9–1630), Church of England clergyman and divine', *ODNB*.
28. Below, 245–7, 384–5.

Catholics, loyal to their sovereign, he was prepared to tolerate.[29] In 1616 the king's fear of puritanism was dominant, and he regarded the laxity of religious discipline in the two universities as the main source of the danger which puritanism presented. In December 1616 he sent a set of nine injunctions to Cambridge and in January 1617 an identical set to Oxford.[30] Their intention was to impose on both universities a rigid Anglican orthodoxy, to be enforced by panels headed by the two vice-chancellors. All those graduating were to acknowledge on oath the royal supremacy in church and state and the authority of the Book of Common Prayer and the Thirty-Nine Articles.[31] All preachers in the town's churches were to be 'conformable' (that is, to the canons of Anglican orthodoxy). All students were to attend sermons at St Mary's, the university church, rather than the town's other churches (where puritanically inclined lecturers might be found). Divinity students were to be directed to read the Fathers, the schoolmen, and histories of the church and its councils rather than compendia and abridgements—in other words, the sources rather than contemporary and probably opinionated 'study aids'. No one either in lectures or in sermons was to maintain any point of doctrine disallowed by the Church of England. Finally, a committee headed by the vice-chancellor was to report annually to the king on the observance of these instructions.

That the king's injunctions were received in Oxford in mid-January 1617 but not backed with proposals for their enforcement by Convocation, the university's senior governing body, until 29 March hints at the consternation which they caused.[32] They represented a degree of royal interference which seemed to be directed as much against the university's Calvinist majority as against the puritan minority whom the king feared. According to Peter Heylyn, Laud's biographer, they were issued in response to the promptings of his hero, whose role is strongly confirmed by Anthony Wood. In favour at court at this time (he had been made dean of Gloucester in 1616), Laud had played on the king's fear of 'presbyterial government', associating it with the teaching of 'Calvinian doctrines' and the destruction of 'monarchical government'. So indistinct was the doctrinal line between orthodox

29. Fincham and Lake, 'Ecclesiastical Policy', 182–6.
30. Wood, *History*, ii. 323–4; *HUO*, iv. 186, 189–90.
31. The injunctions simply refer to 'the three Articles', alluding to Canon 36 of Archbishop Bancroft's canons of 1604, which embodied these three articles: see *The Anglican Canons, 1529–1947*, ed. G. Bray (Church of England Rec. Soc., 6, 1998), 318–21.
32. Wood, *History*, ii. 324, 326.

Calvinists and moderate puritans that their ready confusion was easy enough to exploit. The attempted controls on preaching, teaching, and allegiance could bear down on the one as easily as the other. 'This was the first step', wrote Heylyn, 'towards the suppressing of that reputation which Calvin and his writings had hitherto attained unto in that university.'[33]

It was not a step which Prideaux was prepared to accept. As regius professor, he was a member of the committee set up to consider the king's instructions, but he subsequently joined his father-in-law William Goodwin, dean of Christ Church and former vice-chancellor, and his Calvinist colleague Sebastian Benefield, to ensure that they remained a dead letter.[34] A more forceful riposte came in 1617, when Prideaux 'caused above 18 questions against Arminianism to be publicly disputed on by his fellows in their chapel or hall'.[35] Some of these questions were a direct attack on Arminius's own teachings. Was his analysis of Paul's Epistle to the Romans, chapter 9, to be approved? (answer: no). Others went to the heart of Calvinist convictions. That 'grace sufficient for salvation' was not conceded to all had been one of Prideaux's doctoral theses in 1612.[36] Other questions and responses affirmed predestination, denied the existence of free will to do good after the Fall, and asserted that the regenerate were assured of salvation. In form, they were headings for disputations, but in effect they constituted a fairly full set of Calvinist tenets and anti-Arminian principles. That a copy of these 'Questiones Arminianae' was later found in Laud's study when it was ransacked in 1643 was proof of their interest to the churchman held responsible for the king's decrees.[37]

Part of the significance of these questions lay in their association with Prideaux's College: it was in Exeter, not in the schools, that they were debated, and by Exeter's fellows rather than by any of the numerous other Calvinist scholars in the wider university. To the views of these men and their rector the College's students were regularly exposed via the routine disputations held in the College chapel. The notebook of one such anonymous Exeter student, compiled about this time, throws light on some of their subjects. Most were predictably and starkly anti-Catholic. Is the sacrifice of

---

33. Heylyn, *Cyprianus Anglicus*, 71–2; Wood, *History*, ii. 323–4, 328.
34. Heylyn, *Cyprianus Anglicus*, 72; Wood, *History*, ii. 324.
35. Wood, *History*, ii. 328. The questions are given in W. Prynne, *Canterburies Doome* (1646), 156. Cf. Tyacke, *Anti-Calvinists*, 73.
36. Clark, *Register*, i. 209; above, 38.
37. Prynne, *Canterburies Doome*, 155.

the mass idolatrous? (answer: yes). Was the Blessed Virgin conceived without original sin? (answer: no). But an equal number were quintessentially Calvinist. Was God's will the true, whole, and adequate cause of reprobation? (answer: yes). Does man have free will? (answer: no).[38] That Calvinism and its complement, anti-Catholicism, were so firmly rooted in the College, among students as well as fellows, can only have reinforced the position of the College's rector.

Prideaux had by now emerged as the university's leading theologian controversialist: a role which rested on his learning and forensic skills, his intellectual firepower, the strength of his convictions, and the professorial office which these qualities had brought him. He brought them to bear in arguing against his opponents in religion, whether Remonstrants, Arminians, or Catholics. It was as an anti-Catholic polemicist that, in a reprise of the Casaubon affair, he was appointed about this time, probably by the king, to answer John Barclay's *Paraenesis ad sectarios* (1617), 'a piece of Catholic apologetics' written by a major literary figure once high in James's favour who had subsequently disgraced himself by leaving England for Rome. Prideaux's copy of Barclay's work, unlike most of his books fiercely annotated, survives in Worcester Cathedral Library.[39] But despite this evidence of his interest, the commission never seems to have been executed, perhaps partly because of his laborious involvement in his College's conflict with William Lord Petre at just this time.[40]

The most sustained development of his theological views during these years came in the nine Act lectures which he delivered between 1616 and 1624.[41] Constituting a coherent set, they have sometimes been seen as a barrage directed largely against Arminianism, and certainly there was a strong anti-Arminian thrust to their content. But Stephen Hampton has shown that the lectures embody a much broader, weightier, and less polemical scheme.[42] Although they take issue with a large number of opposing

38. BL MS Harley 977, fos. 81r, 84r, 87r, 93v.
39. Wood, *History*, ii. 328; N. Royan, 'Barclay, John (1582–1621), writer', *ODNB*; Milton, *Catholic and Reformed*, 254–5; WCL, Y.I. 20.
40. For the conflict with Petre, see below, 63–74.
41. The lectures were first published in Prideaux, *Lectiones Novem de Totidem Religionis Capitibus* (Oxford, 1625), and reprinted in 1648 in *VDL*.
42. Tyacke, *Anti-Calvinists*, 74; *HUO*, iv. 587. This and the following three paragraphs largely derive from Chapter 1, 'The Act Lectures of John Prideaux', of Dr Hampton's forthcoming book, *Grace and Conformity*. I am most grateful to Dr Hampton for allowing me to draw on his work, which provides an unequalled account of Prideaux's thought, in advance of publication.

views, Catholic as well as Remonstrant and Arminian, their main purpose was 'to explore the nature and consequences of grace'—grace which may be defined as 'the supernatural assistance of God bestowed upon a rational being with a view to his sanctification [i.e. salvation]'.[43] Prideaux's intention was to provide an account of grace and its work as they were understood by his own Church of England and, perhaps more importantly, to counter any suggestion, by Arminians or others, that redemption owed more to human self-help than to God's grace freely given. He wished to avoid any hint of Pelagianism.

This was theologically a complex task, whose successful undertaking showed the force of Prideaux's intellect as well as the breadth of his reading. Drawing particularly (but by no means exclusively) on St Paul's epistles and on Augustine, he begins by arguing that just as God had predestined some to election and so to salvation, so also, by his absolute decree of reprobation, he had predestined others to damnation (the meaning of 'reprobation'). His decree is 'absolute' in that it proceeds from God alone. Reprobation may result either from God's arbitrary will (his decision not to elect some to grace) or from the sins of the reprobate. But because no one can know whether he is among the reprobate, it is always worth acting well. God has foreknowledge of all human decisions, but this does not undermine human freedom (his foreknowledge does not imply that an action is predetermined) or make God the author of sin, which he merely foresees. Within this framework, grace allows the human will to make the right choices. God's assistance, freely given as grace, is necessary to bring about the salvation of the elect, but the doctrine of absolute reprobation means that it is not conceded to all. Christ's sacrificial death, the atonement, was sufficient to extend salvation to all, but in effect it extended only to the elect (the doctrine known nowadays as 'hypothetical universalism'). Divine predestination is reconcilable with human free choice: grace enables the recipient to make a right choice, the choice which God has desired us to make, but in the absence of grace another choice might have been made. The recipient of grace is active in the process of his salvation, since the believer assents to his salvation through Christ; but grace might be inefficacious if the recipient dissents from it. Faith alone allows the believer to understand and benefit from Christ's atonement. On a related subject, perseverance, Prideaux held fairly conventional views. Despite his sins, the believer cannot fall away from

---

43. The definition of *ODCC*, 700.

grace completely and so be deprived of salvation, and the faithful can be assured of their salvation, their faith preventing their fall from grace and conferring that assurance.

The theology of grace as expounded in these lectures was closely linked to Prideaux's views on the role of the church, for it was only through and within the church that salvation could be obtained. Pagans and non-Christians of all kinds could not achieve it. Outside the church, and possessing only reason and their natural qualities, they lacked the necessary faith, for which both knowledge of Christ and membership of his church was essential. This led on to a discussion of the historicity of the Protestant churches, which Prideaux found in pre-Reformation times—in the primitive Apostolic Church, not yet tainted by papal corruption, in those within the Catholic Church who had pressed for reform, and in the heretical sects, such as the Hussites, who had defied the Church of Rome.[44] The Reformation had not created a new church but decorrupted an old one. The effect of these arguments was to strengthen the claims of the Protestant churches, including the Church of England, to the allegiance of their members.

Prideaux's first nine Act lectures, their conclusions no more than baldly summarized above, represented a remarkable tour de force. Interlinked, closely reasoned, and closely referenced, they justified the title of his later Act lecture 'on the use of logic in theology'.[45] Arid and fanciful though some of their arguments may now seem, they were bound together by a secondary purpose more humane in its implications than the lecturer's main concern to set down the orthodox teaching on grace. That purpose was pastoral. The doctrine of predestination and absolute reprobation might easily seem alarming, conducive both to despair and to an antinomian rejection of the moral law. This Prideaux implicitly denied. Without endorsing a Pelagian view of justification by works, he could still argue that moral behaviour might turn aside reprobation; that God's foreknowledge did not undermine man's status as a free agent to do good (if so enabled by grace) or ill; that the elect could be sure of the remission of sins; and that faithful membership of the church was a halfway house to salvation. Here he took a more liberal and optimistic stance than some stricter puritan predestinarians; and here too was his Christian ministry in action. Since many clergy, including local priests, were present at the Act, his pastoral lessons

44. Prideaux's views on the origins of the Protestant churches are examined below, 199–204.
45. Prideaux, *VDL*, 215–29; below, 210–13.

could be conveyed through his lectures to the church at large and to its constituent parishes. It was in the parishes, perhaps surprisingly, that the doctrine of predestination was often preached, but with the comforting provisos put forward both by Prideaux and by fellow divines such as John Davenant.[46]

Prideaux's lectures were given in an Oxford which remained broadly and deeply sympathetic to Anglican Calvinism. Arminian well-wishers were by no means absent from the local scene. Laud remained as president of St John's, holding the headship of his College in tandem with the deanery of Gloucester from 1616 until 1621, when he became bishop of St David's; and he remained an influence at court. An ally, John Howson, was appointed bishop of Oxford in 1618, and Richard Corbett, another Arminian (and poet), dean of Christ Church in 1620, in succession to the Calvinist William Goodwin.[47] But the prevailing ethos was firmly set against this minority. Until about 1623 many of the theses defended at the Act maintained such Calvinist doctrines as perseverance and the absence of free will after the Fall. A more covert influence was probably that of William Herbert, earl of Pembroke, elected as the university's chancellor in 1617. Pembroke, whose relations with Prideaux will be considered later, was a Calvinist and the patron of Calvinists, and his election by Convocation was itself another indication of the university's collective frame of mind. It gave him the *ex officio* authority to nominate the vice-chancellor, the university's effective working head, and those whom Pembroke nominated—Goodwin from 1617 to 1619, Prideaux from 1619 to 1621 and from 1624 to 1626, and William Piers from 1621 to 1624—were all themselves Calvinists.[48] All in all, Prideaux's professional life at this time was set against an assured and favourable background.

2. The Synod of Dort and the Spanish Match

By this time the international politics of religion had begun to impinge on Prideaux's career. Although he was directly involved in neither, two

---

46. A. Hunt, *The Art of Preaching: English Preachers and their Audiences, 1590–1640* (Cambridge, 2010), 342–89 *passim*, esp. 346–56. For those present at the Act, see below, 206–10.
47. Milton, 'Laud'; *HUO*, iv. 581.
48. Below, 72–4, 250; Wood, *Fasti*, i. 370, 379, 386, 392, 395, 404, 410, 414, 422.

episodes are particularly important in their bearing on his character and reputation: the Synod of Dort and the Spanish Match.[49] The Synod of Dort, a great international conference of representatives of the British and Continental Protestant churches, met at Dordrecht in the winter of 1618–19. It grew out of attempts to settle differences within the Dutch church between the Remonstrants and their Calvinist counterparts, the Counter-Remonstrants, who in most respects shared common theological ground with the Calvinists dominant within the Church of England. Of the four original delegates making up the British party, three were probably chosen by the king, who gave the delegates their instructions and had a strong interest in the synod's outcome. Although there were differences between the British delegates and the Dutch Counter-Remonstrants, the British rejecting the extreme Calvinism of the Dutch, that outcome was a joint anti-Arminian victory for these two parties. The final canons, published in England in translation in 1619 but never formally ratified, reaffirmed Calvinist doctrine on such central matters as predestination, election, perseverance, and free will.[50] Entirely acceptable to James, they reinforced the Calvinist control of the English church. But although the results of the synod apparently set back the progress of the Arminians, they nevertheless, and to a degree paradoxically, helped to promote their formation as a group and to give them a sense of shared identity in opposition to the Calvinist majority.

Prideaux might well have been chosen as one of the four British delegates. Two of the four, John Davenant, master of Queens' College, Cambridge, and Samuel Ward, master of Sidney Sussex College, Cambridge, were, like him, royal chaplains and rootedly Calvinist in their views. A third, Joseph Hall, dean of Worcester, a more moderate Calvinist, had, like Prideaux, been one of Prince Henry's chaplains. The fourth, George Carleton, bishop of Llandaff, was the choice of the Calvinist Archbishop Abbot.[51] Prideaux was a more distinguished theologian and controversialist than any of these, and for a time it had seemed that he might be chosen. In August 1618, before

---

49. For the remainder of this paragraph, see esp. Tyacke, *Anti-Calvinists*, 87–105, and *The British Delegation and the Synod of Dort (1618–19)*, ed. A. Milton (Church of England Rec. Soc., 13, 2005), xvii–lv. For the nuances of theological opinion at Dort, see esp. Milton, *Catholic and Reformed*, 418–22.

50. Milton, *Catholic and Reformed*, 421–2. For the substance of the canons, see *British Delegation*, ed. Milton, 296–319.

51. Tyacke, *Anti-Calvinists*, 91–2.

the formal appointment of the delegates in September, he was warmly commended to Sir Dudley Carleton, British ambassador at The Hague, by Sir Henry Savile, warden of Merton College and the most intellectually distinguished of the Oxford heads. Carleton, who was himself a Calvinist,[52] may have been looking for names to put before the king. Savile wrote:

> Upon your ecclesiasticall busyness I cold doe no lesse than to give you notice of a most fitt person for your service, Doctor Prideaux, rector of Exceter College and publicke reader of the university, a man very well seene [versed] in modern controversies and especially in this of yours, a learned and ready [skilled, knowledgeable] man.

Savile went on to say that Prideaux would give Carleton 'better assistance . . . than any you named, as I remember, in eyther university'.[53] When, in the course of the synod, illness caused Hall to withdraw from the delegation, Carleton took up Savile's suggestion and recommended Prideaux to Abbot as Hall's successor:

> I will take the boldnes to putt your Grace in minde of Dr Prideaux, for the sufficiency of the man (which I have onely by report, for I know him not) as likewise for the reputation of the university of Oxford, which is not yet so much as named in this Synod.

Abbot, in reply, supported Carleton's wish for an Oxford man, but said that Dr Goad, Abbot's chaplain and by now Hall's replacement, was 'neare at hand, whereas Dr Prideaux cannot be provided on the sudden'.[54]

Although it thus seems to have been chance that deprived Prideaux of a place on the Dort delegation at this secondary stage, it was perhaps surprising that he had not been appointed in the first place. Savile's letter survives to testify to his theological expertise and general reputation. But his doctrinal position was rather more extreme than that of one delegate, Samuel Ward,[55] and after his failure in the previous year to implement James's directions to the university for the suppression of puritanism, he may have moved to the edge of royal favour. Even though he had not been present at Dort, however, there was no doubt where he predictably stood on the points at issue. Writing to him on 11 December 1618, his friend George Hakewill

---

52. Ibid., 89.
53. TNA, SP 14/98, fo. 117; Tyacke, *Anti-Calvinists*,74. Tyacke goes beyond the evidence in saying that Carleton was advised to consult Prideaux 'on the finer points of the Arminian dispute'.
54. *British Delegation*, ed. Milton, 15–8.
55. For Ward's slightly softer 'hypothetical universalist' views, see Tyacke, *Anti-Calvinist*, 94–7.

enclosed what he said was 'the choise of a middle way betweene the Remonstrantes and the Contraremonstrantes thought to bee Dr Overals'. He probably refers to a widely circulated tract by Dr John Overall, bishop of Coventry and Lichfield, 1614–18, and of Norwich, 1618–19, one of the leading English Arminians, and a supporter of their Dutch counterparts, setting out the main points in dispute between the two sides at Dort and giving only a secondary place to the doctrine of predestination. That this was enclosed, as Hakewill said, for Prideaux's 'perusall and censure' shows the critical reception which Hakewill expected the tract to receive in the rector's lodgings at Exeter.[56]

In his Act lecture of July 1619 Prideaux mentioned the disputes settled at Dort and the synod's happy outcome, later citing and discussing the final canons in his 1622 lecture.[57] In many ways they mirrored the teaching of his Act lectures, particularly in what they had to say about grace as the free gift of God bestowed on the faithful.[58] The canons became for him a sort of shibboleth: both a definition of the central points of the faith and, in so far as they resulted from royal policy, a lasting mark of King James's righteous guardianship of his church. At Dort, he said in one of his early sermons preached before the king, the Arminians 'by Gods providence and your Maiesties especiall furtherance . . . have met with their masters';[59] while in his *Easy and Compendious Introduction for Reading All Sorts of Histories*, written in his last years in the late 1640s, he singled out as one of the memorable events in King James's time his 'advice and aide, availed especially in composing differences abroad among the reformed churches. To this end he sent certain select and worthy divines to the Synod of Dort.'[60] In an angry moment during the disputations at the 1629 Act he would remark fiercely that 'wee are concluded under an anathema to stand to the Synod of Dort against the Arminians'.[61] Although this was not true—there was no such anathema—it illustrates the high place which the synod and its canons occupied in Prideaux's scale of sacred values.

56. *British Delegation*, ed. Milton, xxviii n. 44, 102–3. For Overall's tract, see ibid., 85–92.
57. *VDL*, 48, 95–6.
58. See esp. Canon V: *British Delegation*, ed. Milton, 298.
59. 'Hezechiahs Sicknesse', in *CS*, 19.
60. M. Prideaux, *An Easy and Compendious Introduction for Reading All Sorts of Histories* (Oxford, 1648), 337. For this work, ascribed to Matthias Prideaux on the title page but actually written by his father, see below, 366–7.
61. Lambeth Palace Library MS 943, fo. 133. For the context, see below, 246–7. Cf. *HUO*, iv. 586; Milton, *Catholic and Reformed*, 422.

Like Prideaux, Hakewill had been passed over as a British representative at Dort, although, again like Prideaux, he was well qualified to serve and at one stage apparently expected to do so. It was reported in September 1618 that he was to be one of the delegates, and in July 1619, when all was over, Abbot told Carleton that Hakewill would have been his choice. 'If I had had my will another Oxford man Doctor Hakewell by name had gone in the place of him who played these giddy parts' (probably meaning Samuel Ward).[62]

It was Hakewill too, rather than Prideaux, who was involved in the affair of the Spanish Match, with unhappy results.[63] The issue here was explosive and had wide ramifications. A marriage between Prince Charles, the king's heir after Prince Henry's death, and the Infanta Maria of Spain, daughter of Philip III, had been under discussion since 1614, initially with the object of acquiring a large Spanish dowry to relieve James's financial problems. The match was never a likely prospect, since it would have entailed a substantial measure of toleration for English Catholics and the probability of a Catholic succession. It became still less likely after the outbreak of Continental war in 1618, the ejection of the Protestant Elector Frederick and his wife Elizabeth, James's daughter, from their Bohemian kingdom in 1620, and the subsequent overrunning of Frederick's Palatinate homeland by Spanish troops. Public opinion in England, which is to say Protestant opinion, became violently agitated, and opposition to the Spanish Match, voiced through the parliamentary commons in 1621, was nationwide. Archbishop Abbot was among the scheme's strongest critics, their opposition strengthened by James's concurrent concessions to Catholics, including the suspension of the penal laws.[64] In February 1623, however, Charles and the king's favourite, the duke of Buckingham, set out on a madcap mission to Spain, hoping to conclude the marriage deal; but negotiations, never very practicable, foundered on Spanish demands for Catholic privileges, both for Charles's prospective wife and for English Catholics in general. In October the two travellers returned to England with nothing gained, to be greeted with 'universall joy'. Bell-ringing, bonfires, and thanksgiving sermons marked the conclusive abandonment of the Spanish Match.[65]

---

62. *British Delegation*, ed. Milton, xxviii n. 44, 371.
63. Unless otherwise stated, the remainder of this paragraph derives from Croft, *King James*, 103–22.
64. T. Cogswell, *The Blessed Revolution* (Cambridge, 1989), 20–32; Fincham and Lake, 'Ecclesiastical Policy', 200.
65. Cogswell, *Blessed Revolution*, 6–12.

Some of the fiercest opposition to the match, and to James's temporarily pro-Catholic tendencies in general, came from Exeter men. Hakewill was the most conspicuous of these. Originally high in James's favour, he had prospered through his collation to the archdeaconry of Surrey in 1617. But the king's foreign policy, the domestic benefits which it brought to English Catholics, and the projected marriage proved too much for him. Without the king's knowledge, in August 1622 he presented to Prince Charles, whose chaplain he was, a tract entitled 'The Wedding Ring' which argued force-fully against marriage between Protestants and Catholics, largely on the grounds that Catholics were idolaters. This rash act led to his arrest and temporary imprisonment. Two months earlier he had published a series of sermons, 'King David's Vow', calling for reform at court, criticizing James's concessions to Catholics, and condemning Protestant-Catholic marriages. Hakewill was not alone. Another of Charles's chaplains, Thomas Winniffe, fellow of Exeter from 1595 to 1609, spent time in the Tower for comparing the Palatinate 'to an innocent sheep savaged by a Spanish wolf', while a third Exonian, Sampson Price, who had taken his DD from Exeter in 1617, similarly incurred the king's wrath for preaching on the same theme.[66] These opinions were almost certainly shared by a second former fellow, Lewis Bayly, bishop of Bangor, who was in trouble with the king in 1620 for praying for Frederick and Elizabeth as king and queen of Bohemia, and as victims of Spanish aggression, before James had acknowledged their titles.[67] Although Exeter was hardly unique in its strong anti-Catholic bias, it remains striking that a group of James's most outspoken critics came from the same college.

Prideaux, however, was not among them: the strong feelings of the College's past and present members resulted more from the legacy of Holland's teaching than from Prideaux's current leadership. That he detested the prospect of the Spanish Match as much as they did must be certain. Not much can be deduced from his brief and conventional contri-bution to *Carolus Redux*, the slim volume of Oxford verses published to celebrate Charles's return from Spain in 1623, to which Hakewill also contributed. But more telling was the retrospective jubilation which he

66. McCullough, *Sermons at Court*, 201–4; McCullough, 'Hakewill'; Milton, *Catholic and Reformed*, 58; Fincham and Lake, 'Ecclesiastical Policy', 199–200. The manuscript of 'The Wedding Ring' is Bodl. MS Rawl. D 853, fos. 111r–131r.
67. Wood, *Athenae*, ii. 529; Fincham and Lake, 'Ecclesiastical Policy', 199–200.

voiced in the dedicatory epistle to Hakewill prefacing his consecration
sermon for Exeter's new chapel, preached on 5 October 1624—the anniversary, he noted, of the day 'which made England most happy and triumphant by your noble master Prince Charles his returne from beyond the
seas'.[68] He may have been earlier sent Hakewill's 'Wedding Ring': 'a
discourse of mine which I pray yow to reade over and correct as yow see
cause', as Hakewill described it in his letter to Prideaux of 11 December
1618.[69] Yet unlike his colleagues he is not known to have made any other
public comment on the Spanish Match, either in print or in the pulpit or the
schools. His silence may partly have reflected a natural timidity and a wish to
avoid confrontation, qualities also seen at other points in his life.[70] But the
regius professor and king's chaplain may also have felt that his position
inhibited him from criticizing royal policy. Even on matters of personal
conviction, he recognized authority and may have been reluctant to defy it.
Always a royalist, his loyalty to the king was paramount.

3. Foreign students, scholars, and visitors

Throughout Prideaux's early and middle years as rector and professor, his
College acted as host to a succession of foreign students and scholars. Their
presence was another mark of the theological expertise and reputation
which had brought him the regius chair; for Exeter's chief appeal to these
visitors lay in the prospect of Prideaux's company, direction, and teaching.
We have already seen that he was beginning to attract them during his later
years as fellow,[71] but they became a more conspicuous feature of the College
after his election to the rectorship in 1612. Their memorialist was Anthony
Wood. 'Many foreigners', he writes, 'came purposely to sit at his feet to gain
instruction,' They 'had chambers there and diet, purposely to improve
themselves by his company, his instruction, and direction for course of
studies. Some of them have been divines of note, and others meer lay-
men, that have been eminent in their respective countries wherein afterwards they have lived.' He goes on to name twenty-two of these

---

68. *Carolus Redux* (Oxford, 1623), sigs. A2v, I3v; Madan, i. 119; Prideaux, *A Sermon Preached.*
69. *British Delegation*, ed. Milton, 102–3.
70. Below, 244, 279, 305, 308–9, 317.
71. Above, 29–30.

'outlanders', as he calls them,[72] and to these we can add a further five from other sources, including three, Matthias Pasor, John Daniel Getsius, and Louis Cappell, to whom Wood gives separate entries—making twenty-seven in all. We have independent evidence from College and university records of the presence of at least twenty of these at Exeter. But there were, Wood says, 'many more, which shall now be omitted'. Since few matriculated and some left no mark on College records, this seems quite possible.

Most of Exeter's foreign visitors came between 1610 and 1629, after which they largely ceased to appear, for reasons to be discussed. They were to some extent representative figures, part of a general trend which saw many overseas students drawn towards the early seventeenth-century university. Political developments help to explain this. The alliance with the Palatinate forged by the marriage of James I's daughter to the Elector Palatine in 1613, followed by the outbreak of what became the Thirty Years War in 1618, made Oxford a friendly base and a refuge, particularly for Germans from the Palatinate and Bohemia whose homelands had been overrun by Catholic invaders. For them and others like them Oxford promised not only security but also intellectual attractions which Cambridge could hardly rival. They flocked to Sir Thomas Bodley's new library, about half of whose 520 or so foreign readers between 1620 and 1642 were Germans. Opened only in 1602, but by 1620 already possessing some 16,000 books and manuscripts, the library in itself constituted a large part of Oxford's appeal to Continental scholars.[73] The affinities and sympathies between the Church of England, with Oxford as its intellectual powerhouse, and the reformed and largely Calvinist churches of Continental Europe created another bond. More perhaps than at any other time in the university's history before the twentieth century, circumstances made Oxford an international centre.

Yet it was Exeter alone among the colleges which benefited from this influx, and most visitors to the university appear to have had no college affiliation. If Exeter's singularity here chiefly derived from Prideaux's reputation as a scholar and teacher, as Wood indicates, at a secondary level it also reflected his College's reputation as a special bastion of Calvinist orthodoxy. As in the university at large, most of the College's known visitors came from

72. Wood, *Athenae*, iii. 266, 269–70.
73. M. Clapinson, 'The Bodleian Library and its Readers, 1602–1652', *BLR*, 19 (2006), 31; *HUO*, iv. 661, 671.

Germany: some fifteen, compared with four from Denmark, three from Switzerland, and two each from France and the United Provinces. Within the College the Germans were seen as a discrete group. That they had their own quarters within the College, the *aedificium Alemanni*, 'the German's building',[74] hints at a foreign community a good deal larger than the mere three or four named foreigners a year who show up in the College records. Henry Petraeus, a visiting scholar and future professor of medicine at the Protestant University of Marburg, present at Exeter with John Combachius around 1610, could write of the College as 'a lodging and a stage (*theatrum*) for Teutons', and of Prideaux as 'the mainstay of German youth (*Germanae columen . . . juventae*)'.[75] The particular hospitality which it offered to Germans and the particular welcome which they received from Prideaux were thus already recognized.

Exeter's foreigners fell into two broad categories. The first comprised undergraduates, generally young men, who often came for no more than a year or two, usually left without a degree, and had no pretensions to an academic or scholarly career. In all these ways they resembled many English undergraduates, differing only in some cases by their having had prior training at a Continental university. Typical of this group was the German student Paul Amyraut. Born about 1600, he had studied at Heidelberg before matriculating at Exeter in 1619. He took no degree, but nevertheless went on to hold a series of benefices in the Church of England and in Ireland, emerging as a militant anti-Catholic.[76] Equally typical was Mark Zeiglier. Coming from the Palatinate, he was a student at Exeter in 1624–5, appears in the College buttery book for 1624 as paying for his commons, contributes to the volume of university verse compiled for the marriage of Prince Charles and Henrietta Maria in 1625, and then disappears.[77] Several of these undergraduates are listed among the pupils of either Prideaux or one

---

74. ECA, A.III.9 (Rector's Quarterly Accounts, 1614–27, unfoliated). Accepta, 1618–19, 1620; Expensa, 1618, 1620). It is, of course, possible that 'Germans' is being used here as a generic term to cover all Exeter's foreigners.

75. 'Epigramma ad rectorem, sub-rectorem et socios Collegii Exoniensis Oxonii', in J. Combachius, *Metaphysicorum*, 3rd edn (Oxford, 1633), sig. A7v; Madan, i. 166. For Petraeus, see F. Krafft, 'The Magic Word *Chymiatria*—and the Attractiveness of Medical Education at Marburg, 1608–1620', *History of Universities*, 26/1 (2012), 8, 16–17.

76. Boase, *Commoners*, 5; Clark, *Register* ii. 379; S. Wright, 'Amyraut, Paul (b.1600/01), Church of Ireland clergyman', *ODNB*.

77. Wood, *Athenae*, iii. 270, 974; ECA, BB/16 (Buttery book, 1624–5); *Epithalamia Oxoniensia* (Oxford, 1625), sig. D3r–v.

of the fellows, among others, Samuel Hortensius, from Berne, and John Stuckius and John Waserus, both from Zurich.[78]

The second category was made up of more senior figures, men either studying for an advanced degree under Prideaux or—a still more superior group—already holding lectureships or chairs at Continental universities and coming to Exeter specifically to benefit from Prideaux's presence. Nicholas Vignier, for example, one of the College's two Frenchmen, was already the possessor of an MA from the Protestant academy at Saumur when he arrived at Exeter in the early 1620s 'to improve his studies by the hearing and doctrine of Dr. John Prideaux'. He took his BD from Exeter in 1623, staying for some years before retiring to his home town of Blois to serve as a Protestant minister.[79] A comparable career was that of John Hoffmann, another German from the Palatinate, who arrived at Exeter, aged 22, in 1624, took his BA in the same year, presumably by incorporation from another university, went on to gain his BD in 1634, and, like Amyraut, became an Anglican clergyman, dying as rector of Wootton by Woodstock in 1640.[80] His 'Liber Amicorum' in the Bodleian, a sort of autograph book, shows him to have been at the centre of a lively circle of 'exiles' (as they often described themselves) from Bohemia and the Palatinate but also including that former Exeter fellow, George Hakewill.[81] For Amyraut, Vignier, Hoffmann, and others like them, Prideaux's Exeter offered a professional training and a route to a clerical career, whether in the Church of England or in the reformed church abroad.

By far the most interesting group in this category, however, were the more advanced scholars, older men of some intellectual distinction, who often resided at Exeter for several years and made a significant contribution to the academic life of the College and, in some cases, of the university, and whose debt to Prideaux was especially large. Three in particular shared some or all of these characteristics and are particularly well recorded in contemporary sources: Sixtinus Amama, Matthias Pasor, and John Daniel Getsius. Each is worth a rather more detailed account.

Sixtinus Amama (1593–1629) came from West Friesland in Holland. In 1610 he entered the local Protestant university of Franeker, later graduating

78. ECA, H.II.11.
79. Wood, *Athenae*, ii. 521–2; Clark, *Register*, iii. 424; Boase, *Commoners*, 337.
80. Wood, *Fasti*, i. 474–5; Boase, *Commoners*, 160.
81. Bodl. MS Rawl. D 933.

and going on to spend a short time at Leiden in 1614, laying the foundations of a career which would see him emerge as one of the most distinguished Hebrew scholars and theologians of his age. In January 1615 he came to Oxford and to Exeter 'for the sake of Dr Prideaux', writes Wood, 'whose person and doctrine he much admired'.[82] He stayed for only a short while, about fifteen months, leaving in March 1616 to return to Franeker and a chair in oriental languages. During his time at Exeter his status was somewhere between that of an ordinary undergraduate or graduate student, and a visiting scholar with advanced qualifications. He appears in the buttery book for 1615–16, paying for his commons, and in his last term he is listed among the pupils of Nathanael Carpenter, one of the College's most eminent fellows.[83] But during his short stay he also taught Hebrew and possibly Arabic, took part in theological disputations in the College chapel, wrote at least one work subsequently published after his return to Franeker, and lived on easy terms with the fellows.[84] He wrote in several places and with exceptional warmth about his time at Exeter and especially about his debt to Prideaux. Prefacing one of his later works with a dedicatory letter to Festus Hommius, the Dutch Calvinist theologian and opponent of Arminius, he called to mind 'the reverend and excellent man' Dr John Prideaux, 'our common friend', who had read his book and encouraged him to publish it.[85] In another dedicatory letter, this one introducing his edition of Drusius's *De Sectis Judaicis* (1619), he addressed not only Prideaux, 'the most vigilant rector of Exeter College', but also the sub-rector and the whole fellowship, 'formerly the most delightful of companions (*iucundissimi quondam commilitones*)'. Enclosing a copy of the book for the College library, he wrote that every day he recalled their kindness to him.[86] This particular book does not survive in the library, but another of his works, *Censura Vulgatae* (1620) is present, with an inscription recording it as the author's gift. Two of his other works remain among Prideaux's books in Worcester Cathedral Library, inscribed to Prideaux in Amama's hand.[87] In terms of

---

82. Wood, *Athenae*, ii. 443–4; Clark, Register, i. 277; J. E. Platt, 'Sixtinus Amama (1593–1629): Franeker Professor and Citizen of the Republic of Letters', in *Universiteit te Franeker, 1585–1811*, ed. G. T. Jensma et al. (Leeuwarden, 1985), 236–9.

83. Platt, 'Amama', 246, n. 43; ECA, H.II.11. For Carpenter, see below, 170–3.

84. Platt, 'Amama', 242–3, 247 nn. 44, 45; *HUO*, iv. 477; BL MS Harl. 977, fos. 81r, 84r.

85. Platt, 'Amama', 246, n. 45. The book was Amama's *De Nomine Tetragrammato Dissertatio* (1628).

86. The letter is printed in C. W. Boase, *Register of the Rector and Fellows . . . of Exeter College, Oxford*, 1st edn (Oxford, 1879), xxv, n. 1; cf. Platt, 'Amama', 243, 247, n. 49.

87. Platt, 'Amama', 246–7, n. 45; ECL, PE 20; WCL, H.D. 18.

learning and scholarly exchange, this was almost a relationship between equals.

Although he wrote very little, Matthias Pasor (1599–1658) made a more permanent mark on the Oxford scene.[88] Like Amama, Pasor was primarily a linguist, but much else besides. Born at Herborn in Germany, he studied at the Calvinist academy there, and then at Marburg and Heidelberg, where he was appointed professor of natural philosophy in 1619 and of mathematics in the following year. After the sack of Heidelberg by the Imperial-Spanish army in 1622, he led a wandering life, visiting Oxford in 1624 and then arriving for a longer stay in the spring of 1625. According to his autobiography, it was Prideaux who persuaded him to come to Exeter. His special value to the College and the university lay in his knowledge of Arabic, and he tells us that he gave instruction in Arabic to Prideaux himself and to Thomas Clayton, the regius professor of medicine.[89] Under Prideaux's patronage he was given pupils and College employment. He taught mathematics to John Robartes, one of Exeter's aristocratic undergraduates, he presided at theological disputations in College, and he was welcomed too by George Hakewill, who on one occasion took him on an adventurous expedition into Hakewill's native Devonshire, in company with another Exeter fellow, Laurence Bodley.[90] Like Amama, he was thus thoroughly embedded in Exeter society.

But his accomplishments found a broader outlet within the university at large. This was particularly so with his teaching of Arabic. He provided public lectures and tutorials in Arabic, giving an inaugural lecture in 1626 which became his only published work, and teaching, among others, the young Edward Pococke, later the first Laudian professor of Arabic. Although his knowledge of the language was fairly superficial, he created a university-wide interest in the subject and in its value for the study of Scripture, for which Arabic, like Hebrew a Semitic language, provided a guide to the meaning of many obscure Hebrew words from the Old Testament.[91] Both within and without the university, Pasor had a wide circle of intellectual

88. For brief accounts, see Wood, *Athenae*, iii. 444–5, and J. van Maanen, 'Pasor, Matthias (1599–1658), linguist and philosopher', *ODNB*.

89. *Parentalia in piam memoriam reverendi et clarissimi D. Matthiae Pasoris . . . Vita Matthiae Pasoris ab hoc ipsomet vivo plenius consignata* (Groningen, 1658), 38–9, 42. G. J. Toomer, *Eastern Wisedome and Learning: The Study of Arabic in Seventeenth-Century England* (Oxford, 1996), 98–101.

90. *Parentalia*, 42; *The Theological Works of the Learned Dr Pocock*, ed. L. Twells, 2 vols. (London, 1740), i. 2; *HUO*, iv. 370; Feingold, *Mathematicians' Apprenticeship*, 83.

91. *Works of Pocock*, ed. Twells, i. 2; *HUO*, iv. 479–80; Toomer, *Eastern Wisedome*, 98.

friends and correspondents, including Henry Briggs, professor of geometry, and Thomas Lydiat, mathematician and astronomer.[92] In 1627 he collaborated with Briggs in raising money for the relief of the distressed Protestant ministers of the Palatinate.[93] He returned to the Continent in 1629—against, he says, the wishes of the Oxonians[94]—to take up the chair in moral philosophy at Groningen. As well as fostering his reputation as something of a polymath, his four-year residence at Exeter had left its mark on the development of the university. Prideaux's initial invitation to him was a tribute to the rector's talent-spotting skills.

Our third scholar, John Daniel Getsius (1591/2–1672) was another refugee from war-torn Germany.[95] Getsius came from the Palatinate and studied at Marburg, alma mater to several of Exeter's 'outlanders'. There he gained his degree in philosophy in 1618. After various wanderings occasioned by the war, he moved first to London and then to Cambridge, taking his BA in 1621. During a short stay at The Hague in 1623 he secured the support of the exiled Elector Palatine and, partly as a result of this, he and four other Germans had by 1624 secured pensions of £18 a year from the University of Oxford, thanks largely to the further backing of the chancellor, Pembroke. It is highly likely, however, that Prideaux, then vice-chancellor, also weighed in behind this small group; and all the more likely, since not only Getsius but two more of his pensioner compatriots, John Hoffman and Mark Zeiglier, all took up residence in Exeter. That three out of these five settled in Exeter confirms what we already know about the College's hospitality to foreigners and especially to Germans. We have already seen that Zeiglier contributed to *Epithalamia Oxoniensia*, the volume of university verse compiled for Prince Charles's marriage in 1625, and so too did Getsius and Hoffmann.[96]

Getsius remained at Exeter for about five years, In the *Epithalamia* both he and Zeiglier appear as students of theology, presumably reading for the BD. Neither seems to have taken the degree, though Getsius may have incepted as Master of Arts. During these years he was kept afloat not only by

---

92. Feingold, *Mathematicians' Apprenticeship*, 139, 148–52.
93. Bodl. MS Tanner 72, fos. 228, 247, 308; Milton, *Catholic and Reformed*, 511 (where Briggs's sentiments are misattributed to Pasor).
94. *Parentalia*, 44–5.
95. For brief accounts, see Wood, *Athenae*, iii. 973–6, and J. T. Young, 'Getsius, John Daniel [formerly Johann Daniel] (1591/2–1672), Church of England clergyman and writer', *ODNB*.
96. *Epithalamia Oxoniensia*, sigs. D2v, D3r, D3v. Cf. Boase, *Register*, cvii, note 1.

his pension but also by teaching Hebrew 'in which he had good skill' (says Wood), and by taking in pupils, 'which privilege was allowed him in Exeter College by doctor Prideaux . . . who had a good respect and kindness for him'. His earnings supported his studies until 1629, when he was ordained priest in Exeter Cathedral[97] and, on Prideaux's advice, moved to Dartmouth in Devon, there to earn his bread as a schoolmaster and preacher, before obtaining the nearby living of Stoke Gabriel in 1636 and marrying an Englishwoman shortly afterwards. Exeter College and Prideaux's patronage had been the twin pivots which turned the impoverished German refugee into the anglicized country parson.

One other foreign visitor, Louis Cappell, deserves a brief biography, both because of the detail which we have on his Oxford career and because of his later eminence as a scholar. We have already been introduced to him as a pupil of Prideaux's during the latter's fellowship years.[98] Cappell was born in 1585 at Sedan in north-east France into a French Protestant family. After studying theology at Bouillon in Lorraine (now Belgium), he later moved to Bordeaux, where by 1610 he had become a member of the local Huguenot community, living under the supervision of John Cameron, the Scottish theologian and the community's pastor. It was Cameron who advised him to study abroad and raised the money to enable him to do so. In that year he travelled to Oxford, attracted by the reputation of Prideaux.[99] As 'Louis Capellus, a Frenchman, a most scholarly young man (*juvenis studiossimus*)', he was admitted to the Bodleian on 12 July 1610.[100] By the time he left Oxford, probably in September 1612, he was very highly regarded by the university's leading men. The testimonial which he received on his departure was signed by the vice-chancellor, the regius professor of divinity (Robert Abbot), the regius professors of law and medicine, ten heads of houses (including Prideaux), Bodley's librarian (Thomas James), the two proctors, and various other professors and doctors.[101] Their listing of his character traits and

---

97. CCEd, Person ID 97156.
98. Above, 29.
99. 'Ludovici Capelli . . . de Cappellorum Gente', the partly autobiographical preface to *Ludovici Cappelli S. Theologiae in academia olim Salmuriensi Professoris Commentarii et Notae Criticae in Vetus Testamentum* (Amsterdam, 1689), sig. **3r–v; Wood, *Athenae*, iii. 463–5; L. W. B. Brockliss, 'Cameron, John (1579/80–1625, Reformed minister and theologian', *ODNB*. But note that Cappell's connection with Exeter rests solely on Wood's word. His name does not appear in any College document.
100. Clark, *Register*, i. 268.
101. 'Ludovici Capelli . . . de Cappellorum Gente', sig. ***.

activities gives us an outline of his Oxford career. He had completed two years in the university and had lived modestly, quietly, and without giving rise to scandal. He had attended church regularly, taken communion, and been present at sermons. He had sedulously attended public disputations in theology, participating in them sometimes as proponent and sometimes as opponent (a detail corroborated in the university records). He had pursued his studies in private and in the library, presumably the Bodleian, to which we know he gave books.[102] To this valuable record of a visitor's routines, Cappell's own autobiography adds a further achievement: it was when he was at Oxford that he also learnt Arabic.

Cappell's ventures into Arabic suggest that during his Oxford years he was already fully conversant with Hebrew, the primary language of biblical scholarship, and this conclusion is confirmed by his next move. When he left Oxford it was to take up the chair of Hebrew at Saumur.[103] His mastery of the language and his originality of mind were shown in 1624, when he published his most famous work, the *Arcanum punctuationis revelatum*. The focus of his book was on a seemingly obscure but actually highly significant point of biblical scholarship. In it he 'argued forcefully against the antiquity of the vowel points and accents of the Hebrew texts of the Old Testament'.[104] If, as Cappell deduced, these were later additions made by the Masoretes, Jewish grammarians of the early medieval period,[105] then the Scriptures could no longer be considered as wholly God-given, God's literal words, but must be regarded as at least partly man-made. This conclusion came to involve Prideaux too, for in his Act lecture of 1627 he surveyed the whole controversy and came down in favour of Cappell's findings, though at the same time managing to avoid derogating from the authority of Scripture.[106] The master had learnt from one who may have been his pupil.

Amama, Pastor, Getsius, and Cappell all remained at Exeter for substantial periods. But there were also other distinguished foreigners whose visits were more fleeting. We have already noticed Casaubon's visit to Oxford in May 1613, when he and Prideaux conversed in the rector's lodgings with the Jew,

---

102. Clark, *Register*, i. 268.
103. Wood, *Athenae*, iii. 268.
104. *HUO*, iv. 452–3; R. A. Muller, 'The Debate over the Vowel Points and the Crisis in Orthodox Hermeneutics', in R. A. Muller (ed.), *After Calvin: Studies in the Development of a Theological Tradition* (Oxford, 2003), 149–51.
105. Grafton and Weinberg, '*I have always loved the Holy Tongue*', 307–28, esp. 308.
106. J. Prideaux, 'De punctorum Hebraicorum origine', in his *VDL*, 180–98; *HUO*, iv. 456–7.

Jacob Barnet, to draw on his expertise in Hebrew and Talmudic learning.[107] One other such bird of passage was the German theologian and Calvinist scholar Abraham Scultetus, chaplain to the Elector Palatine, who came to England in 1613 for the Elector's wedding and spent some time in Oxford, where—he notes in his autobiography—he met the 'celebrated theologians' Robert Abbot (regius professor), Sebastian Benefield (Lady Margaret professor of divinity), and John Prideaux. It is interesting to see Prideaux thus described well before his promotion, just over two years later, to the regius chair. Scultetus had already encountered another distinguished Exonian, George Hakewill, apparently at court.[108] Prideaux similarly met the young Leiden scholar and budding Hebraist, Constantin L'Empereur, a visitor to Oxford for a few months in 1616.[109] There were probably many other such occasional passers-by.

There is no need to labour Prideaux's qualities as a scholar and teacher. For Continental theologians, biblical scholars, and linguists, often trained and employed in such comparable centres of learning and Calvinist churchmanship as Heidelberg and Leiden, these were the qualities that counted. But there were others. Prideaux's personal kindness, his willingness to help and encourage the College's overseas visitors, and the sympathetic milieu provided by the College itself, all worked to nurture the visitors' studies and to inspire their gratitude. In some cases Prideaux acted as their tutor. John Combachius (the senior scholar from Marburg), Philip Cluvier (the German geographer from Leiden), James Dorville (from Heidelberg), and Samuel Hortensius (from Berne), were all listed among his pupils between 1609 and 1613, after which, fully occupied as rector and then regius professor, he largely gave up undergraduate teaching.[110] As rector, he allocated pupils to Pasor and Getsius, and perhaps to others, enabling them to pay their way and to gain useful teaching experience. He read and commented on Amama's book.[111] He assigned John Hoffmann a room in his lodgings, next to his

107. Grafton and Weinberg, '*I have always loved the Holy Tongue*', 255; above, 37.
108. A. Scultetus, *George Abbott. Explicatio Sex Illustrium Quaestionum . . . Oxoniae anno 1597 in Schola Theologica Proposita, ibidem edita: et nunc primum in Germania recusa* (Frankfurt, 1616), sigs 3r–4r; Milton, 'The Church of England and the Palatinate', 145–52.
109. P. T. van Rooden, *Theology, Biblical Scholarship and Rabbinical Studies in the Seventeenth Century* (Leiden, 1989), 26–7, 201–2.
110. ECA, H.II.11.
111. Above, 56.

own study.[112] The responses of his guests, in the few cases where they are recorded, were warm, sometimes almost devotional. Both Combachius and Amama, on returning to their own universities, dedicated books to him. How grateful he was to have lived with Prideaux, wrote Combachius, sending his *Metaphysicorum* to him from Marburg in 1613 as 'a testimony to the love and friendship which most firmly bind us'.[113] Amama addressed the whole College and its fellows, 'the most delightful of companions', giving them a report on his scholarly activities back in Franeker, which suggests that they would have been interested in his continuing progress.[114] Individual fellows were sometimes singled out for greeting or special praise. Combachius's dedicatory letter mentioned especially the sub-rector, William Helme (Prideaux's former tutor), 'a man of rare piety . . . my dearest friend, who has shown me so much love, favour and goodwill'. His Marburg companion at Exeter, Henry Petraeus, wrote that 'Helme, Hakewil, Vilvaine, Prideaux, survive as friends', naming not only the rector but three fellows, one of them, Vilvaine, distinguished in Petraeus's own field of medicine.[115] Taking his leave of the College in 1629, Pasor spoke of the favour and love he had found among seventeen Oxford friends, including five, the largest group, from Exeter: John Robartes (his former pupil), James Dillon (another well-born undergraduate), Prideaux, and two fellows, Henry Tozer and Joseph Maynard.[116] Even allowing for the emotional overload characteristic of much seventeenth-century personal writing, these are impressive testimonies to a College fellowship, in both senses, which Exeter's visitors found as congenial as the scholar at its head. The bonds of friendship enhanced those of scholarship.

What was the general impact of these foreign students? The influence of scholars and teachers on each other, on their pupils, and on their institutions was and is diffusive and can hardly be measured, and in the case of Exeter's foreigners only a very few provide us with even sketchy records for their complete careers. Yet some points of contact can be identified and some influences traced. Our trio of major figures, Amama, Pasor, and Getsius, all made a contribution to the study of Oriental languages for which Oxford in

---

112. Boase, *Register*, 315.
113. Combachius, *Metaphysicorum*, sig. A5v.
114. Boase, *Register of the Rector and Fellows*, (1879), xxv, n. 1.
115. Combachius, *Metaphysicorum*, sig. A6v, A9r.
116. *Parentalia*, 45.

the seventeenth century became 'a truly major centre'.[117] Pasor in particular, though he was no expert Arabist, nevertheless did much to give Arabic a firm place in the Oxford curriculum. Of all Exeter's 'outlanders', Pasor and Cappell were the most significant. The interests of all four scholars coincided closely with those of Prideaux. No mean linguist himself, Prideaux's know-ledge of Hebrew was deep and extensive, and he seems too to have had at least an acquaintance with Arabic, thanks partly perhaps to the instruction which he received from Pasor.[118] So there was interaction here, to the profit of both parties. For others, a period of study at Exeter was a prelude to ordination and entry into an Anglican benefice. Amyraut, Hoffmann, and Getsius all took this course, as also did Cesar Calandrini, a German educated at Geneva and Saumur, who was given a living in Essex shortly before receiving his BD from Exeter in 1620.[119] Pasor's teaching of mathematics to John Robartes, the teaching of Hebrew by Amama and Getsius, probably to BD students, and the participation of both Amama and Pasor in College disputations all enhanced the educational and intellectual resources of the College. The effects of their Oxford experience on those who returned to their home universities can only be surmised. But the enthusiastic responses of Combachius, Petraeus, Pasor, and Amama to their time at Exeter suggest that it was not time wasted, and something of what they had learnt at Exeter will have been passed on to another generation of foreign students. Here was the republic of letters in action.

4. William Lord Petre v. Exeter College

The most difficult problem facing Prideaux in his early years as rector arose not from religious issues but from his and his College's conflict with William Lord Petre, son of Sir John Petre, and grandson of Sir William Petre, the College's refounder. Lasting from November 1613 to December 1618, the conflict overshadowed all Exeter's affairs, absorbing much of the College's corporate energy and a substantial portion of its income. As Exeter's head and representative, Prideaux was involved at every stage, and so too were some of the highest in the land, including the king himself, his councillors

---

117. *HUO*, iv. 449.
118. *HUO*, iv. 457; above, 57. See also below, 197–8.
119. O. P. Grell, 'Cesar Calandrini (1595–1665), Reformed minister', *ODNB*.

and judges, and a few peers, notably William Herbert, earl of Pembroke. Yet for all its salience, local and to some extent national, the episode has remained almost entirely unknown.[120]

What was in its day a miniature *cause célèbre* arose from inconsistencies in the College's refoundation documents and their unscrupulous exploitation by Sir John Petre. In a supplement to his new statutes probably issued in June 1566, at the same time as the statutes themselves, Sir William Petre had given himself and his son John the right to nominate to the seven new Exeter fellowships (later raised to eight) for which his new endowment was to provide. After the deaths of the two men that right was to revert to the College. But in the last clause of the supplement Sir William implicitly qualified his earlier stipulation by empowering both himself and his son to amend the statutes; a prerogative denied to all other parties. The provisions of this supplement were clearly regarded as equivalent to the statutes, and the whole document was copied into the College's book of statutes. The ambiguity here was obvious. In statutorily limiting the right to nominate to fellowships to the lives of the two Petres, while at the same time giving to John Petre the right to amend the statutes, Sir William Petre unwittingly allowed his son to overturn the first of these provisions, potentially to the permanent advantage of his family. Sir John was quick to exploit the opportunity thus offered him. At some point between 1575 and 1583, after Sir William's death, he inserted a new decree in the College statute book. Citing the power given to him by his father to amend the statutes, he conferred on his son William (born 1575) and his male descendants the right to nominate to the eight Petrean fellowships in perpetuity.[121] In several later documents bearing on the case it was claimed that the insertion of this new decree in the statute book had been carried through secretly or in an underhand way or with the connivance of a faction among the fellows, presumably while the book was in Sir John's possession.[122] Thereafter the decree remained in place, the threat which it represented temporarily dormant but constituting an explosive charge liable to detonate on Sir John's death.

120. There is a passing reference in Boase, *Register*, viii.
121. ECA, A.I.2 (Statutes, unfoliated).
122. ECA, A.I.1 (Statutes, unfoliated); A.I.5, 255; F.IV.7, no.2 (Documents re Exeter College v. William Lord Petre).

Sir John Petre died on 11 October 1613. It was almost certainly the two fellows who visited his heir at Ingatestone, his Essex home, to deliver a volume of memorial verses who brought back the bad news that William Petre intended to pursue his supposed rights.[123] In reaction, and no doubt in consternation, on 12 November Prideaux and five senior fellows wrote to William Cotton, bishop of Exeter, the College's Visitor, to express their concern and to explain the dilemma which they now faced. They were bound on oath to obey the College statutes; but they had to disregard either Sir William's statute, which had the consent of the then bishop of Exeter and which gave the right to elect to the College after the death of the second Petre, or Sir John's statute, inserted into the statute book (they pointedly said) they knew not how, which gave the right to Sir John's male heirs. Threatened with perjury whichever alternative they chose, they asked the bishop for a ruling, and it was a satisfactory one that they obtained. The bishop came down in favour of the College: Sir John's statute lacked authority and could not override its predecessor.[124]

This was the first round in a long contest. The fellows next wrote to Petre citing the bishop's ruling and asking him to recognize that his father's supplementary statute was 'framed upon a mistake'. Petre stalled, apparently intending to seek legal advice.[125] The College meanwhile wrote to seek the support of some very eminent men: George Abbot, archbishop of Canterbury, Thomas Baron Ellesmere, the university's chancellor, John King, the Calvinist bishop of London, and the lawyer Sir John Dodderidge, a former member of the College and now justice of King's Bench. The case presented to each of them was the same: that Sir John's statute went against Sir William's original statute, that the bishop of Exeter had confirmed the original statute, and that the fellows could not fall into line behind Sir John's statute without perjuring themselves.[126]

After a long interval Petre wrote again to the College on 1 June 1614.[127] This time his tone was decisive and peremptory. He claimed without qualification to have the right to nominate to the eight Petrean fellowships, one of which, he had heard, would shortly fall vacant. To fill it he nominated one Philip Franklin, requiring the College to admit him. As long as the

123. A I.5, 253; A. C. Edwards, *John Petre* (1975), 100.
124. ECA, A.I.1.
125. ECA, A.I.5, 259.
126. Ibid., 256–9.
127. Ibid., 255, 260.

eight Petrean fellowships were occupied, the crisis in relations with Petre could be deferred. But once a fellowship became vacant a conflict between the two sides became inevitable. It seems, however, that Petre had been misinformed: the fellowship was not vacant, as the fellows told Petre in a letter of 8 June. Petre accepted this, but demanded that Franklin should be elected to the next vacant Petrean fellowship. But the respite produced by his retreat was short-lived. On 30 June, at the mid-year College meeting, two Petrean fellows resigned their fellowships, and the College elected two other men to take their place.[128]

This was to throw down the gauntlet, and Petre responded forcefully. In the autumn of 1614 he sent his agents to the Oxfordshire properties which formed the core of the Petrean endowment of the 1560s. There, by way of distraint, they proceeded to seize the carts, draught animals, and ploughs of the College's tenants. In an undated letter the rector and fellows protested vigorously at this, telling Petre of the tenants' complaints that his men had 'attempted an entry upon those impropriations and lands which your grand-father, our honorable benefactor of ever blessed memory, gave unto our colledge'.[129] They could not give way to Petre's claims, they said 'without manifest periury': an implicit appeal to their oath to observe the original Petrean statutes. As a means to a settlement, they suggested that counsel for each party should meet to discuss the issues, and then, if no settlement could be reached, proceed to law.

Eventually, after further fruitless negotiations with Petre, the case went forward to the court of Common Pleas. It thus became a public issue, moving out of the ambit of private negotiations and onto a larger stage. A Latin narrative of what followed was written for the College register by Prideaux himself, who acted as the College's representative throughout, together with Everard Chambers, senior bursar and a Petrean fellow.[130] On 3 May 1615 Prideaux and Chambers met the lawyer William Noye in London to plan their tactics. A former undergraduate of the College, this 'most perspicacious and knowledgeable man', as the rector called him, later to be Charles I's Attorney General, was to act as the College's chief legal adviser during the remaining years of its contest with Petre. Heard before Sir Henry Hobart, chief justice of Common Pleas, the case opened on the

---

128. Ibid., 251, 263; Boase, *Register*, 96.
129. ECA, A.I.5, 263–4.
130. Ibid., 264–6.

following day. The proceedings, which seem to have been brief, turned on the various documents concerning the College's refoundation by Sir William Petre and on his grandson's more recent attempts to nominate to fellowships. The jury found for the College and against Petre, who was ruled to have unjustly seized the possessions of the College's tenants. This was, however, largely an empty victory. Despite the verdict, the judge asked the College to give way on the grounds that to contend against a benefactor was to show ingratitude: a blatantly partisan intervention. But Prideaux declined to do so, arguing that this would be to commit a double perjury, breaching the fellows' oaths to obey both the statutes and Bishop Cotton's ruling, which had vindicated their cause. Next, he visited Petre in person, but again neither party would compromise. 'And so' wrote Prideaux, 'we retired.'

The affair now moved into an even more confrontational stage. On 21 June 1615 Petre once again demanded the admission of his candidate Philip Franklin to a fellowship. The College once again refused: 'We see noe ground for such authority and hold ourselves bound by oath to stand against it.' Petre retaliated by demanding for a third time that Franklin should be admitted and, going further, by forbidding the rector and fellows to use any of the profits of the lands conveyed to the College by Sir William Petre, intended for the support of the Petrean fellows, for the maintenance of their own elected fellows.[131] Unstated in the background lay the implicit threat that Sir William Petre's endowment might be resumed by Sir William's grandson.

This was far from the end of the dispute, and a new court case followed. Alluded to in the College's reply to Petre's letter of 21 June,[132] its course unfolds through a dossier of items in the College archives comprising documents setting out the College's case, evidently prepared for and perhaps by the College's counsel, and other letters to and from the College and its allies. In the main these documents reiterated the points already made earlier in the dispute. They laid stress on Sir William Petre's decree that after his son's death the Petrean fellows were to be chosen by the College; they pointed to the clandestine insertion into the College statute book of Sir John's amendment to his father's statute, never 'open, fair and acknowledged by the Rector and major part of the scholars'; they argued that in any

131. Ibid., 267–8.
132. Ibid.

case the power given by Sir William to his son to amend the statutes was intended to allow him only to amend the arrangements for the Petrean fellows and not to 'infringe the general statute of election'; and they cited the Visitor's ruling of November 1613 which had upheld the College's interpretation. To accept William Petre's case would amount to a double perjury, as a breach of the fellows' oaths to observe both the statutes and the Visitor's interpretation: a point already made by Prideaux when he met Petre soon after the hearing in Common Pleas.[133]

The sequence of events in this second phase of the College's dispute with Petre is difficult to work out with any precision, but two features are nonetheless clear. First, the case had now come to involve some of the most prominent members of Jacobean political society, including the king himself. And, second, the College's consistent wish was for a fresh public trial at common law, while Petre's was for a small judicial tribunal sitting in private. The first of these features was clear from the outset. Our earliest indication of the revival of the lawsuit introduces us to a man close to the centre of James's court. On 1 March 1616 Sir Ralph Winwood wrote to Prideaux to tell him and his counsel to prepare for a hearing before the king's commissioners (unnamed) on 4 April. He, Winwood, would summon Lord Petre and William Paynter—an aged former fellow who would later write to the College to testify to Sir William Petre's intentions[134]—to see 'that your colledge may be put to no unnecessary trouble'. An Oxford man, with Oxonian sympathies and many Oxford friends, Winwood was one of James's leading diplomats and had recently been appointed his principal secretary of state.[135] The tone of his letter, supported by later references in correspondence to his work for the College,[136] suggests that Prideaux had found a useful ally. That the king himself was now involved is confirmed by a casual final sentence in Paynter's later letter to the College: he much liked, he said, 'the course you have taken to present a petition to his majestie who no doubt by the inclination of those noble personages will with favour respecte the good of your colledge and bring the busyness to a good end'.[137]

133. ECA, F.IV.7, esp. nos. 1, 2, 4; A.I.5, 266.
134. ECA, F.IV.7, no. 2. Paynter had been a fellow at the time of Sir William Petre's benefaction in the 1560s.
135. Ibid., no. 13; M. Greengrass, 'Winwood, Sir Ralph (1562/3–1617), diplomat and secretary of state', ODNB.
136. ECA, F.IV.7, nos. 18, 9.
137. Ibid., no. 2.

But a still more powerful ally than Winwood was about to come on stage. A draft letter in Prideaux's hand to a certain 'right honourable', probably written in 1617, was almost certainly addressed to William Herbert, earl of Pembroke.[138] In the letter Prideaux noted the previous verdict in favour of the College in the Common Pleas and stated that Petre had now persuaded the king that a further trial should be held before the two chief justices, whereas the College wanted a public trial, preferably in King's Bench. A private hearing before the justices alone 'cannot chuse for many reasons but to bee most preiudicall unto us'. It was probably feared that two justices, sitting in private, might be easily suborned. A further approach to the king himself was made in June 1617, when John Balcanquall, a Scot whom James had intruded into an Exeter fellowship, visited the king in Edinburgh—with favourable results, as Balcanquall reported in a letter to Prideaux. James agreed to halt proceedings before the chief justices and to allow the case to proceed at common law, while Pembroke, to whom Balcanquall delivered letters from Prideaux, also promised his support.[139]

But, like some of the College's other victories in this long-drawn-out war, this was no more than a temporary gain. In late October or November 1618 a group of thirteen fellows headed by Nathanael Carpenter, the sub-rector, wrote directly to Pembroke to tell a tale of hopes thwarted and then revived.[140] Their letter took up the story at the point where Balcanquall's had left off. Thanks to Pembroke's kindness when the king visited Scotland in the previous year, the College had been rescued from an unjust legal arrangement. He had ensured that their case should be heard, not 'by the secret judgement of a few men', but in a public examination. But then, by unknown means (though Petre's hand is implied), that decision had been revoked. By royal letters drafted in June, yet received by the College only in October, they had been summoned to appear before a private tribunal on 1 December, which left very little time for them to prepare their case, scrutinize their documents, and consult lawyers, who were now fully engaged. Of the three privy councillors appointed to hear the case, one had supported Petre in the earlier lawsuit, while another had acted as his counsel and spokesman. They were very concerned to see that bribery and influence were not brought to bear on the final judgment. But they were

138. Ibid., no. 18.
139. Ibid., no. 9; A.I.5, 246; Boase, *Register*, 96.
140. ECA, F.IV.7, no. 12.

grateful that Pembroke himself was to head the panel (though they still desired a public hearing), and they knew how much store he set by the welfare of 'your university men (*academici tui*)': an allusion to Pembroke's role as chancellor and the university's benevolent patron. Leaving nothing to chance, the same group wrote, probably about the same time, to a 'most celestial marquis', who can only have been James's favourite, George Villiers, marquis of Buckingham since January 1618, explaining their case and asking for his support.[141]

The endgame was now approaching. Shortly after 21 October the rector and fellows had received a summons issued in response to instructions from the king dated on 15 June to attend at Whitehall on 3 December for 'the hearing of the difference between the Right Honourable the Lord Petre and the Rector and scholars of Exeter College'. They were to come either with or without their counsel.[142] These were the royal letters whose long delayed delivery—presumably a tactic by Petre's party—the fellows were to complain about in their letter to Pembroke, written shortly afterwards. The letters were signed by Pembroke (the first signatory), H. Montagu, and Henry Hobart. This was precisely the partisan panel which again was to be the subject of the fellows' complaint; for 'H. Montagu' was Henry Montagu, chief justice of King's Bench, who, as a serjeant-at-law, had acted as one of Petre's counsel in the Common Pleas trial of 1615, while Henry Hobart, chief justice of Common Pleas, was the judge in that case who had sought to upset the jurors' verdict against Petre by attempting to persuade Prideaux to give way despite that verdict.[143] Both could be regarded as Petre's men.

The College thus had good reason to be apprehensive. Yet they did not trust to Pembroke's headship of the commission in vain. The summons and the fellows' letter to Pembroke complaining about its terms are the last items in the dossier concerning the case, and we have no formal record either of the hearing or of its outcome. For this we have to go to an entirely unrelated source. In a letter of 26 January 1619 Sir John Acland, Devon landowner and College benefactor, wrote to Prideaux about the financing of his current work in building the College's new hall. 'And I muche reioice', he added almost as an afterthought, 'of the good sucksesse you latelye founde in the

141. Ibid., no. 14.
142. Ibid., no. 16c.
143. ECA, A.I.5, 265–6; above, p. 66.

suttee [suit] with my Lord Peeters.'[144] That nothing more is heard of Petre's claim to nominate to the eight fellowships is confirmation of the College's victory. The claim was to be unsuccessfully revived by his grandson, Thomas, the sixth Lord Petre, under James II;[145] but from 1618 onwards the Petres were effectively excluded from any role in the College's governance.

Sub specie aeternitatis, Exeter's conflict with William Lord Petre may seem to have been no more than a minor storm in a college teacup. Yet at the time the defeat of Petre's claims was a matter of vital importance. The acceptance of those claims would imply that the College statutes were 'changeable and controllable without restriction at the pleasure of the Lorde Petre and his successors, soe that in name onlie and not indeede it should remaine a college, which the rector and fellowes holde stupiditie and periurie to suffer' (as the College stated in one of its legal submissions).[146] If Sir William Petre's statutes could be arbitrarily changed by an external authority, then the whole existence of the College as an independent corporation would be under threat. William Paynter, in his letter to the College, had pointed out other objections. In the hands of Petre and his descendants a perpetual right to appoint would introduce to the College men who lacked its approval and who might be 'sottish and simple' and 'never like to speed'. If Petre's heirs happened to be minors, the right to nominate might pass to the great men whose wards they were and who might treat the fellowships merely as a source of patronage, 'as they doe with their lyvings'.[147] Nor was the moral case for resistance negligible, lying as it did behind the rector and fellows' persistent appeals to their oaths. Once the bishop of Exeter had given his ruling in favour of the College, at the start of these proceedings, any acceptance of Petre's claims would involve a double perjury—a breach of the fellows' oaths both to observe the statutes and to obey the interpretations of the Visitor.[148] No doubt the pleading of oaths was a tactical convenience, but it also represented a moral obligation which could not be abandoned. Perjury, after all, was a sin.

Yet resistance to those claims posed comparable dangers. Petre had sought to enforce his supposed rights by distraining on the property of the College's

---

144. ECA, H.III.11, no. 9 (Correspondence re buildings). For Acland, see below, 129–36.
145. Boase, *Register*, cxxi–cxxii.
146. ECA F.IV.7, no. 5.
147. Ibid., no. 2.
148. *The Statutes of Exeter College, Oxford* (1855), 32.

tenants and by forbidding the income from his grandfather's endowment to be used for the maintenance of the non-Petrean fellows.[149] Underlying these provocative actions lay the much greater threat of the confiscation of the whole Petrean endowment. Petre's claim, therefore, had to be not merely countered but conclusively defeated at law. This was very expensive. Between 1614 and 1617 legal and associated expenses were higher than at any other time in Prideaux's rectorship, amounting to £74 in 1616, 21 per cent of the year's total expenditure.[150] Travel expenses, including those for Balcanquall's long journey to Scotland, added to the bill. Other costs were less quantifiable. Although there were periods of inactivity, the Petre affair overshadowed and disrupted the work of the College for five years. When, in 1614, the Rector and fellows asked Petre 'for a fair and speedy trial by law', they gave as their reason 'that so freed from such troubles we might bestow our time and means in those studies which are more proper to our profession'. In 1617, when they thought that they had won their way to the trial by law which they wanted, they wrote in their later letter to Pembroke of their hope of having time again 'for the study of good and liberal letters'.[151] While there were books to be read, lectures to be prepared, and undergraduates to be taught, the worry of a protracted lawsuit with an uncertain outcome was a diversion which this scholastic community might well want to avoid.

One substantial force denied Petre the success that he sought: the earl of Pembroke's support for the College. Although the installation of Buckingham at James's court in 1615 had weakened his position, Pembroke remained one of the court's leading figures and thus well placed to influence the king's decisions. His appointment as chamberlain in December 1615, the holder now of one of the most senior court offices, gave him responsibility for supervising the king's chaplains, of whom Prideaux was one; and it may have been in this way that the relationship between the two men either began or perhaps blossomed after an earlier start. They had much in common. Pembroke's fierce Protestant convictions, Calvinist, anti-Catholic, and anti-Arminian, which led to the Venetian ambassador's describing him in 1616 as 'head of the Puritans in England', were, of course, shared by

---

149. ECA, A I.5, 263, 268; above, 65–6.
150. A.II.9 (Rector's Accounts, 1564–1639) fos. 219v, 224r, 228r, 232r, 236r. For total College expenditure, see ibid., fos. 217–44.
151. ECA, A.I.5, 264; F.IV.7, no. 12.

Prideaux, while Pembroke's concern for the university was well known, and led to his election as its chancellor in January 1617.[152] Pembroke had shown the direction of his sympathies in backing the College's request for a public trial in June 1617, and still more so in securing the headship of the small commission which, in December 1618, declared for Exeter. The two chief justices, both Petre's supporters, could not stand against the great noble. It was a mark of Pembroke's respect for Prideaux that within a few months, in July 1619, he appointed Prideaux as his vice-chancellor. From this time onwards the rector's ties with both the Herberts, Philip earl of Montgomery as well as his elder brother William, became exceptionally close, as we shall see.[153] What proved in later years to be Prideaux's almost subservient willingness to do Pembroke's bidding may have owed something to Pembroke's own service to the College in conclusively quashing Petre's long-pursued claim. Prideaux, and Exeter, had much to be grateful for.

The College's vindication of its rights represented a corporate effort, in which the fellows fully participated. Yet Prideaux was pre-eminent throughout. Sir William Petre's statutes had bound the rector to maintain and defend the college in lawsuits, and this Prideaux had done, attending legal hearings in London, engaging with the College's counsel, drafting much of its correspondence, and writing up a narrative account of its case. The threat from Petre must have been his constant preoccupation during these years, overshadowing the preparation of his Act lectures, his relations with visiting foreign scholars, and his College teaching. That he had thought long and hard about the moral problems raised by the conflict is suggested by the apposite and timely pair of sermons which he preached in 1615 on 'Christ's counsel for ending law cases', where he urged the need for 'brotherly reconciliation' and condemned as un-Christlike 'the going to law of Christians, where a good ende in private may be hoped'.[154] An appeal to law was both a last resort and a measure of moral desperation.

Yet the eventual outcome of the lawsuit marked one of the greatest triumphs of his career. The judicial defeat of William Lord Petre gave the

152. V. Stater, 'Herbert, William, third earl of Pembroke (1580–1630), courtier and patron of the arts', *ODNB*; McCullough, *Sermons at Court*, 73; M. Brennan, *Literary Patronage in the English Renaissance: The Pembroke Family* (1988), 164–5; B. O'Farrell, *Shakespeare's Patron: William Herbert, Third Earl of Pembroke: Politics, Patronage and Power* (2011), 45, 210.

153. Below, 251, 318, 329–30.

154. J. Prideaux, *Christ Counsell for ending law cases as it hath been Delivered in Two Sermons upon the 25th verse of the 5th of Matthew* (Oxford, 1615), 3, 11; Madan, i. 104.

College full command of the eight Petrean fellowships, freed it from outside interference, and conferred on it the full autonomy which had been lacking since the Petrean refoundation of the 1560s. It now enjoyed all the advantages of Sir William's generosity with none of the drawbacks. Barring the unforeseen, the College's continuance and the support of the Petrean endowment were both guaranteed. In Exeter's rise under Prideaux, the legal verdict of 1618 marked a signal moment.

5. Responsibilities and rewards

Prideaux's conduct of Exeter's case against William Lord Petre may have been the most onerous of his internal responsibilities during this period, but other external commitments, if rather less stressful ones, soon followed the College's victory. Chief among these was the vice-chancellorship of the university, to which he was nominated by Pembroke, the chancellor, in 1619 and 1620 and again in 1624 and 1625. His two periods in office, covering four years, were matched by no other vice-chancellor during Pembroke's term as chancellor from 1617 to 1630: a mark of confidence which rested both on Prideaux's personal qualities and on the religious sympathies which both men shared. Informing Convocation of his initial appointment in 1619, Pembroke wrote that his 'soundnes in religion, wisedome and great learning are knowen unto you all', words which he more or less repeated in 1624. At the same time he was aware of the burden placed on his candidate by his dual role as regius professor and vice-chancellor. Signing Prideaux off in 1621, 'Howe troublesome', he wrote, 'these last two yeares have beene to Dr Prideaux whilest he hath bene enforced to supply two such eminent places, each of them of waight inoughe to require a whole man.'[155]

The vice-chancellorship was indeed no sinecure. Its holder was responsible to the chancellor for the general management of the university. Fortunately for Prideaux, he was on the best of terms with Pembroke, who was mostly a laissez-faire governor, interfering only rarely in the day-to-day running of his institution. But even without pressure from above, the routine duties of the vice-chancellor were onerous enough. He presided in Convocation and Congregation, the university's two governing bodies, and

---

155. OUA, NEP/supra/Reg. N (Register of Convocation, 1615–28), fos. 77r, 120r, 190r.

in the Chancellor's court, which met weekly and where he was expected to sit in person (though with assistants); he formally admitted students to the university, graduands to their degrees, and principals to the headship of their halls; and he kept and presented the university accounts.[156] Before, during, and after his vice-chancellorship, Prideaux also served on many committees, chairing those which met, usually in his lodgings at Exeter, during his time in office. In 1620–1, for example, he headed committees to audit and examine accounts relating to the building of the new schools, to decide on presentation to a benefice, to deal with the endowment of a lectureship in moral philosophy, and to scrutinize the fees payable to the university bedels.[157] As vice-chancellor he also acted *ex officio* as Justice of the Peace, though he had already begun to sit on the bench earlier in his career and continued to do so when he had left office. Assiduous and conscientious in attendance, he sat at quarter sessions on nearly fifty occasions between 1616 and 1632.[158] Routine though most of the commitments were, they entailed a large expenditure of time and energy. Biblical exegesis in the schools and the defence of Anglican orthodoxy may have provided Prideaux's public life with its guiding principles, but they by no means filled all his working hours.

By the time he became vice-chancellor for the first time in 1619 Prideaux was on the way to becoming a wealthy man and one who could consider himself well rewarded for his multifarious activities. It is true that after 1613 he largely gave up the undergraduate teaching which had probably provided his main income during his fellowship years, finding no doubt that his duties as rector and then as regius professor left him with little time to spare. But from the mid-1620s he once again began to take on pupils, almost all of them the sons of the nobility and upper gentry. This cannot but have been extremely lucrative. John Aubrey reckoned that William Browne, the Exeter poet, made five or six thousand pounds from his appointment by Pembroke as tutor to Robert Dormer, ward of Pembroke's brother Philip, earl of Montgomery, during Dormer's time at Eton and Exeter between

156. M. Underwood, 'The Structure and Operation of the Oxford Chancellor's Court, from the Sixteenth to the Early Nineteenth Century', *Journal of the Society of Archivists*, 6 (1978), 18, 21; Clark, *Register*, i, 5–6, 48, 282; *HUO*, iii. 117–18, 401–2; Wood, *Life and Times*, i. 75–6.
157. OUA, NEP/supra/Reg N, fos. 93v, 104r, 112r, 121r–v, 152r.
158. *Oxford Quarter Sessions Order Book, 1614–1637*, ed. R. Blades (OHS, n.s., 29, 2009), 19, 53, and *passim*.

1623 and 1625.[159] These figures are hard to credit; but the Herberts were very rich. How much did Philip, now earl of Pembroke, give Prideaux when the rector was tutor to Philip's two sons, Charles and Philip, during their time at Exeter between 1632 and 1635?[160]

Set against his likely income from tuition, at least from the 1620s, his ordinary College income was trivial. His annual College stipend, twice that of a fellow, was a mere £2 13s. 4d. To this has to be added the value of free board and lodging. Much more valuable were the irregular but frequent payments resulting from College entry fines. When a new lease on a College property was drawn up or an old lease renewed, the tenant paid a large entry fine, the proceeds from which were divided between rector and fellows. As with his stipend, the rector usually received twice the sum payable to each fellow. In 1619, for example, when land in Garsington was leased to John Wallis for a fine of £66 13s. 4d., the rector received £6 7s. and eighteen fellows £3 3s. 6d. each.[161] Since, thanks largely to Petre, the College held a substantial portfolio of properties, none of whose leases under Sir William's statutes could run for longer than twenty years, income from such entry fines was a more than occasional windfall. In a good year fines and corn rents between them might bring in a substantial sum. The six leases drawn up in 1635, together with corn rent dividends for Kidlington and other properties, produced £34 14s. 9d. for the rector and £17 16s. 10d. for Henry Tozer, to name a sample fellow.[162]

Prideaux's most regular and substantial income, however, came from none of these sources but from his benefices. He was a pluralist on a large scale. Two of the seven benefices which he held by the late 1620s, all but one in Oxfordshire, had come to him by virtue of his regius chair. The rectory of Ewelme and a cathedral prebend at Christ Church had both been attached to the chair by James I in 1605: a mark of James's respect for learning and one which Prideaux remembered with gratitude when he addressed the king at Woodstock in 1624. He had to wait to take up his Christ Church prebend until 1617, when the existing holder was made to step down in his favour, and until 1629, when the sitting tenant died, to

159. John Aubrey, *Brief Lives*, ed. K. Bennett, 2 vols. (Oxford, 2015), i. 253, ii. 1386; M. O'Callaghan, 'Browne, William (1590/91–1645?), poet', *ODNB*. For Prideaux's aristocratic pupils, see below, 95–102.
160. ECA, A.I.22 (Caution Book, 1629–86), 16.
161. ECA, A.I.6, fo. 1v.
162. ECA, A.III.10 (Dividend Book, 1628–60, unfoliated).

profit from Ewelme.[163] Other benefices he held in his own right: one of three vicarages in the parish of Bampton, secured for him in 1614 from the dean and chapter of Exeter by Laurence Bodley, canon of Exeter and uncle of another Laurence Bodley, chosen (by what is unlikely to have been a coincidence) as the College's fellow-chaplain in the same year;[164] the vicarage of Chalgrove, where he succeeded his father-in-law William Goodwin in 1620;[165] and the rectory of Bladon with Woodstock, which he held by grant from the Crown in 1625. The Bladon rectory and the Bampton vicarage, one of the best endowed in the county, were each worth about £80 a year.[166] Probably next in value was the vicarage of Kidlington, settled on the rector of Exeter by Sir William Petre in 1566 and leased out, with its lands, tithes, and house, by Prideaux in 1622 for £50 a year.[167] A final benefice was more distant. In 1620 the king appointed him to a prebend in Salisbury Cathedral formerly held, like Chalgrove, by William Goodwin.[168] According to Prideaux's own account, written in 1637, he owed his Chalgrove vicarage to the intervention of the Lord Chancellor, Sir Francis Bacon, and his Salisbury prebend to that of 'Mr Treasurer (my own noble favourer)', by whom he meant Sir Thomas Edmondes, treasurer of the royal household: a pointer to significant court connections otherwise unknown.[169] It was a nice touch that one of the two proctors appointed by Prideaux to take possession of the prebend on his behalf was William Helme, his former tutor and old friend, and by then the holder of a Wiltshire living.[170]

It would be wrong to be too censorious about Prideaux's pluralism. This was 'the normal and necessary system' which enabled heads of houses to maintain themselves and their families: Samuel Ward, master of Sidney Sussex College, Cambridge, and Prideaux's Calvinist counterpart in the

163. J. Le Neve, *Fasti Ecclesiae Anglicanae, 1541–1857*. Vol. VIII: *Bristol, Gloucester, Oxford and Peterborough Dioceses*, comp. J. Horn (London, 1996), 97–8; *VCH Oxfordshire*, xviii. 225, 228; J. Prideaux, *Alloquium Serenissimo Regi Iacobo Woodstochiae Habitum 24 Augusti. Anno 1624* (Oxford, 1624), sig. A2r; TNA, SP 16/348, fo. 115.
164. CCEd, Person ID 14698; J. Prideaux, *Ephesus Backsliding*, sig. *3r; below, 90, 177.
165. *VCH Oxfordshire*, xviii. 151–2.
166. *VCH Oxfordshire*, xii. 31–2, 408, xiii. 49.
167. Maddicott, *Founders*, 272, 286–7; B. Stapleton, *Three Oxfordshire Parishes: A History of Kidlington, Yarnton and Begbroke* (Oxford Historical Soc., 24, 1893), 39.
168. Le Neve, *Fasti*. Vol. VI: *Salisbury Diocese*, comp. Horn (London, 1986), 72.
169. TNA, SP 16/348, fo. 115; below, 301.
170. Salisbury Cathedral Archives, DA/1/5/17.

other university, held a similar string of benefices.[171] The system did not lead to neglect of the parishes, since parochial work was carried through by curates or chaplains, supplemented by occasional preaching visits from the holder of the benefice. Prideaux preached regularly at Bladon and Woodstock, as, from time to time, did other Exeter fellows such as George Hakewill and Henry Tozer. The entertainment and gifts which the rector and sometimes his wife received when he preached at Woodstock suggest that the occasional presence of so eminent a man was appreciated and his non-residence uncontentious.[172] Nor did he cling to these resources, for two of his benefices were later made over to his relatives and dependents, while his generosity to a much larger group, the poor, commented on by his biographer, shows how income withdrawn from the parishes might return in other and more diffuse ways.[173]

At its maximum, in years which yielded a large crop of entry fines and aristocratic pupils, and when his benefices were at their greatest yield, Prideaux's income may well have totalled several, perhaps many hundred pounds. If, looking ahead, we need an explanation for his ability to pay for college buildings, to accumulate an impressively large library, and to support some indigent relatives, we should seek it in what can be pieced together about his financial circumstances.[174]

At the time of Prince Charles's return from Spain in October 1623, Prideaux would have had good reason to feel satisfied both with the condition of the church and with his own situation and achievements. The canons of the Synod of Dort had endorsed his theological principles, while the failure of the Spanish Match had ended the threat of an alliance with Catholic Spain and the promotion of the Catholic cause in England which it would have brought. Within the church at large, and the university in particular, Calvinism remained the dominant orthodoxy. It is true that this orthodoxy was potentially under challenge, as it had been for some time. A small group of anti-Calvinist bishops, including Laud at St David's, was now well established; James I's fear of puritans, men whose beliefs both overlapped

---

171. See the comments by H. R. Trevor-Roper, *New York Review of Books*, 35/12, 21 July 1988, 44.
172. *VCH Oxfordshire*, xii, 32, 408; *Woodstock Chamberlains' Accounts, 1609–50*, ed. M. Maslen (Oxfordshire Rec. Soc., 58, 1993), 123, 124, 153, etc.
173. Below, 301–2; Lloyd, *Memoires*, 537.
174. Below, 122, 154–5, 216–17, 301–2.

and formed a spectrum with those of middle-ground Anglican Calvinists, now outweighed his earlier concerns about Catholics; and in his 'Directions concerning Preachers', published in 1622, he had decreed that only bishops and deans should preach on such Calvinist topics as predestination and election and that, with opposition to the Spanish Match in mind, preaching on 'matters of state' was altogether prohibited.[175] Yet Oxford's Calvinists remained relatively untouched by these slow shifts in religious policies and opinions. In restricting those allowed to deal with Calvinist topics, James's 'Directions' had made an exception for 'learned men' handling such topics in the schools, and Prideaux's Act lectures continued to follow a Calvinist programme throughout the early 1620s. Those on the other side might be harshly treated. In January 1623 Gabriel Bridges, an Arminian preacher who had attacked Calvinist doctrine on predestination and spoken out in favour of universal grace, was brought before a vice-cancellarial committee and forced to recant. Prideaux was among the committee's members.[176] It may have been equally pleasing to him to see the provisions of the Synod of Dort published at Oxford for the first time in 1623 and selling enough copies to warrant a reprint in 1624. Oxford remained the well-defended home of a by no means lost cause.[177]

Prideaux's domestic circumstances in both home and College were equally stable and prosperous. As we shall see later, by 1623 his marriage had produced seven children, all living, and he had a growing income to support them. He had seen off the threat to his College posed by the demands of William Lord Petre, established the College's independence, and secured the support of Pembroke, whose chancellorship was in itself a guarantee against anything more than minor Arminian encroachments on Calvinist territory within the university. Prideaux's alliance with Pembroke was a mainstay of his position. His reputation as a theologian and man of learning, signified early on by his commission from Archbishop Abbot to refute the slanders of Casaubon's opponent, had been capped by his appointment as regius professor and confirmed by the resort of foreign scholars to Exeter for his instruction and company. It was a reputation which meant

175. T. Fuller, *The Church History of Britain* (1655), Part II, 109–10; Cogswell, *The Blessed Revolution*, 32–5; Fincham and Lake, 'Ecclesiastical Policy', 34.
176. Wood, *History*, ii. 348–9; Tyacke, *Anti-Calvinists*, 74–5.
177. *Articles agreed on in the Nationall Synode of the Reformed Churches of France* (Oxford, 1623); Madan, i. 119, 121; Tyacke, *Anti-Calvinists*, 75; Milton, *Catholic and Reformed*, 422.

that he could reasonably expect a bishopric before too long. In these years too he had overseen the rebuilding of his College,[178] and at the time of Charles's return from Spain, the new College chapel, the final item in the building programme, was rising towards completion. Its dedication to St James was a self-conscious gesture of homage to a king who had facilitated its building and whom he saw as the revered defender of the national church.[179]

So in the last months of 1623 Prideaux could feel that the sun had shone, and continued to shine, on all his enterprises. The next ten years were to place much of this in jeopardy.

178. Below, 119–56.
179. Prideaux, *Alloquium*, sig. A2v.

PART II

Topics

3

Rector Prideaux and his College

1. Reputation and requirements

We have already seen something of Prideaux's direction of his College in a time of prolonged crisis. Yet the conflict with William Lord Petre was altogether exceptional and hardly typified the activities and routines of Prideaux's normal College life. That life covered a very long span. A member of the College for almost forty-six years, Prideaux was its rector for thirty: elected on 4 April 1612, in the middle of James I's reign, he resigned on 3 August 1642, on the eve of the Civil War. During that time the management of the College, its fellows, students, and finances, was his daily preoccupation, probably absorbing more of his time than the regular and predictable duties of the regius professor or even than the reading and study which were the foundation of his learning. In this chapter we shall look at the structure of the College, at the ways in which it differed from other colleges, and at Prideaux's impact on both. For much of his career, the history of his life is inseparable from that of his College.

By some near contemporaries Prideaux's rule as rector was seen to underlie the exceptionally high reputation which Exeter came to enjoy. 'In the rectorship of his College', wrote Anthony Wood, 'he carried himself so winning and pleasing by his gentle government and fatherly instruction that it flourished more than any other house in the university with scholars, as well of great as of mean birth.' Wood's view was later echoed (and perhaps paraphrased) by a later fellow of Exeter, John Walker, who remarked that 'during his government of the College the fame of his learning had brought it into such repute that it became the residence of more great and learned men, especially foreigners, than any College in the university had ever been

Between Scholarship and Church Politics: The Lives of John Prideaux, 1578–1650. John Maddicott, Oxford University Press. © John Maddicott 2022. DOI: 10.1093/oso/9780192896100.003.0003

before'.[1] More valuable still, because more strictly contemporary, is the witness of Samuel Austin, Cornish poet and Exonian. Dedicating his long poem *Urania*, published in 1629, shortly after he graduated, to 'the especiall favourer of my studies Mr. Dr. Prideaux . . . the most deserving Rector of Exeter Colledge', he went on to supply a second dedication 'to that famous nursery of learning and religion, my mother Exeter Colledge . . . Great Mother of the Muses (thou whose fame/ Hath long times been more glorious by the name/ Of thy learned'd Rector)'.[2] These words have been echoed by more recent historians. To Montagu Burrows Exeter was 'the Devonshire College, already famous under Holland and Prideaux'. 'As one of the more eminent and successful seventeenth-century tutors', writes Feingold, 'Prideaux . . . brought Exeter College to unprecedented fame.'[3] Ancients and moderns agree that Exeter's standing in the university owed almost everything to the virtues of its rector.

What was the rector expected to do? The formal requirements for the office had been laid down by Sir William Petre's statutes of 1566. Some were personal. The rector was to be a man of strict morals, chaste life, and unblemished character, devout, and learned in the Scriptures. Others were more practical, calling for a leader experienced in financial affairs and estate management who would administer the College's revenues, present its annual accounts, represent it in lawsuits, and allocate College rooms.[4] But despite his standing and broad responsibilities, no more than any other college head could he govern autocratically. At the mid-year College meeting elections to fellowships were settled by the rector and a majority of the fellows, though the rector enjoyed two votes.[5] Elections to College offices were decided by an inner ring comprising the rector and five senior fellows, and the same group, often joined by the sub-rector and the dean, sat in judgment when fellows had to be disciplined.[6] Other meetings punctuated the year. The College was not a democracy, but the fellows shared in its government. These arrangements generally worked well. We know of only one episode which set Prideaux against the fellows, and the general absence

---

1. Wood, *Athenae*, iii. 266; J. Walker, *The Sufferings of the Clergy* (1714), part ii, 78.
2. S. A[ustin], *Austins Urania or, The Heavenly Muse* (1629), sigs A1r, A4v.
3. *The Register of the Visitors of the University of Oxford, 1647–1658*, ed. M. Burrows (Camden Soc., 1881), xlv (see pp. xvii–xix for Burrows's encomium on Prideaux); Feingold, *The Mathematicians' Apprenticeship*, 57–8.
4. *Statutes of Exeter College*, 22–3; Maddicott, *Founders*, 271–2.
5. *Statutes*, 29.
6. ECA, A.I.5, 279.

of intervention by the College's visitor, the bishop of Exeter, testified to a period of equable and united governance. The internal peace which had characterized the College under Holland was maintained under his successor.[7]

Yet Prideaux's steersmanship of a well-run vessel, held on a steady course, will hardly explain the fame which his College achieved. There was more to this than routine. In part it rested on the sanctuary which Exeter offered to foreign scholars and students, attracted by the scholar at its head. But these men never made up more than a small minority, and much more significant *in toto* were the College's junior members, comprising both undergraduates and graduates. To understand Exeter's distinctiveness, and Prideaux's responsibility for it, we must look first at their numbers.

2. Undergraduates and graduates: Numbers

In the late sixteenth and early seventeenth centuries the numbers attending the university underwent a huge expansion, peaking in the 1630s, when new enrolments reached heights not seen again until the 1870s.[8] Exeter shared in this expansion, but to an exceptional degree. It was already evident under Rector Holland, when the construction of new rooms from 1597 onwards pointed to the pressures being put on accommodation by growing numbers. It was under Holland that some 109 undergraduates took the oath of allegiance demanded by James I's government in 1610, more than any other college except Magdalen (147), Christ Church (*c.*142) and Brasenose (112).[9] From this time onwards numbers did not rise steadily but remained for the most part consistently high, with one or two peaks and troughs. After a fall-off to about 60 to 80 resident undergraduates between 1615 and 1617, they rose to a first peak between 1619 and 1622, reaching about 110 at maximum. It was one further sign of the demand for undergraduate places in these years, and its exceeding the supply, that the College was able to be selective about those whom it accepted. When the mayor and council of

7. Above, 32. For the falling out, see below, 260–2, 379–80.
8. Stone, 'Size and Composition', 17; *HUO*, iv. 33.
9. The figures cited and trends deduced in this and the following paragraph derive from: OUA, SP E/6/1 (lists of oath-takers, 1610); ECA, A.IV.9 (Bursars' Accounts, 1587–1630, recording annual admissions); ECA, BB/07–30 (Buttery Books, 1608–42, recording numbers in residence); Clark, *Register*, ii. 385–403 (matriculations, 1621); OUA, SP 2 (matriculation register, 1615–47).

Exeter complained, probably in 1618, that candidates from the city had been turned down Prideaux replied that their rejection did not result from 'the aversenesse of our societye but the backwardnesse and negligence of such as come short of their parts, or will not use the meanes'.[10] In other words, they were not up to it. Prideaux's haughty response may have been tactless; but it showed that his College could afford to discriminate.

A reversal came in the mid-1620s, with a sharp fall in numbers between 1623 and 1627: years marked by epidemic disease, high mortality, and presumably their deterrent effects on applications, when resident undergraduates may have numbered no more than fifty-five to seventy. The same downward trend can be seen in other colleges.[11] But in the 1630s numbers again expanded rapidly, as they did throughout the university. In 1630 a maximum of 116 undergraduates were receiving tuition; in 1631, seventy-nine matriculated, the highest number in a single year for the whole period; and in 1638 fifty-one commoners and battelers were admitted, a number exceeded only in 1621.[12] By the late 1630s, and up to 1642, there may have been as many as 120 to 130 resident undergraduates: a number greater than at any point before the 1850s.[13] Here Exeter mirrored the general trend.

Still more striking than these tentative figures for resident undergraduates are the comparisons to be made with other colleges. Such statistics as there are regularly show Exeter to have been among the most populous. Corroborating the records of the 1610 allegiance oath, the university census of the following year ranks Exeter third in size, with 188 members, behind only Christ Church (214) and Magdalen (211), but in front of Brasenose (178).[14] These exceptionally large figures almost certainly include all College members—fellows, graduates, and possibly servants as well as undergraduates, though the last group will have been by far the largest. In the decade 1600 to 1610 Exeter was second in the number of its matriculants, behind Brasenose but ahead of Queen's, Christ Church, and Magdalen Hall. In the 1630s Exeter had more matriculants than any other college, with Magdalen Hall, Christ Church, Brasenose, and Queen's following behind.[15] The

10. HMC, *Records of the City of Exeter* (1916), 99–100.
11. R. Darwall-Smith, *A History of University College, Oxford* (Oxford, 2008); 135; C. Hopkins, *Trinity: 450 Years of an Oxford College Community* (Oxford, 2005), 87.
12. ECA, H.II.11; OUA, SP 2, fos 209r–210v; ECA, A.IV.9.
13. For nineteenth-century numbers, see *VCH Oxfordshire*, iii. 111.
14. Wood, *Life and Times*, iv. 150–1.
15. *HUO*, iv. 35, 41.

Protestation Returns of 1642, recording college by college and hall by hall, the names of those taking or due to take the parliamentary oath of Protestant loyalty, tell a similar story. With 136 names, Exeter comes behind Christ Church (196) and Magdalen Hall (145), but ahead of Brasenose (120), New College (106), Magdalen (105), and all other colleges and halls. Like the figures for the earlier oath of 1610 and the 1611 census, these include all college residents.[16]

One other group of College residents has often been overlooked: the bachelors. In most years Exeter admitted about fifteen bachelors: the maximum number was twenty-nine in 1621, coinciding with a peak in undergraduate numbers, and the minimum a single bachelor in 1632. The majority will have been reading for the MA and some for the BD, a higher degree awarded to a few Exeter men in most years.[17] The annual figures for the bachelor intake point to no particular trend, but there is some evidence to suggest that Exeter's bachelors may have been unusually numerous. In 1610 twenty-seven Exeter bachelors took the allegiance oath, a larger number than in any other college except for Brasenose (thirty-five). Even if we discount the seven among the twenty-seven who were already fellows of the College, the remaining twenty still outnumbered those of all other colleges bar Brasenose.

Exeter's consistently high position in these league tables is all the more remarkable in view of the much greater wealth and larger sites for expansion available to some of its main competitors, such as Christ Church and Magdalen. In terms of numbers it punched well above its weight, and had done so even before Prideaux's time, in the later years of Rector Holland. How is this to be explained? The answer lies in a congeries of related factors: the strength of the College's connections with Devon and to a lesser extent Cornwall; the local interests and religious sympathies of its rector; and the comparable allegiances of the College's recruiting ground.

Exeter was by no means unusual in having strong links with a particular region. Jesus's ties with Wales, Queen's with Cumberland and Westmoreland, and University College's with Yorkshire all provide parallel examples.[18] But Exeter's ties with the West Country were exceptionally

---

16. *Oxfordshire and North Berkshire Protestation Returns and Tax Assessments, 1641–42*, ed. J. Gibson (Oxfordshire Rec. Soc., 59, 1994), 149–172.

17. The figures, recorded because bachelors paid admission fees, are given in ECA, A.IV.9 and A. IV.10 (Bursars' Accounts, 1687–1797).

18. *HUO*, iv. 60.

broad and deep. In most years between 1600 and 1642, 40 to 50 per cent of those matriculating at the College came from Devon and 16 to 17 per cent from Cornwall, while in thirteen years over half came from Devon alone, up to a maximum of 69 per cent in 1609.[19] There were no formal limitations on entry, and Exeter's undergraduates could come from any county. In 1622, for example, twenty-eight out of fifty-two matriculants came from Devon, but the remaining twenty-four were drawn from Wiltshire, Derbyshire, Gloucestershire, Kent, Northamptonshire, and elsewhere. Yet the predominant bloc was always from Devon.

This was only to be expected. Exeter's foundation, by a bishop of Exeter and for the benefit of a diocese comprising Devon and Cornwall, ensured that the College's traditions were firmly rooted in West Country soil. But the strong Devonian bias of its early seventeenth-century membership was due to more than history and sentiment. It also reflected some of the county's leading characteristics: its high population, its prosperity, and its social constitution. In 1600 Devon was the most populous of the English counties after Yorkshire and Middlesex (which included London).[20] Vastly more wealthy than it had been in the Middle Ages, it was enjoying a period of economic growth which stimulated a broadly based prosperity sufficiently deep and widespread to support exceptional numbers of gentry families: a group more numerous and, in the absence of many resident nobles, one even more dominant than in most early modern counties. Between 1623 and 1642 the county's knights and upper gentry are estimated to have numbered some 360 to 400 men, and the lesser parish gentry about 1,500.[21] Though they were never in a majority, these two groups supplied the College with substantial numbers of recruits. Twenty of the JPs active in the county between 1625 and 1640 had been educated at Exeter.[22]

It was the College's ability to draw on a Devonian reservoir of aspiring young men which helps to account for its burgeoning numbers. It had firm

19. 1600, 1602, 1604, 1609, 1612, 1622, 1627, 1634, 1635, 1637, 1638, 1639, 1641. The figures can be worked out from the matriculation registers: see Clark, *Register*, ii. 238–405, and OUA, SP 2.

20. E. A. Wrigley, *The Early English Censuses* (Oxford, 2011), 104. Cf. the muster rolls of 1569, which suggest that Devon was the most populous of all the counties (but the Yorkshire returns are missing): E. E. Rich, 'The Population of Elizabethan England', *Econ. Hist. Rev.*, 2nd ser., 2 (1950), 254.

21. W. G. Hoskins, 'The Estates of the Caroline Gentry', in W. G. Hoskins and H. P. R. Finberg, *Devonshire Studies* (1952), 334; M. Stoyle, *Loyalty and Locality: Popular Allegiance in Devon during the English Civil War* (Exeter, 1994), 20.

22. M. Wolffe, *Gentry Leaders in Peace and War: The Gentry Governors of Devon in the Early Seventeenth Century* (Exeter, 1997), 23–4.

ties with one of the largest and most affluent of the English counties, many of whose families were able to afford the considerable costs of an Oxford education.[23] Once there, their sons would have found a congenial ambience and many College members with a similar local background: for example, their tutors. Although the regional qualifications for Exeter fellowships had been enlarged by Sir William Petre's reforms, eight of the College's twenty-two fellowships were always reserved for Devonians, and even the eight Petrean fellows, who might come from any county where Sir William Petre held land, were often from Devon.[24] So there was always a substantial Devonian presence on the high table as well as among the College's juniors. Some, perhaps many, undergraduates had broad Devon accents, as John Aubrey noted. 'The Exeter Coll: men in disputations,' he wrote, 'when they allege *Causa causae est causa causati*, they pronounce it *caza caza est caza cazati*; very ungracefully.'[25] For these students it must have been important that they had tutors who could understand their ungraceful speech (and who may well have spoken in a similar way). One of the College's leading tutors and scholars, Nathanael Carpenter (fellow, 1607–28), was a Devonian, and in his *Geographie Delineated*, the work for which he is best known, he went out of his way to praise 'the sweet hive and receptacle of our westerne wits . . . our Devonian confines', which had produced so many great men.[26] That within Exeter there was a self-consciously Devonian community, its members regarded as a large but discrete group, is suggested by the bursar's collection of debts in 1621 from 'Cornishmen or Devonians *(Devonienses)*' and by an entry in the accounts kept by Walter Tuckfield, a graduate from Little Fulford in East Devon, which records his spending on 'a Devonshire supper', evidently a regional celebration, in 1626.[27] Exeter was a college where men from that prosperous and populous county would have felt thoroughly at home.

All the more so because the rector himself was Devonian to the core, and proud of his local origins. To some extent he and his colleagues flaunted those origins. 'Our renowned Rector Dr Prideaux' was one of several Devon

23. For costs, see *HUO*, iv. 81–7.
24. Maddicott, *Founders and Fellowship*, 294; below, 104–5.
25. Bodl. MS Aubrey 1, fo. 23v. The phrase is a legal tag meaning 'The cause of the cause is the cause of the effect'. Cf. A. Fox, *Oral and Literate Culture in England, 1500–1700* (Oxford, 2000), 63; Darwall-Smith, *University College*, 154 and n. 57.
26. Boase, *Register*, 92–3; N. Carpenter, *Geographie Delineated Forth in Two Bookes*, 2nd edn (Oxford, 1635), 262–3. For Carpenter, see below, 170–3.
27. ECA, A.I.6, fo. 4; Devon Heritage Centre, Z1/53/Box 9/2.

'heroes' praised by Carpenter in his *Geographie*, but more telling still is the evidence for Prideaux's self-identification with his native county. The opening line of the inscription on his Bredon memorial, which he himself composed, styles him 'Johannes Prideaux Devoniensis', while at the end of the prefatory letter to his *Tyrocinium ad Syllogismum*, the beginner's guide to logic, written before he became rector, he signs himself, rather eccentrically, 'Johannes Prideaux Anglo-Devoniensis'.[28] The fullest expression of his Devonian loyalties came in the 'Epistle Dedicatory' to Laurence Bodley which preceded his sermon *Ephesus Backsliding*, published in 1614. Bodley, a canon of Exeter and brother of the great Sir Thomas, had apparently obtained for him the Oxfordshire vicarage of Bampton, then in the gift of the dean and chapter of Exeter, and in an effusive letter of thanks Prideaux wrote that he was 'with this favour of yours . . . the more affected, because it comes from my native countrey [i.e. county], to which my best services were otherwise devoted'.[29] One of the very few local references in his multitudinous writings was to a familiar Devonshire custom. In a section on 'Exercises and recreations', part of his *Hypomnemata*, an educational miscellany published in 1648, he wrote of the habit among stronger men, 'especially our Devonians (*praesertim Devoniensibus nostris*)', of fighting with javelins, staffs, and cudgels—while the Cornish preferred the sport of wrestling.[30] Prideaux's second marriage in 1628, to Mary Reynell, daughter of Sir Thomas Reynell of East Ogwell, aligned him still more closely with the county and with the Devonshire gentry who supplied so many of his College's students.[31]

But more important than any of these factors in explaining why so many south-westerners went to Exeter at this time were the bonds of religion. By the start of Prideaux's rectorship the religious allegiances of many Devonians closely matched those of Prideaux himself, of Exeter's fellows, and of the College in general: allegiances to the Church of England, but lying towards

---

28. S. P. T. Prideaux, *John Prideaux: In Piam Memoriam* (Salisbury, 1938), 13; *Tyrocinium ad Syllogismum* (Oxford, 1629). This tract occurs as the second part of the second edition of Prideaux's *Tabulæ ad Grammatica Graeca Introductoriæ*, first published in 1607, but without the *Tyrocinium*. The latter, however, with its prefatory letter, must have been written early in Prideaux's Exeter career, since he describes himself as 'fellow of Exeter College', not as rector. Both parts were reprinted in 1639. See Madan, ii. 146, 215–16.
29. Prideaux, *Ephesus Backsliding*, sig. *3r.
30. J. Prideaux, *Hypomnemata, Logica, Rhetorica, Physica, Metaphysica, Pneumatica, Ethica, Politica, Oeconomica* (Oxford, [1648]), 363. For this work, see below, 214, 365–6.
31. Below, 161.

the puritan end of the spectrum constituted by the Church's members. This was a relatively recent development. In the late sixteenth century both county and College had followed the same reverse religious trajectory, from strong Catholic loyalties up to the 1570s to an equally emphatic Protestant-puritanism by 1600.[32] By the early seventeenth century Devon had become 'one of the most Puritan counties in England'.[33] Puritanism was particularly widespread among the Devon gentry,[34] and at a time when the influx of gentry into the university at large was at its peak, the Exeter of Holland and Prideaux, marked as the College was by its evangelical-Protestant tone, provided a natural home for the sons of those from Devon. John Barnard, a fellow of Lincoln in the 1640s and later the biographer of Peter Heylin, epitomized it as 'the common nursery of West Country men in puritan principles'.[35] Nor was it only among the gentry that puritanism took root in Devon. The godly were also numerous at a lower social level, among yeomen, husbandmen, and craftsmen. With gentry support, and partly as a result of gentry patronage of parish churches and the consequent presentation of puritan ministers, puritanism flourished in the countryside.[36] So it did too in some, probably most, towns. By the early seventeenth century, for example, the city of Exeter was 'deeply touched with something of the Puritan spirit',[37] and it was from this milieu, the rural parishes and the towns, that a large number of Exeter's humbler members came. Their families lay outside and below the more exclusive ranks of nobles, gentry, and higher clergy; and it is safe to assume that just as the puritan gentry were drawn towards a puritan college, so too were their puritan social inferiors. We have Prideaux's word for it that in 1631 seven fellows of the College and more than twenty undergraduates came from one Exeter school.[38] Aspiring young men from puritan families of no great social consequence, often destined for a career as parish clergy or schoolmasters, lived side by side in College with the sons of the gentry.

32. For this process in the county, see Hoskins, *Devon*, 236–7, and Stoyle, *Loyalty and Locality*, 22–3, and in the College, Maddicott, *Founders*, 299–307.
33. J. T. Cliffe, *The Puritan Gentry: The Great Puritan Families of Early Stuart England* (1984), 92.
34. Stoyle, *Loyalty and Locality*, 22, 262 n. 85; Cliffe, *The Puritan Gentry*, 237–40.
35. J. Barnard, *Theologo-historicus, or The True Life of the Most Reverend Divine and Excellent Historian Peter Heylin, D.D., Sub-dean of Westminster* (1683), 112–13.
36. Hoskins, *Devon*, 237–8; Stoyle, *Loyalty and Locality*, 22.
37. W. T. MacCaffrey, *Exeter, 1540–1640: The Growth of an English County Town* (Cambridge, MA, 1958), 199–200; M. Stoyle, *From Deliverance to Destruction: Rebellion and Civil War in an English City* (Exeter, 1996), 18–25.
38. TNA, SP 16/182, fo. 8; H. Lloyd Parry, *The Founding of Exeter School* (Exeter, 1913), 49–50.

If Devon's puritan sons were attracted to Exeter partly for religious reasons, the same was true, though to a proportionately lesser extent, of those from Cornwall. Like Devon, Cornwall had undergone a religious transformation towards the end of the sixteenth century. From being a strongly Catholic county, it had become, by the early 1600s, one which contained only a few Catholic recusants but a much larger 'thriving and extremely vocal group of Puritans'. By the 1620s, for example, about half the county's JPs were probable puritans.[39] Exeter was predictably the preferred college for the Cornish, especially for the sons of the gentry. Of the 336 Cornish gentlemen who are known to have gone to Oxford (91 per cent) or Cambridge (9 per cent) between 1595 and 1665, 194, or 58 per cent, came to Exeter.[40] In one particularly illuminating case we can show the direct effect of Prideaux's moral and religious standing on recruitment from the county. Frances Lady Robartes, wife of Richard Robartes, first Baron Truro, was a famously godly woman and the head of a godly household, as Hannibal Gamon, himself a puritanically inclined minister and anti-Arminian, took pains to emphasize in the sermon which he preached at her funeral in 1626. She had, said Gamon, corresponded with Prideaux, 'that learned professor in our famous universitie', about the education of her only son, John Robartes, desiring Prideaux to fit him 'with worthy matches out of religious families', to adorn him 'with the richest endowments of grace and learning', and 'to have the fruit of her body become the fruit of the spirit'.[41] John Robartes had matriculated at Exeter in the year before his mother's death, and in 1627–8 he was among the little group of aristocratic pupils of whom Prideaux took personal charge. He went on to marry the daughter of Robert Rich, second earl of Warwick and another prominent puritan, to become the proponent of 'godly reform' in the House of Lords, and, in the Civil War, to lead a regiment in the parliamentary army.[42]

Prideaux's reputation thus had a tentacular reach which did much to strengthen the College as a natural resort for puritans, and so to enhance its

39. A. Duffin, *Faction and Faith: Politics and Religion of the Cornish Gentry before the Civil War* (Exeter, 1996), 38, 110.
40. Ibid., 26.
41. H. Gamon, *The Praise of a Godly Woman. A Sermon Preached at the Solemn Funerall of the Right Honorable Ladie, the Ladie Frances Robartes, at Lanhide-rock Church in Cornwall, the Tenth of August 1626* (1627), 27; Duffin, *Faith and Faction*, 50, 54–5. The fullest account of Gamon is M. Purcell, *The Library at Lanhydrock* (National Trust Libraries I, n.p., n.d.).
42. ECA, H.II.11; A. Duffin, 'Robartes, John, first earl of Radnor (1606–1685), politician and army officer', *ODNB*.

numbers. His appeal was not confined to West Country puritans. Wood cites the career of Nathaniel Homes, later 'a severe Calvinist', who came from Kingswood in Gloucestershire and matriculated at Magdalen Hall in 1617 but who soon migrated to Exeter 'for the sake of John Prideaux whom he much admired'.[43] Prideaux himself was far from being a radical puritan and was often to be critical of the narrowmindedness of the godly and their subversive tendencies.[44] But there was a sufficiently large overlap between the beliefs of moderate Calvinists and of puritans for Prideaux and his College to attract those whose doctrines and practices were more precise (as contemporaries would have said) than his own. On matters such as predestination, justification by faith, and the iniquities of Rome, there was little to separate them. Prideaux himself was to prove vulnerable to the charges laid by his Arminian enemies that he was a puritan sympathizer, if not an actual puritan. But from the College's point of view this blurring of the boundaries served only to attract men from one of the most puritan parts of England, which was also Exeter's traditional recruiting ground.

3. Undergraduates: Hierarchies and status

When an undergraduate arrived at Exeter he would have found himself in a college which in some basic ways was like any other. He took his place in a society notably hierarchical, like that of all colleges, and in which hierarchy was defined by terminology. This was evident in two forms, the first relating to the university and the second to the College. First, the university's matriculation register recorded the status of each entrant's father, whether the son of a peer or knight, an esquire (*armigeri filius*), a gentleman (*generosi filius*), a cleric (*clerici filius*), or, as Prideaux had been, a mere plebeian *(plebei filius)*. The father's status was notified by the entrant himself and was generally not open to doubt, though since matriculation and other fees varied according to status, there may have been a tendency for some well-born entrants to depress their father's rank.[45]

43. Wood, *Athenae*, iii. 116–18; K. Gibson, 'Homes [Holmes]. Nathaniel (1599–1678), Independent divine', *ODNB*.
44. Below, 39, 232–3, 271–6, 319–20, 379.
45. Clark, *Register*, i. 6–7, 165; *HUO*, iv. 50–2.

College status was a trickier business. In most colleges undergraduates fell into four groups: gentlemen commoners (known at Exeter as 'fellow commoners'), commoners (*commensales* or sometimes 'sojourners'), batteters (*battellari*), and poor scholars or servitors. The fellow commoners, mostly the sons of peers, baronets, and knights, were a privileged elite and paid their tutors and the College accordingly; the commoners, a wealthy group, mainly the sons of the gentry, were so called because they paid for their commons (i.e. food and drink); the batteters, less wealthy, paid for only a portion of their commons, earning the rest through service, often service in the College hall, while the poor scholars were primarily dependent on paid service to see them through their College years.[46] This often meant personal service to the rector, fellows, fellow commoners, and commoners, though for some it might entail serving in hall, as it had for Prideaux himself in his undergraduate years. These categories were more subjective than those recorded at matriculation, and the choice of category might cause tension between fathers and sons, with sons wanting the status and privileges which came with high rank, and fathers wanting to save money and curb the opportunities for the indulgence which rank also afforded. When Peter Heylin, later to be Prideaux's most vicious critic, went up to Broadgates Hall in 1615 his father wanted to enter him as a batteter because his brother, a commoner, 'had been suffered to take too much libertie', but in the following year he was gratified to be entered at Hart Hall as a commoner.[47] At Exeter, as in almost all colleges, the commoners formed the largest group. There was, predictably, a strong correlation between the *filii generosorum* of the matriculation register and the colleges' commoners, just as there was also a correlation between sons of plebeians and batteters and poor scholars.[48] In Prideaux's time as fellow and rector, some 50 per cent of those matriculating at Exeter came from upper-class, mainly landed families (peers, baronets, knights, esquires, and gentry), while some 36 per cent were classified as the sons of plebeians, and some 14 per cent as clergy sons. The proportion of the upper-class and landed was rather higher, and the proportion of plebeians rather lower, than the university average.[49]

46. For helpful definition of, and comments on, these grades, see A. Hegarty, *A Biographical Register of St John's College, Oxford* (OHS, n.s., 43, 2011), lxiii, lxvi, lxxiv–lxxv.
47. P. Heylin, *Memorials of Bishop Waynflete* (Caxton Soc., 14, 1851), xii (Heylin's autobiographical memoranda); *HUO*, iv. 53.
48. *HUO*, iv. 53–4.
49. Clark, *Register*, ii. 238–405; OUA, SP 2; *HUO*, iv. 55.

How were these hierarchies reflected in the internal structure of Prideaux's Exeter? At the apex of undergraduate society, as in other colleges, was a small elite of fellow commoners, with an entry of about four to eight in most years. As in Trinity and Oriel, they had become a feature of the College before 1600, preceding their introduction to Lincoln in 1606, Balliol in 1610, and—probably the last in line—New College in 1677.[50] In some ways their rank was indistinguishable from that of the ordinary commoners. All were initially known as *commensales* and all paid a standard admission fee of one pound on entering the College. (By contrast, battelers paid 13s. 4d. and poor scholars nothing.[51]) What defined the fellow commoners was not only their distinction of birth, though this again might not be very different from that of some commoners, but also the privilege which they enjoyed of dining at the fellows' table in hall. To be admitted to the fellows' table was to be a fellow commoner. From 1610 each had to pay a further pound for this privilege, to be spent by the College on the purchase and repair of books for the library.[52]

Within the ranks of the fellow commoners a still smaller elite was formed by the sons of the nobility and of a few particularly wealthy knights: never more than about half a dozen men at any one time. Exeter's nobles and Prideaux's responsibility for their presence contributed powerfully to the College's reputation and distinctiveness. It was not only Wood who remarked on the scholars 'of great as of mean birth' whom he brought to the College. In 1650 the anonymous preacher of Prideaux's funeral sermon also spoke of the former rector's adroitness in attracting the upper classes (*optimates*) and the nobility—men whom he instructed in polite literature and religion.[53] The presence of such grandees in the colleges of the early Stuart university was unexceptional and has often been noticed. The education, cultural polish, and social contacts provided by colleges for their noble members conferred respect and status in a social and political world which placed a high value on both learning and civility.[54] Yet Exeter *was* exceptional in the degree to which it attracted the aristocracy: witness the

50. *HUO*, iv. 36–7; Hopkins, *Trinity*, 65; Green, *Lincoln College*, 158–9 and n. 7; J. Catto (ed.), *Oriel College: A History* (Oxford, 2013), 100.
51. ECA, A.IV.11 (Liber Bursariatus), 48.
52. ECA, A.I.5, 238.
53. Above, 83; Bodl. MS Jones 56, fo. 22r; below, 376.
54. See, e.g., *HUO*, iv. 25–6; O'Day, *Education and Society, 1500–1800*, 88–99; Stone, 'Size and Composition', 27–8.

university's matriculation register for 1615 to 1647, which contains a folio of signatures by members of the nobility, marked up with the signatories' colleges and their matriculation dates. Exeter's twelve signatories, all signing between 1624 and 1642, and including Charles, Philip and William Herbert, sons of Philip, fourth earl of Pembroke, Robert Lord Dormer, son of Baron Dormer of Wing, Philip Lord Wharton, his brother Thomas, John Robartes, and Anthony Ashley Cooper, are outnumbered only by the thirteen from Christ Church. None of the other seven colleges listed accounted for more than three names.[55] It was a subsidiary mark of Exeter's distinction that six of the signatories were among the country's leading nobles painted by Van Dyck: a total unlikely to have been exceeded even by the aristocrats of Christ Church.[56]

Exeter was thus unusual in the degree to which it attracted the upper classes; doubly so, in that it was by no means a smart and wealthy college like Christ Church. What accounts for this? As we might expect, the sons of the nobility did not conform to the Devon and Cornwall pattern of recruitment common to the undergraduate body as a whole. Their fathers' seats were scattered across southern and midland England; John Robartes, from Cornwall, was an exception. Yet some are likely to have been drawn to the College by the same factors which drew in so many West Country undergraduates. The two Whartons and the three Herberts as well as John Robartes were all from notably godly families. They would have been very much at home in the College's Calvinist-puritan milieu.[57] Others were sent by patrons or relatives to separate them from unwholesome Catholic connections and to steep them in the salvationary Protestantism purveyed by Prideaux and his colleagues. Robert Dormer, with a recusant mother and from a family with many Catholic links, was brought up as a ward of Philip Herbert, then earl of Montgomery. He was sent to Exeter in 1624 and next year married Anne Herbert, Philip's daughter, after the young couple had been instructed in religion by Prideaux, who also conducted the

---

55. OUA, SP 2, fo. 18r–v.
56. Admittedly, four of the six—Charles, Philip, and William Herbert, and Robert Lord Dormer—appear in a single painting, Van Dyck's famous depiction of the Herbert family at Wilton. The brothers Philip and Thomas Wharton have separate portraits. See S. J. Barnes et al., *Van Dyck: A Complete Catalogue of the Paintings* (New Haven, CT, 2004), 572–3, 612–13, 615–16.
57. S. Kelsey, 'Wharton, Philip, fourth baron Wharton (1613–1696), politician', *ODNB*; G. F. Trevallyn Jones, *Saw-Pit Wharton* (Sydney, 1967), 16–18; D. L. Smith, 'Herbert, Philip, first earl of Montgomery and fourth earl of Pembroke (1584–1650), courtier and politician', *ODNB*; Duffin, 'Robartes'; above, 92.

marriage ceremony. Prideaux's religious convictions, well known to his godly guardian, had clearly brought this young noble to Exeter.[58] A parallel example was that of James Dillon, son of the Irish earl of Roscommon. He too was sent to Exeter, in his case by Archbishop Ussher, 'to reclaim him from the superstitions of the Romish church' under the supervision of George Hakewill, as committed a Calvinist scholar as Prideaux himself.[59] For both rich and poor, the religion of the rector and fellows was high among their College's attractions.

For most of the nobility and their parents another factor ranked equally highly: Prideaux's reputation, not only as a famous divine and scholar, but also as a skilful and conscientious tutor who could be relied on to take special pains with his well-born pupils. About 1614, shortly after his election as rector, when he largely gave up teaching ordinary undergraduates, he continued to supervise small groups of the nobility and upper gentry.[60] He noted the point himself. Offering to act as tutor to an unnamed kinsman of Archbishop Ussher in 1638, he wrote that 'I have resolved . . . to make your kinsman one of my peculiar, and tutor him wholly my self; which I have ever continued to some especial friends, ever since I have been rector and doctor'.[61] Clusters of men sent up by these 'especial friends' were particularly conspicuous between 1624 and 1639. In 1626, for example, Prideaux was tutoring the two Wharton brothers; Robert Dormer; the two brothers Sydney and Francis Godolphin, sons of Sir William Godolphin, one of the richest men in Cornwall;[62] and Thomas Dacres, son of Sir Thomas Dacres of Cheston, Herts.[63] In 1632 he was tutor not only to the two elder Herbert brothers, Charles and Philip, but also to John and Francis Poulett, sons of Sir John Poulett, a leading Somerset landowner.[64] Occasionally these privileged

58. *Stuart Dynastic Policy and Religious Politics, 1621–1625*, ed. M. C. Questier (Camden 5th ser., 34, 2009), 352 and n. 1122; Boase, *Commoners*, 89–90; I. Roy, 'Dormer, Robert, first earl of Carnarvon (1610?–1643), royalist army officer', *ODNB*.

59. Ussher, *Correspondence*, ii. 437; Boase, *Register*, cii; J. McGuire and J. Quinn, *Dictionary of Irish Biography*. Vol. 3: *D-F* (Cambridge, 2009), 318.

60. Unless otherwise stated, all subsequent references to Prideaux's tutoring of named pupils are taken from the lists of tutors and their pupils in ECA, H.II.11. Although this manuscript, which covers the years 1606 to 1630, is unpaginated, it is arranged in columns by year and term, facilitating the checking of references.

61. Boase, cii; Ussher, *Correspondence*, ii. 743–4; below, 181.

62. Duffin, *Faith and Faction*, 24; Duffin, 'Godolphin, Sidney (bap.1610, d.1643), poet and courtier', *ODNB*. Sidney was to achieve fame as a poet and leading member of the Great Tew circle, and Francis as the dedicatee of Hobbes's *Leviathan*.

63. Boase, *Commoners*, 80.

64. Ibid., 259; *Peerage*, x. 615–17.

groups might be joined by an undergraduate from a more humble back-ground but to whom Prideaux had taken a liking and whose talents he had spotted. Dedicating his poem *Urania* to Prideaux in 1629, Samuel Austin, a budding literary man but no more than a Cornish plebeian in origin, wrote effusively and gratefully that 'you have vouchsafed to take me into your owne divine tutorage, and honor'd me (beyond all desert) with the privi-ledge of usuall disputes before your selfe, amongst those that were your noble scholers'. Sure enough, Austin had appeared five years earlier among Prideaux's pupils, alongside Robert Dormer, William Dormer his cousin, the two Godolphins, and Hugh Portman, son of Sir John Portman.[65]

In dining on the fellows' table the nobility and other fellow commoners enjoyed a privilege common to their class in all colleges.[66] But at Exeter the elite enjoyed some additional privileges. Prideaux himself tells us that they were lodged apart from the other undergraduates, either in the rector's lodgings or in a new building erected at Prideaux's own charge behind the chapel, where Robert Dormer, John Robartes, the two Whartons, and Lorenzo Cary, son of Henry Viscount Falkland, were all to be found in the mid-1620s, or in the grand and newly built Peryam's Mansions (as it came to be known), where Lorenzo Cary, Thomas Dacres, and James Dillon were housed in 1629.[67] It must have been further conducive to their comfort that they were not subject to corporal punishment for their misde-meanours, unlike their Exeter inferiors and unlike gentlemen commoners (so Aubrey says) in some other colleges.[68] Their indulgent treatment by Prideaux was a less formal privilege. In 1640 Archbishop Laud, the uni-versity's chancellor and always a stickler for firm discipline and good order, was angered by the misconduct of the Irish peer Lord Caulfield, then at Exeter. 'I am very much scandalized at the liberty which is given to these young men . . . noblemen's sons,' he wrote, before going on to lay the blame on Caulfield's unnamed tutor (Prideaux) and the head of his house (also Prideaux).[69] Anthony Ashley Cooper was another occasional offender. Son of a Dorset baronet and later to become famous as earl of Shaftesbury and as

---

65. A[ustin], *Urania*, sig. A1r; Boase, *Commoners*, 9; N. Jagger, 'Austin, Samuel (b.1605/6), poet', *ODNB*; ECA, H.II.11.
66. Cf. *HUO*, iv. 36–7; Boase, *Register*, cx, n. 2.
67. Boase, *Register*, ciii, 312; ECA, C.II.4 (Prideaux's Survey, 1630), fos. 28r–29r.
68. BL MS Sloane 3827, fo 169; Ryan, *An Obscure Place*, 30; J. Aubrey, *Brief Lives*, ed. A. Clark, 2 vols. (Oxford, 1898), ii. 171; Pantin, *Oxford Life in Oxford Archives*, 62.
69. *Works of Laud*, v. 264–5. It is not clear that Laud knew the identity of Caulfield's tutor and head.

Dryden's 'Achitophel', he was resident at Exeter in 1637–8, when his lifestyle epitomized that of the wealthy young nobleman, keeping his own horses and servants and with the liberty to do more or less as he pleased. Recalling in his autobiography a College escapade, 'the old doctor', he wrote (meaning Prideaux), was 'always favourable to youth offending out of courage' and ready enough to overlook his disorderly conduct.[70]

As in other colleges, very few of Exeter's fellow commoners took degrees; and it was mildly paradoxical that the one class of undergraduates allowed entry to Sir Thomas Bodley's new library comprised the sons of 'great men and nobles' and of parliamentary peers—the group least likely to take advantage of this additional privilege.[71] Most studied for a maximum of three years, and in many cases for no more than one or two, before moving away, often to one of the Inns of Court as a further stage in their 'finishing' process. Ashley Cooper had already been entered at Lincoln's Inn before his departure from Exeter in July 1638. But within the College Prideaux saw to it that the education of the nobility was by no means neglected; their studies were taken seriously. In Exeter, as in other colleges, the upper classes followed a curriculum common to all students, though often in a necessarily abbreviated form.[72] We have Samuel Austin's word for it that Prideaux acted as moderator in the formal disputations between his 'Noble Scholers' in which Austin was allowed to participate and which played a similarly large part in the mental training of all undergraduates.[73] Henry Ford, a fellow commoner from a Devonshire landed family, who entered Exeter in 1634, was said by his friend John Prince to have 'followed his studies with happy success', 'conquered logick before he left the university', and acquired some skill in natural philosophy, 'a tang whereof . . . adhered to his conversation ever after'.[74] James Dillon, another fellow commoner, was able to pass on a collection of logic books to his friend Ralph Verney after leaving the College.[75] Those who showed a more pronounced aptitude for their studies might go much further. John Robartes, for example, always a favourite with Prideaux, was taught mathematics by Matthew Pasor, one of the College's

70. Boase, *Commoners*, 292; Boase, *Register*, cx–cxii (extracts from Ashley Cooper's autobiography).
71. Clark, *Register*, i., 262–3; Clapinson, 'The Bodleian Library and its Readers', 33.
72. Cf. *HUO*, iv. 216–17.
73. Above, 98.
74. Prince, *Worthies of Devon*, 379–82; Boase, *Commoners*, 110.
75. N. Tyacke, 'An Oxford Education in the Early Seventeenth Century: John Crowther's *Musae Faciles* (1631)', *History of Universities*, 27 (2013), 10–11.

visiting scholars from the Continent, and went on to take both the BA and the MA, while in the 1640s Prideaux addressed a Latin tract to this Presbyterian former pupil in an attempt to persuade him of the virtues of episcopacy. The extensive library at Lanhydrock, Robartes's Cornish seat, remains today to testify to a talent for learning which had begun at Exeter.[76]

Prideaux's teaching of Robartes and his peers extended beyond the formal confines of the arts syllabus to take in a broader range of subjects in the humanities. These subsidiary studies, a general feature of an Oxford education in the early seventeenth century, were especially relevant for the nobility, providing as they did a diversified cultural background for the country's future governors. Prideaux's Exeter produced its own advertisement for this informal syllabus. Exeter College MS 285 is as a substantial manuscript notebook helpfully titled 'Pridaux Tironum Institutio', 'Prideaux: Instruction for Beginners'. Though not in Prideaux's hand, it appears to have been compiled under his direction for Anthony Ashley Cooper, a fellow commoner at Exeter in 1637–8, and to have once been in the library of his family seat at Wimborne St Giles in Dorset. Its various sections provide a panoramic survey of basic knowledge, beginning with the Bible and biblical chronology, and going on to cover, among much else, British and European history, geography, including the regions of Europe, Asia, and America, and the various types of law (natural, civil, canon, etc.). Each section follows the university's normal scholastic method by providing *quaestiones* for disputation—'whether the story of Brute be a monkish fable', for example. Although little more than a well-ordered compendium of elementary information, it bears witness to Prideaux's concern for the general education of the young nobles in his charge and to the pains which he was prepared to undertake on their behalf; and in doing so it does something to explain the reputation which he enjoyed as a teacher.

Prideaux's supervision of his aristocratic pupils is likely to have entailed regular contacts with their fathers, men keen to know that their money was being well spent and that their sons were making progress.[77] We have one

<hr/>

76. Boase, *Commoners*, 274; Twells, *The Theological Works of the Learned Dr Pocock*, i. 2; Feingold, *The Mathematicians' Apprenticeship*, 83; J. Prideaux, *Reverendi in Christo Patris Joannis Prideaux D. Episcopi Vigorniensis ad Nobilissimum Dominum D. Joannem Roberts, Baronem Truro, de Episcopatu Epistola* (1660); Purcell, *The Library at Lanhydrock*.

77. There are some particularly illuminating letters on this theme in the contemporary correspondence between Sir Bevill Grenville (at Exeter, 1611–14), his son, and his son's tutor at Gloucester Hall: see R. Granville, *The History of the Granville Family* (Exeter, 1895), 205–11, 223–6.

particularly informative instance of such contacts. On 25 November 1629, Prideaux wrote to Henry Cary, Viscount Falkland, himself an Exeter alumnus, in response to an earlier letter from Falkland about the progress of his son Lorenzo, then in his third year at Exeter. Prideaux's reply, almost wholly unknown, is worth giving in full:

> I have been confined to my chamber under the phisitians hand this month by a burning fever [wrote Prideaux] & yet am not freed, your letter could not choose but move mee, wherein is expressed the hearty zeale of a father for the well-doing of a carelesse sonne; but upon right information I make no doubt but faults shalbe layd on them to whom they belong, & those excused who never neglected to doe their best. I held it very reasonable that yo'r sonne should accompany his brothers & sisters at his grandmothers funeral to which purpose he was furnished. It was in the vacation, when publique exercises cease among us, & gentlemen usually take some recreation abroad. It was my chance then to be commanded by my Lo: Chamberline to waite my monthe at the court as his Ma'ties chaplaine of w'ch advantage was taken by yo'r sonne to keepe off from his study, w'ch willingly he attends not without constraint; at my returne he was not neglected, some excuses were made for the enjoying the company of his brothers & sister w'ch he had not a long time seene; he returned fortnight since, I made him acquainted w'th yo'r L'ds letter & added that sharpnes of reproof w'ch I thinke might move any man; corperall punishments we use not to inflict on noble mens sonnes in this place, his fellow-pupills were my Lo: Wharton & his brother w'th my Lo: Robarts eldest sonne; all these I thanke God so thrived that their friends have been thankful unto mee, & yet I may truly say for yo'r sonne only hath been more than for them all; *he is capable of all kinds of learning but I can fasten no goodnesse in him having a better brayne than heart*, w'ch hath beene a continuall vexation unto mee; but that yo'r Lo:p may be thoroughly informed of all particulars, I have taken order with his tutor that the next weeke he shall take a iourney of purpose to attend yo're hone: & give you full account of all passages. So I tender my best service; rest yo'r hone:
>
> In Christ to be commanded Jo: Prideaux[78]

Prideaux took seriously his responsibilities to the young and their families. Clever, but also idle and deceitful, Lorenzo Cary was a type of student whom all tutors would recognize. His mentor did not hesitate to show his

---

78. BL MS Sloane 3827, fo. 169, printed, with minor errors and no source cited, in Ryan, *An Obscure Place*, 29–30. The italicized portion is underlined—by Falkland?—in the original MS.

anger at his behaviour and would, it is implied, have imposed a corporal penalty had this been the custom in Exeter. His tutor was consulted and Cary was sent home to explain himself. Prideaux's concern for the right education of those in his charge was thus as much moral as pedagogical—and even a young nobleman might be forced to mend his ways.

Troublesome though some nobles' sons might prove, as a group they were clearly viewed as an asset—an elite of which both the College and its head might be proud. Prideaux's tone was almost boastful when he told Ussher in 1638 that the archbishop's unnamed Irish kinsman whom Prideaux was happy to take on as his pupil 'hath (three) fellow pupils which are sons to earls, together with his country-man, the son of my Lord Caulfield'.[79] The rector loved a lord. But however high their standing, and however highly they were valued, the sons of the nobility remained a very small group by comparison with the bulk of the ordinary undergraduates. The structure of this larger body is most helpfully revealed by the payment of caution money, the cash sum handed over by each undergraduate on entry to the College and returned to him at his departure, minus any deductions for debts, damage to College property, and so on. Caution money had been introduced into Exeter in 1610, at a time when its usefulness as a security for undergraduate debt was coming to be generally appreciated throughout the colleges. The tariff of payments in Exeter was then fixed at £4 for a commoner, £3 for a batteler, and 30s. for a poor scholar. There was thus no separate rating for fellow commoners, who paid £4 each along with the ordinary commoners, in line with the identical admission fee of £1 paid by members of both groups.[80] But in 1629, when the first caution book began to record the names, payments, and tutors of all caution-money payers, together with the dates of their payments and of their money's return, not only were the rates increased but the fellow commoners were separated from the ordinary commoners. Fellow commoners now paid £6, commoners £5, batteler £4, and poor scholars £2: a formal recognition of the fellow commoners' superiority (and superior wealth) which went beyond the ancient line of demarcation set by their dining privileges.[81]

---

79. Boase, *Register*, ciii; Ussher, *Correspondence*, ii. 743–4. The three earls' sons were almost certainly Henry, Philip, and George Stanhope, sons of the earl of Chesterfield: see Boase, *Commoners*, 306.

80. ECA, A.I.5, 238; A.III.9.

81. ECA, A.I.22, preliminary page (Caution Book, 1629–86).

The social divisions set out in the caution book took on a physical form in the College's seating arrangements. As in so many other societies and circumstances, public seating was a reflection of priority and status. In 1619 Prideaux drew up in his own hand a schedule governing the seating arrangements for the College's grand new hall, recently completed. The fellows and fellow commoners, he laid down, were to return to their old places on the high table. The commoners were to be seated on the tables on the right-hand, north side of the hall, and the battelers on their own table on the south side. The poor scholars (we learn from a later source) had their own table, but were to dine 'without sitting'. Here was the College hierarchy, visible for all to see.[82]

Both the caution money payment and the hall seating plan emphasize the division between the majority comprising the fellow commoners and commoners and the minority of battelers and poor scholars. It was a division reflected in their future prospects. Those in the first group tended to stay for a short time, often for less than two years, rarely took a degree, and in many cases went on to the Inns of Court before returning to their estates. Those in the second group resided for longer, usually took the BA, and in many cases went into the church or became schoolmasters. The fellow commoners and commoners provided the College with prestige and social weight, but they were essentially birds of passage, for whom the College was a staging post leading eventually to a career in public life, whether in politics or in the localities. The battelers and poor scholars, on the other hand, were united in their relative poverty, and despite their different College rankings there may not have been much to separate them. We might recall Thomas Middleton's 'Pierce Pennyless, exceeding poor scholar that hath made clean shoes in both universities, and been a pitiful battler all thy lifetime'.[83] Such men were stayers, providing the undergraduate body with continuity and ballast, and themselves with the degree qualification which was becoming essential for a clerical career. The contrast is beautifully brought out in Anthony Ashley Cooper's account, given in his autobiography, of the 'rent strike' which he led at Exeter in 1637 or 1638. When the fellows proposed to dilute the College's exceptionally strong beer, Ashley Cooper retaliated by persuading his friends to remove their names from the College's buttery book, effectively resigning their College places and so threatening the fellows' income

82. ECA, B.IV.16/2 (Prideaux's Notebook), fos. 21v, 56v. Where did the bachelors sit?
83. Above, 17.

from their wealthiest and most rewarding pupils. At the same time he advised 'all those [that] were intended . . . to get their livelihood by their studies, to rest quiet and not appear'. Dashing young bucks could afford to risk their College places; poorer students, dependent on the success of their studies for their future living, could not. As for the beer, it was restored to full strength.[84]

4. Fellows and tutors

The College's twenty-two fellows, under the headship of the rector, formed the central stem around which its corporate life revolved. With the help of C. W. Boase's biographical register, we can reconstruct the fellowship in Prideaux's time both in general terms and in statistical detail.[85] Between 1601 and 1642, during Prideaux's years as fellow and rector, the typical fellow came from a plebeian background in Devonshire. He matriculated at the College aged about 17, took his BA after three or four years, was elected to a fellowship at the age of 21 or 22, went on to take the MA and most commonly the BD, and held his fellowship for about ten years before resigning either to marry or to take up a parish in his native county—or in many cases to do both.

This pattern was representative rather than unvarying. The regional origins of the fellowship were largely determined by the College's original statutes, which since Stapeldon's day had provided for eight fellows from Devon and four from Cornwall, and, since the 1350s, two from the diocese of Salisbury. The wild cards were the eight additional Petrean fellowships established by Sir William Petre in the 1560s, whose holders had to come from any of the thirteen counties, including Devon, where Petre held land.[86] Even after 1614, when the College first successfully challenged the right of Petre's grandson to nominate to the eight fellowships, this land restriction still applied. Yet it is worth noting that of the twenty-five Petrean fellows elected between 1614 and 1642, a majority, fourteen, came from Devon. When Sir John Petre, Sir William's son, had possessed the right of nomination between 1572 and 1613, his fellows from Devon had been in a small minority, which

---

84. Boase, *Register*, cxi.
85. Ibid., 89–107, for fellows elected in this period.
86. *Statutes*, 28–9; Maddicott, *Founders*, 272–3.

suggests a marked bias towards Devonian candidates from 1614 onwards. Perhaps not surprisingly, an existing Devonian majority tended to elect other Devonians even when there was no obligation to do so.

Most successful candidates for fellowships were 'home-grown'. They had matriculated at Exeter in their late teens and rarely came to their fellowships from other colleges or halls. The matriculation details are known for seventy of the eighty-two fellows elected in Prideaux's time as fellow and rector. Of these, only ten, or 12 per cent, had matriculated at other colleges or halls. In other colleges across the university some 36 per cent of those elected were outsiders,[87] which suggests that Exeter was an exceptionally self-contained College and one reluctant to look for fellows beyond its own ranks. Of the eighty-two fellows elected between 1601 and 1642 a small number gained their fellowships before they had taken the BA: nine out of thirty-eight, for example, between 1621 and 1640. In the medieval College, election before inception as BA had been the norm, but by the early seventeenth century it was highly unusual in most colleges to elect undergraduates to fellowships, and in many cases it was expressly forbidden by college statutes; so here again Exeter went its own way.[88] A few other elections resulted from royal intervention, particularly under James I. John Balcanquall, one of James I's Scottish followers, was effectively intruded into a Petrean fellowship by the king in 1613, just as Richard Amye, Solomon Hext, and—a much more distinguished name—Nathanael Carpenter had been under Rector Holland in 1604. But Exeter suffered less from these intrusions than some colleges, and in Balcanquall's case the intruder proved his value by his role in helping to defeat William Lord Petre's claims to nominate to his grandfather's fellowships.[89]

What of social origins? Of the seventy fellows whose matriculation status is recorded, the two largest groups comprised twenty-five plebeians (36 per cent) and twenty-four *generosi*—knights, esquires, and gentry (34 per cent). Of the rest, seventeen (24 per cent) were sons of the clergy, followed by a short tally of merchants' sons. In general terms the proportion of fellows with plebeian origins was higher, and the proportion with *generosi* origins lower, than among the larger undergraduate community. This is likely to have meant that those fellows who were tutors often found themselves

87. *HUO*, iv. 81.
88. Ibid.
89. Boase, *Register*, 91, 96; *HUO*, iv. 191–2; above, 69.

teaching pupils whose families were socially superior to theirs. Once elected, few held their fellowships for more than the usual span of ten years or so. Between 1601 and 1642 only eight fellows exceeded twenty years, among whom Joseph Maynard (elected 1625, vacated 1653, rector 1662–6) and Henry Willett (elected 1624, vacated 1652) were the leaders.[90] For these two and for a very few others a College fellowship became something like a career for life, but for most it was a staging post, providing the opportunity to acquire qualifications which might lead to better things. Prideaux's own record of forty-two years' service, first as fellow and then as rector, was unequalled.

A few fellows stood out from the rest as outstanding scholars whose written works would have distinguished them in any company. Heading this category were two men, George Hakewill and Nathanael Carpenter, whose careers are considered in a later chapter.[91] There were no other fellows in Prideaux's day who were of the same intellectual calibre. A few published sermons; most published nothing. But a greater number excelled, as did Carpenter, in another important role: that of tutor. The late sixteenth and early seventeenth century was the heyday of the college tutor, a time when his role was at its most expansive, extending well beyond his pupils' tuition.[92] He was both a moral guardian and a financial caretaker, charged with supervising both his pupils' conduct and their spending. Often tutor and pupils shared the same room, an indication not only of pressures on space in increasingly crowded colleges but also of a relationship which transcended the merely pedagogic. When young William Chafin, son of a Wiltshire gentry family, arrived at Exeter in April 1603, his tutor William Helme (who had been Prideaux's tutor) saw to it that he was able to take over his predecessor's bed, advanced him money to buy a map of the world in four sheets, and tried unsuccessfully to persuade him to buy 'a book of viiis. pryce called Orthelius', judged by Chafin, who was clearly a rather prim young man, to be suitable only for a courtier and 'not accademicall or for a university scholler'.[93]

---

90. Above, 104; Boase, *Register*, 100.
91. Below, 167–73.
92. *HUO*, iv. 64–8, provides the best account of the tutor's work. For the tutor's financial role, see below, 115.
93. Wiltshire and Swindon History Centre, Chippenham, MS 865/501 (letter from William Chafin to his father). 'Orthelius' may be the cartographer Ortelius.

At the heart of a tutor's relationship with his pupils lay his work as a teacher, piloting his charges not only through the basic arts course, with its stress on Aristotelian logic and natural philosophy and on the mind-sharpening disputations which had always been a central part of university life, but also through the informal syllabus in the humanities set out in the Ashley Cooper manuscript. How were tutors selected for this arduous and important job? In some cases a particular tutor might be approached directly by a parent or guardian. When in 1627 Sir Walter Pye handed over his son, another Walter, to the 'charge and tuition' of Henry Tozer, young Walter's entry to the College rested on an unlikely friendship between this wealthy Herefordshire landowner, lawyer, and civil servant and one of Exeter's most able fellows. It was a similar friendship between Archbishop Ussher and George Hakewill that placed the young James Dillon in Hakewill's care in 1628.[94] More frequently, however, and, as was usual in all colleges, the choice of tutors lay with the head of house. Prideaux was an especially conscientious selector of tutors and took exceptional pains to appoint the right men. 'So zealous he was also in appointing industrious and careful tutors', says Wood, 'that in short time many were fitted to do service in the church and state.'[95] The same qualities were apparent in Prideaux's letter of 1638 to Archbishop Ussher. Offering to tutor the archbishop's kinsman himself, he remarked that 'Young tutors oftentimes fail their pupils for want of experience and authority (to say nothing of negligence and ignorance).'[96] It was never the case in any college that all fellows were tutors, but in Rector Holland's Exeter and in Prideaux's early years as rector the number of tutors had been large, averaging thirteen, a majority of the fellowship. But from about 1617 onwards, in what looks to have been an act of deliberate policy, the number was cut to about eight.[97] Discarded, probably, were the drones about whom Sir Bevill Grenville grumbled when he reminisced to his son about his years at Exeter from 1611 to 1614. In 1637 Grenville wrote:

94. H. Tozer, *A Christian Amendment Delivered in a Sermon on New Yeares Day 1631 in St Martines Church in Oxford* (Oxford, 1633), sigs. A2r–A6r; Boase, *Commoners*, 264; V. Larminie, 'Tozer, Henry (c.1601–1650), Church of England clergyman', *ODNB;* I. Atherton, 'Pye, Sir Walter (bap.1571, d.1635), lawyer', *ODNB;* below, 181–2.
95. Wood, *Athenae*, iii. 266.
96. Ussher, *Correspondence*, ii. 744; Boase, *Register*, ciii.
97. All information on numbers of tutors and pupils in this and the following paragraphs derives from the lists of tutors and pupils in ECA, H.II.11.

There was a nation of ancient seniors (and I doubt not but there is a succession of them unto these days) who, having gotten a convenient stock of learning in their youth to make them good company, did employ their parts to nothing but the encrease of good fellowship, and changed from the better study to the worse. They were my destruction and many others in my time.[98]

Prideaux was wise in the ways of the negligent. Summing up tersely the defects of various groups in a sermon of 1614, 'Tutors for carelesnesse, schollers [undergraduates] for dissolutenesse', he remarked.[99] It was this ancient regime which he sought to change by reducing the College's tutors to a more select company.

The number of pupils assigned to each tutor varied widely. The busiest and most hard-worked might have twenty to twenty-five pupils, though in any one year there were never more than one or two tutors with as many. The norm was about eight to twelve, and some had only two or three.[100] The ability to nominate tutors and to allocate pupils placed extensive powers of patronage in the rector's hands. Pupils were a valuable commodity. In most colleges a pupil paid fees to his tutor according to the pupil's status, with battelers paying £2 to £3 a year, commoners £4, and fellow commoners proportionately more. Unfortunately, few student accounts have survived from Exeter to substantiate these general figures, but we know that John Tuckfield, a Devonshire fellow commoner in 1641–2, paid his tutor Robert Snow, the College chaplain, £3 for the half year; and since it was normal to reside for only three of the year's four terms, he is likely to have been paying Snow about £4 to £5 annually.[101] A tutor's total income from his pupils might be considerable. In 1635, for example, Henry Tozer took on five new pupils—two fellow commoners, one commoner, and two poor scholars. In 1636 his freshman pupils comprised another fellow commoner, two commoners, two battelers, and one poor scholar.[102] Assuming that the 1635 group continued as his pupils in 1636 and that poor scholars paid nothing, providing service in place of fees, Tozer's income from these two year-groups would have been about £28 in 1636. A head of house who

---

98. Granville, *History of the Granville Family*, 206; cf. 224 for another complaint.
99. Prideaux, *Ephesus Backsliding*, 27.
100. Figures derived from the tutor-pupil lists, ECA, H.II.11.
101. *HUO*, iv. 85, 89; Devon Heritage Centre, ZI/53/Box 9/2 (accounts of Walter and John Tuckfield); Boase, *Commoners*, 332; ECA, A.I.22, 81. In March 1641 Snow was appointed to the Tuckfield living of Morchard Bishop: CCEd, Person ID 17077.
102. ECA, A.I.22, 36–47.

could put his fellows in the way of a good cash income disposed of a large measure of power.

All tutors had a large moral role to play in the education of their pupils, beyond the provision of teaching, to which that role was closely allied. At its core lay the imposition of discipline on unruly and sometimes indolent adolescents. Here rector and tutor often worked together. Concluding his letter to Lord Falkland about the unsatisfactory behaviour of his son Lorenzo, Prideaux added that his tutor (Henry Tozer) would shortly visit his father to provide a full report.[103] If discipline was the prerequisite of good learning, it also offered a necessary training in virtuous living.[104] It was a means to securing orderly conduct, sobriety in dress and deportment, the avoidance of alehouses and the drunkenness which they encouraged, and, above all, diligent application to academic work. All Exeter undergraduates took an oath, probably on admission, to apply themselves to the College's 'ordinarie exercise' (i.e. the syllabus of studies, especially disputations), to accept punishment for their faults, and to conform 'to the good orders and discipline of this Colledge'.[105] In the 1630s these local injunctions were powerfully complemented by the determination of Laud, as chancellor, to enforce order and discipline throughout the university, particularly with regard to dress, deportment, and drinking.[106] In the university the key enforcers were the vice-chancellor and the proctors, and in the colleges, the tutors, whose close supervision of their pupils would, it was hoped guarantee their conduct.[107] When pupils shared chambers with their tutors, even sleeping in the same room, as they often did, the opportunities for kicking over the traces might be limited.

How far did Prideaux's College conform to these general ideals? The rector certainly had a reputation as a disciplinarian. John Conant, a fellow under Prideaux, and elected to the rectorship after the disorders brought by the Civil War, set about restoring 'that ancient and wholesome discipline for which Exeter College had been so famous under the government of Dr. Holland and Dr. Prideaux'.[108] Yet the record was mixed. As we have seen,

---

103. Above, 100–2; ECA, A.II.9, fo. 303v.
104. *HUO*, iv. 230; L. Stone, 'Social Control and Intellectual Excellence: Oxbridge and Edinburgh, 1560–1983', in N. Phillipson (ed.), *Universities, Society, and the Future* (Edinburgh, 1983), 6–13.
105. ECA, A.I.19, 66 (Book of statutes).
106. K. Sharpe, 'Archbishop Laud and the University of Oxford', in H. Lloyd-Jones et al. (eds.), *History & Imagination: Essays in Honour of H. R. Trevor-Roper* (1981), 152–4.
107. Stone, 'Social Control and Intellectual Excellence', 6–9.
108. Conant, *Life of Conant*, 12.

the rowdiness of the nobility was often tolerated, as it was in other colleges, though the example of Lorenzo Cary suggests that even the sons of peers were not permitted to neglect their studies.[109] Their social inferiors might be more vigorously punished, even for minor infractions of unwritten rules and often by public shaming. We know that corporal punishment might sometimes be used, since Prideaux's letter to Lord Falkland tells us specifically that noblemen's sons were exempt from its rigours. In 1633 Robert Waring, a commoner, was told to cut his hair (very much in line with Laudian imperatives) and then to confess publicly in hall his offence in leaving the College without his tutor's permission, while the same public penalty was imposed on another undergraduate, Ambrose Rous, whose name was to be removed from the College books until he had seen the rector.[110] Though not precisely a disciplinary measure, the dilution of the College beer, against which Ashley Cooper and his friends launched their successful protest, may have derived from another Laudian aspiration, the curbing of drunkenness. A variety of methods could thus be used to enforce discipline, some no doubt more painful than others. One of Prideaux's many roles was that of headmaster

5. Wealth

The early seventeenth century was a time of growing prosperity for most Oxford colleges.[111] Rising numbers of students added both to corporate wealth and to fellows' incomes; generous benefactions funded new buildings; the Corn Rent system offset the effects of inflation on rents;[112] and a long period of peace fostered a generally benign economic climate. Exeter shared in the profits of expansion and growth. It was never among Oxford's richest colleges, and it remained in the lower half of such contemporary valuations as there were. When the colleges were taxed for Queen Elizabeth's visit in 1592, Exeter, with an estimated rental income of £200

109. Above, 100–2.
110. ECA, B.I.16/2, fo. 55v; Boase, *Commoners*, 345; Stone, 'Social Control and Intellectual Excellence', 10–11.
111. See *HUO*, iv. 773–4.
112. By the Corn Rent Act of 1576 one-third of the rent on future college leases at Oxford and Cambridge was to be paid in an agreed quantity of grain or in the cash equivalent of that quantity at current market prices, thus providing a hedge against inflation: see *HUO*, iii. 535–7, and Darwall-Smith, *University College*, 153.

a year, was placed tenth, on a par with Trinity and Oriel and above only Lincoln, Balliol, and University College. A comparable rating to raise money for the fortification of Oxford in 1643 again placed Exeter tenth, above the same three colleges and also above the three newcomers to the list, Wadham, Jesus, and Pembroke, but well below the three richest colleges, Christ Church, Magdalen, and New College, the skyscrapers of wealth in the early modern university.[113]

Yet although the College may have been relatively poor, it was far from impoverished.[114] The rector's accounts record a surplus in every year of Prideaux's rectorship, except 1624–5, when there was a small deficit of £15; but the mid-1620s marked a time of general difficulties in other colleges, probably caused by outbreaks of epidemic disease and a consequent fall-off in undergraduate numbers which we have already noticed.[115] The College's average annual income for the whole period was £423, with peaks in the mid- to late 1630s (1634, £598; 1638, £559; 1639, £516) and a trough in the mid-1620s (1624, £306; 1625, £286; 1626, £337). The peaks and troughs coincided with those for undergraduate numbers, showing a clear relationship between undergraduate numbers and annual income: more students, more income. The end-of-year surplus was carried forward to augment the revenues for the following year: a piece of prudent management always followed at Exeter, but one contrasting with New College, where the annual surplus was shared among the fellows.[116] The average annual surplus over the whole period amounted to £119, with the largest surpluses, predictably, in the late 1630s: 1637, £217; 1638, £211; 1639, £232. The College had never been more populous, nor consequently more prosperous, than in the years leading up to the Civil War.

Exeter's main source of revenue comprised rents from property. Its most valuable properties were the four Oxfordshire rectories (Kidlington, Yarnton, South Newington, and Merton), together with other minor

---

113. *Registrum Annalium Collegii Mertonensis, 1567–1603*, ed. J. M. Fletcher (OHS, n.s., 24, 1976), 287; *The Dean's Register of Oriel, 1446–1661*, ed. G. C. Richards and H. E. Salter (Oxford, 1926), 299–300; *HUO*, iii. 559. For comparable listings for the early sixteenth century, see Maddicott, *Founders*, 191–3.

114. Unless otherwise stated, all the following statistics derive from the rector's accounts: ECA, A. II.9 (1564–1639) and A.II.10 (1639–1734). Figures are given to the nearest £. In calculating the annual revenue, the surplus carried forward from the previous year, customarily added to receipts, has been deducted, so providing figures only for revenue raised within the year.

115. Above, 86; Darwall-Smith, *University College*, 135; Hopkins, *Trinity*, 75.

116. Maddicott, *Founders*, 132; J. Buxton and P. Williams (eds.), *New College, Oxford, 1379–1979* (Oxford, 1979), 53.

holdings in Oxfordshire and Somerset settled on the College by Sir William Petre in the 1560s.[117] In 1611–12, the year in which Prideaux was elected to the rectorship, the Petrean properties brought in £246, or 48 per cent of the total receipt of £519; and in 1638–9, £180, or 35 per cent of the total receipt of £519.[118] South Newington rectory, one of the most valuable properties, yielded a steady £58, and Kidlington often more: some £67 in 1638–9. Petre had also done the College a good turn in laying down firm rules for the management of its estate: no reversionary leases, no leases for more than twenty years, no leases to rector or fellows, tenants to bear the cost of repairs, and so on.[119] Prideaux and his colleagues were the fortunate inheritors not only of the Petrean endowment but of Petre's provisions for careful husbandry.

Most of the College's other revenues came from its older properties, Gwinear and Menheniot in Cornwall and Long Wittenham in Berkshire, from urban properties in Oxford, from room rents, and from admission charges collected from fellows at the time of the election, from bachelors at the time of their graduation, and from fellow commoners, commoners, and battelers at the time of their entry (There were no charges for poor scholars.) Rather surprisingly, room rents, usually raising between £30 and £70 a year, were never a major item in the College's total budget, though, like admission charges, they rose in value with rising numbers. By far the largest single item on the other, debit side of the account was for expenditure on fellows' commons and the additional spending on food and drink, over and above the statutory allowances, known as 'decrements'.[120] In 1611–12 spending on commons and decrements amounted to £178, 36 per cent of the total outgoings of £502, and in 1638–9 to £136, or 23 per cent from a total of £595. Payments to fellows for stipends and clothing were also substantial: £59 in 1611–12, £56 in 1638–9. Most of the remaining expenditure went on repairs to buildings, payments to the main College servants (cook, gardener, etc.), rents to other colleges and to the city for Oxford properties, and lawsuits.

In some respects, however, the rector's accounts, indispensable though they are as a guide to getting and spending, offer a flawed picture of the

---

117. Maddicott, *Founders*, 283–7.
118. Account for 1611–12: ECA, A.II.9, fos 213r–216r. For 1638–9: ibid., fos. 352r–356v, summarized in Boase, *Register*, 345–8.
119. *Statutes*, 44–5; Maddicott, *Founders*, 277–8.
120. For decrements, see Maddicott, *Founders*, 196.

College's finances. Exeter's modest annual revenues and its lowly position in the taxation tables by comparison with other colleges—essentially a comparison of rentals—fails to take account of other gains and benefits, great and small, which did not always enter the accounts. The introduction of caution money in 1610, for example, provided the College with a store of cash which could be drawn on as occasion required. The forty undergraduates who entered the College in 1635 paid altogether £166 in caution money, and at any one time the 'caution bag', as it was called, must have contained several hundred pounds. This reserve was used by the bursar in 1617 to pay for the furnishing of the new Peryam's Mansions and for repairs to the same building in 1626–7.[121] These caution-money loans to the College, for that was what they were, thus provided a useful way of resolving temporary cash flow problems. Sometimes the College could also draw on the affection in which it was held by old members to secure services gratis for which it would otherwise have had to pay. Offered a fee by Prideaux to advise on the lease for the College's property at Merton in 1629, that rising young lawyer John Maynard courteously rejected the offer: 'I am so much bounden [to the College] as I could not accept thereof, my poor abilitys being indetted for themselves to that House, and therefore I desire you to do me that favor as to suffer some small payment of my dett in acknowledging it.'[122] The generosity of Maynard, son of a Devonshire squire, and a former commoner of the College, shows why such men were worth cultivating during their undergraduate years. But the benefits which they provided were hardly quantifiable and made no mark on the accounts. Much greater benefactions, from old members and others, helped to finance the College's building campaign between 1617 and 1624.[123]

Prideaux was thus fortunate in ruling a College which, although not among the wealthiest, faced few financial crises. Much was due here to Prideaux's inheritance. If the Petrean endowment and the Petrean statutes provided a foundation for later prosperity, some of Holland's innovations, notably the introduction of caution money, also enhanced Exeter's position. But Prideaux too made his own contribution to that prosperity, and not only by attracting to Exeter the wealthy undergraduates from aristocratic and gentry families who could help the College to pay its way. His particular

121. ECA, A.I.22, 36–42; B.I.16/2, fo. 16v; A.II.9, fo. 292v.
122. Boase, *Register*, 334.
123. For an extended account of the building campaign, see below, 119–56.

role in this and other aspects of College government is considered in the final section of this chapter.

6. A 'hands-on' rector

Prideaux was heavily involved in the affairs of his College at every level: very little was entirely outside his purview. The range of his responsibilities extended well beyond those defined in Petre's statutes—to enforce the same statutes, to defend the College in lawsuits, and so on—and even beyond his non-statutory work in appointing tutors and representing the College in its external relations with the Crown, with old members, with benefactors, and with undergraduates' parents. Something of a superior general factotum, he engaged with the internal life of his College in three broad areas: in finance, in relations with undergraduates, and in the supervision of domestic arrangements. All three overlapped and were closely related.

His financial role stemmed from a statutory duty to present the College annual accounts. This entailed a mass of time-consuming subsidiary business which Prideaux was unwilling or unable to delegate. The rector's quarterly account book, running from 1614 to 1627 and the only surviving example, compiled in Prideaux's own hand, shows the sort of minutiae which occupied his day, noting as it does the income from rooms, with the location of each room, and spending on such trivia as coal for the hall, a cloth for the high table, and ironwork for locks and keys. A separate memoranda book, again in his own hand, shows him receiving room rents, setting down the division of fines between rector and fellows, and recording rents owed by rural tenants and the need for repairs to their properties, among much else.[124] In terms of cash he was usually the collecting agent, acting as a conduit for the transmission of money to the College's two bursars and the College treasury. Much of what we might nowadays regard as bursarial business fell to his charge.

Financial questions also comprised a large part of his dealings with undergraduates. From the start of his career as a fellow he had given a large part of his time to their welfare, both educational and moral. The textbooks which he compiled for them, one specifically dedicated 'to the neophytes of Exeter

---

124. ECA, A.III.9, *passim*; B.I.16/2 *passim*.

College', were a mark of the first, some of the notes in his memoranda book a mark of the second. 'To be inquired whether all the women be excluded from making beds' runs an entry of 1622, penned in his own hand.[125] Students were not to be unhealthily exposed to whatever temptations women bed-makers might present. He clearly had a good knowledge of the qualities and foibles of particular undergraduates. He spotted the intellectual talents of that budding poet, the young Samuel Austin; and when his friend Bishop Ussher asked him to give a character reference for another undergraduate, Richard Holditch, he was able to oblige: Holditch 'demeaned himselfe very well all the time of his abode at Oxford; save only that he coulde not keep himselfe within the compass of that allowance which his frendes had allotted unto him, which was the originall of his discontentedness'.[126] His comment on young Lorenzo Cary—'He is capable of all kinds of learning but I can fasten no goodnesse in him having a better brayne than heart'—suggests both a similar perceptiveness, expressed through a sharp judgement, and a real concern for his pupil's academic progress.

Prideaux's regard for the young was often hard-headed and far from sentimental. Not least was this true in matters of finance. One of the perennial problems facing the College was the tendency of undergraduates to run up debts and then leave them unpaid at their departure—a problem exacerbated in Prideaux's early years as rector by a corrupt and inefficient bursar, Everard Chambers, who allowed undergraduate debts to accumulate for years. Tutors, who were ultimately answerable to the College for the debts of their pupils, were sometimes equally at fault. In 1627, for example, Prideaux made a note that a letter should be written to Thomas Chafin, who had resigned his fellowship six years earlier, 'to pay his battles for himself and schollers'.[127] Prideaux himself was deeply involved in the College's debt-collecting campaign which followed Chambers's departure in 1623, though this was no new task. Delinquent undergraduates unable to pay their battels might find themselves summoned before the rector and asked for an explanation. In 1614 he noted 'De Illidg omnia sunt dubia [concerning Illedge all is in doubt], he hath payd no battles. Sicknes of cattle with his uncle.' (James Illedge was the 'poor blind scholar' admitted to the College in 1612 at Prince

125. Prideaux, *Hypomnemata*, sig. ¶1r; ECA, B.I.16/2, fo. 31r.
126. Above, 97–8; Ussher, *Correspondence*, i. 90–1.
127. ECA, B.I.16/2, fo. 36v; Boase, *Register*, 93.

Henry's request.)[128] Sometimes the debtor laid the onus of payment on his tutor, who held money in trust from his pupils' parents: 'Batshill hath not payd his battles for 2 quarters. He sayeth that his tutor shall.'[129] In 1621 'Bond requested that he might have till Mr Dod his tutors return from London, at which time all shall be payd.'[130]

Particularly interesting is the light thrown by these memoranda on the financial difficulties faced by poor scholars. If they had no College employment, the rector might tell them to find themselves masters—fellows, fellow commoners, or commoners who would pay them for their services. They might be quite roughly handled: 'Turney hath tyme to provide him a master till Saturday sevennight the 15th of July [1614] and to pay his battles, otherwise to depart.'[131] In December 1612 Prideaux called all the poor scholars and servitors before him and put to each a series of questions, evidently with a view to determining their financial credentials. Who were their masters and tutors? Who vouched for them? What maintenance did they have? Where did they stay and lodge?[132] But in some cases he acted more charitably, dipping into his own pocket to help out the poor but deserving. 'Knapman oweth the house for his degree 6s 8d which I layd out for him.' 'Luscomb at his going into ye country. 1617. September 29 . . . I payd for his books—o. 4. 0 I gave him in his purse—o. 5. o. I layd out for his clothes for hose and shoes—o. 6. o.' Thus seen on his way, Richard Luscombe went on to take his BA, to be ordained priest in 1618, and eventually to become curate of the delectable parish of Ashprington on the river Dart in South Devon.[133] In helping out such students Prideaux may have had in mind his own difficulties as a poor scholar and young bachelor whose labours to maintain himself through service in the College buttery had made it difficult for him to concentrate on the study needed for his advancement.

The domestic business which came the way of the rector was more miscellaneous and hard to classify. It might include determining the seating arrangements in the new hall (as we have seen), setting out the duties and allowances of the bible clerk, manciple, and under-butler, and, in 1619,

128. ECA, B.I.16/2, fo. 5r; above, 31.
129. ECA, B.I.16/2, fo. 5r.
130. Ibid., fo. 30r.
131. Ibid., fo. 5r.
132. Ibid., fo. 29r.
133. Ibid., fos. 5v, 14r; Boase, *Commoners*, 199; CCEd, Person ID 99123.

scheduling regular meetings at 9 a.m. every Saturday morning after disputations, where the Rector (or sub-rector), the dean, the two bursars, the five
senior fellows, the butler, and the cook, were to meet to discuss, inter alia,
the payment of battels and 'any extraordinary thing that shall be thought use
[sic] for the good of the colledge'. Minutes were to be taken.[134] Like other
entries in the quarterly accounts and the memoranda book, these arrangements confirmed that Prideaux possessed the orderly mind and the head for
business which Petre's statutes had demanded of the College's rector.

Prideaux was by no means solely responsible for the flourishing state of his
College, to which Anthony Wood later bore witness. Exeter's rise had
begun under his predecessor, Thomas Holland. His rectorship had seen
the consolidation of the College's Protestant allegiance, the education of
many future leaders of the church, an increase in undergraduate numbers,
the beginnings of physical expansion through new building, and some useful
administrative innovations, such as caution money. It was Prideaux, however, who set a still larger mark on the College. Not only did his learning
and international reputation create an academy for foreign scholars and
students, but his Protestant-Calvinist loyalties and his vaunted links with
his native county raised its numbers still further, while his skills as a teacher,
his care in selecting tutors, his appeal to the nobility, whose presence in the
College added to its status, and his general concern for the welfare of the
young all built an impressive structure on Holland's solid foundations.

Prideaux was thus very much a 'hands-on' rector, involved in every aspect
of his College's corporate life. It is unlikely that he was unique among
contemporary Oxford heads, though the collegiate activities of others have
not been sufficiently explored to allow many useful comparisons. But,
thanks to John Aubrey, we know, for example that Ralph Kettel, Trinity's
eccentric president from 1601 to 1642, also befriended the young, supervised
their academic exercises, scolded the idle, gave money secretly to the
impoverished, and was reckoned to be 'an excellent governour'.[135] In all
these ways his management of Trinity paralleled that of Prideaux in Exeter.
But there was a major difference between the careers of the two men.
Kettel was no scholar. He wrote no books and was famed for his odd habits
and his devotion to his College rather than for his learning. Prideaux, by

---

134. ECA, B.I.16/2, fos. 28v, 29r, 24r.
135. Aubrey, *Brief Lives*, ed. Bennett, i. 174–83. Cf. Hopkins, *Trinity*, 70–99, for Kettel's other
    activities, e.g. in building and fundraising.

contrast—and by contrast with almost every other head—was not only a highly active head of house but also the university's leading theologian, the holder of the regius chair with its many obligations, five times vice-chancellor, a Justice of the Peace, and, as the king's chaplain, a man with duties at the royal court which regularly took him away from Oxford. It was the successful mastery of these multiple roles which helped to give him his distinctive place in early seventeenth-century Oxford. Not the least of Prideaux's talents were his capacity for hard work and his ability to organize his time.

4

The Rebuilding of Exeter College

1. Intentions

One of the landmarks of Prideaux's rectorship lay in his rebuilding of his College: a minor facet of his long career, but one marked by more success than his better-known defence of the Protestant traditions of the English church. Between 1615 and 1624 his College acquired a new set of lodgings for the rector and his family, a grand new residential block, a new hall, and a new chapel, the whole ensemble making up an impressive new quadrangle. Amounting to the wholesale reorganization of the College site, the building campaign which he promoted and over which he presided revealed 'the operation of a master-mind'. Its results attracted the admiration even of Prideaux's enemies.[1]

He was not alone in his building ambitions and achievements. Early seventeenth-century Oxford saw a general building boom which extended across both the university and the colleges. Between about 1607 and 1624 Sir Thomas Bodley's library was enlarged, the adjacent Schools quadrangle constructed, other new quadrangles built at Lincoln and Merton, 'total rebuilding' begun at Oriel, a new chapel completed at Jesus, and St John's substantially rebuilt on Laud's initiative. Two entirely new colleges, Wadham and then, from 1626, Pembroke, also rose from the ground. Expansion was made possible by the growing prosperity of the colleges and by an across-the-board campaign of efficient fundraising.[2] Behind this

---

1. *HUO*, iv. 144; below, 151.
2. Ibid., iv. 135–45, 155–8.

Between Scholarship and Church Politics: The Lives of John Prideaux, 1578–1650. John Maddicott, Oxford University Press. © John Maddicott 2022. DOI: 10.1093/oso/9780192896100.003.0004

activity lay in part the need to provide more accommodation for a rising undergraduate population, a need in which Exeter shared. But for Prideaux's College a second motive was equally important: the desire to make good the College's physical and visual deficiencies. Possessing among his other qualities a sharp aesthetic sense, Prideaux was very conscious of these. The layout of its buildings, put together piecemeal over the centuries, was 'inchoate', or, as Prideaux himself was to write, 'the whole colledg was but a confused number of blynd streats'.[3] Ranges of buildings stood some in parallel, others at right angles to each other, a mere collection lacking any coherence. What Exeter most obviously lacked was a quadrangle, which by this time almost all colleges possessed and which would bring form and order to an otherwise ungainly assemblage. [4] Prideaux's intention was not only to provide more rooms for students but to supply this lack. In an appeal for funds to the city of Exeter he wrote of his hope that 'we shall at length see Exeter Colledge in a square as other colledges are'.[5] The driving force behind much of his programme was thus the need to acquire a quadrangle in keeping with his College's rising reputation in the university.

Our knowledge of that programme rests mainly on two sources, both in the College archives. The first, generally known as 'Prideaux's Survey', written in Prideaux's own hand in 1630, provides a topographical guide to the rebuilt College, building by building and room by room. But it is also valuably discursive, commenting on the physical state of the College, revealing much about the history of the various buildings and the benefactors who largely paid for them, and intended as much as anything to record with tacit pride Prideaux's own achievement in reordering his College. It bears witness to Prideaux's methodical and practical cast of mind, to his interest in the College and its past, and to his awareness of the need to provide more accommodation.[6] A second source is equally valuable and still more unusual. It comprises a collection of fifteen letters written by, to, and about the College's main external benefactors, John Peryam and Sir John Acland, some of them penned by the College's ex-fellow and

---

3. G. Tyack, *Oxford: An Architectural Guide* (Oxford, 1998), 52; Boase, *Register*, 319. For a plan of the medieval College, see Maddicott, *Founders*, 140.
4. Maddicott, *Founders*, 144, 222.
5. HMC, *City of Exeter*, 101.
6. ECA, C.II.4, fos. 32r–43v, for Prideaux's Survey. This was mostly printed in Boase, *Register*, 311–20, but from a partial transcript made by Rector Stinton (1785–97), now ECA, L.I.1. The original includes some important material omitted by Stinton. Boase's edition includes Stinton's comments, which are not always easy to separate from the text of the transcript.

intermediary Isaiah Farrington, and some surviving as drafts, in Prideaux's hand, of his and his College's replies, together with other miscellaneous letters relating to the rebuilding.[7] Filed on a contemporary thong, they were clearly preserved by Prideaux himself as a record of his campaign. Hitherto unknown, they reveal as much about Prideaux's motives, methods, and beliefs as they do about the material progress of the rebuilding.

2. The rector's lodgings

The rebuilding of the College had begun before Prideaux's rectorship, but in a largely uncoordinated and piecemeal fashion and driven chiefly by the need for new accommodation rather than by any burgeoning aestheticism. From 1596 to 1613 two rows of wooden cocklofts, as they were known, had been built over the library, along the east range of what would become the main quadrangle, and a few enterprising fellows built similar cocklofts over their rooms, presumably to house their pupils.[8] The only more permanent addition to the College site was a new tower gateway opening on to Turl Street, built by Everard Chambers, the College bursar, in 1605–6 and extended southwards by a short residential range towards what became the College kitchen. During Prideaux's rectorship, Chambers's tower became the main entrance to the College, taking the place of the old northern entrance marked by the gatehouse known as Palmer's Tower, and providing, with its southerly extension, an initial contribution to the quadrangle envisaged by Prideaux.[9] But there was nothing systematic about the building which took place under Rector Holland. The product of private enterprise rather than collegiate or rectorial initiative, it was intended to profit its sponsors as much as to provide new accommodation.

The point of transition came with the building of the rector's lodgings a few years after Prideaux's election to the rectorship. In the fifteenth and sixteenth centuries the rector had been housed in Palmer's Tower, with further rooms for his use in the adjacent ranges to east and west. Tower lodgings were common for the heads of other colleges, though the rector's

7. ECA, H.III.11 (Correspondence re building).
8. ECA, C.II.4, fo. 38; A.I.5, 180, 183–4; A.II 9, fos. 175v, 176r; Boase, *Register*, 85–7, 317; *VCH Oxfordshire*, iii. 116.
9. Boase, *Register*, 85, 320; ECA, A.II.9, 191r, 195v, 197v, 198r, 222r.

rooms in Exeter seem to have been abnormally few and spartan.[10] A turning-point within the university came when heads of houses were allowed to marry, effectively from Elizabeth's reign. In Exeter this seems to have made no immediate difference to the rector's domestic arrangements. Prideaux's two predecessors, Glasier and Holland, had both been married, but Glasier may have lived in the town, where he had a large house at the north gate.[11] Holland's arrangements are unknown, though evidence produced during the trial of Anne Gunter suggests that he lodged in College.[12] Prideaux's own marriage, to Anne Goodwin, daughter of the dean of Christ Church, probably took late in 1614 or early in 1615, and this event, followed by the birth of the couple's first child, William, in December 1615, undoubtedly provided the stimulus for the building of the new lodgings.[13] In this first act of Prideaux's building campaign, family comfort was the prime consideration.

The lodgings were constructed between 1615 and 1617, partly at the College's cost, amounting to just over £63, and partly at the rector's. Prideaux's Survey describes a moderately large building, comprising cellars, a hall, a panelled parlour, a master bedroom, at least three studies, and a panelled 'great dining room' on the first floor, as well as the rector's former rooms in the tower.[14] By the 1630 date of the survey the whole ensemble had already undergone some internal rearrangement. Its site marked an important change of direction in a literal sense. The new lodgings stood where the chancel end of the nineteenth-century chapel now stands, and abutted Palmer's Tower, to which the occupants had direct access. But unlike the old lodgings in the tower and the adjacent range, which looked north across Somenor's Lane, running parallel to and just inside the city wall, Prideaux's lodgings faced south, across what would soon become the main quadrangle, leaving the area along the lane to constitute what Prideaux called 'the rector's back side'.[15] This not only allowed the front rooms of the lodgings to enjoy the sun but also made a powerful contribution to the developing quadrangle, blocking its north-east corner and assisting the College's transition from a Somenor's Lane college to a Turl Street college.

10. *HUO*, iii. 623–7; Maddicott, *Founders*, 202–3.
11. *HUO*, iii. 627; H. E. Salter, *Oxford City Properties* (Oxford, 1926), 235, 241.
12. Sharpe, *Bewitching of Anne Gunter*, 111–12; above, 23–5.
13. For the marriage, see above, 39, and below, 157–9.
14. ECA, A.II.9, fos. 232r, 236r; Boase, *Register*, 314–16.
15. Boase, *Register*, 312.

The new lodgings, with a front door facing the quadrangle, can be seen in Loggan's view (see Figure 3). When the new chapel was built in 1624, the northern range would be almost complete. This was partly at the expense of the lodgings, whose three original western windows were stopped up by the east end of the chapel, which cut out the light. There was a second loss in the abandonment of the 'garden and private walks' which had formerly enhanced the north and west side of the old lodgings. But these losses, Prideaux thought, were 'more than recompensed by the fitness of the place for his own private entrance to it [i.e. the chapel], and the separated seats for his family'.[16] In addition, the new lodgings made a contribution towards easing the College's accommodation problems by providing rooms for a few favoured undergraduates, mainly visiting scholars and the well-born. 'He billets in my lodgings,' Prideaux wrote reassuringly in 1638 to the patron of one such sprig.[17] As a private convenience, a family home, and a public component of the developing College site, Prideaux's lodgings were a pleasing achievement (see Figure 1).

3. Peryam's Mansions

The next building in the sequence was to contribute on a much grander scale both to the College's accommodation and to Prideaux's plans for its physical reordering. Peryam's Mansions, as it soon became known, now Staircase 4, extended from the south end of the library range to the College boundary against Brasenose Lane. Its junction with the old library building can be clearly seen in Loggan's view. It took its name partly from the man whose generosity made it possible, but partly too, says Prideaux, 'in regard of the firmnesse and magnificence of it'.[18] It was the first of the new buildings whose financing and construction we can follow in some detail and the first to be funded by an external benefactor.

That benefactor was John Peryam. Born in 1541, Peryam was a leading member of one of the great merchant families of Tudor and early Stuart Exeter. Both his father, another John, and his grandfather had been mayors of the city, and Peryam himself was mayor in 1587–8 and MP for Exeter in

16. Ibid., 314.
17. Ussher, *Correspondence*, ii. 744; Boase, *Register*, ciii. For other examples, see ibid., 315.
18. Boase, *Register*, 317.

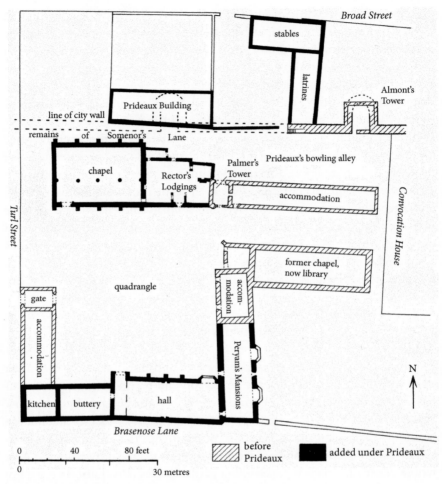

Figure 1. Plan of Rector Prideaux's rebuilt College.

1589 and 1593.[19] Two immediate factors lay behind the younger John Peryam's generosity to the College: his family connections and his religion. His family connections with the College were diverse and multiple. Although he himself had not studied at Oxford, his elder brother, Sir

---

19. For the Peryams, see W. G. Hoskins, 'The Elizabethan Merchants of Exeter', in S. T. Bindoff et al. (eds.), *Elizabethan Government and Society: Essays Presented to Sir John Neale* (1961), 168–70, 176, 177, 185, 186; MacCaffrey, *Exeter, 1540–1640*, esp. 260, but also 63, 109, 150, 172, 197, 214, 223, 253, 262; and *Hist. Parl., 1558–1603*, iii. 208–9.

William Peryam (1534–1604), had been a fellow of Exeter for a short time in 1551;[20] his sister, Thomasina, married to John Hakewill, another prominent Exeter merchant, was the mother of both George Hakewill, fellow of the College from 1596 to 1611, and of William Hakewill, briefly a student in 1600 before going on to become a famous parliamentary lawyer;[21] his cousins included Sir Thomas Bodley and Laurence Bodley senior, a canon of Exeter cathedral, who in 1614 had secured for Prideaux his first living at Bampton in Oxfordshire, while his second cousin, Laurence Bodley junior, son of a third Bodley brother, Miles, was fellow and chaplain of the College from 1614 to 1632.[22] This tangle of relationships, friendships, and patronage was of more consequence than its involved details might suggest. It points to the extensive contacts and connections between Exeter College and the merchant families and mercantile wealth of Exeter city, and it provides one central reason for John Peryam's interest in the College. These were all links which Prideaux was able to exploit.

Religion provided a second and equally important bond between Peryam, his family circle, and a College whose head was fiercely committed to a Calvinistic Protestantism. Peryam came from a zealously Protestant family whose faith had, by the end of the sixteenth century, taken on a distinctively puritan colouring. His father, John Peryam senior, was the brother-in-law of John Bodley, father of Thomas, Laurence, and Miles, and may well have been with John Bodley as a Protestant exile in Geneva during the reign of the Catholic Queen Mary.[23] Our John Peryam gave financial support to an Exeter city lectureship at a time when such lectureships were becoming a mark of municipal puritanism, while his brother, Sir William Peryam, was also among the godly. Said by a contemporary 'to profess the holy gospel of Christ', he was sneeringly referred to by Sir Walter Raleigh in 1596 as 'my

20. J. A. Hamilton, revd. D. Ibbetson, 'Peryam, Sir William (1534–1604) judge', *ODNB*.
21. For the Hakewills, see MacCaffrey, *Exeter, 1540–1640*, 218, 262 (where Thomasina is incorrectly said to have been the daughter of the second John Peryam rather than the first); P. E. McCullough, 'Hakewill, George (bap.1578, d.1649), Church of England clergyman and author', *ODNB*; W. R. H. Hakewill, 'A History of the Revd. Dr. George Hakewill', typescript in ECA, L.III.6 (Members' personal affairs).
22. F. B. Rose-Troup, 'Biography of John Bodley, Father of Sir Thomas Bodley', *Trans. Devonshire Assoc.*, 35 (1903), 167–97; Rose-Troup, 'The Pedigree of Sir Thomas Bodley', ibid., 713–29; Boase, *Register*, 97; S. Wright, 'Bodley, Laurence (1547/8–1615), Church of England clergyman', *ODNB*; above, 90.
23. T. Gray, *The Chronicle of Exeter, 1205–1722* (Exeter, 2005), 95, 106; C. D. G. Littleton, 'Bodley, John (c.1520–1591), religious radical and publisher', *ODNB*; Hoskins, 'Elizabethan Merchants', 168–9.

lord puritan Peryam'.[24] The two Laurence Bodleys, uncle and nephew, were also supporters of city lectureships, indicating godly principles.[25] But if both family and faith inclined Peryam towards a generous benefaction for the College, so too did personal circumstance. By 1617, the year of his first recorded negotiations with the College, he may have been affected by the sort of apprehensions which have often overshadowed the last years of elderly, devout, and wealthy men. Aged about 77, and already described six years earlier as 'an aged, weak and sickly gentleman',[26] he must have known that he had not long to live. The imminent fate of his soul, as concerning a prospect for puritans as for Catholics, is likely to have been a pressing anxiety, and one which a munificent gift in furtherance of religion, learning, and the church was probably intended to influence.

Prideaux had known of Peryam since at least 1614, when William Orford, a fellow of the College until that year, had been presented to the Devonshire church of Clyst Hydon by Peryam, its patron.[27] Patron and priest were evidently close, and Orford was to play a key role in Peryam's dealings with the College. By June 1617 Peryam's new building was under construction. Writing in that month to Prideaux, in the first of a sequence of letters, Peryam could refer to 'that small pittance which I have given for buyldinge of chambers in your colledge', adding that 'next unto God' the gift should be imputed to William Orford, who must have introduced Peryam to the College's needs.[28] The subsequent negotiations raised several minor problems, all of them successfully overcome. At the outset Peryam asked Prideaux to conceal his identity, for 'I have children and children's children many', who, as potential heirs, he clearly feared might obstruct his wishes. This Prideaux promised to do, in an emollient letter of effusive gratitude.[29] With so many children and relatives, it was extraordinary that he should have chosen to enrich a poor college, 'and that upon so small inducements, in so bountefull a manner, without any reflective respects or conditions furder than God's glory and the church's good'. Later, in September 1617,

---

24. W. Jones, 'Sir William Peryam, Lord Chief Baron of the Exchequer', *Devon and Cornwall Notes and Gleanings*, 3 (1890), 114; *Hist. Parl., 1558–1603*, iii. 209.
25. Wright, 'Bodley, Laurence'; TNA, PROB 11/125/273; MacCaffrey, *Exeter, 1540–1640*, 198; HMC, *City of Exeter*, 92–8.
26. HMC, *City of Exeter*, 85.
27. Prideaux, *Ephesus Backsliding*, sig. *3r; Boase, *Register*, 81; CCEd, Person ID 94432.
28. ECA, H.III.11, letter 5. Henceforth the letters under this archive call number will be referred to only by the number of each letter, written in the top right-hand corner.
29. Letter 4.

Peryam wrote to Orford, who was clearly acting as go-between, about another problem.[30] It had been reported that Everard Chambers, the bursar in charge of the building works, was 'not much beloved in the house' and that he was planning to make a personal profit from his role. Given Chambers's later reputation for corruption, this was probably all too true. Peryam was, however, reassured by receiving from Prideaux what he termed 'a testimoniall touchinge Mr Everard Chambers'. In the same letter Peryam provided a significant insight into College politics by noting that he had been 'moved that the fynes and benefitt of the chambers might goe to the fellowes, but my intention was, is and shalbe that it goe to the treasurie and benefit of the colledge'. But if some fellows wished to see future room rents divided between them, that prospect was decisively quashed by Prideaux. It was:

> so far from proceeding from us that it is generally distasted of us all. God forbid that wee should convert these to a private gayne which is so worthyly intended to a publique use . . . Our joynt subscriptions [the letter was signed by the fellows] may argue our unitye, and our united prayers for you and yours show our thankfulness.[31]

Throughout 1617 the work proceeded rapidly. A 'Note of Charges' drawn up on 24 September records a total expenditure of nearly £566, of which £500 had by then been received from Peryam, with a further £60 following in October. The total cost amounted to £700, the balance being made up by the College. The largest item, for stone and masons' wages, came to £351.[32] Writing to Peryam on 21 November, in the final letter of the series, Prideaux thanked Peryam for his additional gift. 'Wee make no doubt but the effect shall make good that your liberalitie hath bene well employed, and our joynt prayers shall be unto God that he will repaye that which wee shall never be able.'[33] Peryam must have died within a year, for his will, which made no mention of the College, was proved in October 1618, a few months after the building had begun to be occupied from June onwards.[34]

Peryam's Mansions marked a new departure in Exeter's history. In its rootedness, permanence, and spaciousness it contrasted strongly with the College's generally ramshackle residential buildings. 'Outside it was solid and magnificent

---

30. Letter 17.
31. Letters 2, 1. For Chambers, above, 115.
32. (Letter) 12.
33. Letter 2.
34. TNA, PROB 11/132/381; ECA, A.II.9, fo. 239r.

and inside it contained an orderly arrangement of chambers with two small studies opening into each.'[35] There were eight sets of these chambers, almost all of them reserved in this first year for fellows and some of them later made over to Prideaux's aristocratic pupils. When the first full room list appears, in the accounts for 1618–19, Laurence Bodley, Peryam's second cousin occupied the second set, and Everard Chambers another. In the first year of occupation, when two sets of rooms were still vacant, the six occupied sets yielded the very large sum of £28 in rent.[36] Since the fellows would normally have expected to occupy their rooms gratis, the rent payments may indicate that the rooms were sub-let by tutors to their pupils, with whom they probably shared accommodation, as was normal in other parts of the College. Payments which the tutors made to the College would then have been recovered from their pupils. A similar practice obtained at St John's College, where fellows sometimes paid room rents on behalf of those for whom they acted as tutors.[37]

Peryam's benefaction of £560 was the largest that the College had received since its re-endowment by Petre in 1566, and perhaps the third largest since the foundation. It helped to make possible the expansion in undergraduate admissions which marked the years around 1618.[38] In his survey, Prideaux had good cause to write warmly of Peryam's generosity:

> He never saw what he had done for us; nor required account of the money he gave; neither conditioned with the colledg in any sort for the disposing of the lodgings with reference to himself or any of his. A worthy benefactor. God rayse us many such to follow his example.[39]

Yet Prideaux himself was also responsible for their warm and beneficial relationship, marked as it was by a thoroughgoing goodwill on both sides. Peryam did not use his wealth as a lure to exact favours and was willing to accept all that Prideaux put to him, while Prideaux took care to keep his patron informed, to answer his doubts, and to show deference when it was needed. Harmony was the keynote, founded on a common, if usually tacit belief in the College's religious purpose and on the unstated sympathies which bound the two parties to a shared ideal of Protestant churchmanship.

---

35. *VCH Oxfordshire*, iii. 116. All the information in the remainder of this paragraph is drawn from the accounts for 1617–19: ECA, A.II.9, fos. 239r, 243v.
36. ECA, A.II.9, fos. 240v, 243v.
37. Hegarty, *Biographical Register of St John's*, xxxv.
38. Above, 85–6.
39. Boase, *Register*, 318.

And, of course, there was William Orford, former fellow and now local priest, to act as go-between. The result was a fine building, which still stands. It went some way to provide both the new rooms which the College needed and the new quadrangle which it was Prideaux's ambition to create.

4. Sir John Acland's hall

As Peryam's Mansions were going up, another project was well in hand. The benefactor here, on an even larger scale than Peryam, was Sir John Acland. A leading member of the Devonshire gentry, he was to prove a more demanding patron than his gratifyingly complaisant fellow Devonian. Acland came from one of Devon's oldest landed families.[40] Born about 1552 in the north of the county, he had moved to the south by about 1590, buying an estate at Columbjohn in the parish of Broadclyst, some five miles north-east of Exeter. Acland's move into Exeter's hinterland involved him quite closely in the affairs of the city, where he was elected a freeman in 1607. But his main field of activity was the county. Justice of the Peace from 1583, knighted in 1604, MP for Devon in 1607, and sheriff in 1608–9, he pursued a trajectory in county government typical of his social group.

Why did Acland become a benefactor of Exeter College? We can point to three probable reasons. First, Acland himself was a former member of the College. Prideaux tells us as much in his survey, but a more precise confirmation comes from a letter written by Acland in 1618 and discussed below.[41] Though he lacked Peryam's multiplicity of family links with the College, in this particular respect he was closer to it. Secondly, Acland was wealthy but childless. Adding to a rich inheritance from his mother, whose favourite son he was, successive marriages to two prosperous widows had brought him further riches but no children.[42] Combined with his lack of direct heirs, his money had enabled him to become a benefactor to many local causes, and his generosity to the College was an extension of an already generous pattern of conduct. Finally, his religious sympathies, in so far as they can be gauged, lay firmly in a puritan direction, and his activities reveal

---

40. Unless otherwise stated all the material relating to Acland in the following paragraphs will be found in M. Wolffe, 'Acland, Sir John, (c.1552–1620), politician and benefactor', *ODNB*; and *Hist. Parl., 1558–1603*, i. 327.
41. Boase, *Register*, 318; below, 131.
42. For Acland's wealth, see esp. Prince, *Worthies of Devon*, 2.

several puritan traits. For his estate chapel at Columbjohn, which he rebuilt, he endowed a preaching ministry, providing a stipend for the minister to enable him to preach on Sundays and to hold services in the week; and among the initial trustees of his charities was Ignatius Jordan, the famous 'Archpuritan', mayor of Exeter in 1617–18, during Acland's last years, and a firebrand Protestant reformer of his city.[43]

In his Oxford education, his later tenure of local office, his puritan affiliations, and to a lesser extent in his philanthropy, Acland was representative of his class and its members' role in his county. But one facet of his many-sided career was less typical: his interest in building. Following his move from north Devon, he had built himself a grand house at Columbjohn, repaired the chapel there, and, in his later years, constructed his own funeral monument in florid Renaissance style in the parish church at Broadclyst, where it can still be seen—'one of the most sumptuous Jacobean monuments in Devon'.[44] As we shall see, his dealings with the College suggest that he had some considerable expertise in (and certainly definite views on) matters of design, construction, and site management. Here he differed from Peryam, and perhaps not always to the advantage of easy relations with the College.

Acland's involvement with Exeter's building plans is first made plain in a letter written to Prideaux by Isaiah Farrington. It introduces us to a loyal son of the College and one who was to be more responsible than any other for securing Acland's benefaction. Born in Exeter (as he himself tells us), Isaiah Farrington had come to the College as a 'plebeian' undergraduate in 1583. Elected to a fellowship in 1590, he resigned in 1604 after having been presented to the rectory of Lympstone, a waterside parish on the Exe estuary a few miles south-east of Exeter.[45] He was on close and friendly terms with both Prideaux and Acland, and ideally placed, as William Orford had been in Peryam's case, to act as the College's local agent. The relations between the three men first emerge in Farrington's letter to Prideaux, written in March 1618, at a time when the building of Peryam's Mansions was nearing completion. The letter makes it clear that Acland had already expressed his intention to provide a new hall for the College. But it is also clear that Acland was an awkward customer, prone to changing his mind and creating

---

43. For Jordan, see Stoyle, *From Deliverance to Destruction*, 19–37.
44. B. Cherry and N. Pevsner, *The Buildings of England: Devon* (1989), 51, 215.
45. Letter 11; HMC, *City of Exeter*, 101–2; Boase, *Register*, 83.

difficulties which it would take all Farrington's persuasiveness and Prideaux's tact to resolve. At first, reported Farrington, Acland had said that he could not go forward with the project. But then, after Farrington had 'used the most favouriblest persuasione and reasons to hold one his purpose as it pleased God to putt in my mynde', he had promised some £200 for stone, timber, and masons to get the work started. Completion was seemingly hoped for in the long vacation of 1618. In a spirit of helpful optimism, Farington promised Prideaux that 'I wilbe your tongue and remembrancer.'

At first all went well, and in a letter of 4 April 1618 Farrington reported to Prideaux on the favourable outcome of a recent visit to Acland.[46] He had spoken of the need to gather stone and timber for a start in the following spring (suggesting that the original timetable had slipped a little). The old hall and the kitchen must be replaced together, 'it being your purpose to make a quadrangle of that part, which pleaseth him well'. This is the first explicit reference in our sources to the creation of the new quadrangle. He wanted Prideaux to supervise the whole project and would shortly send the £200 already promised, with further payments to follow. He had approved the plan and elevation of the new hall: 'the windowes on the side towards the colledge, and so for the windows towards the lane next Lincolne Colledge and the formes of them, gives good content'. Prideaux, continued Farrington, should do all he could to please Acland, writing to thank him with all speed and keeping a close eye on costs. Acland's own expertise as an amateur builder was clearly on view. But his generosity was not to be taken for granted, and a certain touchiness can already be sensed in his dealings with the College.

This was less evident in a warm letter which Acland himself wrote to Prideaux about this time. He was all the more willing to support the work, he told Prideaux, 'to testifie my thankfulness unto God for the many blessings he hathe bestowed one me and also because I was some three or four yeares a poure member of the same house above fortey yeares sithence [since]': an explicit reference to Acland's undergraduate days at Exeter, probably in the 1570s. But he wanted his benefaction to be kept secret and his purpose to remain undisclosed. This Prideaux promised to do in an effusive but dignified letter of thanks shot through with religious feeling.[47] 'God who hath put this into youre heart to honour him with your

46. Letter 5, 10.
47. Letters 13, 6.

substaunce will plentifully repaye you out of his hidden treasure . . . Our college, so founded as it were anew by such favoriall liberalety, shall remayn unto you in place of many sonnes and daughters'—a not entirely tactful allusion to Acland's lack of children. 'In the meanwhilst', he concluded, 'all that we can do is but to pray to God for you and beseech him to pursue that work which he hath begun in you, which we shall trust most singularly to perform.'

Problems, however, were on the horizon. Reporting on a further visit to Acland, Farrington told Prideaux that he hoped Sir John would disapprove of nothing 'except such courses as tend to the overmuch increase of the charge'.[48] Concerns about costs were voiced still more strongly in Farrington's next letter, undated, but probably written in May 1618.[49] 'You must frame your building (I mean the haule)'—writes Farrington, speaking for Acland—'to the proportion of 700[li] and not exceed that'. As for the cloister (a new project broached here for the first time):

> it was more than was mentioned of before unto the gentleman and he will by no means meddle with it, affirminge that it will take up half his charge and he cannot see how it wilbe any ornament, especially being within the colledge, and therefor bid me write that absolutly he will beare no charge of it.

This striking piece of information suggests that Prideaux's ambitions may have ranged well beyond the construction of a new hall and quadrangle. The building of a cloister, a covered walkway extending around the interior of the quadrangle, would have matched Exeter with New College and Magdalen, two much richer and grander colleges.[50] But this was not the only point at which Acland jibbed. He objected to the dimensions of the planned cellar under the hall. He thought that the masons' wages, at 16d. a day, were excessive, but if the work could be carried through for £700, the College could do as it wished. 'No overplus of charge will he have to rise upon him.' He did not think that the exterior of the hall need all be of wrought stone (i.e. ashlar, stone squared and shaped), but again he was content for them to do as they wished, provided that the total cost was not exceeded. He saw no case 'for private buttery and cellars' and would not pay for this 'because there

---

48. Letter 16.
49. Letter 15.
50. For the cloisters at these colleges, see Tyack, *Oxford: An Architectural Guide*, 46–7, 63–4. A cloister was also projected at University College in the 1630s but never built: Darwall-Smith, *University College*, 162.

was nothing entreated of him but the building of a hall, which he is content to do and to afford something towards the righting of buttery and kitchen'. It must have been a relief to find that he was pleased with the dimensions of the projected quadrangle, 140 feet in length and 126 feet in breadth: it 'giveth him much content and encouragement'.

Acland clearly felt that his generosity was being exploited by a College seeking to go well beyond the scheme originally provided for. He was not to be treated as a milch cow, the provider of unlimited funds to support the College's rising ambitions. Farrington cautioned Prideaux to do all that he could to keep Acland happy: 'I beseech you that the best care may be had of the work to give him all good content. He was in a good vein not long since and he manifested unto me to doe some other good for the colledge.' But a particular cause of likely trouble was Acland's relatives: 'I lately have been a witness how much he is troubled by some of his kindred, and one nearer him, for undertaking this, and he dares not manifest without great vexation to them what he will give.' There was even some doubt about whether he could be held to provide the £700 promised. Farrington did not dare to tell him how much the College had spent on timber, 'it being thought to be much more than wilbe imployed in that worke, and yet I will trie him for a hundred pound more to be sent in some convenient time'. Here Farrington must have been successful, for Acland's eventual contribution to the hall amounted to £800, a hundred pounds more than he had originally promised.[51]

Further dire warnings came in a final surviving letter from Farrington to Prideaux, written from Lympstone on 12 October 1618.[52] Farrington wrote that he had recently been with Acland, who had given him £50 for the furtherance of the building:

> which money as all the rest he hath very willingly afforded and takes more ioye and comfort in the worke undertaken than in any earthly thinge he ever did in his life, and wishes that it may be for the glorie of God and great benefit of your house, which he much respecteth.

But he had told Farrington 'that you must by no means exceed the sum of 700^{li} . . . it must serve to perfect [complete] the building'. Should the College exceed it, 'so that for want of supplie the building should stand unperfect, he will hold it as great a wronge done to him as your colledge can

51. Boase, *Register*, 318.
52. Letter 7.

offer and would not sustayne the disgrace thereof for more than he is worth'. But to offset his cantankerous demands and requirements Acland had another generous purpose in mind. He intended, wrote Farrington in the same letter, to found two scholarships at the College, setting aside £16 for such a purpose 'out of a chest which he hath imployed to good and pious uses'. He must, however, have rooms for the two scholars, to be built from the surplus timber left after the building of the hall 'in the vacant space near the back gate'. But this space was reserved for a new building which it was hoped that the citizens of Exeter would fund,[53] as Farrington had told Acland, who had agreed to a delay. The nomination of the scholars was to be reserved to Sir John and Lady Acland during their lives—'which cannot be long', Farrington added realistically if ungraciously. After his death the two were to be chosen by the College. Prideaux should let Acland know what he thought of the scheme: 'I promised him to make it knowen to you and the societie and doe desire you to nourish his good purpose herein.'

Acland was emerging as a somewhat difficult friend—insistent on the strict limits to his generosity, uttering veiled threats if the limits were not observed (though in the end he agreed to raise them), and knowledgeable enough about building matters to take an interfering interest in what was proposed. But his second letter to Prideaux, dated 26 January 1619 and the last in the whole series, was much more reassuring.[54] Acland thanked Prideaux for his 'sundry kinde letters' and for the 'kinde care' which he had for the prosecution of the work. 'I muste very truly confesse (I thanke God) that I take as great joye and comforte of that work as of any I ever tooke in hand. And for that I have a longinge desire to have the same to be finished with all convenyent speed', he had sent a further £150, which he hoped they had by now received. Mentioning as he did 'my late trouble-some sickness', he may have been all too aware of his approaching death. To speed up the work, he advised that it would be 'a verye good course to sell some of the windowes and tymber worke at tauske, so as the same be well husbandered in the selling thereof'. The suggestion here that windows and woodwork should be contracted for at piece rates, as long as good terms could be struck, typifies once again Acland's concern for economy and his familiarity with building practices; he must have been used to dealing with

53. Below, 136–42.
54. Letter 9.

masons and joiners. He ended his letter by saying how happy he was to hear of Prideaux's success in the College's lawsuit with Lord Petre.[55]

Acland died on 14 February 1620.[56] He had been a generous if somewhat capricious benefactor. Despite his adamantine insistence that £700 was the absolute upper limit to his gift, he had in the end donated a further £100, as Prideaux stated in his Survey. Writing there of 'that worthy knight Sir John Acland of Devon', he noted that Acland, like Peryam, never saw what he had built and that in addition he had given £16 a year 'for a pension to be paid unto 2 poor scholars to be chosen out of Exeter School' (this last a detail unrecorded by Farrington). Acland's enhanced gift for the hall, however, was still insufficient to pay for its completion, to achieve which the College had to contribute a further £200.[57] The hall's general style, with its three-light Perpendicular-style traceried windows perhaps modelled on the almost identical fifteenth-century chapel windows at All Souls, conformed to the Gothic mode prevailing in early seventeenth-century Oxford and was clearly approved by Acland, whose conservative tastes mirrored those of the fellows. If the design which he chose for his tomb at Broadclyst was much more in the Renaissance manner, that showed only that different styles were thought appropriate for different purposes.[58]

The chronology of the hall's building cannot be followed with any precision, since no accounts survive beyond a few entries in the regular series of rector's accounts. Most of the work was probably undertaken in the summer of 1618, though Acland's final letter of January 1619 shows that the windows and timberwork, presumably for the interior panelling, screen, and roof, remained to be completed. Prideaux's scheme for seating arrangements in the new hall, drawn up on 19 July 1619, suggests that its opening was imminent.[59] A final minor payment to Hobbs the plumber in 1620–1 'for putting up the great pype of the hall', probably the main drain pipe, may have added the final touch.[60] Much greater expense must have been incurred in the carving and erecting of the elaborately decorated screen, still *in situ*. This goes unmentioned in any account, but it has been suggested

55. For the College's lawsuit with Petre, see above, 66–71.
56. Wolffe, 'Acland'.
57. Boase, *Register*, 318.
58. Tyack, *Oxford: An Architectural Guide*, 103; J. Sherwood and N. Pevsner, *The Buildings of England: Oxfordshire* (Harmondsworth, 1974), 35, 135; above, 130.
59. ECA, B.II.16/2, fo. 21v; above, 103.
60. ECA, A.III.9.

that screen and cresting were the work of John Bolton, the Oxford joiner, since the work at Exeter is so similar to that for Wadham's hall, where Bolton is known to have been employed. Bolton's certain responsibility a few years later for much of the woodwork in Exeter's new chapel makes this all the more likely.[61]

It was not until 1632 that the hall's necessary adjuncts, a new buttery and kitchen, were completed immediately to its west, where the kitchen has been sited ever since. They replaced a fellow's room and two studies, joining up with the southward-extending tower range built by Chambers in 1605 and so completing the south side of the planned quadrangle. The work was largely paid for by donations from former fellows, including William Orford, parson of Clyst Hydon and friend of Peryam, and Robert Vilvaine, fellow from 1599 to 1611 and later a wealthy physician in Exeter, his home town. Each gave £10, and Prideaux himself made up the sum needed to complete the building.[62]

With the construction of Peryam's Mansions, Acland's hall, and the new kitchen, the south side of the projected quadrangle was thus complete.

5. Negotiations with the city of Exeter

Running alongside the College's dealings with Sir John Acland in 1618–19 were parallel negotiations with the city of Exeter. In these too Isaiah Farrington played a leading role, and with the same object in view: to raise money for building. Any Exeter money that might be forthcoming Prideaux intended to use for the construction of a new range extending northwards from the west tower on Turl Street towards what would soon become the west end of the chapel. His general aim, emphasized throughout the negotiations, was both to put in place another section of his projected quadrangle and to provide more rooms for the College's expanding body of students—and in approaching the city he had good reasons to hope for success.

---

61. *HUO*, iv. 157; below, 146.
62. Boase, *Register*, 319. Wood, *Colleges*, i. 112, adds the names of Richard Napier and William Helme to those contributing to the building of the kitchen; cf. Boase, *Register*, 269.

England's fourth largest provincial city under the Tudors,[63] Exeter was prosperous and its leaders wealthy. The links between city and College had always been close, as Prideaux would later remind the city council during the course of their negotiations, and rarely more so than during the years preceding his own rectorship. Between 1599 and 1604 the fellowship included at least four men who came from the city,[64] and the succession was maintained under Prideaux by Laurence Bodley junior, who was, like Hakewill, a member of a prominent city family. In the 'Epistle Dedicatory' to Laurence Bodley senior which preceded his sermon of 1614, Prideaux had written that

> it stands with a kind of conveniencie (in my desires at least) that Exceter College especially should bee patronized from Exceter, from which it first had its name and founder, and for which it hath bred (as by God's grace it shall continue to doe) so many men of worth.

At a less exalted level Exeter's high school provided the College with a regular stream of undergraduates: in 1631 no fewer than seven of the College's fellows and more than twenty commoners and others had been educated there.[65] Equally important in explaining the College's expectations of support was the city's religion. The family histories of the Peryams and the Bodleys, as well as the city's support for preaching lectureships, all point towards its standing as a puritan stronghold, its oligarchy 'determined to have its own way in the refashioning of the city's religious life'.[66] At the time when the city was first approached by the College in 1618, its mayor was Ignatius Jordan, the 'Archpuritan', reformer, zealous sabbatarian, and moral scourge of the city. He was followed in the mayoralty by another puritan, Thomas Martin, who was to prove a willing, if ineffective friend to the College's cause.[67]

These bonds of presumptive sympathy between city and College, as well as their historic links, meant that it was not unreasonable to suppose that the city would play its part in rebuilding a College with which it had so many close connections. So at least thought Isaiah Farrington in a letter written to

63. Hoskins, 'Elizabethan Merchants', 164.
64. Isaiah Farrington, Simon Baskerville, George Hakewill, and Robert Vilvaine: Boase, *Register*, 83, 85, 87, 88; HMC, *City of Exeter*, 99–100.
65. Prideaux, *Ephesus Backsliding*, sig. *2/1–3; CSPD, *1629–31*, 473; Parry, *The Founding of Exeter School*, 49–50.
66. MacCaffrey, *Exeter, 1540–1640*, 20; above, 123–6.
67. Above, 130; TNA, PROB 11/135/675. For Martin, see also *Hist. Parl., 1604–1629*, v. 274.

Prideaux on 20 March 1618 which marked the start of the negotiations.[68] Acting once again as the College's agent, he had approached 'the chiefest of the city', stressing the benefits which many of the city's sons had received at the College, 'both for the good of the church and benefit of the common-welth', and the College's need for money either for a new building 'to bring it unto some uniformitie' or for general funds Farrington thought that there was much goodwill towards the College and suggested that it would be helpful if Prideaux were to write 'some moving letter' to the mayor, aldermen, and Twenty-Four (the council) in an appeal for funds 'for the bringing of your College into some decent uniformitie'. Farrington would do all that he could to further the College's cause, and ended by pointing to the desirability of citing Peryam's generosity as a good example.

Prideaux followed Farrington's suggestions almost precisely in a long, carefully worded, and persuasive letter written in April 1618 and signed by thirteen of the fellows.[69] It was addressed to the mayor, aldermen, and Twenty-Four. It might seem strange, said Prideaux, that now, 300 years after the College's foundation, they should be approaching the city 'to be at length finished'. But never before had there been so good an opportunity and such assurance of success. He mentioned the College's foundation by a bishop of Exeter, the College's longstanding connections with the city, and the many Exeter men educated at the College who had returned 'furnished to do service in church and country'. The College's revenues were 'meaner in regard of the company than any other college' (perhaps true in view of the rising numbers of undergraduates), and it was 'also the most unseemly for buildings and scanted for lodgings'. The citizens now had a chance 'to bring it to an uniformity which never before this time could be hoped for, and now by your good means may conveniently be accomplished'. 'Our worthy benefactor Mr John Periam' had already supplied 'one vacant place' and a second would shortly be filled by 'another of our countrymen, whose work will make him shortly knowne, to be never here after forgotten'. This was, of course, an allusion to Peryam's Mansions and Acland's hall, the latter's sponsorship still a secret and both contributing to the making of the new quadrangle. 'By divine providence' a third space was left for them to fill. 'If God so move your harts we shall at length see Exceter Colledge in a square, as other colledges are.' Mr Farrington, 'a learned, sincere and truly religious

---

68. Letter 11.
69. HMC, *City of Exeter*, 100–1. Letter 3 is a draft of this letter in Prideaux's hand.

man, once a worthy member of our Colledge', would be on hand to tell them how this could best be achieved. It would be a comfort and credit to their children to 'lodge in those buildings which their auncestors have founded'. Finally, he hoped that 'the Lord . . . will (wee trust) direct your respects to such a publique good rather then to private excuses and prosper that worthy corporation for which we shall never cease to pray'.

In its appeal to the citizens' sense of honour, to their self-interest, and to their city's ancestral links with the College, as well as in its invocation of the will of God, this was a most skilful piece of drafting, and one which showed clearly where Prideaux's priorities for his College lay: in the acquisition of new rooms and in the achievement of the 'uniformity' which the completion of the quadrangle would confer. Writing again to Prideaux, probably in May 1618, Farrington reported that the citizens had received his letter 'long since' and had had a meeting about it. 'I been informed that there is some hope, but such men are of no speedie resolution. God grant in the end we may obtayne our desire.'[70] Nor did Farrington's next report, on 12 October 1618, move matters much further forward.[71] The College's appeal had been put to the citizens 'sundrie tymes at their meetings'. It had not been rejected but had made little progress, since the councillors were arguing about internal matters. Farrington advised that the best course would be to set the whole matter aside for a while and wait for a better opportunity. He had conferred with the new mayor, Thomas Martin, and found him very favourably disposed to the College, but this was not among his priorities.

It is clear that, despite Farrington's best efforts and the goodwill of the new mayor, the College's cause was faltering. Yet, going counter to his own advice, Farrington would not let the matter rest, even temporarily. On 27 October 1618 he wrote to Martin, whom he rightly saw as a potential ally.[72] After noting how the mayor had 'lamented the evil of these times' and the general reluctance to promote 'any commendable or pious work', and after assuring Martin that 'your love towards Exeter College shall not be forgotten', Farrington came to the meat of his message. He had that morning determined to write 'to the whole body of your Chamber, to stir them up unto so good and necessary a work . . . I hope the labour will not be in vain,

---

70. Letter 15.
71. Letter 7.
72. DHC, Exeter City Records, L. 184, summarized in HMC, *City of Exeter*, 101; *Hist. Parl.*, *1604–29*, v. 274.

and if I may be any way a poor instrument of God's glory I have my full desire'. He enclosed a copy of his letter for the mayor's criticisms and comments 'because you have more often felt the pulse of their affection than myself have', and he asked Martin to deliver the letter to the council. 'That which lately I desired I do with all humbleness entreat you to set it forward.'

Like Prideaux's earlier letter, Farrington's appeal to the Exeter Chamber was well constructed, persuasive, and carefully designed to emphasize just those points which might be expected to weigh with a puritanically inclined council.[73] He stressed the absence so far of any support from the city, the slimness of the College's resources ('the state of maintenaunce of their house is verie meane'), the College's physical defects ('the want of form in their buildings, some scattered here, others there, with which other colledges are excellently squared'), and the lack of rooms, which set limits to their student numbers and their revenues. Then came an appeal to the councillors' Christian consciences: 'gifts bestowed for piouse and publike uses are like the first fruits dedicated to the Lord'. The letter ended with a stirring peroration in which Farrington aligned himself with the city, and the city with the cause of true religion and the public good:

> Laboured I have to stirre you up unto this worke, who ame by birth a citizen, by affection a citizen, in hart a citizen, and do desire the greatest honor of your city that your selves can desire. With me in this petition doe joyne learning, religion, the sound profession of the gospel, which papists slander. . . . The Lord hath been exceedingly merciful to your city; beyond many which I know in raising up to you worthy benefactors who have given many things, many excellent things for most profitable uses. Now in this suit the Lord knocks at your heart to prove what your city will do for him towards the maintenance of learning and religion.

This was a remarkable rhetorical performance. It equated the College's practical needs with the will of God and the cause of true religion, the religion of the Gospel, 'which papists slander'—a forthright appeal to puritan susceptibilities. Indeed, the appeal was very largely grounded on religion, on the qualities of charity and conscience which religion embodied, and on the moral obligations which sprang from the councillors' position as wealthy men. The citizens' self-interest, in terms of honour and of the remembrance and blessings of posterity, took second place.

---

73. DHC, Exeter City Records, L. 185, summarized in HMC, *City of Exeter*, 101–2.

It was, however, a performance in vain. The College's case, so fully set out in Farrington's letter, was vigorously backed by the mayor in a speech to the Chamber in October or November 1618. Citing the good examples set by 'a worthy freeman of this city, Sir John Acland' and of 'a worthy citizen, Mr Peryam' as 'liberal benefactors' to the College, he urged them to emulate these worthy men, before going on to cite the more distant precedent of Nehemiah urging the Jews to build the walls of Jerusalem. They should not risk the judgement set on the unjust steward. A committed supporter of the College's cause, Martin was also a man with the Scriptures at his puritan fingertips. But one further letter from Prideaux to Martin shows that his words had fallen on stony ground.[74] Dated 15 January 1619, it allows us to glimpse the debates within the council and shows something of the reasons for its rejection of the College's appeal. After thanking the mayor for his exertions on behalf of the College, Prideaux cited two objections which he had heard to have been put forward: the College's unwillingness to admit the city's candidates, and 'corruption in the admitting'. He denied both charges, naming some distinguished Exeter men who had come to the College—'Dr Baskervill, Dr Hakewell, Dr Vilvayne and some others of good note'. If they had had no successors from the city, 'it is not the averseness of our societye but the backwardnesse and negligence of such as come short of their parts or will not use the meanse'. (For all his other qualities Prideaux could be tactlessly combative and rarely unwilling to give offence.) As for corruption, he simply denied it, writing that he would leave his place if it were proved. He still hoped that the city might do something for the College, citing yet again the examples of Peryam and Acland.

This was the end of the road. We have no record of any further contacts between College and city, and certainly no money was forthcoming. Throughout Prideaux's time the space along Turl Street remained vacant. The hope that it might yet be filled was not abandoned. It influenced the design of the new chapel a few years later, when the chapel's lack of a west window and its blank west wall allowed for the erection of a new building against its west end.[75] A further appeal for building funds in 1637 to the lawyer and old member John Maynard, and probably to others, fell on deaf

---

74. HMC, *City of Exeter*, 99–100. Cf. *CSPD, 1629–31*, 508.
75. 'From that the space between the walls, keeping of the same breadth to the city walls, the ground was not consecrated, but was reserved so in case benefactours might be led by God to build lodgings there; which was also the consideration that the chapel hath no west window' (Prideaux's Survey, in Boase, *Register*, 311–12).

ears; and it was not until 1672 that the residential block which Prideaux had envisaged for the site began to materialize.[76]

In Prideaux's building scheme for the College, and more specifically for the construction of the new quadrangle, the gap remaining between the Turl Street tower and the new chapel represented the one setback.

6. Hakewill's chapel

Following on from the building of Acland's hall, Exeter acquired a new chapel. Built between 1622 and 1624, it survived until its demolition in 1856. The main impulses behind its building were certainly religious: it was, Prideaux wrote in the 'Epistle Dedicatory' to its founder prefacing his sermon preached at the chapel's consecration, to be 'a fit house for God's service'. But they were also utilitarian and practical, meeting the needs which underlay Prideaux's whole scheme for the rebuilding of the College to provide for rising numbers and to complete the construction of a quadrangle comparable to those of other colleges. The old chapel, built in Stapeldon's day, was 'too scant for the company, and otherwise very incommodious'.[77] The building of the new chapel allowed its predecessor to be converted into a library, and the old library, forming the eastern range of the quadrangle, to be converted into the rooms which the College desperately required. The new chapel itself, extending westwards from the rector's lodgings, which it adjoined, and standing opposite Acland's new hall, more or less completed the quadrangle's north range, leaving, as we have seen, only the projected Turl Street range to fill the remaining gap and to seal off the chapel's western end. In all ways it made a harmonious contribution to the College's refashioning.

The first we hear of the College's intention to build a new chapel comes in a letter sent by James I to Oxford's city council on 2 November 1622 and subsequently transcribed in the College register. Since Henry VIII's reign Exeter had leased from the city a section of the old Somenor's Lane, the narrow roadway lying between the College's northern boundary and the city wall. Earlier attempts by the College to close this off had been rebuffed by the council. But James's letter brought success. The king directed the city

76. Boase, *Register*, cvii, n. 2, 271, 358; Wood, *Colleges*, i. 111.
77. Prideaux, 'Epistle Dedicatory' to *A Sermon Preached*.

to extend Exeter's lease, then nearing its term, and to permit the College to enclose the lane, 'intendinge to buylde a chapell thereupon'.[78] According to Prideaux himself, the College owed its good fortune to the intervention with the king of James Hamilton, earl of Arran and later marquis of Hamilton, who had been an undergraduate at Exeter for a few months in 1621 while also in James's favour at court: a prime example of how the special place which aristocratic undergraduates enjoyed in Prideaux's Exeter might bring dividends.[79]

The city's compliance with the king's direction marked an important stage in the steady northward expansion of the College site in the early seventeenth century, discussed in more detail below. The possible length of the new chapel was severely limited by the new rector's lodgings, which stood at its east end, and by the need to leave space at its west end for the new residential range which it was still hoped to build along Turl Street. Hence, if the chapel was to accommodate the College's rising numbers, the need for the extra breadth now made available by the enclosure of the lane. The result was a chapel which possessed two aisles, (the northern and wider one sometimes called the nave) and which was broader but shorter than its Victorian successor. The two aisles formed a square, but the building was lengthened into an oblong by an antechapel at its west end which provided an entry to both aisles. That Exeter's was the only college chapel at either Oxford or Cambridge to have a double aisle was thus wholly due to the limitations imposed by the exigencies of the site.[80] The bulk of the chapel lay over the old lane, but it also covered part of the 'garden and private walkes' formerly attached to the lodgings, as Prideaux noted, with a touch of ruefulness, in his survey. The remnant of the lane, in the form of a narrow alley, continued to give access to Turl Street.[81]

The man whose generosity brought the chapel into being was George Hakewill: third son of an Exeter merchant, John Peryam's nephew, fellow

---

78. ECA, A.I.6, fo. 8v; Salter, *Oxford City Properties*, 272–3; Salter, *Oxford Council Acts, 1583–1626* (Oxford, 1928), 313; Boase, *Register*, 312–13.

79. Boase, *Register*, 312–13; Boase, *Commoners*, 138; J. J. Scally, 'Hamilton, James first duke of Hamilton (1606–1649), politician', *ODNB*. Hamilton's influence with Charles I also promoted Prideaux's appointment as bishop of Worcester in 1641: see below, 331.

80. *HUO*. iv. 146; G. Tyack, 'Gilbert Scott and the Chapel of Exeter College, Oxford', *Architectural History*, 50 (2007), 126. The contrast between the broad north aisle and the narrower south aisle may be seen in Loggan's view (see Figure 3) and in the first plan of the College, dating from 1733, in W. Williams, *Oxonia Depicta* (Oxford, 1733).

81. Boase, *Register*, 314.

of Exeter from 1596 to 1611, Calvinist and anti-Catholic churchman, and the most intellectually distinguished of the seventeenth-century fellows The suggestion for a new chapel apparently originated with Hakewill himself. He was by far the most munificent of the three benefactors who contributed to the College's building scheme, giving £1,200 for the building of the chapel, to which the College added a further £200 to complete the work.[82] The source of his wealth remains a mystery. It was so to Prideaux, who hardly looked beyond divine providence to explain Hakewill's generosity:

> They that view and consider the worke [i.e. the new chapel] will hardly be perswaded that it was erected at the sole cost of one, Fellow of Exeter College, not preferred, as many are, and having two sones of his own to provide for otherwise. But where God inlargeth the heart, such difficulties restraine not the hands.[83]

As the third son of a middling Exeter merchant, it is unlikely that Hakewill had much family money, nor is his career in the church, where the arch-deaconry of Surrey represented the height of his progression, likely to have brought in a large income. It is possible that he benefited substantially from his short marriage, 1615–18, to Mary Delbridge, the daughter of John Delbridge, one of the leading merchants of early Stuart Barnstaple and five times MP for the town, who had made his fortune from trade with the Continent and the Americas.[84] We cannot be sure; but if we are to account for the wealth which Hakewill made available for his chapel, we might look ultimately to his links with the seafaring merchant class of North Devon.

The foundation stone of the chapel was laid by Hakewill himself on 11 March 1623, and the finished building was consecrated on 5 October 1624. The consecration ceremony, one of some splendour and more solemnity, lasting four hours, was presided over by John Howson, bishop of Oxford, while Prideaux himself gave the consecration sermon on the text 'My house is a house of prayer'.[85] This was the final act in a process which cannot be

---

82. Prideaux, 'Epistle Dedicatory' to *A Sermon Preached*; Boase, *Register*, 314.
83. Prideaux, 'Epistle Dedicatory' to *A Sermon Preached*.
84. For Delbridge and his family, see A. Grant, 'Breaking the Mould: North Devon Maritime Enterprise, 1560–1640', in T. Gray et al. (eds.) *Tudor and Stuart Devon: Essays Presented to Joyce Youings* (Exeter, 1992), 129–38; Grant, *Atlantic Adventurer: John Delbridge of Barnstaple, 1564–1639* (Instow, 1996), *passim*; and *Hist. Parl., 1604–1629*, iv. 38–44.
85. ECA, A.I.6, fo. 6r; Boase, *Register*, cviii–cix; Dublin, Trinity College, MS 533/3, fos. 58v–66r. I am very grateful to Michael Reeve for drawing my attention to this document and for providing me with a transcript.

Figure 2. Watercolour by Joseph Nash, painted *c.* 1845, showing the interior of Hakewill's chapel. Note the elaborate (and expensive) woodwork and the grand pulpit with its twisted columns, a monument to the dominance of the Word in the Protestant Exeter of Prideaux and Hakewill.

followed in any detail. As was the case with the hall, there are no separate accounts for the chapel's construction, nor did it generate any correspondence, of the kind which charts the progress of Peryam's Mansions and Acland's hall. Since Hakewill was frequently present in College and took an active role in supervising the work—'all succeeded the better through your owne carefull presence and direction', says Prideaux[86]—letter-writing can hardly have been necessary. It cannot be said that the work was well done, at least with regard to the main structure of the building. If surveyors' reports on the chapel, submitted independently in 1842 and 1843, can be believed, the walls were bulging as a result of 'original faulty construction, the walls not being of sufficient strength to resist the lateral pressure, of the kind of roof placed upon them', and the building was in an altogether

86. Prideaux, 'Epistle Dedicatory', to *A Sermon Preached.*

dangerous state.[87] This verdict was the prelude to the chapel's demolition just over ten years later.

The chapel was nevertheless a grand and impressive addition to the rebuilt College. Its great traceried windows, four on the north wall and four on the south, though they did not follow the precise form of the hall windows, were of the same Perpendicular Gothic design. Their magnitude, and the light which they admitted, had to compensate for the lack of either an east or a west window, the former precluded by the abutment of the rector's lodgings on the east end, and the latter by the continuing hope for a Turl Street range extending across the chapel's west end. There were some Renaissance features, notably the main doorway with its broken pediment, the round arches of the screens, and the blank round-arched arcading of the panelling behind the stalls.[88] The most striking feature of the interior must have been the ubiquitous, elaborate, and beautiful woodwork: pulpit, stalls, wall panelling, central arcade, and screens to north and south aisles, each screen surmounted by intricate strapwork bearing Hakewill's arms. Much of this was the work of 'Symes the joiner', and of John Bolton, whom we have already identified as the probable maker of the hall woodwork. The chapel had too 'an unusual plaster ceiling embellished with patterning in the form of late Gothic rib vaults'.[89] It seems highly likely that a large part of the cost of the whole project lay in these ornate interior fittings, perhaps to the detriment of spending on the structural framework and so to the building's soundness. The College's contribution of £200, one-seventh of the total cost, was wholly spent on panelling and painting the south aisle, the smaller of the two aisles, while the recorded payments to Bolton and Symes for 'wainscoting' amounted to nearly £97.[90] As much as the chapel's exterior, its interior contributed to the reordering and beautification of the College which Prideaux aimed to achieve (see Figure 2).

---

87. ECA, E.V.5 (Chapel Box); Tyack, 'Gilbert Scott', 130. But see Boase, *Register*, clv, and W. K. Stride, *Exeter College* (1900), 197–8, for the possible exaggerations in these reports and for the difficulty found in demolishing the old chapel.
88. E. A. G. Lamborn, 'The Woodwork of Hakewill's Chapel, Exeter College', *Notes and Queries*, 23 Sept. 1944, 137. The interior of the old chapel is depicted in Figure 2 above and in a lithograph of c.1850 reproduced in F. Cairncross (ed.), *Exeter College: The First 700 Years* (2013), 43. For the location of what survives of the woodwork, see Lamborn, 'The Woodwork', and Tyack, 'Gilbert Scott', 126, 129.
89. Tyack, 'Gilbert Scott', 126.
90. ECA, A.III.9; Boase, *Register*, 314.

These fittings reflected the religious ideals of Prideaux's Exeter. Chief among them was the magnificent pulpit, 'raised high above the stalls and surmounted by an elaborate carved baldacchino with barley-sugar twisted columns, thus emphasising the supremacy of God's Word, as interpreted by His ministers in homilies and sermons'.[91] The twisted columns were particularly striking, since, assuming the pulpit to be an original part of the work, they predate by thirteen years the similar stone columns which adorn the porch of St Mary's, the university church, and may be the earliest example in England of this architectural device. Thought at the time to derive from the columns of Solomon's temple, they embodied a deliberate biblical allusion.[92] The Bible was accorded a more overt supremacy in the great brass eagle lectern or 'brazen desk', which stood at the east end of the north aisle and which was given later by one of the fellows, John Vivian. It survives in the present chapel. The chapel had no separate chancel, which would have divided the priest from his congregation in the Catholic manner, and the communion table at its east end was set east–west, in the approved Anglican tradition, and not north–south as an altar: a feature unique among the Oxford college chapels and one which attracted complaints from the Catholic James, duke of York, soon to be James II, when he visited the College in 1683.[93] Nor were the windows filled with anything but Protestant plain glass, so spurning the painted glass depicting biblical scenes which was already a feature of Wadham's new chapel and which would later appear in the chapels of University College and of Lincoln. This aspect of the 'beauty of holiness', stigmatized by at least one puritan preacher as 'idolatrous and blasphemous pictures in church windows' and soon to be characteristic of Archbishop Laud's Arminianism, was not for Calvinist Exeter.[94] A final mark of respect for evangelical and Protestant religion came with the chapel's dedication to St James. But if it marked a clean break from the old chapel's papistical dedication to the Blessed Virgin, St Peter, and St Thomas the Martyr, better known as Thomas Becket, it was also intended to honour King James, whose action in closing Somenor's

91. H. Parham, 'Building the College', in Cairncross (ed.), *Exeter College*, 42–3. According to Stride, *Exeter College*, 192, the pulpit 'is said to have run on wheels when first erected' (no source cited).
92. Tyack, *Oxford: An Architectural Guide*, 112.
93. Wood, *Life and Times*, iii. 52–3; *HUO*, iv. 606, 890.
94. *HUO*, iv. 168; Darwall-Smith, *University College*, 162–3; Green, *Lincoln College*, 167–8; Collinson, *The Religion of Protestants*, 147–8.

Lane had made the new building possible. Always keen to win a patron's favour, Prideaux took pains to point this out to the king himself.[95]

The building of the new chapel thus had multiple significances. If it made a large contribution to the creation of the quadrangle which was at the heart of Prideaux's plans, it also provided indirectly for the accommodation of more undergraduates through the transformation of the former chapel into the library, so allowing the old library to be converted into rooms. But more important were the religious attributes of the new chapel. In its interior fittings it stood for the Protestant emphasis on preaching and the Bible and on the reduction of the symbolic distance between priest and people characteristic of Roman Catholicism and of what would soon become Laudian worship. The abandonment of the old chapel, built in the Catholic Middle Ages and possessing an outmoded dedication, was a final episode in Exeter's rejection of its pre-Reformation traditions which had begun with the appointment of the Protestants Thomas Glasier and Thomas Holland to the rectorship in the last decades of the sixteenth century. If the chapel's Gothic form represented the perpetuation of that tradition, the link owed more to the prevailing architectural fashion in early seventeenth-century Oxford than to religious continuity. In the nineteenth century 'Gothic' would come to mean 'Catholic'. But that point had not yet been reached.

7. Expansion northwards

Prideaux's plans for the College's material reordering went beyond the creation of a quadrangle. They also came to include, though in a largely piecemeal way, the College's expansion beyond its medieval northern boundary along the south side of Somenor's Lane. The building of the new chapel across part of the lane was only one aspect of this expansion, as the College took over parts of the city wall and even moved beyond the wall, up to the line of the present Broad Street. All these additions to the College site, comprising what Prideaux called its 'outworkes or suburbs',[96] were held on lease from the city.

The process of expansion was followed through as opportunities arose and need not be described in detail. Once again the initiating force, Prideaux

---

95. Boase, *Register*, xxvii–xxviii; Prideaux, *Alloquium*, sig. A2v.
96. Boase, *Register*, 313.

himself was the gainer as much as the College. In 1612 he bought the lease of a tower on the city wall from Thomas Holland's widow, converting part into a kitchen, building lodgings over it, and adding a completely new block to its rear, soon to be known as 'Prideaux Building'. This, 'the German's building', was first used to house the College's foreign students and later Prideaux's aristocratic pupils. In front of the tower Prideaux built himself a house, almost certainly the 'messuage or tenement . . . being neare unto Exeter Colledge' which he left to his son-in-law Henry Sutton in his will of 1650.[97] Still more utilitarian was his purpose in gaining permission from the city council in 1613 to make a doorway through the city wall. This gave access from within the College curtilage to a new set of latrines, a more salubrious replacement for the privies within the College bounds, which had probably occupied the same site since Stapeldon's day. This was a considerable undertaking, costing £200, but it provided additional value for money by paying due respect to the College hierarchy: the rector had one compartment for his private use, the fellows another, and 'the company of the house' a third.[98] Finally, the College took over a second tower on the wall, lying east of the first, and to which the College stables, probably also Prideaux's work, were adjacent.[99] Tower and stables may be seen in the top left-hand corner of Loggan's 1675 view (Figure 3).

The College's expansion beyond its former northern boundary, which occurred almost wholly during Prideaux's rectorship, was undramatic. The only part of the process which facilitated his master plan for the creation of a new quadrangle was the closing of Somenor's Lane, thus creating a space for the erection of the north aisle of Hakewill's chapel. Since nothing now survives of the buildings constructed on this northern site, Prideaux's achievements here are easy to overlook. Yet, contributing as they did to the solution of the general problems facing the College in these years, they were not negligible. The reconstruction of the west tower on the wall, the creation of Prideaux Building, and the making of the new latrines were all ways of alleviating the difficulties posed by rising numbers. But perhaps equally important, at least in Prideaux's eyes, was the enhancement, even

97. Boase, *Register*, 312; Salter, *Oxford City Properties*, 281; ECA, C.IV.29 (H. Hurst, 'The Old Buildings of Exeter College'), Plans A and B; A. Vallance, *The Old Colleges of Oxford* (1912), 28; Butcher, 'Dr John Prideaux', 24; above, 54.
98. Salter, *Oxford Council Acts*, 231; Hurst, 'Old Buildings', Plan D; Boase, *Register*, 311, 313; Salter, *Oxford City Properties*, 283; ECA, A.II.9, fos. 219v, 224r.
99. Boase, *Register*, clxxvii, 313; *Oxford City Properties*, ed. Salter, 275–6, 284.

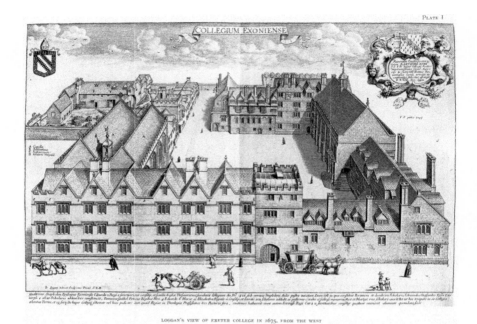

LOGGAN'S VIEW OF EXETER COLLEGE IN 1675, FROM THE WEST

Figure 3. Loggan's bird's eye view of the College in 1675, shown from the west. The buildings completed under Prideaux comprise the new hall (on the right hand/ east side), Peryam's Mansions (to the east and north-east of the hall), buttery and kitchen (south of the hall), the new chapel (opposite the hall), with the rector's lodgings at its east end, and the latrines and stables to the north-east of the lodgings.

beautification, of the College's setting which expansion made possible. The movement of the latrines out of College, to a place beyond its perimeter, was one example of this. The taking in of Somenor's Lane effected a much greater change, making possible the creation of a bowling alley on what had been the east end of the lane and creating a pleasant outlook for those with rooms facing north. It 'was no small thing', wrote Prideaux, 'to turn a place so deformed and incommodious (being a stinking unpitched cartway before) to the use it now serves: both for recreation, comelyness, and benefit of the lower chambers that open their windows to it.'[100] The aesthetic sense and refinement of taste which lay behind the reconstruction of the main part of the College were also perpetuated, if to a lesser degree, in the College's 'outworks'.

100. Boase, *Register*, 313; Hurst, 'Old Buildings', Plan D.

8. Achievements and missed opportunities

In *Ephesus Backsliding*, his Act sermon of 1614, Prideaux had spoken enthu-
siastically about the regeneration of the university: 'our library built and
furnished, our schools mounting, so many colleges enlarged!'[101] The history
of his own College over the next ten years vindicated this buoyant mood.
From one that had been 'but a confused number of blynd streats', it had
acquired form and order in its buildings and layout, and the status which
went with them. Even Peter Heylyn, later to be among Prideaux's leading
Arminian opponents, was impressed by the transformation. Writing about
his visit to Paris and its university in 1625, Heylyn compared the
new Exeter to its advantage with the Parisian colleges: 'These colledges
for their buildings are very inelegant, and generally little beholding to the
curiosity of the artificer. So confused and so proportioned in respect of our
colleges in England as Exeter in Oxford was some 12 years since, in
comparison of the rest.' 'Some 12 years since' takes us back almost to the
start of Prideaux's rectorship. Elsewhere Heylin noted that the benevolent
regime of James I had seen 'the reducing of Exeter . . . into form
quadrangular' and the 'adding of a neat [well-proportioned] chappel
and a fair hall'.[102] By 1625 the confusion and disproportion in Exeter's
relation to other colleges, characteristic of its primordial phase, had passed
into history.

As the master planner behind Exeter's rebuilding, Prideaux's primary
achievement was the creation of the quadrangle which the College had
previously and so signally lacked. True, his failure to persuade Exeter city
council to fund a Turl Street range left the quadrangle incomplete at its
north-west corner. Yet Peryam's Mansions, Acland's hall, the adjoining new
kitchen, and the opposing lodgings and chapel, together with the pre-
existing east range of the old library, now converted into rooms, and Everard
Chambers's west tower and south-west range all made for an impressive
ensemble, and one fit for comparison with the quadrangular buildings of
other colleges, with which Heylyn had compared the old Exeter to its
disadvantage. The desire to put Exeter on a par with other colleges in this

---

101. Prideaux, *Ephesus Backsliding*, 36.
102. P. Heylyn, *A Full Relation of Two Journeys: the One into the Main-land of France. The Other into
     some of the Adjacent Ilands* (1656), 82–3 (I am very grateful to Andrew Hegarty for this
     reference); Heylyn, *Cyprianus Anglicus*, 131.

respect had from the start been high among Prideaux's motives. Had he not told the Exeter councillors of his hope to see 'Exeter College in a square as other colleges are'?[103] Upon the scale and regularity of its buildings depended in part both the College's self-respect and its standing in the university.

But not upon that alone. Prideaux's second achievement was to create a substantial stock of new accommodation for the rising tide of undergraduates and senior scholars attracted to the College, in large part by its rector's reputation. As significant a mark of Exeter's heightened place within the university were its burgeoning numbers. By the time of the chapel's completion in 1624, the College had become well placed to provide for this growing population. Although Prideaux was to write in 1618 of its being 'scanted for lodgings', many rooms had already been added in a piecemeal way during Holland's later years. The main additions in Prideaux's time came from Peryam's Mansions, providing eight chambers, each with two studies,[104] and from the rooms created in what had been the old library (forming the east range of the new quadrangle), once the library had been moved into the old chapel. The new accommodation here comprised two rooms and seven studies, yielding an annual rent of £5 in 1631–2, when it is first recorded.[105] To these must be added seven rooms in Prideaux Building, built at Prideaux's own expense but also to his future profit, since the rents for these rooms do not appear in the accounts after 1620–1. Finally, some favoured undergraduates were accommodated in the rector's new and spacious lodgings.[106] New building before Prideaux's time allowed the accommodation of some thirty-five to forty men (who might be fellows as well as undergraduates), with a further thirty-five or so accommodated in buildings constructed or converted during his rectorship. The failure to raise funds for building along Turl Street, north of the tower, almost certainly meant that the College remained cramped for space. But if it had not solved the problem, the work of Prideaux and his predecessors had at least brought about its major alleviation.

The raising of funds which lay behind this achievement, and which was an achievement in itself, had some peculiar features. As far as we can tell,

---

103. HMC, *City of Exeter*, 101.
104. Ibid., 100; above, 127–8.
105. ECA, A.II.9, fo. 317v.
106. Ibid., fo. 257r; above, 61–2, 98.

Prideaux's fundraising efforts were concentrated exclusively on the city of Exeter and on men connected with the city. Peryam was an alderman and former mayor, Acland a freeman and well known in the city, though resident in the nearby countryside, and Hakewill the son of an Exeter merchant. The College's appeal to the Exeter councillors spread the net more widely, but over the same general class. It is easy to see why the College should have concentrated on these potential sponsors. All the major benefactors were closely connected with the College and its fellows, and the city itself had multiple links extending in the same direction, through its history, its bishops, and its student sons. Moreover, in Orford and Farrington the College had two indispensable local agents, the first a friend of Peryam, his patron, the second an Exeter citizen, and both former fellows and resident clergy in the city's neighbourhood. What is less easy to understand, however, is the restriction of fundraising to such a closely defined community, albeit a large and wealthy one. In the fifteenth century the then rector had on at least one occasion toured Devon to raise money from the College's friends, and funds came in from many sources,[107] but no such enterprise followed the failure of the financial appeal to the city. As late as 1630 Prideaux still seems to have believed that the city might yet fund the building of a Turl Street range, though the apparent cessation of contact with the city council after 1619 must have suggested that nothing could now be expected. Only a letter of 1637 from John Maynard to Prideaux, which offered the College two lectureships in place of money for building, suggests that any further appeal was made for funds.[108]

The virtual abandonment of fundraising after the breakdown of negotiations with the city is all the more surprising in view of the rising numbers of old members at this time and of the social predominance among them of men drawn from the nobility and the upper gentry—the College's fellow commoners. Here was a potentially receptive circle for any appeal; yet where were Prideaux's aristocratic ex-pupils when they were needed? Other colleges at this time organized appeals to their wealthy alumni and others in a systematic and comprehensive way. Griffith Powell, Prideaux's contemporary as principal of Jesus, 1613–20, appointed agents in each Welsh county to approach members of the local gentry and 'men of good worth' in order to finance the College's building programme, while William Lewis,

107. Maddicott, *Founders*, 137.
108. Boase, *Register*, 311, 318; above, 141–2.

provost of Oriel, 1618–21, attempted to raise money by sending out 'letters, elegant, in a winning persuasive way' to his college's eminent old members.[109] Prideaux seems to have left this source untapped. That such men might be willing enough to contribute to Exeter's needs was shown between c.1668 and 1682, when they contributed generously to the construction of the northern Turl Street range originally envisaged by Prideaux. Benefactors then included Lord Clifford, then treasurer of England, who, as Thomas Clifford, had been an undergraduate at Exeter in 1647–8 and who now gave £50; thirty-six gentlemen commoners, three of whom were baronets; and at least four former fellows.[110] These were the sort of men who might have been expected to have come to the College's aid some fifty years earlier.

Could the College itself have funded a new building along Turl Street? Perhaps; but it had already given substantial financial support to Prideaux's building programme. Here we have figures, most of them already cited. Towards the completion of Peryam's Mansions the College gave £140; to the completion of Acland's hall, £200; to wainscoting and painting the south aisle of the chapel, £200; and to the new privies beyond the city wall, £200. All this information comes from Prideaux's Survey. The accounts show that an additional £63 was spent on the rebuilding of the lodgings and, according to the survey, an unspecified sum on the new bowling alley and its boundary walls, laid out over what had been Somenor's Lane.[111] Average annual expenditure on building for these twelve years was thus about £62. Since College income for the same period averaged £413 per annum, about 15 per cent of annual expenditure went towards the new work: an indication of 'planned funding' unusual among the colleges, and a testimony to the corporate pride and effort which Prideaux encouraged and on which he was able to draw.[112] Prideaux too was a major contributor to College buildings, erecting Prideaux Building at his own expense (but seemingly to his own ultimate profit), giving 40s. towards the 'Privy Kitchin Buildings' lying towards the west end of the new chapel on land formerly attached to the

---

109. *HUO*, iv. 141–3. But see *Oriel College*, ed. Catto, 120–1, 555–6, for the suggestion that William Lewis's appeal should be more correctly ascribed to John Tolson, his successor as provost.
110. Wood, *Colleges*, i. 111; Boase, *Register*, 271.
111. Boase, *Register*, 312, 313, 314, 317, 318; ECA, A.II.9, fos. 232, 236.
112. These figures derive from calculations made from the rector's accounts, ECA, A.II.9. For 'planned funding', see *HUO*, iv. 144.

lodgings, and paying for work on the lodgings and for the conversion of the western tower on the wall into a kitchen with room above. In addition, he joined former fellows in giving money for the new kitchen adjacent to the hall.[113] Never wholly reliant on external benefactors, neither the College nor its rector was negligent in supporting their own projects. Yet Prideaux and his colleagues may have flinched from a further heavy commitment of College resources to a Turl Street building. To judge by what was given in the 1670s, even the southern section of such a building might have cost more than £500.[114] An intention to spend on anything like this scale might have been judged imprudent: better to see if the citizens of Exeter would eventually do their duty by the College or to await the appearance of some other as yet unknown benefactor.

The rebuilding of the College has been described here in material terms: money raised, rooms gained, form and order achieved in planning and architecture. Yet there were other considerations which transcended the material. By all who participated in it, Exeter's reconstruction was seen as a religious enterprise. At one level the appeal to religion was a rhetorical device designed to open the purses of co-religionists. Hence Farrington's letter to the Exeter city councillors reminding them (vainly, as it turned out) that their wealth could be put to no better use than the support of the College, which was to 'the good of learning, the good of religion, the good of the church, the good of the common welth'.[115] But these and similar sentiments should also be taken at face value. The enlargement of the College, the provision of new buildings and of more accommodation, and the promotion of the College's status within the university were all means towards the furtherance of learning and the moral as well as intellectual training of the young, on which the wellbeing and defence of church and state were seen to depend. Behind a material facade lay a greater and, in some respects, even a spiritual good.

Shared religious sympathies underlay the largest part of Exeter's fundraising operations. The language of divine providence, divine intervention, and godly ends suffused the correspondence between Prideaux, Farrington, Peryam, Acland, and the Exeter city council. The ends were defined by Peryam when he wrote, in his first letter to Prideaux, that he desired 'of God

---

113. Boase, *Register*, 311, 312, 313, 315, 319.
114. The amount collected in the 1670s was £515: Wood, *Colleges*, i. 111.
115. HMC, *City of Exeter*, 101; above, 138.

that all may be to his glorie and to the good of his church'.[116] It mattered greatly here that the College, its benefactors and potential benefactors, and its emissaries Orford and Farrington stood on common religious ground, defined by an assertive Protestantism and a fierce anti-Catholicism. Prideaux's view of the need 'to hate the abominations of popery' found an echo in Farrington's appeal to the Exeter councillors to support 'the sound profession of the gospel, which papists slander'.[117] Naturally there were shades of difference. Prideaux's gibes against the puritans, among whom he would never have numbered himself, would perhaps not have been well received by Ignatius Jordan, the 'Archpuritan' mayor of Exeter or by the puritan backers of Exeter's city lectureships.[118] But all sides possessed shared beliefs which were the common property of Protestants and of Protestantism's puritan wing: in the Calvinist doctrines of election and predestination, in Scripture as an infallible guide to faith and conduct, and in the efficacy of preaching as a means of spreading and interpreting Scripture. Even Thomas Martin, Exeter merchant and Jordan's successor as mayor, could quote the Bible to some effect. A common Protestantism veering towards puritanism helps to explain both the College's attraction for the sons of puritan West Country families and the concentration of its fundraising efforts on the city of Exeter and its wealthier members.

The rebuilding of Exeter College should thus be seen as a response to both external and internal stimuli, to the problems posed by rising numbers and to the need to create a modern college which had cast off its medieval formlessness and could hold up its head among the other new and newly rebuilt colleges of the university. But it was also an enterprise which was underlain by Protestant convictions and which had at its centre the urge to promote Protestant teaching and habits of thought. Prideaux embodied both these ideals. If the rebuilt College revealed 'the operation of a master-mind',[119] it was also a living monument to his beliefs. In that most moribund of clichés, but here hard to avoid, the rebuilt College was a sermon in stone.

116. Letter 5; above, 126.
117. Prideaux, *Ephesus Backsliding*, 37; HMC, *City of Exeter*, 102; above, 140.
118. Above, 130, 137.
119. *HUO*, iv, 144.

5

Prideaux's Circle

1. Family

Prideaux's life and career can hardly be considered in isolation, for much was contributed to both by his intimates, friends, and sympathizers. Closest to him came his family, then his Exeter colleagues, and finally his allies in the church, particularly in the English church but also among the reformed churches of the Continent.

Of these three groups, it was only natural that his family should have been the foremost. The foundation of his family affections and affiliations lay in his two marriages, each of them bound up with his interests, religious and cultural. His first wife, Anne Goodwin, was the daughter of William Goodwin, dean of Christ Church from 1611 until his death in 1620.[1] Goodwin and Prideaux had natural affinities beyond the headships of their respective houses. Like Prideaux, Goodwin was a royal chaplain and a thoroughgoing Calvinist. His one published work, a sermon preached before the king at Woodstock in 1614, was rabidly anti-Catholic, denouncing the papacy for its temporal claims and its threats to royal government: 'While there is a devil in Hell, a pope in Rome, murders, massacrings, treason shall never die.'[2] He was, however, more learned than this single publication might suggest. If he lacked Prideaux's scholarly range, the preacher at his funeral could still speak of him as 'a holy glutton of books', his study lined with the works of the Fathers.[3] Like Prideaux too, he cut a figure in the university.

---

1. W. F. Wentworth-Shields, rev. V. Larminie, 'Goodwin, William (1555/7–1620), dean of Christ Church, Oxford', *ODNB*; *HUO*, iv. 189, 568.
2. W. Goodwin, *A Sermon Preached before the Kings Most Excellent Maiestie at Woodstocke Aug. 28 1614* (Oxford, 1614), 36.
3. T. Goffe, *Oratio funebris habita in ecclesia Cathedrali Christi Oxon in obitum viri omni aevo dignissimi Gulielmi Goodwin* (Oxford, 1620), sig. A3v.

Between Scholarship and Church Politics: The Lives of John Prideaux, 1578–1650. John Maddicott, Oxford University Press. © John Maddicott 2022. DOI: 10.1093/oso/9780192896100.003.0005

Vice-chancellor to two successive chancellors, Ellesmere and Pembroke, he held the office four times between 1615 and 1619, serving in his last year as Prideaux's immediate predecessor.[4] Even without the extra bond provided by the marriage, the two men were well matched and, on occasion, political allies, joining together in 1617, for example, to thwart the king's 'Directions' for the suppression of puritanism in the university. It comes as no surprise to find that in 1620 Prideaux was one of the two witnesses to the nuncupative will of his dying father-in-law.[5]

But it was not only the standing and convictions of Anne's father which made her a suitable wife for Prideaux. Her mother Mary had a comparable, if more vicarious distinction as the daughter of Rowland Taylor, one of the Marian martyrs executed for his Protestant faith in 1555. Prideaux himself took pride in recording his wife's illustrious descent. In his *Euchologia*, addressed to his two surviving daughters shortly before his death, he wrote of 'that famous martyr, Dr Rowland Taylor, (which should take the more with you because by your mother you are lineally descended from him)', adding that Taylor had had a hand in 'contriving . . . the chain of pearl . . . the Book of Common Prayer'.[6] Through his wife Prideaux was thus linked with the early and heroic days of English Protestantism and with one of its key texts: a link which must have fortified his Anglican-Calvinist credentials and which brought him indirectly into association with the Protestant elite.

The date of the couple's marriage is unknown. But the their first son, William, was baptized on 28 December 1615,[7] so the likelihood is that it took place in 1614 or early in 1615, a few years after Prideaux's election as rector. Anne's personality is almost as elusive as the date of her marriage. Writing much later to his two daughters 'about your long deceased mother', Prideaux says that she was 'a religious and modest matron in all the course of her life, extraordinarily addicted to prayer'.[8] This was no doubt true, but it does not take us much beyond the stock image of the pious materfamilias. Most of her married life must have been taken up with childbearing and children, as one child followed another in quick succession. William's birth,

---

4. Wood, *Fasti*, i. 365, 361, 369, 379, 385.
5. Wood, *Annals*, ii. 324; above, 42; Microfilm. OUA. OU Arch. Wills (Cozens-Ho). HO 235.000. Reel 002.
6. J. Prideaux, *Euchologia, or The Doctrine of Practical Praying* (1656), sig. A4v–A5r. Taylor's part in the making of the Book of Common Prayer seems to be otherwise unknown.
7. Anthony Wood, *Survey of the Antiquities of the City of Oxford*, ed. A. Clark, 3 vols. (OHS, 15, 17, 37, 1889–99), iii. 201.
8. Prideaux, *Euchologia*, sig. A3v.

coming as it did in the same month as his father's nomination to the regius chair, is likely have been a cause of special celebration. Then came Mary (baptized February 1617), Anne (March 1618), Sarah (December 1619), Elizabeth (March 1621), the twins John and Matthias (September 1622), and Robert (May 1624). All except William were baptized in the College's parish church of St Michael at the Northgate.[9] At midsummer 1624, when the family was at its largest, William would have been 9, Mary 6, Anne 5, Sarah 4, Elizabeth 3, John and Matthias 1, and Robert barely more than a month. The building of the new lodgings for the rector between 1615 and 1617, partly at Prideaux's expense, owed much to the need to accommodate this prospective houseful of children.

Soon, however, the family began to shrink, as death came for some of its youngest members. The mid-1620s were a particularly unhealthy time in Oxford, and it was probably epidemic disease which carried off first Anne (buried September 1624, aged 6), then Mary (December 1624, aged 7), and lastly Matthias (February 1625, aged 2). A second Matthias was born at some point in 1625, his baptism unrecorded. But this, the couple's ninth child, was to be the last, for Anne herself died in August 1627, leaving Prideaux a widower with six children under the age of 12. Two more deaths followed during the period of his rectorship. Robert died, aged 3, in 1627, and John, twin brother of the dead Matthias, aged 13, in 1636. Matthias's burial was the first in the College's new chapel, where Robert and John were also buried, while the two girls and their mother were buried in the church of St Michael at the Northgate, where all three are commemorated on a surviving memorial.[10] It was clearly thought inappropriate to bury females in the chapel.

We can only imagine the effect of these multiple deaths on Prideaux and his wife, and then on Prideaux alone. In an age of high child mortality their losses were hardly exceptional, but they were, nonetheless, deeply felt, for all their parents' faith in their childrens' salvation in the afterlife. Something of their emotional impact comes through in the inscriptions on the small memorial brasses for the three boys still preserved in the present College chapel. They were no doubt written by Prideaux himself. For Matthias, the first to die, the inscription (in translation from the original Latin) reads: 'Do you seek to find out what the little child is saying? Read, you will die, as did

9. Wood, *Survey*, iii. 249.
10. Ibid., iii. 160, 249; Butcher, 'Dr John Prideaux', 7–9.

Matthias Prideaux, the rector's son, who was the first to be buried in this chapel after its foundation, February 17 1624 [i.e. 1625].' For Robert, the victim of accidental poisoning: 'How suddenly, how certainly, believe one who has had experience, Robert Prideaux, younger brother of Matthias, who unhappily swallowed poison and died wretchedly (*misere*) in less than ten hours on September 14. 1627.' Most moving of all is the inscription for the 13-year-old John: 'Here lies in his funeral shroud John Prideaux, his father's most precious gem (*patris optima gemma*), twin brother of Matthias, who prematurely followed his brothers, August 1st A.D. 1636.'[11] The deaths made their mark, too, beyond Prideaux's immediate circle, partly perhaps because it was so unusual for a college head to preside not only over his college but also over a houseful of small children. Something may also have been owed to the character and attractiveness of the children themselves. Anne, Robert, Matthias, and most notably the 7-year old Mary were all commemorated in verse elegies by the university's poets, including a former member of Exeter, William Strode, whose poem 'On Mistress Mary Prideaux dying young', a work of real poetic merit, has recently been reprinted. Through these outpourings, surely more than conventional, Prideaux's children made their own adventitious contribution to the literary culture of the period.[12]

What of the survivors? The eldest was William, Prideaux's firstborn child. As a precocious 10-year-old he contributed four lines of Latin verse to *Epithalamia Oxoniensia*, the volume of university verse compiled for the marriage of Prince Charles and Henrietta Maria in 1625. Here he describes himself as a' talkative boy (*garrule puer*) . . . son of the doctor from Exeter College'. Since his father was vice-chancellor at the time and contributed the introductory verse to a volume which he probably edited, here, almost certainly, was a proud parent using his position to draw attention to the talents of a clever son. But young William was not to have an academic career. We hear little more of him until the 1640s, when, having married Ellen Crosland, 'a very great beauty' and daughter of a Yorkshire landowner, he was wealthy enough to raise a regiment for the king, for whose

---

11. The Latin inscriptions are given in Wood, *College*, ii. 118, and Butcher, 'Dr John Prideaux', 7–8. I have generally followed Butcher's translations.
12. M. A. Forey, 'Elegies on the Children of Dr John Prideaux, 1624–5', *The Seventeenth Century*, 30 (2015), 301–16; Forey, 'Strode, William (1601?–1645), poet and playwright', *ODNB*; *The New Oxford Book of Seventeenth Century Verse*, ed. A. Fowler (Oxford, 1991), 356.

cause he died fighting at Marston Moor in 1644.[13] The second son, Matthias, more of a scholar, matriculated at Exeter, aged 15, in 1640, and was elected to a fellowship within a year: a promotion surely procured by his father. By 1645 a captain in the royalist army, he died of smallpox in the following year.[14] His death left Prideaux only with his two daughters, Sarah and Elizabeth, both of whom survived him. Sarah married William Hodges, a fellow of the College, in 1634, while Elizabeth married Henry Sutton, an Oxford doctor of divinity and prominent Worcestershire cleric, in 1642. They were, Prideaux wrote poignantly in his *Euchologia*, 'the only survivors of the nine children that God had blest me with'.[15]

In August 1628, just a year after the death of Anne, his first wife, Prideaux married again. His new bride, Mary Reynell, came from a Devon landed family, and it was in Devon, in the middle of the long vacation, that the marriage took place. The diarist Thomas Crosfield, of Queen's College, who tells us this, comments wittily but allusively that 'the second edition [was] larger than the first', perhaps suggesting a contrast between bulky Mary and petite Anne.[16] Whatever were Mary's physical qualities, Prideaux's almost unseemly haste to marry again must have been largely driven by the needs of his six young children. A new wife would provide them with a new mother.

If Prideaux's first wife had linked him with Oxford's academic aristocracy—few more aristocratic than the dean of Christ Church—his second took him in an entirely different direction, towards the upper ranks of the Devonshire gentry. Living at East Ogwell, near Newton Abbot in South Devon, the Reynells were entrenched among the county elite. Mary was one of the eight children—three sons and five daughters—of Sir Thomas Reynell II (1555–1618) and his first wife, Frances Aylworth: 'a worthy gouvernour in his country', as he was styled in the sermon preached at his funeral. The date of Mary's birth is unknown, but her two elder brothers, Richard and Thomas III, were born in 1584 and 1589 respectively, while her mother died in 1605; so she is likely to have been in her late

13. *Epithalamia Oxoniensia* (Oxford, 1625), sig. F4r; *The Family Memoirs of the Rev. William Stukeley, M.D.*, ed. W. C. Lukis, 3 vols. (Surtees Soc., 1882–7), i. 3–4; Butcher, 'Dr John Prideaux', 8–9.

14. Boase, *Register*, 105; Prince, *Worthies of Devon*, 660; Butcher, 'Dr John Prideaux', 8; Hegarty, 'Prideaux'.

15. Prideaux, *Euchologia*, sig. A3r; Butcher, 'Dr John Prideaux', 10–12. For the later careers of Hodges and Sutton, see below, 356–8.

16. '[1628. August] 15 . . . Regius noster Theologiae professor fit uxoratus Devon. 2a editio priore auctior': Queen's College, Oxford, MS 390, fo. 36v.

twenties or thirties at the time of her marriage.[17] But although she must have been of an age to have children, her marriage with Prideaux produced none. At the time of the marriage he was 49, at least ten and possibly as much as twenty-five years older than his new wife.

Mary's family had multiple connections with Prideaux's Exeter: few families can have sent so many of their members to the same college over two or three generations. Through her Exonian brothers and cousins, socially and regionally typical of the sons of the Devonshire gentry drawn to Exeter in the early seventeenth century, Mary is likely to have been known to Prideaux long before their marriage. Her two brothers, Richard and Thomas Reynell, both matriculated at Exeter in 1602 (the year after Prideaux's election to a fellowship), aged 15 and 12 respectively, and both left within a few years, without taking degrees, to go on to the Middle Temple.[18] With the younger brother, Thomas, his own brother-in-law after his second marriage, Prideaux's links evidently remained close. In 1648, forty-six years after Thomas matriculated at Exeter, Prideaux dedicated his *Easy and Compendious Introduction for Reading all sorts of Histories* (supposedly written by the young Matthias Prideaux but actually by his father[19]) to 'the right worshipfull Sir Thomas Reynell and the virtuous Lady Katherine his wife: for the use of their towardly young sons Mr Thomas and Mr Henry Reynell'. A third brother, Walter (1591–1627), was almost certainly the Walter Reynell who matriculated at Oxford in 1610 at an unnamed college, who is recorded simply as 'Reynell' in the list of Exeter undergraduates taking the oath of allegiance in that year, and who appears among Prideaux's pupils from 1610 to 1612.[20] If so, Prideaux was the tutor of his future wife's brother.

Numbers of Mary's other male relations spread their wings at Exeter during Prideaux's time. Her half-brother Edward was a fellow commoner at Exeter from 1629 to 1632;[21] her two cousins, Carew and John Reynell, were both undergraduates in the years around 1620; and Thomas Reynell, her nephew, was a fellow commoner from 1640 to 1642. At some stage

---

17. J. Preston, *The Patriarchs Portion, or The Saints Best Day. Delivered in a Sermon at the Funerall of Sir Thomas Reynell of Ogwell in Devon. Knight. April 16. 1618* (1619), 68; *Visitations*, ed. Vivian, 644; M. Wolffe, 'Reynell Family (*per.*1540–1735), gentry', *ODNB*. I have followed Wolffe's numbering of the various Thomas Reynells.
18. Clark, *Register*, ii. 255; Boase *Commoners*, 270; *Hist. Parl., 1604–29*, vi. 25.
19. Wood, *Athenae*, iii. 199; below, 366–7.
20. Clark, *Register*, ii. 315; OUA, SP E/6/1; ECA, H.II.11.
21. Boase, *Commoners*, 270.

Prideaux lent him money, for in his will, made in 1650, he left to Mary his wife two bonds for the payment of £500 'due from Thomas Reynell of Ogwell in the countie of Devon esquire'.[22] It was with Mary's aunt and namesake, however, that Prideaux had the most personal link. The sister of Sir Thomas Reynell II, the elder Mary was the 'good gentlewoman' of Ugborough, who, as Lady Fowell, had been Prideaux's patron in his early years and had paid for his schooling.[23] She and her second husband, the lawyer and country gentleman, Edmund Prideaux of Netherton in East Devon, were the dedicatees of Prideaux's *Eight Sermons*, published in 1621, and in his dedicatory letter Prideaux had written not only of 'the many kindnesses I have heretofore received from you both', but also of the couple's exemplary religious life which 'my selfe to my great comfort, have often observed, both in private prayers, duely continued in your well-ordered family, and publike esteeme of the Word, and its true professors': words which suggest that Prideaux had spent time in Edmund and Mary's godly household (and may indeed have been an occasional guest of other gentry families in his native county).[24] Was it perhaps on one such visit to Netherton that he met Mary Prideaux's niece, his future wife?

The Reynell family thus intersected with Prideaux's life and career at many different points. This elevated connection was one in which he clearly took a good deal of pride. Celebrated in a minor way through the dedication to *Eight Sermons,* it was more publicly vaunted in heraldry. The arms of Prideaux impaling Reynell, with the initials 'PR' and the date 1637, appear in a panel of painted glass now set in the east window of the upper reading room in the Bodleian Library and formerly in the possession of the Prideaux family, while the Reynell arms figure separately on Prideaux's tomb at Bredon in Worcestershire.[25] To the relationship celebrated here the bonds of religion were integral. The Reynells exemplified that moderate puritanism which was typical of the Devonshire gentry in the early Stuart period and which overlapped substantially with Prideaux's own Calvinistic Protestantism. It is best illustrated in the life of Mary's father, Sir Thomas Reynell II, whose funeral sermon, preached by the local rector, had put on record

22. Boase, *Commoners*, 269; Boase, *Register*, 276; Wolffe, 'Reynell Family'.
23. Above, 5–6.
24. J. Prideaux, *Eight Sermons* (1621), sigs. A2r–v.
25. *Royal Commission on Historical Monuments: An Inventory of the Historical Monuments in the City of Oxford* (London, 1939), 2a; Butcher, 'Dr John Prideaux', 6. For the early history of the glass panel, see G. Prideaux, 'Prideaux Queries Continued', *Gentleman's Magazine*, May 1865, 625.

both his religious habits and his practical virtues: his detestation of 'all poperie and superstition'; his strict attention to sermons, at which he customarily took notes, his devotion to the works of William Perkins, the master theologian of middle-of-the-road Puritanism; his fair dealings with his tenants; his hospitality and generosity to the poor; and his tireless 'composing of controversies and ending suits of law'.[26] No more in funeral sermons than in lapidary inscriptions is a man upon oath; yet there is enough here that is detailed and circumstantial (particularly perhaps the specific mention of Perkins) to carry conviction. There are indications too that some members of the family were notably learned. The monument to Sir Richard Reynell of Forde, Mary's uncle, in Wolborough church, adjacent to East Ogwell, mentions 'his heavenlie learning' and, more strikingly, his knowledge of Hebrew,[27] while another uncle, the Oxford-educated Josias Reynell, was said to have been 'so studious that [at Oxford] he excelled many of his ranke'. He was a good grammarian, writing and speaking good Latin, 'a good phylosopher, a good historian, some Grecian, a man well read in physicke', and a scholar deeply versed in the Bible and its ancient and modern commentators.[28]

The Reynells, then, were far from unlettered country squires. Had Mary shared in their religious and bookish interests, she would have been a woman after Prideaux's own heart. But equally important were the links which she and her many relations provided with Prideaux's native Devonshire. His second marriage reinforced the local ties and allegiances which we have already explored and which qualify any view of his life as exclusively rooted in the Oxford where he had made his career.

In this context it would be easy to overlook Prideaux's natal family, whose leading members remained firmly settled in his birthplace. His continuing relations with them were an important part of his life. With his elder brother Thomas, the head of the family and in charge of the Stowford farm, his long widowed mother Agnes, living at Stowford until her death in 1626, and his remaining five brothers and three sisters, his links were almost certainly closer than the surviving evidence allows us to say. Prince tells us

26. Preston, *The Patriarchs Portion*, 62–5.
27. M. O'Hagan, *A History of Forde House, Newton Abbot, Devon* (Newton Abbot, 1990), 16. A knowledge of Hebrew cannot have been a common accomplishment among the Devon gentry. Had Sir Richard been to Oxford and acquired it there?
28. J. Preston, *A Sermon Preached at the Funerall of Mr Josiah Reynel Esquire, the 13. of August 1614, in East Ogwell in Devon* (1615), sig. D2v.

Figure 4. Monument to Prideaux's parents, erected by Prideaux in 1639 for their parish church at Harford, Devon, and also showing the couple's seven sons and three daughters. Prideaux is shown as the fourth son, wearing a doctor's gown.

that even after he became rector of Exeter and regius professor, he would often come from Oxford to visit his family, sometimes taking them by surprise, and he may have been on one such visit when Laud found him absent from Oxford and 'gone into the west' in the long vacation of 1630.[29] Similar long vacation expeditions, such as those which saw his ordination at Silverton in East Devon in September 1609 and his second marriage in August 1627, may well have been his usual custom. Probably he took some of his children with him; at any rate, his mother Agnes left to William, his eldest son and her grandson, 'my best cuppe with a silver cover' when she made her will in 1620.[30] The monument which he set up to his parents in their parish church at Harford, showing their seven sons and original three daughters and listing the titles of the originator of 'this final remembrance', was an act of filial piety but also one intended to signify how far their fourth son had travelled (see Figure 4).[31] Erected in July 1639, it commemorated another long-vacation visit to his native county. When his three brothers, Thomas, Richard, and Hugh, drew up a deed in 1639, there was a certain stiffness in their reference to 'our brother the doctor in Oxford', suggesting a measure of distancing in their relationship.[32] But Prideaux himself never lost a strong sense of attachment to his parents and his first home.

2. Colleagues

Apart from his family, those to whom Prideaux was closest were his colleagues: the twenty-two fellows of Exeter who resided in the College and whom he must have encountered daily. During the period of his rectorship, 1612 to 1642, some sixty-two men were elected to fellowships. We have already seen something of their routine duties and activities, particularly as tutors, with responsibility for their pupils' education and moral welfare. Since Prideaux was, unsurprisingly, closer to some than to others, it is worth trying to identify those colleagues for whom he seems to have had an especially high regard and to locate the qualities which drew him to them. They can often be recognized by the college offices which

---

29. Prince, *Worthies of Devon*, 658; *Works of Laud*, v. 28.
30. Prideaux, *Prideaux*, 116. For the Prideaux family relationships, see ibid. 92.
31. Above, 1, 165.
32. Prideaux, *Prideaux*, 117.

they held and by the large numbers of pupils whom they taught. Speaking generally, fellows holding the major offices for long periods or with unusual frequency and fellows with numerous pupils were men whom the rector especially trusted and respected and who might in some cases be regarded as personal friends.

Prideaux's closest relationship was with one who met few of these criteria. Described by Peter Heylin's biographer as 'the intimate friend of Dr Prideaux', George Hakewill has already been introduced as the nephew of the College benefactor John Peryam, Archbishop Abbot's candidate for a vacancy on the English delegation to the Synod of Dort, the diehard anti-Catholic opponent of the Spanish Match, and the financier of the College's new chapel.[33] While most of those considered here were considerably younger than Prideaux, Hakewill (1577/8–1649) was almost his exact contemporary. Theirs was a relationship of equals, in age as in intellect and in a partisanship of belief which drew both men into anti-Arminian battles with Peter Heylin.[34] Strictly speaking, Hakewill should be excluded from the reckoning here, since he held his fellowship from 1596 to 1611, resigning in the year before Prideaux became rector to take up a living at Heanton Punchardon in North Devon. During his time as fellow the only major College office which he held was that of dean, from 1608 to 1611, while in the period covered by the pupil lists from 1606 onward, he never had more than four or five pupils. Yet even after 1611 he remained a kind of supernumerary fellow, often resident in the College, supervising the building of the chapel, retaining a room, and dining in hall.[35] But he was far from being a merely local figure, operating along an Oxford-Devon axis. He was, like Prideaux, the master of a pan-European range of learning, partly informed no doubt by a four-year sojourn abroad between 1604 and 1608 among the reformed churches of Germany and Switzerland, and a winter spent in the Calvinist city of Heidelberg: a foreign experience denied to Prideaux, who never went out of England.

Like Prideaux, Hakewill wrote extensively—sermons, anti-Catholic polemic, treatises on confirmation and Sunday observance, and much else.[36]

---

33. Barnard, *Theologo-Historicus*, 124; above, 125, 50–2, 143–4.
34. Milton, *Laudian and Royalist Polemic in Seventeenth-Century England: The Career and Writings of Peter Heylyn* (Manchester, 2007), 31–2, 40 n. 129, 64, 68, 140 n. 45.
35. For Hakewill's sojourns in college, see ECA, C.II.4, fo. 29r; BB/21, 23, 24; Boase, *Register*, cii; Prideaux, 'Epistle dedicatory', in *A Sermon Preached*; DHC, Z1/53/Box 9/2.
36. McCullough, 'Hakewill'.

But his magnum opus, *An Apologie of the Power and Providence of God*, published in 1627, republished in a slightly expanded version in 1630, and again in 1635, this time greatly enlarged, was a work of a different kind from any of these, standing 'in the first rank of philosophical and literary achievement in the early Caroline period'.[37] It examined the idea of progress and sought to controvert the view of Godfrey Goodman, then bishop of Gloucester, that the world was in a state of perpetual decline and decay. Hakewill's counter-argument, worked out over nearly five hundred pages, was that change was often cyclical. Especially in matters of the intellect and the arts, efflorescence was followed by fading and decline, but then by resurrection and revival. In general, however, Hakewill observed improvement on all sides since the times of the ancients. In divinity, medicine, law, philosophy, and much else, as well as in navigation and printing, progress was undeniable, and to argue the reverse was to deny God's providence. It was not only the breadth and cogency of the argument that was remarkable about Hakewill's thesis, but the range of the scholarship and learning deployed to support it. His thoughts on man's stature and proportion from ancient to modern times, for example, are buttressed by a learned disquisition on ancient weights and measures, while nature's circularity is illustrated by the homely and local observation that the alluvium carried by rivers to the sea is returned to the earth as a fertilizer 'which in some places, and namely in the north part of Devonshire is found to be marvellous great commoditie for the inriching of the soyle'. More elevatedly but with comparable virtuosity he surveyed Roman history, and in particular the vices of the Romans, to show that Christianity had brought a beneficial 'reformation of manners' which was yet another mark of God's providence.[38]

In its learning and in the substance of its argument Hakewill's *Apologie* was the most distinguished work produced by any seventeenth-century fellow of the College. If Prideaux was equally learned, it was over a rather narrower field, at least as demonstrated by his publications. Hakewill's book and the

---

37. Poole, 'The Evolution of George Hakewill's *Apologie*', 1. Poole provides an excellent survey of Hakewill's life and of the evolution of his text. For the content, see esp. R. F. Jones, *Ancients and Moderns: A Study in the Rise of the Scientific Movement in Seventeenth-Century England*, 2nd edn (Gloucester, MA, 1961) 22–37, and V. Harris, *All Coherence Gone*, 2nd edn (Chicago, 1966), 47–85.
38. G. Hakewill, *An Apologie of the Power and Providence of God in the Government of the World* (Oxford, 1627), 130, 17–83, 301–433.

Figure 5. Portrait of George Hakewill, Fellow of Exeter College, 1596–1611, Prideaux's successor as rector, 1642–9, and the College's most distinguished writer and thinker. Artist unknown. Now hanging in the Exeter Senior Common Room.

acclaim which it brought to him[39] and his College must have weighed with the fellows when they elected him as Prideaux's successor in 1642. It was another mark of his colleagues' pride in his achievements, as well as his role as a benefactor, that 'in honour to his memory' his portrait was painted for his College, where it still hangs (see Figure 5).[40]

39. The second edition of *An Apologie* contained testimonials from, among others, Archbishop Ussher, the bishops of Hereford and Gloucester, the regius professor of medicine, and the professors of Hebrew and astronomy.
40. Wood, *Athenae*, iii. 256.

Almost as distinguished as Hakewill, though in rather different ways, and almost as close to Prideaux, was another fellow, Nathanael Carpenter. His distinction was measured both by his College activities and by his intellectual achievements. The son of an East Devon parson, Carpenter matriculated at St Edmund Hall in 1605 and was elected to an Exeter fellowship in 1607 at the early age of 18.[41] His later *cursus honorum* as an office holder was remarkable. He was sub-rector, and thus Prideaux's deputy, from 1618 to 1621 and again from 1624 to 1626, while he also acted as dean, effectively the director of the College's teaching, from 1614 to 1617 and from 1621 to 1623. With the exception of the year 1623–4, he thus held one or other of the College's two main offices from 1614 to 1626: an unequalled record. He was similarly prominent as a tutor. Between 1613 and 1626 he often had more pupils than any of his colleagues, while Prideaux's high opinion of him was shown by his being given charge of some of the illustrious foreigners who came to Exeter in these years, including James Dorville (whom Carpenter took over from Prideaux himself) and, in 1616, Sixtinus Amama.[42] In his day he was the College's leading man.

Prideaux would have thought him especially sound on religion. Carpenter was called by Wood 'a zealous Calvinist . . . by the generality of scholars cried up for a very famous preacher'. With this, predictably, went a virulent anti-Catholicism. The whole religion of the Roman church, he wrote in one of his sermons, was 'little other than a politike hypocrisie', and he went on to denounce 'Pelagius and his latter spawne the Iesuites and Arminians' for their belief in free will.[43] It was in keeping with these views that in 1616 he should have been chosen by Matthew Sutcliffe as a fellow of Sutcliffe's Chelsea College, along with three other Exonians, Prideaux, Matthias Styles, and Nathaniel Norrington: the largest contingent from any college. Dedicated to the production of anti-Catholic propaganda, the college provided an appropriate forum for this little band of Exonian Calvinists.[44] It was, too, Carpenter's Calvinistic zeal which led him to attach himself to Archbishop Ussher, whom he accompanied back to Ireland in 1626 as the archbishop's chaplain, there to act as a schoolmaster to the king's wards,

41. Ibid., ii. 421–2; J. Benedict, 'Carpenter, Nathanael (1598–1628), Church of England clergyman and philosopher', *ODNB*.
42. ECA, A.I.5, 250, 273, 274, 281; A.I., fos. 1r, 2r, 3r, 5v, 8r, 9r; H.II.11.
43. Wood, *Athenae*, ii. 422; N. Carpenter, *Achitophel, or The Picture of a wicked politician*, 2nd edn (1629), 12, 30.
44. Wood, *History*, ii. 324–5. For Chelsea College, see below, 186–8.

charged with converting the sons of Catholic parents into model Protestants. He died in Dublin, without apparently resigning his fellowship, in 1628.

Carpenter's reputation outside the College rested not so much on his religion as on his writings and the independent thinking which they embodied. His earliest work, *Philosophia Libera*, first published in Frankfurt in 1621 and followed by a new Oxford edition in 1622, was dedicated to James, marquis of Hamilton, then an undergraduate at Exeter, and had a preface addressed 'to the young men of the most flourishing university of Oxford'. It was in part a primer for students,[45] thus resembling several of Prideaux's works. Both men, experienced tutors that they were, had the needs of the young very much in mind. But Carpenter's book went well beyond the basic instruction which Prideaux's textbooks tended to provide. It constituted an attack on the blind acceptance of authority and in particular on the usual reverential and uncritical approach to Aristotle—a plea for philosophical freedom and for investigation, observation, and experiment, rather than servile submission to the ancients. Drawing on the teaching and practices of William Gilbert, the discoverer of magnetism, and probably of Francis Bacon, Carpenter thus made his own contribution to the development of scientific method in contemporary Oxford.[46] He also wrote more directly on a scientific subject in his treatise on optics, still in manuscript and still unstudied.[47]

Carpenter's *Philosophia Libera* was followed in 1625 by a much larger work, *Geography Delineated*. Dedicated to William Herbert, earl of Pembroke, this was a comprehensive survey of the earth, its features and characteristics, and its relation to the heavens, and, like his first book, it called once again for experiment and observation.[48] His remaining two works, *Achitophel, or the Picture of a Wicked Politician* (1627), and *Chorazin and Bethsaidas Woe*, published posthumously in 1633, were more conventional sermons, but ones distinguished by their almost Johnsonian sense of psychological penetration and by the occasional beauties of their prose: 'Our intellectuall gifts we commonly value above our morall vertues.' 'Seasonable and acceptable words . . . hang like apples of gold in pictures of silver.'

45. Cf. *HUO*, iv. 395.
46. The best account of Carpenter's work is Jones, *Ancients and Moderns*, 65–71, 288–9. See also *HUO*, iv. 388, 395, 118; and Tyacke, *Aspects of English Protestantism*, 248–9.
47. Bodl. MS University College 153; Feingold, *Mathematicians' Apprenticeship*, 74 and n. 89.
48. N. Carpenter, *Geography Delinated Forth in Two Bookes*, 2nd edn (Oxford, 1635). See Jones, *Ancients and Moderns*, 68–71; *HUO*, iv. 388, 395.

'Death is the common destinie of mankind; to feare or wish for death, is the mark of a coward and shame of a man. To end our course of life in a warm bed is natures tribute and the crown of silver haires.'[49]

Carpenter was much admired by his contemporaries, for his integrity as much as for his intellectual gifts and his scholarship. The anonymous 'N. H.' who wrote the preface to *Chorazin*, and who tells us that he was both Carpenter's pupil and a close relative, says of him that:

> hee was a microcosme, a little world within the hemisphere of this greater, that seemed for his naturall endowments of knowledge, reason, judgement, wise-dome, and all supernaturall gifts, to outstrip many of his equall-contemporaries and superiors both in age and place. He it was whom Oxford so much admired for industry, ingenuity, rationability, and judicious solidity in things pertaining to the liberall sciences.[50]

One personal quality which may have appealed to another fellow Devonian, the rector of his College, was Carpenter's pride in his county of origin. Towards the end of his *Geographie*, his demonstration that what he calls 'our mountainous provinces of Devon and Cornwall' was not to be censured for 'blockishnesse or incivility' becomes a peg on which to hang a long hymn of praise for 'mine own countrey of Devon' and its famous men: its seamen, its patrons of learning, its lawyers, and, of course, its divines. Singled out for special praise are Matthew Sutcliffe for his 'learned conflicts with our pernicious Romanists' and for his foundation of Chelsea College, and Prideaux himself, 'in whom the heroicall wits of Iewell, Rainolds, and Hooker, as united into one, seeme to triumph anew and threaten a fatall blow to the Babilonish Hierarchie'.[51]

Carpenter in many ways prefigures the later Oxbridge ideal: that of the scholar and man of learning who is also an outstanding tutor and, in his acceptance of administrative responsibilities, a good citizen. That he was also 'a meticulously businesslike person' was shown by the agreement which he made with the Oxford printer for the printing of his *Geographie* on very

---

49. Carpenter, *Achitophel*, 61–2; Carpenter, *Chorazin and Bethsaidas Woe* (1633), sig. B9r.
50. Carpenter, *Chorazin*, sig. A2v. 'N. H'. may well be Nathaniel Holmes, who took his BA at Exeter in 1620 and his BD in 1633, and later won fame as a 'severe Calvinist' and puritan divine: see Boase, *Commoners*, 162; Wood, *Athenae*, iii. 1168.
51. Carpenter, *Geographie Delineated*, 2nd edn (Oxford, 1635), 260–3. Cf. P. Slack, *The Invention of Improvement Information and Material Progress in Seventeenth-Century England* (Oxford, 2015), 37 n. 117.

favourable terms.[52] These were all qualities which would have commended him to Prideaux, who possessed them himself. Going beyond Prideaux in his capacity for independent and scientific thinking, he showed in his career that a rational and wide-ranging intellect was not at all incompatible with the rigid adherence to the Calvinist orthodoxy which again he shared with Prideaux.

The third of the Rector's leading colleagues, Matthias Styles, resembled Carpenter in his College activities and to some extent in his public reputation, but differed from him in his lack of publications and of any obvious aptitude for original scholarship. Born about 1591 into a Devon gentry family, Styles had a career at the College which largely ran in parallel with that of Carpenter. Matriculating in 1606, he was elected to a fellowship in 1610 and left the College in 1624 to become chaplain to Sir Isaac Wake, ambassador to Venice.[53] The two men were close to each other. According to 'N. H.' in his preface to Carpenter's *Chorazin*, Styles was 'the authors most indeared and intimate friend',[54] and for much of their time together at Exeter they divided the main College offices between them. When Carpenter was sub-rector from 1618 to 1621, Styles was dean; when Styles was sub-rector from 1621 to 1624, Carpenter was dean for the first two of those years. Like Carpenter too, Styles was a particularly busy tutor. From 1614 to 1624, he had numerous pupils, about fifteen to twenty in most years—figures rivalling those for Carpenter.[55] His holding university office as proctor in 1621–2, when he was also sub-rector, tends to confirm the capacity for administrative business of this reliable workhorse. He resigned his fellowship following his marriage in 1628.[56]

Since Styles wrote nothing, his religious position is less well evidenced than Carpenter's. But we need not doubt that he shared in the Calvinist assumptions and anti-Catholic fixations of both Carpenter and Prideaux. Their friendship was marked by Prideaux's gift to him in 1619 of a valuable book, an edition of the works of the early Christian apologist Lactantius

---

52. I. G. Philip, 'A Seventeenth-Century Agreement between Author and Printer', *Bodleian Library Record*, 10 (1978–82), 69.
53. Clark, *Register*, i. 289; Boase, *Register*, 94.
54. Carpenter, *Chorazin*, sig. A3r.
55. ECA, A.I.5, 281; A. I. 6, fos 1r, 2r, 3r, 5r, 6v, 8r; H II.11.
56. Boase, *Register*, 94.

published in Paris in 1525.[57] Nominated by Sutcliffe for a fellowship at Chelsea College in 1616, along with his friend Carpenter, as we have seen, he remained a fellow in 1629: proof enough of his longstanding anti-Catholic credentials.[58] He was described by 'N.H.' as 'that famous and learned divine', words justified by his BD in 1623, his DD in 1638, and his later membership of the Westminster Assembly of 1643, which marked him out as an anti-Laudian reformer. By that time he held several livings in and around London. Wood calls him 'an eminent minister in London, an excellent grammarian and casuist [an expert in cases of conscience and moral conduct]'.[59] In his younger days he would have fitted perfectly into the religious milieu of his College.

The fourth among this select group of Prideaux's special colleagues, Henry Tozer, was the leading College figure in the second half of Prideaux's rectorship, as Carpenter had been in the first. Born in 1602 at North Tawton in mid-Devon, he matriculated at Exeter in 1621 as a plebeian and took his BA in 1623, when he was also elected to a fellowship. He held his fellowship until 1648, a twenty-five year span exceeded by only two other fellows in the first half of the seventeenth century.[60] Tozer's distinctiveness partly lay in his consistently high place in the College hierarchy. He was sub-rector in 1630–1, 1636–8, 1642–4 and 1646–8, presiding over the College for most of the difficult Civil War period following Prideaux's departure, when his successor as rector, George Hakewill, was largely absent. He was also dean in 1629–30. But it was as one of the College's two bursars that Tozer was most prominent. He was joint bursar from 1632 to 1636, 1638 to 1639, 1641 to 1642, and 1644 to 1646.[61] That he had a good head for business and a zest for efficient management was confirmed by his compilation of the still surviving *Liber Bursariatus*, 'Directions for the Bursar and Butler', in 1636: an invaluably detailed account of the College's domestic organization and accounting procedures, covering everything from the proper keeping of the

---

57. *Divina Opera L. Coelii Lactantii Firmiani Divinarum Institutionum libri vii*, now Beinecke Library, Yale, Me 35 L120 525, inscribed by Styles 'Matthias Stile. Ex dono clarissimi viri Johannis Prideauxii Collegii Exon Rectoris et vicecancellarii dignissimi. Septemb 20. 1619'.

58. Wood, *History*, ii. 324–5.

59. Boase, *Register*, 94; Wood, *Fasti*, i. 502.

60. Wood, *Athenae*, iii. 273; Prince, *Worthies of Devon*, 737; Boase, *Register*, 99; V. Larminie, 'Tozer, Henry (c.1601–50), Church of England clergyman', *ODNB*.

61. ECA, A.I.6, fos 14r, 16r, 18r, 19r, 19v, 20v, 21r, 22v, 25r, 25v, 26v, 27r, 34v, 36r, 38v, 39v. For Tozer's activities in the 1640s, see *Register of the Visitors*, ed. Burrows, lxxv, cx–cxi, 13–14, 60, 91, 113, 115, 137–8, 211, 217, and *HUO*, iv.728, 760.

buttery books to the fellows' special menu—roast beef—on 'Powder-treason day', 5 November.[62] Supremely practical and competent, for long periods, and especially in the rudderless mid-1640s, he held the College together.

Like our other fellows who were virtuoso administrators, Tozer was also an outstanding tutor and teacher. According to Wood, he was 'a useful and necessary person in the society to which he belonged by moderating in the hall, reading to the novices [i.e. tutoring undergraduates], and lecturing in the chapel'.[63] His busy career as a College officer did not obviously reduce the time which he gave to teaching. From 1626 onwards he had consistently high numbers of pupils, in 1629–30 more than any other fellow.[64] As a tutor he had a particular predilection for—or perhaps Prideaux was particularly inclined to send him—the sons of the aristocracy. His first book, *Directions for a Godly Life* (1628) was dedicated to his (far from satisfactory) pupil, Lorenzo Cary, son of Viscount Falkland, and a later work, *Christus* (1634), to Charles and Philip Herbert, current undergraduates and sons of the earl of Pembroke.[65] Two further works, one dedicated to a former pupil, Sir Walter Pye of Herefordshire, and another to Robert Ker, earl of Ancrum (never an Exeter man) are suggestive of a further range of high-ranking contacts, not all of them confined to the College.[66]

For a fellow of Calvinist Exeter, Tozer's religious opinions were conventional enough. Wood calls him 'a most precise puritan in his looks and life', and the town lectureship which he held at St Martin's church in Oxford marks him out as a puritan sympathizer. But, given the large overlap between the views of middle-of-the-road Anglican Calvinists and those of the puritans—for example, on the virtues of evangelical preaching—it is probable that Tozer was no more puritan than Prideaux. His four published works (two sermons and two devotional tracts) were uncontroversial.[67]

62. ECA, A.IV.11.
63. Wood, *Athenae*, iii. 273.
64. ECA, H.II.11; A.I.22.
65. H. Tozer, *Directions for a Godly Life: Especially for Communicating at the Lord's Table* (Oxford, 1628); Tozer, *Christus: sive dicta et facta Christi* (Oxford, 1634). The first of these works was in its tenth edition by 1680: Madan, i. 141. For Lorenzo Cary's failings, see above, 101–2.
66. H. Tozer, *A Christian Amendment Delivered in a Sermon on New-Yeares Day 1631 in St Martin's Church in Oxford* (Oxford, 1633); Tozer, *Christian Wisedome, or the Excellency, Formes and Right Meanes of True Wisdom* (Oxford, 1639).
67. Larminie, 'Tozer'.

Prideaux's links with Tozer did not end with the rector's resignation and departure from the College. In 1649 Prideaux published his *Fasciculus Controversiarum Theologicarum*, a theological compendium of basic instruction. By this time stripped of his see, he returned to Oxford both for the book's writing and publication and probably also to draw on the assistance of Henry Tozer, deprived of his fellowship by the parliamentary visitors but allowed to keep his rooms in College. In the introduction to what was to be the last book published in his lifetime, Prideaux expressed his appreciation of 'the fidelity, erudition and industry' of his friend, 'always a very dear son to me', who had lent him books from his library and compiled the indices to Prideaux's own book.[68] It was the swansong to a relationship stretching back over more than twenty years. Prideaux died on 29 July 1650. Tozer left Oxford in 1648 or 1649 to become minister to the company of Merchant Venturers at Rotterdam. There he died on 11 September 1650, less than two months after Prideaux. In his will he remembered two fellow Exonians, William Standard, a fellow from 1644, and John Hitchens, a poor scholar who had probably been Tozer's pupil. To each he bequeathed books, with the residue of the books and goods in his College rooms going to the rector and fellows.[69] Dying in exile and, like Prideaux, a casualty of the Civil War, he did not forget his College.

The fifth member of this group, William Hodges, was Prideaux's favourite as much as his colleague. By comparison with the preceding four, Hodges held his fellowship only for a short time, from 1628 to 1634, but during these few years he became closer to Prideaux and his family than any other fellow. Coming from Slapton, on the South Devon coast, Hodges had matriculated in 1625, aged 20, not at Exeter but at Hart Hall. He was elected to a fellowship at Exeter within eighteen months of taking his BA in 1627 and soon established himself in the College hierarchy.[70] Bursar in 1630–1 and again in1632–3, he was dean in the intervening year, and throughout these early years he also served as a hard-working tutor, in most terms with twelve to twenty pupils, well above the average for a fellow.[71] These were the usual marks of Prideaux's patronage. But in Hodges's case they were not the greatest or the most significant. On 22

---

68. J. Prideaux, *Fasciculus Controversiarum Theologicarum ad Juniorum Captum* (Oxford, 1649), sig. ¶¶2r.
69. TNA, PROB 11/215/64; Larminie, ' Tozer'.
70. Boase, *Register*, 101.
71. ECA, A.I.6, fos 14r, 15r, 15v; H.II.11.

June 1634 he married Sarah, the elder of Prideaux's two surviving daughters, then aged 14½; on 30 June he resigned his fellowship; and in the following month he was put into the vicarage at Bampton, held by Prideaux since 1614 and now vacated by him in Hodges's favour. William and Sarah went on to have twelve children before Sarah's death in 1652 and to continue to benefit from their influential connection during Prideaux's time as bishop of Worcester in the 1640s.[72]

The qualities which drew Prideaux to Hodges, besides his capabilities as administrator and tutor, are beyond recovery. He had scholarly aspirations, returning to Oxford to take his BD in 1640 and his DD in 1661; yet he wrote nothing. His Calvinistic preaching landed him in serious trouble in 1631, when one of his sermons touched on forbidden themes, which resulted in censure from the king himself and the threat of his dismissal from the university.[73] But the personal traits which marked out this particular fellow as a suitable son-in-law for the head of his College remain elusive.

The two final members of this inner circle among Prideaux's colleagues, Laurence Bodley and John Conant, may be treated more briefly. Bodley, College chaplain and fellow from 1614 to 1632, and son of John Peryam's cousin, Miles Bodley, was clearly a man of supreme competence and some considerable moral weight. That at one time or another he held all the major College offices (bursar, 1624–6, 1628–9; sub-rector, 1626–7, 1629–30; dean, 1627–8) and that he was allocated an exceptionally large number of pupils, in some terms in 1620, 1621, 1626, and 1627, more than any other tutor, were both marks of Prideaux's regard for him.[74] His anxiety to see the Exeter city lectureship founded by his uncle and namesake, the canon of Exeter who was Prideaux's early patron, filled by 'a preacher whose piety and zeale shall hold pace with his learning and science' and his place in the family and religious circle of John Peryam were twin guarantees of the evangelical credentials which would also have commended him.[75] He died in 1634 as rector of the Devonshire living of Shobrooke, his character sketched in the funeral sermon preached by a neighbouring parish priest:

> I need not tell you who or what he was; you all have known't in part, though best the University, where the glasse of his better time was most runne out, and

72. Butcher, 'Prideaux', 10; Wood, *Fasti*, iv.261; Boase, *Register*, 101; below, 356–7.
73. Below, 263, 266–7.
74. ECA, A.I. 6, fos. 8r, 9r, 11r, 11v, 12v; H.II.11.
75. HMC, *City of Exeter*, 98; above, 125–6.

where as a noted pattern of much worth and good, he shined as another moone amid other luminaries . . . piety, learning, liberality, a sweet lovingness of disposition towards every man, concurr'd all in him their centre . . . Gods church in him hath lost a good minister, this parish a good pastor, his wife a good husband, schollers a good patron, the poore a good friend, and we all a good neighbour.[76]

As with all funeral sermons, the usual caveats apply. But one of Bodley's most obvious qualities and one which would have counted for much with Prideaux was surely his example as 'a noted pattern of much worth and good'. In the end the two men fell out in a bitter dispute.[77] But for almost all Bodley's years as a fellow, they appear to have lived on the best of terms.

John Conant owed his place in Prideaux's circle to rather different qualities. Born at Yettington in south-east Devon, an undergraduate pupil of Laurence Bodley, a fellow of the College from 1632 to 1647, and later rector, Conant was, like Bodley, a highly successful tutor, but, unlike Bodley, only an occasional office holder. Of the major College offices, he held only the deanship, and that for a single year in 1641–2.[78] It was primarily his prowess as a scholar and disputant, as well as his moral rectitude, which appealed to Prideaux—'who, by an allusion to his name (*Conanti nihil difficile*) signified the good opinions he had of his parts and industry'.[79] He was particularly assiduous in his study of the Semitic languages, knowledge of which was essential for scholarly work on the Bible; and his linguistic skills are likely to have contributed to his nomination as regius professor of divinity, Prideaux's former post, in 1654. In religion he was anti-Catholic, a more moderate Calvinist than some of his Exeter contemporaries, and a particularly conscientious and frequent preacher.[80]

A survey of Prideaux's closest colleagues throws light on his own character in showing the qualities which he most valued in others. Besides the Calvinistic and anti-Catholic convictions shared by all six of those identified here, the one factor which all had in common came from accidents of birth: all were born and bred in Devon. Given that Devonians formed the largest single group among the fellows, there was perhaps nothing surprising in this.

76. R. Peck, *Christs Watch-word* (1635), 1.
77. Below, 260–2.
78. Conant, *Life of Conant*, 1–4; ECA, A.I.6, fo. 25v.
79. Conant, *Life of Conant*, 4. 'Conanti nihil difficile' translates as 'To him who tries/Conant, nothing is difficult': a typical Prideaux pun.
80. Conant, *Life of Conant*, 5–21; D. D. Wallace, jun. 'Conant, John (1608–1694), college head', *ODNB*.

Even so, Prideaux's own strong Devonian allegiances may have led him to look especially favourably on those who came from his own county. More material was the prominent role of the majority of the six as office holders and tutors, in most cases combining the two roles. Service to the College was both a mark of and a way to Prideaux's approbation. Distinction in scholarship and learning might also do much to earn his respect, as in the cases of Hakewill, Carpenter, and, particularly perhaps, Conant. This was, after all, the defining mark of his own reputation. But beyond these measurable assets and virtues there must have been others less tangible and now irrecoverable: good humour, unselfishness, charm of manner, grace of personality, and all that went to make up attractiveness of character. We get a hint of the possible importance of these qualities in the funeral sermon for Laurence Bodley. The odd man out among our six was William Hodges, from 1634 Prideaux's son-in-law. Was it these characteristics, among others, which gave this this relatively undistinguished fellow a place both in Prideaux's family circle and in the inner circle of his colleagues?

3. Allies

We may guess that a large sector of Prideaux's circle comprised his fellow clergy within the Church of England; yet his links with these men are surprisingly difficult to trace. Lacking extensive letter collections, we cannot easily identify those with whom he had most to do or distinguish friends from mere contacts. Hence it is best to speak of allies: those with whom he shared a common point of view, who came together in mutual support during times of tension, such as that following Richard Montagu's publications,[81] and who may in some cases have been on closer terms with him than the evidence reveals. Almost all who fell into this category were, predictably, senior Calvinist divines, men in varying degrees vigorously opposed both to Catholics and to radical puritans, as was Prideaux. Until about 1630 they represented the dominant group within the church. Yet even the group's most prominent members hardly seem to have been particularly close to the scholar who was the Church of England's leading Calvinist theologian.

A case in point is George Abbot, archbishop of Canterbury from 1611 to 1633. Abbot has been accurately described as 'an evangelical Calvinist,

---

81. For Montagu and the controversy which his publications provoked, see below, 231–9.

embracing the doctrine of double predestination and implacably opposed to the teachings and practices of the Roman church'. Exactly the same was true of Prideaux. Like Prideaux too, Abbot was both an expert theologian who had gained his DD in 1597 and no mean controversialist. Prideaux may have attended his lectures in the 1590s, when the future rector was an undergraduate and the future archbishop a fellow of Balliol, and is likely to have come to know him better between 1600 and 1611, when Prideaux was a young don and Abbot the master of University College.[82] Abbot's respect for Prideaux had been shown in 1613, when archbishop and king jointly appointed Prideaux to answer Eudaemon-Joannes's scandalous tract attacking Casaubon and defending a renegade Catholic priest. Prideaux's response, published in 1614, was prefaced by a dedicatory letter to Abbot, 'the ornament and stay of church and state, protector and glory of our university of Oxford'.[83] But after that the trail of connections disappears. It was Hakewill rather than Prideaux whom Abbot wished to propose as a delegate to the Synod of Dort,[84] and although we can assume that Prideaux and Abbot were very much in sympathy—both, for example, opposed the Spanish Match—we lack any proof of regular contact between them.

James Ussher was another kindred spirit, but one whose connections with Prideaux, though only patchily evidenced, are more visible in the sources than those of Abbot. Born in Ireland in 1581, educated at Trinity College Dublin, and from 1625 archbishop of Armagh and primate of Ireland, Ussher had become by his later years the most learned Briton of his age, with a scholarly range, 'spanning the Bible, theology, patristics, Irish history, ancient history, ancient languages, chronology and the calendar', a good deal wider even than that of Prideaux.[85] From about 1606 the young Ussher paid regular visits to England to make use of the libraries of the two universities and, in London, that of Sir Robert Cotton,[86] and it was on one of the visits that he was introduced to the young Prideaux. The two men had certainly met by December 1612, when Ussher mentioned in a letter his conversation with Prideaux about an Exeter graduate in whom

82. K. Fincham, 'Abbot, George (1562–1633), archbishop of Canterbury', *ODNB*.
83. Above, 36; Casaubon, *Correspondence*, iii. 416; Prideaux, *Castigatio*, sig. ¶2r–¶4r.
84. *British Delegation*, ed. Milton, xxviii n. 44, 371; above, 50.
85. A. Ford, 'Ussher, James (1581–1656), Church of Ireland archbishop of Armagh and scholar', *ODNB*.
86. A. Ford, *James Ussher: Theology, History and Politics in Early-Modern Ireland and England* (Oxford, 2007), 33, 104.

Ussher had an interest.[87] Besides scholarship and learning, common religious opinions provided the main grounds of their association. Like Prideaux (and like Abbot), Ussher was a thoroughgoing Calvinist, fiercely anti-Catholic, a believer in the Pope as Antichrist, an opponent of Laud and the Arminians in the 1630s, and in politics an episcopalian royalist. 'All through the rule of Laud, the frustrated defenders of Elizabethan Protestantism—Dr Prideaux in Oxford, Dr Ward in Cambridge, and their pupils throughout England—had seen him as their spiritual leader.'[88]

Yet for all that they had in common, Prideaux and Ussher seem to have been in contact only very intermittently. The modern edition of Ussher's correspondence contains no letters from Ussher to Prideaux and only one from Prideaux to Ussher. That one, however, implies more about their relationship than is superficially apparent.[89] Writing in August 1638, Prideaux welcomed the news conveyed in Ussher's recent letters of the impending publication of his 'Ecclesiastical Antiquities' (the *Brittanicarum Ecclesiarum Antiquitates,* which was perhaps Ussher's greatest scholarly achievement); advised that 'our Oxford presses' were unsuitable for Ussher's forthcoming edition of 'Ignatius'[90]; said that he regarded it as a favour that Ussher intended to send 'your kinsman' to Exeter; passed comment on the frequent failings of young tutors; and undertook to tutor the archbishop's candidate himself, along with Prideaux's other noble pupils, including the son of the Irish peer Lord Caulfield. The tone of the letter is informal, familiar, almost chatty, and suggests a more engaged and intimate relationship than the otherwise meagre sources reveal.

Ussher's contacts appear to have been as much with Prideaux's College as with Prideaux himself. Two fellows left Exeter to become his chaplains. Nathanael Carpenter (fellow, 1607–28) accompanied him back to Ireland in 1626, while Richard Parr (fellow, 1642–49) served as his chaplain during Ussher's final years in England and became his eventual biographer.[91] With

87. Ussher, *Correspondence*, i. 90–1.
88. Ford, 'Ussher'; H. Trevor-Roper, 'James Ussher, Archbishop of Armagh', in his *Catholics, Anglicans and Puritans* (1987), 148–9.
89. The letter was first published in R. Parr, *The Life of the Most Reverend Father in God, James Ussher Late Lord-Archbishop of Armagh* (1686), 398–9, and thence in Boase, *Register*, ciii; see now Ussher, *Correspondence*, ii. 743–4. Parr, followed by Boase, misdated it to 1628, but Boran, in her edition of the *Correspondence*, correctly dates it to 1638.
90. This refers to Ussher's edition of the writings of Polycarp and of Ignatius of Antioch published at Oxford in 1644: see Madan, ii. 363–5.
91. Benedict, 'Carpenter'; A. Ford, 'Parr, Richard (1616/17–1691), Church of England clergyman', *ODNB*.

one other Exonian, George Hakewill, Ussher had similar links. In 1628 Hakewill wrote to Ussher to thank him for placing a young Irishman, James Dillon, under his charge, and to say that he had appointed Laurence Bodley as his tutor.[92] Two years later, in 1630, Ussher headed the list of those contributing their commendations to the second edition of Hakewill's *An Apologie of the Power and Providence of God*, additionally thanking Hakewill 'for the many cortesies I received from you at Oxford'.[93] Known to several of the fellows as well as to Prideaux, Ussher appears to have been a relatively frequent visitor to the College. Leaving Ireland for England in 1640, permanently as it turned out, and joining the royalists in 1642, he took up residence at Prideaux's invitation in the rector's house adjacent to the College so as to pursue his studies in the Bodleian, Prideaux himself by this time having left Oxford for his Worcester see. On at least one occasion during his stay he preached in the College chapel. All this was justification enough for Parr's description of Prideaux as Ussher's 'good friend'.[94]

Any sympathies between Prideaux and Ussher are likely to have been strengthened during the 1630s by the dominance of Laud. When, in his letter of 1638 to Ussher, Prideaux wrote that Ussher's forthcoming work on 'Ecclesiastical Antiquities' would 'put a period, I trust, to the troublesome fancies which of late have been set on foot', it was probably the 'fancies' of Laud and his followers that he had in mind; here, more especially, their views on the debt of the early English church to Rome rather than to indigenous British Christianity.[95] In the same camp was another prelate familiar to Prideaux, Joseph Hall. A graduate of Emmanuel College, Cambridge, Hall gained his DD in 1610, by which time he had become a chaplain in the staunchly Protestant circle which formed Prince Henry's household. This is the most likely setting for his introduction to Prideaux, his fellow chaplain.[96] But the two men were also part of another overlapping circle, that of the Calvinist enthusiasts who looked to William Herbert, earl of Pembroke, for patronage and for political leadership in the anti-Catholic and anti-Spanish cause. Prideaux's links with the two Herberts have already been touched on, and Hall too belonged to the same connection, dedicating

92. Boase, *Register*, cii; Ussher, *Correspondence*, ii. 437.
93. Ussher, *Correspondence*, ii. 541–2.
94. Parr, *Life of Ussher*, 48.
95. Trevor-Roper, 'James Ussher', 147.
96. R. A. McCabe, 'Hall, Joseph (1574–1656), bishop of Norwich, religious writer and satirist', *ODNB*; Cranfield, 'Chaplains in Ordinary at the Early Stuart Court', 142.

(for example) his 1623 sermon 'The Best Bargain' to William Herbert, 'the great patron of learning, the sincere friend of religion and rich purchaser of truth'.[97]

Although Hall was 'rabidly anti-Catholic',[98] his Calvinism generally was of a more moderate and conciliatory kind than Prideaux's. Yet their views on many current topics coincided. It was hardly surprising that both were opposed to the Spanish Match, an abomination to all right-thinking Protestants, and both too set themselves against Richard Montagu in the storm which followed the publication of his two books in 1624–5. Hall, ever the eirenicist, veered towards the middle ground in his assessment of Montagu's case, but both he and Prideaux were thought by Montagu to have been responsible for his being called to answer before Parliament. If this was so (and it seems quite likely), it would have been the first known instance of cooperation between the two men.[99]

Hall was consecrated as bishop of Exeter in 1627: a promotion which he may well have owed to Pembroke's influence and a position for which Prideaux himself had been a fancied candidate.[100] His new office made him the College visitor, with ultimate jurisdiction over its affairs. In general, Hall seems to have been benevolently non-interventionist; and if his one known instance of decisive intervention worked very much to Prideaux's disadvantage, he could hardly have acted otherwise, so clearly in this case was Prideaux in the wrong.[101] There is much to suggest a warm relationship between the two men in Hall's episcopal years. Shortly after becoming bishop he published *The Olde Religion* (1628), in which he asserted, rather injudiciously, that Rome was 'a true visible church', meaning that it held to the essentials of Christian belief, even though it was full of error and corruption. Such was the offence which this caused to 'radical protestant opinion' that Hall had to issue an apology and explanation, *The Reconciler*

---

97. *The Works of the Right Reverend Joseph Hall*, ed. P. Wynter, 10 vols. (1863), v. 150; O'Farrell *Shakespeare's Patron*, 88–9, 93; P. Lake, 'The Moderate and Irenic Case for Religious War: Joseph Hall's *Via Media* in Context', in S. D. Amussen and M. A. Kishlansky (eds.), *Political Culture and Cultural Politics in Early Modern Europe: Essays Presented to David Underdown*, (Manchester, 1995), 78.

98. Lake, 'The Moderate and Irenic Case', 62.

99. Ibid., 70–7; Tyacke, *Anti-Calvinists*, 148–9, 212; McCabe, ' Hall', *ODNB*; *The Correspondence of John Cosin, D.D.*, ed. G. Ornsby 2 vols. (Surtees Soc., 52, 55, 1868–72), i 50.

100. Tyacke, *Anti-Calvinists*, 168; O'Farrell, *Shakespeare's Patron*, 179; R. Cust, *The Forced Loan and English Politics, 1626–1628* (Oxford, 1987), 74; *Cosin Correspondence*, ed. Ornsby, i. 98, 100.

101. Below, 261–2.

(1629), which received supporting testimony from four Protestant divines, including Prideaux.[102] Hall approached Prideaux with humility and deference:

> All our little world here takes notice of your worth and eminency, who have long furnished the divinity chair in that famous university with mutual grace and honour . . . I suffer, and the church is disquieted: your learning and gravity will be ready to contribute to a seasonable pacification.

Prideaux replied with warmth and generosity in Hall's support: 'For who perceives not, that your lordship leaves no more to Rome than our best divines ever since the Reformation have granted?'[103] In aligning himself with Hall, and against Hall's conservative critics with whom he might have been expected to side, Prideaux showed his respect for one who might be regarded both as an ally and a friend.

By this time another connection had been established. In 1628 Hall's third son, George, entered the College. Taking his BA in 1631, he was elected to a fellowship in the following year, holding it until 1638. Eventually, in 1662, he became bishop of Chester and later by his will a generous benefactor to his old College.[104] George was followed to Exeter by Hall's fourth son, Samuel, who matriculated in 1631 and held a fellowship from 1634 to 1639; by his fifth son, John, a commoner from May 1635 to December 1636; and by his sixth son, Edward, who matriculated in 1635, with his brother John, and held a fellowship from 1638 until his death in 1642.[105] As with Philip Herbert, whose three sons were also at Exeter in the 1630s, so, with Joseph Hall, the dispatch of sons to Exeter was a mark of confidence in Prideaux, his College, and the continuing cultivation there of Calvinistic Anglicanism in a local and national world which the Arminians seemed set to dominate. The further election of three of Hall's sons to fellowships probably marked not only a wish to accommodate the College's visitor but also a real and continuing bond of sympathy between rector and bishop.

Prideaux's relations with another fellow Calvinist and anti-Laudian, Daniel Featley, are equally difficult to trace in any continuous way. Featley's early career ran in parallel to that of Prideaux. Coming from a humble

---

102. Milton, *Catholic and Reformed*, 141–6; Lake, 'The Moderate and Irenic Case', 58–9.
103. *Works of Hall*, ed. Wynter, viii. 743–5.
104. Boase, *Register*, 102–3; J. D. Ramsbottom, 'Hall, George (bap.1613, d.1668), bishop of Chester', *ODNB*.
105. Boase, *Register*, 103, 105; Boase, *Commoners*, 136.

background (his father was a college servant at Magdalen), he entered
Corpus Christi College, Oxford, in 1594, graduated BA in 1601, and was
elected to a probationer fellowship at Corpus in 1602, a year after Prideaux's
election to a fellowship at Exeter. Thereafter their paths diverged. In 1610
Featley became household chaplain to Sir Thomas Edmondes, the English
ambassador in Paris, before returning to Oxford to take his BD in 1613.
Although Prideaux and Featley may have known each other when they
were young fellows of their respective colleges, their first recorded encounter came in 1617, the year in which Featley gave up a remote Cornish living
to become one of Archbishop Abbot's chaplains (proof enough of his
Calvinist credentials). We shall see later how, during Featley's exercises for
his doctorate in that year, he came under attack from Prideaux, then
moderating as regius professor.[106]

This quarrel was composed by Abbot, and from then on Prideaux and
Featley were invariably on the same side. Like Prideaux, Featley was a
vigorous controversialist in the anti-Catholic and anti-Arminian cause.
One of his many publications, Clavis mystica (1636), a sermon collection,
was censored by Laud's chaplain, who removed the passages directed against
papists, Jesuits, and Arminians. Like Prideaux too, Featley was an exceptionally learned and skilful theologian who won the respect of the reformed
churchmen and scholars of France and the Netherlands.[107] In 1624–5 these
qualities brought the two men together against Montagu, who suspected
that Prideaux and 'that urchin' Featley had joined forces against him and
who, in a letter of May 1625, denounced Prideaux as 'this patron of
Featley'.[108] One final point of contact lay in the respect and admiration of
both men for William Herbert, to whom Featley dedicated his Grand
Sacrilege of the Church of Rome. 'The crown of your glory and our ioyes',
wrote Featley, was 'the safe custodie of that pretious depositum of saving
truth, no way clipt by schisme, nor adulterated by popish heresie, nor
embased by any semipelagian alloy,'[109] Prideaux's view of Pembroke
would have been the same.

106. A. Hunt, 'Featley [Fairclough], Daniel (1582–1645), Church of England clergyman and
religious controversialist', ODNB; J. Featley, Featlaei Paliggenesia (1660), 8–9; Wood, Athenae,
iii. 158; below, 245. For Edmondes, Pruideaux's patron, see above, 77.
107. Hunt, 'Featley'.
108. Cosin Correspondence, ed. Ornsby, i. 22, 34, 50, 69.
109. D. Featley, The Grand Sacrilege of the Church of Rome (1630), sig. A3r–v; Tyacke, Anti-
Calvinists, 79.

Two letters from Featley to Prideaux, dating from 1628–9, point to a closer relationship than that stemming merely from membership of the same group. In the first, evidently written during the controversy sparked by the publication of Hall's *Olde Religion*, with its assertion that Rome was in some sense a true church, Featley begged Prideaux not to go too far in support of Hall: 'I entreat you to be carefull so to state the question that the Romanists take no advantage.'[110] In the second, more gossipy letter, he wrote to Prideaux about a possible attempt to secure the election of the Arminian and anti-Calvinist Thomas Jackson as president of Corpus Christi, Featley's own college, and ultimately his possible nomination as regius professor of divinity, 'there to spawne yong Arminians', if Prideaux could be removed by preferment, presumably to a bishopric. In this second letter Featley also spoke of 'my love to you my most honoured father' and signed himself 'your affectionate sonne'.[111] Not much can be built on the terms of address in seventeenth-century letters. Nevertheless, Featley's words suggest a closer connection, one of friendship as much as of mere alliance, than the scanty evidence directly reveals.

The career and aspirations of one other ally, Matthew Sutcliffe, intersected with those of both Prideaux and Featley. Sutcliffe was by some way the oldest member of this circle. Born about 1549, he had graduated from Trinity College, Cambridge, in 1568, gone on to take a doctorate in law, and held a number of administrative posts in West Country dioceses before becoming dean of Exeter in 1588. This cathedral office he held until his death in 1629.[112] His early writings were chiefly aimed at the radical puritan supporters of Presbyterianism, but the main thrust of his theological animus soon came to be directed against the Catholics and those whom he regarded as their halfway associates, the Arminians. Of all those in Prideaux's clerical circle, Sutcliffe was the most virulently anti-Catholic, even arguing in one of his tracts that it was better to be a Turk than a papist.[113] His will, made in 1628, contained an extraordinary opening diatribe against both Catholics

---

110. Bodl. MS Rawl. D. 47, fo. 15v; Milton, *Catholic and Reformed*, 142–3. Both this and the following letter appear to be drafts.

111. Bodl. MS Rawl. 47, fo. 16r; A. J. Hegarty, 'Jackson, Thomas (bap.1578, d.1640), dean of Peterborough', *ODNB*; T. Charles-Edwards and J. Reid, *Corpus Christi College, Oxford: A History* (Oxford, 2017), 160–6.

112. N. W. S. Cranfield, ' Sutcliffe, Matthew (1549/50–1629), dean of Exeter'; *ODNB*; CCEd, Person ID 66203.

113. Ibid.; Milton, *Catholic and Reformed*, 33, 52, 56, 58, 63 n. 101, 115 n. 72, 122–3; Tyacke, *Anti-Calvinists*, 215.

and Arminians, 'those false teachers alsoe among us that palliate popish heresies, and under the name of Arminius, seeke to bringe in poperie'. His main practical efforts against both papists and neo-papists were vested in his foundation of Chelsea College in 1610: a London-based institution, strongly supported by James I and staffed by a provost and twenty fellows, who were intended to use their time in writing in defence of the Church of England and against the Church of Rome—or, as Sutcliffe put it in his will, 'for the maintenance of the true Catholike, Apostolicke and Christian faith' and 'against the pedantry, sophistrie and novelties of the Jesuits and other the pope's factors and followers'.[114] It was hardly surprising that, holding these views, Sutcliffe should have opposed the Spanish Match, for which he earned himself a few months imprisonment in 1621, or that he should have been one of the many orthodox churchmen who went into print to denounce Montagu's writings in the mid-1620s.[115]

As dean of Exeter, the cathedral of Prideaux's home diocese and one historically associated with his College, Sutcliffe must have been known to Prideaux from an early stage in the latter's career. The first evidence of their connection comes in a letter of February 1610 from Sutcliffe to that other Protestant zealot, Thomas James, Bodley's Librarian: 'Commend me to Mr Prideaux and Mr Hakwill of Exeter College', wrote Sutcliffe to James. 'I would have written to them but that I hope to doe it shortlie to good purpose.'[116] Clearly the two men were already on familiar terms, perhaps brought together by regional ties as well as by religious sympathies. But it is only many years later, towards the end of Sutcliffe's life, that we find proof of their closeness. By 1629, and probably earlier, Prideaux was a fellow of Sutcliffe's college at Chelsea, a position to which he had been nominated by Sutcliffe himself.[117] More indicative of their relationship, however, were the arrangements set out in Sutcliffe's will for the transmission of his property. Under the terms of the will Sutcliffe's extensive lands in Devonshire—rich

114. D. E. Kennedy, 'King James I's College of Controversial Divinity at Chelsea', in D. E. Kennedy (ed.), *Grounds of Controversy: Three Studies in Late 16th and Early 17th Century English Polemics* (Melbourne, 1989), 97–126; McCullough, *Sermons at Court*, 187. For Sutcliffe's will, see F. B. [Rose-]Troup, 'Biographical Notices on Doctor Matthew Sutcliffe, Dean of Exeter, 1588–1629', *Trans. Devon Assoc.*, 23 (1891), 186–9.

115. Cranfield, 'Sutcliffe'.

116. *Letters Addressed to Thomas James, First Keeper of Bodley's Library*, ed. G. W. Wheeler (Oxford, 1933), 55.

117. T. Faulkner, *An Historical and Descriptive Account of the Royal Hospital, and the Royal Military Asylum, at Chelsea* (1805), 31. For the right of the provost, in this case Sutcliffe, to nominate the fellows, see Bodl. MS Tanner 142, fo. 54v.

man that he obviously was—were left for the support of his college, and two trustees, named by Sutcliffe as Dr John Prideaux and Dr Thomas Clifford, an Exeter graduate and canon of Sutcliffe's cathedral, were appointed to put this disposition into effect.[118] Prideaux's nomination is evidence enough of Sutcliffe's confidence in him both as a man of business and as a responsible and reliable friend.

The administration of the will did not go smoothly. On Sutcliffe's death Daniel Featley was appointed as provost of Chelsea College on Sutcliffe's prior recommendation, but the provisions of the will in the college's favour were immediately challenged by Sutcliffe's family, and in 1630, after a law suit in chancery, Prideaux and Featley, now acting as joint trustees, were forced to accept £340 for the college in lieu of what was obviously a much more valuable collection of properties. The college was declining financially well before this, and its poverty was among the factors which led to its final demise in the mid-1640s. Sutcliffe had set aside a separate parcel of properties to be divided between his grandchildren and Exeter College if Chelsea College should fail. A striking indication of his interest in Prideaux's College, otherwise unevidenced, this provision bore no fruit, and neither property nor money came the College's way.[119]

Prideaux's dealings with Sutcliffe illustrate some of the difficulties in coming to conclusions about his circle of friends and allies and in judging the quality and closeness of his relations with its members. Between Sutcliffe's cheerful injunction to Thomas James to commend him to Prideaux and Hakewill in 1610 and Prideaux's appearance as Sutcliffe's trustee in 1628 we have no information whatever about their contacts or links. Yet Prideaux's role as a trustee suggest that the two men knew each other well—well enough at least for Sutcliffe's to have a high regard for Prideaux's probity and abilities. Given the common ground which they shared, in opposition to Catholics and Arminians, in their objections to the views of Richard Montagu, and in their comparable activities as scholars in defence of traditional Anglicanism, their coming together, whether in visits or in correspondence, would hardly have been surprising. Nothing of this survives. There may be a richer world of relationships here than our exiguous sources reveal.

118. [Rose-]Troup, 'Biographical Notices', 182–3; Boase, *Commoners*, 63.
119. [Rose-]Troup, 'Biographical Notices', 182–3, 195; Faulkner, *An Historical and Descriptive Account*, 34–41; Kennedy, 'King James I's College', 114, 118; Bodl. MS Tanner 142, fo. 53v.

Abbot, Ussher, Hall, Featley, Sutcliffe: these men, Prideaux's associates and occasional correspondents, had some obvious characteristics in common. All were Calvinists, representatives of the mainstream beliefs of the Church of England and of the Protestant faith as it had taken shape under Elizabeth. It followed that all were anti-Catholic and anti-Arminian, and opposed to the more liberal Anglicanism which they saw as veering towards Rome and which was developing under Laud's guidance in the years around 1630. The degree of their anti-Catholicism varied, with Hall on the moderate wing arguing for the recognition of Rome as a true church and with the more extreme Sutcliffe asserting that it was better to be a Turk than a papist. Nevertheless, both Hall and Sutcliffe (as well as Featley) entered the fray against Montagu and all were bound together by their Calvinist convictions. All too might reasonably be described as church-puritans, firmly episcopalian, favouring the predestinarianism and evangelical practices of the moderate puritans, but strongly opposed to the presbyterian doctrines and rejection of ceremony professed by the radicals.

Beyond these few, the extent of Prideaux's academic circle and the intensity of his relationships with its members are difficult to gauge. Both, however, are likely to have been much greater than the surviving evidence indicates. Had his correspondence survived, we would be better able to assess his place in the republic of letters. As it is, we can draw only on this small muster of divines, surely a group more representative than comprehensive. Some indication of what may be missing comes from the correspondence of Samuel Ward, which *does* survive. Ward was the oracle of the church-puritans at Cambridge as Prideaux was at Oxford—in effect, Prideaux's opposite number.[120] After taking his DD from Sidney Sussex College in 1610, he went on to become one of the English representatives at the Synod of Dort, a master theologian, the greatest scholar of his generation in the university, the opponent of Catholics and Arminians, and the unswerving adherent of such Calvinist doctrines as predestination and perseverance.[121] Like Prideaux, he was elected to the headship of his college, holding the mastership of Sidney Sussex from 1610 until his death in 1643, and, again like Prideaux, he filled one of his university's two theology

---

120. Trevor-Roper, 'Laudianism and Political Power', 76, 82.
121. Unless otherwise stated, the rest of this paragraph relating to Ward derives from M. Todd, 'Ward, Samuel (1572–1643), theologian and college head', *ODNB*. See also M. H. Curtis, *Oxford and Cambridge in Transition, 1558–1642* (Oxford, 1959), 208–11; R. Humfreys, *Sidney Sussex: A History* (Cambridge, 2009), 63–93.

chairs, the Lady Margaret professorship of divinity. Like Prideaux's Exeter, his college had a justifiable reputation as a puritan establishment, though of the church-puritan and anti-Presbyterian kind. But equally striking, and by apparent contrast with Prideaux, was the range of Ward's contacts. He exchanged letters with a number of Calvinist bishops, among them John Davenant of Salisbury, Thomas Morton of Durham, and Arthur Lake of Bath and Wells; with some leading scholars at Oxford, including Sir Henry Savile, warden of Merton, Henry Briggs, Savilian professor of geometry, Matthias Pasor, proto-Arabist, and Thomas James; and with many local clergy. Archbishop Usher had a still wider circle, to judge by his published correspondence, which runs to some 679 to-and-from letters. Prideaux is likely to have been at the centre of a similarly large and varied group of friends and fellow-scholars.[122] The only surprise is to find not a single Prideaux letter among Ward's correspondence and only one letter from Prideaux among Ussher's. Yet he was close to Ussher and very probably to Ward also.

The same near absence of letters makes it equally difficult to assess Prideaux's relations with like-minded foreigners: those Continental churchmen, mainly Dutch Calvinists, Contra-Remonstrants to a man, with whom he shared so much theological ground. Prideaux's European reputation as one of England's leading theologians and teachers is vouched for by the number of Continental students and scholars who came to sit at his feet— men such as John Combachius, Sixtinus Amama, and Matthias Pasor, whose fortunes we have already surveyed and who often kept in touch with their English master after they had returned home.[123] Another such was Egbert Grim, a German Calvinist who, like Amama, studied at the university of Franeker and moved on in 1626 to work under Prideaux before returning to Leiden in 1629. A copy of his first work, the *Disputatio theologia inauguralis,* published at Leiden in that year and warmly inscribed to Prideaux, his 'master, friend, and patron', survives among Prideaux's books at Worcester.[124]

---

122. Most of Ward's correspondence will be found in Bodl. MSS Tanner 72–6. For a listing of Ussher's correspondents, see Ussher, *Correspondence*, i. vii–xviii.
123. Above, 29, 55–8.
124. WCL, Sel. A. 57. 2(4). For Grim, see J. Machielsen, 'When a Female Pope Meets a Biconfessional Town: Protestantism, Catholicism, and Popular Polemics in the 1630s', *Early Modern Low Countries*, 3 (2019), 8–10.

Some evidence survives for his contacts with others more eminent than Grim, particularly with a group of leading participants in the Synod of Dort. It is perhaps not surprising that Prideaux's library contained at least seven works by Franciscus Gomarus, four by Sibrandus Lubbertus, and two by Johannes Polyander, all of them among the most learned scholars of the Dutch church and holders of chairs in theology at either Leiden (Gomarus, Polyander) or Franeker (Lubbertus).[125] More interesting are the tenuous signs of Prideaux's personal contacts with other members of this group. Festus Hommius, one of the official secretaries at Dort and prominent as a theologian and an especially fierce Contra-Remonstrant at Leiden, was described by Amama, in a dedicatory letter to Hommius preceding one of his works, as the 'common friend' of both Amama and Prideaux. It was Prideaux too, in conjunction with the earl of Pembroke, who secured an honorary Oxford doctorate for Hommius when he visited England in 1620, bringing with him the Acts of the Synod for presentation to the king.[126] A further link, this time between Prideaux and Johannes de Laet, another Dutch delegate to the Synod, is suggested by a copy of de Laet's *Commentarii de Pelagianis et Semi-Pelagianis* (1617) inscribed by the author 'to the most famous and learned man Doctor John Prideaux . . . respected master and friend'. De Laet's book, the work of a Contra-Remonstrant, but also a much more wide-ranging scholar, here largely directing his fire against the Dutch Arminians, is certain to have been sympathetically received by the 'master and friend' who shared his views.[127]

Some of Prideaux's admirers and fellow-scholars were based in Germany rather than the Netherlands. The only letter to him from a Continental source so far discovered came from Frankfurt and was written by Theodorus Ebertus, professor of Hebrew there.[128] Dated 20 July 1628 and addressed to Prideaux as 'most excellent theologian', Ebertus's letter praised Prideaux's lectures, which he had read and which had elucidated the Scriptures in many

125. For Prideaux's copies of books by Gomarus, see WCL, U.K. 7, X.H. 17, Y.E 6, 69, Y.I. 32–4; Lubbertus—U. F. 17, X.G. 10, Y.E. 47, Y.I. 40; Polyander—H.D. 21, Y.I. 12.
126. Platt, 'Sixtinus Amama', 246 n. 45; P. J. Wijminga, *Festus Hommius* (Leiden, 1899), 312; Milton, *Catholic and Reformed*, 421.
127. The presentation copy of De Laet's book, additionally signed by Prideaux, is University of Toronto, Thomas Fisher Rare Book Library, Rare Book forbes 00593. For De Laet, see R. H. Bremmer jun., 'Laet, Johannes De [Johannes Latius] (1581–1649), merchant and scholar', *ODNB*.
128. The letter is attached to WCL, R.D. 11, Prideaux's copy of *Scitorum Talmudicorum Centuria Secunda*, by Jacobus Ebertus, father of Theodorus.

places. He went on to mention his contacts with the two leading Oxford Hebraists, William Langton and Edward Meetkerke, and to ask Prideaux if he could supply certain listed English books which were not to be found in their libraries; and he enclosed a copy of his own recently published work, the *Poetica Hebraica*. Not the least significant part of the letter was its final sentence, in which Ebertus asked Prideaux to accept the bearer, a very learned man, as his student and to allow him to share his company. In part a letter of recommendation, Ebertus's missive shows one route by which a foreign student might find his way into the circle of Prideaux's Oxford acolytes.[129]

It is thus possible to piece together an admittedly slender framework of personal contacts between Prideaux and his Continental allies, though the number and quality of the students who came to work with him in Oxford stands as a fuller testimony to his European reputation than the fragmentary evidence of book presentations and the occasional letter or allusion to friendship. What impresses in general is the diversity of Prideaux's circle. Centred on Oxford, the base for his inner family, his College associates, and his fellow university theologians, it extended eastwards overseas to take in the scholars of the Dutch universities of Leiden and Franeker, some of them prominent at the Synod of Dort and most of them engaged in the propagation of Calvinist theology and biblical scholarship—and then westwards to include his outer family in Devonshire and some of the gentry households of the same county, from that of Edmund Prideaux and his wife to those of the multitudinous Reynells. Prideaux remained first and foremost a theologian, scholar, and teacher; but the world of academia was not the only one which he inhabited.

129. Cf. Milton, *Catholic and Reformed*, 374.

6

Prideaux the Scholar

1. Reputation

A fine contemporary portrait of Prideaux, the only one known, shows the
scholar interrupted at his studies.[1] He sits at his desk, his left hand resting
lightly on the arm of his chair, the other holding a pen poised over an open
notebook propped on an ornate lectern. To his right stands another open
book; more books lie piled on the desk, with larger folios and quartos
shelved on the wall. The sitter, spade-bearded and ruffed, alert but baggy-
eyed, glances to the left at the artist, impatient, one imagines, to get back to
work. He looks to be about 50, which would date the picture to the
late 1620s. The artist is unknown. The portrait was painted for Prideaux
himself and his family, and not for the College in whose hall it now hangs.
First mentioned in the will of his grandson, Prideaux Hodges (d. 1699),[2] it
probably had as its distant exemplar one of the many similar portraits of
either St Jerome or St Augustine in their respective studies by such Renaissance masters as Dürer and Ghirlandaio: a model which may well have
appealed to Prideaux the patristic scholar. But whatever its inspiration, the
portrait contrasts strongly with those of other contemporary heads, almost all
of whom are shown formally either in dark clerical dress or in academic
gowns or in the lawn sleeves of the bishops who many of them later became.
Among all these Prideaux's portrait stands out. It is unique.[3]

---

1. See frontispiece to this book.
2. 'My grandfather Prideaux's picture': Butcher, 'Dr John Prideaux', 18.
3. All portraits of heads are reproduced in *Oil Paintings in Public Ownership in Oxford University*, 2
   vols. (The Public Catalogue Foundation, 2015). For typical portraits, see, e.g., those of Samuel
   Radcliffe (Brasenose: i. 33) and Brian Duppa (Christ Church: i. 111). The College's portrait of
   Prideaux (Exeter: i. 134) is incorrectly described as a later copy rather than the original.

Between Scholarship and Church Politics: The Lives of John Prideaux, 1578–1650. John Maddicott,
Oxford University Press. © John Maddicott 2022. DOI: 10.1093/oso/9780192896100.003.0006

It is worth dwelling on Prideaux's portrait not only because of its pecu-
liarities but because it suggests a perception of himself as an *érudit*, a man of
learning, which was widely shared. Prideaux was famously learned, after the
death of Sir Henry Savile in 1622 more so than any other figure in the early
seventeenth-century university. He attracted marvelling comments from all
sides. For David Lloyd, author of an early biographical compendium and of
the best general sketch of Prideaux's character, he was 'an encyclopoedy and
miscellany of all learning'.[4] Writing in 1652, Walter Charleton, who had
come under Prideaux's influence as an undergraduate at Magdalen Hall in
the 1620s and would later become a leading light of the late seventeenth-
century scientific movement, spoke of him as 'that not long since vitall
library, Bishop Prideaux', esteemed 'not only in respect of his insatiable
native capacity, stupendious acquisitions and inestimable benefits to the
republick of learning'.[5] Thomas Bradley, who matriculated at Exeter in
1617, later a DD and one of Charles I's chaplains, wrote in similar terms:
'I will cite you a whole library of fathers and schoolemen, and all in one,
who was himself a living library. I meane the late learned and revered Lord
Bishop of Worcester Doctor Prideaux.' To call a leading scholar 'a living
library' was becoming almost a contemporary cliché, but in Prideaux's case it
was fully justified.[6] Even John Barnard, biographer of Prideaux's enemy
Peter Heylyn, had to admit that he was, 'to give him his due, a right learned
man . . . profoundly admired by the junior masters'.[7] An author much closer
to Prideaux, Nathanael Carpenter, fellow of Exeter, turned his praise in a
slightly different and more specific direction: 'I could offer to your admiration', he wrote, 'the worth and workes of our renowned Rector, Dr
Prideaux, His Maiesties learned professor of divinity in our university, in
whom the heroicall wits of Iewell, Rainolds and Hooker, as united into one,
seeme to triumph anew.' It was no small thing to be seen as the triumphant

4. Lloyd, *Memoires*, 536.
5. W. Charleton, *The Darknes of Atheism Dispelled by the Light of Nature* (1652), sig. b1v; L. Sharp,
    'Walter Charleton's Early Life, 1620–1659, and Relationship to Natural Philosophy in Mid-
    Seventeenth-Century England', *Annals of Science*, 30 (1973), 313–14; Feingold, *Mathematicians'
    Apprenticeship*, 58.
6. T. Bradley, *Elijah's Nunc Dimittis, or The Author's own Funerall Sermons* (York, 1669); S. Lee,
    revd. J. McElligott, 'Bradley, Thomas (1599/1600–1673), Church of England clergyman',
    ODNB; K. Thomas, 'The Life of Learning', *Proceedings of the British Academy*, 117: *2001 Lectures*,
    202–3.
7. Barnard, *Theologo-historicus*, 112.

embodiment of the intellectual heavyweights of the post-Reformation Eng-lish church.[8]

Most of these encomia came posthumously, after Prideaux's loss of his bishopric and death in relative poverty had made him into something of a martyr figure. Even so, the wide acknowledgement of Prideaux's excep-tional learning may seem surprising. His written output was limited. He edited no texts, unlike his friend James Ussher, who produced a pioneering edition of Ignatius's letters, or his fellow head of house, Sir Henry Savile, warden of Merton and editor of an eight-volume edition of St John Chrysostom. He published no sustained work of religious controversy, unlike his fellow Protestant and collaborator Isaac Casaubon, whose unfin-ished *Exercitationes* set out to demolish the Roman Catholic history of Cardinal Baronius. He attempted no large-scale essay in philosophical reflection, unlike his friend and Exeter colleague George Hakewill, whose *Apologie of the Power and Providence of God* put forward a classic case for progress in history. By contrast to the achievements of such intellectual giants as Savile and Casaubon, Prideaux's may seem limited. We might reasonably ask whether his reputation was deserved.

2. The substance of Prideaux's learning

For a guide to the substance of Prideaux's learning we must look to his publications. These were largely of two sorts: first, lectures, sermons, and 'orations', published at intervals and gathered together most comprehen-sively in his *Viginti-duae Lectiones* of 1648; and, second, works of basic instruction on a variety of subjects—Greek grammar, logic, history, theology—intended mainly for undergraduates and for those proceeding to higher degrees in theology.

Most of the works in the first category, which provide the fullest evidence for the range of Prideaux's learning, could best be described as *pièces d'occa-sion*: writings originally delivered orally, in the form of sermons at court or of lectures at the university's annual Act or of addresses to those graduating in arts or proceeding to higher degrees in divinity. They sprang essentially from Prideaux's offices as regius professor of divinity and royal chaplain, just as his instructional books in the second category sprang from his work as a college

8. Carpenter, *Geographie Delineated*, ii. 263.

tutor. Genre was determined by role. Although these sorts of enterprise are easily depreciated by comparison with those of editors and of more prolific authors, they almost certainly reached a wider public. This was particularly true of those delivered at the Act, an event widely attended by the lay gentry as well as the clergy.[9] We should also remember that Prideaux's reputation depended too on his routine lectures, given as part of his duties as regius professor but never printed, and so less easily assessable for the qualities of erudition which they may have displayed.

To appreciate the range of Prideaux's learning we have to turn to its content. The main purpose of all Prideaux's published lectures and sermons was to expound, defend, and propagate Protestant Christianity and to confound those whom he saw as its enemies, primarily Roman Catholics but also such deviants as the Socinians.[10] This in turn necessitated an intimate knowledge of the Bible, for it was upon the accurate interpretation of the Bible that theological truth depended. For all Protestants the Bible as the Word of God was a far greater source of authority than the tradition of the church,[11] and, like other seventeenth-century divines, Prideaux must have known the Bible almost by heart. His Act lectures and orations contain some 670 referenced citations from almost every book of the Bible; St Paul's Epistle to the Romans, the key source for the Protestant doctrine of justification by faith, tops the list with sixty-six citations.[12] But the Bible was not a simple text. Its meaning was often unclear, and its interpretation depended on a close familiarity with the several languages in which it was written and paraphrased. For the most part, this amounted to vulgar or 'common' Greek for the New Testament and Hebrew for the Old. But sections of the Old Testament—passages in Ezra and Daniel—were written in another Semitic language, Aramaic, usually known in Prideaux's day as 'Chaldee', which became the spoken language of the New Testament era. It came to be used by Jewish teachers in the early Christian centuries to produce the so-called targums, Aramaic paraphrases of parts of the Hebrew scriptures. Finally, a knowledge of two other Semitic languages was essential for any biblical expert: Syriac, a form of Aramaic used in early translations of the Bible, and Arabic, whose cognate status in relation to Hebrew meant that it could

---

9. Below, 206–10.
10. For the purposes of theological learning, see esp. Thomas, 'Life of Learning', 203–12. For Prideaux and the Socinians, below, 280–5.
11. Thomas, 'Life of Learning', 206.
12. 'Index Scripturarum', unpaginated but following 'Oratio XIII', in *VDL*.

sometimes be used to elucidate the many obscure words and passages in the Hebrew text of the Old Testament.[13] And, of course, it went almost without saying, as Prideaux himself pointed out, that the true scholar needed to be conversant with the main European languages, especially French, Spanish, and Italian.[14]

Prideaux's command of all these languages was widely recognized. Besides the general comments of David Lloyd ('his skill in tongues was great') and Anthony Wood ('esteemed . . . an excellent linguist'), we have the more specific testimony of the anonymous 'R. C.', who had sat at Prideaux's feet in the Oxford schools and who preached his funeral sermon. 'He gave instruction to all', says 'R. C.', 'in Chaldee, Arabic, Syriac and Hebrew, as though each language were his native tongue.' Prideaux's accomplishments were not unique. The learned Miles Smith, one of the translators of the King James Bible and Prideaux's contemporary as bishop of Gloucester, was also said to have been 'perfect in the Greeke, the Hebrew, the Chaldee, the Syriacke and the Arabicke tongues'. But as such comments on both men suggest, they were certainly regarded as unusual.[15]

There was undoubtedly some exaggeration in these accounts, and particularly in what 'R.C.' had to say about Prideaux's expertise in Arabic. He was certainly acquainted with the language. He may have been among the pupils of the Coptic Arabist Abudacnus, resident in Oxford from 1610 to 1613, and we know that he was instructed by Matthew Pasor during Pasor's Oxford years in the mid-1620s. Although Pasor's own grasp of Arabic was hardly more than superficial, his residence in Exeter gave Prideaux more opportunities than most to learn what he could from this wandering scholar.[16] There are enough casual allusions in Prideaux's works to suggest that he picked up at least a smattering of this difficult language. He was able to cite the Koran, to provide the Arabic equivalent of a Greek phrase, and to name the Arabic vowel points (Fatha, Kasra Damma) which served as

13. *HUO*, iv. 471; *ODCC*, 96, 318, 745–6, 1581, 1588; A. Hamilton, 'The Semitic Languages in the Bible and the Renaissance', in E. Cameron (ed.), *The New Cambridge History of the Bible*. Vol. 3: *From 1450 to 1750* (Cambridge, 2016), 17, 21; J. Barton, *A History of the Bible* (2019), 35–7, 443.

14. 'Concio III', 29, in *VDL*.

15. Lloyd, *Memoires*, 536; Wood, *Athenae*, iii. 267; Bodl. MS Jones 56, fos. 21r–v; T. Roebuck, 'Miles Smith (1552/53–1624) and the Uses of Oriental Learning', in M. Feingold (ed.), *Labourers in the Vineyard of the Lord: Scholarship and the Making of the King James Version of the Bible* (Leiden, 2018), 330.

16. *HUO*, iv. 477, 479–81; Toomer, *Eastern Wisedome*, 98–101; above, 57.

substitutes for vowels in that language, though it is possible that he drew here on the writings of Erpenius, Leiden professor and prince among Europe's Arabists.[17] His skill in all the Semitic languages was evident throughout. He frequently explicated Hebrew material in his lectures and was able to deal critically with other passages in Aramaic/Chaldee. Commenting on one of the targums in a court sermon whose display of learning would surely have delighted James I, he opined that 'widest from the mark is the Chaldy paraphrase of R. Ioseph Caecus, who, without the least warrant from the words, thus blindly renders it [a translation from particular Hebrew quotation] . . . '.[18] In another court sermon he could discuss whether the original Greek word, in a passage from St Luke's Gospel, was best rendered as 'But' or 'And': 'The original . . . (which we expresse by the exceptive, But) is rendered in the vulgar Latine, Syriack, Arabique and Munsters Hebrew translation in S. Matthew by the copulative And'.[19] In his Act lecture of 1632 he was able to adduce evidence from the Syriac, Arabic, and Ethiopic scriptures, as well as from Luther's German Bible, on a point concerning the Trinity, so adding Ethiopic to his known tally of languages.[20]

These bravura displays of linguistic virtuosity, across half a dozen ancient languages, were far from being merely pedantic or ostentatious. Behind them lay the scholar's quest to establish an uncorrupt biblical text, free from error, without which no valid moral and religious exegesis and instruction would be possible. In an uncharacteristically lyrical passage Prideaux told a court congregation that 'Precepts, practise, promises, and prophecies, like the foure rivers of Paradise, streame out of the fountaine of holy writ, and compasse all that therein is contained.' On another occasion, after passing in review the opinions of seven theologians on a single Hebrew quotation, he could say, almost apologetically, and perhaps to a weary audience, 'Such criticismes (I knowe) are harsh in a sermon, but the text must bee cleared that the ground bee sure.'[21] A correct text was the *sine qua non* of theological discussion.

17. 'Oratio III', 25, in *VDL*; 'Concio IV', 32(2), in *VDL*; *VDL*, 189.
18. 'The Draught of the Brooke', 4, in *CS* (separate pagination). For another comment on a targum in a sermon preached before the king, see 'Perez Uzzah', 4, in *CS*.
19. 'Wisedomes Justification', in *CS*, 4.
20. *VDL*, 267. The only text available for him to draw on was the Ethiopic New Testament published at Rome in 1548–9: see B. M. Metzger, *The Early Versions of the New Testament* (Oxford, 1977), 228–9. There was no copy of this book in the Bodleian. Where would Prideaux have found one?
21. 'The Christans Expectation', 8; 'A Christians Free-will Offering', 20, both in *CS*.

But if the text's establishment was a necessary condition for drawing out the lessons of Scripture, it was not a sufficient one. That depended on a comprehensive knowledge of the whole field of theological writing, past and present: primarily the works of the Greek and Latin Fathers from the second to the sixth centuries, but also those of the medieval schoolmen and the post-Reformation commentators. Prideaux was the master of all this material. The range of his learning was nowhere better shown than in his 1623 Act lecture 'On the salvation of non-Christians (*De Salute Ethnicorum*)', where he began by citing the views of the Fathers (Clement of Alexandria, Augustine, Origen, Eusebius, Gregory of Nazianzus, John Cassian, Prosper of Aquitaine, Fulgentius, and Gregory the Great) before proceeding to those of the *scholastici*, the schoolmen (Peter Lombard, Alexander of Hales, Hugh of St Victor, Bonaventure, Aquinas, and Duns Scotus).[22] His command of the Reformation and post-Reformation literature was equally assured, taking in not only the works of the Reformation giants, Luther, Calvin, and Beza, but also of a multitude of lesser figures. In discussing the identity of the Antichrist in another Act lecture he listed a large number of Protestant reformers who believed, wrongly in Prideaux's view, that the Turk rather than the Pope should be seen as this apocalyptic terror. They ranged from such major reformers as Melanchthon, Oecolampadius, Zanchi, and Bishop Jewel to the less well-known Johannes Draconites, Andreas Hyperius, Stephen of Szeged, Simon Grynaeus and Paul Fagius, whose works he must have read.[23]

The extent of Prideaux's learning in other fields can best be illustrated from two related topics: his thoughts on the pre-Reformation ancestry of the Protestant churches and on the pre-Reformation Roman Catholic church and its enemies. In both cases he drew on extensive historical evidence to support a firm confessional line. Like the theological writings of other Protestant *érudits*, men such as Casaubon and Grotius, his scholarship was far from objective or neutral but was rather intended to confront and confute the errors and follies of the old church and to demonstrate the verities and virtues of its newer opponents. Members of the European republic of letters, such as Prideaux was, did not by their membership

---

22. *VDL*, 113–14.
23. 'De Antichristo', in *VDL*, 178. I have assumed that the 'Fatus' of Prideaux's list is a misprint for 'Fagius'.

transcend confessional differences but often reinforced them. Scholarship enabled them to set out the Protestant case. [24]

In discussing the origin of the Protestant churches Prideaux put forward few original ideas and needed none. Many had already set out the arguments. Like other Protestant thinkers, he found himself facing 'the perennial Romanist demand: "Where was your church before Luther?"' It was a question to which he gave the whole of his 1624 Act lecture. Although he put forward a variety of related answers, one strand was dominant, as it was for other contemporary divines.[25] For a thousand years after Christ a true church had persisted. But then, around the year 1000, but more especially in the time of Hildebrand, Pope Gregory VII, Satan had been unleashed, as foretold in Revelations, the Bible's final book.[26] From that point onwards, and under an Antichrist papacy, the church had fallen into corruption. But the true church was precariously preserved through the appearance of heretical sects, especially the Waldensians, the Wycliffites, and the Hussites, groups whose opposition to, and persecution by, the church of the popes testified to their Christian integrity. Their heir was Luther, and through him and his successors the Protestant reformers had begun to rid the church of corruption and, in an alternative form, to return it to its true roots.[27]

These themes had been most fully set out by Prideaux's friend Ussher in his *De Successione* of 1613, but they also permeated Prideaux's own works. Their restatement rested not only on precedent, but on Prideaux's scholarship and his wide and deep reading in the sources. The standard account of the heretical succession was one which he both drew upon and augmented.[28] In that account Wyclif was a subject of particular interest to him, not only as the 'morning star of the Reformation', the forerunner of Protestantism, but probably also as an Oxford man and the sometime head of

---

24. This is the theme of N. Hardy, *Criticism and Confession: The Bible in the Seventeenth-Century Republic of Letters* (Oxford, 2017); see esp. the introduction, 1–20. See also J.-L. Quantin, *The Church of England and Christian Antiquity: The Construction of a Confessional Identity in the 17th Century* (Oxford, 2009), *passim*.

25. 'De Visibilitate Ecclesiae', in *VDL*, 127–43; Milton, *Catholic and Reformed*, 270, 304; Quantin, *The Church of England and Christian Antiquity*, 68–71.

26. 'De Mille Annis Apocalypticis', in *VDL*, 209; 'Oratio III', 29, in *VDL; 'The Christians Expectation', 25, in CS.

27. Milton, *Catholic and Reformed*, 281–3; E. Cameron, 'Medieval Heretics as Protestant Martyrs', in D. Wood (ed.), *Martyrs and Martyrologies*. Studies in Church History, 30 (Oxford, 1993), 185–207.

28. Ford, *James Ussher*, 72–6. For Prideaux and the heretical succession, see 'De Visibilitate Ecclesiae', in *VDL*, 137–8; 'Oratio I'. 8, in *VDL* (where Prideaux's cites Ussher's work); 'Perz-Uzzah', in *CS*, 15–17; *A Sermon Preached*, sig. A5r.

an Oxford college. At three points in his lectures and sermons Prideaux cites Wyclif's greatest philosophical work, the *Trialogus*, once to state Wyclif's views on the perseverance of the elect, once to acquit him of error in a dispute relating to tithes, and once to quote him on the nature of God. In the second of these instances Prideaux states that he has consulted the text of the *Trialogus* both in its printed version and in various manuscripts.[29] He extends his range in a sermon, citing a sentence from what he calls 'Wickliffs Psalter', meaning the Wycliffite Bible, here accurately transcribed from its later version, which was then unavailable in print and only to be consulted in manuscript.[30] Prideaux himself owned two fifteenth-century Wycliffite manuscripts, a fifteenth-century English Bible and a *Rosarium Theologie*, a widely disseminated theological commonplace book.[31] Casual references to Ralph Strode, Oxford philosopher and logician, and to William Woodford, Franciscan friar and theologian, both in varying degrees opponents of Wyclif, suggest a close familiarity with the intellectual background to Wyclif's career.[32] Of all the figures and movements from the European past who could be thought to have anticipated Protestantism, Wyclif and his followers were those most central to Prideaux's historical imagination.

He had, not surprisingly, less to say about the Continental heresies which fed into the same stream, but he was nevertheless widely read in, and well informed about, their histories. For his knowledge of the Waldensians, originally the twelfth-century followers of Peter Waldo, he was able to draw on two books, both of which he possessed: Jean-Paul Perrin's history of the Waldenses, translated into English in 1624, and Balthasar Lydius's 1622 edition of some of the main Waldensian texts, their 'Apologies, Confession and Catechismes'. He referred to both in his Act lecture of 1624 'On the visibility of the church', showing how up to date was his

---

29. *VDL*, 78; 'Oratio V', 46, in *VDL*; 'Concio VI', 60, in *VDL*. The printed text must be that published at Basle in 1525, *Io. Wiclefi viri undiquaque piis*. It is not clear where he would have found manuscripts of the *Trialogus* in Oxford. Only a fragment of one manuscript now survives (in the Bodleian): see W. R. Thomson, *The Latin Writings of John Wyclyf* (Toronto, 1983), 79–80.

30. 'The Draught of the Brooke', 5, in *CS*; below, ooo. I am very grateful to Anne Hudson for identifying the source of the passage quoted by Prideaux, and for her comments.

31. Worcester Cathedral MSS Q. 68 and Q. 84: R. M. Thomson, *A Descriptive Catalogue of the Medieval Manuscripts in Worcester Cathedral Library* (Cambridge, 2001), 166, 178. Prideaux's Bible MS is not that from which he cites in 'The Draught of the Brooke' (*ex inf.* Anne Hudson). The extensive notes in the *Rosarium* are not in Prideaux's hand, as Thomson states them to be. For the *Rosarium* in general, see A. Hudson, 'A Lollard Compilation and the Dissemination of Wycliffe's Thought', in her *Lollards and their Books* (1985), 12–29, esp. 16–17.

32. 'De Usu Logices in Theologicis', *VDL*, 224; 'The First Fruits of the Resurrection', 22, in *CS*.

reading on the subject of the heretical succession vital to his argument. [33] For the Hussites he seems to have relied on Aeneas Sylvius's history of Bohemia, published at Solingen in 1624, though he also used Bellarmine's *De Eucharistica*, which had pointed to the degree to which the Bohemian realm had been 'infected' (the word of a hostile Catholic critic) by the import of Wycliffite works: direct evidence, or so it seemed to Prideaux, of the continuity of proto-Protestantism.[34]

Though neither was as prominent in his thinking as Wyclif, two other medieval English churchmen were venerated by Prideaux, in both cases for their seeming anticipation of the ideas and shibboleths of the Protestant reformers in general and of the English Calvinists in particular. They were Robert Grosseteste, bishop of Lincoln from 1235 to 1253, and Thomas Bradwardine, archbishop of Canterbury in 1349, both in their day leading Oxford scholars and intellectuals. Prideaux placed Grosseteste at the start of a sanctified succession of Oxford theologians, running on through Wyclif to Jewel, Hooker, and Rainolds, 'the more celebrated sons of a most fruitful mother'.[35] In Exeter's library he had access to a rare manuscript of Grosseteste's work on free will, *De Libero Arbitrio*, which he cited. Although Grosseteste was prepared to concede a greater degree of freedom to the will than Prideaux, his subject meshed closely with Prideaux's own interest in grace and predestination.[36] But it was Grosseteste's anti-papalism which resonated most strongly with him. In 1253 the bishop's defiance and condemnation of Pope Innocent IV, the head of a corrupt church and a threat to the souls of the faithful, had come close to identifying the Pope with the Antichrist. Had not the work of Grossesteste, Wyclif and others, Prideaux asked, been suppressed because 'they were too free against friers fopperies, popes tyrannies, and Romes unsufferable purloynings and superstitions'?[37]

33. J. P. Perrin, *Luther's Fore-runners, or a Cloud of Witnesses, Deposing for the Protestant Faith*, trans. S. Lennard (1624)—WCL, Y. E. 18; Balthasar Lydius, *Waldensia, id est Conservatio Verae Ecclesiae* (Rotterdam, 1622)—WCL, Y. K. 28; 'De Visibilitate Ecclesiae', *VDL*, 138; 'Perez-Uzzah', 17, in *CS*; Milton, *Catholic and Reformed*, 282 n. 52.

34. 'De Visibilitate Ecclesiae, *VDL*, 138; *Aeneas Silvi Senensis de Bohemorum Origine ac Gestis Historia* (Solingen, 1624).

35. *VDL*, 32, 83.

36. Exeter College MS 28: A. G. Watson, *A Descriptive Catalogue of the Medieval Manuscripts of Exeter College, Oxford* (Oxford, 2000), 41; N. Lewin, 'The First Recension of Robert Grosseteste De libero arbitrio', *Mediaeval Studies*, 53 (1991), 1–88.

37. R. W. Southern, *Robert Grosseteste: The Growth of an English Mind in Medieval Europe*, 2nd edn (Oxford, 1992), 276–85; 'Perez-Uzzah', 14, in *CS*.

For his knowledge of Grosseteste's life Prideaux drew on the work of John Bale, the mid-sixteenth-century 'evangelical polemicist and [Protestant] historian', whose *Scriptorum Illustrium maioris Brytanniae . . . Catalogus* had attempted to trace the ancestry of the English church and had seen Grosseteste's defiance of the papacy as having its own part to play in that story.[38] Equally sympathetic to Grosseteste's anti-papalism was the chronicler Matthew Paris, whom Prideaux several times mentions and who may have supplied him with details of Grosseteste's life.[39] In the case of 'our most learned archbishop Thomas of Bradwardine', on the other hand, Prideaux's interest lay chiefly in the work rather than the life (and the proprietary tone of his reference is striking). In its attack on the 'modern Pelagians' Bradwardine's greatest work, the *De Causa Dei contra Pelagium*, dealt with many of the issues which concerned the later Protestants, notably those of grace, free will, and predestination; and in placing limits on free will and embracing predestination he came close to the doctrines of the reformers. *De Causa Dei* did not appear in print, in the edition by Sir Henry Savile, until 1618. But since Prideaux cited it by chapter and verse in his Act lecture of 1617, as well as in that of 1619, he must have read this gigantic work (running to nearly 900 printed pages) in manuscript, perhaps drawing on the texts to be found at Merton and at New College.[40] If his use of Bradwardine's magnum opus shows his interest in tracing the antecedents of Protestant ideas to the Catholic Middle Ages, it also shows his intellectual stamina.

These two scholars provided an obvious focus for any fellow scholar arguing for the medieval origins of Protestant ideas. But the precursors of Protestantism were to be sought on the Continent as well as at home. Here Prideaux was able to turn not only to the Waldensians and the Hussites, who often had primacy of place in his lectures and sermons, but also to other unrelated dissidents from the early Middle Ages. His treatment of Gottschalk of Orbais is particularly pertinent. Gottschalk was a ninth-century monk, priest, and theologian whose radically unorthodox teachings had led to his condemnation in successive church synods and to a long conflict with

38. J. Bale, *Scriptorum Illustrium Maioris Brytanniae . . . Catalogus*, 2 vols (Basle, 1557–9), i. 204; Cf. J. N. King, 'Bale, John (1495–1563), bishop of Ossory, evangelical polemicist, and historian', *ODNB*.
39. *VDL*, 164; J. Prideaux, *A Synopsis of Councels* (1661), 24; Southern, *Grosseteste*, 291–5.
40. *VDL*, 14, 15, 46; G. Leff, 'Bradwardine, Thomas (c.1300–1349), theologian and archbishop of Canterbury', *ODNB*; J. A. Weisheipl, 'Repertorium Mertonense', *Mediaeval Studies*, 31 (1969), 181.

Archbishop Hincmar of Rheims.[41] His arguments in favour of double predestination, by which some were predestined to eternal blessedness and others to perdition, and his thesis that the benefits of Christ's atonement were confined to the elect, abhorrent though such views were to most of his contemporaries, anticipated the beliefs of many post-Reformation Anglicans, including Prideaux. Gottschalk moved to the forefront of theological discussion in 1631, when Ussher published the first full study of his work and edited his two confessions. Yet well before this date Gottschalk had made an appearance in two of Prideaux's Act lectures in 1619 and again in 1621. Drawing on the fourteen-volume edition of the Fathers, *Magna Bibliotheca Veterum Patrum*, published at Cologne only a year prior to the first lecture, Prideaux was able to provide a short account of Gottschalk's views, of those who opposed and defended him in the various synods, and of the role of Hincmar. In this particular controversy, as in so many others relating to the supposed ancestors of the Protestants, he was well informed.[42] He alludes more briefly to another early medieval dispute, that between Lanfranc, prior of Bec, and the eleventh-century theologian Berengar, in which Berengar sought to modify the church's traditional teaching on the Eucharist in ways which seemed to approach the later Protestant rejection of transubstantiation. There is general agreement among the 'blessed doctors', Prideaux adds (with more than a hint of sarcasm) that 'a heretic is any man who, in matters of faith, departs from the universal Roman church'.[43]

It would be tediously easy to multiply examples of Prideaux's learning: the product of reading which was as wide as that of any man. Whether citing the views of Copernicus, Brahe, and Fracastorius on the relationship between the sun and the planets, or ridiculing the false history found in Pseudo-Turpin's life of Charlemagne and in chivalric romances such as 'Amadis de Gaule', or quoting four lines of verse from the relatively obscure *Fescennina* of the late Latin poet Claudian, he showed that he had a broad span of European literary culture at his command.[44] These displays of erudition were invariably related to his main theological concerns. His astronomical knowledge was needed to interpret a passage from the second

---

41. For a brief account of Gottschalk, see *ODCC*, 699–700.
42. *VDL*, 46, 78. For a further Gottschalk reference, see 'Hezechias Sicknesse', 19, in *CS*.
43. 'Oratio VIII', 78; *ODCC*, 192; R. W. Southern, 'Lanfranc of Bec and Berengar of Tours', in *Studies in Medieval English History presented to Frederick Maurice Powicke*, ed. R. W. Hunt et al. (Oxford, 1948), 27–48; Milton, *Catholic and Reformed*, 290–1.
44. 'Hezechias Sicknesse', 24, in *CS*; 'Oratio IX', 83, in *VDL*; 'Concio V', 43, in *VDL*.

book of Kings relating how the apparent backward movement of the sun signified the approaching end of King Hezekiah's sickness.[45] His disparagement of Pseudo-Turpin and similar confections emerged in the course of a lecture on theological forgeries and works wrongly ascribed to particular authors ('De Pseudoepigraphis'). Only the extract from the *Fescennina*, part of a dedicatory letter of 1626 to Robert Dormer, Baron Wing, Prideaux's former pupil, had a purely secular context. But for the most part what he had to say in his lectures and sermons, however recondite and rebarbative it may seem to the modern reader, was clearly related to his main themes. He rarely digressed.

3. The context of Prideaux's learning

What broader intentions underlay Prideaux's use of his extensive learning? A large part of the answer has already been given: he wished to clarify and elucidate the text of the Bible, to trace the ancestry of the Protestant churches, and to wage theological war against the errors of the church's enemies. But, like so many branches of scholarship in the early modern world, Prideaux's learning was also intended to be more immediately and practically useful.[46] As we have suggested from the lectures already discussed, one of its main purposes was to educate the clergy, and to some extent the laity, in orthodox theology.

Here we need to consider more fully the medium as well as the message. Prideaux's medium, the vehicle for his erudition, comprised his lectures and his sermons. Just as we have no record of the routine weekly lectures as regius professor, so we have none for his parochial sermons, beyond a very few given in Oxford churches, presumably to largely academic congregations, which he later chose to publish.[47] He certainly preached in parishes where he was the incumbent, such as Bladon by Woodstock, probably in others where the College was patron, and perhaps most frequently at nearby Kidlington, where the rector of Exeter was *ex officio* the rector of the parish. Lloyd tells us that his 'parish and popular sermons' were 'catechetical',

---

45. 2 Kings 20, 8–11.
46. Cf. Thomas, 'Life of Learning', 216–19.
47. 'Ephesus Backsliding' (St Mary's, Oxford, 1614); 'The First Fruits of the Resurrection' (St Peter's in the East, n.d.); 'Gowries Conspiracy' (St Mary's, n.d.); 'Davids Reioycing for Christ's Resurrection' (St Peter's in the East, n.d.)—all published in *CS*.

meaning presumably that they offered instruction in the basics of Christianity, without the displays of exegetical skills, learning, and ratiocination which distinguished his performances before university and court audiences.[48] For these our material comes from sources already extensively used: from his public lectures (*lectiones*), his orations (*orationes*), and his sermon-like addresses (*conciones*). All of these that he chose to print were published together in his *Viginti-duae Lectiones*, while a selection of his court and Oxford sermons appeared together in his *Certaine Sermons* of 1637.

The circumstances of their delivery bore directly on the uses of Prideaux's learning. His *lectiones* and *orationes* were delivered at the Act, the university's end-of-year celebrations in early July, and his *conciones* on Ash Wednesday, at the start of Lent. His primary audience at the Act comprised those incepting (that is, taking their degrees), whether as MAs, BDs, or doctors in one of the higher faculties—Theology, Law, Medicine, and, very occasionally, Music. Of these groups, the MAs were by far the most numerous, usually numbering between 100 and 150, followed by the BDs, of whom there were between fifteen and thirty. Among the doctors, the DDs predominated, though there were rarely more than five to fifteen.[49] But the total audience at these Act addresses was much larger than this university assemblage, comprising, as it also did, a large lay element.[50] In all, those present probably numbered several hundred. Prideaux addressed them on two occasions.[51] At the so-called Vesperies, on the Saturday before the Act proper, he gave his *lectio*, his Act lecture. Into the middle of this often dense and complex Latin discourse was interpolated the 'Benedictio', a shorter and less formal address, in the nature of a breathing space, in which the lecturer gave his blessing to all those incepting, often addressing each group in turn. Then, on the following Monday, at the Act itself, he gave his *oratio* to the same audience. Both *lectio* and *oratio* addressed particular but different theological themes. Following on from both came disputations on set topics between those taking degrees, in which the regius professor acted as moderator. By contrast, the *concio*, earlier in the year, was addressed to the determining bachelors and was more circumscribed in its social setting. It too preceded disputations between graduating candidates, which in this case

---

48. Lloyd, *Memoires*, 537.
49. For numbers, see Clark, *Register*, ii. 410–11; *HUO*, iv. 94–5.
50. Below, 208–10.
51. The procedure at the Act is set out by Prideaux himself in his 'Ad Lectorem' preceding the 'Conciones', in *VDL*, 'Conciones', sig. A2r.

lasted through Lent and were a standard component of the necessary exercises for the BA.

These were the occasions when Prideaux's mental powers were most fully on public display. His court sermons, learned though they were, tended to be conventional exegeses of scriptural texts. But his *lectiones* and *orationes*, together with his Ash Wednesday *conciones*, gave him an opportunity to speak more widely on themes of his choice and to move away from the straightforward exposition of the Scriptures which characterized his court sermons and, probably, his ordinary term-time lectures. Those themes were carefully chosen. As we have seen, his first nine Act lectures were largely concerned with the role of grace in the Christian's salvation.[52] Most of the rest were either on topics of current controversy, such as the antiquity of the Hebrew vowel points (*lectio*, 1627) or the observance of the Sabbath (*oratio*, 1622), or were directed against Roman Catholics ('The Equivocation of the Jesuits', *lectio*, 1625) or other enemies of the English church ('The Atonement of Christ', *lectio*, 1634, which had the Socinians as its target). But whatever their themes, these annual lectures and orations shared a common purpose. They were intended to educate and instruct a largely clerical audience in the core doctrines of their faith and so to equip them for their future careers as 'labourers for the Lord's harvest'.[53] Prideaux particularly had in mind those in his audience who were incepting as BDs and, still more, as DDs: these were the future leaders of the church, whether as bishops, deans, or university divines. In several of his lectures he spoke proudly of his success in training such men. In the past twenty-one years, he remarked in his 'Benedictio' of 1633, he had given his blessing to about 140 doctors of divinity, of whom five had become bishops, twice as many deans, and an unknown number archdeacons: 'Thus the seed moulders and the tiny grain of mustard blossoms and triumphs in its offspring.' He struck a similar note in 1637: 'How many of my theologian sons occupy bishops' sees and by their labour give support to the church?'[54] He was not, of course, thinking here solely of his Act lectures and orations, but of the whole course of training for higher degrees in theology. Yet his annual Act performances, the crowning items in the process, played an important part in that training.

---

52. Above, 43–6.
53. *VDL*, 49.
54. Ibid., 279–80, 353. Prideaux's figure for the approximate number of DDs looks to be unduly high.

The impact of Prideaux's learning, however, extended, and was intended to extend, far beyond the small number of men who went on to occupy the church's highest offices. The great majority of those incepting aimed at a clerical career, the MAs as much as the BDs and the DDs, and it was expected by Prideaux that some of the MAs would go on to higher degrees in theology; 'the church invisible' he called them at this early stage in their careers.[55] His annual 'Benedictiones' addressed to these men were in part exhortations. At the 1625 Act they were urged to strike down popery, to trample Arminians underfoot, and to bind the factious, and in 1628 to beware of the enemies of the church: 'the fume of the Antichrist, the deceitfulness of the Remonstrants, the poison of the Schismatics'.[56] But not all those present at Prideaux's Act lectures and orations could be regarded as the church's storm troopers. Also in attendance both at the lectures and at the disputations which followed was a large external audience of local clergy and gentry. For 'country ministers', such as those present when Peter Heylin defended his DD theses at the 1633 Vesperies,[57] the procedures of the Act, disputations as well as lectures, must have provided a sort of 'refresher course' in current theology and current church issues (such as the observance of the Sabbath). Here the educative role of Prideaux's work extended beyond the ranks of the ecclesiastical climbers and would-be professional theologians to give him a vicarious influence in the parishes of England.

In several of his Act performances Prideaux acknowledged this large and socially mixed audience. In his 1626 *oratio* he addressed 'guests who have flocked hither from all around' and 1628 'university men and outsiders'. 'Cambridge men may flock thither,' wrote Laud in 1638, concerned about a possible outbreak of plague at the forthcoming Act.[58] The Act was thus a great social occasion, and particularly so for the lay participants—men such as 'the flower of the nobility and gentry' present when Daniel Featley defended his theses at the 1617 Act, where Prideaux presided.[59] But 'that

---

55. Ibid., 135.
56. 'Oratio IX', 91, 'Oratio XI', 112, in *VDL*.
57. *Works of Laud*, v. 87.
58. 'Oratio X', 92; 'Oratio XI', 103, both in *VDL*; *Works of Laud*, v. 199.
59. 'The Life and Death of Doctor Daniel Featley, in Featley, *Featlaei paliggenesia*, 12; S. Penton, *The Guardian's Instruction*, ed. H. H. Sturmer (1897), 73. The best general account of the Act's social side is A. Geraghty, *The Sheldonian Theatre: Architecture and Learning in Seventeenth-Century Oxford* (New Haven, CT, 2013), 12–15. Cf. Curtis, *Oxford and Cambridge*, 4–5; *HUO*, iv. 30.

solemn season of luxury', as one observer called it, partly given over to
socializing, sightseeing, and carousing, also entailed a more sober attention
to the religious formalities of the Act, including lectures and sermons.
Reporting to his friend Dudley Carleton on the 1602 Act, Sir John Chamberlain noted that there had been 'an excellent *concio ad clerum*' (the sermon
which incepting BDs were required to preach), in which Dr Goodwin—
Prideaux's future father-in-law, then incepting as both BD and DD—
excelled all others.[60] These Latin addresses were not beyond the reach of
the gentry, many of whom must have been university-educated and some
more eminently learned. We have already met Sir Richard Reynell, uncle of
Prideaux's second wife, and a Devonshire country gentleman who even
knew Hebrew.[61] He and his like would have been well able to follow
Prideaux's Latin lectures and orations. That the Act lectures formed an
ordered sequence, with one year's lecture often opening by referring to
the previous year's, suggests that many in the audience, gentry as well as
clergy, were expected to attend regularly, from one year to the next.

On at least one occasion Prideaux's remarks may have been directed at the
first of these groups. His 1620 oration 'On tithes (*De Decimis*)' argued, with a
characteristic display of biblical fireworks, that tithes were not only scrip-
turally justified and essential for the support of the clergy, but that they were
divinely instituted, *jure divino*. Here he took issue with John Selden's *History
of Tithes*, published two years earlier, which had postulated that tithes in
historic times owed nothing to divine right and everything to 'the laws of
particular jurisdictions'.[62] Prideaux's real target, however, was not so much
Selden but rather those who withheld tithes or impropriated them for their
own purposes—'those wicked caytifes', he called them in his consecration
sermon for the College chapel, 'who uniustly detaine the tithes from their
right owners'. That he had the gentry (and the aristocracy) in his sights here
is suggested by his further imprecations against the same men who 'oftentimes allot more cost for a sepulchre to hide their carcasses, than they and all
their progenitors have been at charge to the church it standeth in'.[63]
Through Prideaux's Act oration the duty to pay tithes was thus set out for

60. *The Letters of John Chamberlain*, ed. N. Egbert McClure, 2 vols. (Philadelphia, PA, 1939), i. 159;
    Curtis, *Oxford and Cambridge*, 4–5; Clark, *Register*, i. 136; Foster, *Alumni*, ii. 586.
61. Above, 164.
62. 'Oratio V', 41–9, esp. 46–7, in *VDL*; P. Christianson, 'Selden, John (1584–1654), lawyer and
    historical and linguistic scholar', *ODNB*.
63. Prideaux, *A Sermon Preached*, sig. B2.1.

the instruction of a particular sector of his audience. From a great public occasion came a practical moral lesson.

4. Reason and theology

Prideaux's methods and objects as both a scholar and an intellectual, as well as his powers of argument, can also be illustrated in another way by looking more closely at one particular Act lecture: that which he gave in 1629 'On the use of logic in theological matters (*De Usu Logices in Theologicis*)'.[64] Despite its dry and narrow-sounding title, this lecture ranged widely to consider the large question of the relationship between reason (a much broader concept than logic alone) and theology. This was a topic of much contemporary interest. Luther, Calvin, and the early Protestant reformers had slighted the role of 'philosophy' in theological discussion, but in the late sixteenth and early seventeenth century the interaction between faith, reason, and scriptural revelation was being discussed in a more positive way, and the essential compatibility between these sources of enlightenment emphasized. This approach was particularly well exemplified in the writings of Bartholomew Keckermann (1572–1609), the German Calvinist, theologian, and educator, whose collected works Prideaux possessed and in whose footsteps he partly followed.[65]

In his lecture Prideaux was concerned in the first place to show that the exercise of reason was necessary both to understand the Scriptures in their literal sense and also to draw out their meaning and implications; and, in the second place, to argue that every man had within him the capacity to exercise that reason. Taking his text from Luke 12:57, 'Yea, and why even of yourselves judge ye not what is right?', he went on to cite other passages from the Gospels and the Epistles in which Christ rebuked his disciples and the Sadducees, and Paul his converts, for their ignorance of the Scriptures

---

64. *VDL*, 215–29. This lecture has been almost entirely ignored by historians of theology; but see, for a few useful comments, S. Rehnman, 'Alleged Rationalism: Francis Turretin on Reason', *Calvin Theological Journal*, 37 (2002), 255–69. For a general introduction to the subject, see Muller, *Post-Reformation Reformed Dogmatics*, i. 231–49.

65. B. Keckermann, *Opera Omnia*, 2 vols. (Geneva, 1614): WCL, U.C. 7. For Keckermann, see R. A. Muller, 'Vera Philosophia cum sacra Theologia nusquam pugnat: Keckermann on Philosophy, Theology, and the Problem of Double Truth', *The Sixteenth Century Journal*, 15 (1984), 341–65. Oxford undergraduates would have encountered Keckermann as the author of standard works on logic.

and their teachings. That ignorance was to be deplored and censured. The ability to reason and to discern was a matter of right judgement and was implanted by nature. It did not need learning, but merely the application of a mature, unprejudiced, and industrious mind. In addition, however, for reason to operate most effectively, spiritual enlightenment, the gift of the Holy Spirit, was necessary. Reason might also be directed institutionally, especially in theological controversies, through the judgements of the church, its councils, and its bishops. But essentially the powers of judgement and discernment, exercised through reason, lay with the individual. Bringing to bear these powers on disputes concerning Scripture would ensure their just settlement.

Prideaux went on to consider qualifications, limitations, and objections to his central argument. Reason was not infallible. It might be corrupted or ignored, and there was no means of compelling men to obey its prescriptions. In rejecting the decisions of the Council of Nicaea the Arians had failed to use reason, while the Catholic belief in what was impossible, the doctrine of transubstantiation and the Mass, and the Lutheran belief in ubiquitarianism, the hypothesis that Christ in his human nature was present everywhere (so justifying the further belief in his real presence in the Eucharist), were both contrary to reason. Yet despite the paramount need for right reason, it remained subordinate to theology, an instrument of faith and not faith's superior. Some of the mysteries of the faith, such as the Trinity and the hypostatic union (the union of the divine and human in Christ) rested on revelation: they were not contrary to reason, like transubstantiation, but rather beyond reason's grasp, incomprehensible but not impossible. But there was no war between philosophy (i.e. reason) and theology—a statement in which Prideaux echoed Keckermann[66]—and St Paul's criticisms of philosophy were aimed only at its fraudulent and abusive forms and applications.[67] They were not a condemnation of philosophy *tout court*.

Finally, Prideaux rested his case on a dense network of syllogistic argument in which the terms of the syllogisms were used to elicit conclusions from Scripture, once again pointing to the indispensability of reason in making deductions about matters of faith. In technical language—though

---

66. *VDL*, 228; Muller, 'Vera Philosophia', 350.
67. The *locus classicus* is Colossians, 2: 4–8: 'Beware lest any man spoil you through philosophy and vain deceit.' Cf. Prideaux's citation of this passage, *VDL*, 226.

it should have been intelligible enough to those in his audience who had followed the Oxford arts course—he put his talents as a logician at the service of a higher discipline, one in which he was also an expert. Here once again he was hardly original, but merely following 'the Reformed scholastic view of the proper construction of syllogistic arguments in which both faith and reason provided elements of the proof'.[68]

Two further points are implicit in Prideaux's exposition. Firstly, his lecture—and here it resembled his earlier Act lectures on grace—had an essentially pastoral purpose. That purpose was to direct the hearer or reader towards salvation: 'In matters pertaining to salvation (*in rebus ad salutem spectantibus*) each man can and ought to judge for himself' (that is, through the exercise of right reason).[69] The key to salvation, it is implied, lies in the rational deductions to be made from Scripture about belief and conduct: a further mitigation of the seemingly cruel imperatives of predestination. Here perhaps was a special message for the country clergy present at the Act to take home to their flocks.

Secondly Prideaux's lecture was not only pastoral in intention. It was also aggressively polemical, intended to confound the enemies of the Protestant churches and to a lesser extent those deviants within the church: mainly Catholics, but also Lutheran ubiquitarians, Dutch Remonstrants, such as Johannes and Petrus Geesteranus,[70] and the Socinians. Predictably, it was the Catholics, particularly the Jesuits and members of the Catholic hierarchy, such as Cardinal Perron, whom Prideaux condemned most strongly. They failed to use reason correctly and so veered away from a true interpretation of the Scriptures: 'Professing themselves to be wise, they became fools' (Romans, 1:22). As for the Socinians, their failing was to make reason the sole path to the truth—at the expense, presumably, of revelation and of the mysteries of the faith which were beyond reason's comprehension.[71]

Much of Prideaux's learning and intellectual enterprise, finding their expression through sermons as well as lectures, was directed towards the establishment of an accurate biblical text and of the text's literal meaning. In this lecture he moved in another, but related direction: towards showing

---

68. For Prideaux's use of logic, see esp. *VDL*, 218, 225–7. Cf. Muller, *Post-Reformation Reformed Dogmatics*, i. 246–7.
69. *VDL*, 217, 226.
70. Ibid., 217. For the Geeseteranus brothers, see *The British Delegation at the Synod of Dort*, ed. Milton, 323, 360–1.
71. *VDL*, 223; Muller, *Post-Reformation Reformed Dogmatics*, i. 240–1.

how salvific conclusions might be drawn from that text, to the spiritual profit of its readers.

5. The instruction of the young

In these lectures, orations, and sermons, and in their subsequent publication Prideaux's learning was put to its most public and pedagogic use. But there was another side altogether to his work as a moral instructor and educator. His reputation was built not only on the erudition displayed in his lectures and publications but also on his skills as a teacher of undergraduates. If these skills were reflected in his college activities as a tutor and a selector of tutors, they also bore fruit in a wider world through his writings. He was a notable compiler of undergraduate textbooks, basic introductions to a variety of subjects intended for those taking the arts course. His first book, the *Tabulæ ad Grammatica Graeca Introductoriæ*, was a short and elementary guide to Greek grammar, written 'for the sake of beginners (*in gratiam tyronum*)' and for 'the most excellent young men' whom he addressed in a preface setting out the reasons for their needing to learn Greek. Published in 1607, and running (without the preface) to a mere eighteen pages, it was reprinted twice, in 1629 and 1639. Each of the reprints was paired with an equally short work on syllogisms, the *Tyrocinium ad Syllogismum*, serving as an introduction to logic, the basic component of the arts course. Written, like the *Tabulae*, in 1607 for the particular benefit of three noble youths from Denmark, the first known of Prideaux's many foreign pupils, this beginner's text had evidently remained unpublished for more than twenty years. The 1639 reprint was supplemented by another brief work, the *Heptades*, on the seven divisions of logic.[72]

Other samples of Prideaux's teaching never moved into print, but seem to have circulated in manuscripts presumably deriving from his lectures. Aubrey tells us that during his short stay at Trinity College in 1642–3 he used both Prideaux's logic notes ('as good perhaps as any . . . short and clear'), which he and others learnt by heart, and also a short work on ethics, reputedly by Prideaux, 'well-digested, clear and short'.[73] As a writer for

---

72. Madan, i. 68, 146, 215–16; above, 22–3.
73. *Aubrey on Education*, ed. J. E. Stephens (1972), 116, 120; *HUO*, iv. 296–7.

the young, clarity and brevity were plainly Prideaux's leading characteristics and probably those most likely to commend him to readers and note-takers.

Prideaux's main pedagogical works were published, and probably written, only in the last years of his life. More substantial and broader in scope than his earlier works in the same genre, they covered not only the main elements in the arts course, but also the subsidiary subjects, particularly history and geography, which now formed part of the less formal syllabus, beyond the boundaries of what was required for the degree. The range of knowledge which they embodied was even more miscellaneous than this summary suggests. These works are discussed in more detail below, in relation to Prideaux's activities in the late 1640s, and what follows is no more than a résumé.[74]

The most remarkable of these later productions was Prideaux's *Hypomnemata* [Notes on] *Logica, Rhetorica, Physica, Metaphysica, Pneumatica, Ethica, Politica, Oeconomica* (Oxford, 1648): an encyclopedic guide to knowledge and philosophy. Its first and longest section dealt with logic, but it also covered other subjects relevant to the arts course, such as rhetoric and ethics, as well as the organization and government of the state, and an extraordinary mixture of other subjects, including the natural world (birds, quadrupeds, snakes, etc.). Dedicated 'to the neophytes of Exeter College', it was explicitly a work for undergraduates, intended, as the preface states, to supplement their tutors' teaching. A second work of 1648, the *Easy and Compendious Introduction for Reading all Sorts of History*, was said on its title page to have been compiled 'out of the papers of Matthias Prideaux', but was wholly the work of his father, intended to provide a well-ordered survey of world history, biblical, Greek and Roman, secular and ecclesiastical, English and European. The third and final work was more specialized and aimed at a different readership. Dedicated to the clergy of the diocese of Worcester, the 'Collection of Theological Controversies put together for the Comprehension of the Young and of Post-holders (*Fasciculus Controversiarum Theologicarum ad Juniorum aut Occupatorum Captum sic Colligatus*)' was, as its title suggests, a general survey of theology intended for the instruction of the clergy and also for the *juniores*, probably meaning young men, undergraduates and BAs, who might be contemplating a clerical career.[75]

74. Below, 360, 364–7.
75. Madan, ii. 473, 483–4, 486–7.

The last of his works to be published in his lifetime, it returned Prideaux to his starting-point in theology.

Collectively these works, stretching in date from 1607 to 1649, constituted a substantial achievement. This was especially true of the last three. Prideaux was by no means unique, or even unusual, in turning his hand to the writing of undergraduate textbooks. A good number of other Oxford tutors did the same. The forerunner here was John Case, fellow of St John's from 1568 to 1574, thereafter a private tutor in Oxford, and the author of an extensive range of Aristotelian handbooks;[76] but in Prideaux's own day the most successful such author was Robert Sanderson, fellow of Lincoln from 1606 to 1619 and, much later, Prideaux's successor in the regius chair, whose *Logicae Artis Compendium* of 1615 became 'the most influential English textbook of the seventeenth century'.[77] Nor was the less formal side of the syllabus neglected. For the teaching of history, for example, one standard work was the *De Ratione et methodo legendi historias dissertatio* (1623) by Degory Wheare, Prideaux's former colleague as fellow of Exeter and afterwards the first Camden professor of history.[78] Besides these and similar books, much also circulated in manuscript and only emerged into print much later, if at all. Prideaux's notes on ethics and logic which Aubrey and his friends relied on were paralleled by the manuscript bibliographies which Thomas Barlow compiled for his pupils when he was a tutor at Queen's in the 1630s and 1640s.[79] For those who wanted to learn there was no shortage of 'study aids' or of tutors keen to turn their tutorial notes and college lectures into marketable commodities. The possibility of profit as well as the needs of pupils must have provided a powerful incentive to publish.

Where did Prideaux stand in this crowded field? Resembling other authors in his college teaching experience and knowledge of undergraduates, Prideaux nevertheless had a distinctive place among them in two ways. First the range of his work was much wider than that of any comparable

76. Madan, i. 14–15, 25–6, 32–3, 39, 44, 45; J. W. Binns, *Intellectual Culture in Elizabethan and Jacobean England* (Leeds, 1990), 366–77; Hegarty, *Biographical Register of St John's College*, 31–2; E. A. Malone, 'Case, John (1540/41?–1600), philosopher and physician', *ODNB*.

77. Madan, i. 104; *HUO*, iv. 297; J. S. McGee, 'Sanderson, Robert (1587–1663), bishop of Lincoln', *ODNB*.

78. Madan, i. 128–9; Salmon, 'Wheare'.

79. J. Spurr, 'Barlow, Thomas (1608/9–1691), bishop of Lincoln', *ODNB*; 'A Library for Younger Schollers' Compiled by an English Scholar Priest about 1655, ed. A. de Jordy and H. F. Fletcher (Urbana, IL, 1961), v–xii.

figure. If he wrote most extensively on that most favoured of all subjects, logic, whether in brief in his *Tyrocinium* or at length in the *Hypomnemata*, he also provided guidance on Greek grammar and on history, geography, and theology. His attention to natural history, again in the *Hypomnemata*, an extraordinarily wide-ranging work unparalleled in others' writings, broke new ground in terms of tutorial instruction, while his *Easy and Compendious Introduction* enjoyed 'immense popularity', selling by the thousand until at least the 1670s.[80] Secondly, no other writer of textbooks combined this role with that of an outstanding scholar in the deeper world of learning which constituted the European republic of letters. It is true that all those who wrote textbooks were learned men, John Case and Robert Sanderson particularly so. But none had quite the reputation which Prideaux enjoyed as an *érudit*, a linguist and biblical expert, and a man who drew on his learning to become the foremost defender of what was, until the mid-1620s, Anglican orthodoxy. That the university's leading theologian should also have been one of its foremost instructors of undergraduates was remarkable. It is hard to see comparably learned men—a Savile, say, or an Ussher—settling down to write elementary tracts on syllogisms. Prideaux's *oeuvre* in this field confirms one of the arguments of this book; that much of his achievement lay in his intellectual direction of the young.

6. Prideaux's books

Like that of any other *érudit*, Prideaux's learning was dependent upon his access to a multiplicity of books. We are fortunate here in knowing a good deal about Prideaux's own library, its contents, and its eventual dispersal, for his library must have been the major resource which he drew on for his lectures and his teaching. In his will, drawn up in June 1650, shortly before his death, he divided his books between his two sons-in-law, William Hodges and Henry Sutton, both of them parish priests in Prideaux's former diocese of Worcester. On Hodges's death in 1676 his daughter sold her father's share to Worcester Cathedral library, where the books remain. Although the descent of those left to Henry Sutton is less certain, some of

---

80. *HUO*, iv. 333.

them also came to Worcester after Sutton's death in 1687.[81] But before making his will Prideaux had already sold a large part of his library to alleviate his poverty after the loss of his bishopric in 1646 and of all other forms of support save for the charity of his two sons-in-law. John Gauden, a post-Restoration successor in Prideaux's see, wrote fancifully that 'having first, by indefatigable studies, digested his excellent library into his minde, [he] was after forced again . . . to devour all his books with his teeth, turning them by a miraculous faith and patience, into bread for himself and his children'.[82] So the library at Worcester is only the residue of what must once have been a much larger collection.

It remains, however, a substantial one, comprising some 700 books, each one clearly identifiable by Prideaux's bold signature 'Jo: Prideaux', across the title page (see Figure 6).[83] Taken by itself, a library of this size would put Prideaux among the middle ranks of episcopal and clerical book owners, with fewer books than some archbishops, where Archbishop Bancroft led the field with more than 6,000 books, but rather more than, say, Arthur Lake, bishop of Bath and Wells, who may have possessed about 500. John Rainolds, president of Corpus Christi College and comparable to Prideaux both as a head of house and as a distinguished theologian, possessed about 1,800.[84] But the contents of Prideaux's Worcester library are more significant that the numbers of books in this truncated collection. Predictably, by far the greater part comprised theological works, exegetical, doctrinal, and polemical, published on the Continent, like most such works. They were both Catholic and Protestant. The leading contemporary Catholic writers are represented, for example, by a thirteen-volume set of Baronius's *Annales*, already established as the standard Catholic history of the church, and by three works of Cardinal Bellarmine, a frequent target in Prideaux's

81. Butcher, 'Dr John Prideaux', 16–20. Some of Prideaux's books at Worcester are signed 'Henry Sutton', in very small writing within the loop of the large 'J' in Prideaux's title-page signature, e.g. WCL, G.C. 1, Hospinianus, *De Templis*.
82. J. Gauden, *A Pillar of Gratitude humbly Dedicated to the glory of God* (1661), 13–14.
83. Prideaux's books have been integrated into the general holdings of the cathedral library and are not readily separable. The library has various partial and often inaccurate listings of his books, but there is no comprehensive catalogue. The above figure of *c*.700 is based on a collation of these lists and an examination of many of the books. For a catalogue of the cathedral library, inadequate and inaccurate but better than nothing, see M. Day, *A Catalogue of the Printed Books in the Worcester Cathedral Library* (Oxford, 1880). This lists many of Prideaux's books but does not identify them as such. For a short survey of Prideaux's Worcester books, see Butcher, 'Dr John Prideaux', 20–2.
84. D. Pearson, 'The Libraries of English Bishops, 1600–40', *The Library*, 6th ser., 14 (1992), 225–6.

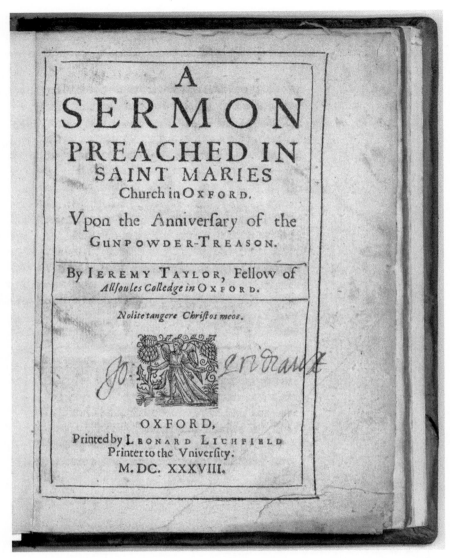

Figure 6. Prideaux's copy of Jeremy Taylor's first published work (1638), signed across the title page by Prideaux in the manner in which he signed all his books. The sermon, dedicated to Archbishop Laud, was 'a virulent and historically detailed attack on the treachery of Roman Catholics' (*ODNB*).

lectures.[85] There were also works by a large number of Jesuit writers, including Eudaemon-Joannes (five volumes), Becanus, Mariana, and the Englishman, Robert Parsons.[86] Among Protestant theologians, the Dutch anti-Arminians were conspicuous, with six works by Franciscus Gomarus and four by Sibrandus Lubbertus.[87] Both men had been present at the Synod of Dort. Prideaux's English co-religionists were still more prominent, with books by Thomas Morton (seven), Sebastian Benefield (three), Hugh Broughton (five), John Day (four), Mathew Sutcliffe (five),[88] and, especially William Ames. Prideaux owned seven works by Ames, a 'radical puritan', to whom he sometimes referred familiarly in his lectures as 'our Ames'.[89] For a Protestant, more fundamental than any of these was, of course, the Bible. At least seven versions remain among Prideaux's books at Worcester, including a Latin Vulgate of 1528, Luther's German Bible, published at Frankfurt in 1580, and the Catholic translation into English published at Douai in 1609.[90]

All these represent the merest sampling of the collection's theological riches. Its remaining contents, perhaps no more than 10 per cent of the whole, were much more miscellaneous. There were a few Greek and Roman classics, including works by Xenophon, Thucydides, Sophocles, and Caesar,[91] and many dictionaries, grammar and lexicons, including the dictionary of eleven languages by the Italian lexicographer Calepinus and a Hebrew grammar by Casper Waser. Some books related to the arts course: a three-volume set of Aristotle's *Physics* (Lyons, 1601) and a much earlier edition of Quintilian's *Orationes* (Cologne, 1527).[92] Mathematics and science made their own showing. Prideaux possessed copies of the *Arithmetica, Logarithmica* (1624), the chief work of the Oxford mathematician and inventor of logarithms Henry Briggs; the *Opera Mathematica* (1561) of the German polymath Johannes Scharus; and the *De Anni Ratione* (1593), the most important calendrical and computational work of the thirteenth-century

---

85. WCL, E.A. 9–13, E.F. 1–8; U.H.8, Y.I. 42, Y.G. 38.
86. WCL, H.D. 16, Y.E. 49, Y.I. 23; Y.I. 135, U.F. 16; C.I. 15; C.C. 1; Y.H. 14.
87. WCL, Y.E. 69, Y.I. 32, 33, 34, U.K. 7; U.F. 17, X.G. 10, Y.E. 47, Y.K. 9. For Lubbertus, see Milton, *Catholic and Reformed*, 398–9, 405, 407 n. 105, 420, 457; for Gomarus, ibid., 411, 419–20, 435, 483–4.
88. WCL, H.I. 11, W.D. 7, W.D. 11, W.F. 13, Y.F. 11, Y.I. 3; Y.K. 10, 11; W.F. 12, Y.C. 21, Y. F. 12; W.G. 15, Y.C. 21; Y.C. 34; Q.I. 8; I.D. 3, W.F. 10, W.H. 3, Y.E. 20, Y.G. 3.
89. WCL, C.E. 6, H.I. 7, H.I. 10, I.D. 7; U.K. 15, X.H. 10, Y.E. 42; *VDL*, 19, 87; Milton, *Catholic and Reformed*, 188.
90. WCL, A.E. 4, W.I. 37–9. For other versions, see A.B. 6–8, A.C. 2–7, A.E. 6.
91. WCL, S.C. 1, S.C. 4, S.K. 10, R.K. 6; R.B. 2, Y.G. 20.
92. WCL, W.F. 17–19, R.G. 10.

astronomer and cartographer Johannes de Sacrobosco.[93] Also present were many pamphlets and some substantial books relating to Reformation history and contemporary politics, for example works on the history of the Waldensians, on the 1609 oath of allegiance to the Crown, and on the Synod of Dort, including its *acta*.[94]

But the two authors most fully represented in the Worcester collection, in terms of the numbers of their works owned by Prideaux, did not quite fall into any of these categories. They were Johannes Alsted (1588–1638) and Otto Casmann (1562–1607). Alsted, a German Calvinist minister and intellectual polymath, was best known for his *Encyclopaedia* (1630), which has been described as 'nothing short of a summary . . . of everything that the mind of European man had yet conceived or discovered'. But he also wrote extensively on logic and theology. Prideaux owned twenty-three of his works, including the *Encyclopaedia*, two books on logic, and most of his theological writings.[95] By contrast, Otto Casmann, a German humanist and professor of philosophy, was a pioneering student of anthropology and psychology who also wrote on the sea and the tides. Prideaux possessed eighteen of his books, including his major *Psychologia* (1594), together with other works on logic, astrology, theology, and marine questions.[96] His extensive collections of both these authors offer one of the best indications of the breadth of his intellectual interests.

Equal in interest to the books present at Worcester are those which we might expect to find in Prideaux's library but which are absent. Particularly noticeable absentees are the works of the Fathers. Athanasius, Bede, and St John Chrysostom are present in *Opera Omnia* form; but not Augustine, Basil, Clement of Alexandria, Cyril, Eusebius, Hilary, Jerome, or Tertullian, to take the works usually found in moderately well-stocked private theological libraries.[97] Of the founding fathers of Protestantism, Prideaux had Luther's Latin works in seven volumes (Wittenberg, 1554–83) and one minor work

---

93. WCL, P.F. 5, U.D. 11, Y.I. 50.
94. WCL, Y.E. 18; Y.E. 8; I.D. 2, C.K. 11.
95. P. Miller, *The New England Mind: The Seventeenth Century* (Cambridge, MA, 1982), 102–3; WCL, B.D. 4, G.I. 3–10, P.I. 10, U.C. 6–6A (the *Encyclopaedia*), U.H. 14, U.K. 13, 14, 17, X. G. 14, Y.C. 48, Y.E. 46, Y.F. 26, Y.I. 17, Y.K. 1, Y.T. 1.
96. WCL, U.H. 9, X.E. 9, X.F. 13, Y.E. 44 (*Psychologia*), 50, Y.F. 39, 40, 48, Y.G. 30, Y.H. 1, 13, 15; Y.K. 12, 21, 39, 41.
97. WCL, D.C. 6, 7; E.B. 3–5; D.B. 7–10, D.E. 1–7. For books commonly found in such libraries, see Pearson, 'Libraries of English Bishops', 228–9.

of Melanchthon,[98] but apparently no Beza, Bucer, or —most surprising of all—Calvin. Of the schoolmen, Aquinas features with one summary work (but not the full *Summa*), and Prideaux also owned Peter Lombard's *Sentences*,[99] but there is no Hugh of St Victor, Bradwardine (whose *De Causa Dei* in Savile's edition of 1618 we would certainly expect Prideaux to have acquired), Duns Scotus, or Ockham. Of the classics, there is no Plato or Cicero. And as striking as the absence of Calvin is the similar absence of books by Prideaux's friends and colleagues. Not a single one of the many works of James Ussher survives among Prideaux's books at Worcester, nor do the major works of the two most intellectually distinguished fellows of Exeter in Prideaux's time—George Hakewill's *An Apologie of the Power and Providence of God*, and Nathanael Carpenter's *Geographie Delineated*. Yet it is almost impossible to believe that Prideaux did not possess both.

An overview of the missing books confirms our initial impression that the Worcester holdings are a relict collection, the diminished remnant of a once much larger library. Evidence for sales of books around the time of Prideaux's death substantiates the remarks of Gauden and points to the main route for the library's partial dispersal. Wood tells us that Thomas Barlow, Prideaux's friend and Oxford colleague, bought at Worcester a manuscript copy of Grosseteste's *Epistolae* which Prideaux had borrowed from Sir Thomas Cotton but failed to return (a reminder both of Prideaux's Protestant interest in the anti-papal Grosseteste and of his library's holding of manuscripts as well as printed books).[100] Two other manuscripts containing works by Roger Bacon and formerly owned by Prideaux were acquired by the Gloucestershire antiquary John Theyer, in 1651.[101] Prideaux's copy of Beza's edition of the Latin New Testament, now in the custody of the National Trust at Blickling Hall in Norfolk, bears the date 'April:1 1649' and two prices '10.6' and '5s'—evidence for a sale some fourteen months before Prideaux's death and, incidentally, for his possession of a book by one of the Protestant Fathers whose works are missing at Worcester.[102] How these books were sold we do not know; but sold they were.

98. WCL, I.H. 1–7, Y.E. 57.
99. WCL, Y.K. 34, G.K. 11.
100. Wood, *Life and Times*, ii. 174 n. 10; above, 202. The manuscript is now Bodl. MS Barlow 49.
101. G. F. Warner and J. P. Gilson, *Catalogue of Manuscripts in the Old Royal and King's Collection*. Vol. I: *Royal MSS 1.A.I to 11.E.XI* (1921), 201–3. For Theyer, see C. Fell-Smith, rev. R. J. Haines, 'Theyer, John (bap. 1598, d.1673), antiquary', *ODNB*. The two MSS are now BL MS Royal 7. F. VII and VIII.
102. National Trust, Blickling Hall Library, NT 3008070.

More information on the library's contents and further piecemeal evidence for its dispersal come from what we know of the books excluded from the Worcester deposit and of their current locations. Some thirty-three books in this category have been found, but no doubt many still await discovery. Perhaps the most significant is Prideaux's set of Augustine, a basic author already noted as missing at Worcester. Prideaux owned the eleven-volume folio edition of Augustine's works printed by Froben at Basle in 1569 and now housed in the Hurd Library at Hartlebury Castle in Worcestershire, formerly the bishop of Worcester's country residence. Since one volume is signed by Henry Sutton as well as by Prideaux, and since the set was given to Hartlebury by a private donor only in 1810, we may guess that the Augustine, a valuable set, was among the books assigned to Sutton in Prideaux's will and subsequently among those dispersed, possibly by sale, after Sutton's death.[103] Two other major works, also in folio, are likely to have been similarly valuable: Sir Henry Savile's huge (916-page) edition of *Rerum Anglicarum Scriptores*, published at Frankfurt in 1601 and now in Hereford Cathedral Library, and *Chronica*, the world history of Marianus Scotus, published at Basle in 1559 and now in the Folger Library.[104]

Other lesser books outside Worcester mix secular and religious themes. Some are scattered through the Oxford colleges: a Latin edition of Machiavelli's *Il principe* (Frankfurt, 1622) at Brasenose; Paulus Manutius's edition of the laws of Rome (Paris, 1557) at Worcester; Brian Twyne's Latin work on the antiquities of Oxford University (1608) at Exeter; Elijah Levita's Hebrew Grammar in a Latin translation by Sebastian Munster (Basle, 1562) at All Souls; and so on.[105] This fairly comprehensive selection emphasizes the diversity of the whole: Prideaux's books were by no means confined to theological themes. A similar diversity characterizes the books which have migrated to North America. In addition to the Marianus Scotus at the Folger, there are, among others, a scriptural chronology compiled by John More (1593), also at the Folger; a collection of sermons by John Rainolds (Oxford, 1613) at the Huntington Library; and William Prynne's first

---

103. Hurd Library, Hartlebury Castle. I am grateful to Chris Penney, the Hurd Librarian, for her help and advice on Prideaux books at Hartlebury.
104. Hereford Cathedral Library 23. B. 5; Folger Shakespeare Library, Washington, 191–808f.
105. Brasenose College Library, Lath. 8. 13. 1; Worcester CL, FF. w.5; Exeter CL, 9M 2440S; All Souls Codrington L, 8: SR. 68c.27.

published work, on predestination theology (1627), at the Union Theological Seminary, New York.[106]

Prideaux's library was thus probably one of exceptional size. It reflected the tastes and interests of one who had some claim to be regarded as a bibliophile, 'a true glutton for books (*verus librorum helluo*)', as Gauden calls him.[107] Some of his bibliophilic traits are evident in his treatment of the books themselves. Not only is each one signed, but smaller and thinner items have usually been bound together as *Sammelbände*, composite volumes, usually in limp vellum and with a numbered list of the various items in Prideaux's hand at the front of each. Although he rarely annotated his books, he quite frequently summarized their contents on the endpapers and sometimes used red crayon to underline or mark up particular passages. Many of the surviving books also bear a number and a letter on the inside cover, which suggests a shelf order and the possible existence of a catalogue. He also possessed some valuable incunabula, which suggests the tastes of a collector,[108] but in general this was a working collection. We are fortunate to know something about its formation. It was largely put together from the Continental sources which published and supplied most theological books to the English universities and to private scholars. Prideaux's copy of the printed 1620 Bodleian catalogue contains a manuscript list in his hand of thirty-four books selected 'from the Frankfurt Spring catalogue 1641'. Like his more famous contemporary Robert Burton, he presumably chose books from the Frankfurt catalogues, a main source for English book imports, for subsequent private purchase from Oxford or London booksellers.[109] On other occasions he may have bought direct from the Continent, as evidenced by a receipt noting his payment, via an agent, of 40 Carolus guilders 'for certain books' purchased from Bonaventura Elzevir, the celebrated Leiden bookseller and publisher, in 1627: a reminder of the cost of

106. Folger Shakespeare Library 18074 copy 2; Huntington Library RB 39644; Union Theological Seminary Library 1627 P 97.
107. Gauden, *A Pillar of Gratitude*, 13.
108. e.g., WCL, INC 1, formerly E.H. 14, Johannes Gallensis, *Summa Collationum* (Argentan, 1479).
109. WCL, Select A. 62. 1; J. Roberts, 'Importing Books for Oxford, 1500–1640', in J. P. Carley and C. G. C. Tite (eds.), *Books and Collectors, 1200–1700: Essays Presented to Andrew Watson* (1997), 317, 324, 328.

Prideaux's library and of the private wealth which made possible its accumulation.[110]

All the evidence indicates that Prideaux's books were collected with discrimination, read with care, treated with respect, and highly valued. His personal library was the armoury of his learning. But his use of books was not, of course, confined to what he owned. He could also draw upon those to be found in the College library and in the Bodleian. The full resources of Exeter's library at this time are unclear, but we know that Sir William Petre's gifts in 1567, including an eight-volume set of Augustine, a four-volume set of Jerome, and Erasmus's edition of Eusebius, had provided the library with some basic works in theology and church history, adding to what may already have been present.[111] Under Rector Holland the rector's accounts occasionally note specific purchases—four untitled volumes by Bellarmine in 1603–4, the *Annales* of Baronius in 1607–8—and, more frequently, substantial payments for purchases from John Bill, the leading London bookseller, and for chains, often in large numbers, for securing the larger books: eleven dozen in 1603–4 alone.[112] Even if titles are usually lacking, a learned college was spending appropriately on the means to learning. But Exeter's resources were soon dwarfed by those of the Bodleian, which already had 2,000 books by the time of its opening in 1602 and 15,000 by the time of its founder's death in 1613.[113] From the sparse records of Bodleian readers, which exist only for 1602–3 and, in a different form, for 1648–9, we can see something of Prideaux's activities here. As a newly elected fellow of Exeter, he visited the library on eleven days between July and November 1602–3, and, as an elderly scholar approaching the end of his life, on at least six days between January and August 1648, largely, it seems, to read books on Welsh and early British history.[114] The intervening years are largely a blank. But we know that he made use of the Bodleian's up-to-date holdings of the latest foreign books when he was

110. WCL, Add. MS. 201 (presumably a stray from Prideaux's papers). The receipt is witnessed by Prideaux's fellow Calvinist scholar, Festus Hommius, 'Coll.Theol. Regens'. For the costliness of books, often beyond the means of scholars, see Quantin, *The Church of England and Christian Antiquity*, 110–11.

111. Maddicott, *Founders*, 291–2.

112. ECA, A.II.9, fos. 182v, 184r, 199v, 203v (purchases from Bill), 207v (purchases from Bill), 224r, 240v, etc. For Bill, who also supplied the Bodleian, see I. G. Philip, *The Bodleian Library in the Seventeenth and Eighteenth Centuries* (Oxford, 1983), 9, 10, 13, 25; *HUO*, iv. 664–5.

113. *HUO*, iv. 660; Philip, *The Bodleian Library*, 14.

114. Bodl. Library Records d. 599, fo. 11r; Bodl. Library Records, e. 544; Clapinson, 'The Bodleian Library and its Readers', 32, 42–3; below, 360–2.

constructing his defence of Casaubon from the calumnies of Eudaemon-Joannes in 1613,[115] and it is safe to assume that he was a regular reader in Bodley's great library throughout his long academic life.

The degree and nature of Prideaux's learning was partly determined by his other roles besides those of scholar and theologian. As both regius professor and college head, he had much to occupy his time besides reading and writing. The obligations which these posts entailed stretched over three-quarters of his Oxford career. If he seems to have achieved less in the way of pure scholarship than a Scaliger or a Casaubon, achievement measured in his day primarily by commentaries, polemical writings, and edited texts, it was partly because of these other commitments. Strong-minded scholars avoided such honorific distractions: witness, for example, Ussher's rejection first of the provostship and then of the chancellorship of Trinity College, Dublin.[116] But it was also the case that Prideaux had different priorities from those of other participants in the republic of letters. His aim was to defend what he saw as Anglican orthodoxy and at the same time to educate future and current members of the clergy, and to a lesser extent future citizens, in their respective duties. His basic text was, as it had to be, the Bible, which he approached with the same skills and methods as those deployed by other textual critics in their editions of the Greek and Latin classics or the Fathers.

Effective textual criticism, and indeed the pursuit of scholarship in general, demanded certain qualities of mind, beyond the mere technical mastery of languages. The only direct comment on Prideaux's particular talents here comes from the biographical memoir by David Lloyd, who praises him for his 'expressiveness and perspicuity', the latter word meaning 'clearness of exposition, lucidity'.[117] Both these characteristics marked out Prideaux's English prose style (more straightforward than that of Clarendon, for example). Carried over into his oral performances and combined with his highly developed powers of reasoning and with a further quality mentioned by Lloyd, an exceptionally retentive memory, they help to explain his success as a teacher. An earlier stage in the scholarly process, from conception to composition, was represented by the historical research which involved Prideaux in work on manuscripts, not only in the Bodleian, but at some point too in the library of Oriel College, where he remembered once seeing

115. Above, 36.
116. Parr, *Life of Ussher*, 11; Thomas, 'Life of Learning', 225 and n. 121.
117. Lloyd, *Memoires*, 536–7.

an ancient manuscript of the Bible.[118] A good scholar needed to be an explorer, searching out new sources. His mental acuteness is a quality more difficult to pinpoint, but it may be judged from many of his textual comments, most strikingly perhaps that on a passage from the Wycliffite Bible cited in his sermon 'The Draught of the Brooke'. He notes here that the Wycliffite quotation (from Psalm 110: 7) 'Of the strond [stream], in the way he dranke' changes the tense of the original—'He shall drink of the brook in the way', in the Authorized Version, following the Hebrew text cited by Prideaux. The future tense has become a past tense, what Prideaux calls the preterperfect, thus altering the whole meaning of a passage which he interprets as a prophetic reference to Christ's future passion: 'The putting of the preterperfect tense for the future intimates rather a thing past than a prophecy somewhat to come.'[119] Prideaux the scholar could deal well enough with the grand themes of his subject: grace, predestination, the descent and authority of the church. But his expertise was grounded in the first place on those minute and pedantic studies in which he was fitted to excel and which no doubt gave him pleasure.[120]

---

118. *VDL*, 194.
119. 'The Draught of the Brooke', 5, in *CS*.
120. Cf. A. E. Housman to Sir Joseph Thomson, 22 Feb. 1925—'those minute and pedantic studies in which I am fitted to excel and which give me pleasure': *The Letters of A. E. Housman*, ed. A. Burnett, 2 vols. (Oxford, 2007), i. 585–6.

PART III

Events, 1624–50

7

The Decline of the Calvinist Cause, 1624–30

1. Background to change

Prideaux's halcyon years can be said to have ended in the later months of 1624. The last two events likely to have given him much cause for satisfaction were the return of Prince Charles from Spain in October 1623, signalling the abandonment of the Spanish Match, and the consecration of Hakewill's new chapel a year later in October 1624. The first marked the end of the threats posed by a Catholic alliance abroad and increased toleration for Catholics at home, and the second the liturgical consummation of the College's building programme. Each provided grounds for rejoicing. But thereafter circumstances deteriorated, locally, domestically, and nationally. The general unhealthiness which seems to have characterized the early to mid-1620s culminated in one of the century's worst plague outbreaks in 1625. Raging in Oxford from July 1625 to January 1626, the plague brought confusion and disaster to town and university, causing the dispersal of undergraduates and dons, the postponement of the start of the Michaelmas term, and the deaths of three Exeter fellows, John Lane, Henry Hyde, and John Maynard.[1] The effect on the College's fortunes of the longer period of malaise which embraced the plague was striking. The average number of annual admissions for the five years from 1623 to 1627 was lower than for any comparable quinquennium since the 1590s, and the College income responded accordingly. In 1624 the accounts showed a deficit for the only time in Prideaux's rectorship, and in 1624–5 receipts reached their lowest for

---

1. Salter, *Oxford Council Acts, 1583–1626*, 330–1, 338; Wood, *History*, ii. 356; Boase, *Register*, xcviii, 98–9.

Between Scholarship and Church Politics: The Lives of John Prideaux, 1578–1650. John Maddicott, Oxford University Press. © John Maddicott 2022. DOI: 10.1093/oso/9780192896100.003.0007

the same period.[2] In retrospect the troubles of the mid-1620s can be seen to have marked only a blip in what was a generally upward trend in numbers and revenues. But contemporaries were denied the advantage of hindsight.

For Prideaux this lengthy mortality crisis had tragic consequences. We have already noticed the concentration of his children's deaths in these few years: the 6-year-old Anne in September 1624, just a month before her father's chapel consecration sermon; the 7-year-old Mary in December 1624, and the 2-year-old Matthias in February 1625. Two further deaths, those of his wife Anne in August 1627 and of another son, Robert, in September of that year point to the years around 1625 as marking an extended break in the history of his family.[3] To conjecture about the emotional effects of these losses would be to indulge in facile psychohistory. But one change is detectable: from the mid-1620s onwards there was an asperity and a harshness in Prideaux's dealings with his inferiors and a timidity in his attitude to his superiors which had been much less evident in earlier years.

It is likely, however, that any mutations in Prideaux's character and behaviour owed more to external religious changes than to any internal convulsions which may have affected him. These changes constitute the main reason for seeing this period as bringing an end to his halcyon years. Despite Archbishop Abbot's continuing headship of the church and the continuing dominance of Calvinism at Oxford, church politics in general was beginning to move in an anti-Calvinist, pro-Arminian direction. From 1618 a small knot of anti-Calvinists had become established in the episcopate, including Laud at St David's, while James I's slumbering fear of puritan subversion and disorder, reawakened by the national agitation against the Spanish Match, was beginning to induce a less hostile approach to the Arminians—men more favourably inclined to the king's pro-Spanish policies than the Calvinist bishops and their academic supporters such as Prideaux and Hakewill.[4] In 1623, wrote Wood, with pardonable exaggeration, 'the Calvinistical opinions disappearing, the tenents of Arminius

2. ECA, A.II.9, fos 273r–v, 277v, 281v.
3. Above, 159–60.
4. S. Lambert, 'Richard Montagu, Arminianism and Censorship', *Past and Present*, 124 (1989), 40–1; K. Fincham and P. Lake, 'The Ecclesiastical Policies of James I and Charles I, in *ESC*, 34–5; Fincham and Lake, 'The Ecclesiastical Policy of King James I', 201–2; Tyacke, *Anti-Calvinists*, 102–3.

(as they were called) began to gather head'.[5] Prideaux and his colleagues could no longer feel that their doctrines and principles had the king's unqualified support.

2. The affair of Richard Montagu

Tensions came into the open with the publication of two sensational books, both written by Richard Montagu, patristic scholar, royal chaplain, canon of Windsor, holder of two rich livings in Essex and Sussex, and proto-Arminian. Montagu's *New Gagg for an Old Goose* (1624) and its sequel, *Appello Caesarem* (1625), written in response to its critics, caused a furore. The reason lay in their Romanizing and anti-Calvinist tendencies. The *New Gagg* was ostensibly a statement of Church of England doctrine written in response to provocation from a group of Roman Catholics in the author's Essex parish. But in setting out what he saw as true doctrine, Montagu deliberately marginalized Calvinist beliefs on such critical issues as predestination, arguing that these were matters of private opinion and no part of the central tenets of the Church of England, as defined by its Elizabethan Articles and Homilies. In his second book he also disowned the canons of the Synod of Dort. That James approved the publication of both books was an indication of how far his views had shifted in an Arminian direction.[6] The consequences of publication were twofold. First, Montagu's arguments identified Calvinists with puritans; and since the two parties overlapped, sharing common ground on predestination, grace, and other dogmas, this was a plausible point of view. But the effect was to suggest that Calvinist beliefs were in fact heterodox and that both Calvinists and puritans were schismatics. This was to play on and exploit James's growing phobia about the subversive nature of puritanism, to the advantage of the Arminians. To tolerate the puritans, it was implied, was to advocate Presbyterianism, the end of ecclesiastical hierarchy, and with it the undermining of hierarchy in the state. Second, the Church of England was shown to have much in common with the Church of Rome. Once Calvinist beliefs had been set to one side, there remained a body of Christian doctrine on which the moderates of both churches might agree—and that agreement was made

---

5. Wood, *History*, ii. 350.
6. Lambert, 'Richard Montagu', 44.

politically easier by Montagu's wavering on the Pope's standing as Antichrist, a point on which most Calvinists had been rigidly certain.[7]

Prideaux's own opinions were not remotely sympathetic to the extreme puritans whom both Montagu and the king saw as the greatest threat to order and orthodoxy within the church. He was a consistent critic of the godly, and primarily of the minority who wished to separate themselves from the body of the church, 'fanatical spirits' who set themselves apart to 'retire . . . to conventicles from their naturall mother' and who rejected the hierarchy of the church and its bishops in favour of congregational and presbyterial government. 'Paritie [i.e. the absence of any distinction between church ministers] is not puritie,' he wrote in his earliest published sermon.[8] Equally open to criticism was the puritans' use of extemporary prayer rather than those prayers laid down in the Prayer Book—'our puritans . . . brabbling and brawling against our set forms of prayer', those 'sudden and unconcocted flashes' which ran contrary to Scripture, the Fathers, and the practice of all Christian assemblies.[9] They were out of line too in their refusal to observe the decent and reverential customs of the church: standing at the Creed, bowing at the name of Jesus, and so on. These were not 'superstitious fooleries', the marks of popery which were to be spurned, but rather 'warrantable ceremonies'.[10] Comparable to their over nice condemnation of such traditional practices was their absurd cavilling at the naming of churches and chapels after saints, which Prideaux attacked in his consecration sermon for Exeter's new chapel. In that sermon too he highlighted one further point of difference between puritan and orthodox. Preaching and the sacraments (as well as prayer), he repeatedly emphasized, had equal value in providing 'the ordinary and blessed meanes for the begetting and confirming true faith in us'.[11] There were no concessions here to the puritans' doctrinaire exaltation of the Word, which left the sacraments very much in second place.

---

7. Fincham and Lake, 'The Ecclesiastical Policy of King James I', 202–5; Fincham and Lake, 'The Ecclesiastical Policies of James I and Charles I', 35–6; Trevor-Roper, 'Laudianism and Political Power', 63–4; Tyacke, Anti-Calvinists, 47; Milton, Catholic and Reformed, 113, 241–2.
8. Prideaux, Ephesus Backsliding, 10, 26; cf. 24; S. Hampton, 'Mera chimaera: The Reformed and Conformist Ecclesiology of John Prideaux (1578–1650)', The Seventeenth Century, 33 (2018), 287–8.
9. Prideaux, Hezechiahs Sicknesse, in CS, 13, 14; Hampton, 'Mera chimaera', 291–2.
10. Prideaux, Euchologia, 48–9; Hampton, 'Mera chimaera', 293.
11. Prideaux, A Sermon Preached, sigs. A3r, C4v, D1r.

At the heart of all these objections was a plea for both unity and uniformity within the church. The task of those discontented with the church was not 'to scatter with the envious or malcontents' but to seek reform from within; to abandon the questioning of adiaphora, things inessential to salvation, and to stay with the mainstream.[12] Some of these convictions were not so very far from those of Laud, another firm believer in the unity of the church, the need for uniformity in its practices, and the authority of its bishops. Prideaux's views on the twinned importance of preaching and the sacraments took up a middle position between the Laudian stress on the sacraments (and on the sacred role of the clergy who administered them) and the puritan emphasis on preaching.[13] Where Prideaux perhaps differed most from Laud was in paying little or no attention to the supposedly seditious nature of puritanism, its apparent association with resistance to rulers, and other forms of treason, which was a commonplace in the thinking of Laud and his associates such as Heylyn.[14] To Prideaux, the puritans were foolish and misguided, even perverse; less so were they the enemies of church and state.

But while the more radical puritans came under attack from Prideaux, he naturally shared their belief in what were still some of the core tenets of Anglican orthodoxy, such as predestination. It was Montagu's attack on these doctrines and his deliberate confusion of traditional Anglican beliefs with puritan extremism that provoked most outrage. His opinions were controverted and denounced in numerous clerical publications,[15] and Montagu himself was petitioned against in the parliament of 1624, summoned to appear before the Commons in 1625, after the publication of *Appello Caesarem*, and in 1626 found guilty of 'publishinge doctryne contrarie to the Articles of the religion established in the Churche of England'. From the start John Pym took the lead in what became a parliamentary campaign against Montagu.[16] The king, now Charles I, was asked to sanction the suppression and burning of his books. Anti-Arminian sentiment had been

---

12. Prideaux, *Ephesus Backsliding*, 16–17, 26–7; Hampton, '*Mera chimaera*', 294.
13. Milton, *Catholic and Reformed*, 319–20, 471–2.
14. Ibid., 520–3.
15. For writings against Montagu, see *Cosin Correspondence*, ed. Ornsby, i. 100 n; J. Davies, *The Caroline Captivity of the Church* (Oxford, 1992), 111; and K. Sharpe, *The Personal Rule of Charles I* (New Haven, CT, 1992), 295–6.
16. J. S. Macauley, 'Mountague [*sic*], Richard (bap.1575, d.1641), bishop of Norwich and religious controversialist', *ODNB*; Tyacke, *Anti-Calvinists*, 128; C. Russell, 'Pym, John (1584–1643), politician', *ODNB*.

inflamed by the negotiations in 1624–5 for Prince Charles's French marriage, which, in providing England with a Catholic queen and in threatening a relaxation of the recusancy laws, was as objectionable a prospect as the earlier Spanish match. The marriage deal and the arrival of the new queen, Henrietta Maria, in June 1626, with a large Catholic entourage, fanned the parliamentary anti-popery of which Montagu and his books were in part the victims.[17] The York House conference called to debate Montagu's views in 1626 was inconclusive. But he had the king's backing, as had been shown as early as 1625, when Charles attempted to rescue him from the wrath of the Commons by making him a royal chaplain. His promotion to the bishopric of Chichester in 1628 showed that he was by no means the loser from the hostility of the orthodox. Seen increasingly as embodying in his books the general growth of popery and Arminianism, he again came under attack in the parliament of 1629.[18] Ineffective though it was, his prosecution by Parliament, pursued intermittently over a period of four years, was a mark of the Calvinist convictions of many of those who sat there, and his elevation to a bishopric a royal snub to his prosecutors. As Peter Heylyn remarked, his promotion was a 'matter of exasperation to the House of Commons'.[19]

Throughout the storm which followed the publication of Montagu's two books, their author saw Oxford as his enemies' stronghold and Prideaux as the chief of those enemies. Hardly less objectionable to Montagu was Daniel Featley, in his early life an Oxford pupil of John Rainolds, the puritan president of Corpus Christi College, and now Archbishop Abbot's chaplain, Prideaux's friend and ally, and one of Montagu's fiercest critics.[20] Montagu's fears, hatreds, and vigorous opinions come vividly alive in the intimate letters which he wrote to his close friend John Cosin, canon of Durham, anti-Calvinist, and chaplain to the anti-Calvinist Richard Neile, bishop of Durham. 'For those Oxford braggarts I feare them not,' Montagu told Cosin on 30 October 1624, after the publication of his *New Gagg* but before that of *Appello Caesarem*. 'Warrs from Oxford' threatened him in May 1625, shortly after the publication of his second book, while a few days later he reported

---

17. C. Russell, *Parliaments and English Politics, 1621–1629* (Oxford, 1979), 204–8.
18. Ibid., 392, 396, 404, 409, 413; Macauley, 'Mountague', *ODNB*; Gardiner, *History of England*, v. 372–3.
19. Heylyn, *Cyprianus Anglicus*, 185.
20. For Featley, see Hunt, 'Featley'; above, 184–6.

that 'att Oxford they are all on fire'.[21] As for Prideaux, he was 'that Jack-a-napes', 'the bedlam of Ex. . . . never better than a butter-quean to raile downe right ribaldry'.[22] But what had Prideaux done to deserve Montagu's distinctive line in exotic invective? In the first place, his contempt was grounded on Prideaux's position as the leading figure among the Oxford Calvinists, his standing enhanced by his position, his learning, and his role as Montagu's leading opponent. Montagu's opinions, particularly his apparent questioning of the Dort canons and his views that the Roman church was a true church, that predestination and perseverance were no necessary part of Anglican doctrine, and that it was possible to fall from grace,[23] all expressed in his two books, were abhorrent to Prideaux. But more particularly Prideaux seems to have been responsible, along with Daniel Featley, Thomas Goade, and Joseph Hall, for drawing up the articles against Montagu presented in the parliament of 1624 and thus initiating his prosecution. The articles listed the various ways in which Montague had deviated from the orthodox Calvinist line, the chief of them listed above. His four opponents were all Calvinists. Goade and Hall had been among the British representatives at Dort, while Goade, like Featley, was one of Abbot's chaplains. All four were accused by Montagu of putting in 'Informations against mee att Parlement', and in consequence Featley's name was exposed to the same sort of vituperative fusillade—'that urchin', 'that hobby-horse'—that Prideaux had met with.[24]

In various other ways Prideaux participated in Montagu's pursuit. Some of these were indirect. In May 1625 George Palmer, an Oxford graduate disputing for the BD, argued formally that the regenerate could be totally and finally excluded from grace: a proposition which ran directly counter to the Calvinist doctrine of perseverance. In doing so he drew not only on the standard Anglican texts but also on Montagu's recently published *Appello*—only to be met with a crushing put-down from Prideaux, who, as regius professor and moderator of the disputation, accused Palmer of being more concerned with words than substance and of perverting the church's Articles and Homilies. He followed this up with a general warning to the whole

21. *Cosin Correspondence*, ed. Ornsby, i. 23, 68, 69.
22. Ibid., 69, 77. A 'butter-quean' was a scolding female butter-seller.
23. Tyacke, *Anti-Calvinists*, 125–8; Russell, 'Pym', *ODNB*.
24. *Cosin Correspondence*, ed. Ornsby, 34, 50, 69, 79, 100; E. Allen, 'Goade [Goad], Thomas', (1576–1638), theologian', *ODNB*; Hunt, 'Featley'; Tyacke, *Anti-Calvinists*, 147–9; Lambert, 'Richard Montagu', 46, 49.

company to be wary of Montagu's book and to stick to the catechisms in their initial study of divinity. Prideaux's bullying manner was in keeping with his treatment of other disputants with whose arguments he disagreed.[25] But the episode also showed his extreme sensitivity towards the doctrinal issues raised by Montagu's book and his awareness of the broad attack which they seemed to constitute on the traditions of the Elizabethan and Jacobean church.

It was not only by picking on individuals that Prideaux sought to shore up the Calvinist defences against these assaults on their integrity. In 1626 he licensed the publication of a book by George Carleton, bishop of Llandaff, the most important of several such books which joined battle against Montagu—in Carleton's case, *inter alia*, by accusing him of denying the doctrine of perseverance and by exposing his sleight of hand in identifying Calvinists with puritans.[26] It might have been expected that Prideaux himself would join the crowd of critics who attacked Montagu in print. Montagu himself expected this. 'Prideaux hath threatened to write against me', he told Cosin on 24 October 1624, before adding scornfully, 'but I thinck he distrusteth himself at his pen.'[27] In fact, Prideaux wrote nothing directly against Montagu. In 1625, however, he published his *Lectiones Novem*, the nine Act lectures which he had given between 1616 and 1624 and which had set out the fundamentals of Anglican-Calvinist beliefs on such matters as grace, justification, and perseverance. These were republished in the following year, with the addition of a tenth lecture, as *Lectiones Decem*.[28] Both books were clearly intended as a restatement of Prideaux's position and of what he regarded as orthodox doctrine, in opposition to Montagu, as the extended title to both works strongly hints: they were lectures 'concerning the heads of religion disputed especially at this time'— items in a polemic. Montagu was prepared to be unimpressed. 'I here say Dr Prideux' 9 eggs are rotten', he wrote on 7 February 1625, apropos the *Lectiones Novem*.[29] Although the battle of the books which seemed likely to

---

25. Wood, *Annals*, ii. 354; *Cosin Correspondence*, ed. Ornsby, 77, n *; below, 245–7.
26. *Cosin Correspondence*, ed. Ornsby, 100; G. Carleton, *An Examination of those Things wherein the Author of the late Appeal holdeth the Doctrines of the Pelagians and Arminians to be the Doctrines of the Church of England* (1626), 1, 5, 14, 78, 95–6; Tyacke, *Anti-Calvinists*, 155–6.
27. *Cosin Correspondence*, ed. Ornsby, i. 22.
28. J. Prideaux, *Lectiones Novem de Totidem Religionis Capitibus praecipue hoc tempore controversis prout publice habebantur Oxoniae in Vesperiis* (Oxford, 1625); Prideaux, *Lectiones Decem* (Oxford, 1626); Madan, i. 127, 130–1; above, 43–6.
29. *Cosin Correspondence*, ed. Ornsby, i. 53.

develop went no further, the publication of Prideaux's lectures, in conjunction with Montagu's animus against him, confirmed his position as the leader of the Calvinist cause. To that extent the Montagu affair marked a milestone in his career.

Prideaux's *Lectiones Novem* and *Lectiones Decem* were major contributions to a series of publications during these years, in terms of authorship the most productive of his life before its final phase in the late 1640s. In addition to the two sets of lectures, he published five separate works between 1624 and 1626. Four were single sermons or addresses: two delivered before King James at Woodstock, a third the sermon preached at the consecration of Exeter's new chapel in 1624, and the fourth another sermon addressed to the graduating Bachelors of Arts on Ash Wednesday 1625. Two were in English—one of the Woodstock sermons and the 'chapel' sermon—and the other two in Latin.[30] More substantial was the fifth, the set of nine *Orationes* delivered at the Act between 1616 and 1625 to those about to incept as doctors. Dedicated to the earl of Pembroke, the 'orations' constituted a further blast against the perversities of Montagu: 'Who today', wrote Prideaux in his preface, 'does not begin to perceive clearly Gog and Magog applying battering-rams to the defences of the church?'[31]

Prideaux's publication record during these years was thus directly related to the Montagu controversy, to which both the *Lectiones* and the *Orationes* contributed. But it may also have been intended to reinforce a claim, not to be realized for many years, for promotion to a bishopric. Montagu's correspondence makes it clear that Prideaux was seen as a likely candidate: 'But let him [Prideaux] passe for a puritan', he wrote on 24 October 1624, 'yet God graunt he, nor any such, come to the bishop of Gloucester' (the former bishop, Miles Smith, having died four days earlier). The identification of Prideaux as a puritan—one which he himself would have repudiated— is characteristic of Montague's deliberate elision of the distinctions between Calvinists and their relatives to the left. Nearly two years later, in June and

---

30. J. Prideaux, *Alloquium serenissimo regi Jacobo Woodstochiae habitum 24 Augusti 1624* (Oxford, 1624); Prideaux, *Perez-Uzzah: or The Breach of Uzzah as it was delivered in a sermon before His Majesty at Woodstock August the 24 Anno 1624* (Oxford, 1625); Prideaux, *A Sermon Preached on the fifth of October 1624: at the consecration of St James Chappel in Exceter Colledge* (Oxford, 1625); Prideaux, *Concio habita Oxoniae ad Artium Baccaulaureos in Die Cinerum Feb. 22 1626* (Oxford, 1626); Madan, i. 122, 127, 130.

31. J. Prideaux, *Orationes Novem Inaugurales de Totidem Theologiae Apicibus, scitu non indignis, prout in Promotione Doctorum Oxoniae publice Proponebantur in Comitiis* (Oxford, 1626), sig. ¶3r; Madan, i. 131.

July 1626, Montagu voiced similar fears about Prideaux's possible promotion to the see of Exeter, vacant since the death of Valentine Carey in June 1626.[32]

The prospect of such a step was entirely plausible. After all, Prideaux's predecessor in the regius chair, Robert Abbot, brother of the archbishop, had gone on to the see of Salisbury in 1615, while Prideaux's learning, reputation, and place as a royal chaplain, now reinforced by his publications in defence of established doctrine, all gave him excellent qualifications for promotion. In Montagu's fears of that happening there was a strong undercurrent of personal rivalry, for he too was angling for a bishopric. In February 1625 he had his eye on Exeter (at that time still held by Carey) and, later in the year, on St David's, should Laud vacate the see. As late as January 1627 he still had in view the now vacant see of Exeter.[33] Via his friendship with Laud, whose position as chaplain to the duke of Buckingham gave him access to the duke's great fount of court patronage, Montague stood every chance of satisfying his ambition, though in the event he had to wait until 1628 before he secured the see of Chichester.[34] Prideaux meanwhile was passed over. Gloucester went to Godfrey Goodman, a moderate Arminian, and Exeter to Joseph Hall, Prideaux's fellow Calvinist. Prideaux does not seem to have been among the several candidates considered for Gloucester,[35] nor do we know that he was ever in the running for Exeter. Despite his royal chaplaincy, he lacked the court connections available to Montague at a time when the Arminians were gaining ground generally and the Calvinists were out of favour with the new king. Had James I lived, he might have enjoyed better fortunes.

Prideaux's main source of support, besides his fellow Calvinist churchmen, lay in Parliament. Between Prideaux and the members of the Commons, the majority of them probably Calvinist,[36] there was a natural affinity which went beyond the responsibility of Prideaux and his Calvinist allies for putting before Parliament the original 'Informations' against Montague. Some members would have been known to him personally, notably perhaps Sir John Eliot, one of the leading parliamentarians of his generation, who

32. *Cosin Correspondence*, ed. Ornsby, i. 22, 95–6, 98, 100.
33. Ibid., 60, 79, 106.
34. Russell, *Parliaments*, 11–12; Macauley, 'Mountague', *ODNB*.
35. N. W. S. Cranfield, 'Goodman, Geoffrey (1583–1656), bishop of Gloucester', *ODNB*.
36. Tyacke, *Anti-Calvinists*, 128. For the anti-Arminianism of the Commons, another side of the same coin, see Russell, *Parliaments*, 404.

had matriculated at Exeter in 1607 and sat in every parliament from 1624 to 1629. In 1625, during Prideaux's time as vice-chancellor, he was given the opportunity to encounter others when plague in London caused Parliament's adjournment to Oxford, where it sat from 5 to 12 August. On the first day of the Oxford session, Exeter College chapel was appointed as the place for the Commons' Sunday communion: a largely Calvinist body directed towards a Calvinist sanctum.[37] The College's rector was seen by some in Parliament as one of the victims of Montague's gibes, in his *Appello Caesarem*, against those whom the Commons regarded as the heroes of Protestantism. In 1625 one of Montagu's offences was said to have been 'the slighting of the great and reverent divines as speaking of Calvin, Beza, Perkins, Whitaker, Reynolds, etc. . . . or Dr Prideaux, with little or no respect at all'. Here his accusers erred, for Montagu had taken care to avoid identifying his contemporary opponents by name, though, as he told Cosin, he certainly numbered Prideaux and Featley among them.[38] The Commons returned to the same point in the 1626 parliament. Montagu, they said, 'does disgrace and despise the learned divines of our Church', but this time they pointed to a critical allusion in the *Appello*: 'Everyone that prates, reads, lectures, preaches or professes must not look to have his *Theses, Lectiones, Harangues* or discourses taken as the dictates or doctrines of our church': a glancing blow, it was thought, at Prideaux's recently published *Lectiones Novem* and its extended defence of the Calvinist position.[39]

There was, however, one episode, unrelated to religion, in which the Commons ruled against Prideaux.[40] On 17 January 1626 an election was held at Oxford for the return of the university's MPs to sit in the parliament summoned to meet on 6 February. It took place in Convocation, over which Prideaux, as the current vice-chancellor, presided. The 'establishment' candidate, backed by the court, by Archbishop Abbot, and by the earl of Pembroke, was Sir Thomas Edmondes, treasurer of the king's household.

37. *CJ*, i. 810.
38. *Proceedings in Parliament, 1625*, ed. M. Jansson and W. B. Bidwell (New Haven, CT, 1987), 343; *Cosin Correspondence*, ed. Ornsby, i. 34.
39. R. Montague, *Appello Caesarem. A Just Appeale from Two Uniust Informers* (1625), 49; *Proceedings in Parliament, 1626*, ed. M. Jansson and W. B. Bidwell, 4 vols. (New Haven, CT, 1991–6), iii. 8–9.
40. For the remainder of this paragraph, see especially M. B. Rex, *University Representation in England, 1604–1690* (1954), 75–7, 107–11, 356–9; and also Wood, *Annals*, ii. 356–7; *Proceedings in Parliament, 1626*, ed. Bidwell and Jansson, ii. 300–2; *CJ*, i. 826, 837–8, 843, 846; *Chamberlain Letters*, ed. McClure, ii. 629–30; *HUO*, iv. 197.

He was also backed by Prideaux, acting for the court interest, and seemingly by Convocation's senior members, the doctors. But a majority among the electors, particularly those whom Wood calls 'the juniors', Masters of Arts and Bachelors of Divinity, favoured another candidate, Sir Francis Stuart. Unlike Edmondes, Stuart was an Oxford graduate. The election was confused and disorderly, partly because the method of electing, whether by scrutiny (i.e. counting votes) or viva voce (i.e. crying 'Placet' or 'Non placet'), was disputed. But it resulted in Prideaux's declaring Edmondes elected in the face of an apparent majority for Stuart. Two further Convocations followed in which Prideaux refused to resile from his earlier decision. The losing party, the Stuartites, obviously sure of their ground, then petitioned Parliament for a remedy. Prideaux was summoned to appear before the Commons' committee of privileges, which he did on 16 March 1626. He was (said John Chamberlain in a letter to Sir Dudley Carleton) 'to answer in returning Master Treasurer Sir Thomas Edmondes for the universitie whereas yt is pretended [asserted] Sir Fraunces Steward had more than double so many yoyces, as the schollers themselves offer to prove and make good'. The outcome was the overturning of the declared result. The election of Edmondes was pronounced void and on 23 March Sir Francis Stuart was declared elected. This was confirmed by the Commons on 4 April.

Prideaux's conduct of the 1626 election did him no favours. He had almost certainly acted at the behest of Pembroke, his patron, and chancellor to his vice-chancellor, whose letter to the electors desiring them to 'make choice of Thomas Edmondes' he had read out at the start of the first Convocation.[41] He had met the points made against him in the dissenters' petition with aggressive denials—' absolutely false . . . most false . . . no such matter . . . intolerable calumny'.[42] That his reputation suffered from this episode is suggested by a letter sent from London on 26 April 1626 by Alexander Gill, formerly of Trinity College and currently a schoolmaster at St Paul's, to his Oxford friend William Pickering, then resident in Trinity. Amid much gossip, Gill made a cutting comparison between Prideaux and Sir Thomas Bodley: 'But that the name of Prideaux should be more gratious [liable to find favour] than the name of Bodley, one having done somuch

---

41. Rex, *University Representation*, 76, 356. For Pembroke's letter, see *Proceedings in Parliament, 1626*, ed. Bidwell and Jansson, iv. 247–8.
42. Rex, *University Representation*, 356, 357, 358.

good to the universitie, and the other somuch mischeife, this indeed is Academiae naevus [a mole on the body of the university]'.[43] Gill had almost certainly favoured the candidature of Stuart, for both men were opposed to the king's favourite, the duke of Buckingham.[44] Since he wrote within a few weeks of the Commons' decision against Prideaux and in Stuart's favour, it is most likely that Prideaux's role in the disputed election lay behind the remarks in his letter. For all his qualities, Prideaux was far from being universally popular on his home ground. When the see of Exeter became vacant a little later in the summer, it may have been Prideaux's failure to secure the election of the court candidate at Oxford, his conduct of the election, and his subsequent humiliation in Parliament, which contributed to his being passed over.

Prideaux's role in the Montagu affair had been twofold. First, in laying information against Montague in the 1624 parliament and in defining the doctrinal positions on which he erred, he and his fellow Calvinists had provided the academic ammunition for the parliamentary attack on Montagu, so linking the university and the Commons as the twin centres of resistance to Arminian innovation. Second, he had confirmed his own position as the university's leading defender of Calvinist orthodoxy. It was surely this that Pembroke had in mind when, on allowing Prideaux to retire after two years as his vice-chancellor in July 1626, he wrote to Convocation of his 'keeping by his sound doctrine the fountaine cleare from the errone-ous tenets and opinions, which are apt to disturb the peace and quiet both of the Church and Commonweale, wherein I cannot enough commend his care and integritie'.[45] Before Montagu there had been few such 'erronious tenets and opinions'. Neither the university nor the Commons could in the end impede Montague's rise. He floated forward on an Arminian tide, buoyed up by the protection which he enjoyed from the king. But Prideaux had at least done what he could to distance orthodoxy from its opponents.

---

43. TNA SP 16/25, fo. 113. For Gill, see G. Campbell, 'Gil, Alexander the Younger (1596/7–1642?), headmaster and poet', *ODNB*; Hopkins, *Trinity*, 85–6, 94.

44. In 1628 Gill was imprisoned for drinking the health of Buckingham's assassin: Campbell, 'Gil'. For Stuart's opposition to Buckingham, see D. H. Willson, *The Privy Councillors in the House of Commons, 1604–1629* (Minneapolis, MN, 1940), 184–5, and Rex, *University Representation*, 107, 109–11.

45. OUA, NEP/supra/Reg. N, fos. 226v–227; Tyacke, *Anti-Calvinists*, 76–7, where 'theare' should read 'cleare'.

3. Prideaux embattled, 1627–30

In the late 1620s the Calvinist cause at Oxford was kept afloat, perhaps surprisingly, in the face of an increasingly Arminian church establishment. The theses debated at the Act often continued to engage with such Calvinist shibboleths as predestination and perseverance, while one Calvinist replaced another when Samuel Fell succeeded Sebastian Benefield as Lady Margaret professor of divinity in 1628.[46] Although there were Arminians among the heads of houses—William Juxon at St John's was one, John Bancroft at University College another—there was no sudden change in Oxford's doctrinal direction. This stability owed much to the Calvinist sympathies of Pembroke, that 'consistent supporter of godly Protestantism',[47] still the university's chancellor, and, as Daniel Featley put it, 'the custodian of that pretious *depositum* of saving truth', unadulterated by popery or Arminianism. The contrast lay with the other university, where there had been no such custodian and where the election as chancellor of the Arminian sympathizer, the duke of Buckingham, in 1626 had led to 'the muzzling of Cambridge Calvinism'.[48]

But within the church at large Oxford's Calvinists were becoming ever more isolated. Montagu's promotion to Chichester in 1628 was only one symptom of a general trend towards Arminianism. A clutch of other sees fell to Arminians about the same time: Winchester to Richard Neile in 1627, York to George Montaigne in 1628 (following on from the Calvinist Toby Matthew), and Durham to John Howson in the same year.[49] More significant still for the future of the church and the university was the rise of Laud. Moved from St David's to the richer see of Bath and Wells in 1626, and thence to London in 1628, he owed his rapid ascent not only to his own abilities and ambitions but also to the friendship of Charles and Buckingham and to the declining fortunes of George Abbot, the archbishop of Canterbury. Abbot's authority had never fully recovered from his accidental killing of a huntsman in 1622, and by the late 1620s his old-fashioned Calvinism was increasingly out of favour at court. Ill health hastened his political decline. In 1627–8 he lost his powers of jurisdiction for a period of fifteen months as a

---

46. Tyacke, *Anti-Calvinists*, 76–7; above, 230.
47. Russell, *Parliaments*, 13.
48. Featley, *The Grand Sacrilege of the Church of Rome*, sig. A3v; Tyacke, *Anti-Calvinists*, 48–9.
49. Tyacke, *Anti-Calvinists*, 161, 181; Fincham and Lake, 'The Ecclesiastical Policies', in *ESC*, 37–8.

result of Charles's displeasure at a supposed offence. Laud meanwhile had already been promised in 1626 the reversion of Abbot's archbishopric, and he was a member of the committee which exercised the displaced archbishop's legal powers in 1627–8. New appointments in 1627 as dean of the chapel royal and privy councillor consolidated his position at the centre of affairs.[50] Seen with justification as an Arminian by his enemies, he was emerging as the unofficial leader of the church.

In the long term the most damaging assault on the Calvinist position came with the two decrees published by the king's orders in June 1626 and November 1628. Rooted in the need to pacify the clashes and controversies produced by Montagu's two books, these declarations aimed to restrain the free expression of clerical opinion on matters of doctrine. The first decree placed a ban on the voicing of 'any new inventions or opinions concerning religion' which departed from Anglican orthodoxy, while the second, more specifically, prohibited any deviation from the Elizabethan Articles of Religion.[51] The decrees were to apply both to preaching and to printing. According to Heylyn, the first was largely ineffective because its publication was restricted to market towns. The second, however, was attached to the Articles themselves. Not only was it more widely published, along with the Articles, but it expressly forbade the expression of speculative opinions in the universities and their colleges, by heads of houses, among others; and it is difficult not to think that Prideaux was the head whom the king had most in mind.[52] The universities were clearly regarded as the main engines of intemperate theologizing. The decree may have been aimed impartially at the extremism of both Arminians and Calvinists,[53] but it was certainly seen as an attempt to rein in the Calvinists alone and to prevent the discussion of such unfathomable subjects as predestination, the property of Calvinists rather than Arminians. That responsibility for its drafting, and probably for

50. Milton, 'Laud'; N. Tyacke, 'Archbishop Laud', in his *Aspects of English Protestantism*, 214–15; Trevor-Roper,'Laudianism and Political Power', 64.
51. 1626 decree: J. P. Kenyon, *The Stuart Constitution, 1603–1688* (Cambridge, 1966), 154–5. 1628 decree: *The Constitutional Documents of the Puritan Revolution, 1625–1660*, ed. S. R. Gardiner, 3rd edn (Oxford, 1906), 75–6. Cf. Heylyn, *Cyprianus Anglicus*, 154; Tyacke, *Anti-Calvinists*, 48–9, 77.
52. Heylyn, *Cyprianus Anglicus*, 187–9.
53. Cf. Sharpe, *The Personal Rule of Charles I*, 281–3; Davies, *The Caroline Captivity* 115–19; Tyacke, 'Anglican Attitudes: Some Recent Writings on English Religious History from the Reformation to the Civil War', in his *Aspects*, 189–90.

that of the first decree too, lay with Laud, the known supporter of Montagu, gave some colour to this view.[54]

How did Prideaux respond to the burgeoning influence of the Arminians and the parallel restraints on freedom of expression? Although his new wife, Mary Reynell, whom he married in August 1628, may have brought him domestic stability and personal happiness, his public life was one of disappointments. The rise of Laud and the crop of Arminian promotions to sees must have made it seem increasingly unlikely that he would secure the bishopric for which his eminence qualified him—though speculation on the matter still persisted. Writing to Prideaux in 1628, Daniel Featley reported a rumour that, should he achieve preferment, the Arminians plotted to secure the regius chair for one of their own, Thomas Jackson, 'there to spawne yong Arminians'. Although nothing came of this, it showed that the Arminian interest, paradoxically and for reasons of its own, might well have favoured Prideaux's promotion.[55]

By contrast with the Act disputations, often on Calvinist themes, Prideaux's formal public statements on theological matters were strikingly cautious: a result perhaps of the king's two decrees as well as of a natural timidity in the face of potentially hostile authority, which we shall see at other points in his career. His Act lectures in these years were uncontroversial. In 1627 he lectured on the Hebrew vowel points, an academically charged but politically neutral subject; in 1628, on the Apocalypse; in 1629, on the use of logic in theology; and in 1630 on the safely anti-Catholic topic of the invocation of saints.[56] Visiting Oxford in 1629 and reporting to Laud on proceedings at the Act, Robert Skinner, royal chaplain, Arminian, and Laudian partisan, could find nothing worse to say about Prideaux's lecture on logic and divinity than that the lecturer treated his subject 'very slackly and very taediously to litle purpose', taking unnecessary issue with the papists.[57] There was no suggestion that he had breached the 1628 decree or veered from the Articles. His 1626 lecture on the Antichrist was perhaps marginally more contentious; but his identification of the Antichrist with the Pope and not the Turk, whose credentials for the role

54. Heylyn, *Cyprianus Anglicus*, 187–9; Milton, 'Laud', *ODNB*.
55. Bodl. MS Rawl. D. 47, fo. 16r; Tyacke, *Anti-Calvinists*, 78.
56. *VDL*, 161–244.
57. Lambeth Palace Library, MS 943, fo. 133. Skinner refers to Prideaux, 'De usu logices in theologicis', *VDL*, 215–29.

had been toyed with by Montagu,[58] was traditional enough. The standard Calvinist topics—grace, justification, election, perseverance—in any case dealt with already in earlier lectures, were left untouched.

It was in his conduct of disputations rather than in his lectures that Prideaux showed most clearly both his underlying beliefs and his frustrations at the successes of the Arminians. As regius professor of divinity, he acted as moderator when candidates for the BD and DD defended their degree theses and when theological theses were disputed at the Act. But some of his interventions, angry or sarcastic, were hardly those of an impartial referee. This was no new trait. His shortness of temper had already been shown well before this period in his treatment of the young Daniel Featley, as an anti-Catholic and anti-Arminian a natural ally for Prideaux. If Featley's nephew and biographer can be believed, Featley's performance at his doctoral disputation in 1617 was distinguished by 'acuteness of learning, sharpness of wit, solidity of judgement, smart answers and undainted [sic] courage': qualities which Prideaux seems to have seen as both an intellectual challenge to himself and a threat to his position. His objection to Featley's thesis led to a quarrel which had to be composed by the archbishop. He did not appreciate rivals.[59]

So far as can be judged, Prideaux's quarrel with Featley did not spring from differences on points of theology, and the two men soon became firm allies. But in the late 1620s a series of comparable confrontations occurred, all of them arising from theological arguments which Prideaux found abhorrent. We have already noticed his fierce criticism of George Palmer, who had made the mistake of drawing on Montagu's *Appello* when he defended his thesis in 1625.[60] Two similar incidents followed in 1627. In the first, Christopher Potter—no novice but the 37-year-old provost of Queen's College—argued at his DD disputation against God's absolute decree of reprobation (a Calvinist commonplace), only to be berated by Prideaux for views which may have seemed Arminian but were clearly put forward as part of an exercise, a formal contribution to a formal debate. Shaken by the forcefulness of Prideaux's reaction, Potter remembered for

58. Milton, *Catholic and Reformed*, 113.
59. 'The Life and Death of Doctor Daniel Featley', in *Featlaei paliggenesia*, 12–13; Wood, *Athenae*, iii. 156–7.
60. Above, 235–6.

years what he regarded as an unjust attack.[61] The second incident involved Peter Heylyn, fellow of Magdalen and soon to become (though not yet) one of Laud's most fervent disciples. In April 1627, while going through an exercise towards the completion of his BD, Heylyn maintained that the Church of England was in continuous descent from the eastern churches and the western provinces of Christendom subject to the Pope, and not from the pre-Reformation heretical sects, which he took to be Prideaux's view. He cited in his defence the writings of Cardinal Bellarmine, the great Jesuit theologian of the Counter-Reformation. For this piece of imprudence he was denounced by Prideaux, 'calling him' (says Heylyn himself), 'by the odious names of papicola [pope worshipper], Bellarminianus, Pontificius [papist] and I wot not what'. This was a partisan account which misrepresented Prideaux's position. But it was also the first incident, and probably a causal one, in what was to become a long-running feud between the two men.[62]

Two further victims of Prideaux's intemperate tongue were Gilbert Sheldon and Thomas Laurence. A future archbishop of Canterbury but at this time a junior fellow of All Souls, Sheldon had the temerity at his BD disputation in 1628 to deny that the Pope was the Antichrist: the first public denial in Oxford of 'this fundamental axiom of the Calvinist establishment'. Prideaux, obviously astonished, wondered if he had heard aright, and, when told that he had, remarked sardonically that the Pope owed Sheldon much and that he did not doubt that he would give him a cardinal's hat.[63] Thomas Laurence, another fellow of All Souls, was treated still more harshly, as Robert Skinner reported to Laud in the same letter which contained his comments on Prideaux's 1629 Act lecture. Laurence came before Prideaux at the Act to defend his BD thesis that 'the definition of controversies belongs to synods' and not to the laity. According to Skinner, he argued perspicaciously and judiciously, winning the plaudits of the whole audience

---

61. The Queen's College, Oxford, MS 390 (Thomas Crosfield's diary), fo. 46; A. J. Hegarty, 'Potter, Christopher (1590/91–1646), college head and dean of Worcester', *ODNB*; Hegarty, 'Prideaux'.

62. P. Heylyn, *Examen Historicum* (1659), ii. appendix, sigs P3v–P4r; Wood, *Athenae*, iii. 553; Milton, *Catholic and Reformed*, 303–4; Milton, *Laudian and Royalist Polemic in Seventeenth-Century England: The Career and Writings of Peter Heylyn* (Manchester, 2007), 20–2.

63. T. Barlow, *The Genuine Remains of that Learned Prelate Dr Thomas Barlow, late Lord Bishop of Lincoln* (London, 1693), 191–2; J. Spurr, 'Sheldon, Gilbert (1598–1677), archbishop of Canterbury', *ODNB*; Milton, *Catholic and Reformed*, 117; R. A. Beddard, 'Sheldon and Anglican Recovery', *The Historical Journal*, 19 (1976), 1007 n. 10.

for his manner and for his mastery of the authorities. Prideaux, however, denounced him, breaking out 'in such a passion, with such a challeng upon poore Mr Laurence as was wonderfull to us that were present'. After contradicting a point which Laurence had never made, 'the Doctor of the Chair goes on in a rage (for I must tell you it was a meer rage)—You talk of synods, wee are concluded under an anathema to stand to the Synod of Dort against the Arminians: why doe not you and your fellowes stand to it?' But since the rulings of the Synod of Dort had never been formally adopted in England, Prideaux was wrong here. Even allowing for the partisan nature of our source—a Laudian writing to Laud—his conduct of the disputation appears to have been outrageous.[64]

Prideaux's irascibility, his intolerance of opposition, and his tendency to browbeat and bully his juniors, fellow scholars ill-placed to answer back, were all persistent failings, seen at other points in his career. He was a better and more equable manager of undergraduates and college colleagues than of other theologians engaged in debate. Yet we should also make allowances for his sense of frustration and of growing impotence in the face of advancing Arminianism. It was surely no coincidence that all four of these episodes— Palmer, Potter, Sheldon, and Laurence —occurred in the mid- to late 1620s, years when the Arminians, with a firm base at court, were riding high. Prideaux's slapping down of what he regarded as pernicious opinions represented a kind of rearguard action fought in an arena where such contests were still possible. Although the 1628 decree had specifically prohibited heads of houses and other university men from veering from orthodoxy in (among other fora) 'any public disputation', it would have covered Prideaux's role only in his 1629 conflict with Laurence and not the three earlier incidents. In any case, this provision of the decree may have been overlooked. Skinner had ended his letter to Laud by noting that the vice-chancellor had concluded the Act 'with due commemoration of his Maiesties high desert in settling the peace of the university': a probable allusion to the 1628 decree, but with no suggestion that it had been contravened either by Laurence's thesis or by Prideaux's forceful responses.

---

64. Lambeth Palace Library, MS 943, fo. 133; Tyacke, *Anti-Calvinists*, 78; *HUO*, iv. 209, 586; V. Larminie, 'Skinner, Robert (1591–1670), bishop of Worcester', *ODNB*; Milton, *Catholic and Reformed*, 422. For the non-adoption of the Dort rulings in England, see *Works of Laud*, vi. 246.

In the background to these quarrels stood the watchful figure of Laud, of all the Arminians the one with the closest ties to Oxford.[65] Although president of St John's College from 1611 to 1621, Laud was probably non-resident for much of his time, and his successive external church appointments, together with his attachment to the court, maintained his distance from the Oxford scene. Despite his absences, however, Laud remained well informed about events in Oxford and about Prideaux's part in them, and Robert Skinner was not his only agent. Thomas Turner, fellow of St John's, had written to him about the regius professor's harsh treatment of George Palmer in 1625 and his warning against the use of Montague's book, and Laud may have intended to take action against him in consequence—or so Prynne thought.[66] William Juxon, president of St John's in succession to Laud, vice-chancellor from 1626 to 1628 in succession to Prideaux, and Laud's long-time supporter, was another who is likely to have kept him *au courant* with university affairs.[67] That the king was now firmly convinced of the need for reform of both universities, and in particular for the imposition of order and discipline, was a further stimulus to the local intervention of one who was now well established at Charles's court. Busy (and busybodying) as always, Laud took the initiative in devising a new proctorial cycle for the colleges in 1628 and in initiating the revision of the university's statutes in 1629. Prideaux's membership of the large committee of sixteen set up to consider the revision tells us little about his attitude to this Laudian enterprise, which he was later to oppose.[68] As regius professor and head of house, he could hardly have been left out.

Prideaux's antagonism towards Laud and his associates was strongly implied by his role in another dispute. In 1627 one of the fellows of Wadham College, James Harington, was at loggerheads with the college's warden, William Smyth.[69] Their differences hinged on Harington's claim to be allowed to continue to receive an annuity of £40, despite a college statute limiting a fellow's independent income to £10 a year. The grounds for this

65. For what follows, see Trevor-Roper, *Archbishop Laud*, 37–58, esp. 43–4, 57 n. 3; Milton, 'Laud'.
66. Prynne, *Canterburies Doome*, 157–8; *Cosin Correspondence*, ed. Ornsby, 77.
67. B. Quintrell, 'Juxon, William (bap.1582, d.1663), archbishop of Canterbury', *ODNB*.
68. Wood, *Annals*, ii. 360–4; *HUO*, iv. 198–9; below, 286–90.
69. There is an admirable summary of the dispute in *The Further Correspondence of William Laud*, ed. K. Fincham (Church of England Rec. Soc., 23, 2018), xlvii.

claim lay in Harington's supposed dispensation from the statute by a ruling of Dorothy Wadham, the College's co-founder; but the truth of this was challenged by Warden Smyth. Harington's response, in October 1627, was to appeal to Laud, who, as the current bishop of Bath and Wells, held the office of Wadham's Visitor and so possessed ultimate jurisdiction in matters of this sort.[70] Harington then went further and, judging perhaps that he was unlikely to obtain a favourable verdict from Laud, secured from the Court of Requests the appointment of a superior commission of five to try the case. The commission was headed by Prideaux, whose membership of Gray's Inn since 1625 may have seemed to give him some legal qualification to serve. He was the choice of Harington himself.[71] The commission met in Oxford in early December and took statements from some of the Wadham fellows, but Laud, furious at this attack on his authority, petitioned the king and quickly secured its suppression. It was formally revoked in January 1628, and the case was finally closed by Harington's submission a few months later.[72]

It would be easy to overlook the significance of this trivial episode. Though apparently only a minor college altercation, and one soon settled, it showed up some bitter rivalries. It set Prideaux against both Laud as Visitor and Smyth as warden in what was a direct challenge to Laud's visitatorial jurisdiction, and it is highly likely that Harington had petitioned for Prideaux's appointment knowing of his hostility to both men. Smyth's later alliance with Laud was probably no more than embryonic in 1627. But Prideaux had long known him, not only as an Exeter alumnus, but also as a protégé of the Catholic Petres and one who had actively sided with William Lord Petre in the latter's dispute with the College in 1614. Holding the 'home' Petre living of Ingatestone in Essex from 1619, and entrusted at Wadham with the education of the son of the crypto-papist Sir Richard Weston, the treasurer, Warden Smyth bore all the marks of a Catholic fellow traveller or even a crypto-papist himself.[73] He saw the commission as part of a personal vendetta: it was sued out, he told Laud, 'as much to wrong me as to right Mr Harington'.[74] Prideaux thus had a major role to play in a minor engagement which formed a part of his developing conflict

70. Ibid., 28–9.
71. Ibid., 31–2; *The Register of Admissions to Gray's Inn, 1521–1889*, comp. J. Foster (1889), 175.
72. *Further Correspondence*, ed. Fincham, 32–3, 38–9.
73. ECA, A.I.5, 261; Hegarty, 'Smyth', *ODNB*.
74. TNA, SP 16/86/95.

with Laud and the Arminians. But it was also one which, through Smyth's partnership with Laud, may have seemed to confirm Calvinist suspicions of their enemies' dangerously pro-Catholic sympathies.

One phase of this conflict came to an end with the death of Pembroke on 10 April 1630. This proved to be a major reverse for Prideaux and a turning-point in his career. As we have seen, Pembroke's chancellorship had provided the informal protection which had allowed Oxford Calvinism to survive in a world where church and court were increasingly dominated by Arminians. But Pembroke had also been Prideaux's particular patron, even friend. For Prideaux's College, and for Prideaux himself, he had in 1618 performed the signal service of quashing William Lord Petre's claims to nominate to his grandfather's fellowships, thus saving Exeter from a per-manently intrusive presence.[75] In return, Prideaux had been a compliant and ever helpful agent. As vice-chancellor, he had not only attempted in 1626 to impose Pembroke's parliamentary candidate on the university, at some cost to his own reputation, but also, in an earlier and comparable episode, forced the fellows of Jesus College into accepting Pembroke's kinsman and chap-lain, Francis Mansell, as their principal.[76] At the root of this mutually beneficial relationship lay the common ground of religion. Although Pem-broke did not share all the usual Calvinist convictions—he viewed predes-tination, for example, as 'a most pernicious doctrine'—he was soundly anti-Catholic, anti-Arminian, and anti-Spanish (and had been against the Spanish Match).[77] It was entirely in order that Prideaux's *Orationes Novem*, his theological orations at the Act, published in 1626, should have been dedicated to Pembroke. The earl and the professor had every reason to see eye to eye.

Pembroke's death struck hard at Prideaux's position within the university. But what followed weakened him still further, setting the scene for the further Calvinist retreat which marked the remainder of the decade. Within two days of the death, Laud had been elected as the university's new chancellor—but by a narrow majority of only nine votes and in the teeth of an opposition party which had put forward as its candidate Philip Herbert, the former earl of Montgomery, now earl of Pembroke, the brother and heir

75. Above, 70–1.
76. Above, 239–41; Clark, *Register*, i. 289, 291–3; *VCH*, iii. 264–5.
77. Sharpe, *Personal Rule*, 294; O'Farrell, *Shakespeare's Patron*, 21, 45; Stater, 'Herbert, William, third earl of Pembroke'.

of the dead man.[78] The victorious party had a strong base in St John's, Laud's college, although it was led by Accepted Frewen, president of Magdalen and the current vice-chancellor. The opposition, the 'Calvinian Party', as Heylin called them, included Prideaux (who may well have been its leader), some other unidentified heads of houses, and Bishop John Williams of Lincoln, Laud's long-time enemy, together with the four colleges of which he was Visitor. The election was immediately challenged on the grounds that it had not been conducted in a properly constituted Convocation, but an appeal to the king on those grounds got nowhere.

The truth was that Pembroke was a weak candidate and Laud a much stronger one. Although a lavish patron of building and art, Philip Herbert, unlike his brother, had no interest in learning, and although James I had appointed him high steward of the university in 1615, he had shown no particular affection for it. Though inclining towards 'godly protestantism', he lacked his brother's religious commitment, while his general roughness of manner and reputation for violence can hardly have commended him to scholars and divines.[79] He had, however, been close to Prideaux, who had taken charge of the Exeter education of his noble ward, Robert Dormer, celebrated Dormer's wedding to Anne Herbert, Philip's daughter, and in 1626 dedicated a published sermon to him. In it he wrote of the earl of Montgomery as 'a most honoured Maecenas to me', suggesting unspecified reasons for gratitude, perhaps financial in nature; his responsibility for Dormer's education may have helped to make him a rich man.[80] Prideaux's leadership of the pro-Pembroke faction in 1630 would have been natural enough. But his candidate could in way match Laud for suitability. Laud was already the university's patron, former president of St John's, munificent donor of manuscripts to the Bodleian, and inaugurator of much needed reforms, and his love for Oxford could hardly have been doubted. However

78. For the election, see Heylin, *Cyprianus Anglicus*, 208; Wood, *Annals*, ii. 368; Trevor-Roper, *Archbishop Laud*, 113–15; Trevor-Roper, 'Laudianism and Political Power', 77; Tyacke, *Anti-Calvinists*, 79; Sharpe, 'Archbishop Laud and the University of Oxford', 155.
79. Smith, 'Herbert, Philip'.
80. T. Birch, *The Court and Times of James the First*, 2 vols. (London, 1848), ii. 503; *Stuart Dynastic Policy and Religious Politics, 1621–25*, ed. Questier, 352; Roy, 'Dormer', *ODNB*; Prideaux, *Concio habita Oxoniae* (Oxford, 1626), reprinted in 'Conciones', *VDL*, 43–4.

considerable a figure Philip Herbert may have seemed to the 'Calvinian Party', they had, if understandably, plumped for the wrong man.

In his will, made shortly before his death in 1650, Prideaux stated that he died 'in the true Christian Faith, firmly beleevinge and houlding the doctrine, worshipp and discipline established and professed in the Church of England in the raigne of Queen Elizabeth, King James and the beginninge of the reign of the late Kinge Charles'.[81] The last phrase was the most telling: the established modes of the Church of England had lasted until 'the beginning of the reign of the late King Charles'. Prideaux gave no indication as to when he thought that 'beginning' had come to an end, but 1630 would have been as good a year to choose as any. Although Charles's accession in 1625 had tipped the balance of religious forces firmly in an Arminian direction, accelerating the move away from Calvinism which had marked his father's last years, until 1630 Calvinism had survived at Oxford under the earl of Pembroke's protective mantle. The Calvinist content of disputations was maintained, and the two restrictive decrees of 1626 and 1628 had had little noticeable effect. Despite the growing strength of the Arminians at court and in the episcopate, all was not lost. But with Pembroke's death and Laud's election as Oxford's chancellor, and still more with his appointment to Canterbury in 1633, this was to change. About this time, so Prideaux thought, the 'doctrine, worshipp and discipline' of the church ceased to be 'established and professed'. We shall now see how far, during Prideaux's remaining time at Oxford, this was true.

81. TNA, PROB 11/213/611, transcribed in Butcher, 'Dr John Prideaux', 24.

8

Rector Prideaux and Chancellor Laud, 1630–6

1. The new broom

Laud's chancellorship lasted from his election in April 1630 until his resignation in June 1641.[1] From 1633 the powers deriving from his office were augmented by his standing as archbishop of Canterbury in succession to Abbot, a position which, in 1636, allowed him to propose a metropolitical visitation of the university. That this was never carried through may have resulted from Laud's already having effective supervision of university affairs. Had the visitation taken place, its purpose would have been to enhance the drive for reform, order, seemliness, and, above all, religious uniformity which formed the guiding principles behind Laud's activities throughout his time as chancellor.[2] Here his ideals coincided closely with those of the king. If James I's relations with the university had been those of a patron and scholar, Charles I's were more those of a disciplinarian, and Laud was fortunate to enjoy the king's support in what was a further reinforcement of his position. As chancellor, archbishop, and royal counsellor, he possessed unprecedented authority over the university.

To attempt to put his ideals into practice entailed a high degree of direct control, and to a greater extent than any of his predecessors Laud was an active chancellor whose energetic tenure was very different in style from that of the benignly laissez-faire Pembroke. The best example of Laud's reforming spirit was seen in the new statutes for the university presented to

---

1. For Laud's activities as chancellor, see esp. *HUO*, iv. 200–10, and Sharpe, 'Archbishop Laud and the University of Oxford', *passim*.
2. *HUO*, iv. 204; Milton, 'Laud', *ODNB*.

Between Scholarship and Church Politics: The Lives of John Prideaux, 1578–1650. John Maddicott, Oxford University Press. © John Maddicott 2022. DOI: 10.1093/oso/9780192896100.003.0008

Convocation in 1636, for which Laud was the inspiration and to a large extent the author.[3] The best example of his methods of control lay in his weekly exchange of letters with his vice-chancellor;[4] for he was not, of course, resident in Oxford and had to rely on written directions to carefully chosen subordinates in order to make his wishes known. The chancellor's power to appoint the vice-chancellor was all-important here. The main obstacle to reform lay in the independence of the colleges and their heads, but that too could be sapped by the visitatorial powers which Laud was able to gather into his hands. As chancellor he was the visitor of three colleges, University, Jesus, and Pembroke; as Abbot's successor at Canterbury he was the visitor of two more, All Souls and Merton; and when Bishop John Williams of Lincoln fell from grace in 1637, he became temporary visitor of a further four, Balliol, Oriel, Lincoln, and Brasenose. Those bishops who were both allies and visitors of other colleges gave him influence over most of the rest.[5] In Bishop Williams's colleges he may have been reluctant to meddle,[6] but in others he was less diffident, telling the warden of All Souls in 1634, for example, to appoint only senior fellows as deans and bursars and to see that the fellows did not wear boots under their gowns or—a favourite topic with Laud—cultivate 'long undecent hair'.[7] His ability, and often his willingness, to intervene, either directly or vicariously, subjected the university and its colleges to a form of overlordship.

The religious changes within the university were part and parcel of the same programme. Intended to secure general conformity to what Laud saw as a purified Anglicanism, neither puritan nor papist, they entailed the elevation of the sacraments above preaching, the use of decorous ceremony in liturgy and worship, and a broad emphasis on that 'beauty of holiness' which it was Laud's ambition to impose on the church at large. The university's role as a training ground for Anglican priests gave these policies a special relevance in Oxford and a special part in the Laudian programme. The restraints on preaching imposed by the royal decrees of 1626 and 1628 were rigidly enforced, and many college chapels were refurbished to give the altar a prominent place at the east end, to fill the windows with painted glass, and to repave the floors. Most heads of houses aligned themselves with the

---

3. Below, 285–90.
4. e.g. *Works of Laud*, v. 47–9. Cf. *HUO*, iv. 202; Milton, 'Laud', *ODNB*.
5. *HUO*, iv. 205; Trevor-Roper, 'Laudianism and Political Power', 77–9; below, 310.
6. *Further Correspondence*, ed. Fincham, xxii–xxiii.
7. *Works of Laud*, vi. 387–8.

chancellor. Brian Duppa, dean of Christ Church from 1628 to 1638, had helped to secure Laud's election; Thomas Jackson, elected president of Corpus Christi in 1631, was effectively intruded into office by Charles I and the Arminian bishop of Winchester, Laud's ally Richard Neile; and Christopher Potter, provost of Queen's and once a Calvinist, now bent in the direction of the prevailing wind.[8] We get a particular indication of the heads who favoured Laud and whom he trusted from the list of those whom he chose as his vice-chancellors—William Smyth, warden of Wadham and Laud's former ally in the Harington case, from 1630 to 1632; Brian Duppa from 1632 to 1634; Robert Pinck, warden of New College, from 1634 to 1636; Richard Baylie, president of St John's, from 1636 to 1638, Laud's chaplain and particular friend; Accepted Frewen, president of Magdalen and the man largely responsible for Laud's election, from 1638 to 1640; and Christopher Potter from 1640 to 1641. All were *ipso facto* Laudians and to varying degrees Arminian, with Jackson, Smyth, and Baylie perhaps the most committed among the latter group. Since it was the heads of houses alone who could impose order and discipline on the colleges, the presence of this corps of sympathetic lieutenants carried Laud some way towards the implementation of his policies.[9]

The upshot of all these changes was that a university which had been predominantly Calvinist in complexion swung towards what contemporaries saw as Arminianism. Laud's chief aims may have been order and uniformity, but to those who remained unreconciled to the new regime his policies were heavily tainted with the popery with which Arminianism had long been associated. Laud was aware of his vulnerability here and was by no means sympathetic to Rome; but he could easily be seen to have been. In this changed environment Prideaux was increasingly isolated. He was the leading survivor of the old order, a grand relic of the Elizabethan and Jacobean church in which he had been brought up. He was not the only remaining Calvinist head: Samuel Radcliffe of Brasenose, Paul Hood of neighbouring Lincoln, and John Wilkinson of Magdalen Hall, on the

---

8. *HUO*, iv. 164–9, 205–8, 585–6, 589; Tyacke, *Anti-Calvinists*, 80–4; Sharpe, 'Archbishop Laud and the University of Oxford', 157–8; L. W. B. Brockliss (ed.), *Magdalen College: A History* (Oxford, 2008), 165–71; Charles-Edwards and Reid, *Corpus Christi College*, 160.
9. For examples of Laud's directions to heads of houses, conveyed through his vice-chancellor, see *Works of Laud*, v. 16, and Bodl. MS Twyne 17, pp. 129–30.

extreme puritan wing of the Calvinist party, all shared his views.[10] But his chair, his learning, and his international reputation made him by far the most eminent, and it was his eminence that made him irremovable. His position in the university was nevertheless downgraded. Vice-chancellor for five years under Pembroke, at no point during Laud's chancellorship was he appointed to the same office, nor does he seem even to have held the lesser post of pro-vice-chancellor. His administrative skills and long experience were no doubt still valued, and he continued to serve on many university committees.[11] But from some of the more important ad hoc committees he was excluded. When in 1633, for example, Laud set up a committee of scholars to decide which Bodleian manuscripts should be printed, its members included the vice-chancellor, Laud's nominee (Duppa of Christ Church), four Laudian heads of houses (Pinck, Frewen, Smyth, and Baylie), and Peter Turner, Laud's ally at Merton.[12] None of these had scholarly credentials to match those of the absent Prideaux. His professional life suffered too, for as regius professor he now had to avoid controversial points of theology and religion in his sermons and lectures, which thus compounded his decline in influence.[13] In most ways he had effectively been sidelined.

Prideaux's position nevertheless remained entrenched. It was protected not only by his prestige as a scholar, but also by the invulnerability of his College to Laudian penetration.[14] Exeter now stood out as the largest Calvinist island in an expanding Arminian sea. Its Visitor, Joseph Hall, a Calvinist like Prideaux, if more moderately so, was beyond Laud's reach, so freeing Exeter from the visitatorial intrusions which helped to consolidate Laud's power in other colleges. It was another mark of Exeter's resistance to the new Laudian norms that its chapel escaped the refurbishment common in other colleges and continued to be dominated by a grand and elevated pulpit, symbol of the centrality of the Word in Calvinist practice.[15] But still

---

10. Sharpe, 'Archbishop Laud and the University of Oxford', 156, 158; Tyacke, *Anti-Calvinists*, 73; J. M. Crook, *Brasenose: The Biography of an Oxford College* (Oxford, 2008), 44–5, 49–50; Green, *Commonwealth of Lincoln College*, 174; Brockliss (ed.), *Magdalen College*, 145–6, 152–4.

11. *HUO*, iv. 209–10; OUA, NEP/supra/Reg. R, fos 50r, 81r.

12. A. Hegarty, 'The University and the Press, 1584–1780', in Gadd (ed.), *OUP*, 60 and n. 48. For Turner, see Trevor-Roper, *Archbishop Laud, 1573–1645*, 3rd edn (Basingstoke, 1988), 278, 355, and E. J. Carlyle, rev. H. K. Higton, 'Turner, Peter (1586–1652), mathematician', *ODNB*.

13. Below, 305.

14. Cf. Trevor-Roper, 'Laudianism and Political Power', 78–9.

15. Above, 147.

more important was Exeter's continuing reputation as a puritan college, at a time when the terms 'puritan' and 'Calvinist' had become elided and when most other colleges had turned in another direction. For the sons of the puritan nobility and gentry, particularly the overwhelmingly puritan gentry of Devonshire, the College thus exercised an exceptionally strong attraction, offering what was decreasingly available elsewhere. In the 1630s numbers rose and, with numbers, prosperity.[16] Exeter's head may have been out of favour, but, in a mildly paradoxical way, Prideaux's marginalization in the university contributed to Exeter's strength and so to Prideaux's own survival.

It was Prideaux's weakness, however, that the sorts of men who sent their sons to be educated at Exeter were now absent from the national stage. Charles I's dissolution of Parliament in March 1629 inaugurated eleven years of personal rule, facilitating a more authoritarian style of government and largely silencing public criticism of the Crown's ecclesiastical policies. For Prideaux and those diminishing numbers in the church hierarchy who thought like him, the absence of Parliament meant the absence of potential allies. In the assemblies of the late 1620s the Commons had vigorously, if ineffectively, prosecuted Richard Montagu, attacked what they saw as Catholicizing tendencies in church and state, and spoken out against the rise of Arminianism. As the object of Montagu's scorn, Prideaux had several times elicited their sympathy.[17] But with Parliament in abeyance, his position was more isolated. With no concerted voices to defend the common beliefs of the Elizabethan and Jacobean church, now increasingly branded as puritanism, Laud and his policies had something like free rein.

It would be easy to assume from all this that Prideaux's relationship with Laud would have been one of unbridled antagonism. But this was by no means the case. The two men often clashed, as we shall see, but equally often Prideaux, prudent to the point of timidity, showed himself unwilling to offend Laud and ready enough, perhaps after some initial opposition, to fall in with his wishes. Christopher Potter, provost of Queen's, even opined in 1631 that Prideaux might have wanted to modify his extreme Calvinist views had this not been made impossible by his long-standing commitment to them.[18] Personal ambition may have been a factor here, for Prideaux

16. For numbers and the College's position in the 1630s, see above, 85–7, below, 310–11.
17. Above, 238–9.
18. *Crosfield's Diary*, ed. Boas, 51; Milton, *Catholic and Reformed*, 537.

might not yet have given up all hope of the bishopric which he was eventually to obtain, under very different circumstances, in 1641.[19] His stance and attitudes were not always consistent or easy to fathom.

2. Conflicts: With Laud and the College

Prideaux's dealings with the new chancellor started badly. The initial provocation came from the pulpit. In May 1630, within a few weeks of Laud's election, he noted in a letter to the vice-chancellor's deputy that 'one of Exeter College' had preached a 'disorderly' sermon, inveighing against 'all reverence in churches, and all obeisance, or any devout gesture in or at the receiving of the communion'. The sermon had clearly been directed against the decorous ceremonialism in worship which was integral to Laud's reforming ideals but which his opponents saw at best as Arminian in tendency and at worst as rank popery. The preacher, he wrote, deserved a severe reprimand for his 'ill example'.[20] Even at this early stage in Laud's chancellorship two persisting themes had begun to emerge: his determination, following the king's edicts, to control the public expression of religious opinion, and his difficult relations with Exeter College.

A second episode was no more than a minor irritant in Laud's early dealings with Prideaux, but is worth recounting for the light which it throws on the attitudes of both parties. It arose from the practice known as 'accumulation', that is, the custom of allowing two degrees to be taken on the same occasion, often the BD and the DD, without the interval required by the university's statutes. The purpose was usually to save the candidate the trouble and expense of returning to Oxford, from what might be a remote country parsonage, for a second visit in order to take a second degree.[21] Laud disliked this custom, as he did all dispensations from the statutes, and, while acknowledging its antiquity, he gave notice during the early months of his chancellorship of his intention to prohibit it. In consequence of his impending prohibition, Prideaux wrote to him in October 1630 to raise the difficult case of John Bayly, a former fellow of Exeter (1612–19) and son of another Exonian, Lewis Bayly, bishop of Bangor. Having qualified for both the BD

19. Sharpe, *Personal Rule*, 363–4; *HUO*, iv. 209; below, 330–2.
20. *Works of Laud*, v. 15.
21. For accumulation, see Clark, *Register*, iii. 146, 147; iv. 12.

and the DD, Bayly wished to take both degrees together and so to avoid a second journey from North Wales, where he held several livings. Prideaux supported him in this and asked Laud, in a distinctly deferential letter, to permit this instance of accumulation. Laud replied with some haughtiness that Bayly had already pestered both him and the vice-chancellor about the matter and asked Prideaux to 'chide him into better temper'. But he admitted that he might not have given sufficient notice of the new prohibition, and he left a final decision to the vice-chancellor. In the event the affair ended without acrimony. Prideaux wrote a mollifying letter to Laud, welcoming his intended reform of the university, acknowledging that proper notice had been given of the new ruling, and adding that Bayly had been 'well chid'. The university records show that Bayly went on to take both degrees together in December 1630.[22]

Trivial though this case might seem, it was nonetheless revealing. At its centre lay Laud's determination to rid the university of what he regarded as abuses but what others might see as sensible and time-honoured customs, even if they derogated from the statutes which for Laud defined good practice. Prideaux for his part, while pleading for one who must have been a former pupil, was clearly anxious to stay on the right side of Laud, and his tone throughout his correspondence with the chancellor was respectful, placatory, even ingratiating. In response to Laud's accusation, made at the same time as his ruling on accumulation, that the regius professor had permitted an inappropriate subject for disputation at the Act (no doubt seen by Laud as a breach of the king's prohibition of contentious theological debates), Prideaux adopted an almost servile tone: 'Now I understand by your loving and fatherly advertisement, what will be expected of me, I shall by God's grace take a care hereafter that no such occasion of exception be given.' At the same time he sought Laud's favour by drawing attention both to 'the neglect of divinity disputations' on the part of those who should have come forward to dispute and to the rising numbers of those proceeding to degrees in law, to the prejudice of divinity. These were problems ripe for the chancellor's attention.[23] Prideaux's zeal in thus exposing abuses suggests that, whatever his private opinions of Laud's churchmanship, he was determined to do what he could to keep in with him.

22. *Works of Laud*, v. 25–32; OUA, NEP/supra/Reg R, fo. 29r; Boase, *Register*, 95.
23. *Works of Laud*, v. 28, 31–2.

The minor wrangle over accumulation was easily resolved, and the other early differences between Laud and Prideaux over the Exonian's disorderly sermon and the inappropriate subject for disputation did not amount to much. Nor perhaps did the chancellor's further complaint in September 1631 about the regius professor's failure to deliver his statutory number of lectures.[24] Yet inconsequential though these episodes may seem, they amounted cumulatively to an interface of friction between the two men which was not replicated in Laud's relations with any other head of house, so far as can be seen from the evidence of Laud's letters and his later history of his chancellorship. Laud's repeated rebukes, growing from his characteristically meddlesome style of management, must have rankled with their recipient. But following on came two other disputes which were much more serious and, for Prideaux, much more damaging. The first was largely an internal College matter, the second significant for the whole university, and both were to a degree linked.

The College issue sprang from two contested elections.[25] In the summer of 1631 two Exeter fellowships lay vacant. One had been formerly held by William Hyde, a Sarum fellow from the diocese of Salisbury, and the other by Nathaniel Norrington, a Devonshire fellow. Hyde had died in November 1630 and Norrington in January 1631. Under the statutes each fellowship had to be filled by a candidate from the previous holder's region. The elections to fill both fellowships took place at the usual mid-year College meeting on 30 June 1631, and they immediately revealed a sharply divided College. In the case of the Sarum fellowship, ten of the fellows present, the majority, voted for Francis Goddard, born in Wiltshire, and so within the diocese, while the minority, the rector and six fellows, voted for one Thomas Hyde. In the case of the Devonshire fellowship, the same majority voted for John Conant, a former undergraduate of the College and now a resident BA, and the same minority, again led by Prideaux, for Robert Snow, also an Exeter BA. Having thus been thwarted in his choices, Prideaux then took matters into his own hands. Apparently genuinely misled by a certificate forged by Hyde's party in the locality which denied

---

24. Ibid., v. 48.
25. The course of the dispute is best followed in the record compiled for the College visitor: ECA, L.II.1 (Visitor's Decrees, 1613–74). The entry in the College register for the meeting of 20 June 1631 records the election of both Hyde and Snow, the rector's candidates, with both entries subsequently deleted: ECA, A.I.6, fo. 15. For Goddard and Conant, see Boase, *Register*, 102, 103.

Goddard's Wiltshire birth, he declared Hyde, the minority candidate, to be duly elected. He similarly denied the claim of John Conant, asserting later that there was no proof of his Devonshire origins. Since Conant had been a member of the College since 1627, was well known to have been born in Devon, and was recorded in the university's matriculation register as coming from that county, Prideaux's assertion was disingenuous, not to say downright dishonest. Retribution followed. At some stage, probably immediately after the votes had gone against him, by a brazen misuse of his authority and in defiance of the College statutes, Prideaux dismissed his ten opponents from their fellowships.

The rector's extraordinary actions naturally provoked a furore. Edward Goddard, father of the disappointed Francis, immediately launched a petition on his son's behalf.[26] Noting that the admission of Hyde was contrary to the College statutes and that his son's ten supporters had been pronounced 'nott fellowes', he appealed for redress to Joseph Hall, bishop of Exeter, the College Visitor. Hall, however, probably embarrassed by this call to intervene against his friend and religious ally, passed the buck and declared that Goddard's appeal was a matter for the chancellor. But Laud also declined to act, doubting whether the College statutes gave him the right to intervene. Finally, in desperation, Goddard appealed to the king, asking him to appoint Laud or some other person as arbiter. In the end any measures which Charles might have contemplated were forestalled by the Visitor's decision to take action. On 5 September Hall gave notice to the College of his intention to hold a visitation and at the end of the month he appointed his commissary (i.e. legal officer), George Parry, to act for him, thus sparing himself any personal embarrassment. By this time the expelled fellows had been restored to their places.[27] The case was heard in the College chapel, before Parry and in the presence of Prideaux and fourteen of the fellows, on 6 and 7 October 1631. Laurence Bodley, who had been Conant's tutor,[28] acted as spokesman for the ten-strong majority and their rejected candidates, while the grievances of both Goddard and Snow, together with Prideaux's responses, were submitted in writing. A verdict was soon reached. By the decree of the commissary Goddard, having produced a certificate proving that he was

26. TNA, SP 16/171, fo. 92; *CSPD, 1629–31*, 317. For the dismissal of the fellows, see also TNA, SP 16/198, fo. 72.
27. Bodl. MS Jones 17, fos. 308v–309r.
28. Conant, *Life of John Conant*, 3.

Wiltshire-born, was declared duly elected in place of Hyde, while the proceedings of the second election, which had set Bodley's Conant against Prideaux's Snow, were declared null and void. On the same day Goddard was admitted to Hyde's fellowship.[29] The Devonshire fellowship remained vacant until the following year, when it was filled by Conant's election in June 1632. Later that year a place was also found for Snow, who was nominated as College chaplain by the dean and chapter of Exeter in place of Laurence Bodley, recently departed for a Devonshire living.[30] His quarrel with Prideaux may well have hastened his departure.

These events were deeply humiliating for the rector. His two choices for fellowships had been overturned, his highhanded and bullying ways all too clearly demonstrated, and his authority within the College weakened by successful opposition from nearly half the fellowship. His leading opponent, Laurence Bodley, was no cipher but one of Exeter's mainstays—nephew of the great Sir Thomas, a senior fellow, the College chaplain, and a particularly distinguished tutor.[31] Prideaux's arbitrary decisions in College matters had been exposed before both the king and the chancellor, neither of them previously particularly well inclined towards him. Just why Prideaux acted as he did and why his preferences for Hyde and Snow were so strong are impossible questions to answer. One clue may lie in a pointed remark in Edward Goddard's petition noting that Thomas Hyde, who had displaced Goddard's son, 'hath 80 li per annum left him by his friends'. Was Prideaux attracted by the prospect of taking on a relatively wealthy fellow? If Hyde was the son of Sir Laurence Hyde of Salisbury, as seems likely,[32] the magnetism of pedigree may have been added to that of wealth.

This was not the first episode to show Prideaux in an unfavourable light: his conduct of the 1624 parliamentary election was closely comparable. Nor would it be the last. Running in parallel with Exeter's local conflict through the summer of 1631 were other less parochial disputes whose resolution marked a defining moment in Prideaux's exercise of his religion and Laud's of his chancellorship.[33] They originated in four provocative sermons

29. ECA, A.I.6, fo. 15.
30. Ibid., fo. 15v; Boase, *Register* 103.
31. Above, 177–8.
32. The failed Exeter candidate was probably the Thomas Hyde who had matriculated at New College in 1627 and was the son of Sir Laurence Hyde: see Foster, *Alumni*, ii. 783.
33. The chief sources are Laud's history of his chancellorship (*Works of Laud*, v. 49–71), followed in part but also augmented in Wood, *Annals*, ii. 372–81, and the official account of proceedings before the king at Woodstock in August 1631, Bodl. MS Jones 17, fos. 300r–309v. See also

preached in St Mary's, the university church, by Thomas Hill of Hart Hall (on 24 May), Thomas Ford of Magdalen Hall (on 12 June), Giles Thorne of Balliol, and William Hodges of Exeter. The last of these we have already met as Prideaux's favoured colleague and future son-in-law.[34] All four sermons were broadly directed against Arminianism and its adherents, slightingly described as Pelagians or semi-Pelagians by some of the preachers. Opposition to the replacement of communion tables by altars in college chapels, changes in line with Laud's views, provided a particular local theme.[35] Individual preachers ranged more widely. Thorne and Hodges attacked what they saw as innovations in the church; Hill accused his opponents of using Scripture to defend popery;[36] Hodges spoke out against the king's ecclesiastical appointments; and Ford cited the Scriptures against the doctrine of universal grace denied by the Calvinists.[37] Preaching on these subjects blatantly contravened the king's declaration of 1628 against the public airing of theological and religious controversies; and since all four sermons came within the space of a few weeks, it looks almost as if they constituted a planned campaign against the rise of Arminianism in the university. Laud himself thought that this pulpit rebellion was linked with other attempts to obstruct the reform of the university's statutes, a project which he had initiated in conjunction with Pembroke, his predecessor as chancellor, and which was then going forward.[38]

Among the quartet of delinquent preachers, Thomas Ford soon emerged as the leading culprit. His recklessly contumacious behaviour following on from his sermon seemed to strike at all those principles of order and hierarchy within the university which Laud sought to enforce. On the day when Ford preached, the vice-chancellor, William Smyth, Laud's ally, had asked to see a copy of his sermon. Ford refused, repeating his refusal several times in response to Smyth's repeated demands. Smyth then committed Ford to prison for contempt, but Ford declined to go, saying that the vice-chancellor had no power to commit him. Eventually on 6 July he finally

Prynne, *Canterburies Doome*, 172–6; Heylyn, *Cyprianus Anglicus*, 214–15. For comment, see Trevor-Roper, *Archbishop Laud*, 116–17; Tyacke, *Anti-Calvinists*, 82; *HUO*, iv. 200; Davies, *Caroline Captivity*, 120–2.

34. Above, 176–7.
35. E. Calamy, *The Nonconformist's Memorial*, 2nd edn, 3 vols. (1802), ii. 27–8.
36. Ibid.; Wood, *History*, ii. 372, 374–5.
37. MS Jones 17, fos. 301v, 305r–v.
38. *Works of Laud*, v. 49; Wood, *History*, ii. 372; MS Jones 17, fos. 303v–304r.

gave in and submitted his sermon for the vice-chancellor's inspection. This did him no good, however, since he was again remanded to prison for contumacy.[39] Probably a little before this both Ford and Thorne had appealed to Congregation for justice, and the two proctors had accepted the appeal. This they had no right to do, since the preachers' offences constituted a breach of the peace, which the proctors lacked the statutory authority to settle.[40] The committee set up by the proctors to hear the appeal then found that neither man was guilty of disturbing the peace.[41] At this stage, with the vice-chancellor facing open defiance, the university in turmoil, and the implicit threat of a wider mutiny against the royal and Laudian ordering of the church—all set out in a letter from Brian Duppa, dean of Christ Church, to Laud—Vice-Chancellor Smyth appealed to the king. His appeal came before king and council at Woodstock on 22 August 1631, in the presence of the chancellor, the vice-chancellor, many heads of houses, including Prideaux, and three of the four offenders, Ford, Thorne, and Hodges. The hearing was in the nature of a trial and provided the final act in this little drama.[42]

In that drama Prideaux had a central role, as indeed he had throughout the affair of the sermons. Laud saw him as the leader of the dissidents, 'the head of all these tumultuous stirs', and if, as he said, he refrained from naming the chief culprit out of respect for his office, Antony Wood had no such qualms: 'he means . . . the Regius Professor of Divinity'.[43] Two specific charges were made against Prideaux at the Woodstock council. First, that on being asked by Ford whether he should show his sermon to the vice-chancellor, he had failed to advise him to do so. Here Prideaux equivocated, not denying the charge, but saying that he had been ill at the time and that in general he thought preachers should show their sermons. Laud, however, continued to hold him responsible for Ford's contempt.[44]

The second charge raised broader issues and suggested a wider conspiracy which Prideaux may have headed. He was accused of allowing the committee appointed by the proctors to consider Ford's appeal to degenerate

39. Wood, *History*, ii. 374–5.
40. *Works of Laud*, v. 51–3; Wood, *History*, ii. 375; MS Jones 17, fo. 305r.
41. *Works of Laud*, v. 50–3; Wood, *History*, ii. 375.
42. *Works of Laud*, v. 49–51; Wood, *History*, ii. 375–6.
43. *Works of Laud*, v. 49; Wood, *History*, ii. 372.
44. MS Jones 17, fos. 302v–303r, 308r.

into disorder.[45] But behind this accusation lay various related questions which the charge did not explicitly bring forward. The two proctors who had accepted the appeal, Atherton Bruch of Brasenose and John Doughtie of Merton, were both Calvinist in religion and anti-Laudian in outlook.[46] Prideaux and the four preachers may well have seen the year of office of these two potential sympathizers, which began in March 1631, as offering a special opportunity to allow the unhindered expression of their views on the state of the church; and indeed the two proctors, in illicitly accepting Ford's appeal, had shown their anti-Arminian colours. These were still more clearly revealed by the constitution of the committee which the proctors set up to hear the appeal. This was a thoroughly partisan body, 'rather parties than judges', as Duppa noted in his letter to Laud.[47] Besides Prideaux, the delegates included Samuel Radcliffe, principal of Brasenose, and Richard Hill, a fellow of Brasenose, both Calvinist-puritan members of a Calvinist-puritan college; John Wilkinson, principal of Magdalen Hall, another puritan; and Paul Hood, rector of Lincoln, 'a decided Protestant with some Puritanical opinions'.[48] It was not surprising that such a body acquitted Ford of any breach of the peace. The committee had no appointed chairman, but Prideaux, its senior member, might have been expected to control the proceedings, as the king pointed out at the Woodstock council. Instead, he permitted the 'tumultuary behaviour' of some of its members, including the Brasenose Calvinist Richard Hill, who, in a subsequent letter to Laud, blamed Prideaux for having drawn him into subverting the vice-chancellor's authority.[49]

Laud later wrote that these 'tumultuous stirs' resulted from the 'secret plottings' of factious men,[50] and it is difficult to doubt that a plot of sorts lay behind the whole episode. The concentrated sequence of anti-Arminian sermons, the exploitation of the proctors' sympathies, the packing of the committee, and its verdict in Ford's favour all suggest a coordinated attempt to defy the king's declaration against contentious preaching, to challenge the authority of both the chancellor and the vice-chancellor, and to roll back the

45. Ibid., fo. 308r.
46. Crook, *Brasenose*, 44; J. Morgan, 'Doughtie, John (1598?–1672), Church of England clergyman and religious writer', *ODNB*.
47. *Works of Laud*, v. 50.
48. Ibid., 53; Crook, *Brasenose*, 44; Brockliss (ed.), *Magdalen College*, 145, 152–3, 165–6; Green, *Commonwealth of Lincoln College*, 174.
49. MS Jones 17, fos. 308r–v; *Works of Laud*, v. 64.
50. *Works of Laud*, v. 49.

advances of the Arminians within the university. But if these were the dissidents' intentions, they failed completely. At the Woodstock council Laud's opponents were crushed and his policies vindicated. The two proctors were made to resign for entertaining Ford's appeal contrary to the statutes and for contributing to the general disorder. Ford, Thorne, and Hodges were expelled from the university. Thomas Hill, the preacher of the first sermon, had already submitted and asked for pardon, and played no part in the proceedings.[51]

Prideaux's case was a special one. The rector of Exeter was clearly viewed as the chief encourager, if not the ringleader, of the dissidents. To Laud's charge, backed by the king, that he had in effect encouraged Ford to withhold his sermon from the vice-chancellor and tolerated the disorderly conduct of the delegates when he could have used his authority to suppress it, Prideaux replied insouciantly with a Latin tag: 'Nemo mortalium omnibus horis sapit', 'No mortal is wise at all times'. 'It was the best answere he had yet heard from him,' the king retorted, perhaps with a touch of sarcasm. As the trial moved to a conclusion, with Prideaux now the central figure among the accused, Laud added fuel to the flames which now lapped about him by reminding Charles of Edward Goddard's petition regarding Prideaux's unjust dismissal of his son's claim to an Exeter fellowship. Prideaux's statement that the dispute was now before the College Visitor and that the dismissed fellows had been restored soon set this question aside—but not before Laud had sourly observed that the ten dismissed were the only honest men in the College save Hodges.[52] The raising of this secondary conflict can have done nothing to enhance Prideaux's reputation.

This was the moment of Prideaux's greatest danger, when he came close to being stripped of his regius chair: 'the king himself then publicly declared that Dr Prideaux deserved to lose his place more than any of the rest'. He was spared only because he was the king's 'ancient servant', because it was hoped that 'he would look better to himself for the future' (a chastening humiliation for the regius professor), because of his 'Nemo mortalium . . .' admission, and above all because Laud interceded for him, 'upon his knees', says the account of the trial.[53] Prideaux's old ally and patron, Philip Herbert,

---

51. MS Jones 17, fos. 308v–309v; *Works of Laud*, v. 56–7.
52. MS Jones 17, fos. 308r–309r; *Works of Laud*, v. 57.
53. MS Jones 17, fos. 308v–309v; *Works of Laud*, v. 56–7.

earl of Pembroke, present at the council, may also have spoken up for him.[54] Nevertheless, Laud recorded in his diary that 'Dr Prideaux . . . received a sharp admonition.'[55] Hodges was equally well served. Not only was he one of the College's 'honest men', according to Laud, but during the council Laud also put in a further plea for him: he was 'a man of very good partes and learninge . . . an honest and sober man', who had willingly shown his sermon to the vice-chancellor. It must have been largely Laud's doing that resulted in the commutation of Hodges's original sentence. Instead of permanent banishment, the fate of Ford and Thorne, he was put on probation for a year, and after a full recantation and a grovelling submission to the king, he was restored to his place in the College and university in September 1632.[56]

Laud's successful intervention on behalf of Prideaux and his favoured fellow William Hodges did not spring from softheartedness. It demonstrated his influence with the king, confirmed his authority as chancellor, and, perhaps most important, placed Prideaux under an obligation, making him in a sense Laud's subject. In all these ways it served Laud's purposes. About the scale of Laud's more general victory there could be no doubt. He had ensured that for the remainder of his chancellorship no member of the university would dare openly to challenge the norms of Laudian religion. The Woodstock council had shown that behind Laud stood the king, and that dissidents setting themselves against the university authorities or challenging the king's declaration of 1628 could expect to be punished. Two royal decrees issued at the council's conclusion completed this victory. The king ordered that in future all sermons were to be delivered to the vice-chancellor if he should so demand, while the 1628 declaration was to be sent to the heads of all colleges and halls for reading aloud.[57] This was to prevent anyone pleading ignorance of the declaration—as Ford had done[58]—as an excuse for stepping out of line. The effect of all these measures was to shut down public controversy over religion within the university: an outcome more damaging to the university's Calvinists than to the Arminians. They also meant that the reform of the statutes, Laud's major objective, could now

54. Crosfield's Diary, ed. Boas, 56.
55. Works of Laud, iii. 214.
56. MS Jones 17, fos. 305r, 309r; Works of Laud, v. 66–7, 70.
57. MS Jones 17, fo. 309r; Works of Laud, v. 58–60.
58. MS Jones 17, fo. 301v.

go forward unhindered.[59] If the dissidents had hoped to disrupt this process, as Laud suspected, they had failed there too.

In his diary Laud devoted a long entry to these 'great disorders', and in the brief list of outstandingly memorable events in his life which prefaced the diary he included 'the great hearinge of ye disorders at Woodstock. Aug: 23. 1631'.[60] He was right to place so much emphasis on the outcome of events which had worked so greatly to his advantage and to his schemes for the reform of the university. As for Prideaux, he had had a narrow escape. Its narrowness, together with the king's ban on controversial preaching and publishing, which extended to university lectures, contributed both to his vulnerability and to his frustrations in the ensuing years. Despite his intellectual eminence, far greater than that of any other of the university's theologians, he was in a sense on probation. The king's declaration was, of course, a two-edged sword, to be held over Arminians as well as Calvinists and sometimes to be wielded by Prideaux himself. When Robert Rainsford of Wadham preached an Arminian sermon in St Mary's in August 1632, favouring universal grace and election through faith, Prideaux reported him to the vice-chancellor, who forced Rainsford to recant. But, as Wood astutely noted, Rainsford's recantation was made privately in the vice-chancellor's lodgings and not publicly on bended knee in the Convocation house, the humiliating procedure imposed on the three Calvinist delinquents of the previous year.[61] The declaration may not have been aimed exclusively at Prideaux's party,[62] but its enforcement was certainly weighted against them.

3. Conflicts: With Heylyn

Prideaux's exposed position, after his chastening experiences at Woodstock and under the Laudian regime more generally, was shown by two further episodes in 1633 and1634. Both brought him up against an old adversary, Peter Heylyn, a man whose resentments against both Prideaux and his College went back a long way. In 1617, when he was still an undergraduate

59. *Works of Laud*, v. 49, 59.
60. Ibid., iii, 130, 214. Cf. Davies, *Caroline Captivity*, 121.
61. Wood, *Annals*, ii. 382.
62. Cf. Davies, *Caroline Captivity*, 121–2; Milton, 'Laud'.

at Magdalen College, Heylyn had been a contender for the minor university post of collector, but he lost the contest, 'being betrayed by Exeter Coll.', whose 'perfidious dealings' rankled with him for years.[63] Much more humiliating was his public dispute with Prideaux over the nature of the church during his BD exercises in 1627, when he had been verbally roughed up and abused by the regius professor for his supposedly papistical views.[64] By 1633, however, Heylyn was a much more formidable opponent than he had been six years earlier. He had now been taken up both by the king, whose chaplain he had become in 1630, and by a new patron, Chancellor Laud, while his position in the church had been strengthened by the acquisition of a prebendal stall in Westminster Abbey. Aptly termed the 'Laudian Rottweiler', from this time onwards he began 'to be put to work as a hitman against the regime's opponents',[65] a role for which his scheming and vindictive temperament, his lack of scruple, and his anti-puritan convictions made him admirably suited.

Prideaux was one of Heylyn's first targets. At the Act ceremonies of July 1633 the two men clashed for a second time. Heylyn then appeared not only before Prideaux but also before the large public audience customarily present at the Act, just as he had done in 1627, this time to offer the defence of three theses required for his progression to DD.[66] His theses all concerned the rights of the church, which, Heylyn maintained, had the authority to determine controversies concerning the faith, to interpret Scripture, and to decide on rites and ceremonies.[67] For what immediately followed we have only Heylyn's word, set down in writing much later in 1659, after Prideaux's death. Although the details are circumstantial, his account is *parti pris* and may not be entirely accurate. According to Heylyn, he went on to cite in defence of his thesis Article 20 of the Thirty-Nine Articles, which did indeed declare that 'the church hath power to decree rites and ceremonies, and authority in controversies of faith'. Prideaux, however, denied that this was correct, asserted that Heylyn had 'falsified the publike doctrine of the Church', and proceeded to read aloud the Article in question—but from

63. Heylyn, *Memorial of Bishop Waynflete*, ed. J. R. Bloxam, xiv. For collectors, see Clark, *Register*, i. 74, and *OED*, s.v. 'collector'.
64. Above, 246.
65. K. Fincham and P. Lake, 'Popularity, Prelacy and Puritanism in the 1630s: Joseph Hall Explains Himself', *EHR*, 111 (1996), 877; A. Milton, 'Heylyn, Peter (1599–1662), Church of England clergyman and historian', *ODNB*.
66. The best modern account of this episode is Milton, *Laudian and Royalist Polemic*, 48–50.
67. *Works of Laud*, v. 87; Heylyn, *Examen Historicum*, ii, appendix sigs. P4r–v.

an early version of the Articles, compiled under Edward VI, which omitted the key article. Seeing his opportunity, Heylyn asked a friend to slip out and buy a copy of the current Articles. Observing what was happening, Prideaux wished to move matters on, but he was unable to do so before Heylyn triumphantly produced the Article, read it aloud and then passed the book round the audience to prove his case.[68] Steeped as he was in the liturgy and formularies of the Church of England, it seems unlikely that Prideaux had made such a basic mistake, and it is here that Heylyn's account is at its least trustworthy.[69]

Prideaux's substantive response followed, recorded not by Heylyn alone but in what came to be the official record of the proceedings. He contradicted absolutely Heylyn's view of the church, asserting that the church was a 'mere chimaera', that it could neither teach nor determine anything, and that controversies were better settled by learned men in the universities. During these exchanges the dangerous question of predestination was also raised, upon which Prideaux 'brake into a great and long discourse, that his mouth was shut by authority, else he would maintain that truth *contra omnes qui sunt in vivis* [against all men living]': a clear allusion to the king's decree against theological controversies. At this stage the record of the case, with Heylyn's theses, Prideaux's contrary responses, and his further outburst regarding predestination and his own gagging on the subject (but omitting the dispute over Article 20), was sent to Laud by Heylyn, who had plainly drafted it, for onward transmission to the king. It must have been felt that Prideaux's opinions on the church were too provocatively heterodox to be passed over. The king then ordered that the paper be sent to Prideaux, evidently to give him an opportunity to respond.[70]

Prideaux was next called to answer in person before the king at Woodstock in August 1633, where it seems, from Heylyn's confused account of the proceedings, that he received no further reprimand, though Heylyn was afterwards to remark darkly that if he himself had been present, Prideaux might not have escaped so easily.[71] Prideaux's vindication rested upon his written answers to the points made against him, produced as his justification at Woodstock. He stated that he detested the doctrines concerning the

---

68. Heylyn, *Examen Historicum*, ii, appendix, sigs P4v–P5r.
69. Cf. Hampton, 'Mera chimaera', 281.
70. *Works of Laud*, v. 87; Wood, *History*, ii. 392; Hampton, 'Mera Chimaera', 296 n. 25.
71. Heylyn, *Examen Historicum*, sigs, P2v–P3r.

church which were attributed to him—that the church was a 'mere chimaera', etc.—and that he had proposed them from the chair as formal debating points in a disputation, necessarily in opposition to the candidate's theses. His personal opinion on the role of the universities, for example, was not that they should determine theological questions but that they should thrash them out for later determination in ecclesiastical assemblies. As for his words about predestination, he said that he had spoken out only because a third party had raised the subject, that he had done so briefly, and that he had cut short the discussion 'in obedience to authority'. He ended with a protestation of his loyalty to the Church of England, his determination to defend it against papists, puritans, and any other opponents, his constant support for *jure divino* episcopacy, and his desire only 'for the continuance of my vocation in a peaceable course that after all my pains in the place of his majesty's professor almost for these eighteen years together, my sons especially be not countenanced in my declining age to vilify and vex me.' He intended to spend the remainder of his life in prayer for the king, 'my only master and patron', and for the bishops, and in service to the church 'to whose authority I ever have and do hereby submit myself and studies to be according to God's word directed or corrected': a clever final flourish which returned the argument to its starting point and implicitly acknowledged the orthodoxy of Heylyn's original theses.[72] Heylyn was later to complain that he had been 'disturbed and traduced' by Prideaux's response.[73]

These ill-tempered wrangles disguised important matters. At their heart was the question raised by Heylyn, that of the authority of the church. Heylyn's intention here was to trap Prideaux into a denial of that authority and thus to align him with the radical puritans, Presbyterians who set themselves against bishops and who identified the church, not with a national, overarching body, but with a congeries of local congregations held together by synodical government.[74] Indeed, Heylyn may from the start have had this object in mind, choosing his three theses so as to elicit a formal denial from Prideaux of the church's authority which could be presented as an assertion of his true beliefs. Prideaux was able to escape this trap by pointing out that his counterarguments directed against Heylyn's

72. *Works of Laud*, v. 87–91. The presence of Prideaux's statement among the state papers witnesses to its formal submission: SP 16/245, fo. 18.
73. Heylyn, *Examen Historicum*, ii, appendix, sig. P3r.
74. Cf. N. Tyacke, 'The Fortunes of English Puritanism, 1603–1640', in his *Aspects*, 119–20, 122. For Prideaux's general views on puritans and puritanism, see above, 232–3.

theses were required by the terms of the disputation—as Heylyn's opponent, he was obliged to take the opposing view—while in his concluding protestation he stressed his resolve to maintain the church against puritans as well as papists, his constant defence of the episcopal hierarchy, and his loyalty to the king. But even though he had proved himself orthodox, some harm must have been done to his reputation. For the second time in two years he had been forced to appear before the king to explain himself, while his apparent sleight of hand over Article 20, with what Heylyn alleged to have been the deliberate citation of an incomplete and outdated version of the Articles, left him open to exposure by his opponent and to the criticism of the large audience, including 'country ministers',[75] to whom Heylyn appealed and who constituted Prideaux's natural constituency. To a degree, therefore, his victory was a pyrrhic one.

Prideaux's relations with the puritans and their belief, already raised in this dispute about the church's authority, came more sharply into focus in the course of a further attack on his position by Heylin. Their new conflict arose in 1633–4 from the revival in prominence of the sabbatarian question, which allowed Heylyn once again to undermine Prideaux's reputation. For many years the nature of the Sabbath and the obligations which its observance imposed had been debated both by churchmen and, in Parliament, by the laity.[76] What was the relationship between the Jewish Sabbath and the Christian Sunday? To what extent should Christian practices and prohibitions follow those of the Jews? How was the fourth commandment, 'Thou shalt keep holy the Sabbath day . . . ', to be interpreted? And, most important of all, what recreational activities, if any, were to be permitted on Sundays? These were all thoroughly contentious questions. Although, as K. L. Parker has pointed out, many moderate clergy within the Church of England favoured strict Sunday observance, making little or no allowance for recreations, it was the puritans who were the most uncompromising in their strict adherence to the Mosaic commandment. For them Sunday was a day set aside exclusively for religious exercises. From 1618, however, the official line was more liberal. James I's Declaration of Sports published in that year sanctioned 'lawful recreations' after divine service on Sunday afternoons,

---

75. *Works of Laud*, v. 87, 90.
76. The fullest survey is K. L. Parker, *The English Sabbath: A Study of Doctrine and Discipline from the Reformation to the Civil War* (Cambridge, 1988); see esp. 150–4. But see N. Tyacke, *EHR*, 106 (1991), 1002–3, for criticisms.

including such activities as archery, dancing, and the setting up of maypoles. Only 'unlawful games' such as bear- and bull-baiting were banned. The declaration was partly aimed at recusant papists, whose absence from church now barred them from these recreations, but its main target was the 'puritans and precisians' who prevented the people from enjoying their innocuous Sunday afternoon sports.[77]

This was the current doctrine when, in 1622, Prideaux gave his annual Act *oratio* on the subject of the Sabbath. In his lecture he argued for the distinction between the Jewish Sabbath and the Christian Sunday, branded as 'Judaizers' those who insisted on a literal interpretation of the fourth commandment, with rigorous observance of its Mosaic prohibitions, and denounced both the 'zealots' who complained 'that the Lords day is with us licentiously prophaned' and—the same group—'the Sabbatarians of this age who by their Sabbath-speculations would bring all to Judaisme'. Consistently with these views, and following the lead given by the Declaration of Sports, he allowed Sunday recreations 'of what sort soever which serve lawfully to refresh our spirits and nourish mutuall neighbourhood among us'.[78] His 1622 address was both an academic inquiry into the origins of the divergence between the Christian Sunday and the Jewish Sabbath and a polemic directed against the practices of the more extreme puritans. Not once identified in the lecture by their vernacular label, they were none the less chief among Prideaux's 'zealots' who insisted most rigorously on the literal observance of the fourth commandment and who were most opposed to Sunday recreations. Yet despite its controversial nature, the lecture appears to have caused no particular stir, partly no doubt because it was given in Latin and remained unprinted until 1626, when Prideaux published it in his *Orationes novem inaugurales*, his collected Act orations. Even then it seems to have attracted no notice, passed over perhaps in the more public and bitter controversies arising from the contemporary Montagu affair. In 1633, however, the lecture acquired a new topicality when Charles I reissued his father's Book of Sports. Responding to disorderly festivities in some West Country churches, the king's declaration added a new preface to James's text and a supplementary codicil ordering local justices to prevent

77. James's declaration was incorporated verbatim in Charles I's declaration of 1633: Gardiner (ed.), *Constitutional Documents*, 99–102. Cf. Sharpe, *Personal Rule*, 351–3.
78. J. Prideaux, 'De Sabbatho', in *Orationes Novem Inaugurales*, 130–51, reprinted as 'Oratio VII', in *VDL*; Prideaux, *The Doctrine of the Sabbath* (1634), 4, 14, 18–19, 31, 39.

any interference with 'any of our loyal and dutiful people, in or for their lawful recreations, having first done their duty to God'. The codicil concluded with a further (and more contentious) direction for the reading of the book from the pulpit in all parish churches.[79]

Prideaux's approval of lawful recreations and his disapproval of hard-line sabbatarianism, the related themes of his 1622 lecture, were largely in accord with the newly reissued declaration. Their approach to consonance gave Heylyn his opportunity. He saw here a pretext for translating the lecture into English both to give it a wider circulation and, in a cunning way, to strike at Prideaux's reputation among his natural constituency of moderate but nevertheless sabbatarian puritans. He wasted no time. The king's declaration was published in October 1633 and by January 1634 Heylyn had entered his translation, *The Doctrine of the Sabbath*, at Stationers' Hall. It was accompanied with a new preface which preserved his anonymity: at no point was Heylyn's role acknowledged, either as translator or as author.[80] This preface was a thoroughly tendentious and sometimes dishonest piece of work.[81] Partly a summary of Prideaux's own views, it also embellished them to portray him as an anti-puritan zealot with views far more extreme than those expressed in the original lecture. Heylyn, for example, took care to state, as Prideaux had not done, that in Calvin's Geneva 'all honest exercises', including shooting with a variety of bows, were permitted both before and after the Sunday service, while he also added dancing, shooting, and wrestling to Prideaux's permissible but unspecified 'recreations'.[82] Heylyn also emphasized the support for his views which Prideaux had sought from 'all sorts of papists, Iesuits, canonists and schoolemen'.[83] The general effect was to elide Heylyn's additions with Prideaux's views so as to create the impression that Prideaux's had a thoroughly indulgent attitude towards Sunday sports and also to show him as leaning towards Rome. He was thus converted into a fierce anti-sabbatarian, as zealous for his cause as he had accused the puritans of being for theirs, and one prepared to pray in aid

79. Gardiner (ed.), *Constitutional Documents*, 102–3.
80. Prideaux, *Doctrine of the Sabbath*; E. Arber, *A Transcript of the Registers of the Company of Stationers of London, 1554–1640 AD*, 5 vols. (London, 1875–94), iv. 287. For discussion, see Parker, *English Sabbath*, 166–7, 197–8; Milton, *Laudian and Royalist Polemic*, 51–2; Milton, 'Licensing, Censorship and Religious Orthodoxy in Early Stuart England', *The Historical Journal*, 41 (1998), 648; Davies, *Caroline Captivity*, 203.
81. Milton, *Laudian and Royalist Polemic*, 52.
82. Prideaux, *Doctrine of the Sabbath*, preface, sigs. B3v, Cv.
83. Ibid., sig. B2v.

the traditional enemies of the Church of England, who stood at the opposite pole from the puritans.

As we have seen, until this point Prideaux's followers included many moderate puritans with whose theological opinions on such matters as predestination and grace his own overlapped. Their views on sabbatarianism might diverge, but they had much in common. He was thoroughly set apart only from the radical wing of the puritan camp: Presbyterians, opponents of bishops, advocates of synodical government. But the intention of Heylyn was to destroy Prideaux's reputation among his puritan supporters by any possible means, and in this he seems to have been at least partly successful. His translation, with its insinuating preface, proved popular, going into three editions in 1634–5,[84] and it was Heylyn himself, in his life of Laud, who provided the fullest account of its reception. Still concealing his own identity as the author of the preface, he wrote almost gleefully that:

> The name of Prideaux was so sacred that the book was greedily bought up by those of the Puritan faction, presuming they should find in it some invincible arguments to confirm both the party and the cause. But when they found how much they had deceived themselves in that expectation and that nothing could be writ more smartly against them and their Lords-day-Sabbath; as it did very much cool their courage and abate their clamours: so did it no less tend to the diminution of that high esteem and veneration which before they had harboured of the man.[85]

We have little more than Heylyn's word for the success of his stratagem, and he may have exaggerated. But there is no reason to doubt that his translation did Prideaux a good deal of harm with his natural supporters, as Heylyn had intended. Some such as William Twisse, expert theologian and godly minister par excellence, spotted Heylyn's distortions and, knowing of Heylyn's hatred of Prideaux, suspected foul play. Others, more innocent, were simply bewildered by his apparent change of tack.[86] Nor was it only among the puritans that Prideaux lost support but probably also among the many moderate ministers who were opposed to the sabbatarian permissiveness of the Book of Sports which Prideaux seemed both to have backed and amplified. In what seemed to be an over enthusiastic endorsement of the

---

84. Milton, *Laudian and Royalist Polemic*, 52.
85. Heylin, *Cyprianus Anglicus*, 261.
86. Milton, 'Licensing, Censorship', 648; Milton, *Laudian and Royalist Polemic*, 52.

book's principles, he appeared to have gone some way in a Laudian direction.

4. Relations with the Continental churches

The relations between the Church of England and the Continental reformed churches, mainly those of Germany and the Low Countries, provide further evidence of the more hostile environment in which Prideaux now moved. Here, and by contrast with some among the Arminian clergy, Prideaux was a liberal internationalist—at least until the 1630s. Like others in the universities and among the episcopate, he regarded the Church of England and the Calvinist churches abroad as part of a single community of faith, and he had maintained regular contacts with Continental churchmen and scholars. The more learned English Calvinists and their foreign counterparts formed one branch both of the republic of letters and of an international Protestant church. In a practical expression of these views, Prideaux had made his home an academic base and centre for those foreign scholars and students who sought him out. Between about 1610 and 1630 Exeter College had become something of a theological and philosophical powerhouse, playing host to such renowned men of learning as John Combachius from Marburg and Sixtinus Amama from Franeker. Prideaux's reputation as a scholar of pan-European fame was in part both cause and effect of the hospitality which his College was able to offer.[87] There were, of course, some natural lines of division between the Church of England and its Continental affiliates which Prideaux had to take account of. The absence of bishops in the Continental churches posed the greatest potential problem for one whose views have been called 'unashamedly Episcopalian': Prideaux was never less than a firm believer in the legitimacy and authority of Anglican bishops.[88] But he was able to reconcile his ecumenism with his Anglicanism by arguing that the reformed churches were not in any way opposed to bishops and that in any case their officials were analogous to bishops.[89] There was no insuperable difficulty in the way of good relations.

---

87. Above, 52–63; Milton, *Catholic and Reformed*, 397–8.
88. Hampton, '*Mera Chimaera*', 288.
89. Ibid., 290–1; Milton, *Catholic and Reformed*, 494.

The outlook of Laud was very different. He was cool, even inimical, towards the Continental churches and their claims. Taking as he did a thoroughly uncompromising view of the need for rule by bishops in any true church, he saw the Presbyterian structures of the Continental churches as too close for comfort to the ideals of the more extreme English puritans.[90] Hardly a leading scholar himself, and so lacking Prideaux's contacts with foreign scholars, he had no personal basis for a strong relationship with this group. Although he supported the collections for foreign churchmen, especially the dispossessed ministers of the Palatinate, which were a feature of James I's reign, he thought it necessary to deny that these collections derived from any notion of Protestant unity, while he later sought to impose Anglican ideals and jurisdiction on those foreign churches which had immigrant branches in England.[91] His policies in the 1630s partly reflected political circumstance: he favoured the broader objective of avoiding Continental alliances and of keeping his country's distance from expensive foreign entanglements, where he took his lead from his master the king. But they also reflected an underlying lack of sympathy with those other churches which, like the Church of England, had Reformation roots. The concept of international Protestantism made no appeal to him.[92]

These differences between the views of Prideaux and Laud were of little consequence until the 1630s, when Laud became archbishop of Canterbury and John Dury launched his noble, if chimerical project for reuniting the Protestant churches of Europe. A Scottish cleric who became the apostle of ecumenism, Dury spent much of his life on the move through the states of northern Europe, negotiating with princes, parliaments, and local churchmen in his attempts to bring their churches together.[93] Between 1631 and 1635 he paid three visits to England,[94] but he maintained close contacts at all times through his friendship with Samuel Hartlib, the London-based polymath, writer, projector, and disseminator of information. In England, as

90. Milton, *Catholic and Reformed*, 494.

91. Ibid., 403, 434, 510–15; Trevor-Roper, *Archbishop Laud*, 197–204.

92. Trevor-Roper, *Archbishop Laud*, 200.

93. See in general H. R. Trevor-Roper, 'Three Foreigners: The Philosophers of the Puritan Revolution', in his *Religion, the Reformation and Social Change*, 3rd edn (1984), 237–93, esp. 251–6; A. Milton, '"The Unchanged Peacemaker"? John Dury and the Politics of Irenicism in England, 1628–1643', in M. Greengrass et al. (eds.), *Samuel Hartlib and Universal Reformation: Studies in Intellectual Communication* (Cambridge, 1994), 95–117; and J. T. Young, 'Durie[Dury], John (1596–1680), preacher and ecumenist', *ODNB*.

94. G. H. Turnbull, *Hartlib, Dury and Comenius: Gleanings from Hartlib's Papers* (1947), 132, 156, 169.

elsewhere, Dury looked for support to the powerful and influential and, above all, to well-placed churchmen. With the old guard among the bishops he had some success. John Williams of Lincoln, Thomas Morton of Durham, John Davenant of Salisbury, and Joseph Hall of Exeter, all 'moderate Calvinist episcopalians' and anti-Laudian to a man, were among his supporters, and Hall in particular became an assiduous correspondent, always keen to advise.[95]

With the universities, however, Dury was less successful. Divines such as Christopher Potter, provost of Queen's, Oxford, and Joseph Mede, fellow of Christ's, Cambridge, and a leading biblical scholar, 'displayed a benign interest in Dury's schemes',[96] but no more. Prideaux's international reputation, foreign contacts, and high standing in the Church of England and in Oxford would have made him a more valuable catch than any of these, and Dury pursued him with special vigour; but to no avail. In 1633 or 1634 he sought opinions on a recent conference at Leipzig with the Lutherans from a number of bishops and scholars, including Prideaux. Bishops Morton, Hall, and Davenant, together with Archbishop Ussher and Christopher Potter, all submitted written opinions, but both Prideaux and Samuel Ward, the Calvinist master of Sidney Sussex, Cambridge, failed to do so. In April 1634 Dury twice complained that he had received no letters from Prideaux, and in June he was still hopeful that Prideaux and others might 'perform (as I conceive it) their duty'.[97] Another letter, addressed to Hartlib, Laud, and Sir Thomas Roe, Dury's chief patron and Charles I's roving ambassador in Europe, and written a little later in the last months or 1636 or in 1637, is more directly revealing of the value which Dury set on Prideaux's support:

> As for dr Prideaux if you could bring him to shew either that there is no fundamental difference betwixt us and the Lutherans even in the schoole-questions, or supposing there were a fundamental difference in the same then to shew how that it ought to bee taken away, his judgement might bee of great worth and profit. Also if hee would insist upon the grounds laid in the conference of Leipsigk and shew how that the agreement found there is either sufficient or may further bee accomplished and made up it would be very steadable [helpful]. But all this I leave to his will and Gods disposing.[98]

---

95. Trevor-Roper, 'Three Foreigners', 255–6; Milton, '"The Unchanged Peacemaker"', 98, 104–6; Turnbull, *Hartlib, Dury and Comenius*, 204, 213, 221.
96. Milton, '"The Unchanged Peacemaker"', 108.
97. TNA, SP 16/265, fo. 91; SP 16/269, fo.1; *CSPD, 1633–4*, 547; *CSPD, 1634–5*, 55.
98. SUL, Hartlib Papers, 9/1/49B–50A; Turnbull, *Hartlib, Dury, and Comenius*, 178.

Once again, there is no indication that Prideaux responded.

There are two probable reasons for Prideaux's reluctance to engage with Dury. First, Dury's attempts to secure union with the Lutherans, a main aim of his work in the 1630s, bred distrust among those more hard-line Calvinists who were most closely associated with the puritans. Lutheran errors, as they were seen, on doctrines such as predestination, seemed to bring the German church close to the English Arminians: a factor which may have carried weight with Prideaux, the arch-enemy of the Oxford Arminians, as it did with others who shared his outlook.[99] Dury's letter, just cited, suggests that doctrinal differences with the Lutherans ('the schoole-questions)' were seen by Prideaux as a major obstacle to his participation in the sort of reunion scheme which Dury had in mind.

But this consideration had not deterred the Calvinist bishops from supporting Dury, and probably more important was a second consideration: Laud's tacit hostility to Dury's project and, following from that, Prideaux's fear of implicating himself in another enterprise which might once again put him on the wrong side of the archbishop.[100] Laud paid lip service to Dury's ideals and in 1634 even offered him an English living, but at heart he did not wish to become involved and he gave no active help. The cause of Protestant reunion was a species of Continental entanglement, all types of which both king and archbishop looked to avoid. Laud's lead was followed by the Arminian bishops, none of whom offered help to Dury.[101] In these circumstances, if Prideaux wished for a quiet life beyond Laud's surveillance and in accordance with a natural timidity of character which we have noted earlier,[102] he would have been ill-advised to give Dury his active support. In a letter to Hartlib probably written in 1635 Prideaux's fellow scholar, Joseph Mede, politely declined to assist Dury in words which may have echoed Prideaux's own sentiments. To meddle in such affairs Mede wrote, was to be 'taken notice of for factious and a busi-body; and if he be once this branded, all the waters of the Thames will not wash him clean, if it be to his prejudice'.[103] Timidity was prudence under another name.

99. Milton, '"The Unchanged Peacemaker"', 100–2.
100. Milton, Catholic and Reformed, 508–9.
101. Trevor-Roper, Archbishop Laud, 265–8; Trevor-Roper, 'Three Foreigners', 252, 256; Milton, '"The Unchanged Peacemaker"', 106–8; Davies, Caroline Captivity, 55, 81.
102. Above, 52, 244.
103. The Works of Joseph Mede, ed. J. Worthington, 4th edn (1677), Bk. IV, 865–6; Milton, Catholic and Reformed, 509.

The view that Prideaux was, for whatever reasons, now wary of Continental contacts and projects receives some support from an unexpected quarter. In the 1630s the stream of foreign scholars who, for the past twenty years, had come to study at Exeter and to sit at Prideaux's feet completely dried up. After the departures of Matthias Pasor and John Getsius in 1629, only two foreigners are known to have joined the College: Wibbo Jansonius Artopaeus, a German, present in 1635–6, and Hieronymus Ernesti, also German, from 1638 to 1641.[104] Both were undergraduates (and Ernesti a fellow commoner), who made no mark on the College and left no scholarly imprint. The personal links between Exeter and the great Protestant centres at Heidelberg, Marburg, Leiden, Saumur, and elsewhere had ceased; and if there was correspondence between Prideaux and his former friends at Continental universities, none survives. The chaos of war in Germany may account for something. But this will not explain the absence of scholars from France and the Low Countries, and it is perhaps more likely that the wary relationship between Prideaux and Laud does more to explain the change. From his 'trial' at Woodstock Prideaux may have learnt caution on a variety of fronts.

5. Prideaux and the Socinians

The restraints imposed by the Laudian regime had their most inhibiting effects on Prideaux's public pronouncements. After the royal declarations of 1626 and 1628, and the penalties imposed at the Woodstock council of 1632 on those found to have contravened them, it would have been unwise for him to have continued to speak his mind in lectures and sermons. The staple topics of Calvinist theology were now off limits. His frustration with the new order had been vividly shown during his dispute with Heylyn in 1633, when, at the mention of predestination, 'he brake into a great and long discourse, that his mouth was shut by authority, else he would maintain the truth against all'.[105] Similar restrictions were increasingly applied to printing, where Laud aimed to tighten the university's and its chancellor's control over what came from the press. The formal licensing of books was in the hands of the vice-chancellor, who was, of course, the chancellor's nominee.

---

104. Boase, *Commoners*, 102, 174.
105. *Works of Laud*, v. 87.

Prideaux himself had acted as licenser during his time as vice-chancellor in 1625. Laud, however, intervened in the licensing process in ways hardly seen before, ensuring in 1631, for example, the publication of a book which argued for bowing at the name of Jesus, a practice condemned by some of his opponents as Arminian, and in 1639 prohibiting other works favouring the 'presbyterial government' of the extreme puritans. The authors, William Ames and Festus Hommius, were both men admired by Prideaux.[106] Prideaux himself was very conscious of the limitations under which Oxford printers now worked, complaining to his friend Archbishop Ussher in 1638 that while old-fashioned works on logic and ethics could be freely printed, 'matters that entrench nearer upon true divinity must be more strictly overseen'.[107] Beyond Oxford, there was a tightening control over printing on a national scale in the1630s which curbed the free expression of Calvinist opinion. Predestination in particular became a subject increasingly difficult to raise.[108]

Prideaux himself appears to have come near to a brush with the authorities over his own printed works. In 1637 he published *Certaine Sermons*, a collection of nineteen sermons, nine of which had appeared earlier as single productions or in his *Eight Sermons* (1621), with most of the remainder having been preached at court, almost certainly in the 1630s.[109] This was Prideaux's first publication since his *Lectiones Decem* and his *Orationes Novem* of 1626. Unobjectionable though the sermons' content largely was, someone took exception to various short passages in six of them, notably those alluding to the corruption of the court, the failings of the church, and the haughtiness of some of its bishops, whose lack of humility bred schismatics and puritans. These offending passages were transcribed in a series of 'Exceptions taken to Dr Prideaux his sermons'; and since this document found its way into the state papers it is likely to have come to the attention of, or possibly been solicited by, those in high places—perhaps by Laud or his allies.[110] Nothing seems to have come of this. But the production of

106. Ibid., v. 39–40, 254–5; W. Poole, 'The Learned Press: Divinity', and I. Gadd, 'The University and the Oxford Book Trade' in Gadd (ed.), *OUP*, 354–5, 562–3.

107. Boase, ciii; Ussher, *Correspondence*, ii. 743–4; Milton, 'Licensing, Censorship', 640.

108. Ibid., 636–7.

109. J. Prideaux, *Certaine Sermons preached by John Prideaux* (Oxford, 1637). Although the general title–page to the whole collection, missing in many copies, dates publication to 1637, the title pages of the individual sermons are all dated 1636. The earliest, 'Ephesus Backsliding', had been preached in 1614. See Madan, i. 199–200.

110. *CSPD, 1638–9*, 214; SP 16/406, fos 167–8. Cf. *HUO*, iv. 589; Hegarty, 'Prideaux', *ODNB*.

these 'Exceptions' remains symptomatic of the more watchful, censorious, and ultimately repressive regime under which Oxford's scholars now worked.

The near impossibility of speaking out on the old Calvinist topics and of attacking the old Calvinist enemies does much to explain why, in his lectures and sermons from the early 1630s onwards, Prideaux moved against a different set of opponents whose beliefs were seen as hostile to the whole establishment of orthodox religion and therefore easier to attack than the beliefs of the Arminians. His new target was Socinianism, the set of doctrines originally promoted by the Italian theologian Faustus Socinus (1539–1604) and propagated by his followers, mainly in Poland, from the 1580s onwards. Socinianism represented a revolutionary reworking of Protestant Christianity, and its adherents rejected some of what seemed to orthodox Christians to be among the fundamental tenets of their faith. Most radically and notoriously, they rejected the Trinity as non-biblical, seeing Christ instead as possessing 'a kind of subordinate divinity',[111] his divine nature a matter of function but his person essentially human. These views placed them close to the Arian heretics of the fourth century. They similarly rejected the notion of Christ's atonement, arguing that salvation came through the moral efforts of the individual believer to follow Christ's teaching, and not through his death on the cross. In consequence, they rejected the notion of justification by faith and that of predestination which often went with it, veering instead towards a belief in justification by works which placed them close to another heresy, that of the Pelagians. Against predestination they asserted the existence of free will. But underlying all these particular principles was a more general stress on the role of reason in the Christian religion. Understanding God's revelation in the Bible, and with that understanding a knowledge of how to act, depended not on the authority of the church but on the believer's right use of his intellect.[112]

Socinianism became known in England from the early years of James I, but it was only in the 1630s that it began to impinge on the horizons of English theologians and on Prideaux in particular. Its growing salience owed less to any threat which it offered to the Anglican church (for at this stage

---

111. S. Mortimer, *Reason and Religion in the English Revolution: The Challenge of Socinianism* (Cambridge, 2010), 36.

112. H. J. McLachlan, *Socinianism in Seventeenth-Century England* (Oxford, 1951), 11–17; Mortimer, *Reason and Religion*, 15–18, 22–5, 35–6.

English Socinians were few and far between) than to the tactical advantages which attacks on Socinianism offered to the English Calvinists. Criticisms of Socinian teaching offered an opportunity to expound and defend orthodox doctrine, and at the same time, tacitly and by implication, to indict the Arminians, since some Socinian tenets overlapped with theirs. Both parties, for example, were opposed to the notion of predestination, while the Socinians were closely linked with the Dutch Remonstrants, the disciples of Arminius himself.[113] There were other reasons for taking a strong line against the Socinians, especially perhaps the desire to cultivate good relations with the strongly anti-Socinian reformed churches of the Continent, to which Socinianism presented a more immediate danger. But in general the case against Socinianism rose to prominence because it allowed those who regarded themselves as orthodox to promote their orthodoxy and to defend conventional doctrine in the face of the rising Arminian tide.[114]

As early as 1614, in his first published sermon, Prideaux had denounced, among other targets, 'Socinus blasphemies, Arminius subtilities': a significant juxtaposition.[115] But it was only from the early 1630s that he became the main public voice of the Socinians' opponents. In his court sermons of the period he dealt them a series of glancing blows, though they were never the main subject of his various discourses. The Socinians were 'all for wresting [perverting] Scripture, without the least respect to antiquity or modern church determinations'. St John had sought to prove 'our Saviours deity' and 'his Godhead (which by the Arians heretofore and now by the Socinians is eagerly and perfidiously opposed)'. 'How dangerously doth Socinus take vantage by affirming that Christ so meriting for himselfe, served his own turne only, and not ours, in that behalf and therefore his doings and sufferings were only exemplary for our imitation, not satisfactory for our redemption. Which cuts off all the assurance & comfort of our salvation.'[116] Prideaux thus attacked some of the central heresies of the Socinians: their reliance on personal interpretation of the Scriptures and their rejection both of the divinity of Christ and of the doctrine of the atonement. The court congregations who heard him preach and who may have included the king

---

113. Mclachlan, *Socinianism*, 127; Mortimer, *Reason and Religion*, 25.
114. Mortimer, *Reason and Religion*, 10, 53, 55–6; *HUO*, iv. 587–8.
115. Prideaux, *Ephesus Backsliding*, 16.
116. 'Heresies Progresse', 22; 'The Great Prophets Advent', 26; 'The Draught of the Brooke', 18, all in *CS*. The court sermons lack dates for their preaching.

could have been left in no doubt as to where he stood on the Socinian question—or of the preacher's impeccable orthodoxy.

What was alluded to merely in passing in Prideaux's court sermons was treated more comprehensively in the six Act lectures which he gave between 1632 and 1637. Unlike his court sermons, these were delivered in Latin to a mixed audience of clergy and laity, and attempted a more systematic demolition of the main Socinian positions.[117] In his first lecture Prideaux took aim at the Socinians' central heresy, their denial of the Trinity (*De Sancta Trinitate*, 1632). In subsequent lectures he defended the divinity of Christ and the doctrine of the atonement (*De Christi Deitate*, 1633, *De Christi Satisfactione*, 1634), argued for the divine nature of the Holy Spirit (*De Spiritus Sancti Deitate, et Personalitate*, 1635), expounded the nature of original sin (*De Peccato Originali*, 1636), and, in a particularly meaty final lecture, emphasized the authority of the church in matters of faith against the Socinians' stress on individual reason as a guide to interpreting the Scriptures and the settlement of disputes arising from them (*De Authoritate Ecclesiae in Rebus Fidei*, 1637). The weight of learning which he deployed against his enemies was immense. He was clearly familiar with all the works of Socinus himself and of his most prominent disciples, and he was able to answer them point by point, often quoting chapter and verse. His main ammunition, predictably, was provided by the Bible, the Fathers, the medieval school-men, and the post-Reformation Protestant theologians, whom he cited systematically and often chronologically. It was a sustained and bravura performance, and one which elicited at least one admiring comment. In 1635 John Houghton, a graduate of Leiden temporarily resident in Exeter, wrote to his cousin John Walker full of praise for the head of his College. Prideaux was 'the glory of Oxford, the brightest light of the Church, the chief defender of Anglican truth; who at the last *comitia* [Act] most learnedly refuted the errors of Socinus and others about the satisfaction [atonement] of Christ'.[118]

---

117. Published in *VDL*, 261–362. For comment of the substance of the lectures, see McLachlan, *Socinianism*, 127–8; *HUO*, iv. 587–8; Mortimer, *Reason and Religion*, 55–6.

118. HMC, *12th Rep., Appendix IX* (1891), 124–5. John Houghton was a commoner at Exeter from 14 October to 26 November 1635: Boase, *Register*, ci; Boase, *Commoners*, 165. He is not to be confused with his contemporary namesake, who was a fellow of Brasenose. In 1648, when, well after the event, these lectures were published, Prideaux seems to have been in some confusion about the years when they were given. In his published text the lecture on the atonement is dated 10 July 1634; but Houghton, writing on 20 July 1635, says that its

Prideaux's Act lectures thus enhanced his reputation and vindicated his Anglican orthodoxy. In undermining Socinian doctrines he reinforced the teaching of the Church in ways to which no party within the Church could take exception. That his last lecture before that of 1632 on the Trinity had been on 'the sacrifice of the mass' indicates how he had shifted his hostility away from the Roman Catholics and those whom the more puritanical Calvinist might consider as their Arminian affiliates.[119] This marked a sharp change in direction, caused no doubt in the first place by Prideaux's genuine abhorrence at Socinus and his teachings. But after the opprobrium which had fallen on him at the Woodstock council of 1631 and at the time of Heylyn's disputation in 1633, the anti-Socinian theme of his lectures may also have represented a bid for respectability and for a return to the favour of king and archbishop. Through his lectures he may have hoped to secure the bishopric which, as Oxford's leading theologian, he had long seemed to merit and which others had long thought might well come his way. In the mid-1620s Richard Montagu had feared that his enemy would soon be promoted to a see, while in 1629 Sir William Trumbull speculated that his preaching before the king might help him 'to carry back a mitre to Oxford'. And in 1636 a satire giving colleges the names of ships had branded Exeter as 'the Repulse because Dr Prideaux shall suffer the repulse if hee sue for bishopricke'—which suggests that Prideaux still nursed episcopal ambitions even if they stood small chance of being realized.[120]

6. Laud's apogee: The new statutes and the king's visit

The summer of 1636 marked the zenith of Laud's career as Oxford's chancellor. In June, the new statutes, embodying Laud's model of a reformed university, were finally published and gratefully accepted by Convocation, while two months later the king's visit to Oxford allowed the chancellor to act as host and impresario on what was a grand state and

---

subject was treated by Prideaux 'at the last Act', i.e. in 1635. Similarly, his Act lecture on the authority of the church is dated 10 July 1637. But the presence of pestilence in Oxford caused the cancellation of the Act in that year: see *Works of Laud*, v, 175, 184.

119. *VDL*, 244–60.
120. Above, 237–8; Sharpe, *Personal Rule*, 364; NUL, MS Cl C 84; *HUO*, iv. 209.

academic occasion. Both events served to emphasize Laud's authority within the university and, in a more minor way, the degree to which Prideaux now stood in isolation against him.

The revision of the statutes had begun in 1629. On Laud's initiative and with Pembroke's support, Convocation had established a large committee of sixteen, including eight heads of houses, to carry through the work. Prideaux was one of the eight heads.[121] But in 1633, when Laud was chancellor, his impatience with the committee's slow progress led him to replace it with a smaller body of four to speed on the reforms.[122] Chaired by Robert Pinck, warden of New College, the new committee's leading and most active member was Brian Twyne, antiquarian, scholar, expert on university and college records, and from 1634 keeper of the university archives. A draft set of statutes was prepared by August 1633 and minutely vetted both by the larger committee and by the Hebdomadal Council, the weekly meeting of heads of houses under the chairmanship of the vice-chancellor, Brian Duppa. Clearly acting on Laud's directions, he then persuaded Convocation to hand over the draft to Laud for final correction. This penultimate version, published and circulated throughout the university in 1634, underwent further amendment, mainly through the work of Laud and his Merton ally Peter Turner. So by the time of the statutes' publication in 1636, what had begun as the work of a committee, and of Twyne in particular, had become a more exclusively Laudian product.

It is essential to know something of how the Laudian statutes came into being in order to understand the opposition which they subsequently provoked, from Prideaux among others. They were the chancellor's most lasting achievement and would govern Oxford until the University Reform Act of 1854.[123] Laud had taken the inchoate mass of the university's earlier statutes, which had, in his words, 'lain in a confused heap some hundred of years',[124] and reordered, revised, and augmented them. The new statutes contained much that was salutary and useful: regulations to ensure that lectures were properly delivered and properly attended, to enforce

---

121. Wood, *Annals*, ii. 366; Bodl. MS Twyne, 17, p. 63.
122. *Works of Laud*, v. 83–4. From this point on the process of statute-making is best followed in Twyne's account, Bodl. MS Twyne 17, pp. 63–79. Cf. Madan, ii. 179; *HUO*, iv. 201; Hegarty, 'The University and the Press', 164–5. The above account simplifies a complicated story.
123. The statutes are printed in *Statutes*, ed. Griffiths, and translated in *Oxford University Statutes*, trans. G. R. M. Ward, 2 vols. (1845), Vol. I.
124. *Works of Laud*, iii. 253, iv. 187.

residence, and to substitute oral examinations for disputations in the final stages of the arts degree, for example. Prideaux's own divinity chair was also regulated, the times and days of the regius professor's lectures laid down, and his audience defined, while his various roles at the Act, in moderating disputations and in giving sermons, were all precisely set out.[125] But if the statutes were in many ways beneficial, there was also much in them that was less easily accepted. The powers of the chancellor were greatly enhanced and so—but to a lesser degree—were those of his deputy, the vice-chancellor, while those of Congregation, the university's junior governing body beneath Convocation, were diminished. The existence of the Hebdomadal Council, the weekly gathering of heads of houses, was put on a statutory footing and its work expanded to allow it to initiate legislation and to function as a court (and by this stage those who comprised it were largely Laudian and Arminian in allegiance). The result of both these changes was to accelerate the oligarchical direction in which the university was already moving.[126] Perhaps of particular interest to Prideaux was one further clause prohibiting sermons which contained material dissenting from or contrary to the doctrine and teaching of the Church of England, and demanding that offenders should hand over any such sermons to the vice-chancellor for judgement. Founded ultimately on the two royal declarations of 1626 and 1628, and clearly alluding to the furore caused by the anti-Arminian sermons of 1631, when Thomas Ford had refused to surrender his sermon, this clause gave new statutory force to the existing restrictions on preaching. Laud may have taken some pleasure in laying down, in the same clause, that if the regius professor had been present at any sermon thought to have offended, he should be one of the six doctors of theology who were to advise the vice-chancellor on the sermon's content.[127]

The statutes were published in Convocation on 22 June 1636; after their reading, all heads of colleges and halls swore to observe them.[128] Almost from the start of the statute- making process there had been an undercurrent of opposition to Laud's work and methods. In 1631 Giles Thorne, another

125. Sharpe, 'Archbishop Laud and the University of Oxford', 148–50; HUO, iv, 202–3; Statutes, ed. Griffiths, 40, 70, 74, 80, 158.
126. Ibid., 129–30,142; Sharpe, 'Archbishop Laud and the University of Oxford', 148–50; HUO, iv, 202–3. For the distinction between Convocation and Congregation, see especially Hegarty, 'The University and the Press', 160–1.
127. Statutes, ed. Griffiths, 161.
128. Wood, History, ii. 403–4.

of the Calvinist sermonizers, had spoken out in Convocation 'in a factious and tumultuous manner' against the 'reordering' of the statutes in an apparent attempt to secure the dissolution of the statutes committee,[129] though his actions were probably grounded on nothing more than his dislike of the arch-Arminian who was the chief promoter of the scheme. There were wider complaints from 1634 onwards that the business of reform had been effectively removed from the purview of the committee and the supervision of Convocation, and handed over to Laud, which was true enough, though Convocation had given its consent. This may have been among the factors which in 1635 led Thomas Crosfield of Queen's to consider 'what exceptions could be made against' the statutes.[130] More concerted and broadly based criticism greeted the statutes' publication and the rapid dissemination of their contents in the following year. According to Wood, 'the Anti-Arminians and Puritans' immediately took exception to several passages, especially an apparently favourable reference in the preface to the reign of the Catholic Mary: a passage which had not been written by Laud and whose implications he subsequently showed to have been mis-construed.[131] A more weighty and damaging broadside, probably presented to the Commons in Parliament, came only after Laud's fall in 1641. It set out a long list of charges against the statutes: their imposition on the university without proper consent; their enhancement of the chancellor's powers (for example, to nominate university officials); their curtailing of the right of appeal to Congregation and Convocation; and the general weakening of the authority of these bodies, while that of the Hebdomadal Council was expanded.[132] How many of these complaints were immediately current is hard to say; but the less democratic and more top-down system of university government embodied in the general thrust of the statutes was probably seen as an abuse from the start. It was an accurate indication of Laud's aims.

On the day following publication Convocation met again, this time formally to give thanks to king and chancellor for the statutes. Prideaux had signed the statutes on 22 June, along with the other heads,[133] but it is

---

129. Bodl. MS Jones 17, fo. 303v; *Works of Laud*, v. 49.
130. *Crosfield's Diary*, ed. Boas, 77; Sharpe, 'Archbishop Laud and the University of Oxford', 155–6.
131. Wood, *History*, ii. 391; *Works of Laud*, iv. 324.
132. Bodl. MS Bodley 594, fos 139v–146r; Sharpe, 'Archbishop Laud and the University of Oxford', 156.
133. The sheet bearing his and their signatures is reproduced in facsimile in *Statutes*, ed. Griffiths, facing page 1.

only at this point that we can see something of how he regarded them. In a letter to his uncle, Francis Cheynell, fellow of Merton and noted anti-Arminian, describes what happened.[134] First, the public orator, William Strode, read aloud his letter of thanks to Laud, written on the university's behalf. Couched in exceptionally fulsome and obsequious language, it opened by going so far as to place their benefactor on a level with the angels. Prideaux objected vigorously to the tone and content of this letter, apparently the only one of those present to do so. 'The Reverend Dr disliked that hee should preferr him before an angell', wrote Cheynell, 'and told him that there was no rhetorike and as little truth in the expression, hee desired him to express our thanks not our flattery.' Prideaux went on to make a lengthy distinction between the various sorts of angels (one imagines to the growing impatience of his audience). At one point he spoke of 'ministringe angells which are sent on messages for preservinge of the elect or confusion of reprobates', thus bringing forward Calvinist allusions now banned from public discourse in an arena where he must have known that he would be immune from prosecution. Without naming either party he then made a veiled but probably cognizable comparison between Laud and the over-mighty Cardinal Wolsey, a comparison which was later to become a puritan commonplace.[135] He finished by making a further attack on the public orator for thanking Laud for freeing those present from the perjury of which they and their predecessors had been guilty. This obscure statement is elucidated by some words of Laud at his later trial, where he explained that the former statutes had been so jumbled and inconsistent that men taking their oaths to different sets could not but commit perjury, since an oath to one statute was incompatible with an oath to another.[136] Prideaux, however, took umbrage at Strode's anodyne remark, telling him that 'it was not fitt that we should accuse our fathers or our selves', when they themselves had signed and sealed the new statutes.

Prideaux's interventions here were extraordinary, and it is perhaps not surprising that Cheynell offered no supporting comments, despite his own strong anti-Arminian views. Captious and intemperate, his words betrayed a deeper dissatisfaction with the current state of affairs which went beyond the

---

134. NUL, MS Cl. C 73; *HUO*, iv. 589. The public orator's letter, briefly mentioned by Cheynell, appears in full in *Works of Laud*, v. 138–40, and in the Register of Convocation, OUA, NEP/supra/Reg R, fo. 127v.
135. Trevor-Roper, *Archbishop Laud*, 52–3; cf. *HUO*, iv. 589.
136. *Works of Laud*, iv. 187, v. 91, 139.

relatively trivial points he had raised in Convocation. Frustration at his enforced silence on doctrinal topics was one element in that dissatisfaction, but more important was his tacit detestation of Laud and his statutes, expressed in his disgust at the adulation heaped upon the chancellor and his works. If his attitude is understandable, it nevertheless reflected a certain small-minded unwillingness to recognize the new statutes for the monumental and beneficial reforms that they undoubtedly were.

'The universal triumph of Laud in Oxford . . . was consecrated in the summer of 1636 by the visit which the King and Queen made to Oxford to inspect his handiwork.'[137] Following shortly after the publication of the statutes, the visit combined spectacle and ceremony to glorify the Stuart monarchy and one of its leading servants, Oxford's chancellor, in a sort of elaborate and extended masque. It began on 29 August with a speech of welcome from the vice-chancellor and a procession of university and town dignitaries sent out to meet the royal party as they came in from Woodstock.; and it continued with an escorted journey to Christ Church, a speech from the public orator, William Strode, and, by way of evening entertainment, a play written by Strode. Next day came a morning sermon from the senior proctor, Thomas Browne, canon of Christ Church, followed by a meeting of Convocation, where honorary degrees were conferred upon Prince Rupert, the king's nephew, and the Elector Palatine, Rupert's brother. The whole party then moved off to St John's, Laud's college, to look over the chancellor's new buildings and to enjoy a sumptuous feast in Laud's new library and a further play, before a return to Christ Church and yet another play. After the king's departure on 31 August, Laud gave a celebratory dinner, again in St John's, for the doctors, the proctors, the heads of houses, and a few friends: 'We were merry and very glad that all things had so passed to the great satisfaction of the king and the honour of that place.'[138]

Prideaux played a minor part in these proceedings and then only as one of a group. Along with other heads of houses, he was summoned to join the procession at the king's entry into Oxford,[139] and he presumably attended Laud's post-festal dinner, again with other heads. There were aspects of the

---

137. Trevor-Roper, *Archbishop Laud*, 287. Ibid., 287–94, for a full account of the visit; *Works of Laud*, v. 148–55, and NUL MS Cl C 84/1, for contemporary accounts. Cf. Wood, *History*, ii. 407–13; *HUO*, iv, 204–5; Sharpe, 'Archbishop Laud and the University of Oxford', 150–1.
138. *Works of Laud*, v. 154–5.
139. OUA, NEP/supra/Reg. R, fo. 133r.

visit which would have displeased him, besides its exaltation of Laud. The initial speech of welcome by William Strode, whose flattery of Laud at the preceding Congregation had already drawn fire from Prideaux, spoke of Charles as *Homo-Deus*, 'Man-God', words regarded as almost blasphemous by their reporter, Francis Cheynell, and no doubt by Prideaux too.[140] Nor would he have been placated by Thomas Browne's sermon, which had not only attacked the puritans but had also taken a swipe at other Calvinists by criticizing the Calvinist doctrine of reprobation ('they who say God is gloryfyed by the damned in hell'). Laud, however, regarded the sermon as 'excellent' and shortly afterwards appointed Browne as one of his domestic chaplains.[141] Prideaux may have been more heartened by a 'very neat' speech made before the king by an Exeter undergraduate, William Herbert, the 14-year-old son of the earl of Pembroke, Prideaux's patron. 'Delivered with a well-tempered spirit', says Cheynell, 'the king was much affected with it, and taken with him.'[142]

More striking than Prideaux's absence from the narratives of the king's visit, in common with almost all other heads of houses, was his absence from two committees set up in advance of the visit, one to supervise its planning and the second to advise on the arrangements for the new chair in Arabic founded by Laud and conferred on Edward Pococke in 1634. Both committees were appointed on the same day, 8 August, and had the same membership.[143] They mainly comprised Laudians and Arabists, with some overlap between the two categories. The Laudians included four, possibly five, heads of houses (Pinck of New College, Jackson of Corpus, Potter of Queen's, Clayton of Pembroke, and Escott of Wadham, the last of these possibly a Laudian); Peter Turner of Merton, both Laudian and Arabist; and a few other notable Arabists, such as John Bainbridge and Henry Stringer.[144] The only theologian on the two committees was Samuel Fell, Lady Margaret professor and the junior of the two divinity professors, no scholar but a good man of business.[145] Prideaux, Fell's senior, a much more distinguished scholar and a notable linguist (though not an Arabic specialist), was omitted.

140. NUL MS Cl C 84/1; *HUO*, iv. 210.
141. NUL, MS Cl C 84/1; *Works of Laud*, v. 149–50; *HUO*, iv. 207–8.
142. *Works of Laud*, v. 151–2; NUL MS Cl C 84/1; Boase, *Commoners*, 153.
143. OUA, NEP/supra/Reg R, fos 130v, 131r, 132r–135r.
144. For the allegiances of these men, see above, 255; *VCH Oxfordshire*, iii. 295 (for Clayton). For Pococke and the Arabists, *HUO*, iv. 481–2 (Pococke), 486–7 (Bainbridge and Turner), 489 (Stringer); *Works of Laud*, v. 108, 146, 230 (Escott).
145. Hegarty, 'Fell'.

After his ill-tempered and anti-Laudian eruptions in the preceding June Convocation, this was perhaps not surprising. Nevertheless, his absence illustrates the extent to which he had now been sidelined and power in the university lay in the hands of Laud's friends and allies.

For Prideaux himself these great public events were overshadowed by a private tragedy. On 1 August 1636, just a few weeks before the king's visit, John Prideaux, his father's sixth child, died, aged 13. He was later buried in the new chapel. The twin brother of Matthias, who had died in 1625, and the fifth of Prideaux's children to die, John seems to have been his father's favourite, described on his surviving memorial plate in the present chapel as *patris optima gemma*, 'his father's most precious gem', who 'prematurely followed his brothers'. These unusual emotional touches remind us that Prideaux had a personal life largely hidden from us and lying beyond the affairs of the university and his difficult relationship with its chancellor. At the time of John's death, his eldest surviving brother, William, was aged 20, his second brother, Matthias, about 11, his eldest surviving sister Sarah (married to William Hodges), 16, and his second daughter, Elizabeth, 14, so Prideaux still had children at home.[146] The father's grief for his son's death brings into focus the human figure who lived beside the dogmatic theologian and university politician.

Prideaux's career between 1630 and 1636 may appear to have been one of episodes. The daily routines which linked those episodes—the routines of College management, university business, and professorial duties—are largely invisible and have to be taken for granted. Yet the episodes themselves also have an underlying theme: that of conflict, with Laud, with Heylyn, and to some extent with the king. The instability of Prideaux's relationship with Charles in these years is easy to overlook. But any defiance of Laud was almost *ipso facto* a defiance of his master and backer, while sometimes that defiance might be more direct. The support of Prideaux, 'the head of all these tumultuous stirs',[147] for the dissident preachers of 1631 amounted to an open challenge to the royal declarations of 1626 and 1628 prohibiting theological contention. Only slightly less direct were his objections to the new statutes of 1636. Since these had been presented to Convocation by Sir John Coke, the king's secretary, were sealed by

---

146. Wood, *Colleges and Halls*, i. 118; Butcher, 'Dr John Prideaux', 7–9.
147. *Works of Laud*, v. 49; above, 264.

Charles I, and were intended to be received as royal legislation,[148] Prideaux's cavilling remarks, ostensibly directed at the public orator, could be seen as an implied criticism of the Crown itself. For his part the king treated Prideaux with an occasional disdain. Perhaps surprisingly, he remained a royal chaplain.[149] But he was barred from the bishopric for which his eminence qualified him, and his vulnerability to royal displeasure had been show at the conclusion of his Woodstock 'trial' in 1631, when he came close to dismissal. Appointed by the king, the regius professor could lose his title by the same route.

'The beginning of the raigne of . . . King Charles', when, in Prideaux's later words, 'the doctrine, worshipp and discipline established and professed in the Church of England' had flourished, was now well and truly over.[150] In the face of a rising tide of Arminianism and of Arminians who increasingly sought to brand conventional Calvinists as subversive puritans, Prideaux's adherence to what had been the mainstream doctrines of the church of England and the convictions of his youth was greatly to his disadvantage, though we may doubt Christopher Potter's opinion that he would have moderated his views if he could have done so without harm to his reputation.[151] Yet the expression of those views often made him his own worst enemy. Both his treatment of Thomas Laurence at the 1629 Act and his differences with Heylyn at the 1633 Act clearly antagonized his public audience, while his petty interjections in Convocation at the presentation of the statutes are likely to have raised eyebrows among a more restricted but more influential gathering. The respect earned by Prideaux's learning, theological acumen, and double status as regius professor and head of house was not unshakeable, and if he found himself increasingly isolated within the hierarchy of the university and the church, the reasons did not entirely lie with the rise of Arminianism.

148. Sharpe, 'Archbishop Laud and the University of Oxford', 146–7.
149. Ryan, 'An Obscure Place', 29–30; Cranfield, 'Chaplains in Ordinary', 143–4.
150. The quotation is from Prideaux's will: Butcher, 'Dr John Prideaux', 24.
151. *Diary of Thomas Crosfield*, ed. Boas, 51; above, 257–8.

9

From Laud's Apogee to Laud's Decline, 1636–40

1. A recusant puritan?

In the four years between the king's visit to Oxford in August1636 and the summoning of the Long Parliament in September 1640, the beginning of the prelude to the Civil War, the dominant theme of Prideaux's public life continued to be his relations with Laud. These were brought into focus within months of the visit by a small and apparently trivial episode. One of the many university matters with which Laud busied himself at this time related to the form and conduct of the Latin Communion service celebrated in the university church before the start of every term (a custom which continues today). On 26 November 1636 he voiced his concerns about this service in a letter to Richard Baylie, his vice-chancellor. His chief concern lay with the question of language. While the Communion sermon was quite properly delivered in Latin, the prayers were in English 'as if Latin prayers were more unfit for a learned congregation than a Latin sermon'. This practice, Laud wrote, was contrary to Queen Elizabeth's direction and to the wishes of the king, whom he had consulted, and henceforth the whole service was to be in Latin, a decision to be enforced by the vice-chancellor and to be communicated to the heads of houses The letter to Baylie was accordingly read out in Convocation on 19 December.[1]

Laud's instructions, and others which followed in the same letter about the correct vestments for the celebration and the need to ensure that the choristers were able to sing in Latin, provide one further example of his obsession with strict adherence to decorum and correct form in matters of

---

1. *Works of Laud*, v. 156–8.

Between Scholarship and Church Politics: The Lives of John Prideaux, 1578–1650. John Maddicott, Oxford University Press. © John Maddicott 2022. DOI: 10.1093/oso/9780192896100.003.0009

liturgy and worship; Latin prayers were a peripheral element in the beauty of holiness which the Laudians promoted. More interesting than this familiar trope, however, was Baylie's reply to his superior's letter, written on 16 January 1637, following the first service under the new order.[2] After dealing with other items of university business, Baylie wrote that 'the Latin prayers had the success that was desired'. The choir had sung tunefully and the congregation had followed the rubric, so that Drs Prideaux, Fell, Morris and Clayton, had they been present, could have found no fault. The four men thus named were among the university's leading professors and scholars: Prideaux and Fell the two theology professors, Morris the regius professor of Hebrew, and Clayton the regius professor of medicine. But they were also men whose failure to appear for the service put them under suspicion, for after noting their absence, Baylie added in parentheses 'I hope they yet bee not recusant puritans'.

Baylie's comment, casual but malicious, was no doubt intended to arouse or confirm Laud's misgivings about the allegiances of this little group.[3] It is safe to assume that all four were Calvinist in their convictions, as Prideaux and Fell certainly were, and for this reason men who might have been expected to boycott Latin prayers which could be thought to run counter to the vernacular traditions of the reformed church or even to be papist The public language of Protestantism was the language of the people. The Latin Communion, also introduced in some colleges, would later be condemned in 1641 by the reforming parliamentary subcommittee headed by Bishop John Williams and including Prideaux, on the justifiable grounds that 'some young students and servants of the colledge doe not understand their prayers'.[4] Prideaux is very likely to have disapproved of this Laudian innovation; but 'recusant', a term usually applied to non-churchgoing Catholics, was one now being potentially applied to loyal Anglicans. Prideaux and Fell were in no sense puritans, except in so far as all those adhering to the norms of the Elizabethan and Jacobean church were increasingly condemned as such. Since puritans were now viewed as dangerous radicals, Baylie's slur, perpetuating as it did the their elision with the Calvinists which had taken off

2. *CSPD, 1636–7*, 368; SP 16/344, fo. 35.

3. Since so little is known about John Morris (see *HUO*, iv. 456, 463), his appearance here is a valuable indication of his possible religious allegiance.

4. W. A. Shaw, *A History of the English Church during the Civil Wars and under the Commonwealth, 1640–1660*, 2 vols. (1900), ii. 290; S. Hampton, 'A "Theological Junto": The 1641 Lords' Subcommittee on Religious Innovation', *The Seventeenth Century*, 30 (2015), 442; below, 326–7.

with Montague's writings in 1624–5, hinted at what was now seen as the subversive character of traditional Calvinism. In Laud's eyes, and probably in those of the king with whom Laud shared his hopes and fears, it may have helped to push Prideaux a little further towards the margins of religious respectability.

2. The Chillingworth affair

Despite the implications of Baylie's remark, Prideaux's standing in the university and his reputation as a scholar meant that he could not easily be dispensed with; indeed, in one further episode, a famous one, Laud had to draw on these qualities in order to further his own plans. At issue was the publication of William Chillingworth's book, *The Religion of Protestants*. Chillingworth was both a native of Oxford and an Oxford graduate. Born in 1602, the son of a prosperous Oxford mercer and, more importantly, the godson of Laud, he had gone up to Trinity College in 1618 and had rapidly established a name for himself as the cleverest man of his generation and the best disputant in the university. He was elected to a fellowship at Trinity in 1628 and remained close to his godfather and patron, acting as one of Laud's informants on university affairs.[5] But in the following year his upward progress had been halted by his conversion to Roman Catholicism and, in 1630, by his journeying overseas to take up residence at the Catholic seminary at Douai. This phase did not last. Within a year he had returned to England and Protestant orthodoxy, apparently won back by Laud's persuasions. From 1634 he was often to be found at Great Tew in Oxfordshire, in the circle of writers and thinkers which gathered around Lucius Cary, second Viscount Falkland, and it was there, in a milieu characterized by intense intellectual debate and eirenic reflection, that he set to work on his great book.[6]

The Religion of Protestants was written in response to a tract by the Jesuit Edward Knott and it took issue with one central doctrine of the Catholic church, that of Roman infallibility. Although it was far from being a standard

---

5. Wood, *Annals*, ii, 369.
6. R. R. Orr, *Reason and Authority: The Thought of William Chillingworth* (Oxford, 1967), 1–44; W. Chernaik, 'Chillingworth, William (1602–1644), theologian', *ODNB*; *Further Correspondence*, ed. Fincham, 67–8.

piece of anti-Catholic polemic, in other superficial ways it was conventional enough. At the apex of its thesis lay Chillingworth's famous declaration of his credo: 'The BIBLE, I say, the BIBLE only, is the religion of Protestants!'[7] But the Bible, Chillingworth argued, was to be interpreted in a spirit of rational inquiry, through the individual's use of his reason and under the guidance of his conscience, without recourse to the authority of the church. In controversies on matters of faith it was for the individual, drawing on the resources of reason and conscience, and not the church, to decide. There were clear dangers in this approach. Though Chillingworth professed ortho- dox beliefs on the Trinity (albeit it seems with reservations) and the atone- ment, the two doctrines on which the Socinians deviated most sharply from convention, his stress on the role of reason in religion otherwise placed him perilously close to their camp. In the narrow sense, Chillingworth was not a Socinian, a denier of the Trinity and the atonement. But in the broader sense, as an exponent of the primacy of reason in religious debate, he was.[8] Like the Socinians too, but also like most Arminians, he had no time for the doctrine of predestination, a belief which he saw as running counter to a less harsh and more plausible doctrine of individual responsibility.[9] So Chilling- worth's book, the product of a particularly agile and original mind, could give comfort to no particular party within the church, least of all perhaps to Calvinist-puritans. It was *sui generis*. If the Bible was 'the religion of Prot- estants', it was not the Bible as they knew it.

Long before the book's publication Laud had got wind of his godson's project, and what he heard made him uneasy. Yet he wished to forward the work of one for whom he felt some responsibility and of whom, as Chilling- worth's deliverer from the snares of Rome, he was probably proud. Torn two ways, he found a solution in seeking approval for the future book from the scholar best qualified to give or refuse it. On 3 March 1637 he approached Prideaux. 'You know', he wrote, ' that Mr Chillingworth is answering of a book, that much concerns the Church of England; and I am very sorry that the young man hath given cause why a more watchful eye should be held over him and his writings.' Here he almost certainly had in mind the short-lived Roman Catholic phase in Chillingworth's career.

7. Orr, *Reason and Authority*, 71. The remainder of the paragraph draws on Orr, *Reason and Authority*, 45–182, esp. 79, 97–8, 105 133; Mortimer, *Reason and Religion*, 65–82, esp. 74–5; Trevor-Roper, 'The Great Tew Circle', in his *Catholics, Anglicans and Puritans*, 199–209.
8. Trevor-Roper, 'The Great Tew Circle', 188.
9. W. Chillingworth, *The Religion of Protestants* (Oxford, 1638), 387–8.

'I would willingly desire this favour from you in the Church's name', he wrote later in the letter, 'that you would be at the pains to read over this tract, and see that it be put home in all points against the Church of Rome, as the cause requires.' If Prideaux wished to make reasonable amendments, he was sure that Chillingworth would not object. Always aware of the need to distance himself from the anti-Arminian charge that he favoured the cause of Rome, Laud here voiced a palpable anxiety. He apparently had no additional misgivings about his protégé's possible Socinian tendencies; it was Rome that concerned him. At this stage he clearly knew nothing of the book's contents and had only his suspicions to guide him. Prideaux responded by readily agreeing to what was asked of him, and in a letter of 6 March (to which we shall return) he wrote to Laud to tell him so: 'In that or anye other thing wherein my poor indeavours may be serviceable for the church or the common goode, no man shall be moer willing or readye to receive your graces directions and exequete your commands.'[10]

Prideaux was as good as his word. When Chillingworth's book was finally published in the early months of 1638, it contained a preliminary imprimatur from Prideaux and others from Richard Baylie, Laud's vice-chancellor, and Samuel Fell, Lady Margaret professor of divinity. Prideaux's stated (in Latin) that he had read the book thoroughly 'in which I find nothing contrary to the doctrine or teaching of the Church of England, but much which adds lustre to the orthodox faith and . . . destroys opposing interpretations'. Baylie and Fell wrote in similar terms. Although the licensing of Oxford books was not a novelty, this was the first time that a licence naming the examiners had been printed as part of the final book: another indication of Laud's anxieties about the book's content and his concern to have it endorsed at the highest level by the university's senior official and its two leading theologians.[11]

Prideaux's apparent willingness to commend *The Religion of Protestants* is astonishing.[12] His six Act lectures had shown that he was opposed to most of the main theological positions adopted in Chillingworth's book and to the Socinian doctrines which they seemed to embody. The author's acceptance

---

10. *Works of Laud*, v. 165–6; SP 16/349, fo. 86; *CSPD, 1636–7*, 486.
11. Chillingworth, *Religion of Protestants*, sig. S4v; Poole, 'The Learned Press: Divinity', 354–5.
12. This point was first made by R. M. Krapp (later 'Adams') in his *Liberal Anglicanism, 1636–1647: An Historical Essay* (Ridgefield, CT, 1944), 27–9, and subsequently in his review of Trevor-Roper's *Catholics, Anglicans and Puritans*, in the *New York Review of Books*, 14 April 1988, 28–30. The ensuing controversy, which contains much of value, can be followed in *NYRB*, 16 June 1988, 48–9, and 21 July 1988, 44–5.

of the atonement and his support (albeit lukewarm) for the Trinity gave no grounds for dispute, but most of his other positions had been specifically controverted by Prideaux in his lectures. They were most radically at odds on the broad questions of individual reason and church authority: while Chillingworth exalted the first and depreciated the second, Prideaux depreciated the first and exalted the second. In Chillingworth's opinion, 'Naturall reason is the last resolution . . . unto which the Churches authority is but the first inducement.' In Prideaux's opinion, set out in his Act lecture 'On the authority of the church on matters of faith', the Socinians were heretics 'who create a tribunal of reason in order that questions of faith may be determined by the uncertain judgement of nature'.[13] Prideaux's lecture had been due for delivery on 10 July 1637, but the cancellation of that year's Act from fear of an impending epidemic must have prevented its actual delivery.[14] If his imprimatur was given around 13 October, the date of Fell's licence (the only one to bear a date), only a short interval supervened between the conclusions reached in the lecture and his approval of the book's opposing conclusions. A number of Chillingworth's other deviations from orthodoxy were picked out in a letter from a fellow of Brasenose, Thomas Sixsmith, written in February 1638 to another Brasenose man. Some things in the book, wrote Sixsmith, are:

> very well done, but at others I cannot but boggle: in my poore iudgment . . . hee overthrowes the popish cause, but [on] grounds which indanger the shakinge of our owne . . . to talke of natural reason for grace, never to mention originall sinne, nor grace neither (having so often occasion) in the true notion of it, that hee hath a twange of the puritain in ascribing nothinge to the present Church, and the libertine too, who would bee tyde to no form of faith.

'I conceive him', Sixsmith summed up, 'to smell too much of the Socinian.'[15]

There are several possible explanations for the unlikely imprimatur which Prideaux conferred on Chillingworth's book. If he conceived of his task as being to search the book for any leanings towards Roman Catholicism, a task certainly deducible from Laud's letter of commission, then he could honestly say that he had found none. Indeed, the book's strong anti-Catholic thrust,

---

13. Chillingworth, *Religion of Protestants*, 65; *VDL*, 347; Adams, *NYRB*, 14 April 1988, 30; *HUO*, iv. 588.

14. For the Act's cancellation in three successive years, 1636–8, see above, 284 n.118; below, 306.

15. Brasenose College, Oxford, MS B2 a. 38, 34–5; *HUO*, iv. 588–9.

seen above all in its denial of the Roman church's infallibility,[16] would have commended it to him—and might have been thought to outweigh its Socinian deficiencies. A more plausible explanation is given by Sixsmith in another part of his letter. Sixsmith records that he had 'much parlee' with Prideaux about the book and 'I am sure that Dr Prideaux (whose approbation you find in the front) now much dislikes it . . . his best excuse is, that they have dealt fouly with him in printing passages which he expunged.' That Prideaux subsequently came to detest the book is confirmed by Francis Cheynell, fellow of Merton, and admittedly an inveterate enemy of Chillingworth, who wrote that, among his friends, Prideaux 'would liken it to an unwholesome lamprey, by having a poysonous sting of Socinianism throughout it, and tending in some places to plain infidelity and atheism'.[17] Prideaux had certainly been asked by Laud to correct the book. Yet it seems unlikely that amendments made by such an authority would simply have been ignored by the printers or that any such blatant disregard of Prideaux's direction would have passed without a public protest from their originator. Nor is it easy to see how a book whose deviations from orthodoxy were often more pervasive than particular could have been revised without wholesale rewriting.

There is, however, another possible explanation for Prideaux's complaisance. The outlines of what is a complicated story can partly be reconstructed from a letter written by Prideaux to Laud on 27 February 1637, shortly before he agreed to read and revise Chillingworth's text.[18] At the story's centre was a petition directed against Prideaux, presented to Laud, and forwarded by Laud to Prideaux prior to the latter's writing his February letter. The petition itself does not survive and is known only from Prideaux's letter intended to answer the petition's claims. The petitioner was Prideaux's brother-in-law, brother of his deceased wife Anne Goodwin and one of the five children of William Goodwin, the former dean of Christ Church. Although his first name is nowhere recorded, this brother-in-law was almost certainly Matthew Goodwin, known to have been William's son, who had matriculated at Christ Church in 1621, taken his BA in 1623, and had

---

16. Orr, *Reason and Authority*, 46.
17. BNC, MS B2 a 38, 35; Wood, *Athenae*, iii. 91, 706.
18. SP 16/348, fo. 115; *CSPD, 1636–37*, 469.

subsequently been ordained.[19] This Goodwin was a particularly disreputable character, a rogue who had long troubled Prideaux and whose unedifying career Prideaux set out in some detail in his letter to Laud. Goodwin had been expelled from Christ Church, said Prideaux, not for debt, as he claimed, but for 'misdemeanours too well knowen that made him unfitt for any society'. He had then roamed around England and Ireland 'in a scandalous way to the disgrace of his dead father, myself and of the ministry', one of those indigent, untitled, and itinerant priests whose habits Laud particularly disliked.[20] He had pretended that Prideaux had promised to get him a living, either from the lord keeper or in Oxford or on reversion from Exeter College. 'All this is malitiously forged', wrote Prideaux, and based on no more than a visit to Prideaux, when, 'in his begging way', he had impudently told the Rector that it was within his power 'to procure him something, either from my lord keeper or otherwise'. Prideaux had replied 'that if he would reforme himself and make himself fitt, I should doo the best I could to furder him and not otherwise'.

As this suggests, Goodwin claimed to have some call on Prideaux's patronage. The letter shows that Goodwin wanted to make it appear that this obligation stemmed from dispositions made by King James or by William Goodwin, the petitioner's father. Prideaux denied that any such dispositions had been made. At stake here were two particular benefices, a prebend at Salisbury Cathedral worth £16 a year and the Oxfordshire living of Chalgrove, both formerly held by William Goodwin, Prideaux's father-in-law. Both had come to Prideaux after Goodwin's death in 1620, the prebend, Prideaux stated, through the mediation of the university's then chancellor, the earl of Pembroke, and of the household treasurer, Sir Thomas Edmondes, 'my own noble favourer', while the church of Chalgrove had come from the lord chancellor, Francis Bacon.[21] He stressed that he had acquired both properties entirely legitimately and without conditions, though he judged that his benefactors had hoped that he would use their proceeds to help his widowed mother-in-law and her five children. This he had done. He self-effacingly declined to give any details, but we know from another source that in 1625 he generously passed on Chalgrove

19. Foster, *Alumni*, ii. 585.
20. *Works of Laud*, vi. 327–8. The absence of Matthew Goodwin from CCEd suggests that he never held a living.
21. Prideaux does not locate the prebend at issue, but it is clear from the context that Salisbury is meant. Cf. Krapp. *Liberal Anglicanism*, 30.

to John Goodwin, William's eldest son, just as he would later pass on his vicarage at Bampton to his son-in-law, William Hodges.[22] He was open-handed with what was his to give. But now apparently his brother-in-law was claiming in his petition to have a good title to the prebend and in his wanderings had been putting forward the petition 'as a breife [document] to cheate by'. The petitioner had been disowned by his mother, who had complained of his disobedience and had acknowledged how much she and her family owed to Prideaux. 'There is scarce a passage in [the petition] that may in honesty be justified'. Prideaux ended by saying that he depended on Laud's goodness and justice 'that I may peaceably hold myne owne'.

What Prideaux thus wanted was Laud's rejection of Goodwin's petition, which would effectively confirm him in his rights. This he speedily obtained. On 3 March, four days after Prideaux had written his letter, Laud wrote to ask him to read and revise Chillingworth's book, as we have seen. He must at the same time, and almost certainly in the same letter,[23] have notified him of his dismissal of Goodwin's case, for when Prideaux replied on 6 March, he began by expressing his gratitude to Laud for his verdict: 'I was confident that my brother Goodwin would prevayle little in such a cause, before such a judg, after true information once given, for your gracious acceptation of which, and favourable expression, I hold myself to be ingaged to be always thankful.' After expressing his willingness to help Goodwin if he mended his ways, he went on to accept Laud's commission with regard to Chillingworth's book. His letter was endorsed by William Dell, Laud's secretary, 'Dr Prideaux his undertaking to revise Mr Chillingworths book'.[24]

It is difficult not to see a connection between Laud's verdict against Prideaux's bête noire Goodwin and Prideaux's subsequent verdict in favour of Laud's protégé Chillingworth. Goodwin had clearly been a pestilential nuisance to Prideaux. An embarrassment to his extended family, including Prideaux, he had spread malicious lies about his mistreatment by Prideaux,

---

22. For John Goodwin's tenure at Chalgrove, see *VCH Oxfordshire*, xviii. 152. Hegarty, 'Prideaux', mistakenly identifies John Goodwin as Prideaux's miscreant brother-in-law, but John Goodwin was dead by September 1636, before Prideaux's correspondence with Laud: see his will, proved 26 Sept. 1636, Oxfordshire History Centre, Wills Inventory, 199.252.

23. Laud's letter of 3 March, copied in the 'History of his Chancellorship of Oxford' (*Works of Laud*, v. 165–6) is a partial transcript only, which begins 'I had almost forgotten a business to you of greater consequence than this.' 'This' can hardly refer to anything except Laud's rejection of Goodwin's petition.

24. SP 16/349, fo. 86; *CSPD, 1636–7*, 486.

his claims on Prideaux's resources, and his right to Prideaux's property. He was a threat both to his brother-in-law's reputation, his income, and his peace of mind. Laud's dismissal of his petition must have come as a huge relief to Prideaux, as his letter of 6 March suggests, and it appears to have ended the whole affair. We hear no more of Goodwin and his claims. In this light Prideaux's undertaking to review Chillingworth's book was a minor quid pro quo offered to Laud in return for a major favour received. If he also saw Laud as Chillingworth's patron and mentor, not only his godfather but his saviour from the perils of Roman Catholicism, he may have been ready to go further and to please Laud more handsomely by sanctioning his godson's book. He could do so the more easily, since Laud had asked him to keep 'a watchful eye' open for Catholic tendencies, and he had found none. He may have been prepared to overlook Chillingworth's Socinianism, apparently unsuspected by Laud, in order to secure the book's publication: a major thanks-offering to Laud, who had freed him from the incubus of Goodwin.

We cannot rule out the possibility that Prideaux had made amendments to the text which were subsequently ignored. But it seems more likely, indeed almost certain, that in return for private advantage—the securing of his property and the quashing of Goodwin's claims—Prideaux had been prepared to compromise his principles and his integrity by turning a blind eye to what could be seen as the heterodoxy inherent in Chillingworth's vision of Protestantism. His book's three examiners had been carefully chosen by Laud, and over each of them he had some hold. Apart from Prideaux, Baylie, the vice-chancellor, was Laud's friend, chaplain, relative by marriage, and president of his college, while Fell had hopes of Laud's favour, possibly in the form of a bishopric, at just this time. Prideaux, of course, was in his debt for a favour already received.[25] From each Laud had reason to expect the positive verdict on his godson's book carefully set down in print in the book's imprimatur. If Prideaux was the most distinguished theologian of these three, and for that reason the examiner whose support Laud valued most, he was also the one best qualified to recognise the book's Socinian tendencies. That he tacitly declined to do so was *trahison des clercs* indeed.

We have one surviving physical memento of Prideaux in the year when Chillingworth's book was published—a fine medal now in the British Museum and struck in 1638 by the famous French engraver and medallist

---

25. Hegarty, 'Baylie'; Hegarty, 'Fell'.

Figure 7. Medal image of Prideaux by the French medallist Claude Warin, 1638, and one of a group of medals by Warin mainly showing members of Charles I's court.

Claude Warin, then midway through a sojourn in England lasting from about 1633 to 1646 (Figure 7). Warin's medal for Prideaux shows him in profile, straight-nosed, moustached, spade-bearded, the whole face characterized by *gravitas* but not severity, recognizably the same man who appears in his earlier portrait. The inscription around the medal's edge advertises his position in the university: 'IO. PRIDEAUX S.T.P. REG. OXON. AETAT. SVAE. 58. 1638'.[26] Since such a medal would have been commissioned by the sitter,[27] Prideaux must have intended this to serve both as an enduring memorial and as an emblem of his high office in the university. During his time in England, Warin produced at least ten similar medals, almost all of them for men associated with the royal court: figures such as Richard Weston, earl of Portland, the treasurer, and Hubert le Sueur, the sculptor. To find Prideaux in such company is surprising. Despite his differences with both Charles and Laud, he may have continued to be an identifiable presence in the king's circle.

26. 'John Prideaux Regius Professor of Divinity at Oxford, in the fifty-eighth year of his age. 1638': M. Jones, *A Catalogue of the French Medals in the British Museum*, 2 vols. (1989), i. 258–69.
27. Jones, *A Catalogue*, i. 9.

3. University and College

Throughout these later years of the Laudian regime Prideaux's standing remained high. One William Johnson, writing from Cadiz in May 1638 in an improbable attempt to convert him to Catholicism, spoke of 'your profound learning and estimation in England as the oracle of the university and the overlooking eye of the nation', while John Dury, writing to Samuel Hartlib in October 1640, told him that the rector of Bremen University 'doth highly esteem of Dr Prideaux', whose lectures he was 'very desirous to see'. He had written to Prideaux himself a few months earlier, in May 1640, both to seek copies of his works for the *Bremenses theologi* and to ask more generally for his spiritual guidance.[28] But for all these marks of Prideaux's standing at home and abroad, his reputation greatly exceeded his influence on events. In a university overseen by a watchful and censorious chancellor, whose religious views differed sharply from his own, Prideaux's marginalization was perhaps to be expected. Yet there were other, special reasons for his submergence at this time. In particular, he lacked a public voice. This was only in part a result of the continuing ban on controversial preaching and publishing which affected all the university's members. It was in August 1638 that Prideaux complained to Archbishop Ussher about this imposed silence: 'We can print here *Smiglecius* the Jesuits Metaphysical Logick and old John *Buridane's* ploddings upon the Ethicks. But matters that entrench nearer upon true divinity, must be more strictly overseen.'[29] Prideaux himself published nothing between his *Certaine Sermons* in 1636–7 and his *Nine Sermons* in 1641. After the exception apparently taken to some of the opinions voiced in *Certaine Sermons* he may have been wary of again exposing himself in print until, with the fall of Laud in 1640, he felt that he could do so with impunity.[30] As with so many of his actions, his silence may have been underlain by his natural timidity.

28. Bodl. MS Eng. Misc. e. 226, fo. 14; SUL, Hartlib Papers, 2/2/41A, 5/20/1A–2B.
29. Boase, cii; Ussher, *Correspondence*, ii. 743–4; Smiglecius, *Logica*, had been printed at Oxford in 1634 and was reprinted in 1638, while Buridan, *Philosophi Trecentis Retro annis celeberrimi Quaestiones in Decem Libros Ethicorum Aristotelis ad Nicomachum* was printed at Oxford in 1637: Madan, i. 181, 196, 210. Both were standard works for the arts course: see *HUO*, iv. 294–6, 321, 322, 325.
30. Madan, i. 199–200, ii. 158; above, 281–2; below, 327–8.

A more fortuitous reason, and one already referred to, lay in the absence for three successive years of the platform normally given to him by the university's Act celebrations. In 1636, 1637, and 1638 the presence of plague in regions close to Oxford (though never apparently in Oxford itself) led to the cancellation of the Act.[31] For Prideaux these cancellations meant that for three years he had no opportunity to address and influence, via his Act lectures, either his domestic university audience or the much more heterogeneous collection of outsiders who usually attended. The Act lectures which he subsequently published, nominally for the years 1636 and 1637, must either have been given at other times or to a more restricted academic audience, or possibly never delivered but merely printed.[32] Fate as well as church politics thus imposed on him a degree of silence. He presumably lectured at the Act in subsequent years until he left the regius chair in 1642; but if so, he did not publish.

His isolation was further emphasized by two promotions which took place in 1638. Vacating the Lady Margaret chair of divinity, Samuel Fell was elected as dean of Christ Church, while Laud's intervention secured the chair for a favoured son, Thomas Laurence. Fell seems to have been a mild Calvinist and no friend to the chancellor, though perhaps willing enough to cultivate him when advancement seemed in the offing, as over the licensing of Chillingworth's book. Laurence, on the other hand, was an outright Arminian, a critic of predestination and a supporter of Laud's views on the altar and the sacraments. Humiliated by Prideaux at the 1629 Act, where he had been accused of popery, he had no reason to love his Calvinist colleague in the regius chair. In the previous year he had been elected as master of his old college, Balliol, again probably through Laud's intervention, replacing the largely absentee John Parkhurst, who, as George Abbot's former chaplain and protégé, had certainly been no Laudian. This double promotion of Laurence could not fail to strengthen Laud's hand in the university and to create a further counterweight to any influence which Prideaux might continue to exercise.[33]

---

31. 1636: Wood, *History*, ii. 407; Madan, ii. 131. 1637: *Works of Laud*, v. 175, 184, 187, 199; Madan, ii. 134. 1638: *Works of Laud*, ii. 199; Madan, ii. 138.

32. *VDL*, 327, 346.

33. *Works of Laud*, v. 185–6; A. J. Hegarty, 'Laurence, Thomas (1597/8?–1657), college head', *ODNB*; V. Larminie, 'Parkhurst, John (1563–1639), Church of England clergyman', *ODNB*; Tyacke, *Anti-Calvinists*, 78, 83, 84, 184, 221; J. Jones, *Balliol College: A History, 1263–1939* (Oxford, 1988), 92, 99.

Laud's appointments bolstered his attempts to impose on the university, and increasingly on its colleges, the order and discipline which he saw as essential to the university's well-being as an ark of religion and learning. Between 1637 and 1639 there was no let-up here in a campaign which marked the whole period of his chancellorship, and even his most petti-fogging instructions have to be seen as a means to this end. Wealthy undergraduates were not to go about booted and spurred on pretence of attending riding schools; unlicensed alehouses were to be suppressed (perhaps the most recurrent of all these directions) and undergraduates were not to spend time in these unwholesome dens; and heads of houses were not to tolerate drunkenness and disorder in their colleges.[34] Laud's instructions were often more honoured in the breach than in the obser-vance, and he was never able to secure the degree of placid conformity and decorous behaviour which he desired—partly because he could not easily intervene within college walls. Arminian heads might do their best to enforce the rules and often succeeded, but such few Calvinists as there were proved more recalcitrant.[35] Exeter's undergraduates came especially to Laud's attention in various unfavourable ways. In 1639 he was told of an Exeter student whom the Jesuits had seduced into Roman Catholi-cism, and of two others, poor scholars, who had stolen some of the College plate and then either fled or been expelled for their crime.[36] Rowdiness was a more general problem. It sometimes took the form of 'coursing', when formal academic disputations between undergraduate members of rival colleges broke down into riotous fighting beyond the control of the proctors. The coursing between Exeter and Christ Church during the Lent disputations of 1638 mentioned by Wood became notorious and led the vice-chancellor to prohibit all further disputations between the two col-leges. The strong aristocratic presence at Exeter aggravated these disorders. The ungovernable Lord Caulfield, an Irish peer and a gentleman com-moner at Exeter from 1638 to 1640, was accused by Laud of being both disorderly and a bad influence on others, and he instructed the vice-chancellor to tell his tutor and the head of his house (the unnamed Prideaux) 'that if he mend not his manners, he shall not stay there to corrupt others'. Prideaux's own son William was similarly involved in a

34. *Works of Laud*, v. 173–4, 179, 201, 262–3; Wood, *Annals*, ii. 419.
35. Sharpe, 'Archbishop Laud and the University of Oxford', 157–9.
36. *Works of Laud*, v. 215, 232.

quarrel, probably due to drink, with a Christ Church undergraduate, the young earl of Downe, which Laud, noting the role of 'Dr Prideaux's son', regarded as a 'disaster'.[37]

After the short-lived rapprochement brought about by the Chillingworth affair, Prideaux's indulgence towards the aristocracy may have contributed to the further cooling of his relations with Laud. An item from Samuel Hartlib's papers next casts a bright light on their relationship. In August 1640, between the dissolution of the Short Parliament and the meeting of the Long Parliament, Constantine Adams provided Hartlib with an interesting report on Prideaux's mental state. Adams, who took his MA from Lincoln College in 1638 and was later to become fellow and vice-principal of Jesus,[38] might be expected to have been a good witness to the affairs and opinions of the Turl Street colleges, Exeter, Lincoln, and Jesus. Writing about John Dury's attempt to enlist Prideaux's support for his ecumenical schemes, he reported that:

> He seemeth to bee much affected with all Mr Durrys his endeavours & intentions; but having certain information dass der Ertzbishof [Laud] does not altogether [word deleted, no doubt meaning 'approve'], he is affraid to encounter [oppose], as walking now under the cloud, and having many spies set about him for to prie into all his actions.

To 'shake off this needlesse feare', Adams had cited the examples of Archbishop Ussher and Bishops Davenant and Morton, all of whom had 'given great encouragement to the worke by their learned advice'. They were Dury's allies, as they had been earlier. Prideaux had promised to confer with Ussher, but, so far as we know, nothing came of this.[39]

The reasons for Prideaux's fears are not immediately apparent. But he may have had in mind the fate of another of Laud's enemies, John Williams, bishop of Lincoln. Williams was 'the most celebrated anti-Laudian of the entire 1630s'.[40] Thoroughly secular in his way of life, ambitious, wealthy, lavish in his hospitality, lord of England's largest diocese, perpetually sailing close to the legal wind, and a confirmed Calvinist in religion, this prince of

37. *Works of Laud*, v. 261, 263–5.
38. Foster, *Alumni*, i. 5.
39. SUL, Hartlib Papers, 15/8/3A–4B. Cf. Turnbull, *Hartlib, Dury and Comenius*, 207, n. 3; Milton, *Catholic and Reformed*, 509 (where 'restlesse feare' should read 'needlesse feare'); above, 277–8.
40. J. Adamson, *The Noble Revolt: The Overthrow of Charles I* (2007), 170. For Williams, see especially Trevor-Roper, *Archbishop Laud*, 52–6, 58–62, 114–15, 179–84, 325–32, 357–8, and B. Quintrell, 'Williams, John (1582–1650), archbishop of York', *ODNB*.

the church had built up for himself an almost unrivalled position of power within its structures. Dean of Westminster as well as bishop, and the holder of many livings, he was as far from the Laudian ideal of a model churchman as could be imagined. But in 1637 he had been brought down by a series of charges laid against him in Star Chamber. They included perjury, the suborning of witnesses, embezzlement, and revealing the secrets of the Privy Council; and they resulted in the imposition of a huge fine and Williams's committal to the Tower. Later, in February 1639, while he was still in custody, further charges were brought against him, this time involving his support for libels and insults directed against Laud. Further fines resulted. From this great struggle Laud had emerged victorious. But only temporarily: by the spring of 1641 it was Williams who was at liberty and Laud who was in the Tower.

Prideaux's cautious mentality and sober way of life were very different from those of the flamboyant Williams. Nevertheless, the two men had much in common, most obviously their Calvinism and their opposition to Laud. Though Williams was a Cambridge man, a one-time fellow of St John's, he had a permanent footing in Oxford through his episcopal visitorship of four colleges, including Exeter's neighbour, Lincoln. Through his ties with these colleges he had attempted in 1630 to mobilize opposition to the election of Laud as chancellor and to promote the cause of Laud's rival, the earl of Pembroke, an attempt in which he was partnered by Prideaux, Laud's leading opponent in residence.[41] Both men retained their links with Pembroke, some of whose sons spent time both in Williams's household and at Exeter College.[42] In the mid-1630s both men too crossed swords with the egregious Heylin, Laud's venomous chaplain. Prideaux's various clashes with Heylin were paralleled by the fierce debate between Williams and Heylin over the arrangement of church furniture. Here Williams took a predictably anti-Laudian position, arguing for the placing of the communion table east-west within the body of the church or chancel, rather than as an altar at the east end, as Laud would have it. Williams's views on the subject were said by his biographer to have been spoken of 'reverendly' by Prideaux, and they were supported again in his Act lecture of 1631, in what amounted to an implicit attack on Laudian policy. These differences led to a

---

41. Wood, *Annals*, ii. 368; Heylin, *Cyprianus Anglicus*, 208; above, 250–1.
42. Adamson, *Noble Revolt*, 170; above, 96, 291.

bitter pamphlet war between Williams and Heylyn in 1636–7.[43] So both in their ecclesiastical politics and in their churchmanship Prideaux and Williams shared a good deal of common ground. For this reason Williams's conviction after his trial in 1637, leading as it did to the suspension of his Oxford visitorships and to his replacement by Laud in all four,[44] is likely to have come as a particular blow to Prideaux. It strengthened still further the chancellor's hand within the university.

If, therefore, by 1640 Prideaux was 'walking under a cloud', too fearful to support Dury's schemes, and wary that a watch might be set on him, he may have been all too well aware that Williams's opposition to Laud had brought him to the Tower. Of course, no criminal charges comparable to those levelled against Williams could possibly have been laid against Prideaux. Yet any help to Dury could have been construed as anti-Laudian, and the Williams affair had shown that Laud and his allies could act ruthlessly against their enemies. Prideaux's fears, aggravated though they may have been by a temperamental nervousness, were perhaps not wholly unreasonable.

In these years of disappointment and frustration there was one major consolation for Prideaux: his College flourished. We have already seen that undergraduate numbers reached a peak in the late 1630s, coming to exceed those of all other colleges, and with a concomitant effect on corporate income, which in several years exceeded £500.[45] Quantity was matched by quality. It was in 1638 that Prideaux mentioned to Archbishop Ussher that he had three 'sons to earls' billeted in his lodgings (probably the three sons of the earl of Chesterfield), and this period also saw the presence at Exeter of William Herbert, third son of the earl of Pembroke, following in the footsteps of his brothers Charles and Philip, of Anthony Ashley Cooper, of Tobias and Robert Caulfield, sons of the Irish peer William Lord Caulfield, and of Lionel Carey, Lord Leppington, son of Henry Carey, earl of Monmouth.[46] If the price to be paid for housing and educating the nobility was a measure of disorder and the possible wrath of the chancellor, the sons

---

43. J. Hacket, *Scrinia Reserata* (London, 1693), part ii, 102; Milton, *Laudian and Royalist Polemic*, 56–60, 75 n. 54; *HUO*, iv. 165. For a dissenting view which argues that the differences between Williams and Laud on the altar question have been exaggerated, see Sharpe, *Personal Rule*, 336–7.

44. *HUO*, iv. 205.

45. Above, 86, 111.

46. Boase, *Register*, ciii; Ussher, *Correspondence*, ii. 744; Boase, *Commoners*, 53, 54, 152–3, 292, 306.

of the aristocracy also formed an elite which enhanced the College's status. The boastful tone of Prideaux's remark to Ussher told its own story.

For the College this was also a time of profitable projects and new departures. The first of these involved building. In 1634 Laud had initiated the building of a new Convocation House to replace the use of the university church for meetings of Convocation and for the Act ceremonies, seen by Laud as the profanation of a sacred space. The purpose-built replacement, opened in 1638, stood against the east end of the Divinity School and occupied land formerly part of Exeter's garden and outbuildings sold by the College to the university in 1634 for the agreeably large sum of £264.[47] Besides raising more than half a year's income, Exeter's participation in this project marked the College's willingness for once to fall in with Laud's schemes—a minor means perhaps to a more equable relationship between College and chancellor.

But more important still, because more permanent in their consequences, were two other projects, each intended to augment the College's academic resources. In the mid-1630s Charles I founded fellowships for scholars from the Channel Islands, one at Exeter, another at Pembroke, and a third at Jesus. His intention was to reinforce religious orthodoxy. Both the king and Laud hoped that Channel Island clergy, hitherto often looking to the Protestant academies at Saumur and Geneva for their education, would now be diverted to Oxford before returning home 'to purge that old leaven [of Calvinism] out of the islands', in Heylyn's words, though if the intention was to inoculate the scholars against Calvinism, the choice of Exeter was a peculiar one. Exeter's first Channel Island fellow, John Poindexter, was elected in 1636, and although the whole scheme was soon disrupted by the Civil War, it marked a welcome reinforcement of the College and the first addition to the fellowship since the election of Ralph Sherwin as the eighth Petrean fellow in 1568.[48] A second benefaction should have contributed still more to the College's teaching strengths. In 1637 John Maynard, an old member and now a successful barrister, settled £40 a year on his former College to fund two new lectureships, one in divinity and another in Hebrew, turning down Prideaux's request for money for building in order

47. Geraghty, *The Sheldonian Theatre*, 15–25; OUA, SEP/F/6–9, 11 (documents relating to the university's purchase of land from the College).
48. Heylyn, *Cyprianus Anglicus*, 356–8; Boase, *Register*, cxiv, 104; Trevor-Roper, *Archbishop Laud*, 349.

to support causes which Maynard clearly regarded as more worthwhile. The College, however, used the money to promote existing fellows to the two lectureships. Joseph Maynard, John's brother, to the divinity lectureship and John Conant to that in Hebrew, so failing to provide the infusion of new blood which Maynard had seemingly wanted.[49] The College's resources had, nevertheless, been enhanced and a new impetus given to subjects central to its scholarly work.

There was one more circumscribed event which is likely to have given Prideaux more personal pleasure than either of these two benefactions. On 3 July 1640 his second surviving son Matthias, then aged 15, matriculated at the College, and on 30 June 1641, less than a year later, he was elected to a fellowship.[50] Election at such an early age, and well before graduating, was by this time very unusual, and no doubt Prideaux had pressed his son's claims—perhaps all the more strongly since his elder son, William, had no academic credentials. But young Matthias, 'esteemed by his contemporaries an ingenious man', was capable enough to go forward for his BA in 1644 and to have some plausible claims to authorship.[51] His father's favour may have been deserved.

So within the College there were compensations for the restraints which Laud and circumstance had imposed on Prideaux's external freedoms.

4. The affairs of the nation

In the late 1630s the parochial affairs of College and university were set against a background of rising national discontents which would lead eventually, though by no predestined path, to civil war.[52] The central link between the local and the national was provided by the personality and policies of Laud, chancellor and archbishop. Laud's attempts as chancellor to impose discipline, order, and decorum on the university were paralleled in the church at large by principles and practices which elevated the status of

---

49. ECA, A.I.6, fos. 20v (printed in Boase, *Register*, cviii), 22v, 23v; Conant, *Life of Conant*, 5.
50. Boase, *Register*, 105; Butcher, 'John Prideaux', 8; Hegarty, 'Prideaux'.
51. Wood, *Athenae*, iii. 199; below, 000.
52. The brief factual account which follows draws on Gardiner, *History*, viii. 304–92, ix. 1–217; C. Russell, *The Fall of the British Monarchies, 1637–42* (Oxford, 1991), 27–205; A. Woolrych, *Britain in Revolution, 1625–1660* (Oxford, 2002), 91–148; M. Kishlansky, *A Monarchy Transformed: Britain, 1603–1714* (1996), 134–41.

the clergy, threatened the interests of the landed laity in matters such as tithes and impropriations, and seemed to conformist Anglicans, and still more to puritans, to be aligning the Church of England with the Church of Rome. But Laud's government of the church was only one half of a system of royal government which was seen to be moving in an increasingly authoritarian direction. The use of the prerogative courts of Star Chamber and High Commission to pursue the recalcitrant, and the king's drawing on prerogative expedients for raising money—forest fines, fines for refusing knighthood, and, most of all, ship money—impinged on a wide range of interests and pointed to a less 'constitutional' and more arbitrary style of rulership. It was in 1637 that John Hampden was prosecuted for refusing to pay ship money and that Prynne, Bastwick, and Burton were tried in Star Chamber for attacking Laud's policies and the whole order of bishops. Their subsequent cruel punishment exemplified the seeming alliance of church and state in the suppression of dissent.

The absence of a parliament meant that the grievances produced by Caroline rule, wanting both focus and coordination, might have gone without a remedy had it not been for the problem of the Scottish church. The fundamental structure of the church in Scotland was Presbyterian, with bishops lacking the diocesan supremacy which they enjoyed in England. In 1637 Charles and Laud had attempted to impose the English Prayer Book on the Scots, in a move which typified both Laud's drive for uniformity within the church and the masterful temper which seemed increasingly to characterize its government. This led to fierce resistance. The immediate results were the drawing up of a National Covenant binding its members to resist religious innovations and, in December 1638, a vote in the Scottish General Assembly of clergy and laity, the governing body of the Presbyterian kirk, in favour of abolishing episcopacy. The resulting tension between England and Scotland culminated in March 1639 in the First Bishops' War, while the negotiated peace which ended the war in June opened the way for the Scots to strengthen their administrative and military control of their country. In order to counter these developments and to renew the war Charles needed money, which could only be obtained in sufficient quantities from parliamentary taxation. But the Short Parliament, the first since 1629, sitting for three weeks in April–May 1640, failed to grant it. Instead, its members used the occasion to air the national grievances which had accumulated during the eleven years of Charles's personal rule. The onset of war and the summoning of Parliament had shattered that rule. The Convocation of the clergy met in parallel with Parliament but continued after Parliament's dissolution, by the king's order and contrary to constitutional custom. It attracted further opprobrium by passing canons which seemed to confirm some of the ceremonial changes of the 1630s, regarding, for example, the placing of the altar, and by imposing the so-called *et cetera* oath, which appeared to bind both the clergy and senior university graduates to oppose any innovations in the government of the church and to accept other principles which were left undefined. To the oath's hostile critics it seemed both to imply that unspoken changes to that government were in the air and at the same time 'to involve a blanket endorsement of the new Arminian status quo'.[53]

While Convocation was in session, there were riots in London directed against Laud, and an attempt to lay siege to his palace at Lambeth. Associated with arbitrary rule, with ceremonial innovations in religion which could be seen as popish, and with the Catholicism of Charles's queen Henrietta Maria and her circle, Laud was an easier and more vulnerable target than the king whom he served. Meanwhile, Scotland was in process of becoming a self-governing state and a military power to be reckoned with. In the Second Bishops' War, English forces mustered in June 1639 failed to prevent a Scottish army moving south of the border and, in August, capturing Newcastle. With the Scots still in possession of their conquered territory, Charles in September summoned another parliament to meet in two months' time. The Treaty of Ripon, which ended the war in October, not only left the invaders securely established in northern England but also bound the English to pay £850 a day for their army's maintenance, at a time when the English army also had to be similarly maintained. These were the desperate financial imperatives which confronted what was to become the Long Parliament when it assembled on 3 November 1640.

Before 1640 these events made little public impact in Oxford; how far and in what terms they were discussed in private we do not, of course, know. We do know that the Scottish issue was a sensitive one, particularly with Laud. An indelicate question proposed for debate in the (subsequently cancelled) 1638 Act and asking whether 'the additions and alterations in the Scottish liturgy give just cause for scandal', a question to which 'no' was the

---

53. Tyacke, *Anti-Calvinists*, 240. For Convocation and the canons, see also Gardiner, *History*, ix. 108, 142–8; Russell, *Fall*, 136–9; *HUO*, iv. 688–9; Sharpe, *Personal Rule*, 878–84; Davies, *Caroline Captivity*, 251–87; B. Worden, *The English Civil Wars, 1640–1660* (2009), 29.

intended and correct answer, was promptly quashed by Laud, who saw it as likely to endanger his own reputation, presumably as the promoter of the new Scottish Prayer Book. His letter to Richard Baylie, his vice-chancellor, on this ultra-sensitive point was notable for the ferocity and anger of its tone. Wood clarified the chancellor's fears by noting that the topic was put forward by 'the Anti-remonstrants, commonly called the Faction'—that is, the more extreme Calvinist-puritans within the university, who might have been expected to sympathize with the Scots.[54] Since Wood elsewhere includes Prideaux in this group, it is just possible that he may have been among them, though his abhorrence of Presbyterian government within the church makes this unlikely. Clearly any public discussion of English policy towards Scotland within the university was regarded as both divisive and potentially seditious.

But it was only in 1640, with the April meeting of the Short Parliament and the Second Bishops' War which followed, that the increasingly rapid motion of national affairs began to impinge directly on and even to threaten the university. 'This year', wrote Wood, 'presents unto us many troubles and tokens of approaching ruin.' For him these 'troubles and tokens' meant chiefly the insubordinate behaviour of the Oxford townsmen and their disrespect for the rights and privileges of the university, both of which he ascribed to the waning power of Laud, the university's 'great and renowned patron'.[55] Religion, however, was now the overriding issue and would remain so until the outbreak of war in 1642. In the Short Parliament the whole Laudian programme of the 1630s came under fire. John Pym led the attack, just as he had led that on Montague in the parliaments of the 1620s. The emerging leader of the Commons, he denounced 'the encouragement . . . of the popish religion', the failure to enforce anti-Catholic legislation, the publication of popish books, the introduction of 'popish ceremonyes', such as bowing towards the east, and the prosecution of ministers for failing to read the Book of Sports in their churches. The substitution of railed east-end altars for communion tables set east-west came in for particular criticism. In what was to become a common theme, another speaker criticized the use of the word 'puritan' by Catholic sympathizers as a

---

54. *Works of Laud*, v. 198–9; Wood, *History*, ii. 417, 424; *HUO*, iv. 590.
55. Wood, *Annals*, ii. 420; cf. *HUO*, iv. 688.

term of abuse to describe those who were mere Protestants.[56] Taking as its target what was seen as the whole Romeward drift of the past decade, the debate amounted to 'a comprehensive condemnation of the Laudian church'.[57]

In that condemnation the universities, and Oxford in particular, were included. They were seen as nests of popery infecting the whole church through the clergy which they trained. The chapels of the universities, said Pym, were 'a fountayne of ill spirits flowing to all parts'.[58] He spoke out against 'the publishing and preaching of many popish poynts in pulpitts and disputed in schools in the Universities and there mayntened for sownd doctrine', while Sir Thomas Littleton retailed rumours that there was 'a nurserye of Jesuites' at Oxford. Pym responded that 'he had heard that the Masse was said at Oxford', but that the vice-chancellor 'durst doe nothinge in it because it received countenance from above'.[59] This barb can only have been aimed at Laud, although he had, in fact, taken great care to suppress any Catholic tendencies within the university and to hunt down any possible Jesuits.[60] The whole charge sheet was a *mélange* of exaggerations and irrational fears, a part of the rising tide of virulent anti-Catholic sentiment which was to mark the next few years. But there were enough highly placed Oxford Arminians, among them heads of houses and most of them owing their positions to Laud, to make the accusations seem plausible. The change in the attitude of the Commons since the previous parliaments of the late 1620s is a notable feature here. Then, the divines of Oxford, Prideaux included, had been seen as honest Protestants, traduced by the Arminian Montagu as puritans, and men with whom the Commons sympathized.[61] Now, many of them were seen as crypto-papists, Arminian sympathizers serving an Arminian master, whose ten years of manipulative overlordship had overthrown the Protestant character of the university as part of a more general attack on the traditions of the church.

---

56. *Proceedings of the Short Parliament of 1640*, ed. E. S. Cope and W. H. Coates (Camden 4th ser., 19, 1977), 147, 150–1, 254–5; *The Short Parliament (1640) Diary of Sir Thomas Aston*, ed. J. D. Maltby (Camden 4th ser., 35, 1988), 87; Russell, *Fall*, 114–15, 105–7.
57. Ibid., 115.
58. *Short Parliament*, ed. Maltby, 91.
59. *Proceedings of the Short Parliament*, ed. Cope and Coates, 151, 182; Wood, *Annals*, ii. 425; Russell, *Fall*, 106.
60. *Works of Laud*, v. 181, 215, 242, 269–70; Cf. Wood, *History*, ii. 434.
61. Above, 238–9.

There is not enough evidence for us to gauge Prideaux's responses to these events. His known opposition to the Arminians and his fierce hatred of popery should have meant that he had nothing to fear from the rhetoric deployed against the universities in the Short Parliament. In the summer months which followed the parliament, it was the continuing hostility of Laud and not the anti-clerical zeal of the Commons which Prideaux saw as the main threat to his position. As late as August 1640, between the meetings of the two parliaments, Prideaux was reported by Constantine Adams to be afraid to stand against the archbishop, 'as walking now under a cloud and having many spies set about him to prie into all his Actions'.[62] Prideaux's apprehensions were perhaps surprising in view of his enemy's decline since the dismissal of Parliament. It was not only Laud's policies which the Parliament had condemned: he was also popularly (though unjustly) blamed for the dissolution of Parliament, for the continuance of Convocation after the dissolution, and especially for the formulation of the *et cetera* oath.[63] The subsequent demonstrations against him in London were a sure mark of his increasingly fragile position and would have been inconceivable before Parliament's meeting.[64] Yet if Adams's letter can be believed, the waning of Laud and Laudianism had done little to allay Prideaux's concerns about Laud's ability to harm him. He remained a worried man.

The election of the university's members for what became the Long Parliament, summoned on 24 September 1640 to meet on 3 November,[65] soon gave Prideaux an opportunity to show his continuing opposition to Laud. The Oxford election took place in Convocation on 17 October, just over two months after Adams had reported on Prideaux's fears. Our chief source, Anthony Wood, tells us that there was unanimous support for one candidate—Sir Thomas Roe, the most experienced diplomat of his day and one of the most loyal servants of the early Stuart state. For the second seat, however, there were two candidates. The majority plumped for John Selden; yet, says Wood, 'some few there were with Dr. Prideaux of Exeter and Dr. Hood of Lincoln College, of the Antiarminian or Puritan party, that were chiefly for Sir Nathan. Brent, Knight, warden of Merton College, but

62. Above, 308.
63. Davies, *Caroline Captivity*, 285–7.
64. Trevor-Roper, *Archbishop Laud*, 385–93; Milton, 'Laud', *ODNB*.
65. Gardiner, *History*, ix. 207–8.

being out-vied with votes, sate down in peace'. 'The puritan faction', wrote Dr Thomas Read, a New College contemporary, 'prevailed not.'[66]

That Nathanael Brent was Laud's enemy provides the most plausible reason for Prideaux's supporting him. Despite the implication of Wood's remark, there is little evidence that, at this stage in his career, Brent was particularly anti-Arminian. In the 1620s and early 1630s he had been Laud's vicar-general and so his active agent in the enforcement of the Laudian reforms in the dioceses. What then turned Laud against his former ally was his gross misgovernment of Merton College, where Brent had been warden since 1622 and where Laud was Visitor. Prompted by an informer within the college, in 1638 Laud had initiated an inquiry into the various goings-on at Merton, which revealed a deplorable state of affairs. Brent was shown to have embezzled college funds, submitted false claims for expenses, failed to collect debts owing to the college, and awarded postmasterships (scholarships) through graft and bribery. The subsequent injunctions, sent down to the college in July 1640, attempted a thorough reformation, in part by curbing the powers of the warden. But they also turned Brent into Laud's bitter enemy. At the archbishop's trial in 1643–4 he appeared as a witness for the prosecution.[67]

This was the candidate whom Prideaux and his ally Hood put forward as the university's second representative in Parliament. It is probable that they were covertly supported by the earl of Pembroke, whom both Brent and Prideaux had backed against Laud for the chancellorship in 1630 and who was unsuccessfully to promote Brent as his candidate for the vice-chancellorship (in succession to Prideaux) in 1642.[68] Pembroke was always a shadowy force in the background to Prideaux's affairs. But the votes of the majority went to a very different sort of man. John Selden was the country's most learned legal historian, a savant deeply versed in Jewish as well as British history, an exceptional linguist, an experienced parliamentarian who had sat in the parliaments of the mid- and late 1620s, and a cosmopolitan figure with an irreproachable reputation. But he was also Laud's friend and may indeed

66. Wood, *History*, ii. 424; M. Strachan, 'Roe, Sir Thomas (1581–1644), diplomat', *ODNB*; Rex, *University Representation*, 145.

67. Wood, *Athenae*, iii. 333–4; Trevor-Roper, *Archbishop Laud*, 146, 192–6, 353–7, 420–1; G. H. Martin and J. R. L. Highfield, *A History of Merton College* (Oxford, 1997), 199–203; A. J. Hegarty, 'Brent, Sir Nathanael (1573/4–1652), ecclesiastical lawyer and college head', *ODNB*.

68. *Clarendon State Papers*, 3 vols. (Oxford, 1767–86), ii. 145; Trevor-Roper, *Archbishop Laud*, 114; Rex, *University Representation*, 144–6; *HUO*, iv. 691–2; Hegarty, 'Brent'.

have been the chancellor's candidate for the Oxford seat.[69] That Prideaux should have backed the unprincipled (but anti-Laudian) Brent against Selden, the scholar and public man, says much about his detestation of Laud and his willingness to pursue personal feuds at the expense of the public good. His unsuccessful campaign for Brent also emphasizes what had been evident for the past few years: his relative isolation within the university. Wood named only one other head of house who supported him—and their candidate got nowhere.

5. Prideaux and Laud: A retrospect

The relationship between Prideaux and Laud, the theme of the preceding two chapters, is difficult to characterize. Prideaux's hostility to Laud is hardly in doubt. He had regularly sought to thwart him, though rarely with any success. His challenge to Laud's jurisdiction as Visitor of Wadham in 1627, his opposition to Laud's election as chancellor, his objections to the Laudian reform of the university statutes, and his support for Laud's enemy, Nathanael Brent, in the parliamentary election of 1640 all point to an active and long-standing antipathy. Differences in personality and circumstance—between Laud, the fussy, ever-busy, and unsociable pedant, and the more humane Prideaux, grounded in family and community—may account for something.[70] But their antagonism was more firmly rooted in religious differences springing from divergent views of the destiny of the Church of England. Was its purpose, beyond its evangelizing mission, to preserve and hand on the Calvinistic certainties which had solidified under Elizabeth and held their own until James I's last years? Or was it to be a regenerated church in which the search for, and statement of, doctrinal truths took second place to discipline, sacramental and reverent worship, a well-ordered and well-supported clergy serving their congregations in well-maintained buildings, and all else that was meant by 'the beauty of holiness'?

For all their differences, however, Prideaux and Laud saw eye to eye on a good many points of ecclesiastical practice and principle, to a degree not always appreciated. Like Laud, Prideaux was an anti-Presbyterian, a believer in *iure divino* episcopacy (though prepared to make an exception for

69. Trevor-Roper, *Archbishop Laud*, 336–7.
70. For Prideaux's personality, see below, 383–5.

Continental Protestants), and no friend to what he saw as the subversive tendencies of the extreme puritans. He favoured, too, the 'warrantable ceremonies', such as bowing at the name of Jesus by which Laud set such store, but which the radicals regarded as papist superstition.[71] Again like Laud, he gave due weight to the sacraments as a means of access to faith, though to this end he put them on a par with preaching, where Laud gave them superiority.[72] He was also fiercely critical of neglectful lay patrons, insistent that church buildings should be properly maintained, and emphatic that tithes should be paid for the clergy's upkeep: all key points in Laud's programme for ecclesiastical regeneration.[73] Close to the puritans in some aspects of his Calvinism, Prideaux nevertheless shared much common ground with his adversary.

'Dr Prideaux was wont to say, tho' Arch-Bishop Laud and he could never understand [agree with] one another, yet he reverenced no man more before his death, that he had wisely foreseen what lay hid to many of them.' Prideaux's opinion of Laud, a unique expression of his views, was recorded by a reliable source: Sir Philip Warwick, the trusted servant and later secretary of Charles I, whom Prideaux must have encountered at Charles's court.[74] It was obviously voiced after Laud's execution in 1645, when the chaos of religious libertarianism engulfing the church had conferred on Laud a measure of posthumous respectability denied him in his lifetime. Yet even before 1640, and despite their bitter differences, it may have been true that to some degree Prideaux 'reverenced' Laud. His deference to him in the minor altercations of 1630, his willingness to please him by giving his approval to Chillingworth's book, and his unwillingness to displease him by offering support to John Dury or, possibly, by continuing to receive foreign students at his college all blended a nervous apprehension with a respect grounded on Laud's authority as both archbishop and chancellor and on the weight of his churchmanship. At no point did he endorse the accusations of crypto-popery increasingly made by Laud's enemies. How far his attitude to his superior may have been affected by his hopes for a bishopric is hard to say. It is true that we lack hard evidence to show that he harboured any such hopes,

---

71. Prideaux, *Euchologia*, 48–9; above, 232.
72. Prideaux, *A Sermon Preached*, sig. D1r.
73. Ibid., sig. B3r; Trevor-Roper, *Archbishop Laud*, 96; C. Hill, *Economic Problems of the Church* (Oxford, 1956), 82, 143–4; 101–2, 107–8, 126, 322–31; Milton, 'Laud'.
74. P. Warwick, *Memoires of the Reign of King Charles I*, 3rd edn (1703), 88–9; D. L. Smith, 'Warwick, Sir Philip (1609–1683), politician and historian', *ODNB*.

though it must be almost certain that he did. But if, from the mid-1620s onwards, and possibly earlier, he was seen by others, and probably by himself, as a likely candidate, he must have known that promotion would depend on an abandonment, or at best a modification, of the Calvinist principles which had governed his life. He was supremely qualified for a bishopric and may well have coveted this prize. But as long as the Laudian regime lasted, it was unattainable without a grand surrender which he was unwilling to make.

If Prideaux's possible hopes could not be realized, his fears may have been equally misplaced. By 1640 those fears had reached a pitch of almost neurotic intensity as he envisaged 'many spies set about him to prie into all his actions'—'needless feare', according to Hartlib's correspondent, Constantine Adams.[75] Prideaux's strength lay in his rectorship, where Laud could hardly touch him. He was the successful head of a large, prosperous, and (except for one episode in 1631) united College whose prestige was at its height in the 1630s. Laud's powers stopped at Exeter's walls; nor were they enhanced by the visitatorial role which he enjoyed at some other colleges. It is worth noting that he had been unwilling to intervene when, in 1631, the father of the disappointed candidate in Exeter's fellowship election appealed to him to do so.[76] He recognized the limits on his authority. Although Prideaux's alliance with the forces of anti-Arminianism in 1631 may have placed his tenure of the regius chair in jeopardy, and he remained to an extent on probation after the Woodstock 'trial' which had ended that crisis, his position as rector was unassailable. It remained a bulwark to set against the tensions of a difficult relationship.

These were some of the complexities which underlay the rector's dealings with the chancellor. They cannot easily be reduced to the simple issue of Prideaux versus Laud.

75. Above, 308.
76. Above, 261.

IO

Prideaux Redivivus and the Road to Civil War, 1640–2

1. The early stages of the Long Parliament, 1640–1

In the early months of the Long Parliament from November 1640 onwards, Prideaux's career was transformed as he moved in from the margins of both church and university and began to take on a role in affairs denied him during Laud's later years as Canterbury's archbishop and Oxford's chancellor. There were three reasons for his improved position. First, the fall of Laud removed what had been the main block to his advancement. Second, his expertise as a theologian came to be in demand outside the academy, as the reform of the church rapidly emerged as one of Parliament's main objectives. And, thirdly, his standing as an old-school Calvinist divine untainted by Laudianism allowed him to escape the offensive Arminian and, by association, popish imputations which compromised so many of the bishops and Oxford college heads. The way was thus prepared for his own promotion to a bishopric in 1641.

Like the Short Parliament, its successor was summoned by the king in the hope of obtaining a grant of taxation. Having invaded the north of England in August 1640, the Scots were now established in arms at Newcastle, where, by the terms of the Treaty of Ripon drafted in October, Charles's government had obliged itself to provide financial support for their army.[1] Yet when Parliament met, the king's needs took second place to the venting of grievances, above all grievances concerning religion. Between Parliament's convening in November 1640 and the outbreak of civil war in August 1642, religious issues formed the central strand in the deliberations of both Lords

1. Russell, *Fall*, 162–3; Woolrych, *Britain in Revolution*, 145–8.

Between Scholarship and Church Politics: The Lives of John Prideaux, 1578–1650. John Maddicott, Oxford University Press. © John Maddicott 2022. DOI: 10.1093/oso/9780192896100.003.0010

and Commons. Pym, the Commons' chief spokesman, led the attack on innovation in the church and on the popish practices by which it was feared that the church was being subverted. Anti-Catholicism, founded on the presence of Catholics at court, on the seemingly papistical practices which Laud had sought to impose, on suspicion of his ultimate intentions, and on the nebulous fears of a general Catholic conspiracy came almost to obsess those present in Parliament. This was still more true after the outbreak of the Catholic rebellion in Ireland in October 1641, when obsession moved towards hysteria. Laud was an early victim of these understandable delusions. Impeached for high treason in December 1640, he was sent to the Tower in the following March. His rule of the church, in partnership with the king, was seen not only as having given rise to offensive innovations in ceremonies and modes of worship, but as another facet of Charles's misgovernment of his kingdom. Laud's political activities—for example, on High Commission and in Star Chamber—largely justified this view. [2] As much as his Arminian government of the church, his association with the instruments of authoritarian rule was the cause of his downfall.

Laud's authority in the universities, particularly at Oxford, meant that their loyalties and religious affiliations soon came under parliamentary scrutiny. The budding hostility shown to the universities in the Short Parliament burgeoned in the Long. But now it took on an organized form. In November 1640 one of the first acts of the newly assembled Commons had been to set up a subcommittee to consider 'abuses in the universities of Oxford and Cambridge'. It was later elevated to a full committee and in June 1641 its remit was extended to cover abuses in colleges and halls.[3] Within a few weeks of its establishment, the new body was in action. In September 1640 Henry Wilkinson, divinity lecturer at the notoriously puritanical Magdalen Hall, had preached a contentious sermon in St Mary's, the university church. Anti-Laudian, critical of church ceremonies, and apparently sympathetic towards the Presbyterian Scots, the sermon had been condemned by Oxford's Arminian vice-chancellor Christopher Potter, and Wilkinson had been suspended from his lectureship.

2. Trevor-Roper, *Archbishop Laud*, 162–6, 322–5; Sharpe, *Personal Rule of Charles I*, 142–5.
3. *CJ*, ii. 55, 184; *The Diary and Papers of Henry Townshend, 1640–1663*, ed. S. Porter et al. (WHS., n. s., 25, 2014), 55; *The Journal of Sir Simonds d'Ewes from the Beginning of the Long Parliament to the Opening of the Trial of the Earl of Strafford*, ed. W. Notestein (New Haven, CT, 1923), 82 n. 34. Cf. H. Kearney, *Scholars and Gentlemen: Universities and Society in Pre-Industrial Britain, 1500–1700* (1970), 99–100.

Wilkinson had then appealed to Parliament and subsequently appeared before the new committee, which had not only restored him to his lecture-ship but ordered the printing of his sermon, while it was Potter who was now called to answer before the committee for his actions.[4] Although this was a storm in a teacup, it showed both the bias of the Commons and the novel vulnerability of the universities to parliamentary intervention.

Prideaux, as anti-Laudian (if with a touch of ambiguity) and anti-Catholic as any man, had little to fear from any such intervention. But the university's leaders were anxious to defend themselves from any possible accusation of popery, and in response to an earlier rumour that the Mass was commonly celebrated in Oxford 'and frequented by university men', the heads of houses wrote a joint letter to Parliament on 14 December 1640 to certify that 'we neither know, nor can probably suspect any member of our university to be a papist, or popishly addicted'. The signatories included such Laudian stalwarts as the vice-chancellor, Potter of Queen's, Frewen of Magdalen, and Baylie of St John's, as well, of course, as Prideaux. That Laud included this letter in his history of his chancellorship showed his continuing anxiety to defend himself from any charge of popish sympathies. He and his supporters might be Arminians, but they were not papists—though it was easy and convenient enough for the Commons to elide the two.[5] But despite the heads' declaration, William Hawkins, the London agent of the earl of Leicester, reported to his master that all were summoned to London about this time, presumably to explain themselves, while the painted glass windows in most of the colleges were voluntarily dismantled and the altars turned into tables and set east-west: outward and visible signs of the parliamentary-inspired reaction against Laudianism.[6]

The state of the universities was only an aspect of the larger question which preoccupied the members of the Long Parliament, that of the reform of the church. The issues which particularly concerned them, both arising out of Laud's rule, were the status of the episcopate and the changes in worship introduced in the 1630s. The first of these was particularly divisive and the divisions were to persist throughout the early years of the

---

4. *Works of Laud*, v. 287–9, 297; Wood, *Athenae*, iii. 1038–9; Wood, *History*, ii. 423–5; *CJ*, ii. 64; *Journal of Sir Simonds d'Ewes*, ed. Notestein, 182, 228; J. Spivey, 'Wilkinson, Henry (1610–1675), Church of England clergyman and ejected minister', *ODNB*.
5. *Works of Laud*, v. 297–8; Wood, *History*, ii. 425.
6. Letter from Hawkins to Leicester, 14 Jan. 1641: HMC, *De L'Isle and Dudley MSS*, Vol. VI (HMSO, 1966), 364.

parliament. The Root-and-Branch petition, presented in December 1640 and probably originating with the godly clergy of the city of London, had called for the abolition of episcopacy, but this radical step was one which only a small minority in the Commons was as yet prepared to take, possibly and partly in an attempt to placate the Scots.[7] Robert Baillie, covenanting minister and chaplain with the Scottish commissioners in London, reported from the capital on 2 December that the people and their preachers favoured abolition. No one from the universities had yet spoken out on the subject, but nothing was expected from 'Holsworth, Ward, Feitly, Bromerik, Prideaux, or any famous for learning'. There was, though, 'great appearance that God will doe his own work, without these rabbies help'.[8] So these leading divines, Prideaux included, were expected to stand by the bishops.

Abolition was only the main plank of the Root-and-Branch petition, which had ranged more widely over such contentious matters as the position of the communion table and the general Rome-ward drift of the church under Laud's direction. It was followed by a flood of other petitions from the counties, almost all of them anti-Arminian and many favouring abolition.[9] Public opinion was emerging as a destabilizing political force. With all these questions still unresolved, the Lords in March 1641 set up a committee 'to take into consideration all innovations in the church concerning religion' and shortly afterwards its powers were devolved upon a subcommittee headed, like the superior body, by Bishop John Williams, Laud's old adversary, released from the Tower in November 1640. The subcommittee's members included three bishops besides Williams and a number of university divines and other clergy. All were Calvinists; some were puritans; one was Archbishop Ussher; and another was Prideaux.[10]

The first sign of Prideaux's rehabilitation had appeared a few months before the establishment of the subcommittee. In early January 1641 William Hawkins records that he had been offered the vacant bishopric of Waterford in Ireland, 'but he hath the king's leave to return againe to Oxford and refuse it'. This he obviously did, since we hear no more about

7. *Constitutional Documents*, ed. Gardiner, 137–8; Gardiner, *History*, ix. 247–8; Russell, *Fall*, 180–2; J. Morrill, *The Nature of the English Revolution* (1993), 77–8.
8. *The Letters and Journals of Robert Baillie. A.M., MDC.XXXVII–MDC.LXII*, ed. D. Laing, 3 vols. (Edinburgh, 1841–3), i. 275. The four named besides Prideaux were Richard Holdsworth, Samuel Ward, Daniel Featley, and Ralph Brownrigg, all well-known Calvinist clerics. 'Rabbi' is a derogatory term for a person in religious authority.
9. A. Fletcher, *The Outbreak of the English Civil War* (1981), 92–7.
10. *LJ*, iv. 174, 180; Russell, *Fall*, 271–2; Hampton, 'A "Theological Junto"', 433–6.

the offer. His refusal was hardly surprising. With the Commons and the country turning strongly against the bishops, this was hardly a propitious time to become one. Even the much wealthier and more dignified archbishopric of York, also vacant, was eliciting no interest from possible candidates.[11] A remote Irish bishopric in a strongly Catholic region, Waterford was hardly a tempting prospect for one accustomed to the scholarly resources and congenial company of Oxford, particularly since the previous bishop, the disreputable John Atherton, popularly thought to have committed incest with his niece, had been found guilty of buggery and hanged on 5 December 1640.[12] A newcomer would have had much work to do. Yet although the king's offer was the barest of compliments, it marked the beginning of a revival in Prideaux's fortunes. He was no longer a forgotten man.

Prideaux's appointment to Bishop Williams's subcommittee was a greater accolade than the offer of a bishopric in distant Ireland. It gave public recognition to his eminence as a theologian, to the respect which he enjoyed in Parliament, and to his entitlement to a central place in the counsels of the Church of England. Besides Ussher, some other old friends and allies of Prideaux, notably Joseph Hall, Daniel Featley, and Ralph Brownrigg, as well as Samuel Ward, master of Sidney Sussex College, also sat with him. All were theologians and scholars loyal to the king and the conservative ideals of the Elizabethan and Jacobean church in which they had been brought up; and all save Ussher and Hall had been named by Baillie as men likely to come down in favour of bishops. In terms of reputation and learning, Ussher and Prideaux were the most distinguished of the group and the best qualified to provide intellectual underpinnings for any programme of reform. Both indeed were singled out by the Huguenot and anti-Catholic physician Louis du Moulin in his parallel proposals of 1641 for a reforming synod comprising '40 or 50 English divines, men . . . such as be unpartiall, learned and uncorrupt in their lives and doctrine, such as Dr Usher. Arch. B. of Armach, Dr. Prideaux, Dr Twisse and the like'.[13]

The subcommittee's task and main achievement was to provide a programme for the reform of the church. It was one marked by moderation and

11. De L'Isle and Dudley MSS, Vol. VI, 359.
12. A. Clarke, 'Atherton, John (1598–1640), Church of Ireland bishop of Waterford and Lismore', ODNB.
13. [L. du Moulin], Vox populi, Expressed in XVIII Motions to this Present Parliament for Reforming the Church of England (1641), 1–2; Ford, Ussher, 229.

compromise. Although the Ussher-Prideaux group (by no means the whole body) rejected what they called 'the whole grosse substance of Arminianisme', they did not mount an across-the-board attack on Laudian innovations.[14] The setting of the communion table 'altarwise', excessive bowing in church, and the introduction of occasional services in Latin were all condemned. In matters of theology Calvinism was reasserted in an attack on the doctrine of universal grace and in approval for that of perseverance. An assertion of the authority of the church in matters of faith may have come directly from Prideaux, since the same point had been raised in his 1633 dispute with Heylyn.[15] But altar rails, images, and stained glass, all essential elements in Laud's 'beauty of holiness', were spared criticism. The main propositions were signed off by seven men, including Ussher, Williams, Prideaux, Ward, and Featley, the old Calvinist establishment. It was the puritans on the subcommittee who were disappointed, for nothing was done towards the reform of episcopacy, let alone towards its abolition on which the radicals had set their sights, though Ussher's contemporary plan for 'reduced episcopacy' did attempt a synthesis between episcopal government and the synodical government favoured by the puritans.[16] The division between the subcommittee's steering group of moderate reformers and its puritan members, which mirrored the similar division emerging in the Commons, was one reason for the subcommittee's demise. The wishes of the more extreme puritans for a more Presbyterian form of church government could not be accommodated.[17] Lasting through April and May 1641, the subcommittee's proceedings were cut short by the introduction of the Root-and-Branch Bill in the Commons at the end of May. In the end it proved a damp squib, more important as a stage in Prideaux's return to the centre of church affairs than in changing the course of the church's history.

It was another sign of Prideaux's reviving fortunes that at some point in 1641 he was able to venture on a new publication. His *Nine Sermons Preached upon Severall Occasions* (Oxford, 1641) comprised an apparently random selection from the twenty which he had published in 1637 as *Certaine*

---

14. The reforming propositions are set out in *A copy of the proceedings of some worthy and learned divines appointed by the Lords to meet at the Bishop of Lincolnes in Westminster* (1641), reprinted in Shaw, *A History of the English Church*, ii. 287–94. For comment, see Hampton, 'A "Theological Junto"', 437, 440–1; Ford, *Ussher*, 247–8.
15. Hampton, 'A "Theological Junto"', 439; above, 269–70.
16. Shaw, *History of the English Church*, i. 71–2; Ford, *Ussher*, 244–7; Russell, *Fall*, 249–50.
17. Hampton, 'A "Theological Junto"', 447–9.

Sermons.[18] The nine were reprinted word for word 'without any alterations', as the title page stated, and with no apparent principle behind their selection. Permeated by a passionate anti-Catholicism, denunciations of the Pope as Antichrist, and hostility to the puritans as sectaries and fanatics, they shared the characteristics of many of Prideaux's sermons. But more important than their content, which seems to have served no special contemporary purpose, was the fact of their publication. Since 1637, during Laud's later years as chancellor and archbishop, Prideaux had published nothing. The excerpts from six of his 1637 sermons filed among the state papers and headed 'Exceptions to Dr Prideaux his sermons' point to the offence taken by Charles I's government at his preaching, and it was probably the threat of further intervention which deterred him from further publication.[19] Three of the six sermons which had produced such 'exceptions', 'Ephesus Backsliding', which made some criticisms of the court, 'The first fruits of the resurrection', which attacked the 'proud and factious', and 'Hezekiah's sicknesse', which alluded to 'the unsettled waverings of divers learned men among us', possibly referring to Montagu's books, were reissued in 1641. The republication of all nine must be seen as a mark of Prideaux's novel emancipation. Freed from the shadow cast by Laud, he could publish without fear of censure or reprisals.

Throughout the spring and summer of 1641 Parliament continued to be the cockpit of the nation's affairs, though in August attention shifted towards Scotland, as Charles moved north to conclude a treaty with the Scots. Preventing any repetition of what was seen as the previous excesses of arbitrary royal rule remained high on Parliament's agenda. The earl of Strafford, seen as an exemplar of these abuses, was executed in May, and the abolition of Star Chamber and High Commission followed in July. This latter move should also be seen as an aspect of church reform, since it was partly through the prerogative courts that Charles and Laud had governed the church.[20] Meanwhile there was no progress on that larger and more contentious reforming issue, the future of the bishops. On 1 May the Commons had voted to exclude bishops from Parliament, but this was rejected by the Lords. The Root-and-Branch Bill, which went much further in calling for the abolition of bishops, passed its first reading in the Commons

18. Madan, i. 199–200, ii. 158.
19. *CSPD, 1638–9*, 167–8; SP 16/408, fos. 167–8; *HUO*, iv. 589; above, 281–2.
20. Gardiner, *History*, ix. 368–71, 404–5; Russell, *Fall*, 252.

but then became enmeshed in committees and never reached the Lords, where it would certainly have been rejected.[21]

Oxford had its own interest in these debates. In April 1641 the university had petitioned first Parliament and then the king to preserve both episcopacy and cathedral churches. Both were seen as providing openings and preferment for 'many godly and learned men' and their abolition as threatening the standing of the clergy and 'industry and knowledge in the universities'. They supplied the means to maintain 'many of the learned professors in our university'. Cambridge petitioned in similar terms.[22] Delivered in London on 29 April by the vice-chancellor Christopher Potter and 'certain doctors', who may well have included Prideaux, the Oxford petition provided a banner behind which both Arminians and Calvinists could unite. Their awareness of external threats to their security, as well as their shared loyalties to the king, was coming to provide both parties with newly discovered common ground.

2. Bishop and vice-chancellor, 1641–2

The university's main focus, and with it Prideaux's, soon came to lie elsewhere. On 25 June 1641, writing from the Tower, Laud resigned the chancellorship, thoughtfully timing his resignation to coincide with the end of Christopher Potter's term as vice-chancellor.[23] A week later, on 1 July, Convocation elected as his successor Philip Herbert, earl of Pembroke, who, as Laud bitterly remarked, 'thought it long till he had that place, which he had long gaped for'.[24] We know nothing of any manoeuvres or intrigues which may have preceded his election, but it is highly likely that it owed much to Prideaux's initiative. Prideaux had previously backed Pembroke against Laud for the chancellorship in 1630; three of Pembroke's sons, including his heir, had been educated at Exeter; and in the elections for the Long Parliament Prideaux had campaigned for Nathaniel Brent, who

---

21. Gardiner, *History*, ix. 378–9, 386–92, x. 1; Russell, *Fall*, 342–3; Woolrych, *Britain in Revolution*, 174, 183.

22. Wood, *History*, ii. 429–32; Madan, ii. 154–5; Russell, *Fall*, 255.

23. *Works of Laud*, iii. 242, v. 300–1; Hegarty, 'Potter',

24. *Works of Laud*, iii. 447. For the date, see Wood, *Fasti*, iv. 2. HUO, iv. 690 gives the date as 6 July but cites no source.

was almost certainly Pembroke's candidate for one of the two university seats.[25] Pembroke's wealth, his godly Protestantism, and his opposition to Laudianism in the church may have commended him more widely, but at the same time his demerits were very great. A discerning and generous patron of art and architecture, he was also quarrelsome, untrustworthy, and violent. Anthony Wood's verdict may be only a little harsh. After Laud, he says:

> The University chose another quite of a contrary temper, rather a foe than a friend to them, or any way at all beneficiall to learning, he being an illiterate person, and scarce could write his own name.[26]

By 1641 Pembroke was a marginal figure at court, disliked by Charles's for having voted for Strafford's attainder and lacking much influence in the Lords. He was in no position to help the university; nor, evidently, did he want to do so. In February 1643 the university would complain to the king that he had 'wholly neglected the care and government of the university', 'wilfully betrayed' their privileges, failed to protect them against the parliamentary army (whose side he had by now taken), and called them 'a pack of corrupt knaves' into the bargain.[27] If Chancellor Laud had been a benign busybody, Chancellor Pembroke was to prove a malign mischief-maker.

One of the university's main charges against Pembroke was that for five months (actually three) he had failed to provide them with any deputy, that is, a vice-chancellor. This dereliction was rectified only on 7 October 1641, when Prideaux was nominated to the vacant post.[28] His new promotion to an office which he had last held in 1625–6 under William Herbert, Pembroke's brother, was another mark not only of his reviving fortunes after the fall of Laud, but also of his ties with, and in this case dependence on, the earl of Pembroke. But the sharp and rapid decline of Pembroke's reputation so soon after his election as chancellor and his subsequent swinging towards the parliamentary side are likely to have meant that Prideaux's position was not entirely comfortable.

A second promotion quickly followed. In late October the king nominated Prideaux as bishop of Worcester in place of John Thornborough, who

---

25. Above, 250–1, 318–19, 96–7.
26. Wood, *Annals*, ii. 433.
27. OUA, SP/F/40/8 (Articles against Lord Pembroke).
28. Wood, *Fasti*, ii. 2.

had died in July. He was one of five new bishops appointed to vacant sees at the same time. A bishopric was the prize for which he had been reckoned to have been well qualified since at least the mid-1620s, but denied to him for most of this time by Laud's control of the church.[29] As we have seen, the earlier (and almost derisory) offer of Waterford had been turned down. Yet Prideaux's new appointment was primarily a tactical move on the king's part rather than an overdue recognition of his qualities and qualifications. It was rumoured, says Wood, that he owed his see to what had been 'endeavoured' on his behalf by James, marquis of Hamilton, his old pupil, and there may be something in this, since Hamilton was with Charles in Scotland at the time of the appointment.[30] But a more powerful initiative undoubtedly came from Sir Edward Nicholas, Charles's acting secretary of state and a man whose 'unwavering service and honest opinions' gave him the king's trust.[31] On 19 September 1641 Nicholas had written to Charles to suggest that he should confer the several bishoprics then vacant 'upon persons of whome there is not the least suspicion of favouring the popish partie, such as may be Dr Prideaux [and three others]'. Such appointments would counter the widespread belief that the clergy and the court favoured popery, secure the king in the 'esteeme and affeccion' of his people, give assurance that he intended to maintain the Protestant religion, and strengthen the votes for episcopacy in the Lords. Nicholas reinforced this with a further letter of 3 October: 'There is no one thing that you can now doe that will better rectify the jealousies of your good people, more satisfie their mindes, and settle their affeccions to your Majesty, than the good choyce of such as your Majesty shall now appoint to be bishops.'[32]

The king took his secretary's advice. Prideaux was the first of the bishops to be formally nominated by Charles, with the dispatch of the king's notification to the dean and chapter of Worcester, his new see, on 10 November.[33] The four others appointed with him—Ralph Brownrigg to Exeter (also recommended by Nicholas), Thomas Winniffe to Lincoln, Henry King to Chichester, and Thomas Westfield to Bristol[34]—were, like

---

29. Above, 237–8, 285, 320–1.
30. Wood, *Athenae*, iii. 266; Scally, 'Hamilton'. Heylin, *Cyprianus Anglicus*, 497, says the same. Hamilton had been an undergraduate at Exeter in 1621–2.
31. S. A. Baron, 'Nicholas, Sir Edward (1593–1669), government official', *ODNB*.
32. *Diary and Correspondence of John Evelyn, FRS*, ed. W. Bray, new edn, 4 vols. (1857), iv. 71–2, 79.
33. Wood, *Athenae*, iii. 266 n. 3.
34. Richard Holdsworth, vice-chancellor of Cambridge, had been offered Bristol, but declined: Russell, *Fall*, 412; Fletcher, *Outbreak*, 121.

him, strict and respectable Calvinists, men, as Clarendon would later write, who were 'all of great eminency in the Church, frequent preachers, and not a man to whom the faults of the then governing clergy were imputed, or against whom the least objection could be made'. Thomas Fuller said much the same: 'His majesty was most careful to choose them out of the most sound for judgement and blameless for conversation [way of life].'[35] Their appointments were partly a consequence of other equally respectable translations from one see to another made about the same time.[36] Under Laud's regime the new men would have stood no chance of promotion. 'If this Parliament had not happened', commented Sir Simonds D'Ewes in his diary, they 'should assoone have been sent to the gallies as have been preferred to bishoppwricks.'[37] Prideaux must have been particularly pleased by Winniffe's promotion, for he was, like Prideaux himself, a former Exeter pupil of Thomas Holland and had been a fellow of the College from 1595 to 1609.[38] Three of the five, Prideaux, Brownrigg, and Westfield, had previously served on Williams's subcommittee. All these men combined Calvinist respectability with dependable royalism. Anti-Laud but also pro-king, they stood for one side of a growing division emerging in the Commons between conservative reformers and puritan radicals.[39]

The king's appointments, however, had the opposite effect to that intended. When, in the last days of October, the Commons got wind of what was intended, they reacted with fury. The Venetian ambassador saw the king's move as one 'that strikes a blow at the puritans whose sole interest is to uproot the hierarchy, and affords the greatest consolation to the Protestants'.[40] The first of these observations was shrewder than the second. Intermittently through the summer, the Commons had been debating the future of episcopacy. Although opinion was divided, at a minimum they

---

35. E. Clarendon, *History of the Rebellion and Civil Wars in England*, ed. W. D. Macray, 6 vols. (Oxford, 1888), i. 401–2; T. Fuller, *The Church History of Britain*, new edn, 3 vols. (1837), iii. 440. For these appointments, see Russell, *Fall*, 411–12; Woolrych, *Britain in Revolution*, 191–2; Fletcher, *Outbreak*, 120–2; Morrill, *Nature of the English Revolution*, 158; and A. Milton, 'Anglicanism and Royalism in the 1640s', in J. Adamson (ed.), *The English Civil War: Conflict and Contexts, 1640–49* (Basingstoke, 2009), 63–4.

36. Joseph Hall from Exeter to Norwich, John Williams from Lincoln to York, Robert Skinner from Bristol to Oxford, Brian Duppa from Chichester to Salisbury, and James Ussher to Carlisle, to be held *in commendam* with his Irish archbishopric.

37. *The Journal of Sir Simonds D'Ewes, from the First Recess of the Long Parliament to the withdrawal of King Charles from London*, ed. W. H. Coates (New Haven, CT, 1942), 46; Russell, *Fall*, 412.

38. Above, 13–15.

39. Hampton, 'A "Theological Junto"', 435; Fletcher, *Outbreak*, 122–3.

40. *Calendar of State Papers, Venice*, xxv, *1640–42*, 234.

wanted the exclusion of the bishops from judicial positions and their restriction to spiritual functions. At a maximum the Root-and-Branch party wanted the abolition of bishops. But both these plans foundered on the opposition of the Lords, who included a substantial bloc of bishops and whose consent was, of course, necessary for any anti-episcopal legislation.[41] The appointment of the five bishops thus ignited grievances which were already flammable. Even their standing as Calvinistic divines broadly sympathetic to the anti-Laudian reforming views of the Commons majority did nothing to placate their opponents. 'Many who much loved them in their gowns', says Fuller, 'did not at all like them in their rochets.'[42] The filling of the vacant sees was regarded as a provocation, a way of increasing the king's power and also of boosting the voting strength in the Lords of those opposing any moves against episcopacy and so preventing reformation—as indeed it was.[43] The outcome was a decision to set up a committee headed by Oliver Cromwell with the object of submitting a joint petition to the king to halt the making of the bishops. But that this was carried by only seventy-one votes to fifty-three suggests that a substantial minority objected to such potential interference with the royal prerogative.[44]

The Commons' decision had no immediate effect. On 1 November, three days after their debate, news reached them of the outbreak of rebellion in Ireland, and the parliamentary reaction swept aside most other business.[45] So despite the Commons' resolution, the making of the new bishops went forward, with Prideaux first in line. On 22 November he was formally elected and on 19 December he was consecrated in Westminster Abbey by John Williams, now archbishop of York.[46] Laud, who should have officiated (but would no doubt have been pained to do so) was in the Tower. Shortly afterwards, on 7 January 1642, he received the temporalities of his see, an accession which put him in the way of becoming a relatively wealthy man.[47] The laudatory verses which he contributed to a university volume celebrating the king's return from Scotland in November, a volume which Prideaux as vice-chancellor took personally to Charles at Hampton

---

41. Gardiner, *History*, ix. 299, 347, 378–83; Russell, *Fall*, 341–5, 410–12.
42. Fuller, *Church History*, iii. 440.
43. *Journal of Sir Simonds D'Ewes*, ed. Coates, 46; Clarendon, *History of the Rebellion*, i. 402.
44. *CJ*, ii. 298; *Journal of Sir Simonds D'Ewes*, ed. Coates, 54; Russell, *Fall*, 412.
45. *Journal of Sir Simonds D'Ewes*, ed. Coates, 61–102; Russell, *Fall*, 414–24.
46. E. H. Pearce, *Hartlebury Castle* (1926), 130–1, citing Laud's Register at Lambeth. Pearce, himself a later bishop of Worcester, provides an excellent guide to Prideaux's time as bishop.
47. Le Neve, *Fasti*, vii, comp. Horn: *Ely, Norwich, Westminster and Worcester Dioceses* (1992), 107.

Court, may have been heartfelt. Signing himself 'the king's most devoted servant and professor', he was also now the king's bishop.[48]

There could hardly have been a less favourable time for his elevation. The Commons' mounting hostility to the episcopate had been made plain in August 1641, when the lower house had impeached the thirteen bishops supposedly responsible for the Canons of 1640 and the clerical tax granted in the same convocation.[49] The impeachment process was still pending at the time of Prideaux's nomination, partly through the procrastination of the Lords, whose cooperation was essential for the process. The equally fierce reaction to Charles's October appointments was part of the same campaign, and once the initial shock of the Irish rebellion had subsided, the Commons resumed their assault on episcopacy. The Grand Remonstrance, presented in the Commons on 8 November 1641 and very much the work of Pym, called for the removal of the bishops from the Lords and the curtailment of their powers, seeing them as men intent on subverting 'the fundamental laws and principles of government upon which the religion and justice of this kingdom are firmly established' and putting them on a par with 'the Jesuitical Papists', who had the same intentions.[50] One particular incident demonstrated the vulnerability of the bishops to the Commons' anger. On 27 December 1641 a group of bishops seeking entry to the House of Lords was attacked and jostled by a mob shouting 'No bishops! No popish lords!' On the next day, and as a consequence, most were too fearful to take their seats. In their absence, and with the rabble outside very much in mind, a motion was proposed in the Lords that Parliament was no longer free, but this was not carried. Twelve bishops led by Williams then launched a petition of protest to the Lords asking that whatever had been done in their absence should be declared null and void, thus seeming to declare that Parliament was indeed not free, a point of some constitutional importance. For this seeming threat to the constitution the twelve were impeached by the Commons. Ten were sent to the Tower and two taken into custody elsewhere.[51] In making their protest the bishops had overreached

---

48. *Eucharistica Oxoniensia* (Oxford, 1641); Madan, ii. 149–50; Wood, *Life and Times*, iv. 58.

49. *LJ*, iv. 340; *Proceedings in the Opening Session of the Long Parliament: House of Commons: Vol. 6, 19 July–9 September 1641*, ed. M. Jansson (Rochester, NY, 2005), 149, 151; Woolrych, *Britain in Revolution*, 210.

50. *Constitutional Documents*, ed. Gardiner, 204, 206–7, 227 (cl. 170); Gardiner, *History*, x. 59–64; Russell, *Fall*, 424–9; Fletcher, *Outbreak*, 82.

51. *Journal of Sir Simonds D'Ewes*, ed. Coates, 364–8; *CJ*, ii. 362–3; Gardiner, *History*, x. 117–25; Russell, *Fall*, 441–4; Woolrych, *Britain in Revolution*, 210.

themselves. Their aggressive promotion of their right to attend the Lords had been their downfall.

As Clarendon saw, the incarceration of the twelve bishops, now prevented from taking their seats in the Lords, helps to explain the victory won by the anti-episcopacy party when, on 5 February 1642, the lords finally agreed to banish the bishops from their House. By this time the king had withdrawn to Windsor. The effect of the Bishops' Exclusion Bill, reluctantly accepted by Charles on 13 February, was to prohibit bishops and other clergy not only from sitting in Parliament but also from holding all secular judicial offices, such as justiceships of the peace. The bill thus gave a large section of the Commons—though not the Root-and-Branchers—what they had long wanted but had long been resisted by the Lords, a remarkable volte-face, to be explained not only by the enforced absence of many of the bishops but also by the absence of many royalist peers. Pembroke, chancellor of the university and Prideaux's erstwhile patron but now firmly in the anti-royalist camp, probably voted in favour of exclusion. With this issue finally settled, the question of episcopacy largely disappeared from the parliamentary agenda for the remainder of the year.[52]

How did Prideaux respond to these events and to the heavy responsibilities which he now bore? For a few months from November 1641 onwards he held four offices: bishop of Worcester, vice-chancellor of Oxford, regius professor of divinity, and rector of Exeter College. In the university's history there had probably never been such a gathering of important posts into the hands of one man. His new obligations as bishop of Worcester were those which affected him least. After his consecration on 19 December 1641 it was a deputy who stood in for him at his enthronement at Worcester on 14 January 1642, and the first evidence for his presence in his diocese comes on 19 February, when he presided at an institution to a benefice. Five other institutions, apparently conducted by Prideaux in person, were held at Worcester in April, May, and June.[53] The Exeter buttery book shows that throughout this time he was almost always resident in his College.[54] He was largely absent too from the Lords, where his bishopric qualified him for a seat until the exclusion of the bishops in early February 1642. He was not

52. *Constitutional Documents*, ed. Gardiner, 241–2; Clarendon, *History of the Rebellion*, i. 474, 566–8; Gardiner, *History*, x. 163–4; Russell, *Fall*, 471–2; Adamson, *Noble Revolt*, 311, 339–40.
53. Bishop Prideaux's Register, Worcestershire Archives, Worcester, 6716.093. BA 2648, parcel 10 (ii), 49–51, 25; Pearce, *Hartlebury Castle*, 130–3.
54. ECA, BB/30, Buttery Book, 1641–2.

among the twelve bishops whose access to the Lords had been threatened in December 1641, an event which preceded his consecration[55] and which led to his colleagues' impeachment, and he was appointed to only one Lords' committee—that set up on 27 January to consider the king's answers to the Scots negotiators. But his commission had only a few days to run before exclusion and he almost certainly did not act. The only occasion on which he can be shown to have attended the Lords was, significantly, on 5 February, when he was one of three bishops who protested against the Exclusion Bill.[56] He evidently placed a high value on a right of which he had made no use.

Almost as brief as his tenure of a place in the Lords was Prideaux's remaining period as regius professor. On 29 April 1642 the king notified him that he had appointed Robert Sanderson in his place and required him to surrender his own patent of appointment, though he was to continue to perform the duties and to receive the emoluments of the chair until 24 July. Since Sanderson, a Calvinist, an anti-Arminian, and a hater of puritans (though, like other Calvinists, he had much in common with them), was very much in Prideaux's mould, this was perhaps another small sign of Charles's newfound willingness to placate the Calvinists who had risen with Laud's decline. It was also the end of an era. With one short interval from 1612 to 1615, when Robert Abbot had been regius professor, the divinity chair had been in the hands of two successive rectors of Exeter since Thomas Holland's election as rector in 1592. The severing of the link between rector and chair was one of the more minor consequences of the emerging conflict between king and Parliament.[57]

The last months of Prideaux's time as Exeter's rector presented no obvious problems. Until July 1642, when civil war was imminent, there was no fall-off in undergraduate numbers, and the troubles which came upon the College when war finally broke out, bringing with it a sharp decline in numbers and income, were not yet on the horizon. There was, nevertheless, and unsurprisingly, an awareness within the College of rising political tensions and of the growing threats to the king's authority. It must have been a well-read and royalist butler who, one week in January 1642,

55. Fuller, *Church History*, iii. 432.
56. *Journal of Sir Simonds D'Ewes*, ed. Coates, appendix C, 408–11; *CJ*, ii. 362; *LJ*, iv. 546, 564.
57. OUA, NEP/Supra/Reg Sb, 4; Pearce, *Hartlebury Castle*, 131–2; McGee, 'Sanderson, Robert';
    P. G. Lake, 'Serving God and the Times: The Calvinist Conformity of Robert Sanderson', *Journal of British Studies*, 27 (1988), 81–116, esp. 81, 91, 106.

interrupted his dry compilation of the College buttery book by inserting a rhyming couplet adapted from George Sandys's translation of Ovid's *Metamorphoses*:

> All cannot rule, for many rulers bring
> Confusion. Let there be one king.[58]

The butler is unlikely to have been the only member of the College who was thoroughly out of sympathy with the Commons.

In these months of continuing College routine and deepening national divisions, Exeter's everyday management of the College was in the capable hands of John Procter, a fellow since 1623, a former senior bursar, and now, in 1641–2, Prideaux's sub-rector.[59] Prideaux himself was thus free to give a large part of his time to the vice-chancellorship, an office increasingly impinged on by national politics as trust between king and Parliament, always fragile, began to break down completely and both sides sought to secure the loyalties of the university. Charles's attempted arrest, on 4 January 1642, of the Five Members of the Commons whom he had accused of treason—a folly, a constitutional outrage, and a staging post along the road to civil war—led to the opening of a propaganda campaign in which Prideaux, as vice-chancellor, was inevitably caught up. On 17 January, shortly after the impeachment of the Five Members, he wrote to Secretary Nicholas to say that he had summoned all the heads of houses as the king had commanded and told them of the king's intentions to preserve the liberties of Parliament, while at the same time proceeding against 'some Parliament men [i.e. the Five Members] in an unquestionable way' (indicating that their prosecution was still to go forward). He had found 'a most hearty and ready concurrence in all for the king's service', and all were resolved to tell the members of their colleges and halls of the king's intentions so as to forestall any hostile rumours. It was their 'special delight' to be exemplary in their religious loyalty and faithfully to stand by their sovereign.[60]

In Prideaux's response there was no mistaking the deep sense of loyalty to the king which was a constant feature of his career. Here he had shown himself to be the king's faithful agent, ready to sanction Charles's actions and to rally the university in his cause. It is probable that Charles too had a

---

58. ECA, BB/30; G. S[andys], *Ovid's Metamorphoses Englished* (1639). In the original, the conclusion of the second line reads 'Let there be one lord, one king.'

59. Boase, *Register*, 99–100; ECA, A.I 6, fos 19v, 24v, 25v.

60. *CSPD, 1641–43*, 258.

growing appreciation of Prideaux's merits, for in 1642 he was appointed as one of the king's Lenten preachers, along with several other non-Laudians, a novel honour which he had not enjoyed in the previous year and, on Charles's part, another conciliatory gesture towards the radical reformers in the Commons and the country.[61] Prideaux may have owed his new position partly to Pembroke, who, as lord chamberlain, was responsible for appointing court preachers. But shortly afterwards Parliament imposed its own test of another kind. In May 1641 the Commons had drafted a Protestation imposing on all Englishmen an oath of loyalty to the Protestant religion and the Church of England and a declaration against 'all popery and popish innovation'.[62] Designed to flush out Roman Catholics, the Protestation was sent down to Oxford on 18 February 1642. The heads of houses or their deputies were called on to subscribe first. Prideaux was absent at the time, probably prolonging his stay in London after his appearance in the Lords to vote against the Bishops' Exclusion Bill and then journeying to Worcester to conduct his first institution.[63] His subscriber's place as vice-chancellor was taken by John Tolson, pro-vice-chancellor and provost of Oriel, and, as rector of Exeter, by John Procter, the sub-rector. The process of subscription produced an interesting division between seven former Laudian heads, men such as Baylie of St John's, Pinck of New College, and Sheldon of All Souls, potential anti-parliamentarians, who insisted on taking a qualified form of the oath stressing their allegiance to the king and the belief in the wrongfulness of armed opposition to him, and the former anti-Laudians, such as Hood of Lincoln and Wilkinson of Magdalen Hall, who took the oath in its unamended form. Among the latter group were Procter of Exeter and, on 24 February, after his return to Oxford, Prideaux. The old divide between Arminians and Calvinist-puritans was once again visible. But the presence of Prideaux, whose loyalty to the Crown could not be impugned, among the takers of the unqualified oath shows that this was by no means a straightforward division between proto-royalists and proto-parliamentarians. Events had already made clear that anti-Laudians might be as royalist in their principles as Laudians, and Prideaux was decisively among the first group.[64]

61. Milton, 'Anglicanism and Royalism', 64, 253 n. 11.
62. *Constitutional Documents*, ed. Gardiner, 15–16; Woolrych, *Britain in Revolution*, 179–80.
63. The buttery book shows that he was away from the College from 4 to 18 February: ECA, BB/30.
64. *Oxfordshire and North Berks. Protestation Returns*, ed. Gibson, xi–xiii, xvi, 149, 164; Wood, *History*, ii. 437–8; *HUO*, iv. 692–3; Hegarty, 'Prideaux'.

Prideaux's January address to his fellow heads on the king's behalf had shown his office at its most political and its holder at his most commanding. Much of his work as vice-chancellor, however, was more routine. It gave him control over a wide range of minor spending—on travel, building, and printing, for example—some of which would later be called into question by the heads of houses who acted as auditors. It looks as though he had sometimes used the university's money imprudently, though he defended himself effectively enough.[65] But while the censure of the auditors came only in December 1642, after he had left Oxford, a more immediate challenge came with the appointment of a commissary, a deputy, to preside in his place in the chancellor's court. In the early months of his vice-chancellorship Prideaux had managed the business of the court, as was customary for the vice-chancellor, though a surrogate, usually Provost Tolson of Oriel, had sometimes acted for him.[66] But soon after the passing of the Bishops' Exclusion Bill, Giles Sweit, a civil lawyer of no great distinction, had petitioned Pembroke for Prideaux's place on the grounds that the recent bill had barred clerics (such as Prideaux) from exercising secular jurisdiction. This Pembroke conceded about 2 March, an unprecedented overriding of the vice-chancellor's powers which showed that the pre-existing ties between Prideaux and Pembroke stretching back over some twenty years counted for little.[67]

The chancellor's action, in what was seen as 'a matter of so great consequence and moment',[68] caused an outcry. It was the first incident in what became an increasingly bitter parting of the ways between Pembroke and the university. Prideaux himself sought the countermanding of Sweit's commission, for which no university consent had been given. In January 1643 the college heads called on Sweit to resign, which he refused to do, and next month the university divines petitioned Pembroke for their exemption from the Bishops' Exclusion Bill, 'that the vice-chancellor and proctors, having their authority by charter . . . may still execute that authoritie and govern the universitie as in all ages past'. Their petition may have had some effect, for in the same month Sweit was removed. But between March and

65. Wood, *Life and Times*, i. 75–6, 85–6, iv. 58–9.
66. OUA, Chancellor's court papers, 1642.
67. Wood, *Life and Times*, i. 85–6; Wood, *Fasti*, iv. 2; *HUO*, iv. 691.
68. Wood, *Life and Times*, i. 86.

July 1642, during the four months in Oxford that remained to him, Prideaux lacked one of the main attributes of his predecessors' authority.[69]

During the spring and summer of 1642 Prideaux had more to concern him than these local problems. In the country at large a division was emerging between royalists and parliamentarians, as Charles and his allies strove to present the king as the defender of the ancient constitution and the church, and Parliament claimed an increasing—and, to a growing number, an intolerable—degree of control over the executive. The Militia Ordinance, which passed the Lords in March and claimed for Parliament the right to control the county militias, represented what proto-royalists saw as a particularly dangerous intrusion on the king's prerogative. Still more intrusive were the Nineteen Propositions, passed in June, which effectively subjected the executive and the judiciary to parliamentary control.[70] By this time both sides were arming. In this rallying process a large part was played by the stream of royal orders, proclamations, and vindicatory statements issued from Charles's northern headquarters at York.[71] Sent down to Oxford, they represented an attempt to reinforce the already royalist sentiments of most of the university, and to win over waverers. Prideaux, as vice-chancellor, was made responsible by the king for publishing them and for seeing that they were read out in colleges and halls and other public places. To secure the university mattered greatly to Charles, and Prideaux, *ex officio*, was his willing instrument.[72]

But Prideaux's allegiance, already demonstrated by his January summoning of the heads to justify the king's actions and by his February opposition to the Bishops' Exclusion Bill, did not stand in the way of his receiving at least a measure of favour from the Commons. For many months they had floated the notion of an assembly of divines and other churchmen to reform the church's liturgy and government and to clarify its doctrines. Such a notion had assumed a firmer shape in the Grand Remonstrance, in which, 'to effect the intended reformation', the Commons had pressed for 'a general synod of the most grave, pious, learned and judicious divines of this island'.[73] Soon to be known as the Westminster Assembly, it moved a crucial step

69. Wood, *Life and Times*, i. 85–6; OUA, SP/F/40/8; *HUO*, iv. 691–2.
70. *Constitutional Documents*, ed. Gardiner, 245–7, 249–54; Morrill, *Nature of the English Revolution*, 11–13; Woolrych, *Britain in Revolution*, 217–19, 222.
71. For the above summary I have largely followed Woolrych, *Britain in Revolution*, 215–30.
72. Madan, ii. 160–4; *HUO*, iv. 693–4.
73. *Constitutional Documents*, ed. Gardiner, 229, cl. 185.

nearer on 25 April 1642, when the Commons approved the names of two representatives from each county, chosen by the county's parliamentary knights and burgesses, to serve in the assembly. Prideaux was elected for Worcestershire and subsequently approved, the only English bishop among the representatives, though Archbishop Ussher, chosen by the university, was also a member. Prideaux kept company with a little group of past and present fellows of Exeter, among them Henry Tozer, the sub-rector and perhaps Prideaux's closest ally, chosen for Glamorganshire; John Conant senior, fellow from 1611 to 1620, chosen for Somerset; and Matthias Styles, fellow from 1610 to 1628, chosen alongside Ussher for the university. Since the assembly was composed almost entirely of 'self-acknowledged Calvinists', this was a reaffirmation, if any were needed, of the conservative and anti-Arminian complexion of the College in the years leading to the civil war.[74]

Prideaux did not in the end serve, and by July 1643, when the assembly finally met, he had been replaced by another Worcestershire representative.[75] His initial election and approval, however, had shown him to be *persona grata*, with the Commons, perhaps surprisingly so. But if his episcopal status and known royalism had counted against him, his Calvinism, his former opposition to Laud, his ties with the godly Pembroke and, probably most of all, his prestige as a theologian may all have counted in his favour. Then, in July 1642, came a step on the road towards his ejection from the assembly list, a divergence which, from the point of view of the Commons, placed him firmly in the enemy's camp. On 11 July he had received, again as vice-chancellor, one of Charles's most exigent letters. Rumours were being spread, the letter stated, that the king intended to make war on Parliament, and in consequence he was being forced to take measures for his own and his kingdom's defence. Because of his care for 'such nurseries of learning' he had reason to expect help from the university. He appealed, therefore, for monetary assistance in the form of loans both from colleges and from individuals, to be repaid at 8 per cent interest.[76] This plea was immediately put before Convocation by Prideaux, its president, and within a week the huge sum of almost £11,000 had been raised for the royalist cause. Exeter

74. *CJ*, ii. 541; Shaw, *History of the English Church*, i. 124; Russell, *Fall*, 493; C. van Dixhoorn, 'The Westminster Assembly and the Reformation of the 1640s', in *OHA*, i. 430.

75. *The Minutes and Papers of the Westminster Assembly, 1643–1652*, ed. C. van Dixhoorn, 5 vols. (Oxford, 2012), i. 115, 137, 140, 141.

76. Wood, *History*, ii. 438–9.

gave £300 on the day of Convocation's meeting.[77] The parliamentary response was savage and swift. On 12 July John Prideaux, rector of Exeter, Samuel Fell, dean of Christ Church, Christopher Potter, provost of Queen's, and Accepted Frewen, president of Magdalen, were accused of sending treasure to the king, now at York, 'for maintaining of warrs against the parliament and the whole kingdome', and orders were issued for their arrest and appearance before Parliament for this 'high crime and conspiracy against the peace of the kingdome'. They had been summoned, the Venetian ambassador wrote, 'with the idea of punishing and making a severe example of the authors of these acts'.[78] Fell, Potter, and Frewen are known to have given money, either now or later, both for themselves and their colleges, and Prideaux is likely to have done the same.[79] That this quartet was a mixture of former Laudians (Potter and Frewen) and long-standing Calvinists (Prideaux and Fell) suggests the degree to which the heads of houses were now united behind the king. All, however, were to escape the consequences of their actions. Arriving in Oxford on 14 July to make the arrests, Parliament's agents found that the birds had flown. The king's letter of thanks to Prideaux, dated from the court at Beverley on 18 July and directing that any parliamentary summons to his benefactors should be disobeyed, similarly came rather after the event.[80]

Prideaux's flight presumably took him to Worcester. So precipitate had it been that he left behind him much unfinished business, only some of which was terminated during the weeks that followed. The future of the regius professorship was already settled. As we have seen, Robert Sanderson's appointment had been made known in April and was formally confirmed in July, though Sanderson did not take up the office until October 1646.[81] The College was a different matter. Prideaux had presided at what turned out to be his last College meeting on 30 June 1642, when he may have found some satisfaction in the confirmation of his son Matthias's fellowship after his probationary year.[82] A short time before he left, in June or July, he

77. Ibid., ii, 439; OUA, NEP/supra/ Reg Sb, 6 (Register of Convocation, 1642–47); ECA, L.II.6, 8; *HUO*, iv. 694–5.
78. *Calendar of State Papers, Venice*, xxvi, 1642–43, 112.
79. *LJ*, v. 208; Wood, *History*, ii. 440–1; *HUO*, iv. 695.
80. Wood, *History*, ii. 440–1; M. G. Hobson and H. E. Salter, *Oxford Council Acts, 1626–1665* (OHS, 95, 1933), 367.
81. I. Walton, 'Life of Dr Sanderson', in R. Sanderson, *XXXV Sermons*, 7th edn (1681), 18; above, 000.
82. ECA, A.I.6, fo. 27r.

had been called on by Provost Tolson to consecrate Oriel's new chapel, a refreshing hint of normality in a time of crisis.[83] But it was not until 3 August, some three weeks after his flight, that he resigned his rectorship, sending his letter to the College under his seal as bishop of Worcester. Entering his letter in the College register, the scribe noted, almost with a touch of emotion that 'he was rector of this college for 31 years'. It was by far the longest reign of any of Exeter's rectors since the foundation. In June 1642 the king had written to the College to recommend George Kendall, a fellow since 1630, as his replacement. But although Kendall was a zealous Calvinist, very much in the Prideaux tradition, it was a mark of the king's declining authority that his wishes were ignored, and on 29 August the College elected George Hakewill as its rector.[84] In some ways this was an excellent choice, since Hakewill was by far the most intellectually distinguished of the College's fellows and former fellows. But in others it turned out to be an unfortunate one. Hakewill was 64 years old at the time of his election and he was absent for almost the whole of his rectorship, remaining in his North Devon parish until his death in 1649 and leaving much of the College business in the hands of Henry Tozer, sub-rector at the time of Prideaux's departure.[85]

Of wider importance than the rectorship of Exeter was the vice-chancellorship. The suddenness of Prideaux's departure from Oxford had meant that he had had no time to resign the office and in fact he never did so. It then effectively lapsed into the hands of Robert Pinck, pro-vice-chancellor, warden of New College, and a former vice-chancellor in 1634–6. It was left to Pinck to deal with the immediate consequences for the university of the outbreak of war in the autumn of 1642.[86]

This was effectively the end of Prideaux's Oxford career. Its conclusion was not entirely glorious. Although flight was his only option if he was to avoid arrest, he left a headless college and a headless university. Though perhaps a very occasional visitor during Oxford's existence as a royalist encampment for king, court, and army from 1642 to 1646, from this point onwards he was very largely absent. Although he returned periodically

83. Wood, *Colleges and Halls*, i. 135.
84. ECA, A.I.6, fos. 26v, 27r, 28r, 29r; B. Till, 'Kendall, George (bap.1611, d.1663), clergyman and religious controversialist', *ODNB*.
85. Larminie, 'Tozer', *ODNB*.
86. *HUO*, iv. 695; Wood, *Life and Times*, i. 52–4; A. J. Hegarty, 'Pinck, Robert (bap. 1573, d. 1647), college head', *ODNB*.

thereafter, he came as a revenant and college guest rather than an active participant in the affairs of the university. After 1642 his life divided into two phases, as bishop of Worcester and as a retired but still active scholar. In his last eight years, and as we shall see, he was by no means idle.

To assess Prideaux's position and opinions in the years immediately before the Civil War is not easy. He left no public statement of his views and no personal writings, of the sort which engaged him towards the end of his life.[87] His one publication, the *Nine Sermons* of 1641, certainly showed his new-found freedom from Laudian restraints. But it was hardly more than a set of reprints, and in general its author played no part in the explosion of anti-Laudian tracts on such topics as the Sabbath and predestination which marked the two years after the archbishop's downfall. Nor was he a famous preacher able to make a public and self-revealing impact through his sermons, like his fellow Calvinist and Cambridge college head, Richard Holdsworth.[88] His moderate Calvinism, setting him apart from puritans such as William Twisse, remained unchanged and could be glimpsed in his contributions to the work of Bishop Williams's reforming subcommittee. But his convictions, expressed vigorously enough in the late 1620s and early 1630s, remained largely unvoiced at this time.

External events revealed something of what others thought of him. The early offer of the bishopric of Waterford in January 1641 and his appointment to the reforming subcommittee shortly afterwards both testified to his role in the post-Laudian church. The offer of a bishopric, refused in the case of Waterford, accepted in that of Worcester, showed that he was at last judged *papabile* (though that was hardly the word that he would have used). It also showed that he now enjoyed the king's favour, if only a favour bestowed by Charles for expedient reasons. But Prideaux's firm belief in the episcopate, leading up to his own promotion to a see, set him apart from the Commons in Parliament, whose anti-Arminian and anti-Laudian members had initially seemed likely to be his natural allies and sponsors. Their views differed fundamentally. Pym and his fellows judged episcopacy to be at best a human institution and the bishops' jurisdiction to derive from the king, while for Prideaux and other non-puritan Calvinists episcopacy was *iure*

87. Below, 367–70.
88. Milton, 'Licensing, Censorship', 640–2; P. Collinson, 'Holdsworth, Richard (1590–1649), Church of England clergyman and college head', *ODNB*.

divino, established by divine right.[89] As the hostility of the Commons towards episcopacy hardened, culminating in their ineffectual vote of May 1641 in favour of abolition[90] and their fury at Charles's new appointments in October, so the position of the bishops came to seem increasingly endangered. The impeachment of those thought responsible for the 1640 canons, and, in December 1641, of those who had declared that Parliament was not free, were further signs of the threats which they faced. At this pre-war stage the practical and legal limitations on their powers went no further than their exclusion from secular jurisdiction and from their places in the Lords by the Bishops' Exclusion Bill of February 1642.[91] But the portents must have been clear.

For much of this time Prideaux was one of a small group of leading Calvinist divines who broadly held the same views, shared in the same activities, and secured promotion at the same time. In December 1640 the Covenanting Scot Robert Baillie had named Prideaux, Samuel Ward, Daniel Featley, Ralph Brownrigg and Richard Holdsworth as men 'famous for learning' who were likely to favour episcopacy. In March 1641 Prideaux, Ward, Featley, Brownrigg, and Holdsworth had all been active members of Bishop Williams's reforming subcommittee. And in October 1641 Prideaux, Brownrigg, and Holdsworth were among those offered bishoprics. Three members of this group were heads of colleges: Prideaux at Exeter, Ward at Sidney Sussex, and Holdsworth at Emmanuel, both Cambridge. All were men whose fortunes had revived with the fall of Laud. Yet Prideaux stood apart from this group and its Oxbridge subgroup by virtue of his nomination as Oxford's vice-chancellor in October 1641, the same month in which he obtained his bishopric. From then on his local responsibilities in Oxford took priority over all else, including his other obligations as bishop of Worcester. His absence from his enthronement at Worcester in January 1642, his infrequent visits to his diocese, and his permanent residence there only under the stress of events in July 1642 all showed a perhaps excusable insouciance towards his new role. Add to his university duties his continuance in office as Oxford's regius professor of divinity (until April 1642) and as Exeter's rector, and it becomes possible to see Prideaux, even at a time of

89. *Proceedings of the Short Parliament*, ed. Cope and Coates, 152; J. Rushworth, *Historical Collections* (1691), III. i. 35; Milton, *Catholic and Reformed*, 16, 455–6 and n. 23; Hampton, 'Mera Chimaera', 288–90.
90. Russell, *Fall*, 344.
91. Gardiner, *Constitutional Documents*, 241–2; Russell, *Fall*, 471.

widening responsibilities and a gathering national crisis, as a figure still rootedly Oxonian.

Prideaux's final months in Oxford, when, as vice-chancellor, he was called on to rally the university's support for the king, brought together these two worlds of locality and nation. His fundraising activities on behalf of Charles and his gathering army in the north were the prelude to his own hurried departure from the Oxford scene. They brought into focus one of the guiding principles of his whole career: his unwavering royalism. However much he may have disapproved of the government of the church by Charles and Laud in the 1630s, he remained Charles's chaplain, thereby a fringe member of his court, and very much the king's man. In the growing divide between royalists and parliamentarians which marked the summer of 1642 his role as vice-chancellor made it obvious which side he was on; and the same principle was to govern the pattern of his life and conduct until 1649.

11

In Office and in Retirement,
1642–50

1. Bishop of Worcester

Prideaux's time as a diocesan bishop effectively began with his flight from Oxford in July 1642 and ended with his expulsion from Worcester when the city fell to the parliamentary army in July 1646. Before then he had been only an occasional visitor to his see. His 'working' episcopate thus fell almost precisely within the conventional limits of the first civil war, from Charles's raising of his standard at Nottingham in August 1642 to his surrender to the Scots in May 1646 and the fall of Oxford in June. For most of that time, from October 1642 onwards, shortly after the battle of Edgehill, Oxford had been the base for the king, the court, and the royal army. These were hardly years when episcopal authority could be consistently exercised, particularly in a diocese such as Worcester.[1] Comprising the county of Worcestershire and the south-western part of Warwickshire, the diocese lay throughout in the thick of the fighting. Although the loyalties of its citizens were only precariously for the king, Worcester was garrisoned for the royalists throughout the war, and the city underwent two sieges, a brief one by Sir William Waller in 1643 and a much longer one through the summer of 1646, the last major episode of the war. The strategic importance of both city and county drew in marauding armies from both sides. The county was regarded by the royalists as part of the king's sphere of influence, extending westwards from his headquarters at Oxford, some sixty miles away. The city was a main crossing point of the Severn, a 'key staging post' on the road from Wales to

---

1. What follows derives from M. Atkin, *The Civil War in Worcestershire* (Stroud, 1995), 19–54, 67–116, and *Diary of Henry Townshend*, 21–41.

Between Scholarship and Church Politics: The Lives of John Prideaux, 1578–1650. John Maddicott, Oxford University Press. © John Maddicott 2022. DOI: 10.1093/oso/9780192896100.003.0011

Oxford, and part of a major corridor for the transmission of military supplies to Oxford, factors which made the whole region vulnerable to attack. Both sides squeezed the county for taxes and both plundered it remorselessly for cash, crops, and livestock, particularly horses. By the last months of 1645 it was reported that all the county between the rivers Severn and Teme, and all the parishes within four miles of the city, together with the lands around Kidderminster and Bewdley, had been 'eaten up, undone and destroyed' by passing armies. Deserters, bandits, and refugees contributed to the break-down of order. This was no country for an elderly bishop.

Our first record of Prideaux's presence in his diocese after his departure from Oxford comes on 3 August 1642, when, from his palace at Worcester, he made provision for the union of two Warwickshire parishes.[2] He came to the diocese not only as its newly resident bishop but as the king's agent, and on 16 August orders were issued by Charles—who must have known of Parliament's instructions for his arrest—for Prideaux's protection: the sheriff was to assist him in every way and not to allow him to be taken 'forcibly or otherwise' out of the see or county.[3] A simultaneous attempt by the Commons to secure his person was spiritedly rebuffed. As their agent reported:

> He refused to goe with me and told me that he had the king's protection. And that he would not obey the parliament. And that they must send an army for him if they meane to bring him to them ffore he would not be a non-resident, but would remaine where he was.[4]

He was not without other friends and allies. The cathedral chapter was predominantly royalist, and the dean was Christopher Potter, provost of Queen's, ex-Laudian, and once the target of Prideaux's doctrinal wrath, but now his fellow royalist and fellow refugee from parliamentary justice. Both men, now together at Worcester in September, had been among the four heads of houses who had organized the raising of Oxford money for the king in July.[5]

---

2. Prideaux's Register [hereafter 'Register'], Worcestershire Archives, Worcester, 51–7; Pearce, *Hartlebury*, 135–6. Pearce, 130–50, provides the best general survey of Prideaux's activities in his diocese.

3. HMC, *14th Report*, Appendix, Part VIII (1895), 203; Pearce, *Hartlebury Castle*, 135.

4. Bodl. MS Nalson 13, fo. 223r; HMC, *Manuscripts of the Duke of Portland*, Vol. I (1891), 53.

5. Atkin, *Civil War*, 23; *LJ*, v. 208; *Special Passages* [a newsletter], Number 1. 13 Sept. 1642; *Special Passages*. Number 7, Tuesday 20 Sept.–Tues. 27 Sept.

In the chaos of war the king's protection counted for little, and Worcester was to prove a good deal less safe than Oxford. On 23 September 1642, a month after Edgehill, one of the other early engagements of the conflict took place at Powick Bridge, a mile or so south of the city. Although royalist cavalry under Prince Rupert were able to put a small parliamentary force to flight, the prince's subsequent withdrawal to Ludlow allowed the main parliamentary army under the earl of Essex to march into Worcester, which they occupied for a month. During their stay the cathedral was desecrated: the organ destroyed, the stained-glass windows broken, the library rifled, and the horses of the occupiers stabled in the nave, There was also, according to the puritan divine Richard Baxter (who was present), 'some excellent preaching'.[6] Not surprisingly, Prideaux hurriedly moved out, probably about the time of Essex's entry into the city. 'Dr Prideaux, late made bishop, and other popish priests . . . are all run away,' reported Nehemiah Wharton, a sergeant in the parliamentary army.[7] Clearly, in the eyes of the more fanatical parliamentarians, bishops were *ipso facto* papists. But Wharton's information on the bishop's flight was more accurate than his opinion of Prideaux's religion. He is next found at Bridgnorth in Shropshire, well outside his diocese, where, on 27 November, he instituted Henry Sutton, soon to become his son-in-law, to the Worcestershire living of Bredon. When he left Worcester, he may have been aiming to join the king at Shrewsbury, where Charles and his army were based from 20 September to 12 October; and he may indeed have done so.[8] By early December he had moved south again to his episcopal castle at Hartlebury, near Kidderminster, and by 12 December he was back in Worcester, where the cathedral bells rang to mark 'my Lo: Bps returne to Worcester after xi weeks absent since first the rebels entred Worcester'.[9] Shortly afterwards he received a strongly worded letter from the king written from Oxford on 22 December, perhaps with his recent brief but ignominious exile in mind. He was strictly enjoined to attend to his pastoral charge and to remain in his diocesan city, the better to do what belonged to his office—to counter the great increase in Brownists, Anabaptists, and other sectaries ('the principal

---

6. Atkin, *Civil War*, 34–9; W. Dugdale, *A Short View of the Late Troubles in England* (Oxford, 1681), 557; R. Baxter, *Reliquiae Baxterianae* (1696), 42–3.
7. *CSPD, 1641–43*, 397.
8. Register, 57; Pearce, *Hartlebury Castle*, 137–8; S. R. Gardiner, *History of the Great Civil War, 1642–49*, 4 vols (1886–91), i. 30, 43.
9. Pearce, *Hartlebury Castle*, 137 (from Dean and Chapter Treasurer's Accounts).

cause of the said rebellion'), to reform abuses, to correct the 'ill lyves' of the clergy, to advance pious and learned preachers, and to labour for the conversion of any papist priests.[10] Laid out here was an intimidatingly comprehensive programme designed to strengthen orthodox religion, to suppress extremists to left and right, and to facilitate the general reform of the church which might yet win support for Charles's cause.

Prideaux's flight from Worcester had shown how vulnerable he was to the attacks of the king's enemies in a county which was on the point of becoming a major war zone. It soon became clear that his vulnerability was as much economic as military. In March 1643 orders were issued by Parliament for the sequestration of his estates, along with those of thirteen other bishops. The charges against most comprised either taking up arms against Parliament or contributing money or plate to the funding of the king's armies, as presumably in Prideaux's case: his actions as the university's vice-chancellor in July 1642 had not been forgotten.[11] More than any other previous act, the sequestration ordinance marked out Prideaux as an enemy of Parliament. But whether it made much difference to his well-being is unclear. There is nothing to show how the ordinance was implemented, if at all, and any depletion of his income is as likely to have been due as much to the devastation of his diocese by the contending armies as to the sequestration. We can be sure only that the war hit him hard. When he became bishop, he wrote later, 'with much difficulty, by reason of these distracted times, he hath procured a poor livelihood, which now, by ordinance of parliament, is sequestrated'. 'Such was the iniquity of the times', stated one of his earliest biographers, 'and the greedy appetite of those who gaped to devour the remaining revenues of the church' that 'he received very little else from his bishoprick' besides 'the title and the burden of it'.[12]

After his return to Worcester in December 1642 Prideaux remained in his diocese for the duration of the war. It is possible that he paid occasional visits to Oxford, since he was appointed as one of the king's Lenten preachers at court in 1644, one of only two former anti-Laudians appointed and a sure

---

10. Ibid., 138–9, summarized in HMC, *14th Report*, Appendix, Part VIII, 203.
11. *Acts and Ordinances of the Interregnum, 1642–1660*, ed. C. H. Firth and R. S. Rait, 3 vols. (1911), i. 106–17; P. H. Hardacre, *The Royalists during the Puritan Revolution* (The Hague, 1956), 39–40, 44–5; P. King, 'The Episcopate during the Civil Wars, 1642–1649', *EHR*, 83 (1968), 523, 528; J. Morrill, 'The Church in England, 1642–9', in his *Nature of the English Revolution*, 152.
12. *LJ*, viii. 503; Prince, *Worthies of Devon*, 660.

sign that he enjoyed the king's favour.[13] His more usual residence at
Worcester set him apart from his fellow bishops, most of whom either
quietly retired or fled from their sees. Godfrey Goodman, for example,
Prideaux's neighbour at Gloucester, spent much of the war either at his
Berkshire rectory or on his estates in Wales, while John Williams, by this
time archbishop of York, also took refuge in Wales.[14] To judge from the
sparse records of his administration, Prideaux stayed mainly in his palace at
Worcester, with at least one long sojourn at Hartlebury from August to
October 1644.[15] He may have been there when news reached him of the
death of his son William, fighting for the king at Marston Moor on 2 July
1644. With the city garrisoned with royalist troops, crowded with refugees,
and perpetually under threat from parliamentary forces, Worcester cannot
have been a comfortable billet, and still less so after Prince Maurice of
Nassau, Rupert's brother, made the palace his headquarters in 1645.[16]
From the palace Prideaux did what he could to advance the king's cause.
Charles himself paid two brief campaigning visits to Worcester in June 1644
and September 1645,[17] but more usually he communicated by letter from
his base at Oxford. Prideaux was told to ask the clergy of his diocese to lend
money, with a promise of interest at 8 per cent; to thank them for what they
had given and to encourage them to give more; and, more frequently, to
inquire into the activities of various named seditious and rebellious clergy
and, if necessary, to eject them from their livings and to put in the king's
nominees. In raising loans Prideaux was to stress that the money would be
employed only for the defence of the king's person, the true Protestant
religion, the law of the land, and the privileges of Parliament.[18] Not the least
of Prideaux's uses to Charles was his potential service as a propaganda agent.
Occasionally we see him acting on his own initiative, as when (according to
Wood) he excommunicated all those in his diocese taking up arms against
the king.[19]

13. Milton, 'Anglicanism and Royalism', 66, 253 n. 23; above, 343–4.
14. Hardacre, *The Royalists*, 45; Morrill, 'The Church in England', 159; Cranfield, 'Goodman';
     Quintrell, 'Williams'.
15. See the record of Prideaux's institutions in CCEd, Ordinary Tenure ID: 619; and Register, 58,
     59, 60, 62, 63–5, 66, 68.
16. Atkin, *Civil War*, 8; *Diary of Henry Townshend*, 33.
17. Gardiner, *Civil War*, i. 415, ii. 283; Atkin, *Civil War*, 71, 90.
18. Register, pp. 95–8; HMC, *14th Report*, Appendix, 203; Pearce, *Hartlebury*, 139–41.
19. Wood, *Athenae*, iii. 266.

By remaining in his diocese Prideaux was able to maintain at least the rudiments of episcopal administration. Circumstances were hardly favourable. Not only did the war make travel hazardous and the exercise of authority at best sporadic, but numbers of local clergy had fled, leaving vacancies in the parishes Discipline among the laity had broken down. According to the chancellor of the diocese, ecclesiastical laws were disregarded, clandestine and illicit marriages had become commonplace, and legal remedies through the church courts had ceased to be available.[20] Yet the collapse of diocesan machinery seen in other dioceses[21] was less clearly mirrored at Worcester. Meetings of the cathedral chapter continued until 1645; institutions and collations to benefices never entirely lapsed (there were thirteen in 1643, twelve in 1644, eight in 1645; and three in 1646); and some ordinations took place.[22] Prideaux was even among the few bishops who attempted a formal visitation of their dioceses during the war. In his autobiography Thomas Hall, the cantankerous but exceptionally godly curate of King's Norton, recorded that on 23 October 1643, a fast day, 'Dr Prideaux Bishop of Worcester kept his visitation intending to try whose service they preferred Gods or his,' though since Hall also recorded that he absented himself on account of the fast, and apparently suffered no penalty, the visitation may not have been entirely successful.[23] With others among his clergy, especially those untainted by the Presbyterianism which marked Hall's beliefs, he remained on much better terms. His theological handbook, the *Fasciculus Controversiarum Theologicarum*, published in 1649, was dedicated to his two sons-in-law, both now Worcestershire parish priests, to five additional named local clerics, 'and others of the diocese of Worcester . . . pious, learned and prudent ministers of the gospel . . . and fellow workers in the vineyard of the Lord'.[24]

What we know of Prideaux's activities thus suggests that he made a conscientious and brave attempt, at this most difficult of times, both to manage his diocese effectively and to serve its pastoral needs. But all these activities came to a halt in 1646, as the parliamentary forces closed in on

---

20. *The Autobiography and Library of Thomas Hall B.D. (1610–1665)*, ed. D. Thomas (WHS, n.s., 26, 2015), 54–5, 58; Pearce, *Hartlebury Castle*, 140, 145.
21. Morrill, 'The Church in England', 159.
22. K. Fincham and S. Taylor, 'Episcopalian Identity, 1640–1662', in *OHA*, i. 462; Fincham and Taylor, 'Vital Statistics: Episcopal Ordination and Ordinands in England, 1646–60', *EHR*, 126 (2011), 329; CCEd, Ordinary Tenure ID: 619.
23. *Autobiography of Thomas Hall*, 54; Fincham and Taylor, 'Episcopalian Identity', 461.
24. Prideaux, *Fasciculus Controversiarum Theologicarum*, sig. ¶2v.

Worcester. After the king had left Oxford in April 1645, his main army had been shattered at Naseby in June 1645 The last royalist field army had been defeated at the battle of Stow-on-the-Wold in March 1646, and Charles had surrendered to the Scots on 5 May. Worcester and Oxford were now the only royalist bases still holding out. After arriving before Worcester on 25 March, the parliamentary army withdrew to Droitwich, only to return to begin a full-scale siege of the city on 20 May.[25] Prideaux conducted his last institution on 8 May and his fortified and well-stocked country residence at Hartlebury feebly surrendered to the parliamentarians on 16 May.[26] From then on his palace and cathedral became central points in the city's resistance. Guns were mounted at the palace, and the cathedral cloisters were used for the storage of arms and ammunition.[27] On 26 June, after news had come of the surrender of Oxford, the city's governor, Colonel Washington, called an assembly at the palace to discuss a possible treaty with the besiegers. Nothing as yet resulted, and a few days later the palace was struck by a cannon ball while Prideaux was dining in the room below. When provisional terms for a surrender were drafted by the defenders on 1 July, they provided elaborate protection for the bishop's interests: he was to be continued in office, his houses and revenues to be preserved and restored with arrears, and his family and goods kept safe. This draft treaty, favourable in every way to the city, was predictably and contemptuously rejected by Colonel Rainsborough, the commander of the parliamentary forces now on the brink of victory. When the city finally surrendered on 20 July, Prideaux was named as one of the garrison, and when its gentry defenders left on 23 July, it was to Prideaux that they went for a final blessing.[28]

Both the attempt in the draft treaty to protect Prideaux's position and the eagerness of the departing gentry to receive his blessing were a reflection of his standing, even popularity, among the city's royalists. As the eminent and learned defender of their church and religion, and as the ally and agent of their king, he had a totemic significance beyond his diocesan role. But in any case that role was now at an end—formally so after Parliament moved on to abolish the episcopate in October 1646.[29] Prideaux's movements and activities in these few months following the fall of Worcester are uncertain.

25. Atkin, *Civil War*, 101–7, 155.
26. CCEd, Record ID 132866; *Diary of Henry Townshend*, 208–9; Pearce, *Hartlebury Castle*, 151–2.
27. *Diary of Henry Townshend*, 37.
28. Ibid., 230, 241, 242, 244, 251, 261.
29. Gardiner, *Civil War*, ii. 527.

Initially he was presumably given a pass to leave the city, as were all its defenders.[30] He may have done so in some degree of poverty. The defenders were limited in what they were allowed to take with them, and on 24 September Parliament received a petition from Prideaux noting that his bishopric had been sequestered and 'that he hath no personal estate whereby to provide for his wife and children or to subsist himself any longer' and asking for an allowance. The lords agreed to recommend that he be given 'relief and subsistence', and it may have been at this stage that a meagre living allowance of 4s. 6d. a week was settled on him.[31] At the end of November he moved back to his old College for a fortnight's stay, but shortly afterwards he appears as a prisoner in the custody of the Commons' serjeant-at-arms. As a leading royalist, his role in raising an army for the king, in excommunicating his enemies, and in defending Worcester had probably not escaped the notice of his parliamentarian captors. But his incarceration did not last long. On 25 December orders were issued for his release and for the delivery to him of all his books and manuscripts, provided that he remained within twenty miles of London.[32] These terms too were soon relaxed, and in his last years, probably beginning in 1647 but possibly as early as July 1646, after the fall of Worcester, he lived with his daughter and son-in-law at Bredon in his former diocese.[33] It proved to be a surprisingly fruitful retirement.

2. Retirement: Family

The first civil war ended with Charles I's surrender to the Scots in May 1646 and the fall of Oxford to Fairfax's army in the following month. The king passed back into the hands of Parliament's commissioners only in February 1647.[34] Yet his defeat settled little. The national background to Prideaux's last years, from his leaving Worcester in July 1646 to his death almost exactly four years later, remained one of continuing conflict and political instability. The conflict was mainly factional—between different groups, Presbyterians and Independents, within the ranks of the victorious parliamentarians—but

---

30. *Diary of Henry Townshend*, 262; Pearce, *Hartlebury Castle*, 147–8.
31. *Diary of Henry Townshend*, 262; LJ, viii. 503; Boase, *Register*, 95.
32. ECA, BB/33; CJ, v. 29.
33. Prince, *Worthies of Devon*, 661.
34. Woolrych, *Britain in Revolution*, 349. For the remainder of this paragraph, see esp. Worden, *English Civil Wars*, 77–105.

also in part military: the second civil war, in the spring and summer of 1648, saw local risings in the king's favour and an invasion by his new allies, the Scots, defeated by Cromwell at Preston in August. Political instability sprang both from these conflicts and from the persistent but ultimately unsuccessful attempts to reach a settlement with the king, whose duplicity and devious-ness in his negotiations contributed much to his own fate. Of the two main political groupings, the Presbyterians at first led in their efforts to come to terms with Charles, while their opponents, the more fiercely anti-royalist Independents, were increasingly aligned with the New Model Army, which had emerged as a political force in 1647. By June 1647, however, when the king had fallen into the hands of the army, the Independents were prepared to offer him generous terms for a settlement in order to counter the Presbyterians. The army was behind both the purge of Parliament con-ducted by Colonel Pride in December 1648, which saw the ejection of those members lacking the army's approval, and the subsequent proposal to put the king on trial. But Charles's trial and his execution, which followed on 29 January 1649, solved nothing. The revolution was completed by the formal abolition of the monarchy in March 1649 and the concurrent abolition of the Lords, which left an improvised and unstable government in the hands of the Rump Parliament, while Cromwell's invasion of Ireland in August marked the renewal of the war.

The religious situation was similarly fluid.[35] The execution of Laud in 1645, the replacement of the Prayer Book by the Presbyterian Directory of Public Worship in the same year, the abolition of episcopacy in 1646, and the imposition of a new congregation-centred and less hierarchical system of public worship all suggested that the Anglican church as it had evolved under Elizabeth and James I and during Charles's partnership with Laud, had been thoroughly superseded. Yet Anglican norms proved surprisingly resili-ent. Many of the former bishops continued to ordain, though on a much reduced scale, so guaranteeing the propagation of the orthodox clergy; the Prayer Book, though outlawed, continued to be widely used; and the new Presbyterian system was only patchily imposed. Discontent with puritan practices in the parishes, including the suppression of traditional feasts such as Christmas, was a factor in the revival of royalism which contributed to the second civil war. After Charles's death, and partly as its consequence, a new

---

35. For this paragraph, see esp. J. Morrill, 'The Church in England, 1642–9', 148–75; Fincham and Taylor, 'Episcopalian Identity', 461–4.

challenge arose from the sprouting of radical sects, the Fifth Monarchy Men, the Diggers, the Ranters, and their like, whose emergence owed much to the breakdown of centralized religious authority and the demise of the faith's defender. Laud's ideal of uniformity and order had given way to diversity and confusion.

In his last years Prideaux's life touched only obliquely and occasionally on these themes of national history. As an elderly and retired bishop now lacking the status conferred by his former Oxford roles as regius professor, vice-chancellor, and head of house, he could contribute little to the course of events. Instead, he found solace and occupation in two more personal ways: through the company of his family and through a programme of writing and publishing more extensive than at any other period of his life. Neither his energy nor his qualities of mind showed signs of falling off.

By the time of his retirement Prideaux's immediate family was much reduced. He had lost almost all his children, including the only two of his sons to survive to adulthood: William, killed at Marston Moor, and Matthias, a fellow of Exeter but also a royalist officer, who died of smallpox in London in 1646.[36] All that remained to him were his daughters, Sarah and Elizabeth, 'being the only survivors of the nine children that God had blest me with by your long since deceased mother', as he pathetically noted in the devotional tract which he wrote for the two of them.[37] But he found some consolation in his daughters' marriages to two clerics for whom he had a high regard and to whom he was deeply attached. As we have seen, Sarah, the elder daughter, had married William Hodges, a fellow of Exeter, in 1634. Hodges had always been a favourite with the rector, and despite his brush with Laud and the king in 1631 (which had nearly cost him his place in the university), his subsequent career had flourished, thanks largely to his father-in-law. About the time of the marriage Prideaux had resigned his Oxfordshire vicarage of Bampton in favour of his son-in-law, who had necessarily given up his fellowship on marrying. After nine years at Bampton, Hodges had followed his patron to Worcestershire, though still retaining his original vicarage. In 1643 Prideaux collated him to the church of Ripple, a wealthy country parish in the bishop's gift some thirteen miles south of Worcester, and in 1645 he advanced him further to the

---

36. Above, 351; Wood, *Athenae*, iii. 199.
37. Prideaux, *Euchologia*, sig. A3r; below, 368–9.

archdeaconry of Worcester.[38] Until he was ejected from Bampton by the parliamentary commissioners in 1648, his pluralism must have brought him in a comfortable living.

We cannot know much about past marriages, but that of William Hodges and Sarah Prideaux appears to have been an exceptionally happy one. The couple had twelve children, six born during their Bampton years, five of whom survived, and at least another five at Ripple. When Sarah died aged 33 in 1652, giving birth to a stillborn thirteenth, her husband's grief was palpably expressed on her brass memorial plate in Ripple church. She was his 'very sweetest and most grievously missed wife (*coniunx praesuavissima ac desideratissima*)', who had died worn out by her labour 'amid the prayers and embraces of her most deeply afflicted husband'. William married again but apparently had no more children, and in his will, made shortly before his death in 1676, he asked 'to be buryed in the chancell of the Church of Ripple as neere to my first wife as conveniently may be'.[39] Since her memorial plate is now set into his ledger slab, this was presumably done.

Elizabeth Prideaux's marriage followed a closely parallel track to that of her sister. Her husband, Henry Sutton, had matriculated in 1636, aged 17, from that Calvinist college, Brasenose, whose head was Prideaux's anti-Laudian ally, Samuel Radcliffe.[40] But there was more than Sutton's college to commend him to Prideaux. His father, William Sutton, a doctor of divinity, had been chancellor of Gloucester cathedral, and his mother, Katherine, was the eldest daughter of Miles Smith, bishop of Gloucester, an expert linguist, one of the translators of the King James Bible, and a notable Calvinist opponent (according to a contemporary) of 'papists, Arminians and carnal gospellers'.[41] No son-in-law of Prideaux could have had a better pedigree. Henry and Elizabeth must have known each other for some time before Prideaux left Oxford in 1642, for they were married in the bishop's country palace at Hartlebury on 8 December 1642, shortly after Prideaux's arrival in his diocese. A few days earlier Prideaux had collated Henry Sutton to the church of Bredon, like Ripple one of the most valuable

38. CCEd, Person ID 13317; *Fasti Ecclesiae Anglicanae*, comp. Horn, vii. 113; A. G. Matthews, *Walker Revised* (Oxford, 1988), 297; above, 176–7. Ripple was a valuable living, worth £320 a year c.1665 and the third most valuable of those in the bishop's gift: *Diary of Francis Evans, Secretary to Bishop Lloyd, 1699–1706*, ed. D. Robertson (WHS, 1903), 24.
39. The inscription is nowhere in print but may be seen in the church at Ripple. See also Butcher, 'John Prideaux', 10.
40. Foster, *Alumni*, iii. 1443; Crook, *Brasenose*, 42–3, 49–50.
41. Butcher, 'John Prideaux', 11; J. Tiller, 'Smith, Miles (d. 1624), bishop of Gloucester', *ODNB*.

livings in the diocese, across the river Avon about three miles east of his other son-in-law's parish at Ripple.[42] The living was sequestrated in 1646, during what Henry Sutton's monument in Bredon church describes as 'a period of tyrannical usurpation', but Henry was restored in 1660 and lived on as Bredon's parish priest until 1687.[43] Like the marriage of William and Sarah, that of Henry and Elizabeth was exceptionally fruitful. Their first son, Henry, born in 1643, was baptized in the bishop's palace at Worcester; another three children followed between 1644 and 1647; and a good many more before Elizabeth's death in 1659.[44]

After Prideaux's loss of his see, Henry and Elizabeth offered him a home and a refuge at Bredon. Surrounded by his grandchildren and with others across the river at Ripple—'your little ones whom God hath blessed you with abundantly'—he played the part of a benign paterfamilias in a large and growing household.[45] His sons-in-law were men of some learning, and both went on to graduate as DDs after Prideaux's death. Henry in particular also appears to have been a model parish priest, 'the shepherd of a numerous flock' and generous in his hospitality (again according to his monument). Addressing his two daughters, Prideaux wrote of 'your loving husbands . . . whom those that know must confesse to be learned, pious and painful [assiduous, diligent] ministers; and I think you happy to have met with such above divers that hold themselves of a higher pitch in the world'.[46] When he came to publish his *Fasciculus Controversiarum Theologicarum* in 1649, William Hodges and Henry Sutton were the two leaders of the Worcestershire clergy, 'pious, learned and prudent men', to whom he addressed his letter of dedication.

Prideaux's happy family circumstances, and the happiness of his daughters' marriages, provided some compensation for the poverty which also marked his retirement. Since he had lost his bishopric and all his Oxford emoluments, it was not surprising that, as he told parliament in September 1646, 'he hath no personal estate whereby to provide for his wife and children, or to subsist himself any longer'.[47] This was a little disingenuous, since his only

---

42. Pearce, *Hartlebury Castle*, 137–8; T. Nash, *Collections for the History of Worcestershire*, 2 vols. (1781–2), ii. 131.

43. Matthews, *Walker Revised*, 386; Butcher, 'John Prideaux', 11.

44. Bredon parish register, Worcestershire Archives, Worcester; Butcher, 'John Prideaux', 11–12.

45. Prideaux, *Euchologia*, sig. A4v.

46. Ibid.; Butcher, 'John Prideaux', 10–11.

47. *LJ*, viii. 503; above, 000.

two children had husbands to provide for them. But after Henry's living at Bredon was sequestrated, it is hard to know how Henry and his large family, including his father-in-law, survived; Prideaux can only barely have got by on the weekly allowance of 4s 6d conceded to him by Parliament.[48] 'Silver and gold have I none . . . and you know it too well,' he wrote to his daughters. It is true that the evidence of Prideaux's will may seem to gainsay much of this. Made on 20 June 1650, a month before his death, the will left to his wife two bonds for the repayment of £500 owed by Thomas Reynell of Ogwell, a hundred pounds in gold already in her possession, and various chattels. Most of his remaining chattels and all his books were to be divided between his two sons-in-law, whom he named as his executors.[49] Wealth indeed? But bonds represented money owing, not cash in hand; the gold may have been in the nature of capital, a nest egg laid up long since for his wife's sole benefit; and we have already seen that there is good evidence that poverty forced him to sell many of his books.[50] The Civil War had cost him his livelihood.

3. Retirement: Books and writings

His need for money partly (but by no means wholly) explains Prideaux's remarkable record of publications and writings during his retirement. He had published nothing since his *Nine Sermons* of 1641, itself no more than a partial reissue of his earlier *Certaine Sermons* (1637).[51] Now, however, between 1648 and 1650 came three major works. The *chef-d'œuvre* was his *Viginti-duae Lectiones de Totidem Religionis Capitibus praecipue hoc tempore controversis* ('Twenty-two lectures concerning as many chief matters of religion especially disputed at this time'), published at Oxford in 1648. This large and grand volume, published unusually in folio rather than quarto or octavo and running to nearly six hundred pages, was in the nature of a 'collected works', the summation of a lifetime's achievement in theology. Comprising the twenty-two Act lectures of the title delivered between 1616 and 1637, thirteen orations given at the Act between 1616 and 1630, six

48. Above, 354.
49. TNA, PROB/11/213/611; Butcher, 'John Prideaux', 24.
50. Above, 217, 221.
51. Madan, i. 199, ii. 158; above, 327–8.

sermons delivered in Lent to graduating bachelors, and the *Alloquium*, his speech before James I in 1624, the volume reprinted many items—ten of the lectures and thirteen of the orations—first published in 1625 and 1626.[52] But Prideaux and his Oxford publishers were at pains to point out on the book's title page that this was a 'third edition, more free from errors than the earlier editions and almost twice as large (*prioribus emaculatior, et duplo fere auctior*)'. Whether what were clearly intended as selling points actually boosted sales is impossible to say. It may have sold reasonably well in Oxford—there are at least nine copies in Oxford college libraries—but, unlike some of Prideaux's other works from this period, it was never reprinted and its cost may have deterred potential purchasers. That the two smaller sections comprising the thirteen orations and the six sermons were also published separately in the same year, effectively as offprints, suggests that the demand may have been for smaller and cheaper guides to Prideaux's main themes.[53]

Unlike the *Viginti-duae Lectiones*, the second major work of Prideaux's retirement, his *Fasciculus Controversiarum Theologicarum* ('Collection of theological controversies'), published at Oxford in 1649, was a new production and not a mere gathering up of past work. It represented a large-scale survey of Christian theology divided (as so often with Prideaux's writings) into seven parts, covering Scripture, knowledge of God, sin, the church, redemption, the sacraments, and the four last things. The text was not just exposition but also a defence of what its author saw as Anglican orthodoxy against its opponents, whether papists, Socinians, or the dogmatists and fanatics then perturbing the religious scene. It is likely to have been widely read, since two further editions followed in 1652 and 1664.[54] The range of references is characteristically wide; one short section calls in aid some half a dozen of the Fathers, including Ignatius, Justin Martyr, Cyprian, Hilary of Poitiers, Rufinus and Augustine.[55]

It may have been the need, during the book's writing, for access to more books than his own library could supply that took Prideaux back to Oxford for several lengthy periods during these last years. The Exeter buttery books record his residence in College from early October to mid-December 1647

---

52. Ibid., ii. 476–7.
53. J. Prideaux, *XIII Orationes Inaugurales de Totidem Theologiae Apicibus* (Oxford, 1648); Prideaux, *Conciones Sex ad Artium Baccalaureos Habitae* (Oxford, 1648). Neither of these is listed by Madan.
54. Madan, ii. 483–4, iii. 19–20, 188.
55. Prideaux, *Fasciculus*, 114. *HUO*, iv. 597 has some important remarks.

and then from Christmas 1647 to the end of March 1648.[56] The sequence of
buttery books ends in June 1648, but another source fills out the picture of
his Oxford visits. The Bodleian Entry Book for 1648–9 shows Prideaux's
presence in the library on 10 January, 26 February, 17 and 22 March, 17 and
24 July, and 1 August 1648. He may well have been present on other days
too.[57] Occasionally we hear something of his other occupations. The
biographer of George Bull, in later life a revered bishop of St David's, says
that when the 14-year-old Bull arrived at Exeter on 10 July 1648, he
received much help and encouragement from Prideaux, then resident in
College.[58] So it looks as if he spent much of 1647 and 1648 in Oxford,
probably returning to Bredon in the spring and early summer of the latter
year, but otherwise preparing his works for the press, reading in the Bodleian, and perhaps taking up again some of the undergraduate teaching for
which he had once been famous. Since he was also present in Oxford in
October 1648, he may even have been present to hear the inaugural address
by the new regius professor of divinity, Joshua Hoyle, delivered on 16
October, during which Hoyle 'commended Dr Holland and Dr Prideaux
much, and wished he had but half [Prideaux's] spirit'. But, adds the hostile
Wood, 'it appeared to his audience that he had 'not . . . one quarter of it'. [59]

But more interesting than the bare record of Prideaux's later Oxford
activities is the subject matter of his Bodleian reading. The titles of the
books looked out for him suggest a partial shift in his intellectual interests.
The focus of the fifteen or so of these works which can be identified was not
on theology, as we might expect, but on history and particularly on early
British history. They included two works by the sixteenth-century Welsh
antiquary Humphrey Llwyd, his *Commentarioli Britannicae descriptionis frag-
mentum* (1574) and his posthumous magnum opus, the *Historie of Cambria,
now called Wales* (1584), together with John Leland's work on King Arthur,
Assertio inclytissimi Arturi regis Britanniae (1544) and John Hayward's *Lives of
the Three Norman Kings of England* (1613). More local in scope was Brian
Twyne's only book, *Antiquitatis Academiae Oxoniensis Apologia* (1608), a

56. ECA, BB/34.
57. Bodl. Library Records e. 544, fos. 6r, 17v, 20r, 21r, 40r, 41r, 42v; Clapinson, 'The Bodleian
    Library and its Readers, 1602–1652', 42–4, 45 n. 49. I am very grateful to Mary Clapinson for
    identifying the books which Prideaux read.
58. R. Nelson, *The Life of Dr George Bull, Late Lord Bishop of St David's*, 2nd edn (Oxford, 1714),
    11–14.
59. Wood, *Annals*, ii. 607.

riposte to John Caius's *De Antiquitate Cantabrigensis Academiae* (1574), also consulted by Prideaux. Less local was the *Historia Luxembergensis* (1605–6), the first history of Luxembourg, by Johannes Bertelius, and the *Historia Orientalis* (1602) by the sixteenth-century German historian, Reinerus Reineccius. In addition to history, a work by the contemporary logician, encyclopedist, and theologian Johannes Alsted, his *Physica Harmonica* (1616) and another on Ramist logic by Petrus Martinius (1590) may relate to the later stages of the arts course. Prideaux himself owned many of Alsted's works.[60] The only theological works on the list appear to be an untitled Marprelate tract of 1589 and a book by Johannes Schroder (1612) on the fifth-century Christological dispute between Nestorius and Eutyches. The bias towards historical writing is clear and might suggest that Prideaux was contemplating some new contribution to his own repertoire of scholarly writing. Was he perhaps especially interested in the early British church as the predecessor of Rome and the forebear of Protestantism? Whatever his motives, his Oxford reading in 1648 suggests that old age had brought no decline either in his academic vigour or in his intellectual curiosity.

Proof of the importance of Prideaux's College sojourns comes from the preface to the *Fasciculus*, where he emphasizes his debt to 'the fidelity, erudition and industry' of Henry Tozer, 'always an especially dear son to me', and his oldest and closest friend among the fellows. In particular, Tozer had supplied him with books and compiled the index to the *Fasciculus*. Tozer, then governing the College as sub-rector in the absence of Rector Hakewill, was himself under attack from the parliamentary visitors at just this time—for permitting the continued use of the Prayer Book among other offences—and was expelled from his fellowship and from the College in June 1648, after having been pulled from his pulpit by the soldiers of the parliamentary garrison and subsequently imprisoned. This was probably during the period of Prideaux's residence, at a time when half the College's resident fellows joined Tozer in losing their fellowships.[61] The milieu in College and university can hardly have been conducive to concentrated academic work. Both victims of the parliamentary regime, the deposed bishop and the displaced fellow had more in common than their friendship and religious sympathies.

---

60. Above, 220.
61. *Fasciculus*, sig. ¶¶2r; ECA, A.I.6, fo. 41r; *Register of the Visitors of the University of Oxford*, ed. Burrows, 13, 91, 113, 115, 21l; Larminie, 'Tozer'; *HUO*, iv. 728, 730.

Prideaux's purpose in the *Viginti-duae Lectiones* and the *Fasciculus* was not merely to make some money in order to sustain himself and his family. They had a higher purpose and a contemporary relevance, implied in the extended title of the first book, which concerned matters of religion 'especially disputed at this time'. Taken together, they constituted a manifesto, a final statement of his most firmly held beliefs. By the time that he came to publish the *Fasciculus* in 1649 he was 70 years old and physically failing. In his preface he had warm words not only for Henry Tozer but also for his doctor, William Croote, an Exeter graduate, who had laboured to maintain his health and whose kindness and skill he remembered with gratitude.[62] He must have known that not much time was left to him for the declaration of faith which he intended as his legacy. Deeply conservative, he held unwaveringly to the tenets of that faith which he had professed throughout his life. In the *Viginti-duae Lectiones* the subjects of the lectures which he had delivered between 1616 and 1637, among them double predestination, grace, perseverance, the Antichrist, and the authority of the church in matters of faith, now received a fresh endorsement. The *Fasciculus* had a more topical slant, not only setting out Prideaux's long-held views on 'absolute' election and reprobation, and the reservation of grace to the elect, but also defending *iure divino* episcopacy, the authority of the church, the conformity of the Prayer Book to the Bible, and the wrongfulness of resistance to the king. His stand for the Prayer Book, put together as it had been by learned and eminent men, was particularly resolute.[63] These were all doctrines which were anathema to the dominant parliamentary factions and the leaders of the army, to Presbyterians and Independents. They took issue with the main tenets and activities of parliamentary opposition and parliamentary rule since the start of the Civil War.

The two works together thus made their own contribution to the continuity of the Church of England, which is now seen as a half-submerged feature of the years of puritan rule.[64] But they were also a vindication of the position set out shortly afterwards by Prideaux in his will:

> I doe protest that I dye in the true Christian Faith firmely beleevinge and houldinge the doctrine, worshipp and discipline established and professed in

---

62. Prideaux, *Fasciculus*, sig. ¶¶1; Croote had obtained his BM from Exeter in 1642: Boase, *Commoners*, 78.
63. *HUO*, iv. 597; Hampton 'Mera chimaera', 288, 291–2.
64. Cf. Morrill, 'The Church in England, 1642–49', 148–75 *passim;* Hampton, '*Mera chimaera*', 293.

the Church of England, in the raigne of Queen Elizabeth King James and the beginninge of the raigne of the late King Charles as I have always professed, mayntened and defended the same in my severall places and callings.[65]

After 'the beginning of the raigne of the late King Charles', doctrine and practice had changed, first under Laudian rule and then with the upsurge of dissenting groups after 1640. Prideaux, however, had remained a constant in these stormy ecclesiastical seas. A bishop no longer, he yet had the means to defend the traditional teachings of the Church of England and the beliefs which had governed his life.

One further work of a different sort was also the product of Prideaux's retirement. The undated and cumbrously titled *Hypomnemata* ['Notes on'] *logica, rhetorica, physica, metaphysica, pneumatica, ethica, politica, oeconomica* is usually thought to have been published shortly after Prideaux's death,[66] but a copy in the library of Queen's College, Oxford, tells a different story. It carries an *ex dono* inscription recording its gift by Prideaux to Thomas Barlow on 6 October 1648, which suggests both that it resulted from the same concentrated burst of mental energy which gave rise to the two other retirement works already discussed and that Prideaux's summer visit to Oxford in 1648 was either extended into, or repeated in, the autumn.[67] That it was composed 'in the most difficult times' is stated in Prideaux's preface; and the late 1640s would certainly come under that heading. A second surviving copy, this one given by Henry Tozer to Thomas Marshall of Lincoln College in June 1649, hints at a more general distribution of copies about this time.[68] The gift to Barlow is particularly interesting, since it points to a connection otherwise unrecorded—but not an implausible one, since Barlow, fellow of Queen's from 1633 and later provost of his college and Bodley's librarian, was, like Prideaux, an expert on the arts course and, more tellingly, a high Calvinist in religion and a royalist in politics.[69]

---

65. Butcher, 'John Prideaux', 24.
66. Madan, ii. 486–7. Madan thought that the book might have been published at the end of 1650, basing his guess on the author's title-page description simply as 'Jo: P: Coll: Exon:' and not 'bishop of Worcester'.
67. Queen's College Library, FF. g. 830: 'Lib. T. Barlow è Coll. Reg.Oxon. ex dono . . . authoris Jo: Prideaux'. Cf. W. Poole, 'Barlow's Books: Prolegomena for the Study of the Library of Thomas Barlow (1608/9–1691)', *BLR*, 29 (2016), 17 n. 14.
68. Lincoln College, Senior Library, E. 1. 48.
69. Spurr, ' Barlow'.

Dedicated *ad Exoniensis Collegii neophytos*, 'to the neophytes of Exeter College', the *Hypomnemata* was written for undergraduates, to supplement the teaching of their tutors (as Prideaux explicitly stated) and to serve both as a guide to the subjects of the arts course (logic, rhetoric, etc.) and, beyond that, as a general survey of knowledge. It has already been briefly summarized.[70] If it was partly written as a money-spinner, a book which students might want to purchase, it also provides one of the best indications of Prideaux's deep interest in the education of the young, especially those from his own College, and of his qualities as a teacher. It is a work notable for its clarity and its orderly arrangement. Beginning with a lengthy section on logic, at just over a hundred pages the longest in the book, it proceeds through the subjects listed in its title. *Physica* covers natural philosophy, including descriptions of fishes, plants, and animals; *Pneumatica*, the world of religion and spirituality; *Oeconomica*, the household, relations between the sexes, trade and agriculture, and moral behaviour; and *Politica*, the ordering and organization of the state. The work is divided throughout into short numbered paragraph, with each section supplemented by questions for disputation, and the whole accompanied by an excellent subject index. In method and substance, much of it inevitably derives from Aristotle, but it is also full of unusual touches and miscellaneous information. One of the *quaestiones* in *Oeconomica*, for example, asks whether the cultivation of woad and tobacco (the latter a new foreign plant) is more harmful than useful (answer: yes); while the discussion of recreations, under *Politica*, mentions the Cornish predilection for wrestling, and avers that while hawking and hunting are proper recreations for the nobility, walking, archery, and fishing are more suitable for scholars and academics.[71] Parts of other sections bore on contemporary issues. Under *Pneumatica*, Prideaux took aim at his usual religious opponents, Roman Catholics and Socinians, and, under *Politica*, at the current regime, with *quaestiones* affirming that monarchy was the best form of government and that a king with a just title could not on any pretext be deposed or punished by his subjects.[72] Far from being a mere handbook of method and information, the *Hypomnemata* was intended to provide religious, moral, and political guidance to its neophyte readers.

70. Above, 214.
71. Prideaux, *Hypomnemata*, 323, 363, 364.
72. Ibid., 258, 265, 271, 342.

Still more overtly didactic was another work, published at Oxford in 1648: *An Easy and Compendious Introduction for Reading all Sorts of Histories.* Although its title-page ascribes authorship to Matthias Prideaux, we can be virtually certain that it was the work of his father. It was said, writes Wood, that Prideaux senior 'had a considerable hand in it'—a statement confirmed by the Cambridge scholar Thomas Smith in a letter of September 1648 to Samuel Hartlib.[73] The book's preliminary division into seven parts resembles the arrangement of Prideaux's other works (though it has to be said that the division was largely ignored in the text). Even more telling are the parallels between the English history sections of the *Introduction* and those in the volume of Prideaux's teaching notes probably written for or by Anthony Ashley Cooper about 1638.[74] In these sections the *Introduction* supposedly written by the younger Prideaux follows the earlier text verbatim, although Matthias cannot have been more that 13 or 14 when the Ashley Cooper volume was compiled. The Bodleian copy of the *Introduction* bears a contemporary inscription in Prideaux's hand recording his presentation of the book on 12 April 1648, another of the several events associated with his Oxford sojourns in that year.[75] It reinforces the view that this is a commemorative volume, mainly, if not wholly compiled by a grieving father as a public memorial to the prematurely extinguished talents of his last surviving son, a fellow of Exeter before his service in the royalist army.

The *Introduction* provides a compressed but comprehensive survey of world history set out in simple terms, beginning with Adam and concluding with James I. Between these two bounding figures come, among others, the great men of the Old and New Testaments, the Greeks and Romans, the Fathers of the early church, the popes, the leader of the western empire, the rulers of the Franks, the (mythical) British kings, and the English kings from the Anglo-Saxon heptarchy onwards. The approach is almost wholly biographical, and each short section terminates with 'Inquiries', which, like the *quaestiones* of the *Fasciculus* and the *Hypomnemata*, were intended to provoke discussion. Was Nero or Tiberius the more insufferable tyrant? Did Edward

---

73. Wood, *Athenae*, iii. 199; SUL, Hartlib Papers, 15/6/18A–19B: 'from Oxford I heare that there is somewhat Chronologiccall of Dr Prideaux in the presse. That small introduction to History in 4to set out 1648 under the name of Mr Mathias Prid. I am certified thence was the Doctors.'

74. Exeter College MS 235; above, 100. The parallels were first pointed out by Fraser Buchanan, 'Like Father, Like Son', in *Exon*, the Exeter College magazine, Autumn 2017, 25.

75. Bodl. 4P 77 Th.

the son of Ethelred deserve the title of Confessor?[76] The religious tone, also like that of the *Hypomnemata*, was assertively Protestant, anti-Catholic, anti-papal, and anti-heretical. Luther, Melanchthon, and the other Protestant reformers 'maintained God's truth against the Tridentine Engineers of the Romanists and the voluminous Jesuits, their emissaries', while Socinianism was 'an introduction to paganisme and atheisme'.[77] If comments such as these mirror Prideaux's religious convictions, his praise of James I for his liberal patronage of learning and the universities (seen not least in his augmenting the stipend of the regius professor of divinity) closely reflected the views set out in his address to James published in 1624.[78] Here Prideaux senior speaks with his own characteristic voice—and to some effect, for the *Introduction* became a bestseller, going into five editions or reprints between 1650 and 1682.[79]

It seems probable that the *Introduction*, like the *Hypomnemata*, was primarily intended for undergraduate readers. It made a contribution, at the most basic level, to the informal syllabus of general subjects, including history and geography, which was taught largely by college tutors alongside the more formal degree requirements of the arts course.[80] The parallels between the *Introduction* and Prideaux's teaching notes in Exeter College MS 235 point firmly in this direction. But the book was almost certainly meant too for younger schoolboy readers, at a time when undergraduates often came up to the university at 13 or 14 and there was some overlap between these two categories. It was dedicated to Prideaux's brother-in-law Sir Thomas Reynell and his wife Katharine 'for the use of their towardly young sons Mr Thomas and Mr Henry Reynell': 'young sons' who were surely not undergraduates and who are noticeably absent from the records of the College which had found a place for their father and for so many members of his family.[81]

All these books, the *Viginti-duae Lectiones*, the *Fasciculus*, the *Hypomnemata*, and the *Introduction*, were thus largely written for academic readers, whether theologians or undergraduates. Two further works, also the products of

---

76. Prideaux, *Easy and Compendious Introduction*, 209, 312.
77. Ibid., 154–5.
78. Ibid., 340–2; Prideaux, *Alloquium*; Madan, i. 122.
79. 1650, 1654/5, 1664, 1672, 1682: Madan, ii. 474. The 1672 edition numbered 1,500 copies: *HUO*, iv. 333.
80. Cf. Curtis, *Oxford and Cambridge in Transition*, 126–48; *HUO*, iv, 333–4, 467–9.
81. For the Reynells at Exeter, see above, 162–4.

Prideaux's retirement, were altogether more personal and never intended for publication. The *Euchologia* [Prayer], *or the Doctrine of Practical Praying*, and the Συνειδησιλογία [Conscience], *or the Doctrine of Conscience*, were written for members of Prideaux's family, the former for his two daughters, Sarah Hodges and Elizabeth Sutton, and the latter for his wife Mary. They were essentially pastoral works, sharing a common purpose in the advancement of the spiritual welfare of these three women, and they seem later to have gone forward as a pair: both were subsequently published in 1656 by the same London publisher, Richard Marriott, and in the same duodecimo format.[82] Each had been written in Prideaux's last years, and in the case of the *Doctrine of Conscience* in his last days, for the preface to this second work, written by an unidentified 'Y. N.', states that it was begun 'but a little before his fatall sicknesse' and left unfinished at his death. The preface also states that its publication was prompted by Mary Prideaux, 'a most religious matron', who was anxious for the benefits of the work to be available for others. It seems likely too, given the coincidence of the publication details, that the launching of the *Euchologia* was also prompted by the family, if not by both daughters (for Sarah Hodges had died in 1652), then by William Hodges and the two Suttons, husband and wife. In all probability the publication of both works resulted from a family collaboration.

The *Euchologia* remains Prideaux's most personal work. It is entirely concerned with prayer, broadly defined: its necessity, the variety of its occasions (personal, household, assembly), the variety of its types (petitionary, salutations, blessings, lamentations, comminations), and the liturgical prayers of the Psalms and, especially, the Prayer Book. The Book of Common Prayer, the title page states, would 'satisfie upon all occasions, without looking after new lights from extemporal flashes', a shaft aimed at the puritans and their veneration for inspired and extempore prayer. In the text Prideaux takes for granted the dogmas of Calvinistic Anglicanism (we are not to seek through prayer 'the secrets of God in election or reprobation') and makes clear, as he does nowhere else, his anger and bitter distress at the current state of religion in puritan England, writing of 'the irreverent contempt, and worse than heathenish, that is fallen of late upon Gods

---

82. The *Euchologia* was, however, first published in 1655. The title page of the 1656 edition was identical, bar the date. The Bodleian copies of the two 1656 items are bound together as a single volume, which suggests simultaneous and coordinated publication. The 1656 edition of the *Euchologia* appears to differ from that of 1655 only in being printed more compactly and with fewer pages.

worship, under a pretence of exacter teaching, and purer Reformation . . . the shepherds smitten, the flocks scattered' and 'the dismal spectacle of this flourishing Commonwealth, so late famous among neighbor nations and now so ruinated'.[83] Often emotional in his tone of voice, the author of what was intended as a parting gift frequently addresses his daughters directly: 'And thus have you (my dear daughters) the best legacy which my ruined worldly estate, amongst so many distractions could lay together for you.'[84] The language is simple and the references exclusively to the Bible and the Prayer Book, with none of the allusions to the works of the Fathers, the medieval schoolmen, and other theological commentators which characterize Prideaux's academic lectures and sermons. It is also virtually the only one of his writings which contains a personal reminiscence. When he was a boy, he says, in time of plague, 'your grand-father John Prideaux, my dear father', commended to him the collect for the fourth Sunday after Epiphany, 'O God, that knowest us to be in the midst of so many and great dangers . . . '.[85] At the start of the book, in the prefatory letter to his daughters, he had reminded them that on their mother's side they were also descended from Rowland Taylor, their mother's grandfather (and a Marian martyr), who had been one of the makers of Cranmer's Prayer Book. As he came towards the end of his life, he reached far back into the past to present his daughters with a vision of continuity in which family affections and Prayer Book religion were combined.

The second work, the *Doctrine of Conscience*, resembles the *Euchologia* not only in its family context but also in its presentation—in English and in straightforward prose, with references confined again to Bible and Prayer Book. It is, however, more impersonal in tone than the parallel work. Though written for the benefit of Prideaux's wife, she is never addressed personally and is known as the beneficiary only from the book's title page and from Y. N.'s preface. The subject matter is also more austere, leading the reader through the main Christian and Anglican texts and formularies—the Creed, the Ten Commandments, etc.—and showing in question-and-answer form the sorts of moral problems, particularly those of conscience, which they raise. If the Creed is 'a perfect symbole of our faith', why does it have nothing to say about predestination and free will? The Sixth

83. Prideaux, *Euchologia* (1656), 30, 181, 183, 184.
84. Ibid., 280.
85. Ibid., 280–3.

Commandment prohibits murder, but does this also cover suicide?[86] The form, an exercise in casuistry, is very like that of the confessors' manuals of the Middle Ages which had raised and answered the same sorts of difficult questions.[87] Mary Prideaux must have found it morally useful, since she promoted its publication, but it cannot be said to possess the appeal of the more intimate *Euchologia*.

Prideaux's achievement in these last years was remarkable, all the more so in view of 'the most difficult times' and of the writer's age—'after the expiration of three score and ten years (the ordinary date by Moses allotted to mans life)', he remarked to his daughters.[88] In 1648 he published three large books, the *Viginti-duae Lectiones*, the *Hypomnemata*, and the *Easy and Compendious Introduction*, a fourth, the *Fasciculus*, in 1649, while during these two years he also wrote two shorter works, the *Euchologia* and the *Doctrine of Conscience*, published only after his death. It is true that the first of these was largely a reprint of what had been published long before, and that the second, third, and fourth were largely manuals of elementary instruction. Nevertheless, these were substantial works, ranging widely across the two fields of academic theology and undergraduate pedagogy where Prideaux's strengths had always lain. More original were his two ventures into a different field, that of pastoral advice. The *Euchologia* and the *Doctrine of Conscience* dealt with the same issues and problems of worship and morality on which he must often have given oral directions, but on which he had never previously written systematically. If there is an underlying theme beneath these varying productions it lies in his conservative defence of the Church of England as it had been established (he said in his will) 'in the raigne of Queen Elizabeth, King James and the beginning of the raigne of the late Kinge Charles'. Forming the theme of his prefatory letter to *Euchologia*, his defence of the Prayer Book in particular, at a time when its use had been prohibited and it had been replaced by the Directory of Public Worship, was now more than ever necessary. It was a response and antidote to the 'irreverent contempt and worse than heathenish profaneness . . . fallen of late upon Gods worship'.

---

86. *Doctrine of Conscience*, 59, 92.
87. See, e.g., E. Corran, 'Moral Dilemmas in English Confessors' Manuals', *Thirteenth Century England*, 16 (2017).
88. Prideaux, *Euchologia*, sig. A3r.

But he also left behind him an extensive *Nachlass* which similarly contributed to the survival of the old order through the turmoil of the puritan regime. Between 1650 and 1660 at least six other works were published under his name, all of them broadly theological or ecclesiological in content and most of them pedagogical in intention. We do not know when they were written or in what circumstances they were published, but most probably originated during his years as regius professor and were a byproduct of his teaching and lecturing.

First among these posthumous works was the *Conciliorum Synopsis*, published at Oxford in 1651 and republished in translation as *A Synopsis of Councels* in 1654: a listing of biblical assemblies and church councils, eastern and western, papal and national, up to the reign of James I, and of their main acts. For any beginner wanting to know, say, the leading decrees of Innocent III's fourth Lateran council or of the Council of Trent, this was the place to start.[89] The English version generally occurs as a supplement to the *Easy and Compendious Introduction* and its various reprints, which suggests its role as a primer of elementary instruction. Another pointer in the same direction came with the supplementing of each short section by a set of *quaestiones*, often bearing on the highly topical subject of authority within the church: 'whether councells are of divine authority and simply necessary' (answer: no), and so on.[90]

Church history was approached from a different angle in *Scholasticae Theologicae Syntagma Mnemonicum*, another basic guide, in this case providing 'a useful survey of scholastic theology',[91] in which Prideaux considered a series of large theological topics (God, sin, redemption, etc.) through the commentaries provided by the leading schoolmen from Peter Lombard to Aquinas and Ockham. Sharing in the contemporary revival of academic interest in the medieval schoolmen, he showed himself to be as familiar with their writings as with those of the Fathers.[92] Much more substantial than the *Syntagma*, which runs to only thirty-six pages, was his *Manuductio ad Theologiam Polemicam* (Oxford, 1657). Ranging over the whole field not only of theology per se but also of the organization of the church and the claims of Rome, it was yet another beginners' handbook, though of a rather more

89. Madan, iii. 10, 40; J. Prideaux, *A Synopsis of Councels* (Oxford, 1654), 24, 28–9.
90. *Synopsis of Councels*, 4.
91. Madan, iii. 10.
92. Cf. Milton, *Catholic and Reformed*, 292–3.

than usually elaborate sort. As with the *Synopsis of Councels*, one indicator of its purpose lay in the long section of *quaestiones* concluding each chapter and often accompanied by references to the sources which allowed each 'question' to be followed up. According to Anthony Wood, the preface to the book, full of praise for Prideaux's learning and for his defence of orthodoxy, was the work of Thomas Barlow, to whom, as we have seen, Prideaux had previously presented a copy of his *Hypomnemata*.[93] One final work completed this quartet of handbooks and teaching aids. Published in London in 1659, Prideaux's *Sacred Eloquence: or the art of rhetoric as it is layd down in Scripture* provided a guide to the effective oral presentation of prayers, sermons, and speeches in assemblies by defining and describing the various rhetorical devices (tropes, hyperbole, metaphor, etc.) which might be used to this end, Taking as its unspoken starting-point the role of rhetoric in the arts course, *Sacred Eloquence* was an implicit demonstration of the usefulness of undergraduate studies to the propagation of the faith.[94]

One further posthumously published work stood apart from all these: a very short pamphlet of four pages with an inappropriately lengthy title 'A letter of the reverend father in Christ John Prideaux, lord bishop of Worcester, to the most noble lord John Robartes, Baron Truro, concerning the office of bishop' (*Reverendi in Christo Patris Joannis Prideaux D. Episcopi Vigorniensis ad nobilissimum dominum D. Joannem Roberts, Baronem Truro de episcopatu epistola*) (1660). John Robartes, second baron Truro, an Exeter pupil of Prideaux in the 1620s had gone on to become a parliamentary commander in the Civil War. Prideaux's pamphlet was probably written as a personal letter in the early or mid-1640s, when the controversies about episcopacy were at their height. It was intended to confute Robartes's Presbyterian beliefs, to argue for the existence of bishops as a distinct order in the church hierarchy (and thus superior to presbyters), and to put the case on scriptural grounds for *iure divino* episcopacy.[95] According to Clarendon, at the Restoration Robartes was able 'to assure the King, that he was so far from a presbyterian, that he believed episcopacy to be the best government the church could be subject unto'.[96] But his conversion at that particular

---

93. Madan, iii. 69; Wood, *Athenae*, iii. 268; above, 000.
94. For rhetoric in the arts course, see *HUO*, iv. 246–53.
95. Hampton '*Mera chimaera*', 289–91.
96. Duffin, ' Robartes'.

time was probably merely politic rather than a delayed response to the arguments of his former tutor.

4. Last things

Prideaux's main preoccupation during his retirement years at Bredon and Oxford is likely to have been his writings. On these, his finances, his family, his standing as a theologian, and his religious influence were all partly dependent. But his withdrawal from active life was not absolute. He still had a minor role to play on the fringes of national politics, where his office, his reputation, and his known loyalty to the king all combined to give him a place among the parties negotiating for a peace with Charles. In August 1647 the Heads of Proposals, the army's terms for a settlement, sought formally to preserve the bishops but to deprive them of all jurisdiction, thus leaving them in place while denying them coercive power. For Charles, adamant for episcopacy, this posed a perplexing moral quandary on which he sought help. Prideaux was one of several bishops prepared to advise the king that he could in conscience, and in these exigent circumstances, tolerate the exercise of other religions (that is, primarily Presbyterianism) which this paring down of episcopal authority would promote.[97] Along with four fellow bishops and four others, including Robert Sanderson, his successor in the regius chair, and Gilbert Sheldon, warden of All Souls and Charles's chaplain, he signed a statement to this effect on 28 August 1647—which points to his absence from Bredon and his attendance at some otherwise unknown meeting of the king's advisers.[98] In the following year he maintained a tenuous contact with Charles, then a prisoner on the Isle of Wight. Appointed once again as a royal chaplain, and his presence requested by Charles, on 3 November 1648 he was given permission by the Commons, together with Archbishop Ussher and four others, to go to the Isle of Wight and to counsel the king on the religious issues arising from the Treaty of Newport, the negotiations between the king and the parliamentary commissioners. Charles found his conscience once again in play and in need of reinforcement before he made any further concessions on the future of episcopacy. But the negotiations,

97. Gardiner, *Constitutional Documents*, 321; King, 'Episcopate during the Civil Wars', 535–6; Milton, 'Anglicanism and Royalism', 73–5; Woolrych, *Britain in Revolution*, 375.
98. Bodl. MS Tanner 58, fo. 453; MS Sancroft 78, fo. 15.

and Prideaux's projected part in them, came to nothing. He did not go to Newport, prevented from making the journey, so it was said, by his poverty.[99] His public role in these last years, such as it was, was more a testimony to the value which Charles set on his guidance than to his influence on events.

To an equally limited extent he still functioned as a bishop. Like some of his fellow bishops, he continued to ordain. In 1649–50 he ordained three men as priests, but the records are too sparse and patchy to permit a full tally, and he may well have ordained more. This too was a contribution in a minor way to the maintenance of the Church of England during 'the most difficult times'. One of his last public acts was the ordination on 23 May 1650 of Theophilus Cooke, a graduate of New College, whom he had previously ordained deacon in 1644, to a Worcestershire living.[100] Shortly after this he fell ill with what was to prove a fatal fever. On 20 June he made his will, 'being at present in perfect sence and memory, praised bee God'. Most of his personal belongings he left to Mary, 'my beloved wife': his great gilt bible, his prayer book bound up with the Anglican homilies, his episcopal seal, two bonds for debts owed by Mary's brother, a purse containing £100 in gold, his best bed, two beds for her servants, his plate, and his great cedar chest. His linen he left to his wife and his two daughters, his house in Oxford next to Exeter College to Henry Sutton, his books and his remaining chattels to his executors, his two sons-in-law.[101] He lived on for another six weeks, striving no doubt to finish the *Doctrine of Conscience* which was another part of his legacy to his wife, and dying on 29 July in the fine rectory at Bredon next to the church, looking out across the river Avon to the Malvern Hills.[102] He may have been the victim of some general sickness in the neighbourhood, for his faithful doctor, William Croote, died about the same time.[103]

99. *CJ*, vi. 68–9; Rushworth, *Historical Collections*, III. vii. 1315–16; E. Walker, *Historical Discourses . . . together with perfect copies of all the Votes, Letters, Proposals, and Answers relating unto, and that passed in the Treaty held at Newport* (1705), 73, 77; King, 'Episcopate during the Civil Wars', 535–6; Lloyd, *Memoires*, 536.

100. Fincham and Taylor, 'Vital Statistics', 319–44, esp. 329 and n. 39; CCEd, Person ID 134642; Foster, *Alumni*, i. 322.

101. Above, 149; TNA, PROB/11/213/611; Butche, 'John Prideaux', 24.

102. The date of his death is given on his memorial brass at Bredon, transcribed in Prince, *Worthies*, 661, and in Prideaux, *John Prideaux*, 13.

103. Boase, *Commoners*, 78.

Prideaux was buried on 16 August 1650 in the chancel of the church at Bredon, the resting place he had asked for in his will. His funeral was a grand occasion and the setting for a great gathering. Of the many who were present, we know only one name, that of William Chudleigh, a junior fellow of Exeter, whose expenses were paid by the College.[104] No doubt other fellows were present but paid for themselves. Later commentators give a more general impression. There was, says one of Prideaux's earliest biographers, 'such a train of persons of all qualities at his funeral that . . . such as denied bishops to be peers would have conceived this bishop to be a prince'.[105] 'Prideaux his mem'ry lives in the Oxford chair/More than at Wooster', wrote the clergyman-poet Clement Barksdale about the funeral:

> Where he begat so fair
> A progeny of divines that (as they say)
> A hundred of his sons did meet that day.[106]

It was one of this 'progeny' who gave the Latin funeral oration.[107] Identifying himself only as 'R.C.', but titling himself a Bachelor of Divinity, he had evidently been among Prideaux's theological students, rejoicing in his master's forceful lectures (he tells us) for twenty years. More a highly rhetorical panegyric than a sermon, much of what he had to say none the less provides a persuasive review of the reasons for Prideaux's fame. He had instructed the university, worked for a moral reformation in men, encouraged Christians, and refuted heresies. He had been the master of the liberal arts, from logic and rhetoric to music and astronomy. He had explained the enigmas of Scripture and unravelled the sophistries of the Jesuits. He had dispersed the clouds spread by the papacy, allowed the truth of the gospel to spring forth, and waged war week by week against the Jesuits. Moderating at the disputations which were part of the annual Act, he had settled controversy's storm with his syllogisms. A most skilful captain of the ship of the church, he had steered a steady course, so that the ship should neither be swallowed up by the Roman sea of the papacy nor be dashed against the rocks of puritanism. So expert was he in languages that he could speak in their own tongues to the foreigners who flocked in from every region. Chaldean and Arabic, Syriac and Hebrew were as vernaculars to him. Had

104. ECA, A.II.10, unpaginated, expenses, 1649–50.
105. Lloyd, *Memoires*, 538. Cf. Prince, *Worthies*, 661, for a similar comment.
106. C. Barksdale, *Nympha Libethris, or, The Cotswold Muse* (1651), 63–4.
107. Bodl. MS Jones 56, fos. 21r–22v.

he lived at the time of the Fathers of the church, he would have shone brightly among them. He was not dead but lived on, as a controversialist, in sermons, and in the hearts of the funeral congregation. As rector of Exeter, he had conducted himself so adroitly that the College became the muses' home for the gentry and nobility, whom he educated in polite letters and religious practice. In his private life he was a man of prayer, leaving his bed at night to pray recumbent on the ground, as his physician had testified. 'Stupor mundi Prideaux Anglicanus'.

Prideaux's own epitaph, part of his memorial brass still surviving in the church at Bredon and composed by himself shortly before his death,[108] was less effusive but, in a different way, equally impressive. Translated from the Latin, it reads:

> John Prideaux of Devon A.D. 1578, Sept. 17, born at Stowford, an obscure village, but to worthy parents. First a fellow of Exeter College at Oxford, he was then elected rector; which place he held for almost thirty-two years. He occupied the chair of regius professor in divinity for more than twenty-seven years. He attained the dignity of the vice-chancellorship five times in the same most famous university. He was chaplain to Prince Henry, to King James and to King Charles, by the last of whom he was promoted to the bishopric of Worcester (elected November 22, consecrated at Westminster December 19 1641). He died on July 29. A.D. 1650. Aged 72.

Prideaux reached the heights of his profession at a time when he was least able to exploit his new position or to be of use to the church. Promoted to his bishopric by the king in the hope that the election of so prominent an anti-Laudian would appease the parliamentary critics and would-be reformers of the church, he found that his appointment, made at a time when the whole justification for episcopacy was in question, was viewed as a hostile provocation. In his other role as Oxford's vice-chancellor his subsequent organization of the university's financial help for the king branded him more openly as Parliament's enemy. Having fled to his diocese, he was soon made aware that the outbreak of war had ruined his chances of effective rule.

Yet in these impossible circumstances he remained more than a shadow bishop. He sustained the rudiments of diocesan administration, maintained

---

108. Thus, Wood, *Athenae*, iii. 269. The epitaph is printed in the original Latin in A. Wood, *Historia et Antiquitates Universitatis Oxoniensis*, 2 vols. (Oxford, 1674), ii. 99, and in Prince, *Worthies*, 661.

friendly relations with many of his clergy, and did what he could for the king's cause. In personal terms the war cost him much. He lost his two remaining sons and, in 1646, his bishopric, which left him with barely the means to subsist. In his last year poverty proved to be his main affliction. But compensation came from his daughters and their families for whom felt a deep affection and a deep spiritual concern, and probably from that more shadowy presence, Mary Reynell, the 'beloved wife' of his will, to whom he left the bulk of his estate and, in the *Doctrine of Conscience*, spiritual counsel. Intellectual sustenance and satisfaction, and perhaps some financial profit, came from his writings. Although they involved some recycling of old material, most notably in the *Viginti-duae Lectiones*, his publications constituted the main achievement of his later years, embodying the two causes to which he had given much of his life: the defence of the Church of England and its doctrines, and the instruction of the young. The substance of these later works linked back to his time as regius professor and indeed to his still earlier career as a young tutor more than forty years before. Despite the upheavals brought by the Civil War, there were continuities here; and not all was loss.

12

John Prideaux: Life and Afterlife

Throughout his career Prideaux stood out as the most articulate defender of what had been the mainstream beliefs of the Elizabethan and Jacobean church at a time when those beliefs seemed increasingly under threat. This constitutes his chief but by no means his only claim to fame. Resting both on his theological expertise and his university position, his role set him apart from the extremes of radical puritanism on the one side and of the neo-popery which many contemporaries, misguidedly but understandably, saw in Arminianism on the other. In part his defence was that of structures—of the authority of the church vested in synods and other ecclesiastical assemblies, of the *iure divino* authority of its bishops, of the Prayer Book which provided its liturgy, and of the Articles and Homilies which gave legal definition to its beliefs. Perhaps more centrally, that defence was also one of doctrine and especially of the Calvinist doctrine of grace. Prideaux's exposition of the theology of grace, one of his major intellectual achievements, came in the nine Act lectures which he delivered between 1616 and 1624. Here he set his own mark on his doctrinal inheritance by moderating the rigid predestinarian doctrines of fellow Calvinists and puritans through his argument that predestination, dependent on God's foreknowledge, was compatible with a degree of free will.[1] More conventional, but part and parcel of the same territory, was his violent hostility to Catholics and to the papacy, and his condemnation of their church for its gross perversion of its primitive ideals, its irrational beliefs, and its leaders' claimed superiority to secular rulers, with all that claim's subversive implications. This was the common currency of anti-Catholic polemic shared by almost all the divines of the early seventeenth-century Church of England, and Prideaux's views

---

1. Above, 43–6.

Between Scholarship and Church Politics: The Lives of John Prideaux, 1578–1650. John Maddicott, Oxford University Press. © John Maddicott 2022. DOI: 10.1093/oso/9780192896100.003.0012

were remarkable only for the forcefulness with which they were expressed. If Rome was nevertheless a true church, as both Prideaux and his friend Joseph Hall believed, it remained one which was irredeemably corrupt.

Especially notable in both Prideaux's theology and in his related ecclesiology was his consistency. Though muted by the two decrees of 1626 and 1628 in restraint of preaching and publishing, and by Laud's oversight of the university, his opinions varied little throughout his long life. Two of the theses which he defended for his BD in 1612—that grace sufficient was not conceded to all and that the sacraments did not confer grace through human action (*ex opere operato*)—were reasserted in his Act lecture of 1618 and reiterated more than twenty years later in his *Fasciculus Controversiarum Theologicarum* of 1649.[2] Whatever modifications he may have introduced into the Calvinist doctrine of predestination, the views of the retired bishop did not deviate by much from those of the young fellow of Exeter. Christopher Potter, provost of Queen's, speculated in 1631 that Prideaux would have retracted his anti-Arminian views had he been able in all honesty to do so (and as Potter himself was to do);[3] and certainly it might have been to his advantage to change course and put himself in line for a bishopric. But given the adamantine nature of his stated beliefs and the intellectual capital invested in them, it seems highly unlikely that he would have even contemplated such a volte-face. Against the puritans and 'their extemporary brabbling and brawling against our set formes of prayer', he remained, too, a consistent promoter of the Prayer Book. In the 1640s, when the Prayer Book came under open attack before being superseded altogether, his attachment to this 'chain of pearl' became almost as much emotional as doctrinal or liturgical.[4]

But it was not only as a theologian and polemicist that Prideaux stood out. His parallel achievements as college head, teacher, and writer for undergraduates have generally been neglected, or at least underestimated, by comparison with his work as a scholar-theologian. Yet this other role was one which occupied much of his time and which brought him a renown acknowledged by such near contemporaries as David Lloyd and, especially, Anthony Wood. His efficient management of his College, which saw its numbers rise, its income grow, and its buildings magnificently replaced or

2. Clark, *Register*, i. 209; *VDL*, 32–44; Prideaux, *Fasciculus*, 273–81.
3. *Crosfield's Diary*, ed. Boas, 51; Hegarty, 'Potter'; above, 257–8.
4. 'Hezechiah's Sicknesse', in *CS*, 13; Hampton, '*Mera chimaera*', 288, 291–3; above, 232, 369.

renewed, was one of the most notable features of his whole career. It was perturbed only twice, by the claims of William Lord Petre between 1613 and 1618, successfully seen off thanks to Prideaux's close relationship with the earl of Pembroke, and by the contested fellowship election of 1631. The latter marked the sole occasion when Prideaux is known to have fallen out with the fellowship and the sole dispute which required the intervention of the Visitor, by contrast with the frequent visitatorial interventions seen at some other colleges. In general Prideaux's adroit leadership, and the pride taken by fellows such as Nathanael Carpenter in having so distinguished a head, made him the captain of a happy ship.[5]

Prideaux's local activities in his College had a wider bearing on matters of church and state. This was especially true of his teaching. In opening Exeter as an hospitable base for foreign scholars and students who came to enjoy the stimulus of his company and instruction, he strengthened the links of the English church with the great centres of Continental Protestantism, extended the influence of his teaching beyond Oxford, and enhanced his own place in the European republic of letters. His parallel reputation as a teacher of English undergraduates, vouched for by the long lists of pupils assigned to him in his early days as a tutor, is easy to overlook, since the effects of his teaching left few material traces and his tutorial work was largely abandoned after he became rector. If he retained his elite and aristocratic pupils—the Whartons, the Herberts, and others—it was not only because it was socially appropriate for these young nobles to be taught by the celebrated head of their College, but also because Prideaux himself saw his teaching as helping to mould the culture and conduct of the country's future governors. The sentiments which he voiced in speaking to those incepting in theology in 1637—that the curriculum which they studied was a means to their own salvation and to the profit of the church, the commonwealth, and the academy—applied as much to those destined for more secular careers in what could be regarded as public service. Wood said much the same: by his zeal 'in appointing industrious and careful tutors . . . many were fitted to do service in the church and state'.[6] And for all his pupils, sons of plebeians, aristocrats, future clerics, and schoolmasters, he made provision through his textbooks—on elementary Greek, on

---

5. Above, 172. For visitatorial interventions at other colleges, see, e.g., Green, *Commonwealth of Lincoln College*, 169–73; Charles-Edwards and Reid, *Corpus Christi College*, 154–60.
6. *VDL*, 350; Wood, *Athenae*, iii. 266.

syllogisms and logic, and on the encyclopedic miscellany of subjects covered in his *Hypomnemata*, specifically dedicated to 'the neophytes of Exeter College'. He took undergraduates and undergraduate teaching seriously.

What lay behind the rising curve of achievement which took Prideaux from a Devonshire farm to the headship of his College, the regius chair of divinity, and a reputation as perhaps the outstanding theologian of his generation? In the first place, he owed much to good fortune and to the patronage which was its central component. A neighbour, Lady Fowell, had spotted his boyhood talents and paid for his schooling; his Devonian origins had taken him to Devon's own college, where Thomas Holland, another sharp-eyed talent spotter, had given him the chance to excel; Prince Henry had adopted him as a fellow-Calvinist protégé and had brought him his rectorship; King James had made him a royal chaplain, given him the opportunity to shine in answering Eudaemon-Joannes's attack on Casaubon, and subsequently appointed him to the regius chair; and the earl of Pembroke, Oxford's chancellor and Prideaux's sympathetic co-religionist, had nominated him to the vice-chancellorship and supported him more generally. His time as an undergraduate and junior fellow in Holland's Exeter had been particularly important for his future. It placed him at a rising college, brought him into everyday contact with one of the most eminent biblical scholars of the age, and imbued him with the high Calvinist and anti-Catholic doctrines which were to govern his future religious life. With the possible exception of Corpus Christi under its more radically puritan and even more learned head, John Rainolds (Holland's rival for the regius chair in 1589), there could have been no more suitable institution for Prideaux's grounding in scholarship and learning.

Throughout this time, and into his later life, Prideaux's connections with the court may have been particularly important both for his private advancement and for his standing in the church. These connections extended beyond his royal chaplaincy, though it must have been through the court-based chaplaincy that they were forged, and through the Lord Chamberlain, the earl of Pembroke, in charge of court procedures, that they were maintained. Pembroke was by no means his only friend in high places. According to Prideaux's own account, it was the intervention of Sir Thomas Edmondes, treasurer of the household and privy councillor, which brought him his Salisbury prebend in 1620, and the backing of an even greater man, Lord Chancellor Bacon, which gained him the vicarage of Chalgrove in the same year. Nearly twenty years later, his medallion image associated him with a group of court figures portrayed by the French medallist Claude Warin, while in the mid-1640s it was Charles I's secretary, Sir Philip Warwick, who listened to and recorded his opinions of Laud.[7] His links with the court, renewed annually through his month's service as chaplain, reinforced the consistent royalism which was another feature of his public life. Despite his belief that after Charles I's early years the church which the king headed had deviated from 'the doctrine, worship and discipline' established in earlier reigns, and despite the humiliating reprimand which he received from Charles at his Woodstock 'trial' in 1631, his allegiance was never in doubt. In 1642 it was to play a central part in rallying the university's support for the king.

Prideaux's career evinced a willingness to serve and to oblige—whether Prince Henry, King James, or the earl of Pembroke—which stood him in good stead. From the start, he was ambitious, keen to do well, and to advance himself, all aspirations shown in his young man's letter to Kenelm Carter.[8] But he would not have attracted the attention of his patrons and superiors had it not also been for his personal qualities, both native and acquired. These comprised intellectual grasp, a quick understanding, an extraordinary knowledge of books, and powers of argument honed initially by the university arts course and then by undergraduate teaching, by years of moderating disputations as tutor and regius professor, and by the polemical skills burnished through his Act lectures. These powers were underlain by an exceptional capacity for hard work best evidenced by his concurrent mastery of several different roles—in some years, head of house, regius professor, and vice-chancellor. The last two 'eminent places', wrote Pembroke in 1621, when Prideaux held both, were 'each of them of waight inoughe to require a whole man'. According to Lloyd, three men in his College 'lost their own lives by endeavoring to equal his industry', a tall story which embodied a figurative truth.[9] All these assets contributed to his strengths as an *érudit*, controversialist, and a leading Calvinist author. The number and distinction of his theological publications, which extended well beyond the massive *summa* of his *Viginti-Duae Lectiones*, contrasted strongly with the almost empty cupboard left by his one-time master and predecessor Thomas Holland—a scholar but no publisher.

---

7. TNA, SP 16/348, fo. 115; above, 301, 304, 320.
8. Above, 17–19.
9. Above, 74; Lloyd, *Memoires*, 157.

Prideaux had more humane qualities which are easy to overlook but which may also help to account for his appeal to patrons and others. His affection for his family, and to a lesser extent for his native county, provided powerful emotional ties. His mourning for his deceased 13-year old son John, 'his father's most precious gem', his attempt to credit another dead son, Matthias, with a book which he himself had written (the *Easy and Compendious Introduction*), his deep concern for the spiritual welfare of the two final survivors among his daughters, seen in the *Euchologia* which he wrote for them, were all testimonies to the intensity of his family relationships. Both paterfamilias and 'Anglo-Devonian',[10] he had other interests besides those which gave him his place in the world of learning and which commended him to posterity. In his sermons he sometimes showed the same humane and benevolent spirit, setting aside the complex austerities of his lectures to speak simply and in movingly epigrammatic ways. 'All the long art of divinity is comprised in this one short word love,' he said in a sermon of 1615 which combined uncharacteristic pithiness with moral weight.[11] His charitable ideals were exemplified even his non-religious writings, most notably perhaps in the great gallimaufry of his *Hypomnemata*: a husband should hold his wife dear above all others; a wife who errs should be treated with gentleness rather than severity; a son should receive an allowance from his father, just as a daughter receives a dowry; children should support their parents in their old age.[12] What little we know of his private conduct conveys the same impression of compassionate liberality. His relief of the poor, 'which he said he was bound to do as they were God's image', was no doubt accurately reported by David Lloyd and Thomas Fuller ('his constant charity to those in want'), but it was also a cliché in the public story of any Christian life.[13] His more targeted generosity towards his impoverished Goodwin relatives, 'to the almost undoing of my selfe and myne', including the passing on of one of his benefices, he revealed only reluctantly, while the records of his small gifts to indigent undergraduates were jotted down in the privacy of his notebook. His feelings for others were reciprocated, most strikingly perhaps in the comments of the foreign scholars and students whom he entertained and instructed at Exeter, so that John Combachius could write of 'the love

---

10. Prideaux, *Tyrocinium*, sig. A3r; above, 89–90.
11. Prideaux, *Christs counsell for ending law cases*, 5.
12. Prideaux, *Hypomnemata*, 305, 307, 359.
13. Lloyd, *Memoires*, 537; T. Fuller, *History of the Worthies of England*, ed. P. A. Nuttall, 3 vols. (1840), i. 408.

and friendship which most firmly bind us' and Matthias Pasor of the favour and love he had enjoyed from Prideaux and other Exeter friends.[14]

Equally appealing as a mark of his human qualities was his sense of humour (though it might now be thought a rather juvenile one). His skill at punning, recorded by many contemporaries, reflected in a minor key the same verbal dexterity which he showed as a disputant and as a master of syllogisms. Of the notorious Thomas Anian, president of Corpus Christi, '"They say some of us doctors are cuckolds; is *Any one* here?", saith Dr Prideaux at a meeting of the doctors'—alluding rather daringly to Anian's wife, who was reputedly the mistress of John Williams, bishop of Lincoln.[15] Just occasionally we can catch the humour in his tone of voice. 'Jack Conant will have my place', he said about the precociously clever John Conant, later fellow and (as Prideaux had jokingly predicted) rector of Exeter and regius professor of divinity.[16] Despite his fierce devotion to his studies, he was human enough too to have time for recreations. His own were archery and bowls, the former, he thought, particularly suitable for academics. With his own pleasures in mind, he must have planned the new bowling alley adjacent to the rector's lodgings which was a minor feature of Exeter's great rebuilding.[17] Out of sympathy with the joyless austerity of the more extreme puritans, it was not surprising that he should have given his support to the modest Sunday recreations proposed in the *Book of Sports;* nor did he object when some of the College's parishioners at Kidlington wanted to erect a maypole.[18]

Although Prideaux's personal qualities of affection, generosity, and good humour may have made for a certain charm of character and help to explain his attraction for those whom he served, he had some opposing tendencies. They were marked. Notoriously irascible and, on occasion, bullying, he was temperamentally averse to being crossed and liked to get his own way, especially in religious matters but also in secular ones. Those who felt the full force of his displeasure, often bitingly expressed, were mainly aspiring theologians defending their BD or DD theses at the Act—men such as Gilbert Sheldon or Christopher Potter, whose arguments either strayed

---

14. Above, 62, 116, 301–2.
15. Wood, *Life and Times*, i. 154. For other examples, see Boase, *Register*, ci; Conant, *Life of Conant*, 4; Wood, *Athenae*, iii. 55; 'Oratio XIII', 128, in *VDL*.
16. Conant, *Life of Conant*, 4.
17. Lloyd, *Memoires*, 537; Prideaux, *Hypomnemata*, 364; Boase, *Register*, 312, 313.
18. Above, 273–4; Heylin, *Examen Historicum*, 216–17.

too close to Rome or questioned the fundamental tenets of Calvinist belief, in most cases innocently enough, since the process of disputation necessarily involved taking sides either pro or con. The fierceness of his responses often left his juniors shaken and mortified. 'For the doctor was a better disputant than a preacher', wrote the biographer of Prideaux's enemy, Peter Heylyn, 'and to give him his due, a right learned man in his place of regius professor, yet withal so dogmatical in his points that he would not abide to be touched, much less contradicted.'[19]

Outside the schools his determination to override opposition was sometimes marked by a brazen lack of scruple. His attempts in 1627 to secure the parliamentary election of Pembroke's candidate and his own patron, Sir Thomas Edmondes, in the face of majority opinion within the university and in 1631 to secure the College election of his favoured candidates in the face of a majority of the fellows were both cases in point. Marked by his use of authority and office, whether as vice-chancellor or rector, to beat down opposition, both attempts were defeated. His detestation of Laud led him into several similar misjudgements, notably in backing the unworthy Philip Herbert against Laud in the cancellarial election of 1630, in captiously opposing the revised Laudian statutes of 1636, and in supporting Laud's enemy Nathanael Brent in the parliamentary election of 1640. Prideaux's disapproval of Laud's religious policies trumped all other considerations, even the manifest benefits which the chancellor's generosity and patronage had brought to the university. Both in the schools and in public life, personal animosities, in combination with an awareness of his own position and eminence, did something to tarnish his reputation. Nor was he always entirely honest in the decisions which he made. His approval for Chillingworth's *Religion of Protestants*, despite its Socinianizing tendencies and apparently in return for a favour given by Laud, together with the unconvincing reasons which he subsequently gave to justify his action, must surely have lain on his conscience. No more than any man was he a paragon of virtue.

Prideaux's career may seem to have ended in defeat; and no doubt it did seem so to him. By the time of his death, the stage had collapsed on which his achievements in the church and the academy had counted. His university had been subjected to a parliamentary visitation which had resulted in the expulsion of half of Exeter's fellows, including his close friend Henry

---

19. Above, 245–7; Barnard, *Theologo-historicus*, 112. Barnard's remark applied specifically to Prideaux's clash with Heylyn, but it had a wider applicability.

Tozer.[20] The Church of England had been overthrown, its head executed, its episcopate abolished, its wealth and buildings pillaged, and many of its ministers ousted from their livings. The monarchy which Prideaux had served for so long was gone. What was there to contemplate but 'the irreverent contempt, and worse than heathenish profaneness, that is fallen of late upon God's worship' and 'the dismal spectacle of this flourishing Commonwealth, so late famous among neighbor nations and now so ruinated'?[21] Prideaux himself had suffered too, losing his two remaining sons in the Civil War. Stripped of his livelihood and forced to sell many of his books, he had become dependent on the support of his family, who did their duty by him just as he had enjoined in his *Hypomnemata*.

Yet not all was loss. He had been a conscientious bishop and one who had, so far as was possible, stuck to his post through the turmoil of war. The tentative exercise of his powers as diocesan, the few ordinations which he was able to conduct, and the limited encouragement which he was able to give to his Worcestershire clergy all helped to keep the Church of England alive. His defence of Anglican episcopacy, both in his *Fasciculus* of 1649 and in his letter to John Robartes, provided a theological counterpart to his work on the ground.[22] The posthumous publication of new works and the reprinting of old ones bridged the Restoration of 1660 and contributed to the restoration of the church alongside that of the monarchy. His *Fasciculus* went into two new editions, in 1652 and 1664, the entirely new *Manuductio* was published in 1657, and his letter to Robartes in 1660. His reputation survived his death and indeed grew in the dismal circumstances of the 1650s and in the more favourable post-Restoration years. 'After the funeral rites he lives in his writings,' wrote an anonymous versifier.[23] There were good reasons to remember him. Friends, allies, and memorialists saw him as the pursuer and prosecutor of Arminians, Socinians, and papists, and the enemy of the schismatics who had torn the church apart. 'Where shall our bleeding church a champion gain / to grasp with heresie Or to maintain/ her conflict with the devil?' asked another anonymous poet in a set of 'Obsequies', with the sects of the interregnum as the devil in mind. He was 'the great Atlas of religion', 'that pious arch whereon the building stood'.[24] To the preacher of his funeral

---

20. *Register of the Visitors*, ed. Burrows, lxxv, cxii, 499–501.
21. Prideaux, *Euchologia* (1656), 181, 184; above, 368–9.
22. Cf. Hampton, '*Mera chimaera*', 288–90.
23. Fuller, *Worthies*, i. 408.
24. 'Obsequies', in J. Cleveland, *Poems* (1669). This poem is no longer ascribed to Cleveland.

oration, he had refuted heresies, struck out against the Jesuits, and waged war against Cardinal Bellarmine;[25] to David Lloyd, he was the British Hercules, who had fought against Arminians and Socinians; while Thomas Barlow, writing anonymously in the preface to Prideaux's *Manuductio*, saw him as the destroyer of the hydra of Pelagianism (i.e. Arminianism) and Socinianism.[26]

Barlow was almost certainly a key figure in the preservation of Prideaux's teaching and reputation. As a fellow of Queen's from 1633, he had been a friend of his older colleague, the donee of a copy of Prideaux's *Hypomnemata* in 1648, and a purchaser at the sale of his library. A Calvinist Episcopalian, devoted to the Prayer Book, 'one of the most consistently apoplectic anti-Papists of his age', and an outstanding scholar and teacher, in his beliefs and interests he was perhaps closer than any man to Prideaux.[27] He played a leading role in the efflorescence of Calvinism in post-Restoration Oxford and in the church in general; and the vigorous survival of Calvinist doctrine, together with the continuing threat from Socinianism, against which Barlow contended in the 1660s and 1670s, does much to explain the continuing relevance of Prideaux's work and example.[28] Nor was it only in England that Prideaux's reputation was maintained, almost as one of the fathers of the Reformed church. 'As his learning was admired by foreigners, Sext. Amama, Rivet and others,' wrote Wood, 'so were his books, especially those written in Latin.' Lloyd goes so far as to say that 'his reputation [was] greater abroad among foreign ministers than at home'.[29] It was certainly the case that he had been able to attract foreign students and scholars to Exeter from 1610 onwards, before any of his major publications; and it was a further indication of his later standing on the Continent that the most complete edition of his works was published at Zurich in 1672 under the editorship of Samuel Maresius, professor of theology at Groningen and, like Prideaux (whom Maresius may have met during a visit to Oxford in 1625), an avowed enemy of Catholics, Arminians, and Socinians.[30] No comparable edition was ever published in England.

25. Bodl. MS Jones 56, fos. 21r–v.
26. Lloyd, *Memoires*, 538; Prideaux, *Manuductio*, sig. A2v. For Barlow's authorship of this preface, see Wood, *Athenae*, iii. 268; Madan, iii. 69; Poole, 'Barlow's Books', 15 n. 5.
27. Above, 221, 364; Poole, 'Barlow's Books', 17 n. 14, 33; Spurr, 'Barlow', *ODNB*.
28. *HUO*, iv. 593, 601–4, 605, 607–8; Hampton, *Anti-Arminians*, 10–11, 80, 127, and *passim*.
29. Wood, *Athenae*, iii. 267; Lloyd, *Memoires*, 538.
30. J. Prideaux, *Opera Theologica quae Latine extant omnia . . . antehac sparsim edita nunc vero collecta* (Zurich, 1672). This edition comprised all Prideaux's Act lectures, *orations*, and *conciones*, first published in *VDL*, together with his *Fasciculus*, his *Conciliorum Synopsis*, and his *Syntagma*. For Maresius, see Wood, *Athenae*, iii. 446, 595 n. 2.

Other than in the pages of Wood and Prince, Prideaux's reputation did not last much beyond this point. None of his works was reprinted in England after 1672, and in that year only the insubstantial *Synopsis of Councels* and his history textbook, the *Easy and Compendious Introduction*, published together as a single volume.[31] Circumstances did not favour his continuing remembrance. Prideaux's heyday had lain in a period when his talents both as a theologian and a college head could be deployed to best effect. His sermons and his dense and elaborate Act lectures defending orthodox religion and attacking those whom he saw as its enemies—Catholics, Remonstrants, Arminians, Socinians—had been delivered, and subsequently published, at a time when his opinions had practical and polemical value and attracted respect, while his success as a pedagogue had come during the relatively short period between about 1570 and 1660 when English upper-class society set a high value on the humanistic ideals of culture, learning, and intellect which a university education was thought to provide. These social desiderata Prideaux, his college and its tutors, had been able to satisfy—to judge by Exeter's rising numbers and high reputation, more so than most colleges.

But in the years between about 1660 and 1680 less weight began to be set on all these values, theological as well as social. The public appetite declined for academic theology and its Latin literature, the branch of learning in which Prideaux had excelled, in preference for plainer and simpler works in English.[32] About the same time, a parallel cultural change saw a comparable decline in the importance attached to 'good letters'. As cultural ideals, politeness and the social graces began to replace mental training, erudition, and the discipline needed to pursue them.[33] A university education of the sort provided in Prideaux's Exeter gradually ceased to be seen as a desirable training for the sons of the nobility and gentry. A degree of frivolity set in. Part of the same pattern of change was a slackening of standards and discipline in some colleges, particularly at Exeter. It did not emerge immediately. John Conant, Prideaux's protégé and Hakewill's successor as rector from 1654 to 1660, was very much in his master's mould as a scholar-theologian and, as a head, greatly concerned with the quality of his College's tutors and their teaching. After the Civil War, wrote his son and biographer,

---

31. Madan, iii. 270.
32. Hampton, *Anti-Arminians*, 32–3.
33. *HUO*, iv. 233–8.

he recovered 'that ancient and wholesome discipline for which Exeter had been so famous under the government of Dr Holland and Dr Prideaux'.[34] But under his successor, Joseph Maynard, rector from 1662 to 1666, came a general breakdown. 'Debauched by a drunken governor', according to Wood, Exeter gained a new reputation for its rudeness and incivility. It is a minor but telling comment on Maynard that he breaks the succession of rectors—Holland, Prideaux, Hakewill, Conant—thought worthy of an entry in the Oxford Dictionary of National Biography. Nor did the long rule of Maynard's successor, Arthur Bury, rector from 1666 to 1690, do anything to restore the College's standing. It saw Bury in frequent conflict with the fellows, equally frequent interventions by the Visitor, and the rector's publication in 1690 of a scandalous book, The Naked Gospel, which took an anti-Trinitarian and neo-Socinian stance (and which would have horrified Prideaux). Between them, the examples of Maynard and Bury showed how hard it was to sustain a college's reputation beyond one or two exceptional generations.[35]

That after the Restoration Prideaux stood for an old regime which was in process of supersession does something to explain the fading of his reputation. It does not quite explain, however, why he was never the subject of a biography, beyond the summary lives produced by Fuller, Lloyd, Prince, and Wood, A good number of other men who had been his contemporaries as divines and scholars did find their biographers in the post-Restoration years. John Barwick's biography of Thomas Morton, bishop of Durham, was published in 1660; Isaak Walton's of Robert Sanderson, bishop of Lincoln (and Prideaux's successor as regius professor) in 1678; Richard Parr's of James Ussher, archbishop of Armagh, in 1686; and John Hacket's of John Williams, bishop of Lincoln and then archbishop of York, in 1693. Not only had all been bishops, but in three cases out of four, the biography had been the work of the bishop's chaplain. (Walton's life of Sanderson was the exception). It was also the case that all four had, like Prideaux, been conspicuous Calvinists and largely anti-Laudian. Belonging to the same genre, but, of course, belonging too to a very different camp, was Peter Heylyn's biography of Laud, Cyprianus Anglicus, published posthumously in 1668. It is easy to see why Prideaux attracted no similar attention. He had made his name as a university scholar and lived for most of his time as head of his College.

34. Conant, Life of Conant, 10–17.
35. Wood, Life and Times, i. 455, ii. 56; Stride, Exeter College, 70–9.

Heads of houses, living apparently quiet lives and comparatively uninvolved in politics (though neither was entirely true of Prideaux), almost never attracted biographers; John Conant's life of his father and namesake was an exception. Prideaux's subsequent time in office as bishop from 1641 to 1646 was too short and troubled to provide the material for a biography, nor did he have any single disciple or devoted chaplain who might have written one.

No revival of interest came in the mid-nineteenth century, when one might perhaps have been expected. There was no large-scale edition of Prideaux's works, an accolade accorded to his adversary William Laud and to his friends Joseph Hall and James Ussher.[36] The task of producing one evidently appealed to neither side in the Tractarian movement under whose influence so much historical work on the seventeenth-century church was carried through. That the majority of Prideaux's most important writings were in Latin and that no substantial collections of letters survived were further disincentives to an *opera omnia*. It was left to Montagu Burrows, Oxford historian and Chichele professor, to comment on Prideaux's unjustified disappearance from the historical stage. 'A Life of this remarkable man', he wrote in 1881, 'still remains a desideratum.'[37]

It is to be hoped that this desideratum has now been supplied.

---

36. *The Works of the Most Reverend Father in God William Laud, sometime Lord Archbishop of Canterbury*, ed. W. Scott and J. Bliss, 7 vols. (Oxford, 1847–60); *The Works of the Right Reverend Joseph Hall*, ed. P. Wynter, 10 vols. (1863); *The Whole Works of the Most Rev. James Ussher*, ed. C. R. Elrington and J. H. Todd, 17 vols. (Dublin, 1829–64).

37. *Register of the Visitors*, ed. Burrows, xviii.

Bibliography

MANUSCRIPT SOURCES

Bodleian Library, Oxford

Library Records d. 599	Bodleian Attendance Register, 1602–3
Library Records e. 544	Bodleian Entry Book, 1648–9
MS Aubrey 1	
MS Bodl. 594	Charges against Laud
MS Eng. Misc. e. 226	William Jones letter
MS Jones 17	Proceedings before the king, Woodstock, 1631
MS Jones 56	Prideaux's funeral oration
MS Nalson 13	
MS Rawl. D. 47	Daniel Featley letters
MS Rawl. D. 853	Hakewill, 'The Wedding Ring'
MS Rawl. D. 933	John Hoffmann's 'Liber Amicorum'
MS Sancroft 78	
MS Tanner 58	Resolution re religious toleration, 1647
MS Tanner 72–6	Samuel Ward letters
MS Tanner 142	Chelsea College papers
MS Twyne 17	Papers re Laudian Statutes
MS University College 153	Nathanael Carpenter's treatise on optics

Brasenose College, Oxford

MS B2 a. 38	Thomas Sixsmith letter

BRITISH LIBRARY

MS Harley 977	Student Notebook
MS Sloane 3827	Prideaux letter to Viscount Falkland

Coventry History Centre

BA/H/17/A79/36, 106, 108.   Correspondence re James Illedge

Devon Heritage Centre, Exeter

L. 184, 185	Exeter City Records
ZI/53/Box 9/2	Tuckfield Accounts

Exeter College Archives

A.I.1	Statutes
A.I.2.	Statutes
A.I.5	College Register, 1539–1619
A.I.6	College Register, 1619–1737
A.I.19	Statutes
A.I.22	Caution Book, 1629–86
A.II.9	Rector's Accounts, 1564–1639
A.II.10	Rector's Accounts, 1639–1734
A.III.9	Rector's Quarterly Accounts, 1614–27
A.III.10	Dividend Book, 1628–60
A.IV.9	Bursar's Accounts, 1587–1630
A.IV.10	Bursar's Accounts, 1631–1797.
A.IV.11	Liber Bursariatus
B.IV.16/2	Prideaux's Notebook.
BB/01–34	Buttery Books, 1593–1648.
C.II.4	Prideaux's Survey
C.IV.29	College Plans, by H. Hurst
E.V.5	Chapel Box
F.IV.7/2	Exeter College v. William Lord Petre
H.II.11	Tutor-Pupil Lists, 1606–30
H.III.11	Correspondence re buildings.
L.I.1	Rector Stinton's transcript of C.II.4
L.II.1	Visitor's Decrees
L.III.10	College History Box

Exeter College Library

MS 28	Grosseteste, *De libero arbitrio*
MS 285	'Pridaux Tironum Institutio'

Lambeth Palace Library

MS 943   Laud papers

The National Archives

PROB 11   Wills of George Hakewill, Thomas Martin,
                                John Peryam, John Prideaux, Henry Tozer
SP 16   State Papers, Domestic, Reign of Charles I.
STAC 8/4/10   Star Chamber Depositions

Nottingham University Library

MS Cl C 73, 84   Francis Cheynell letters

Oxford University Archives

Chancellor's Court Papers, 1642
OU Arch. Wills (Cozens-Ho.)
HO 235.000. Reel 002   Will of William Goodwin
NEP/supra/Reg. N   Register of Convocation, 1615–28
NEP/supra/Reg. R   Register of Convocation, 1628–40
NEP/supra/Reg. Sb   Register of Convocation, 1642–7
SEP/F/6–9, 11   Documents re the University's land purchase
                                from Exeter College.
SP 2   Matriculation Register, 1615–47
SP E/6/1   Lists of oath-takers, 1610
SP/F/40/8   Articles against Lord Pembroke

The Queen's College, Oxford

MS 390   Thomas Crosfield's Diary

Salisbury Cathedral Archives

DA/1/5/17   Prideaux's presentation to a prebend

Sheffield University Library

Hartlib Papers 2/2/41A,   Letters to Hartlib from John Dury, Constantine
5/20/1A–2B, 9/1/49B–50A   Adams, Thomas Smith, and from Dury to
15/6/18A–19B, 5/8/3A–4B   Prideaux.

Trinity College Library Dublin

MS 533/3   Consecration of Exeter College Chapel

Wiltshire and Swindon History Centre, Chippenham

MS 865/501   William Chafin letter

Worcestershire Archives, Worcester

Bredon Parish registers
6716.093.BA 2648,   Bishop Prideaux's Register
parcel 10 (ii)

PRINTED SOURCES

Academiae Oxoniensis Pietas erga Serenissimum et Potentissimum Jacobum (Oxford, 1603).

Acts and Ordinances of the Interregnum, 1642–1660, ed. C. H. Firth and R. S. Rait, 3 vols. (London, 1911).

Aeneas Silvi Senensis de Bohemorum Origine ac Gestis Historia (Solingen, 1624).

The Anglican Canons, ed. G. Bray (Church of England Rec. Soc., 6, 1998).

Arber, E., *A Transcript of the Registers of the Company of Stationers of London, 1554–1640*, 5 vols. (London, 1875–94).

Articles Agreed on in the Nationall Synode of the Reformed Churches of France (Oxford, 1623).

Aubrey, J., *Brief Lives*, ed. A. Clark, 2 vols. (Oxford, 1898).

Aubrey, J., *Brief Lives*, ed. K. Bennett, 2 vols. (Oxford, 2015).

Aubrey on Education, ed. J. E. Stephens (London, 1972).

A[ustin], S., *Austins Urania or, The Heavenly Muse* (London, 1629).

The Autobiography and Library of Thomas Hall B.D. (1610–1665), ed. D. Thomas (WHS, n.s., 26, 2015).

Bale, J., *Scriptorum Illustrium Maioris Brytanniae . . . Catalogus*, 2 vols. (Basle, 1557–9).

Barksdale, C., *Nympha Libethris, or, The Cotswold Muse* (London, 1651).

Barnard, J., *Theologo-historicus, or The True Life of the Most Reverend Divine and Excellent Historian Peter Heylin, D.D, Sub-dean of Westminster* (London, 1683).

Baxter, R., *Reliquiae Baxterianae* (London, 1696).

Boase, C. W., *Register of the Rector and Fellows . . . of Exeter College, Oxford* (Oxford, 1879).

Boase, C. W., *Registrum Collegii Exoniensis. Pars II: An Alphabetical Register of the Commoners of Exeter College, Oxford* (Oxford, 1894).

Boase, C. W., *Registrum Collegii Exoniensis: Register of the Rectors, Fellows and other Members on the Foundation of Exeter College, Oxford*, new edn (OHS, 27, 1894).

Bradley, T., *Elijah's Nunc Dimittis, or The Author's own Funerall Sermons* (York, 1669).

The British Delegation and the Synod of Dort (1618–1619), ed. A. Milton (Church of England Rec. Soc., 13, 2005).

Calamy E., *The Nonconformist's Memorial*, 2nd edn, 3 vols. (London, 1802).

Calendar of State Papers Domestic.

Calendar of State Papers, Venice, Vols. XXV, XXVI.

Carleton, G., *An Examination of those Things wherein the Author of the Late Appeale holdeth the Doctrines of the Pelagians and Arminians to be the Doctrines of the Church of England* (London, 1626).

Carolus Redux (Oxford, 1623).

Carpenter, N., *Achitophel, or The Picture of a Wicked Politician* (London, 1629).

Carpenter, N., *Chorazin and Bethsaida's Woe or Warning-peece* (London, 1633).

Carpenter, N., *Geographie Delineated Forth in Two Bookes*, 2nd edn (Oxford, 1635).

Charleton, W., *The Darknes of Atheism Dispelled by the Light of Nature* (London, 1652).

Chillingworth, W., *The Religion of Protestants* (Oxford, 1638).

Clarendon, E., *History of the Rebellion and Civil Wars in England*, ed. W. D. Macray, 6 vols. (Oxford, 1888).

Clarendon State Papers, 3 vols. (Oxford, 1773).

Clergy of the Church of England Database, https://theclergydatabase.org.uk.

Combachius, J., *Metaphysicorum*, 3rd edn (Oxford, 1633).

Conant, J., *The Life of the Reverend and Venerable John Conant, D.D.* (London, 1823).

The Constitutional Documents of the Puritan Revolution, 1625–1660, ed. S. R. Gardiner, 3rd edn (Oxford, 1906).

The Correspondence of Isaac Casaubon in England, ed. P. Botley and M. Vince, 4 vols. (Geneva, 2018).

The Correspondence of James Ussher, 1600–1656, ed. E. Boran, 3 vols. (Dublin, 2015).

The Correspondence of John Cosin, DD, ed. G. Ornsby, 2 vols. (Surtees Soc., 52, 55, 1868–72).

Day, M., *A Catalogue of the Printed Books in the Worcester Cathedral Library* (Oxford, 1880).

The Dean's Register of Oriel, 1446–1661, ed. G. C. Richards and H. E. Salter (Oxford, 1926).

Devon Taxes, 1581–1660, ed. T. L. Stoate (Almondsbury, 1988).

Diary and Correspondence of John Evelyn, FRS, ed. W. Bray, new edn, 4 vols. (London, 1857).

The Diary and Papers of Henry Townshend, 1640–1663, ed. S. Porter et al. (WHS, n.s., 25, 2014).

Diary of Francis Evans, Secretary to Bishop Lloyd, 1699–1706 (WHS, 1903).

Dugdale, W., *A Short View of the Late Troubles in England* (Oxford, 1681).

[Du Moulin, L.], *Vox Populi, Expressed in XVIII Motions to this Present Parliament for Reforming the Church of England* (London, 1641).

Epithalamia Oxoniensia (Oxford, 1625).

Eucharistica Oxoniensia (Oxford, 1641).

Eudaemon-Joannes, A., *Responsio ad Epistolam Isaaci Casauboni* (Cologne, 1613).

The Family Memoirs of the Rev. William Stukeley, M.D., ed. W. C. Lukis, 3 vols. (Surtees Soc., 1882–7).

Featley, D., *The Grand Sacrilege of the Church of Rome* (London, 1630).

Featley, J., *Featlaei Paliggenesia* (London, 1660).

Foster, J., *Alumni Oxonienses: The Members of the University of Oxford, 1500–1714*, 4 vols. (Oxford, 1891).

Fuller, T., *The Church History of Britain*, new edn, 3 vols. (London, 1837).

The Further Correspondence of William Laud, ed. K. Fincham (Church of England Rec. Soc., 23, 2018).

Gamon, H., *The Praise of a Godly Woman. A Sermon Preached at the Solemne Funerall of the Right Honourable Ladie, the Ladie Frances Roberts, at Lanhide-Rock Church in Cornwall, the tenth of August 1626* (London, 1627).

Gauden, J., *A Pillar of Gratitude humbly dedicated to the Glory of God* (London, 1661).

The Genuine Remains of that Learned Prelate Dr Thomas Barlow, late Lord Bishop of Lincoln (London, 1693).

Goffe, T., *Oratio Funebris habita in Ecclesia Cathedrali Christi Oxon in obitum viri omni aevo dignissimi Gulielmi Goodwin* (Oxford, 1620).

Goodwin, W., *A Sermon Preached before the Kings Most Excellent Maiestie at Woodstocke, Aug. 28. 1614* (Oxford, 1614).

Gray, T., *The Chronicle of Exeter, 1205–1722* (Exeter, 2005).

Hacket, J., *Scrinia Reserata* (London, 1693).

Hakewill, G., *An Apologie of the Power and Providence of God in the Government of the World* (Oxford, 1627).

Heylyn, P., *A Full Relation of Two Journeys: the One into the Main-land of France. The Other into some of the Adjacent Ilands* (London, 1656).

Heylyn, P., *Examen Historicum* (London, 1659).

Heylyn, P., *Cyprianus Anglicus, or, The History of the Life and Death of the Most Reverend and Renowned Prelate William, by Divine Providence Lord Archbishop of Canterbury* (London, 1668).

Heylyn, P., *Memorial of Bishop Waynflete* (Caxton Soc., 14, 1851).

Historical Manuscripts Commission, *12th Report*, Appendix IX (London, 1891).

Historical Manuscripts Commission, *Manuscripts of the Duke of Portland*, Vol. I (London, 1891).

Historical Manuscripts Commission, *14th Report*, Appendix VIII (London, 1895).

Historical Manuscripts Commission, *Records of the City of Exeter* (London, 1916).

Historical Manuscripts Commission, *De L'Isle and Dudley Manuscripts*, Vol. VI (London, 1966).

Hobson, M. G., and Salter, H. E., *Oxford Council Acts, 1626–1665* (OHS, 95, 1933).

Iusta Oxoniensium (London, 1612).

'John Howson's Answers to Archbishop Abbot's Accusations at his "Trial" before James I at Greenwich, 10 June 1615', ed. N. Cranfield and K. Fincham, in *Camden Miscellany*, 28 (Camden 4th ser., 34, 1987).

Jones, M., *A Catalogue of the French Medals in the British Museum*, 2 vols. (London, 1989).

The Journal of Sir Simonds D'Ewes from the Beginning of the Long Parliament to the Opening of the Trial of the Earl of Strafford, ed. W. Notestein (New Haven, CT, 1923).

The Journal of Sir Simonds D'Ewes, from the First Recess of the Long Parliament to the Withdrawal of King Charles from London, ed. W. H. Coates (New Haven, CT, 1942).

Kenyon, J. P., *The Stuart Constitution, 1603–1688* (Cambridge, 1966).

Kilbye, R., *A Sermon Preached in Saint Maries Church in Oxford March 26. 1612 at the Funerall of Thomas Holland* (Oxford, 1613).

Le Neve, J., *Fasti Ecclesiae Anglicanae, 1541–1857*, comp. J. Horn. Vol. VI: *Salisbury* (London, 1986).

Le Neve, J., Vol. VII: *Ely, Norwich, Westminster and Worcester Dioceses* ((London, 1992).

Le Neve, J., Vol. VIII: *Bristol, Gloucester, Oxford and Peterborough Dioceses* (London, 1996).

Letters Addressed to Thomas James, First Keeper of Bodley's Library, ed. G. W. Wheeler (Oxford, 1933).

The Letters and Journals of Robert Baillie, A.M., M.DC.XXXVII–M.DC.LXII, ed. D. Laing, 3 vols. (Edinburgh, 1841–3).

The Letters of John Chamberlain, ed. N. Egbert McClure, 2 vols. (Philadelphia, PA, 1939).

'*A Library for Younger Schollers*' Compiled by an English Scholar Priest about 1655, ed. A. de Jordy and H. F. Fletcher (Urbana, IL, 1961).

The Life and Times of Anthony Wood, Antiquary of Oxford, 1632–1695, described by himself, ed. A. Clark, 5 vols. (OHS, 19, 21, 26, 30, 40, 1891–1900).

Lloyd, D., *Memoires of the Lives, Actions, Sufferings and Deaths of those Noble, Reverend and Excellent Personages that suffered by Death, Sequestration, Decimation or Otherwise for the Protestant Religion* (London, 1668).

Lords Journals.

Ludovici Cappelli S. Theologiae in Academia olim Salmuriensi Professoris Commentarii et Notae Criticae in Vetus Testamentum (Amsterdam, 1689).

Lydius, B., *Waldensia, id est Conservatio Verae Ecclesiae* (Rotterdam, 1622).

Middleton, Thomas, 'The Black Booke', in *Thomas Middleton: The Collected Works*, ed. G. Taylor and J. Lavagnino (Oxford, 2007).

The Minutes and Papers of the Westminster Assembly, 1643–1652, ed. C. van Dixhoorn, 5 vols. (Oxford, 2012).

Montague, R., *Appello Caesarem. A Iust Appeale from Two Uniust Reformers* (London, 1625).

Nelson, R., *The Life of George Bull, Late Lord Bishop of St David's*, 2nd edn (Oxford, 1714).

Oliver, G., 'Letter of John Prideaux', *Devon and Cornwall Notes and Gleanings*, 5 (1892).

Oxford Quarter Sessions Order Book, 1614–1637, ed. R. Blades (OHS, n.s., 29, 2009).

Oxfordshire and North Berkshire Protestation Returns and Tax Assessments, 1641–42, ed. J. Gibson (Oxfordshire Rec. Soc., 59, 1994).

Oxford University Statutes, trans. G. R. M. Ward, 2 vols. (London, 1845).

Parentalia in Piam Memoriam Reverendi et Clarissimi D. Matthiae Pasoris . . . Vita Matthiae Pasoris ab hoc ipsomet vivo plenius consignata (Groningen, 1658).

Parr, R., *The Life of the Most Reverend Father in God, James Usher Late Lord Archbishop of Armagh* (London, 1686).

Peck, R., *Christs Watch-word* (London, 1635).

Penton, S., *The Guardian's Instruction*, ed. H. H. Sturmer (London, 1897).

Perrin, J. P., *Luther's Fore-runners, or a Cloud of Witnesses deposing for the Protestant Faith*, trans. S. Lennard (London, 1624).

Preston, J., *A Sermon Preached at the Funerall of Mr. Josiah Reynel Esquire, the 13. of August 1614, in East Ogwell in Devon* (London, 1615).

Preston, J., *The Patriarchs Portion, or The Saints Best Day. Deliverd in a Sermon at the Funerall of Sir Thomas Reynell of Ogwell in Devon, Knight. Aprill 16. 1618.* (London, 1619).

Price, D., *Praelium & Praemium* (Oxford, 1608).

Price, D., *Prince Henry His First Anniversary* (Oxford, 1613).

Prideaux, J., *Tabulæ ad Grammatica Graeca Introductoriæ* (Oxford, 1607).

Prideaux, J., *Castigatio Cuiusdam Circulatoris qui R. P.Andream Eudaemon-Johannem Cydonum e Societate Jesu seipsum nuncupat* (Oxford, 1614).

Prideaux, J., *Ephesus Backsliding Considered and Applyed to these Times in a Sermon Preached at Oxford, in St Maries the tenth of July, being the Act Sunday 1614* (Oxford, 1614).

Prideaux, J., *Christs Counsell for ending Law Cases as it hath been Delivered in Two Sermons upon the 25th verse of the 5th of Mathew* (Oxford, 1615).

Prideaux, J., *Eight Sermons, Preached by John Prideaux, Doctor of Divinity, Regius Professor, Vice-Chancellor of the University of Oxford and Rector of Exceter Colledge* (London, 1621).

Prideaux, J., *Alloquium Serenissimo Regi Jacobo Woodstochiae habitum 24 Augusti. Anno 1624* (Oxford, 1624).

Prideaux, J., *Lectiones Novem de Totidem Religionis Capitibus praecipue hoc tempore controversis prout publice habebantur Oxoniae in Vesperiis* (Oxford, 1625).

Prideaux, J., *Perez-Uzzah: or The Breach of Uzzah as it was Delivered in a Sermon before His Majesty at Woodstock August the 24 Anno 1624* (Oxford, 1625).

Prideaux, J., *A Sermon Preached on the fifth of October 1624: at the Consecration of St James Chappel in Exceter Colledge* (Oxford, 1625).

Prideaux, J., *Concio habita Oxoniae ad Artium Baccaulaureos in die Cinerum Feb. 22 1626* (Oxford, 1626).

Prideaux, J., *Lectiones Decem* (Oxford, 1626).

Prideaux, J., *Orationes Novem Inaugurales de Totidem Theologiae Apicibus, scitu non indignis, prout in Promotione Doctorum Oxoniae publice proponebantur in Comitiis* (Oxford, 1626).

Prideaux, J., *Tyrocinium ad Syllogismum* (Oxford, 1629).

Prideaux, J., *The Doctrine of the Sabbath* (London, 1634).

Prideaux, J., *Certaine Sermons Preached by John Prideaux* (Oxford, 1637).

Prideaux, J., *Conciones Sex ad Artium Baccalaureos Habitae* (Oxford, 1648).

Prideaux, J., *Hypomnemata, Logica, Rhetorica, Physica, Metaphysica, Pneumatica, Ethica, Politica, Oeconomica* (Oxford, [1648]).

Prideaux, J., *XIII Orationes Inaugurales de Totidem Theologicae Apicibus* (Oxford, 1648).

Prideaux, J., *Viginti-duae Lectiones de Totidem Religionis Capitibus praecipue hoc tempore controversis* (Oxford, 1648).

Prideaux, J., *Fasciculus Controversiarum Theologicarum ad Juniorum Captum* (Oxford, 1649).

Prideaux, J., *A Synopsis of Councels* (Oxford, 1654).

Prideaux, J., *Euchologia: or, The Doctrine of Practical Praying* (London, 1655).

Prideaux, J., *Synedesilogia [Συνειδησιλογία], or The Doctrine of Conscience* (London, 1656).

Prideaux, J., *Manuductio ad Theologiam Polemicam* (Oxford, 1657).

Prideaux, J., *Reverendi in Christo Patris Joannis Prideaux D. Episcopi Vigorniensis ad Nobilissimum Dominum D. Joannem Roberts, Baronem Truro, de Episcopatu Epistola* (London, 1660).

Prideaux, M., *An Easy and Compendious Introduction for Reading All Sorts of Histories* (Oxford, 1648).

Prince, J., *Danmonii Orientales Illustres, or The Worthies of Devon*, new edn (London, 1810).

Proceedings in Parliament, 1625, ed. M. Jansson and W. B. Bidwell (New Haven, CT, 1987).

Proceedings in Parliament, 1626, ed. M. Jansson and B. Bidwell, 4 vols. (New Haven, CT, 1991–6).

Proceedings in the Opening Session of the Long Parliament: House of Commons, ed. M. Jansson. Vol. 6: *19 July–9 September 1641* (Rochester, NY, 2004).

Proceedings of the Short Parliament of 1640, ed. E. S. Cope and W. H. Coates (Camden, 4th ser., 19, 1977).

Prynne, W., *Canterburies Doome* (London, 1646).

The Register of Admissions to Gray's Inn, 1521–1889, comp. J. Foster (London, 1889).

Register of the University of Oxford. Vol. II: *1571–1622*, ed. A. Clark, 4 parts (OHS, 10–14, 1887–9).

The Register of the Visitors of the University of Oxford, 1647–1658, ed. M. Burrows (Camden Soc., 1881).

Registrum Annalium Collegii Mertonensis, 1567–1603, ed. J. M. Fletcher (OHS, n.s., 24, 1976).

Rushworth, J., *Historical Collections*, Vol. III (London, 1691).

Salter, H. E., *Oxford City Properties* (Oxford, 1926).

Salter, H. E., *Oxford Council Acts, 1583–1626* (Oxford, 1928).

Sanderson, R., *XXXV Sermons*, 7th edn (London, 1681).

Scultetus, A., *George Abbott. Explicatio Sex Illustrium Quaestionum . . . Oxoniae anno 1597 in Schola Theologica proposita, ibidem edita et nunc primum in Germania recusa* (Frankfurt, 1616).

The Short Parliament (1640) Diary of Sir Thomas Aston, ed. J. D. Maltby (Camden 4th ser., 35, 1988).

Special Passages [a newsletter], nos. 1 and 7, September 1642 (London, 1642).

The Statutes of Exeter College, Oxford (London, 1855).

Statutes of the University of Oxford Codified in the Year 1636, under the Authority of Archbp. Laud, ed. J. Griffiths (Oxford, 1888).

Stuart Dynastic Policy and Religious Politics, 1621–1625, ed. M. Questier (Camden 5th ser., 34, 2009).

The Theological Works of the Learned Dr Pocock, ed. L. Twells, 2 vols. (London, 1740).

Thomson, R. M., *A Descriptive Catalogue of the Medieval Manuscripts in Worcester Cathedral Library* (Cambridge, 2001).

Tozer, H., *Directions for a Godly Life: Especially for Communicating at the Lord's Table* (Oxford, 1628).

Tozer, H., *A Christian Amendment Delivered in a Sermon on New-Yeares Day 1631 in St Martines Church in Oxford* (Oxford, 1633).

Tozer, H., *Christian Wisdome, or the Excellency, Forms and Right Meanes of True Wisdome* (Oxford, 1639).

Turner, W., *A Compleat History of the Most Remarkable Providences both of Judgement and Mercy which have Hapned in this Present Age*, 2 vols. (London, 1697).

Vivian, J. L., *The Visitations of the County of Devon* (Exeter, 1895).

Walker, E., *Historical Discourses . . . together with Perfect Copies of all the Votes, Letters, Proposals, and Answers relating unto and that passed in the Treaty held at Newport* (London, 1705).

Walker, J., *The Sufferings of the Clergy* (London, 1714).

Warner, G. F., and Gilson, J. P., *Catalogue of Manuscripts in the Old Royal and King's Collections.* Vol. I: *Royal MSS 1.A.1 to 11.E.XI* (London, 1921).

Warwick, P., *Memoires of the Reign of King Charles I*, 3rd edn (London, 1703).

Watson, A. G., *A Descriptive Catalogue of the Medieval Manuscripts of Exeter College, Oxford* (Oxford, 2000).

Wood, A., *Historia et Antiquitates Universitatis Oxoniensis*, 2 vols. (Oxford, 1674).

Wood, A., *The History and Antiquities of the Colleges and Halls in the University of Oxford*, ed. J. Gutch, 2 vols. (Oxford, 1786–90).

Wood, A., *The History and Antiquities of the University of Oxford now first published in English by John Gutch*, 3 vols. (Oxford, 1792–6).

Wood, A., *Athenae Oxonienses*, 3rd edn, ed. P. Bliss, 4 vols. (London, 1813–20).

Wood, A., *The Fasti*, in Wood, *Athenae*, Vols. 2 and 4.

Wood, A., *Survey of the Antiquities of the City of Oxford*, ed. A. Clark, 3 vols. (OHS, 15, 17, 37, 1889–99).

Woodstock Chamberlains' Accounts, 1609–50, ed. M. Maslen (Oxfordshire Rec. Soc., 58, 1993).

The Works of Joseph Mede, ed. J. Worthington, 4th edn (London, 1677).

The Works of the Most Reverend Father in God William Laud, sometime Lord Archbishop of Canterbury, ed. W. Scott and J. Bliss, 7 vols. (Oxford, 1847–60).

The Works of the Right Reverend Joseph Hall, ed. P. Wynter, 10 vols. (London, 1863).

SECONDARY SOURCES

Adams [formerly Krapp], R., Review of Trevor-Roper, *Catholics, Anglicans and Puritans*, in *New York Review of Books*, 14 April 1988.

Adamson, J., *The Noble Revolt: The Overthrow of Charles I* (London, 2007).

Allen, E., 'Goade [Goad], Thomas (1576–1638), theologian', *ODNB*.

Atherton, I., 'Pye, Sir Walter (bap.1571, d.1635), lawyer', *ODNB*.

Atkin, M., *The Civil War in Worcestershire* (Stroud, 1995).

Ball, B. W., 'Byfield, Nicholas (1578/9–1622), Church of England clergyman and religious writer', *ODNB*.

Barnes, S. J. et al., *Van Dyck: A Complete Catalogue of the Paintings* (New Haven, CT, 2004).

Baron, S. A., 'Nicholas, Sir Edward (1593–1669), government official', *ODNB*.

Barton, J., *A History of the Bible* (London, 2019).

Beddard, R. A., 'Sheldon and Anglican Recovery', *The Historical Journal*, 19 (1976).

Benedict, J., 'Carpenter, Nathanael (1589–1628), Church of England clergyman and philosopher', *ODNB*.

Benedict, J., 'Carpenter, Richard (1575–1627), Church of England clergyman', *ODNB*.

Binns, J. W., *Intellectual Culture in Elizabethan and Jacobean England* (Leeds, 1990).

Birch, T., *The Life of Henry Prince of Wales* (London, 1760).

Birch, T., *The Court and Times of James the First*, 2 vols. (London, 1848).

Bremmer, R. H., jun. 'Laet, Johannes [Johannes Latius], 1581–1649, merchant and scholar', *ODNB*.

Brennan, M., *Literary Patronage in the English Renaissance: The Pembroke Family* (London, 1988).

Briggs, N., 'William 2nd Lord Petre (1575–1637)', *Essex Recusant*, 10/2 (1968).

Brockliss, L. W. B., 'Cameron, John (1579/80–1625), Reformed minister and theologian', *ODNB*.

Brockliss, L. W. B. (ed.), *Magdalen College: A History* (Oxford, 2008).

Buchanan, F., 'Like Father, Like Son?', *Exon*, Autumn 2017.

Butcher, A. V., 'Dr John Prideaux (1578–1650)'. Typescript copies in ECL and WCL.

Buxton, J., and Williams, P., *New College, Oxford, 1379–1979* (Oxford, 1979).

Cairncross, F. (ed.), *Exeter College: The First 700 Years* (London, 2013).

Cameron, E., 'Medieval Heretics as Protestant Martyrs', in D. Wood (ed.), *Martyrs and Martyrologies*, Studies in Church History, 30 (Oxford, 1993).

Campbell, G., 'Gil, Alexander, the Younger (1596/7–1642?), headmaster and poet', *ODNB*.

Carlyle, E. J., rev. H. K. Higton, 'Turner, Peter (1586–1652), mathematician', *ODNB*.

Catto, J. (ed.), *Oriel College: A History* (Oxford, 2013).

Charles-Edwards, T., and Reid, J., *Corpus Christi College, Oxford: A History* (Oxford, 2017).

Chernaik, W., 'Chillingworth, William (1602–1644), theologian', *ODNB*.

Cherry, B., and Pevsner, N., *The Buildings of England: Devon* (London, 1989).

Christianson, P., 'Selden, John (1584–1654), lawyer and historical and linguistic scholar', *ODNB*.

Clapinson, M., 'The Bodleian Library and its Readers, 1602–1652', *BLR*, 19 (2006).

Clarke, A., 'Atherton, John (1598–1640), Church of Ireland bishop of Waterford and Lismore', *ODNB*.

Cliffe, J. T., *The Puritan Gentry: The Great Puritan Families of Early Stuart England* (London, 1984).

Cogswell, T., *The Blessed Revolution* (Cambridge, 1989),

Collinson, P., *The Religion of Protestants* (Oxford, 1982).

Collinson, P., *The Elizabethan Puritan Movement*, new edn (Oxford, 1990).

Collinson, P., 'Holdsworth, Richard (1560–1649), Church of England clergyman and college head', *ODNB*.

Considine, J., 'Casaubon, Isaac (1559–1614), classical scholar and ecclesiastical historian', *ODNB*.

Cooper, T., rev. B. Nance, 'Baskerville, Sir Simon (bap.1574, d.1641), physician', *ODNB*.

Corran, E., 'Moral Dilemmas in English Confessors' Manuals', *Thirteenth Century England*, 16 (2017).

Cranfield, N. W. S., 'Early Seventeenth-Century Developments and Change in the Doctrine of [Episcopacy] and Understanding of the Office of Bishop in the Church of England, 1603–1645' (DPhil thesis, Oxford University, 1988).

Cranfield, N. W. S., 'Chaplains in Ordinary at the Early Stuart Court; the Purple Road', in C. Cross (ed.), *Patronage and Recruitment in the Tudor and Early Stuart Church* (York, 1996).

Cranfield, N. W. S., 'Goodman, Geoffrey (1583–1656), bishop of Gloucester', *ODNB*.

Cranfield, N. W. S., 'Howson, John (1556/7–1632), bishop of Durham', *ODNB*.

Cranfield, N. W. S., 'Price, Sampson (1585/6–1622), Church of England clergyman and religious writer', *ODNB*.

Cranfield, N. W. S., 'Sutcliffe, Matthew (1549/50–1629), dean of Exeter', *ODNB*.

Croft, P., *King James* (Basingstoke, 2003).

Crook, J. M., *Brasenose: The Biography of an Oxford College* (Oxford, 2008).

Cross, F. L., and Livingstone, E. A., *The Oxford Dictionary of the Christian Church*, 3rd edn (Oxford, 2005).

Curtis, M. H., *Oxford and Cambridge in Transition, 1558–1642* (Oxford, 1959).

Cust, R., *The Forced Loan and English Politics, 1626–1628* (Oxford, 1987).

Darwall-Smith, R., *A History of University College, Oxford* (Oxford, 2008).

Davies, J. *The Caroline Captivity of the Church* (Oxford, 1992).

Dent, C. M., *Protestant Reformers in Elizabethan Oxford* (Oxford, 1983).

Doyle, S., 'Hakewill, William (bap.1574, d.1655), lawyer and politician', *ODNB*.

Duffin, A., *Faction and Faith: Politics and Religion of the Cornish Gentry before the Civil War* (Exeter, 1996).

Duffin, A., 'Godolphin, Sidney (bap.1610, d.1643), poet and courtier', *ODNB*.

Duffin, A., 'Robartes, John, first earl of Radnor (1606–1685), politician and army officer', *ODNB*.

Edwards, A. C., *John Petre* (London, 1975).

Faulkner, T., *An Historical and Descriptive Account of the Royal Hospital, and the Royal Military Asylum, at Chelsea* (London, 1805).

Feingold, M., *The Mathematicians' Apprenticeship: Science, Universities and Society in England, 1560–1640* (Cambridge, 1984).

Feingold, M., 'Rainolds [Reynolds], John (1549–1607), theologian and college head', *ODNB*.

Fell-Smith, C., rev. R. J. Haines, 'Theyer, John (bap.1598, d.1673), antiquary', *ODNB*.

Fincham, K., 'Introduction', in K. Fincham (ed.), *The Early Stuart Church, 1603–1642* (Basingstoke, 1993).

Fincham, K., 'Abbot, George (1562–1633), archbishop of Canterbury', *ODNB*.

Fincham, K., 'Lapthorne, Anthony (1572–1658/9), Church of England clergyman', *ODNB*.

Fincham, K., and Lake, P. 'The Ecclesiastical Policy of King James I', *Journal of British Studies*, 24 (1985).

Fincham, K., and Lake, P. 'The Ecclesiastical Policies of James I and Charles I', in *ESC*.

Fincham, K., and Lake, P. 'Popularity, Prelacy and Puritanism in the 1630s: Joseph Hall Explains Himself', *EHR*, 111 (1996).

Fincham, K., and Taylor, S. 'Vital Statistics: Episcopal Ordination and Ordinands in England, 1646–60', *EHR*, 126 (2011).

Fincham, K., and Taylor, S. 'Episcopalian Identity, 1640–1662', in *OHA*.

Fletcher, A., *The Outbreak of the English Civil War* (London, 1981).

Ford, A., 'Parr, Richard (1616/17–1691), Church of England clergyman', *ODNB*.

Ford, A., 'Ussher, James (1581–1656), Church of Ireland archbishop of Armagh and scholar', *ODNB*.

Ford, A., *James Ussher: Theology, History and Politics in Early Modern Ireland and England* (Oxford, 2007).

Forey, M. A., 'Strode, William (1601?–1645), poet and playwright', *ODNB*.

Forey, M. A., 'Elegies on the Children of Dr John Prideaux, 1624–5', *The Seventeenth Century*, 30 (2015).

Fox, A., *Oral and Literate Culture in England, 1500–1700* (Oxford, 2000).

Gadd, I., 'The University and the Oxford Book Trade', in Gadd (ed.), *OUP*.

Gardiner, S. R., *History of England from the Accession of James I to the Outbreak of the Civil War, 1603–1642*, 10 vols. (London, 1883–4).

Gardiner, S. R., *History of the Great Civil War, 1642–49*, 4 vols. (London, 1886–91).

Geraghty, A., *The Sheldonian Theatre: Architecture and Learning in Seventeenth-Century Oxford* (New Haven, CT, 2013).

Gibson, K., 'Homes [Holmes], Nathaniel (1599–1678), Independent divine', *ODNB*.

Graf, W. S., *Ashburton Grammar School, 1314–1938* (Ashburton [1939]).

Grafton, A., and Weinberg, J., *"I have always loved the Holy Tongue": Isaac Casaubon, the Jews, and a Forgotten Chapter in Renaissance Scholarship* (Cambridge, MA, 2011).

Grant, A., 'Breaking the Mould: North Devon Maritime Enterprise, 1560–1640', in T. Gray et al. (eds.), *Tudor and Stuart Devon: Essays Presented to Joyce Youings* (Exeter, 1992).

Grant, A., *Atlantic Adventurer: John Delbridge of Barnstaple, 1564–1639* (Instow, 1996).

Granville, R., *The History of the Granville Family* (Exeter, 1895).

Green, V. H. H., *The Commonwealth of Lincoln College, 1427–1977* (Oxford, 1979).

Greengrass, M., 'Winwood, Sir Ralph (1562/3–1617), diplomat and secretary of state', *ODNB*.

Grell, O. P., 'Cesar Calandrini (1595–1665), Reformed minister', *ODNB*.

Hamilton, A., 'The Semitic Languages in the Bible and the Renaissance, in E. Cameron (ed.), *The New Cambridge History of the Bible. Vol. 3: From 1450 to 1750* (Cambridge, 2015).

Hamilton, J. A., rev. D. Ibbetson, 'Peryam, Sir William (1534–1604), judge', *ODNB*.

Hampton, S., *Anti-Arminians: The Anglican Reformed Tradition from Charles II to George I* (Oxford, 2008).

Hampton, S., 'A "Theological Junto": the 1641 Lords' Subcommittee on Religious Innovation', *The Seventeenth Century*, 30 (2015).

Hampton, S., '*Mera chimaera*: The Reformed and Conformist Ecclesiology of John Prideaux (1578–1650)', *The Seventeenth Century*, 33 (2018).

Hampton, S., *Grace and Conformity* (Oxford, forthcoming).

Hardacre, P. H., *The Royalists during the Puritan Revolution* (The Hague, 1956).

Hardy, N., *Criticism and Confession: The Bible in the Seventeenth-Century Republic of Letters* (Oxford, 2017).

Harris, V., *All Coherence Gone* (Chicago, 1949).

Hart, J. S, jun., 'Noy [Noye], William (1577–1634), lawyer and politician', *ODNB*.

Hasler, P. W., *The History of Parliament: The House of Commons, 1558–1603*, 3 vols. (London, 1981).

Hegarty, A. J., 'Brent, Sir Nathanael (1573/4–1652), ecclesiastical lawyer and college head', *ODNB*.

Hegarty, A. J., 'Jackson, Thomas (bap.1578, d.1640), dean of Peterborough', *ODNB*.

Hegarty, A. J., 'Laurence, Thomas (1597/8–1657), college head', *ODNB*.

Hegarty, A. J., 'Pinck, Robert (bap.1573, d.1647), college head', *ODNB*.

Hegarty, A. J., 'Potter, Christopher (1590/91–1646), college head and dean of Worcester', *ODNB*.

Hegarty, A. J., 'Prideaux, John (1578–1650), bishop of Worcester', *ODNB*.

Hegarty, A. J., 'Smyth, William (1582–1658), college head', *ODNB*.

Hegarty, A. J., *A Biographical Register of St John's College, Oxford, 1555–1660* (OHS, n. s., 43, 2011).

Hegarty, A. J., 'The University and the Press, 1584–1780', in Gadd (ed.), *OUP*.

Hill, C., *Economic Problems of the Church* (Oxford, 1956).

The History of the University of Oxford. Vol. III: *The Collegiate University*, ed. J. McConica (Oxford, 1986).

The History of the University of Oxford. Vol. IV: *Seventeenth-Century Oxford*, ed. N. Tyacke (Oxford, 1997).

Hopkins, C., *Trinity: 450 Years of an Oxford College Community* (Oxford, 2005).

Hoskins, W. G., 'The Estates of the Caroline Gentry', in W. G. Hoskins and H. P. R. Finberg (eds.), *Devonshire Studies* (London, 1952).

Hoskins, W. G., *Devon* (London, 1954).

Hoskins, W. G., 'The Elizabethan Merchants of Exeter', in S. T. Bindoff et al. (eds.), *Elizabethan Government and Society; Essays Presented to Sir John Neale* (London, 1961).

Hudson, A., 'A Lollard Compilation and the Dissemination of Wycliffite Thought', in A. Hudson, *Lollards and their Books* (London, 1985).

Humfreys, R., *Sidney Sussex: A History* (Cambridge, 2009).

Hunt, A., 'Featley [Fairclough], Daniel (1582–1645), Church of England clergyman and religious controversialist', *ODNB*.

Hunt, A., *The Art of Preaching: English Preachers and their Audiences, 1590–1640* (Cambridge, 2010).

Jagger, N., 'Austin, Samuel (b.1605/6)', poet', *ODNB*.

Jones, G. F. Trevallyn, *Saw-Pit Wharton* (Sydney, 1967).

Jones, J., *Balliol College: A History, 1263–1989* (Oxford, 1988).

Jones, R. F., *Ancients and Moderns: A Study in the Rise of the Scientific Movement in Seventeenth-Century England*, 2nd edn (Gloucester, MA, 1961).

Jones, W., 'Sir William Peryam, Lord Chief Baron of the Exchequer', *Devon and Cornwall Notes and Gleanings*, 3 (1890).

Kearney, H., *Scholars and Gentlemen: Universities and Society in Pre-Industrial Britain, 1500–1700* (London, 1970).

Kelsey, S., 'Wharton, Philip, fourth baron Wharton (1613–1696), politician', *ODNB*.

Kennedy, D. E., 'King James I's College of Controversial Divinity at Chelsea', in D. E. Kennedy (ed.), *Grounds of Controversy: Three Studies in Late 16th and Early 17th Century English Polemics* (Melbourne, 1989).

King, J. N., 'Bale, John (1495–1563), bishop of Ossory, evangelical polemicist, and historian', *ODNB*.

King, P., 'The Episcopate during the Civil Wars, 1642–49', *EHR*, 83 (1968).

Kishlansky, M., *A Monarchy Transformed: Britain, 1603–1714* (London, 1996).

Knighton, C. S., 'Brooke, Samuel (c.1575–1631), college head', *ODNB*.

Krafft, F., 'The Magic Word *Chymiatria*—and the Attractiveness of Medical Education at Marburg, 1608–1620', *History of Universities*, 26/1 (2012).

Krapp, R. M., *Liberal Anglicanism: An Historical Essay* (Ridgefield, CT, 1944).

Lack, W., Stuchfield, H. M., and Whittemore, P., *The Monumental Brasses of Devonshire* (London, 2000).

Lake, P. G., 'Calvinism and the English Church, 1570–1635', *Past and Present*, 114 (1987).

Lake, P. G., 'Serving God and the Times: The Calvinist Conformity of Robert Sanderson', *Journal of British Studies*, 27 (1988).

Lake, P. G., 'Lancelot Andrewes, John Buckeridge, and Avant-Garde Conformity at the Court of James I', in L. Levy Peck (ed.), *The Mental World of the Jacobean Court* (Cambridge, 1991).

Lake, P. G., 'The Moderate and Irenic Case for Religious War: Joseph Hall's *Via Media* in Context', in S. D. Amussen and M. A. Kishlansky (eds.), *Political Culture and Cultural Politics in Early Modern Europe: Essays Presented to David Underdown* (Manchester, 1995).

Lambert, S., 'Richard Montagu, Arminianism and Censorship', *Past and Present*, 124 (1989).

Lamborn, E. A. G., 'The Woodwork of Hakewill's Chapel, Exeter College', *Notes and Queries*, 23 September 1944.

Larminie, V., 'Parkhurst, John (1563–1639), Church of England clergyman', *ODNB*.

Larminie, V., 'Skinner, Robert (1591–1670), bishop of Worcester', *ODNB*.

Larminie, V., 'Tozer, Henry (c.1601–1650), Church of England clergyman', *ODNB*.

Lee, S., rev. J. McElligott, 'Bradley, Thomas (1599/1600–1673), Church of England clergyman', *ODNB*.

Leff, G., 'Bradwardine, Thomas (c.1300–1349), theologian and archbishop of Canterbury', *ODNB*.

Lewin, N., 'The First Recension of Robert Grosseteste De libero arbitrio', *Mediaeval Studies*, 53 (1991).

Littleton, C. D. G., 'Bodley, John (c.1520–1591), religious radical and publisher', *ODNB*.

Löwe, J. A., 'Holland, Thomas (d.1612), theologian', *ODNB*.

Macauley, J. S., 'Benefield [Benfield], Sebastian (1568/9–1630), Church of England clergyman and divine', *ODNB*.

Macauley, J. S., 'Mountague, Richard (bap.1575, d.1641), bishop of Norwich and religious controversialist', *ODNB*.

McCabe, R. A., 'Hall, Joseph (1574–1656), bishop of Norwich, religious writer and satirist', *ODNB*.

MacCaffrey, W. T., *Exeter, 1540–1640: The Growth of an English County Town* (Cambridge, MA, 1958).

McCoog, T. M., 'Garnett, Henry (1555–1606), Jesuit', *ODNB*.

McCullough, P. E., 'Buckeridge, John (d.1631), bishop of Ely', *ODNB*.

McCullough, P. E., 'Hakewill, George (bap.1578, d.1649), Church of England clergyman and author', *ODNB*.

McCullough, P. E., 'Price, Daniel (1581–1631), dean of Hereford', *ODNB*.

McCullough, P. E., *Sermons at Court: Politics and Religion in Elizabethan and Jacobean Preaching* (Cambridge, 1998).

McCullough, P. E., '"Avant-Garde Conformity" in the 1590s', in *OHA*.

McGee, J. S., 'Sanderson, Robert (1587–1663), bishop of Lincoln', *ODNB*.

McGuire, J., and Quinn, J., *Dictionary of Irish Biography*. Vol. 3: *D–F* (Cambridge, 2009).

Machielsen, J., 'When a Female Pope Meets a Biconfessional Town: Protestantism, Catholicism, and Popular Polemics in the 1630s', *Early Modern Low Countries*, 3 (2019).

McLachlan, H. J., *Socinianism in Seventeenth-Century England* (Oxford, 1951).

Macleod, C. (ed.), *The Lost Prince: The Life and Death of Henry Stuart* (London, 2012).

Madan, F., *Oxford Books: A Bibliography of Printed Works relating to the University and City of Oxford or Printed or Published there*, 3 vols. (Oxford, 1895–1931).

Maddicott, J., *Founders and Fellowship: The Early History of Exeter College, Oxford, 1314–1592* (Oxford, 2014).

Malone, E. A., 'Case, John (1540/41?–1600), philosopher and physician', *ODNB*.

Martin, G. H., and Highfield, J. R. L., *A History of Merton College* (Oxford, 1997).

Mathews, A. G., *Walker Revised* (Oxford, 1988).

Maxted, I., 'Prince, John (1643–1723), Church of England clergyman and author', *ODNB*.

Metzger, B. M., *The Early Versions of the New Testament* (Oxford, 1977).

Miller, P., *The New England Mind: The Seventeenth Century* (Cambridge, MA, 1939).

Milton, A., '"The Unchanged Peacemaker"? John Dury and the Politics of Irenicism in England, 1628–1643', in M. Greengrass et al. (eds.), *Samuel Hartlib and Universal Reformation: Studies in Intellectual Communication* (Cambridge, 1994).

Milton, A., 'Heylyn, Peter (1599–1662), Church of England clergyman and historian', *ODNB*.

Milton, A., 'Laud, William (1573–1645), archbishop of Canterbury', *ODNB*.

Milton, A., 'Willet, Andrew (1561/2–1621), Church of England clergyman and religious controversialist', *ODNB*.

Milton, A., *Catholic and Reformed: The Roman and Protestant Churches in English Protestant Thought, 1600–1640* (Cambridge, 1997).

Milton, A., 'Licensing, Censorship and Religious Orthodoxy in Early Stuart England', *The Historical Journal*, 41 (1998).

Milton, A., *Laudian and Royalist Polemic in Seventeenth-Century England: The Career and Writings of Peter Heylyn* (Manchester, 2007).

Milton, A., 'Anglicanism and Royalism in the 1640s', in J. Adamson (ed.), *The English Civil War: Conflict and Contexts, 1640–49* (Basingstoke, 2009).

Milton, A., 'The Church of England and the Palatinate, 1566–1642', in P. Ha and P. Collinson (eds.), *The Reception of Continental Reformation in Britain* (Oxford, 2010).

Morgan, J., 'Doughtie, John (1598?–1672), Church of England clergyman and religious writer', *ODNB*.

Morrill, J. S., *The Nature of the English Revolution* (London, 1993).

Mortimer, S., *Reason and Religion in the English Revolution: The Challenge of Socinianism* (Cambridge, 2010).

Muller, R. A., 'Vera Philosophia cum sacra Theologia nusquam pugnat: Keckermann on Philosophy, Theology, and the Problem of Double Truth', *The Sixteenth Century Journal*, 15 (1984).

Muller, R. A., 'The Debate over the Vowel Points and the Crisis in Orthodox Hermeneutics', in R. A. Muller (ed.), *After Calvin: Studies in the Development of a Theological Tradition* (Oxford, 2003).

Muller, R. A., *Post-Reformation Reformed Dogmatics*, 2nd edn, 4 vols. (Grand Rapids, MI, 2003).

Nash, T., *Collections for the History of Worcestershire*, 2 vols. (London, 1781–2).

O'Callaghan, M., 'Browne, William (1590/91–1645?), poet', *ODNB*.

O'Day, R., *The English Clergy, 1558–1642* (Leicester, 1979).

O'Day, R., *Education and Society, 1500–1800* (Harlow, 1982).

O'Farrell, B., *Shakespeare's Patron: William Herbert, Third Earl of Pembroke: Politics, Patronage and Power* (London, 2011).

O'Hagan, M., *A History of Forde House, Newton Abbot, Devon* (Newton Abbot, 1990).

Oil Paintings in Public Ownership in Oxford University, 2 vols., The Public Catalogue Foundation (London, 2015).

Orme, N., *Education in the West of England, 1066–1548* (Exeter, 1976).

Orr, R. R., *Reason and Authority: The Thought of William Chillingworth* (Oxford, 1967).

The Oxford Dictionary of the Christian Church, ed. F. L. Cross and E. A. Livingstone, 3rd edn revised (Oxford, 2005).

Pantin, W. A., *Oxford Life in Oxford Archives* (Oxford, 1972).

Parker, K. L., *The English Sabbath: A Study of Doctrine and Discipline from the Reformation to the Civil War* (Cambridge, 1988).

Parry, H. Lloyd, *The Founding of Exeter School* (Exeter, 1913).

Pattison, M., *Isaac Casaubon, 1559–1614*, 2nd edn (Oxford, 1892).

Pearce, E. H., *Hartlebury Castle* (London, 1926).

Pearson, D., 'The Libraries of English Bishops, 1600–40', *The Library*, 6th ser., 14 (1992).

Philip, I. G., 'A Seventeenth-Century Agreement between Author and Printer', *BLR*, 10/1 (1978).

Philip, I. G., *The Bodleian Library in the Seventeenth and Eighteenth Centuries* (Oxford, 1983).

Platt, J. E., 'Sixtinus Amama (1593–1629), Franeker Professor and Citizen of the Republic of Letters', in *Universiteit te Franeker, 1585–1811*, ed. G. T. Jensma et al. (Leeuwarden, 1985).

Pollard, A. F., rev. P. E. McCullough, 'Winniffe, Thomas (bap.1576, d.1654), bishop of Lincoln', *ODNB*.

Poole, W., 'The Evolution of George Hakewill's *Apologie or Declaration of the Power and Providence of God*, 1627–1637: Academic Contexts and Some New Angles from Manuscripts', Article 7, *Electronic British Library Journal* (2010).

Poole, W., 'The Learned Press: Divinity', in Gadd (ed.), *OUP*.

Poole, W., 'Barlow's Books: Prolegomena for the Study of the Library of Thomas Barlow, (1608/9–1691), *BLR*, 29/1 (2016).

Prideaux, G., 'Prideaux Queries Continued', *Gentleman's Magazine*, May 1865.

Prideaux, R. M., *Prideaux: A Westcountry Clan* (Chichester, 1989).

Prideaux, S. P. T., *John Prideaux: In Piam Memoriam* (Salisbury, 1938).

Purcell, M., *The Library at Lanhydrock* (National Trust Libraries, n. p., n. d.).

Quantin, J.-L., *The Church of England and Christian Antiquity: The Construction of a Confessional Identity in the 17th Century* (Oxford, 2009).

Questier, M. C., 'Loyalty, Religion and State Power in Early Modern England: English Romanism and the Jacobean Oath of Allegiance', *The Historical Journal*, 40 (1997).

Quintrell, B., 'Juxon, William (bap.1582, d.1663), archbishop of Canterbury', *ODNB*.

Quintrell, B., 'Williams, John (1582–1650), archbishop of York', *ODNB*.

Ramsbottom, J. D., 'Hall, George (bap.1613, d.1668), bishop of Chester', *ODNB*.

Rehnma, S., 'Alleged Rationalism: Francis Turretin on Reason', *Calvin Theological Journal*, 37 (2002).

Rex, M. B., *University Representation in England, 1604–1690* (London, 1954).

Rich, E. E., 'The Population of Elizabethan England', *Economic History Review*, 2nd ser., 2 (1950).

Rigg, J. M., rev. V. Larminie, 'Chetwynd, Edward (1576/7–1639), dean of Bristol', *ODNB*.

Roberts, J., 'Importing Books for Oxford, 1500–1640', in J. P. Carley and C. G. C. Tite (eds.), *Books and Collectors, 1200–1700: Essays Presented to Andrew Watson* (London, 1997).

Roebuck, T., 'Miles Smith (1552/53–1624) and the Uses of Oriental Learning', in M. Feingold (ed.), *Labourers in the Vineyard of the Lord: Scholarship and the Making of the King James Version of the Bible* (Leiden, 2018).

[Rose-]Troup, F. B. 'Biographical Notices on Doctor Matthew Sutcliffe, Dean of Exeter, 1588–1629', *Trans. Devonshire Assoc.*, 23 (1891).

Rose-Troup, F. B. 'Biography of John Bodley, Father of Sir Thomas Bodley', *Trans. Devonshire Assoc.*, 35 (1903).

Rose-Troup, F. B. 'The Pedigree of Sir Thomas Bodley', *Trans. Devonshire Assoc.*, 35 (1903).

Roy, I., 'Dormer, Robert, first earl of Carnarvon (1610?–1643), royalist army officer', *ODNB*.

Royal Commission on Historical Monuments: An Inventory of the Historical Monuments in the City of Oxford (London, 1939).

Royan, N., 'Barclay, John (1582–1621), writer, *ODNB*.

Russell, C., *Parliaments and English Politics, 1621–1629* (Oxford, 1979).

Russell, C., *The Fall of the British Monarchies, 1637–42* (Oxford, 1991).

Russell, C., 'Pym, John (1584–1643), politician', *ODNB*.

Ryan, L., *An Obscure Place: A History of Stowford in the Parish of Harford, Devon* (privately printed, Stowford Court, 1973).

Salmon, J. H. M., 'Wheare, Diagory [Degory] (1573–1647), historian', *ODNB*.

Scally, J. J., 'Hamilton, James, first duke of Hamilton (1606–1649), politician', *ODNB*.

Sellin, P. R., *Daniel Heinsius and Stuart England* (Leiden, 1968).

Sharp, L. 'Walter Charleton's Early Life, 1620–1659, and Relationship to Natural Philosophy in Mid-Seventeenth Century England', *Annals of Science*, 30 (1973).

Sharpe, J., *The Bewitching of Anne Gunter* (London, 1999).

Sharpe, K., 'Archbishop Laud and the University of Oxford', in H. Lloyd-Jones et al. (eds.), *History & Imagination: Essays in Honour of H. R. Trevor-Roper* (London, 1981).

Sharpe, K., *The Personal Rule of Charles I* (New Haven, CT, 1992).

Shaw, W. A., *A History of the English Church during the Civil Wars and under the Commonwealth, 1640–1660*, 2 vols. (London, 1900).

Sherwood, J., and Pevsner, N., *The Buildings of England: Oxfordshire* (Harmondsworth, 1974).

Slack, P., *The Invention of Improvement: Information and Material Progress in Seventeenth-Century England* (Oxford, 2015).

Smith, D. L., 'Herbert, Philip, first earl of Montgomery and fourth earl of Pembroke (1584–1650), courtier and politician', *ODNB*.

Smith, D. L., 'Warwick, Sir Philip (1609–1683), politician and historian', *ODNB*.

Southern, R. W., 'Lanfranc of Bec and Berengar of Tours', in R. W. Hunt et al. (eds.), *Studies in Medieval History Presented to Frederick Maurice Powicke* (Oxford, 1948).

Southern, R. W., *Robert Grossesteste: The Growth of an English Mind in Medieval Europe*, 2nd edn (Oxford, 1992).

Spivey, J., 'Wilkinson, Henry (1610–1675), Church of England clergyman and ejected minister', *ODNB*.

Spurr, J., 'Barlow, Thomas (1608/9–1691), bishop of Lincoln', *ODNB*.

Spurr, J., 'Sheldon, Gilbert (1598–1677), archbishop of Canterbury', *ODNB*.

Stapleton, B., *Three Oxfordshire Parishes: A History of Kidlington, Yarnton and Begbroke* (OHS, 24, 1893).

Stater, V., 'Herbert, William, third earl of Pembroke (1580–1630), courtier and patron of the arts', *ODNB*.

Stone, L., 'The Size and Composition of the Oxford Student Body, 1580–1910', in L. Stone (ed.), *The University in Society.* Vol. I: *Oxford and Cambridge from the 14th to the Early 19th Century* (London, 1975).

Stone, L., 'Social Control and Intellectual Excellence: Oxbridge and Edinburgh, 1560–1983', in N.Phillipson (ed.), *Universities, Society, and the Future* (Edinburgh, 1983).

Stoyle, M., *Loyalty and Locality: Popular Allegiance in Devon during the English Civil War* (Exeter, 1994).

Stoyle, M., *From Deliverance to Destruction: Rebellion and Civil War in an English City* (Exeter, 1996).

Strachan, M., 'Roe, Sir Thomas (1581–1644), diplomat', *ODNB*.

Stride, W. K., *Exeter College* (London, 1900).

Thomas, K., 'The Life of Learning', *Procs. of the British Academy*, 117: *2001 Lectures*.

Thomson, W. R., *The Latin Writings of John Wyclyf* (Toronto, 1983).

Thrush, A., and Ferris, J. P., *The History of Parliament: The House of Commons, 1604–1629*, 6 vols. (Cambridge, 2010).

Till, B., 'Kendall, George (bap.1611, d.1663), clergyman and religious controversialist', *ODNB*.

Tiller, J., 'Smith, Miles (d.1624), bishop of Gloucester', *ODNB*.

Todd, M., 'Ward, Samuel (1572–1643), theologian and college head', *ODNB*.

Toomer, G. J., *Eastern Wisedome and Learning: The Study of Arabic in Seventeenth-Century England* (Oxford, 1996).

Trevor-Roper, H. R., 'Three Foreigners: The Philosophers of the Puritan Revolution', in his *Religion, the Reformation and Social Change*, 3rd edn (London, 1984).

Trevor-Roper, H. R., 'The Great Tew Circle', in his *Catholics, Anglicans and Puritans: Seventeenth Century Essays* (London, 1987).

Trevor-Roper, H. R., 'James Ussher, Archbishop of Armagh', in his *Catholics*.

Trevor-Roper, H. R., 'Laudianism and Political Power', in his *Catholics*.

Trevor-Roper, H. R., *Archbishop Laud, 1573–1645*, 3rd edn (Basingstoke, 1988).

Trevor-Roper, H. R., 'Great Tew, Continued', *New York Review of Books*, 35/12, 21 July 1988.

Turnbull, G., *Hartlib, Dury and Comenius: Gleanings from Hartlib's Papers* (London, 1947).

Tyack, G., *Oxford: An Architectural Guide* (Oxford, 1998).

Tyack, G., 'Gilbert Scot and the Chapel of Exeter College, Oxford', *Architectural History*, 50 (2007).

Tyacke, N., *Anti-Calvinists: The Rise of English Arminianism, c.1590–1640*, new paperback edn (Oxford, 1990).

Tyacke, N., 'Anglican Attitudes: Some Recent Writings on English Religious History from the Reformation to the Civil War', in his *Aspects of English Protestantism, c. 1530–1700* (Manchester, 2001).

Tyacke, N., 'Archbishop Laud', in his *Aspects*.

Tyacke, N., 'The Fortunes of English Puritanism, 1603–1640', in his *Aspects*.

Tyacke, N., 'An Oxford Education in the Early Seventeenth Century: John Crowther's *Musae Faciles*, 1631', *History of Universities*, 27/2 (2013).

Underwood, M., 'The Structure and Operation of the Oxford Chancellor's Court, from the Sixteenth to the Early Nineteenth Century', *Journal of the Society of Archivists*, 6 (1978).

Vallance, A., *The Old Colleges of Oxford* (London, 1912).

Van Dixhoorn, C., 'The Westminster Assembly and the Reformation of the 1640s', in *OHA*.

Van Maanen, J., 'Pasor, Matthias (1599–1658), linguist and philosopher', *ODNB*.

Van Rooden, *Theology, Biblical Scholarship and Rabbinical Studies in the Seventeenth Century* (Leiden, 1989).

Victoria County History of Oxfordshire, Vols. III, XII, XIII, XVIII, ed. A. Crossley *et al.* (Oxford, 1954–2016).

Vince, M., 'Isaac Casaubon, Andreas Eudaemon-Joannes, John Prideaux, and Tarnished Reputations: A (not Entirely) Scholarly Controversy', *Erudition and the Republic of Letters*, 4 (2019).

Wallace, D. D., jun., 'Conant, John (1608–1694), college head', *ODNB*.

Weisheipl, J. A., 'Repertorium Mertonense', *Medieval Studies*, 31 (1969).

Wentworth-Shields, W. F., rev. V. Larminie, 'Goodwin, William (1555/6–1620), dean of Christ Church', *ODNB*.

Westbrook, V., 'Authorized Version of the Bible, translators of (*act*. 1603–1613)', *ODNB*.

Wijminga, P. J., *Festus Hommius* (Leiden, 1899).

Wilks, T. V., 'The Court Culture of Prince Henry and his Circle, 1603–1613' (DPhil thesis, Oxford University, 1988).

Williams, W., *Oxonia Depicta* (Oxford, 1733).

Willson, D. H., *The Privy Councillors in the House of Commons, 1604–1629* (Minneapolis, MI, 1940).

Wolffe, M., 'Acland, Sir John (c.1552–1620), politician and benefactor', *ODNB*.

Wolffe, M., 'Reynell Family (*per*.1540–1735), gentry', *ODNB*.

Wolffe, M., *Gentry Leaders in Peace and War: The Gentry Governors of Devon in the Early Seventeenth Century* (Exeter, 1997).

Woolrych, A., *Britain in Revolution, 1625–1660* (Oxford, 2002).

Worden, B., *The English Civil Wars, 1640–60* (London, 2009).

Wrigley, E. A., *The Early English Censuses* (Oxford, 2011).

Wright, S., 'Amyraut, Paul (b.1600/01), Church of Ireland clergyman', *ODNB*.

Wright, S., 'Bodley, Laurence (1547/8–1615), Church of England clergyman', *ODNB*.

Young, J. T., 'Durie [Dury], John (1596–1680), preacher and ecumenist', *ODNB*.

Young, J. T., 'Getsius, John Daniel [formerly Johann Daniel] (1591/2–1672), Church of England clergyman and writer', *ODNB*.

Index